FLORIDA STATE
UNIVERSITY LIBRARIES

MAY 11 2000

TALLAHASSEE, FLORIDA

The Tree
of Commonwealth,
1450–1793

The Tree of Commonwealth, 1450–1793

Whitney R. D. Jones

Madison • Teaneck
Fairleigh Dickinson University Press
London: Associated University Presses

© 2000 by Associated University Presses, Inc.

All rights reserved. Authorization to photocopy items for internal or personal use, or the internal or personal use of specific clients, is granted by the copyright owner, provided that a base fee of $10.00, plus eight cents per page, per copy is paid directly to the Copyright Clearance Center, 222 Rosewood Drive, Danvers, Massachusetts 01923. [0-8386-3837-6/00 $10.00 + 8¢ pp, pc.]

Associated University Presses
440 Forsgate Drive
Cranbury, NJ 08512

Associated University Presses
16 Barter Street
London WC1A 2AH, England

Associated University Presses
P.O. Box 338, Port Credit
Mississauga, Ontario
Canada L5G 4L8

The paper used in this publication meets the minimum requirements of the American National Standard for Permanence of Paper for Printed Library Materials Z39.48-1984.

Library of Congress Cataloging-in-Publication Data

Jones, Whitney R. D. (Whitney Richard David), 1924–
    The tree of commonwealth, 1450–1793 / Whitney R.D. Jones.
      p. cm.
    Includes bibliographical references and index.
    ISBN 0-8386-3837-6 (alk. paper)
    1. Great Britain—Politics and government—1485–1603. 2. Great Britain—Politics and government—1603–1714. 3. Great Britain—Politics and government—18th century. 4. Democracy—Great Britain—History. I. Title.
DA300.J66   2000
941—dc21   99-049988

PRINTED IN THE UNITED STATES OF AMERICA

To A. G. Dickens

Contents

Preface	9
1. Genesis: Roots and Branches	13
2. First Flowering: The Mid-Tudor Commonwealth	33
The Body Politic and its Members 35	
"Reformers of the Commonwealth" 41	
Objectives of Government 63	
3. "The Dormant Years"?: Elizabeth I and the Early Stuarts	85
Elizabeth I 87	
The Early Stuarts 118	
4. Full Blossom: The Mid-Seventeenth-Century Commonwealth	144
"Of Government and Obedience" 145	
"The Godly Commonwealth" 173	
Equity or Equality? 185	
5. Recession and Reparation: 1660–1727	206
A Commonwealth: Ideal or Nightmare? 206	
Religion and Morality 232	
Equity and Social Justice 240	
6. Autumnal Fruits and Falling Leaves: The Eighteenth-Century Commonwealthmen	258
Changing Perspectives 258	
1727–1760 262	
1760–1793 295	
7. Conclusion	322
Notes	329
Bibliography	356
Index	383

Preface

IN A BOOK OF THIS SCOPE AND NATURE A FULL LIST OF PRIMARY SOURCES seems appropriate. This, together with the detail given in the selective list of secondary authorities, makes for commensurate brevity in the notes. Within the notes, few abbreviations are employed but full use is made of unambiguous short titles. In the text itself, all quotations (save for those rendered into modern English, with occasional correction of obvious slips) are as in the source cited; my own interpolations are in square brackets. Inevitably, full consideration of the provenance and genre of each individual work proved impracticable, but the contingent political, religious, and social background is examined in some depth.

My gratitude is expressed to those scholars who generously acted as readers within their specialised fields and whose suggestions led to many improvements: Professor A. G. Dickens, Professor Patrick Collinson, Professor Ivan Roots, Professor Jock Gunn, Professor Gwynne Lewis (Dr. M. Sonenscher also read chapter 6). To Professor Roots my special thanks are owed for his heartening encouragement at a crucial stage, while to Professor Dickens, my friend and mentor for over thirty-five years, I owe more than I can express by a note of dedication.

My thanks for several decades of assistance are extended in particular to the Bodleian Library, the British Library, the National Library of Wales, Cardiff University Library, and the former Mid-Glamorgan Library Mobile Branch. My thanks also to Mr. Julien Yoseloff and his staff for seeing this book through the press. As ever, I owe much to the encouragement and tolerance of my dear wife, Mona.

The Tree of Commonwealth, 1450–1793

1
Genesis: Roots and Branches

IN DECEMBER 1992 A BILL WAS TABLED IN THE HOUSE OF COMMONS that sought to abolish the monarchy in establishing a "democratic, federal and secular" state, entitled the "Commonwealth of Britain" and "dedicated to the maintenance of the welfare of all its citizens." These citizens would exercise "all sovereign power" through a democratic electoral process and also, as individuals, enjoy the protection of a Charter of Rights that established civil, political, social, and economic liberties and entitlements. Perhaps in recognition of unpopular connotations, the term "republic" does not appear, but the title that was proposed marks only the latest of recurrent appeals to a commonwealth ideal. Just over fifty years ago there was a short-lived "Common Wealth" political party; the term has long designated a Commonwealth of Nations. The principles of the abortive bill have for centuries been commonplace elements in social and political thinking—some would argue that many are already in place under a constitutional monarchy. This book will trace the changing nature of notions of the commonwealth, as a crucial yardstick of the progress of social and political thought between 1450 and 1793.

Current skepticism regarding "continuity of ideas" between eras requires a caveat: there will be no attempt to depict a free-standing monolithic commonwealth idea with a life and history of its own, impervious to events. Yet to dismiss the term "commonwealth" as little more than an often-convenient synonym for "realm" flies in the face of the massive evidence of some three-and-a-half centuries. I shall trace the fortunes of what was by far the most significant indicator of *contemporary* assessments of the political, social, and religious values and parameters of society. This book will consider the development of notions of the commonwealth as seen through the eyes of contemporaries, not seeking retrospectively to impose an anachronistic pattern. The device adopted in the title and the derivative chapter headings are clearly contrived, but they furnish a broadly accurate indication of the stages of development in the popularity and connotations of the term commonwealth, providing a framework not a strait jacket.

Indisputably, over the period studied, the term "commonwealth" was recurrently and quite consciously envisaged as embodying a set of values—usually but not always desirable. Those values normally encompassed all aspects of political and social relationships, the part that the church should play, and the nature and duties of government. As to their significance for policy, Quentin Skinner has pointed out that "in recovering the terms of the normative vocabulary available to any given agent for the description of his political behavior, we are at the same time indicating one of the constraints upon his behavior itself."[1] It is the contention of this book that during the early modern era in England the term "commonwealth" was very often normative in a sense in which "realm" was not. For most of the time, enduring notions of social obligation were consciously related to the term. Sometimes it emerged quite clearly as the focus of a passionately expressed ideal; occasionally it was seen as embodying a threat to the social order. Yet the very fact that so many statesmen and writers, in differing circumstances, related their hopes and fears to the concept of a commonwealth must surely establish its enduring significance.

The word itself emerged as a late-medieval equivalent of the term *respublica*—devoid of those anti-monarchical overtones that were to become implicit in the more literal translation, "republic." While space permits no more than an allusion to the classical roots of some aspects of the emergent commonwealth tradition thus suggested, these were acknowledged by English writers right up to the eighteenth-century Commonwealthmen. Cicero's emphasis upon *virtus* and on the aims of education were fully reflected in the "mirror-for-princes" literature. Elyot's *The Gouernour* (1531) was to cite Cicero, while Thomas Starkey was influenced both by Plato's ideas about the virtuous life and the philosopher prince and by Aristotle's notion of balance in a perfect state. Before the mid-sixteenth century the word "state" was in fact rarely used in its modern sense, and it might be argued that "commonwealth" often served instead. But it was never a precise equivalent, conveying a concern for society as a whole as well as for its governmental aspects, and was often the consciously chosen standard of certain social ideals. Several eras of particular tension within English society each evoked an eager contemporary debate as to the nature and values of the commonwealth. The dual usage of the term involves an overlap. Changing perceptions of "commonwealth ideals" are reflected in the implicit assumptions as to the *nature* of the commonwealth when it serves as a synonym. The formal inauguration of a Commonwealth in 1649 stands in stark contrast with its earlier and later rejection—as synonym and as ideal—by some conservative elements.

While continuity is never quite broken, the pattern of commonwealth thought is subject to change as some constituent threads become more and others less important—or as a new thread is occasionally interwoven. It is therefore useful to identify some salient aspects, while recognizing that we are not concerned with a coherent and consistent body of social and political philosophy—for social indignation sometimes looms larger than logical analysis. First in point of time, and arguably of importance, is a belief in the corporate responsibility of society for the welfare of its members. This, originaly coinciding with an organic analogy of society and clearly of religious derivation, will ultimately wane—though destined to reappear much later in the philosophies of collectivism and of the Welfare State. But certainly for Tudor and for mid-seventeenth-century Commonwealthmen it remained a fundamental element of their faith—and faith indeed implies a religious basis.

Clearly linked with the organic or corporeal analogy of society and its members within a Christian context is the notion of equity or social justice. Oddly, this second major criterion was often defined in terms of negatives: that the prince's power is not arbitrary but circumscribed by religious and moral obligations; that no man may pursue his private advantage to the total disregard of his neighbour; above all, that the unquestioned right of *possession* of private property must not be exercised in a selfish fashion or pursued *ad libitum*. More positively expressed, social equity is involved in the injunction that "thou knowest well there is in all things a Measure and a Mean." Those who were endowed with power and property were obligated to behave with due regard to the rights and the welfare of those less fortunate. These, in turn, were entitled to expect just treatment in return for their acceptance of their duties (pre-eminently, those of manual labor) as lower members of the social order in the body politic.

For *equity* did not imply *equality*—although occasional egalitarian aspirations were expressed, as in the medieval couplet;

> When Adam delf, and Eve span,
> Who was then the gentleman?

This was the recurrent nightmare that frightened all responsible and respectable members of society. Significantly, the egalitarianism implied is conceived of in terms of labor and of living standards rather than in those of political participation. For the natural aspiration of the commons was usually taken to be anarchy; their wish was not to reform the law, but to cut the throats of all the lawyers. As we shall see, this above all will change in a way that will totally alter the balance of commonwealth ideals.

Meanwhile, at the outset of the chosen period the accepted expectations of the commons in governmental terms were completely passive: they had the right to be governed well. In general terms this meant that rulers must behave with due regard to equity. More specifically—and here I reach a third major theme in commonwealth thinking—government had both the right and the duty to intervene in what would now be called the economic processes of society to ensure social justice, and in particular to protect the well being of its poorer members. In effect, the early commonwealth idealist thought of government as the conscience of a Christian society equipped with teeth. In post-Reformation England the temporal ruler was increasingly seen as inheriting the role of the late-medieval Catholic Church in inculcating a code of morality in economic and social relationships—though some would urge that this transition itself antedated Henry VIII's break with Rome.

Yet what if the custodian of the social concience should fail, if the prince himself should renege upon his moral, social, and religious obligations? The original reply, that subjects thus injured and neglected should rest their case with God, will gradually change so as to introduce a new, fourth element into commonwealth thought. The contention that a people betrayed by its rulers has the right, first, to take active steps to secure its expectation of being governed well, and secondly to demand and to implement its own active participation in the political process, constitutes a watershed in the history of commonwealth thinking. Indisputably, the right first of resistance and then of participation emerges primarily within a religious rather than a political or a social context. But once the breach in the dyke of quiescent acceptance of quality of governance is made, a whole philosophy of individual rights floods through.

Moreover, many of those rights will later be envisaged in terms of freedom from, rather than reliance upon, governmental intervention. Many mid-seventeenth-century commonwealth idealists advocated political participation avowedly as a means of ensuring governmental intervention in the interests of equity in social and economic affairs. But suspicion of government, almost per se, will emerge as a dominant trait in some eighteenth-century writers. Schematically, the later Commonwealthman looks for an increasing right of participation by the political nation (however defined) in the electoral and governmental process. Yet simultaneously the governmental intervention that was so passionately sought by the Tudor moralist as a necessary guarantor of social equity has become highly suspect to the eighteenth-century Commonwealthman as a potential infringement of individual liberties. The term "commonwealth" itself remains, denoting an ideal. But the late-medieval concept of society as an organic unity—whose members' individual rights are overwhelmingly subsumed within a corpus of duties and of mutual obligations—has gradually been replaced by the view of a society whose members' individual rights must be respected by a government, the powers of which are held in trust from its subjects, to whom it is accountable for any infringement. A sea-change has taken place. The changing concept of the ideal commonwealth in effect embodies evolving notions of the nature, scope and duties of government.

The following chapters will trace these developments between the mid-fifteenth and the late eighteenth centuries. Yet one is constrained by weight of evidence to concentrate especially upon the crucial middle decades of the Tudor and the Stuart eras respectively, and then upon the impact of crises of a different type in the late Hanoverian period. For while the background and the immediate circumstances may change, it was undoubtedly in response to specific crises of government and of society that the keenest discussion and development of the ideal of the commonwealth occurred. But first we must consider its late-medieval roots and in particular its derivation from religious prescriptions. These involve the mutual responsibilities of members of society and the responsibility of the prince overall—quite literally embodied in the organic analogy of society. In this, as in much else, there is a striking continuity between medieval and Renaissance (more specifically, Erasmian) social thinking. A fairly detailed examination, later in this chapter, of the work from which our title derives, Edmund Dudley's *Tree of Commonwealth*, will illustrate the late-medieval nature of the ideal and lead us into the Tudor century. Thereafter, chapter 2 will include the contributions of Wolsey and of Thomas Cromwell to the practical implementation of commonwealth ideals in government. The religious and social impact of the "Revolution in Government" attributed to Cromwell by Sir Geoffrey Elton,[2] combined with subsequent dynastic uncertainty and with several major rebellions, leads into the crises of the mid-Tudor decades. For the coincidence between the dramatic events of the 1530s, 1540s, and 1550s and the spate of contemporaneous discussion, in pamphlets and in sermons alike, of the social and economic aspects of the commonweal was assuredly not random. Admittedly, economic and particularly demographic factors underlay much of the debate; yet the social and economic impact of Crown policies—not only in respect of the takeover of the Catholic Church and its lands but also in regard to such issues as inflation and the problem of poor relief—combines to spin a complex web of causation. The appeal of mid-Tudor commonwealth idealists was to government as the residuary legatee of the late-medieval church in its duties to enunciate and enforce the social aspects of a Christian moral code.

Chapter 3 will consider the fortunes of the concept of the commonwealth during the reigns of Elizabeth I and the early Stuarts. Assuredly, the decades between 1558 and 1603 were not wanting in recurrent dynastic, religious, and social problems. But after the relatively precarious first few years the successive *conjunctions* of such issues that had characterised the mid-Tudor era were absent. It might perhaps be contended that the apparent near-moratorium on publicized discussion of the deeper and more challenging themes of the social and economic duties of government is indicative merely of the fact that such debate was, like Lollardy in an earlier era, driven underground. A sampling of the literature and the public declarations of the period extending into the early decades of the seventeenth century confirms that the absence of much overt debate is no optical illusion. But this is not to say that religious and political developments during these years will not contribute to a change in balance in the concept of the commonwealth when speculation once more bursts forth.

When that at length took place we shall find, exemplified in chapter 4, an intermingling of continuity with change in the declared objectives of those who proclaimed commonwealth principles. The parallel between the conjunction of political, constitutional, and ultimately dynastic crisis with religious upheaval and serious social and economic discontent that characterized England in the 1640s and 1650s and that which distinguished the mid-Tudor decades needs little elaboration. The reprinting circa 1640 of a number of mid-Tudor tracts is totally indicative. But we shall encounter in many of the writings and also in recorded oral debate of this period two elements that had found no favor a century earlier. First is a demand for political rights (and *active* political rights, involving consultation and participation) that certainly envisaged a radical extension of what would later be called the political nation. This sometimes involves an explicit appeal to a more egalitarian standard—a move from *equity* toward *equality*—in respect of the economic and social aspects of the commonwealth. This latter indeed may be traced right back to Piers Plowman, but had been almost unanimously rejected by the commonwealth idealists of the mid-Tudor years. Meanwhile, after the temporary downfall of the monarchy, the term "Commonwealth" became for a short time not just a synonym for realm but the actual title of the English state. Ironically, its effective ruler for most of its duration had scant sympathy with the egalitarian element noticed above.

Across the full range of speculation as to the political, religious, social, and economic objectives of an ideal commonwealth, the mid-Stuart decades unquestionably witnessed the full blossoming of its potential. Yet this ferment of discussion produced more divergence of opinion among those who considered themselves to be commonwealth adherents than had been the case a century earlier. This, together with the memory of constitutional upheaval and of regicide, explains the ambivalence that will concern us in chapter 5, "Recession and Reparation." For the legacy of an association of the very word itself with both an antimonarchical revolution and a dread of social dissolution often made it a synonym for disintegration of the traditional political and social order. The subsequent process, in the late seventeenth and early eighteenth centuries, of divesting the word "commonwealth" from regicidal and egalitarian connotations while reasserting its claim to embody certain political and social ideals was to be protracted.

Thus, while Locke, by 1690, could assert that "by commonwealth I must be understood . . . to mean not a democracy, or any form of government, but any independent community [or] society of men,"[3] Molesworth, just over thirty years later, still felt constrained to protest that "a True Whig is not afraid of the name of a Commonwealthman, because so many foolish People who know not what it means, run it down."[4] Significantly, it has cogently been urged that what happened in and after 1688 was—in contrast with the events of the 1640s—a conservative revolution, prepared to disrupt dynastic continuity only in order to preserve that of the religious, social, and political order. Against this background, Caroline Robbins concludes that "the stream of political invention did not entirely dry up between the English and American revolutions, but it ran slowly and partially underground," and suggests indeed that "redress of grievance was much more difficult to wrest from the entrenched oligarchs than from the Stuarts."[5]

This pattern may well be thought simplistic. Yet beyond doubt the Commonwealthmen of the mid- and late eighteenth century, considered next in chapter 6, were as skeptical of any proposed governmental intervention in social and economic affairs for egalitarian readjustment as they were eager to reassert a burgeoning claim to political involvement. An enhancement of the commonwealth concept of individual political rights was matched by a *recession* of individual socioeconomic expectations from the hand of government. Perhaps the key to this lies partly in the fact that the notion of the state—the commonwealth in its governmental aspect—had by now in effect been very largely secularized. Government was now envisaged as the guarantor primarily not of a collective moral code but of individual rights, with property very near the head of the list. And these individual rights received far more emphasis than social duties. In concluding this brief synopsis one may suggest that, if the eighteenth-century Commonwealthmen (as Caroline Robbins has justly remarked) were to find their memorial in the Constitution of the United States of America,[6] the mid-Tudor and mid-Stuart Commonwealth idealists had to wait for theirs until the philosophies of collectivism and the Welfare State.

Meanwhile, to revert now in more detail to the derivation of the concept, its medieval roots are unmistakable. This is true both of the emergence of the term "commonwealth" itself as meaning something other than the possessions of the temporal prince, and also of the criteria that remained at its heart throughout the Tudor and into the Stuart eras. This emergence must indeed be seen as part of a European development. An increasingly secular approach to the problems of political and social thought has been traced at latest from the writings of Marsiglio of Padua in the fourteenth century. "Increasingly secular" does not imply any antireligious note. More accurately, the increasing complexity of economic and social issues, together with the gradual development of what has been termed the "nation state," brought about a shift in the balance of perceived responsibility for the enforcement of a generally accepted code of Christian values. Accordingly, the unit of temporal governance ceased to be regarded simply as the possessions of the prince. In the use of such terms as *respublica* or *publica utilitas* concern for the body politic, while not in any way displacing reverence for the monarchy as such, found expression in a synthesis of the interests of the king and of the community.

Against a specifically English background, some fifty years ago S. B. Chrimes observed that by the fifteenth century, as political thought became less exclusively a theory of monarchy, there are the clearest indications of the currency of a notion of "*respublica,* commonweal, or State, which transcends theory of a purely monarchical derivation. Talk of the body politic, elaborate anthropomorphic conceits, concern for the *respublica Angliae* and 'the whole weal publique,' and the questions of 'politic governance' " become significant commonplaces of discussion.[7] The emergence of the idea of the realm, body politic, or commonwealth as something that transcended, while still firmly incorporating, the person and the interests of the prince, is incontestably pre-Tudor. Quite recently, Dr. David Starkey has reverted to this emergence of "a new language of politics" in the usage and significance of the word commonweal from circa 1450.[8] Rival factions in the Yorkist-Lancastrian struggle employed it, sometimes as a peg on which to hang personal attacks but occasionally with a somewhat deeper exposition of its meaning, as in the "curious political pamphlet" unearthed by J. P. Gilson as long ago as 1911. This, written admittedly in defence of the proscription of the Yorkists in 1459, relates its charges to the criteria of those "many things by the which the common wealth of a kingdom standeth," condemning such as, in breach thereof, falsely purport to be "protectors or procurours of the common wealth," and commending the objectives of "the good publique" and "the procuring of the public prosperity."[9]

Starkey's supporting evidence for a cogently stated case merits close examination. It is true that William Gregory's *Chronicle of London* relates how the term "common weal" was used when the Kentish rebels entered the capital in 1450; but the context—"and then they entered into the city of London as men that had been half beside their wits; and in that furiousness they went, as they said, for the common weal of the realm of England"[10]—hardly suggests a vehicle of sober reform. Yet the increasing popularity of the phrase seems incontestable. *An English Chronicle* includes a letter written to Henry VI by his rebellious Yorkist earls in 1459 professing their "true intent to the prosperity and augmentation of your high estate, and to the common weal of this realm."[11] The accusations made, elsewhere, against the duke of Suffolk charge him with neglect of recognition of royal responsibilities, including "the fourth, for the common weal, increase and profit of all the land."[12]

Thus, while Elton has questioned the real significance and influence of the commonwealth ideal during the reign of Edward VI as compared with the era of Thomas Cromwell, Starkey has now, perhaps more provocatively and certainly not without some irony, contended that it was in the context of the late-*fifteenth*-century debate that "common weal" had marched hand in hand with governmental reform, whereas during the 1530s the term "ceases to be a *political and governmental* slogan, as it had been in the fifteenth century, and becomes instead the banner for *social* improvement and reconstruction." Predictably, this challenge has not gone unanswered, but exigencies of space preclude fuller consideration of the debate between Elton's identification of a conjunction between commonwealth ideology and governmental and administrative reform in the 1530s, and Starkey's submission that such an identification is far more appropriate to the later decades of the fifteenth century.[13] But one's own reading of the sources suggests that the commonwealth terminology became and remained throughout the first two centuries of our chosen span of study pre-eminently the banner of social amelioration.

It may hardly be too strongly urged that a general transfer of emphasis from the ecclesiastical to the secular unit as a focus of such concern is as much a development from as in any sense a break with medieval social thought. For while enunciating the moral standards and social precepts of medieval Europe the Catholic Church had always looked to the secular arm as guarantor and enforcer of the last resort, in matters ranging from the extirpation of heresy to attempts at regulation of certain aspects of commerce. That church's code, in turn, may not unfairly be described as a Christian interpretation of current political and social realities. It may justly be argued that, in an essentially teleological interpretation of society, the Catholic Church strove for an approximation of political institutions, and also of social and economic realities, to its Christian ideals. In so doing its insistence upon an organic or corporeal analogy was of crucial importance; for differences of function, of status and of rewards within society were explained as but analogous to those most clearly evident within the human body itself. Again within an English context, in a Paul's Cross sermon in 1388 Thomas Wimbledon explained that

> to knighthood it falleth to [prevent] wrongs and thefts to be done, and to maintain God's law, ... to keep the land from enemies of other lands. And to labourers it falleth to travail bodily and with their sore sweat get out of the earth bodily livelihood for them and other parts. Therefore every man see to what state God hath cleped [called] him, and dwell therein by travail according to his degree.[14]

An organic theory of society would clearly stress the mutual interdependence of all the members of the body politic, an interdependence that transcended potential divergences of interest. Undoubtedly this picture idealized the situation, yet its interpretation of the political and social order was broadly in accord with the facts. The Middle Ages had indeed "witnessed the expansion of the Church to a comprehensive, unifying, and reconciling social whole, which included both the sociological circle of religion itself and the politico-religious organisation."[15] In seeking to make contemporary realities relate as closely as possible to fundamental Christian values in individual relationships, much emphasis was placed upon the belief that all material resources—of land, of wealth and of power—were held in trust from God. The church besought Christian conduct within, not a remodeling of, society. In the countryside manorial power entailed responsibilities toward the tenants, obliged in turn to work in dutiful obedience to their lord and to manorial custom. In the towns, the avowed religious and social consciousness of the guilds persisted. In general the approach of the Catholic Church to economic relationships was morally normative rather than analytical. Yet in respect of trade and finance it displayed an occasional flexibility in response to an increasingly complex economy. G. R. Owst's medieval preacher who declared that "God made the Clergy, knights and Labourers, but the Devil made the Burghers and Usurers"[16] still spoke for many in early Tudor England; but he had long been overtaken against the background of the north Italian cities by a more sophisticated recognition of financial practices that proved essential to a developing economy. One specialist has described the scholastic theory of Usury as "an embryonic theory of economics."[17]

Two crucially important aspects of medieval social teachings relate to private property and to poverty and its relief, although these topics were in fact closely connected. A property owner was expected to administer his wealth on principles perhaps best defined in the concept of *liberalitas*: the art of using worldly goods aright, avoiding the extremes of prodigality and ostentatious waste on the one hand, and of avarice or "an immoderate love of having" on the other. Langland's *Piers Plowman* declared that "the word of God assures us, that if men lived in moderation there would be no more famine in Christendom"; for after the well-to-do received sufficient to maintain their appropriate living standards something would be left to relieve the indigent.[18] Thus the *existence* of poverty was seen as a reproach neither to society as such nor to those afflicted. To quote Langland again, "Poverty, if you seek it with joy as a penance, is pure spiritual health to the body. . . . So do not be ashamed to beg and be needy."[19] For while the presence of poverty was not regarded as a defect in the economic functioning of society, its relief was most certainly a bounden duty in any Christian community. The poor, bearing their lot with humility and patience, fulfilled a definite function as the rich man's way to Heaven through his expression of voluntary brotherly love. The poor man was seen as the victim neither of his own laziness, requiring discipline, nor yet of impersonal economic forces over which he had no control, with a legitimate grievance in society. There was little thought of removing the causes of poverty; for by later standards poverty was the norm, and any acute distress could usually be attributed to personal ill-fortune or to natural catastrophe—rather than to "market forces."

In this, as in so much else, the social philosophy of the church combined a reflection of realities with an optimistically idealised assessment of the norm of individual conduct. A similar appreciation would be true of church teachings on the political institutions of the medieval world. Those who bore responsibility for the temporal welfare of society, for good government, defence of the weak against the strong and of the Christian faith against the heathen from without and the heretic within, were surely entitled to the support of the church. Thus secular authority and a largely military ruling caste were subsumed quite naturally within this concept of an essentially interdependent society. In a political as well as an economic and social context, protection entailed submission to overlordship, while for the prince or magistrate power implied responsibility.

A fairly detailed prescription of the ruler's duty was set down in 1411 by Thomas Occleve—in English, despite its Latin title *De regimine principium* (*The Government of Princes*). The expectation of just administration of the laws, avoidance of extremes of avarice and prodigality, and merciful treatment of the weak: all exemplify the assertion that the prince "is set in his realm for his people's ease and relief."[20] Later, in midcentury, Sir John Fortescue, in *The Governance of England: otherwise called The Difference between an Absolute and a Limited Monarchy*, contrasting the poverty-stricken French with his fellow countrymen, declares that "the law of nature will in this case that the king should do to his subjects as he would be done to himself if he were a subject." The theme of the social responsibilities of the prince runs through the book—perhaps more clearly than the explicit commitment to the commonwealth ideal as such discerned by Starkey. Enlightened self-interest is certainly involved, for impoverishment of the commons would weaken archery, the principal weapon of the realm. Moreover, "when any rising hath been made in this land before these days by [the] commons, the poorest men thereof have been the greatest causers and doers therein." Thus, "it is the king's honour, and also his office, to make his realm rich" rather than men should say "that he reigneth but upon beggars."[21]

A couple of decades later, the unknown author of *The Boke of Noblesse*, addressed to Edward IV on his invasion of France in 1475, is much more specific in identifying the "natural love that a prince should have to his people," as being "his true diligence to do that may be to *the common weal of his people* [my italics], which is to be understood in the executing of justice equally." "The common public of a realm" is defined as "vulgarly the common profit"—a phrase that, like "common weal" and *respublica,* recurs several times. Interestingly, "the term of Res publica, which is in English tongue cleped [called] a common profit . . . ought as well [to] be referred to the provision and wise governance of a messuage or a household as to the conduct and wise governance of a village, town, city, country, or region."[22] In such a context it would seem perverse to dismiss the term "commonwealth" as a merely conventional synonym for kingdom or realm, and not to recognize its conveyance of an ideal of *quality* of governance, devoted to the well-being of the prince's subjects. Ironically enough, an early realisation that lip service to such an ideal might serve as a handy cover for selfish interests occurs in William Caxton's translation, in 1484, of *The Curial made by maystere Alain Charretier,* which declares that "the court, to th'end that thou understand it, is a convent of people that, under fantasy of Common weal, assemble them together for to deceive each other."[23]

In seeking for what we may call official employment of the word "commonwealth" the statutes of the late fifteenth century are relevant. Under Edward IV we find only a couple of references to the princely duty to care for the weal of his subjects, and one interesting distinction in expression of concern for "the honour, estate, and prosperity of the King, and also of the commonweal, defence, surety, and welfare of the realm." But it is left to the preamble to the first of the statutes of the much-maligned Richard III to establish a pattern that will persist for a number of decades, declaring his commitment "to the Honour of God, and of holy Church, and for the common Wealth of his Realm of England." In the equivalent preamble under Henry VII, some two years later, the format is slightly changed: to "the Honour of God and holy Church and for the common Profit of his Realm." In subsequent Parliaments "Commonwealth" and "Profit" alternate until they are combined in 1503. While such terminology does not loom large either in the statutes themselves or in Henry's royal proclamations, those instances that occur with some regularity confirm the impression of a qualitative implication of the term, rather than of a mere synonym. Appearing usually in the context of social and economic regulation, such references include the common weal of the monarch's realm, people, and subjects. One very interesting usage alludes to "the advancement of the commonweal of our faith." A statute devoted to shearing of worsted in Norwich condemns such as act "for their own singular Profit, contrary to the common Weal of the said City." On two occasions, the monarch is described as "most desirously intending the commonweal" of his realm and his people.[24]

This theme of the monarch's responsibility for his subjects' welfare, a major constituent of all early commonwealth thinking, runs straight through from late-medieval teaching to Christian humanism, which is perhaps best typified by Erasmus. Indeed, if any one literary influence may be credited with nurturing and enhancing the concept of the Christian commonwealth in England—where he spent a notable proportion of his middle years and made many enduring and important friendships—it is assuredly that of Erasmus. One scholar has even suggested that in Erasmus, who states plainly that "the prince was made for the good of the commonwealth, not the commonwealth for the good of the prince," the social contract theories of Hobbes, Locke, and Rousseau are clearly foreshadowed.[25] If so, it was in a version portraying the prince as of crucial importance. For

> the common people are unruly by nature, and magistrates are easily corrupted through avarice or ambition. There is just one blessed stay in this tide of evils—the unsullied character of the prince. If he too is overcome by foolish ideas and base desires, what last ray of hope is there for the commonwealth?[26]

An English translation of Erasmus's *Enchiridion militis christiani (Handbook of a Christian Soldier*, 1504), appearing in 1533, adjured all rulers and officers that they

> turn not to thine own profit things which are common, but bestow those things which are thine and thine own self altogether upon the commonwealth. The common people oweth very many things to thee, but thou owest all things to them.[27]

Of course, the fullest picture of the Erasmian ideal of statecraft appeared later, in his *Institutio principis christiani (The Education of a Christian Prince)* in 1516. Therein, the analogy of the body politic recurs. The realm or *publica utilitas* is a body composed of sundry members. These include the prince himself, for "what the heart is in the body of a living creature, that the prince is in the state." If sound, it imparts life to the whole, but if diseased brings utter collapse. As to his status in a Christian realm, while the prince is not a priest, in governing correctly he follows the rule of Christ himself. As father to a great multitude, he must always be alert so that others may sleep, and must toil so that others may rest. He must display the highest moral integrity in enforcing laws based on equity and honesty, with no aim other than the advancement of the commonwealth.[28]

In a slightly variant approach, Erasmus answers his own rhetorical question:

> What is the prince but the physician of the state? It is not enough for a physician to have skilled assistants if he himself is not most adept and alert. . . . [For] the parts of the mind are not all equal in importance: some control, others obey. The body only obeys.

Nearest to the prince are the magistrates. These obey in part and rule in part, for they obey the prince but govern the common people, and merit the severest penalties for malpractice and extortion. It is true that "the people are bidden to endure worthless magistrates, so as not to disrupt the order of the state, provided that they perform their duties and do not give orders that are opposed to God." But the good ruler should both give and enforce a good example. In so doing he must spurn the flattery of court sycophants and—remembering that immoderate taxation has provoked many rebellions—must not follow such as "heartlessly extort from the good citizen what they squander on fools." Yet he must also recollect that the great mass of people are swayed by false opinions and resemble those in Plato's cave who mistook empty shadows for the real thing. Again, while the prince must ever attempt to prevent too great an inequality of wealth, and indeed take steps to prevent what should be the wealth of the multitude from being hoarded by a few, he must also remember that "equity does not lie in giving everyone the same reward, the same rights, the same honour."[29]

Our sampling of the seminal influence of Erasmus has carried us into the early sixteenth century where, of course, his was not the only voice expressing such ideas. While his *Institutio* was printed in Latin, a few years later appeared an English version of a very influential work propounding the same ideas: *The booke whiche is called the body of Polycye* (1521), translated from the French of Christine de Pisan. Predictably, the corporeal analogy receives extended treatment. "The nobles and worthy men occupy the places of the arms and the hands of the body of policy"; they must be liberal, show humanity, and love justice. After touching on clerks and students, burgesses and merchants, the author writes of the third estate, which includes common laborers:

> The third manner of the people be likened to the belly, to the feet, and to the legs. For like as the belly receiveth in him all things that comfort

> the head and the members, in like wise the exercise of prince and nobles ought return to the common weal. . . . And like as the legs and feet bear up the weight of a man's body, in like wise the labourers sustain all other estates.[30]

Necessary medicines or prescriptions for the head are closely Erasmian, as is the warning that, if taxation is inevitable, then "the rich ought to support the poor. And not that the rich to be excused nor exempt." Above all, the prince "should love and keep the common wealth of his land more than his own proper." Yet again,

> the body of Policy may not be perfect nor entire if these estates that we have spoken of heretofore be not well joined and assembled all in one, so that every of them may help others, and each of them to exercise that office that they be called to. . . . [For] as soon as any of them faileth, of very necessity all the body shall feel it and be diseased thereby.

The third estate is of special importance, expected to "bear the charge of all the surplus of the said body," and a scenario of the disastrous effects of discord depicts how

> the belly (com)plained sore of the members and said that they thought harm unto him and that they kept him not in ease as they should do. The members on the other side plained on the belly and said that they were very weary for labour

yet could not satisfy belly who should now shift for himself. At this, "belly began to wear lean" and all the members grew feeble. Despite some blurring of roles, the general message is clear![31]

Resemblances have been suggested between de Pisan's book and Edmund Dudley's *The Tree of Common Wealth,* from which this present work derives its title. Before examining what its modern editor describes as the political ideas current among ordinary men of the late fifteenth century, presented in "a medieval allegory carried almost to the length of a parody," a word about its author does not come amiss.[32] For we must at once remark on the irony that, of the three Tudor statesmen whose names, in terms of literature or of statecraft, have traditionally been most closely linked with the concept of the commonwealth—Edmund Dudley, Thomas Cromwell, and the duke of Somerset—all have been accused of personal ambition and rapacity, and all eventually put their heads upon the executioner's block. One might in extenuation apply to most Tudor statesmen the verse from Deuteronomy that, in another context, Denis Brogan placed as the rubric to his chapter on the Senate of the United States: "Thou shalt not muzzle the ox when he treadeth out the corn." Yet Dudley's feeding appears to have outraged even contemporary standards, making him an obvious scapegoat at the start of the reign of Henry VIII. As Speaker of the House of Commons and then a royal councillor toward the end of the reign of Henry VII, Dudley in his ruthless pursuit of the financial interests of the Crown engendered in several influential quarters a vindictive if understandable desire for revenge; in 1509 he was arrested on charges that were manifestly false, and was executed the following year. He left lands in thirteen counties and had undoubtedly used his power to lucrative personal advantage. Nonetheless, his book reflects not only a concept of the commonwealth current in the Gray's Inn in which as a lawyer he had moved, and which, urges D. M. Brodie, "seems to be 'society' rather than 'state,' " but also the practical experience of an able administrator. Written while in the Tower, it should be judged "rather as a manual for the education of a Prince than as a comprehensive political treatise"—although, as a contemporary jested savagely, "this tree of knowledge did not become a tree of life."[34]

In our present context, Brodie's conclusions that Dudley was neither an original nor a profound thinker, and that his book's importance lay in its combination of inherited conceptions of society with a shrewd analysis of contemporary problems of governance based upon practical experience,[35] are all the more significant. For it furnishes an extended example of the fact that the *ideal* of the commonwealth was firmly established very early in the Tudor era. After dealing first with religion and with "holy church, with the which thing every Christian king hath need most to begin," and then with the range of princely obligations, Dudley next enunciates his titular analogy:

> the common wealth of this realm or the subjects and inhabitants thereof may be resembled to a fair and mighty tree growing in a fair field or pasture, under the covert or shade whereof all beasts, both fat and lean, are protected and comforted from heat and cold as the time requireth. In like manner all the subjects of that realm where this tree of common wealth doth surely grow are thereby helped and relieved from the highest degree to the lowest. But for a truth this tree will never long stand or grow upright in this realm, or in any other, without diverse strong roots, and fastened sure in the ground.

Before considering Dudley's lengthy and somewhat contrived enumeration of the roots and fruits of the tree, note his insistence that the monarch's wealth and prosperity resides in that of his true subjects—"for though the people be subject to the king yet they are the people of God, and God hath ordained their prince to protect them and they to obey their prince."[36]

The principal root of this tree is then defined as the love of God and the observation of his commandments. Perhaps surprisingly, but certainly most significantly, "the prince is the ground out of which this root must chiefly grow"; for his own example and his powers of appointment must "enforce and encourage the bishops and other of the spiritualty to be the very lanterns of light." The other four roots are those of justice, truth, concord, and peace. The first, again, must spring from the monarch through his administration of justice; with rigorous standards in appointment and in supervision eliminating bribery, perjury, and injustice. Most notably, the king must prevent extortion by great men: "for out of doubt if his grace look not marvellously well thereto, the poor people of his realm shall be oppressed with their letters, and often times by his servants by the colour of his service."[37]

The root of truth or fidelity must fasten itself in all true subjects, but again chiefly in the monarch himself. For should it fall, what laws or institutions will then endure? But if this root gives nourishment,

> What friendship and confidence shall then be between men and men from the highest degree to the lowest. How kindly and lovingly will merchants and craftsmen of the realm buy and sell together. . . . How diligently and busily will the artificers and husbandmen occupy their labour and business, and how well content will men be, from the highest degree to the lowest, to increase their household servants and labourers, whereby all idle people shall be set awork.

Such euphoria anticipates much of Tudor comment on such issues; but so does Dudley's expression of the perennial lament of the moralist that in this respect, nowadays, "this tree of commonwealth is well-nigh utterly failed and dead!"[38]

The third root is that of concord or unity, in default of which comes disorder "and oft-times rebellion, of whom for a surety cometh Idleness, the very mother of all vice . . . and the lineal grandam of poverty and misery." The Crown's responsibilities herein are analogous to those entailed in the safeguard of justice. But the obligations both of the nobility—to keep good hospitality and be "the helpers and relievers of poor tenants, and also . . . of all poor folks in God's cause"—and of the clergy—"to shew themselves true priests of Christ's Church, by virtuous living and punishment of sin"—are also detailed. Most interestingly, Dudley is quite content that on occasion "the children of poor men and mean folk are promoted to the . . . authority that the children of noble blood should have if they were meet therefor." But as for the commonalty in general,

> these folk may not grudge nor murmur to live in labour and pain, and the most part of their time with the sweat of their face. Let them not presume above their own degree, nor any of them pretend or counterfeit the state of his better, nor let any of them in any wise exceed in their apparel or diet.

Let them also beware "of pollers, pillers and of Westminster Hall, or else their purse will be thin." This thrust at Dudley's own profession is followed by advice for other occupations: rich merchants and wealthy grasiers must not be over-covetous, while businessmen must "beware of usury, both plain and cowled, for both to God be indifferently known," and avoid deceit in the making and the weighing of their wares. Craftsmen, avoiding sloth, must remember that their bellies and their backs are enemies to thrift.[39]

After brief treatment of the root of peace, involving good relationships with other realms, Dudley embarks on an elaborate description of the fruits of the Tree of Commonwealth. As always, measure and discretion must be observed in their plucking and consumption, which must neither be immoderate nor indiscriminate as between the estates of the realm. Hence the commonalty must "not smatter in matters of divinity lest the infection of heresies creep in." The device is now becoming so labored as to diminish its impact, but contemporary insights recur. Thus Dudley again warns the commons, this time against such as would insinuate "that ye be made of the same metal and mold that the gentles be made of. Why then should they sport and play and you labour and till?" Since all are Adam's heirs, bought at an equal price by Christ's blood, why are some of poor estate and others of high degree? Several pages depict the dangerous lure of the banner of Insurrection to "the commonalty of this realm of England, who oft times smarted right sore for such lewd enterprise?"[40]

This work, despite its limitations, has been cited at some length, as adumbrating so many of the ideals and concerns of the Commonwealthmen of mid-Tudor England. Admittedly, its approach almost throughout is that of moralizing reproof at society's failure to adhere to traditional standards. There is little sign of any quest for innovative reform; unsurprisingly, Elton finds "no sense of organic relationship, no notion of change."[41] Quite certainly, it is a far cry to the positive suggestions of the *Discourse of the Common Weal* some forty years later; indeed the inclusion within the commonwealth tradition both of Dudley and of its author, Sir Thomas Smith, is a clear indication that the ideal was not static even within the Tudor period. Yet it will not do to be too sweeping. We have noticed in Dudley a hint of recognition of social mobility, while Skinner suggests that embedded within his "apparently bland terminology" are warnings about the religious duty of the prince that are "virtually Marsiglian in character."[42] This said, it is now appropriate to follow such pointers into the middle decades of the sixteenth century.

2
First Flowering: The Mid-Tudor Commonwealth

A CLOSE COINCIDENCE BETWEEN THE CONCEPT OF THE RELIGIOUS DUTIES of the prince and an increasing emphasis upon the social and economic responsibilities of the temporal power is probably the most distinctive characteristic of the "mid-Tudor Commonwealth." The time span here considered (circa 1514–1558) may best be defined as that during which commonwealth ideals became the subject of urgent advocacy to those entrusted with the government of the realm. In this sense these decades witnessed the first flowering of the commonwealth ideal. While the continuity of many of the ideas encountered in the previous chapter is very evident, the parameters of discussion are now widened as Christian humanism is joined by the impact of the Protestant Reformation in England and by the consequent enhancement of the concept and expansion of the functions of what would now be called the state. This, together with the onset of economic and social developments which engendered the severest tensions within society, furnished the background to increasing urgency in discussion of the commonwealth.

In examining the elements of continuity in the basic nature of that concept this chapter will look first at the persistence of the organic or corporeal analogy in portrayal of the commonwealth. Next we shall encounter the continued insistence upon the notion of equity, as distinct from equality, with its associated virtues of the happy mean and of *liberalitas* as norms of social conduct. This in turn will lead to the issue of deliberate and effective governmental intervention in economic and social relationships in order to realise the ideals of the commonweal. Here one reaches more controversial ground. In the years that have elapsed since the present writer's *The Tudor Commonwealth 1529–1559* appeared in 1970 a number of substantial discussions of aspects of this topic have been published. These have centered, first, upon the significance of any relationship between the writings of those who professed concern for the ideal of the commonwealth and the actual statecraft of those men whose tenure of power gave some opportunity for its implementation in policy. A second preoccupation has been the development of the ideal in itself, ranging between the Erasmian humanist legacy of the early years and the innovatory notions best typified by Sir Thomas Smith's *Commonweal of this Realm of England,* followed by the bland conservatism of the 1560s.

Notable contributors to this debate include Brendan Bradshaw, Sir Geoffrey Elton, David Starkey, and John Guy. Their writings have focused largely upon assessment of the contributions of Wolsey, More, Thomas Cromwell, and the duke of Somerset. Alongside such discussions stand the wider-ranging enquiries undertaken by J. C. Davis and D. W. Hanson into "English utopian writing" and "the development of civic consciousness in English political thought" respectively. The first of these does not purport to show "how ideal-society concepts have influenced political history" but is nonetheless of relevance, while the second is engaged with the emergence of a conscious resolve to translate ideal objectives into political action.[1] More directly contingent is Dr. Joan Thirsk's study of *Economic Policy and Projects in Early Modern England,* with its differently based approach. Most notably, its author is concerned not to "underrate the effectiveness of pamphlets and propaganda, the exhortations of the Commonwealthmen, and the official prodding of politicians and Privy Councillors in establishing projects. Official policy statements and public discussions among the Commonwealthmen so often coincided remarkably with what was actually achieved." Indeed, so far from discerning any midcentury hiatus between the end of the era of Thomas Cromwell and that of William Cecil under Elizabeth I, Dr. Thirsk identifies a continuous chain of influence running from the reign of Henry VIII to the end of the century and beyond, "promoting all the projects that were enumerated in 1549, and continually searching for new."[2]

The issues raised will concern us in some detail later. But two further crucial facets of the mid-Tudor concept of the commonwealth will also demand consideration. Political thinking will focus largely upon the cardinal necessity for good order and obedience within an essentially hierarchical society. And finally, those religious assumptions that underpinned both political and social theory will be surveyed—last but not least because it is precisely here that the beginnings of fundamental change may clearly be discerned. While some religious trends will nurture an increasing emphasis upon the social and economic responsibilities of government within the commonwealth, others will put in question some of the basic assumptions for the exercise of political power itself.

The Body Politic and its Members

To look first at the continuity of traditional elements in the ideology of the commonwealth, survival of the medieval analogy of the body politic is most significant. The term "state" was as yet rarely used in its modern sense. Thomas Starkey indeed, writing (unpublished) as early as circa 1535 alluded to "rulers of the state," while John Ponet in 1556 wrote in identical terms, and Lawrence Humphrey in 1563 made several references to "the state."[3] But such usages were far outweighed by recurrence of an older terminology, not least at an "official" level in the royal proclamations of the early and mid-sixteenth century. Not only did this organic analogy of the commonwealth portray the essential interrelationship and differentiations in function of the members of the body politic, but it served also to depict their shortcomings as ills or diseases of that body. At the same time, a burgeoning realization of the increasing responsibilities of the Crown, in social and economic as well as religious spheres, found strikingly apposite expression in a heightened emphasis upon the powers and duties of the head. Sometimes other similitudes were employed: Erasmus, whose works were immensely influential in England, likened the commonwealth to a ship, while Sir Thomas Elyot's *The Governour* (1531) ingeniously compared the "public weal" to a garden, its rulers to the gardeners, its degrees of people to the beds therein, and the vices and abuses suffered to the damage done by moles![4] But the corporeal analogy was overwhelmingly most popular.

An extended use of the device in Starkey's *Dialogue* defines the body of the common weal as "nothing else but the multitude of people," and explains that "the thing which is resembled to the soul is civil order and politic law, administered by officers and rulers." Thus the heart of a commonwealth is strong when the king, "as fountain of all natural powers," governs well. "For like as all wit, reason, and sense, feeling, life, and all other natural power, springeth out of the heart, so from the princes and rulers of the state cometh all laws, order and policy, all justice, virtue, and honesty, to the rest of this body politic." Its head, with its eyes, ears and other senses, is likened to the prince's officers; the craftsmen and warriors are the hands; and the ploughmen and tillers of the soil are the feet, "because they, by their labour, sustain and support the rest of the body."⁵

Naturally, the device found favor not only with those who wished to endorse the hierarchical nature of society but also with those who sought to enhance the power of monarchy. Starkey's *Exhortation to the people, instructynge theym to Unitie and Obedience*, which was published in 1536, often reverts to the theme that subjects are "members of one body, hanging of one head."⁶ Yet it served equally well, particularly when employed by religiously motivated idealists, to underline the *duties* of the head to the members. To Thomas Becon it was ludicrous for "the inferior members to envy the principal parts of the body,"⁷ while Cranmer asked rhetorically in his "Sermon concerning the Time of Rebellion," "who did ever see the feet and legs divide themselves from the head and other superior parts?"⁸ But their fellow Protestant Hugh Latimer, writing in 1530, was more concerned to admonish Henry VIII himself that "though you be a higher member, yet you must not disdain the lesser."⁹ The ruler's responsibility was often envisaged in an economic and social context: Clement Armstrong, in "Howe to Reforme the Realme in Setting Them to Werke and to Restore Tillage" (written circa 1535/6), complained that in his day "people cannot live in right order one with another, because the king, being the head of his lords, knights and squires, which are his arms, hands and fingers, do not minister to all common people bodily members such gifts of grace as God yearly giveth to them."¹⁰

Divergences of function, of status, and of rewards quite easily found their place. The preacher Thomas Lever was clear that "in the congregation, the mystical body of Christ . . . there must needs be divers members in divers places, having divers duties," and that while "one member ought as well to be provided for, as another: I do not say that one ought to have as costly provision as another."¹¹ In his "Charges" to the Enclosure Commissioners in 1549 John Hales, one of the best-known propagandists for commonwealth ideals, explained that "as it hath pleased God to make the body of divers parts and members, and every part and member hath his distinct and proper office . . . so hath it pleased God to ordain in the common-wealth divers degrees of people"; and unless they work together "the whole body should shortly perish." Hales is also typical in his inclusion of the poor as "necessary members of the common wealth, such as every Christian man is bounden to his power to aid, help, and relieve."¹²

Not surprisingly, the analogy of disease often served to depict the ills of the commonwealth. Indeed, Paul Slack has pointed to the particularly apposite use of this device against the background of recurrent epidemics through the 1540s and 1550s.[13] Starkey compared any weakness in superior officers to a frenzy, lack of concord to a pestilence, depopulation to a consumption, idleness in the realm to dropsy, and the pursuit of idle pleasures to palsy. Bernard Gilpin, preaching before Edward VI, chose the similitude of a great dropsy to depict avarice, and chided his listeners that evil leaders "seem to have brought blindness into the whole body."[14] Logically, the device was extended to the *treatment* of the ills of the body politic. The erudite scholar, Sir John Cheke, warned the rebels of 1549, in *The hurt of sedition*, that "desperate sickness in physic must have desperate remedies, for mean medicines will never help great griefs. So if ye cast your selves into such sharp diseases, ye must needs look for sharp medicines again at your physicians' hands."[15] These included drastic surgery. Even the Homily or Sermon of "Christian Love and Charity" (1547) conceded that "such evil persons, that be so great offenders of God and the commonweal, charity requireth to be cut off from the body of the commonweal, lest they corrupt other good and honest persons; like as a good surgeon cutteth away a putrified and festered member."[16] The humanitarian Tyndale pleaded for mercy in the exercise of such amputation, but Henry VIII himself, alluding to the Pilgrims of Grace in 1536, left no doubt about his intention to "cut away all those corrupt members that with wholesome medicines will not be recovered and brought to perfect health."[17]

Occasionally, in considering the definition of a healthy body politic, the term "public wealth" was preferred to the much more usual "common wealth." But Sir Thomas Elyot was quite untypical in discerning a "like diversity to be in English between a public weal and a common weal, as should be in Latin between Res publica and Res plebeia," and in attributing to *common* wealth the implication that "every thing should be to all men in common, without discrepancy [so that] all men must be of one degree or sort." In fact nearly all his contemporaries would have accepted Elyot's own definition of a "Public Weal" as "a body living, compact of made of sundry estates and degrees of men, which is disposed by the order of equity and governed by the rule and moderation of reason,"[18] as a valid picture of what they called a commonwealth.

Among the complex of social prescriptions essential to a healthy commonwealth, pride of place must surely be given to that of equity. The concept of liberality, the belief that "there is in all things a Measure and a Mean," the tenacious adherence to a social hierarchy: all these were interwoven with an insistence on equity in social relationships. So too were accepted attitudes toward property and also toward the problem of poverty. While any notion of equality was subject to the gravest suspicion, it is no exaggeration to identify that of equity as the principal yardstick by which the Crown was urged to measure its policies in the government of the commonwealth.

Equity in mid-Tudor England may broadly be defined as the application of the idea of natural justice to social relationships. In modern terms, it is not inaccurate to speak of an ideal of social justice—given the parameters of an hierarchical society. In unusually explicit phraseology, a royal proclamation "Pricing Sugar" in 1543 asserted that "his majesty will raise and decrease and default the price of the same as shall stand with reason and equity and for the commonwealth of this his realm."[19] It is no coincidence that the courts of justice that now evolved to mitigate the hardships imposed by the cost, the tardiness, and the shortcomings of existing judicial procedures are identified as Equity Jurisdiction. In a letter to the duke of Somerset, John Hales linked the service of God's Word with a resolve to "set such a stay in the body of the commonwealth, that all the members shall live in a due temperament and harmony, without one having too much, and a great many nothing at all."[20] Edward VI himself defined the duty of the temporal power as the "well ordering, enriching, and defending the whole body politic of the commonwealth, and every part of the whole, so one hurt not the other. [For] no member in a well fashioned and whole body is too big for the proportion of the body."[21] Equity, measure, and due degree are thus typically combined within a familiar analogy—always remembering that in a well-ordered commonwealth distribution of wealth must reflect one's rank and occupation.

The codicil is crucially important. Nothing excited more dread in mid-Tudor England than the nightmare of egalitarian revolt, a specter fleshed out by lurid accounts from Germany of the Peasants' Revolt of 1525 and of the Anabaptist occupation of Münster a decade later. Nor of course were domestic examples of such dangers far to seek. The fullest and most graphic analysis of the threat to society posed by notions of equality is probably that of Sir Richard Morison in *A Remedy for Sedition* (1536):

> I as good as he, why goeth he before, I behind? I as rich as he, what needeth me to labour? The maid as proud as her dame, who milketh the cow? . . . To my purpose, Lords must be lords, commons must be commons, every man accepting his degree, every man content to have that, that he lawfully may come by. . . . Cheese is no medicine to drive away rats: neither sedition a means to make men wealthy. What end of misery

shall there be where no man weareth rich, but an other is made a beggar? . . . What end of robbing and spoiling shall there be, if the poor may evermore rob the rich? If the stronger may pull from the weaker? Must not you abide the same law, that you make your self? Must not you, when you have spoiled them that are rich, and so made your selves wealthy, suffer that they now being poor, spoil you rich? And then must not ye be poor again?

While Morison concedes that "it can not be chosen, but men will steal, though they be hanged, except they may live without stealing," those who see poverty as the only cause of rebellion deceive themselves. Admittedly, the roots of poverty must be sought and cured; but even this does not go far enough. There remains "some other wild worm, that would not suffer mad brains to be at rest": the deep-seated jealousy felt by "the worser sort" toward their superiors.[22]

The concept of hierarchy, in turn, was just as carefully defined and circumscribed; there were no rights without derivative duties. *The Book of Homilies* indeed explained that "every degree of people, in their vocation, calling, and office, hath appointed to them their duty and order."[23] The notion lay at the heart of Tudor social philosophy. Occasional concessions to the ideal of social mobility in the interest of nurturing talent were far outweighed by expressions of derisive scorn of upstarts. Yet gentle birth in itself was a necessary but not a sufficient qualification of true gentility—which displayed itself in the exercise of liberality without ostentation, assessed by the touchstone of measure. This was extolled in works that ranged from John Rastell's *Gentleness and Nobility* (1529) to the anonymous *Institucion of a Gentleman* (1555) and William Baldwin's *A Myrroure For Magistrates* (1559), with its conclusion

> that true gentry standeth in the trade
> Of virtuous life, not in the fleshly line:
> For blood is Brute, but Gentry is divine.[24]

The charge of ostentation and extravagance devoid of true liberality was often levelled at excesses in apparel, in "curious building," and in gluttony. Successive enactments of Sumptuary Legislation were directed at the first, while all were perennial targets of moralizing pamphleteers and preachers.

Cheke indeed defined the whole objective of government in a commonwealth as that of preventing "any excess of unmeasurableness, either of the one side, or of the other."[25] This in turn was embodied in the concept of stewardship in the *Institution of a Christian Man* (1537):

> And to them, to whom thou dost vouchsafe to give more than their own portion necessary for their vocation and degree, give thy grace, that they may be thy diligent and true dispensators and stewards, to distribute that they have (over and above that is necessary, concerning their estate and degree) to them that have need of it.[26]

Yet if true liberality involved such actions, *indiscriminate* charity was not always commended. Moreover, increasing concern with the problem of poverty did not derive solely from an ethos of Christian obligation. In 1526 the Duke of Norkolk, in parley with a body of unemployed and rebellious cloth workers, and seeking to talk to their captain, was told: "Since you ask who is our captain, for sooth his name is Poverty, for he and his cousin Necessity hath brought us to this doing."[27] The incident well indicates the reasons why the mid-Tudor decades saw a gradual shift in emphasis from the still-extant identification of almsgivings as a personal testimony of religious faith, to the belief that organized provision for the poor and an attempt at elimination of the causes of poverty were functions of an efficiently governed commonwealth.

This consideration may also introduce discussion of those related issues that lie at the heart of recent assessments of the mid-Tudor commonwealth: the belief in the duty of government to intervene in social and economic affairs so as to maintain a healthy body politic; the extent to which expression of commonwealth ideals and objectives played any real part in the motivations and policies of leading statesmen; and the shift in balance between traditional and innovatory elements within both the ideals and the policies involved. On the first of these, contemporaries expressed general though not unanimous agreement. Admittedly, Stephen Gardiner voiced his dissent from what he saw as attempts to foist upon government the duty of enforcement in social and economic matters of moral precepts that were more properly the province of the Church. "Slothful, sluggish and idle fellows," he argued, "spoil themselves by their laziness; they infringe God's law, yet they do not touch the commonwealth, nor do they disturb it, still less do they cast it into confusion."[28] Indeed, in "a Machiavellian treatise" Gardiner (circa 1555), while concluding that for a prince "it is safer to be feared than loved," urges readiness to "listen willingly to the complaints of the poor" as a sure way to popular repute[29]—a motivation in stark contrast with that of Erasmus. Meanwhile a more utilitarian argument against governmental intervention was that of Sir John Mason in 1550. Condemning attempts at price controls, he asserted that "ever the end is dearth, and lack of the thing that we seek to make good cheap. Nature will have her course."³⁰ Nevertheless, Gardiner's and Mason's were minority voices.

Far more truly representative of contemporary thinking, and certainly of those who professed commonwealth ideals, is Henry Brinklow's declaration of the ruler's duty "for the common wealth to make and establish politic acts." More fully, Starkey is clear that without such intervention by the monarch the existence of merely material endowments among his subjects is meaningless: "for they shall abuse all such commodities to their own destruction and ruin." In a quintessentially Erasmian pronouncement he declares that "the end of all politic rule is, to induce the multitude to virtuous living according to the dignity of the nature of man."³¹ Apart from such religio-social idealism, there can be no question but that a conjunction of serious economic and social problems—debasement and inflation, enclosures, dearth, and poverty, to mention outstanding examples—made it incumbent upon government to take effective action. These factors, together with religious changes and an element of dynastic uncertainty, made up the background to a spate of speculation both as to the nature of the commonwealth ideal itself and as to the duties of governance. Assuredly, governmental attitudes were sometimes equivocal, as in those adopted toward industrial expansion, and governmental policies were in themselves occasionally harmful, as in the debasement of the coinage. But it will not do to dismiss the approach of government throughout these decades as a compound of drift and of reflex reactions to events.³²

"Reformers of the Commonwealth"

Assessment of such policies—not, of course, necessarily cohering into a consistent unity over forty years—suggests a scrutiny of individual statesmen of particular importance. First, a striking reinterpretation of recent years has been the emergence of much greater emphasis upon the commitment of Cardinal Wolsey *not*, admittedly, to the overt personal expression of commonwealth ideals, but to the practical implementation of paternalist social and economic objectives. His efforts would have elicited the warm approval of the mid-century commonwealth idealists had they not, for the most part, been consumed with bitter resentment toward the cardinal's religious policy and his personal arrogance. Dr. J. A. Guy's *The Cardinal's Court* (1977) depicts Wolsey not only as a statesman pursuing the cause of peace in Europe but also "as a minister of government pursuing the reform of the commonwealth at home."³³ In 1987 Professor J. J. Scarisbrick identified his major preoccupation with agrarian problems, while Slack indeed suggested that "if one man can claim to have been the inventor of Tudor paternalism, that man was Thomas Wolsey," whose interests included social medicine.[34]

Beyond dispute, two statutes of 1514 and 1515 were directed at the problem of enclosures. If, as some have urged, there was at this time no significant upsurge in the incidence of eviction and conversion it is difficult to explain why these acts and the subsequent enquiry of 1517–1518 transpired. A royal proclamation (of circa 1514/15) is quite explicit as to the king's motivation, ascribing it to "the zeal that he hath to the commonweal, desiring to encounter with the uncharitable appetites of enclosers and engrossers, reputing them as enemies of the commonwealth."[35] Adducing evidence not present in Leadam's much earlier enquiry, Scarisbrick points out that the enquiry of 1517–18, remarkable in itself because so ambitious and disinterested, was followed by successful legal proceedings. Between 1518 and Wolsey's fall from power late in 1529, "legal action was taken against 264 persons alleged in the enquiry ... to have offended against the statutes." These involved nine peers, three bishops, thirty-two knights, fifty-one heads of religious houses, and well over a hundred other gentlemen.[36]

Again, between 1526 and 1529 no fewer than five royal proclamations attempted further enforcement of anti-enclosure legislation. The first of these explicitly associates the purpose of "the advancement of the commonwealth" with "the industry and diligence of his most dear and entirely beloved councillor, Thomas, Lord Cardinal ... and Chancellor of this his said realm." The proclamation issued in May 1528 is significant in its charge to all "subjects being relaters and furtherers of the commonwealth of this his realm, that they, by writing and bills, *secretly* [my italics] disclose" the names of engrossers of farms and enclosers of land, "to the hurt of the commonwealth of this the King's realm. And the same Lord Chancellor shall keep secret the same bills." The difficulty of Wolsey's task so clearly implied is the more understandable when we recollect that the Parliament of 1523 had displayed little sympathy with his policies, and had provided loopholes for many offenders to escape financial penalty. Finally, what must one make of the fact that of the eleven peers who signed the articles for the proposed attainder of Wolsey, six had been involved in enclosure litigation?[37]

Different conclusions have been drawn from these events, as also from Wolsey's enhancement of equity jurisdiction, which we shall shortly consider. Elton remains skeptical of "Wolsey's much advertised concern for social justice," concluding that the alleged proof "really demonstrates a crass absence of political sensitivity and an unflinching refusal to look reality in the face"[38]—attributes normally associated with impracticably idealist social reformers! But Scarisbrick, while conceding that "Wolsey finally committed political suicide," ascribes this to a genuine readiness to act "on behalf of underdogs against their social betters." Moreover, he credits Wolsey with transforming the anti-enclosure movement and concludes that "it may be permissible to describe Thomas Wolsey as a begetter, but not the only begetter, of the Commonwealth men.' "[39] Whether he was a conscious "begetter" as distinct from reflecting a basic constituent of paternalist or commonwealth thinking is an open question. But the contention gains additional credibility if we move on to the distinct but closely associated issue of the protection of the poor against the weaknesses and injustices of the existing judicial system.

The notion sometimes encountered in expositions of the "enclosure problem"—that the peasant tenant met his landlord in the Courts of Common Law on equal terms—strains credulity. Certainly, a major theme that ran through the commonwealth literature was the need to restore natural justice, which was all too often lacking in the ordinary courts of the realm. In this context, Wolsey's assertion in 1516 that he intended "to see the law enforced against the powerful" finds a congenial place. The contention that "Wolsey's concern for the poor could at times be little more than an animus against the rich and well-established"[40] is perhaps ungenerous. Whatever its motivations, its implementation would strike a chord among those it was designed to help. As for its practical effect, Sir Charles Ogilvie concluded that "the making of justice accessible to the poorer classes seems, indeed, to have been one of Wolsey's main domestic occupations. . . . He increased, sometimes arbitrarily, the scope of equity." In particular, the Court of Requests exemplifies at once the expansion of conciliar judicial activity, the growth of equity jurisdiction, and Wolsey's interest in "the hearing of poor men's complaints on matters of justice."[41]

A contemporary reference to "Wolsey's great zeal for the reform of the Common Law" accompanied much discussion of projected changes. Whether he really contemplated radical innovations is open to question. What is, however, certain is that his penchant for riding roughshod in judicial matters would not have appealed to Common Lawyers. So too is the unequivocal verdict of Guy in rejecting the assertion that the evidence for the cardinal's concern to enforce justice on the over-mighty is only "slight."[42] It is evident that Wolsey's insistence upon the greater availability of equitable jurisdiction to the poorer members of society was not the least of the reasons for the hatred he aroused among its upper ranks.

Reverting to the cardinal's efforts against enclosure, measured against other such endeavors, one notes Scarisbrick's conclusion not only that nothing so ambitious had previously been attempted but also that "what came later, in the time of Thomas Cromwell or under Edward VI, was probably neither as determined nor as successful."[43] Brendan Bradshaw's review article on "The Tudor Commonwealth; Reform and Revision" arrives at an identical assessment; "in combating rural depopulation, Wolsey's mobilization of the administrative, legislative and judicial machinery of the state to tackle the problem of enclosure looks more impressive than anything Cromwell did."[44] The contemporary Bishop Longland at least was in no doubt that "there was never thing done in England more for the commonweal than to redress these enormous decays of towns and making enclosures."[45]

Any assessment of the contribution of Thomas Wolsey to the emergence of commonwealth idealism must face the caveat expressed by Guy, that his zeal was often combined with paying off old scores and that "there was much arrogance in the man."[46] Yet the resentment engendered among so many leaders of the political nation, together with the hatred aroused in a very different quarter, among so many of the commonwealth idealists who also happened to be Protestant, ensured that such efforts as he made were unlikely to be fairly judged. Assuredly, the evidence of recent scholarship suggests an importance greater than that indicated in the present writer's monograph of 1970 and should not too cavalierly be dismissed. To try to identify, "simon pure," a "Commonwealth statesman" is naïve, inviting demolition. But the description of Wolsey as a begetter of the Commonwealthmen may serve as a salutary reminder that sharp lines of demarcation between paternalism, Erasmian humanism, and commonwealth idealism are well-nigh impossible to draw.

If Wolsey's empathy with commonwealth ideals is arguable, that of Sir Thomas More as statesman is far from unequivocal. His lifelong friendship with Erasmus, the living embodiment of Christian humanism, perhaps obscures the position. That friendship was probably preserved by the fact that for many years in later life the two men did not meet. This masked the steadily increasing divergence between the ideals of the tolerant Erasmus and the harshening policies pursued by More toward suspected heresy. One might indeed perceive a dichotomy between More the freely speculative author of *Utopia* and More the chancellor, subject to the harsh realities of governance. Richard Marius concludes that "More and Erasmus were profoundly different." The latter's *Praise of Folly* is at least in part associated with a sojourn in More's home, while his host's *Utopia* won favorable comment from Erasmus. Yet Marius finds no great resemblance between the two works, suggesting a crucial difference in that "More is a rulesman in *Utopia*—just as he was a rulesman in life." Davis observes the pre-eminent importance of discipline in Utopia, which can claim the name of commonwealth because, nothing being private, selfish interests have little scope.[47]

Nevertheless, in terms of its explicit or implied criticism of so many of the social and economic ills of mid-Tudor England, More's *Utopia* is without doubt a fundamentally important exposition of many commonwealth ideals. Skinner's statement that its author "believes, like Erasmus and the later Commonwealthmen, that these evils are mainly caused by the misuse of private property" is surely unexceptionable. But in going on to say that, in respect of the Utopian solutions proposed in order to establish "the best state of a commonwealth [More] must have meant exactly what he said," he begs some questions.[48] For at the other end of a virtual spectrum of interpretation stand those who consider *Utopia* to be a *jeu d'esprit* whose author knew that it "was nowhere and proves nothing."[49] More's own reluctance to see the work translated (an English version did not appear until 1551) may not be unrelated to his own perception of the gulf between many of its prescriptions and his attitudes and policies adopted as officer of the Crown.

His friends also included such writers and scholars as Sir Thomas Elyot, John Rastell, John Heywood, Pole and Lupset (the two protagonists in Starkey's *Dialogue*), as well as Starkey himself. Pearl Hogrefe, in *The Sir Thomas More Circle*, has suggested that the members of this grouping equated good government with applied Christianity.[50] I have already discussed some of their contributions to the nurturing of the commonwealth ideal. Yet the "startling novelty of the social analysis," accompanied by an urgent suggestion that society's "underlying socio-economic problems be tackled," identified in *Utopia* by Bradshaw,[51] soon gave way to a very different attitude in More as chancellor. In face of the threat of heresy and of social subversion that he discerned in tracts such as Simon Fish's *A Supplicacyon for the Beggars* (circa 1529), More's humanist speculation was quite submerged by a tide of dread of religious heresy, civil disorder, and social anarchy.

In a direct reply, *The supplicacion of soules . . .* (1529), More ascribes to Fish "sedition under the colour of counsel," which threatens "poor and rich, priests, religious, and lay man, prince, lord and people as well quick as dead." Indeed a passage in *Utopia* itself that argues *against* the abolition of private property, painting a picture of "continual sedition and bloodshed" in a state "where all things be common," virtually anticipates the heightened language of its author's reply to Fish, sketching the danger from those who will move on from asking

> to the taking of their alms themselves, and under pretext of reformation
> . . . shall assay to make new division of every man's land and substance, never ceasing if ye suffer them, till they make all beggars as they be themself, and at the last bring all the realm to ruin, and this not without butchery and foul bloody hands.[52]

Nor, as we shall find in discussing religious issues, were More's scathing attacks confined to those perceived as a danger to the *social* order. In the cases of Tyndale and Frith he did not stop short at merely verbal attacks. More may well have been a martyr for religion, but he was also prepared to martyr others.

If recent scholarship suggests that Wolsey has perhaps rather more and Thomas More rather less of a claim to be exemplars of commonwealth ideology, the place of Thomas Cromwell within this canon has also been the subject of successive reassessments. Following the cogent advocacy and erudition of Elton in establishing the concept of a *Tudor Revolution in Government,* and more recently, in *Reform and Renewal* (1973), of Cromwell as the most significant *practitioner* of service to the commonwealth, something approaching an orthodoxy of interpretation was established. The first of these works did not go quite unchallenged (particularly in a notable "exchange of articles" with Dr. Penry Williams), while following the first edition of Elton's *Reform and Reformation* (1977) the thesis that "the 1530s constitute a watershed in the history of the reform of the Tudor commonwealth" has also been questioned. Most notably, Bradshaw's "The Tudor Commonwealth: Reform and Revision," in 1979, and Starkey's more recent contribution noted in the previous chapter, have expressed the view that Sir Geoffrey's predilection for the contribution of Thomas Cromwell to a reformed commonwealth has led him seriously to undervalue both previous and subsequent contributions.[53]

Accordingly, it might prove fruitful to identify the salient features of Cromwell's massive contribution to the English realm and then to relate these to the crucial aspects of the emergent commonwealth ideal. The extension, in every sense, of the English realm itself, most notably by the Crown's assumption of the headship of the church;

the deliberate use of Parliament as the instrument of this change; the increased efficiency, and bureaucratisation, of administration of the state; the nurturing of a greater knowledge of the Scriptures and awareness of the meaning of the Christian faith among the laity; and an extensive program of ameliorative social and economic reform: all these may fairly be presented as striking features of the case for Cromwell as reformer of the commonweal.

Before one looks at these more closely, some general comments may be made. First, devotion to the service of the commonwealth was repeatedly professed by Cromwell himself and recognized by his contemporaries. Not, admittedly, by *all* contemporaries: during the rebellions of 1536, those who had taken an oath supporting "the Pilgrimage of Grace for the commonwealth" specifically singled Cromwell out as a "destroyer of the commonwealth" and a heretic.[54] Assuredly, Cromwell himself declared that "as to the commonwealth, I have after my wit, power and knowledge travailed therein, having had no respect of persons." Yet this last phrase, together with the fact that one testimony to his "great continual business for the common weal" was that of Bishop Longland,[55] who penned a very similar tribute to Wolsey, prompts an interesting reflection. Cromwell has been described, after all, as Wolsey's pupil, and it is worth remembering that in terms of general paternalism on economic issues, of declared commitment to proceed without respect of persons, and indeed of the fact that those who rejoiced in their respective downfalls derided them as upstarts whose conduct infringed the normal hierarchical canons of society, there are close resemblances. There were of course two crucial differences: their attitudes toward religious issues, and their ability to use and manage Parliament. A second general issue: one does well to take note of the cautionary point of B. W. Beckingsale: that "measures which used to be called mercantilist or paternalist are now described in the context of the concept of the commonwealth is indicative of a change of historical perspective. . . . This change of interpretation does greater justice to the moral and idealistic element in the commonwealth thinking of the time but it is in danger of introducing the anachronistic preoccupations of the modern welfare state into an estimation of Cromwell's policy."[56] This caveat has perhaps a wider application.

Beckingsale insists that Cromwell "was not the founder of any school of commonwealth men" and indeed that "in his policies the well worn assumptions of governmental tradition predominated over the ideas of the commonwealth men and the humanists."[57] Nevertheless, it remains a fact that it was overwhelmingly in terms of service to a perceived commonwealth ideal that *contemporary* judgments were made. Moreover, as we have seen, commonwealth terminology was itself already "well worn" by this time in such assumptions. Thomas Cromwell has a prominent place in the assessments of modern scholars who perceive the emergence of commonwealth influences not only upon social thought but also upon attempts to translate its ideals into governmental policies. In particular, Elton demonstrates that "in the eight years of Cromwell's ascendancy a great many new laws were made for the commonwealth, and of that number a good part can be securely linked with him and his men.... In Thomas Cromwell a sincere passion for reform combined with a singular ability to get things done." It is fair to claim that, whatever his personal shortcomings, Cromwell's vision of what should emerge from his "Revolution in Government" and from the Henrician Reformation of the 1530s was indeed "ultimately inspired by a concept of Christian living," and that the notion of a *Christian* commonwealth in England was immeasurably strengthened by certain of his policies.[58]

Important as were the constitutional repercussions of the revolutionary change involved in what was effectively the takeover of the church in England by the Crown, using parliamentary statute as the instrument, its social implications were also significant. It is not without interest that the enormously important statutes that, step by step, arrogated to the Crown control of the church and its wealth in England, are not in any way distinguished by commonwealth language. Indeed, lip service to the "Common Wealth" had been much more strikingly present in a range of statutes on economic and social topics between 1529 and 1532. But Cromwell himself asserted that the Act of Supremacy was "as much for the common wealth of this realm as any act that was ever made."[59] Despite the almost total frustration of the hopes of commonwealth idealists that confiscated church land and wealth would promptly be diverted to ameliorative social uses, most notably in respect of poor relief, the appropriation of the ecclesiastical unit of the parish for purposes of secular administration proved to be symbolic. For in the minds of many people, not only was the prince's status enhanced by headship of the church, but he and his ministers also became in effect residuary legatees of the duties of enforcement in social relationships of certain moral values which had previously been the remit of the Catholic Church.

Elton's portrayal of Cromwell as a bureaucratic reformer has not gone unchallenged. But as to the use of Parliament as the instrument of religious change, his interpretation of its crucial importance for the future of the English realm can surely scarcely be contested. Yet ironically, while Parliament proved a not uncooperative partner in carrying through what is brutally described as the annexation of the church, it proved anything but a pliant agent of Cromwell's projected social and economic reform. A cynic might suggest that, while the first process involved lucrative and readily perceived side effects, the second often posed threats to vested selfish interests; whatever else the Tudor political nation was, it was not altruistic. Even if a bill survived its parliamentary travails, Cromwell, like many before and after him, discovered that legislation was not administration. Hence, perhaps, the frequent resort to royal proclamations—instruments expressive not so much of despotic tendencies as of desperation at nonenforcement.

It is perhaps time to turn to another aspect of Cromwell's service to the English commonweal. Possibly the most striking contrast between modern assessments of Cromwell and those of some sixty years ago is that in which the image of the grim-faced hatchet-man has been replaced by that of the eager purveyor of the Gospel and its teachings. The picture of Cromwell en route to Rome, memorizing Erasmus's Latin New Testament remains, for some, difficult to credit. Yet quite certainly on one occasion Erasmus received a substantial gift from him while minister and also, to his surprise, more than one assurance that the donor, a lover of learning, was a devoted friend to his name.[60] Among those notable writers whose names were associated both with Erasmus (and in particular with translations of his works) and with Cromwell were Starkey, William Marshall, Richard Taverner, and Leonard Cox.[61] When one adds to this the probability that the Commonwealthmen of the midcentury derived as much from the radical Protestant urge toward social reform that characterized so many in their ranks as they did from the Erasmian humanism of More's associates, then Cromwell's religious leanings become of great import.

The precise doctrinal stance of his Protestantism may scarcely be proven, but more important is the singular favor that one contemporary discerned as shown "to the uncloaked and pure teaching of the holy letters and Scripture of God."[62] Professor A. G. Dickens has demonstrated not only the sincere conviction but also the considerable determination and skill that Cromwell brought to the task of providing for the laity the Bible in English.[63] Historians of religion concur in describing the English Bible of 1539 as his memorial. Equally relevant within our present context is the condemnation included in a statute of 1536 of such "Spiritual Men" as were guilty of "never exercising nor practising their Learning to the Example of Virtue and Maintenance of the common Weal."[64] The "Injunctions to the Clergy" of 1536 are as much concerned with social and economic as with any doctrinal issues. Therein the clergy are enjoined to lead and to exhort their parishioners toward behavior tending to the "profit of the common weal." This, predictably, includes hard work and genuine charity, rather than pilgrimages—hence the need for the training of youth either to learning or to some craft or husbandry, by default of which ensues idleness.[65] To Cromwell, "the reformation of the church and of the commonwealth were one and the same thing."[66] The unitary view of the body politic and ecclesiastical that he fostered lies at the heart of the ethos of the mid-Tudor commonwealth.

Yet if the touchstone of sincere commitment to that ethos is the reality of practical achievement of social and economic reform, how does Cromwell fare? Here there is no concurrence between the claims of Elton and Bradshaw's assertion that "the record of the Cromwellian regime does not seem at all impressive in these areas. The evidence will hardly sustain the claim that what was done at this period was either startlingly novel in relation to what had gone before or notably more successful."[67] Before I sample that evidence, it is relevant to say first, that the prescriptions of most commonwealth idealists at this time did not usually demand any startling novelty; and secondly, that the gaps between reformist proposals and successful enactment, and thereafter between parliamentary statutes and their administrative and judicial enforcement, were always painfully evident. Sir Geoffrey himself concedes the limitations of what was actually achieved.[68]

It is as easy to claim too little as too much. The muster-roll of topics extant both in Cromwell's declarations of intent and in his legislative and administrative endeavors resembles any list of "commonwealth idealist" concerns. Yet any attempt to draw a sharp distinction between legislation that is traditionally paternalist, that is "commonwealth idealist," and that redounds primarily to good order and efficiency in the state and the economy, is futile. Cromwell's priority was certainly the good governance and security of the realm. He was also, until his fall, well apprised of the limits of political realities; if Erasmus was not prepared to be a martyr for Luther, no more was Cromwell eager to sacrifice himself upon an altar of impracticable idealism. Beyond question, many prominent commonwealth idealists (as Bradshaw correctly demonstrates) were bitterly disappointed with the meagre fruits of the religio-social reformation of which they had hailed Cromwell as the initiator. But did Cromwell achieve too little, or did they expect too much?

Among the complex of demands by Commonwealthmen are the

prevention of enclosure and expansion of sheep rearing—with the associated outcry against depopulation, decay of housing, and rack-renting; the nurturing of industry and trade, which would preserve employment; control of prices, which—together with a reform of the coinage—would diminish hardship among the poor; the enforcement of standards in manufactures; control or better prohibition of usury; and above all, a systematic and humane provision for the relief of poverty, where its incidence could not be prevented. This list may be extended by pleas for better educational provision, including vocational training, for sumptuary legislation, and also for reforms both in the content and in the administration of the law. In moving to consider a number of related proposals that reached Parliament and sometimes the Statute Book during the 1530s it is as well to remember Elton's conclusion that it is often well-nigh impossible to prove where governmental initiative ends and private initiative begins, or to decide the relative weight of Crown policy and of sectional interests.[69] Yet whether they be attributed to Cromwellian or to other pressures, the quite regular profession of seeking "the common Weal of the King's People" or "the common Wealth of this Realm" in so many pieces of legislation is certain testimony of the real impact during this decade of a conscious pursuit of commonwealth ideals.

Again, the language of the royal proclamations on a range of topics displays a notable continuity in appeals to commonwealth motivation. Sometimes a touch of irony is not lacking. In view of the dismal record of the Crown in terms of debasement of the coinage, a proclamation of July 1538 is interesting in its depiction of the monarch as "more considering the commonwealth of this his realm than the singular profit which his grace might lawfully take"! Even more striking is that issued in the following February, which seems to echo Erasmus in its declaration that "it is the office and duty of chief rulers and governors of all civil commonalties to study, devise, and practice by sundry ways and means to advance, set forth, and increase their commonwealths committed to their cures and charges."[70]

Of those statutory measures that were most demonstrably ministerial in origin, the projects for quite substantial control of sheep rearing and protection of tillage, and for the introduction of a sweeping and in some respects innovatory scheme for poor relief, stand out. Cromwell himself, writing to Henry VIII, besought royal favor for the first of these as "the most noble, profitable and most beneficial thing that was ever done for the common wealth of this your realm."[71] Not only were these arguably the flagships of so much commonwealth writing and influence, but both of them were subject to so much parliamentary obstruction and revision that what was finally enacted might almost be described as an emasculated version of what had originally been projected. Indeed, in relation to Bradshaw's arguable contention that Cromwell "contributed more to the making of Leviathan than to the making of the welfare state," it is ironic that Sir Geoffrey identifies a major reason for the failure of the first bill on poor relief in 1536 as its inclusion of a proposal for financing the scheme by a graduated income tax.[72] For many would identify that device, much later, as the key to the financing of the welfare state itself!

A list of measures receiving parliamentary consideration in this decade—including, as computed by Elton, an all-too-lengthy muster of "failed bills"[73]—is indeed an impressive reflection of the principal subjects of concern in the commonwealth literature. They include proposals (and sometimes enactments) for the two topics just mentioned; for control of certain trades and the setting of acceptable standards of production and of marketing; for the control of prices (a problem that proved well-nigh intractable) and of usury; for the encouragement of manufactures, most notably of cloth, and of trade; for nurturing employment; and sumptuary legislation. Cromwell also showed an interest in another subject on which such writers as Starkey, Morison, and Rastell were often articulate: the need for reform of the law and of the legal system. Setting on one side the discrete issue of the church courts, the record consisted rather more of discussion than of accomplishment. The Statutes of Uses and of Wills were major enactments, but projected law reform as far as concerned most ordinary people fell well short even of any real effort. The most interesting scheme in a commonwealth context, designed to solve the problem of enforcement of statutes directed toward social welfare (which often proved unpopular with vested interests) by the creation of a Court of Justices or Conservators of the Common Weal, did not even receive Cromwellian consideration.[74]

Impractical as it might well have appeared, it indicates none the less a major reason why on several social and economic issues Cromwell's reach proved to be beyond his grasp. Quite simply, those entrusted with local enforcement of such legislation found that all too many clauses ran counter to their personal interests. It is fair to remark that, in the face of such "opposition by default" even after a bill survived Parliament, and amidst the multifarious distractions of the other crucially important facets of his policies, what Cromwell attempted is surely sufficient to warrant his identification as a major exemplar of the influence of commonwealth ideology upon the policymaking of this era. It is ironical that Aske reported of the Pilgrims of Grace that "their especial great grudge is against the Lord Cromwell, being reputed the destroyer of the commonwealth."[75]

Such factors, albeit in a different combination, were also involved in the circumstances and occasion of his fall from power. Alongside the influence of a disastrous miscalculation in terms of foreign policy and marital advice, eagerly seized upon by his enemies, may be set that described by Susan Brigden in "Popular Disturbance and the Fall of Thomas Cromwell." Her suggestion is that Robert Barnes, whose condemnation preceded that of Cromwell, was seen by conservative influences at Court not only as an agent of the hated minister's flirtation with Lutheran embroilment abroad, but also and more immediately as a symbol of a combination of religious heresy and social subversion at home.[76] Insofar as this is true, then the fear of a potentially "subversive" type of commonwealth thinking, tainted with religious heresy and sufficient to appal the established political nation, may well have played a part in the fall of Cromwell, which presaged the circumstances of the downfall of the duke of Somerset a decade later. Certainly the terms of his attainder pointed to Cromwell's alleged disdain of the nobility in order to depict him as engaged in the subversion of a hierarchical society, while the charge of Lollardy sufficed to parade the old association between religious heresy and sedition.

Whether or not it was entirely coincidental that, in the introductory phraseology to several blocks of statutes at this time, "Concord, Quiet and Wealth" replaced "Commonwealth,"[77] the yearning of commonwealth idealists for further progress in religious reformation combined with ameliorative social measures had received a setback. Admittedly, lip service continued to be paid (as in a royal proclamation in 1541) to the monarch's "having special regard to the advancement of the commonwealth of this his realm."[78] Moreover, Erasmian humanism continued to be influential at Court—nurtured by Katherine Parr, the last of Henry's wives. Yet even such a vehicle of moderate reform became suspect to the arch-conservative Stephen Gardiner. Early in the reign of Edward VI, imprisoned in the Tower, he wrote to the duke of Somerset pleading that the distribution of an English translation of Erasmus's *Paraphrases* should be prevented, as a virtual incitement to social and political subversion.[79] But his voice was drowned amid the euphoria of those whose hopes of genuine commonwealth reforms led them to hail the accession to the English throne of Edward VI, the "Young Josiah."

It is worthy of comment that the young king himself was rather more than a mere symbol of such hopes. Educated by tutors steeped in the Erasmian tradition, some of whom were also zealous for continued Protestant religious reforms, Edward's written exercises bear witness to his own inculcated beliefs. Such exhortations as Thomas Cooper's address to the monarch, defining the ruler's task as being "constantly to proceed forth to the advancement of the commonweal: that is, Truly to administer justice, to restrain extortion and oppression, to set up tillage and good husbandry,"[80] coincide with the young king's own definition of "the temporal regiment" in his "Discourse on the Reformation of Abuses" in 1551. The concept of equity combines with the corporeal analogy in his assertion that princely duty consists "in well ordering, enriching, and defending the whole body politic of the commonwealth, and every part of the whole, so one hurt not th'other."[81] The lengthy "Injunctions for Religious Reform" issued by royal proclamation in July 1547, which include the direction that "the *Paraphrases* of Erasmus, also in English, upon the Gospels" be placed in all churches, present a striking blend of the religious and the social hopes of those who now thought to see the Christian Commonwealth become a firm reality. They include prescriptions for the training and education of youth and for scholarship, for morality in personal conduct "with endeavour to profit the commonweal," and for the provision of a "poor chest"—"knowing that to relieve the poor is a true worship of God."[82]

Sadly, the duke of Somerset's anticipation of what might be expected from the king, despite his youth—"in Scripture, Josiah was no old king even when he died"[83]—was prophetic in an unintended sense: by 1553 both the author and the subject of that comment were dead. Discussion of the influence of the commonwealth ideal during Edward's short reign must once more be related to its propagandists, to ministers of the Crown, and to the record. Here again we are on controversial ground. The years that have elapsed since publication of the present writer's *The Tudor Commonwealth 1529–1559* have seen much trenchant reassessment of such issues—and also "revisionism revised." Such reappraisal has centered upon the term "Commonwealth Party," the evidence for the effective influence of commonwealth ideals upon actual policy, and the record and motivations of Protector Somerset and the duke of Northumberland respectively.

First, surely no one would wish to defend any reading of the term Commonwealth Party—accepted as it was in the early 1970s—in the sense in which it has been depicted by its critics. Not only did the mid-Tudor polity know of no parties in any modern political sense, but there was never a coherent, organized body of men with an agreed program that they were determined to translate into governmental policy. Yet the assertion that "the whole concept sprang fully armed from one man's head"[84] surely goes too far. For quite clearly the editor of the *Calendar of State Papers Domestic, 1547–1580* in 1856 was not influenced by A. F. Pollard's overgenerous portrait of Somerset when he summarized a letter of Sir Anthony Aucher to Cecil (22 September 1549) as "apprehensive of the new party called Commonwealths men, thought to be favoured by the Protector."[85] Lemon's ascription, accurate or not, can only derive either from his own reading of the source or from received tradition. The contention that "the very name 'commonwealths men' is nowhere vouched in the record"[86] is equally surprising. Aucher's allusions to "these men called common wealths and their adherents," to "those called common wealths," and to "that Common Wealth called Latimer" as having procured the pardon of rioters who merited punishment, are surely near enough.[87] Again, what other term may one deduce from John Bradford's confession, while in prison awaiting martyrdom, that "this is a sin, dear Father, that I always have been a private more than a commonweal man"?[88] We do not need to cling quite literally to Pollard's identification of "a small but able party"[89] in order to recognize the existence, early in the reign of Edward VI, of a number of like-minded men in several walks of life who sought to influence policy in a "commonweal" direction.

That they looked most hopefully toward the new king and his uncle, Edward Seymour, duke of Somerset, is as clear as is the fact that these in turn nurtured such hopes. Somerset's arrogance, miscalculations, and personal rapacity have been made all too evident by the research most notably of M. L. Bush in *The Government Policy of Protector Somerset* (1975) and of Dale Hoak in *The King's Council in the Reign of Edward VI* (1976). Yet his self-description, immediately before his execution, as having been "ever glad of the furtherance and helping forward of the Common Wealth of this realm,"[90] should not be dismissed as evidence solely of the mid-Tudor tradition that on the scaffold the condemned must "make a good end." Striking testimony of the belief of many Edwardian commonwealth sympathizers that the Protector was the lode-star of their hopes is found in a letter to him from John Hales, on circuit with the Enclosure Commissioners:

If there be any way or policy to make the people receive, embrace, and love God's word, it is only this—when they shall see that it bringeth forth so goodly fruit, that men seek not their own wealth, nor their private commodity, but, as good members, the universal wealth of the whole body.... I am fully persuaded, and certainly do believe in your Grace's sayings, that... it shall go forward, and set such a stay in the body of the commonwealth, that all the members shall live in a due temperament and harmony, without one having too much, and a great many nothing at all, as at this present plainly they have.[91]

Equally significant are the words of a coolly skeptical though not hostile witness, Sir William Paget, written to Somerset at the time of Ket's Rebellion in Norfolk in 1549. He warns the Protector, whom he had indeed supported in establishing his power, that

your pardons have given evil men a boldness to enterprise as they [have done].... I told your Grace the Truth, and was not believed: well now your Grace seeth it what sayeth your Grace? Marry, the King's subjects out of all discipline, out of obedience.... And what is the cause? Your own levity [lenity?], your softness, your opinion to be good to the poor. The opinion of such as sayeth to your Grace, "O Sir, there was never man that had the hearts of the poor as you have. Oh! the Commons pray for you, Sir...."[92]

The equally astringent modern assessment of Dr. Bush concedes that Somerset's "social programme proved to be a cause of insurrection" that, together with his allegedly unwarranted leniency toward the rebels, enabled his enemies to reassess it "as an attack on the traditional order."[93] Such a course was never his intention. Nor should it be forgotten that, vitiated by an overambitious and ruinously costly foreign policy as his projects were, and flawed by overweening personal ambition as he may have been, Somerset stopped short of ruining the realm to save himself in the crisis of 1549. Unlike the duke of Northumberland (whose "rehabilitation" has probably gone far enough), who lacked only the means and support but not the will to fight against Mary Tudor's adherents in 1553, Somerset could very probably have waged war to protect himself in 1549.

To turn now to the Commonwealthmen (a term as valid in the 1540s as in the 1530s), a survey of those who wrote, preached, or submitted memoranda on the reform of the commonweal is as impressive as is that of those who addressed themselves to Thomas Cromwell. Slack concurs that "Edward VI's reign in particular was as much an era of social and economic projects as the years of Cromwell's ministry."[94] Among those of major significance in propaganda and sometimes action for the commonweal was John Hales. A former dependant of Cromwell, Hales was a most zealous supporter of commonwealth ideology among those who held official posts—in his case as MP for Preston in 1547 and as chief spokesman for Somerset's Enclosure Commission in 1549. But the authorship of the most highly thought-of piece of commonwealth literature, *A Discourse of the Common Weal of this Realm of England,* written in 1549 but not printed until 1893 when Elizabeth Lamond attributed it to Hales, is now attributed to Sir Thomas Smith.[95]

This only makes the case for commonwealth influence in Somerset's entourage more striking. For Smith, who entered his service in 1547, became Clerk of the Privy Council and also acted as master of the Court of Requests for poor men's cases, which the Protector established in his own home. Between 1548 and 1549 he was one of the two secretaries of state, and Mrs. Dewar describes him as staking all on Somerset, with whom he fell in 1549. Between October of that year and March 1550 Smith was to suffer imprisonment in the Tower. His loyalty to Somerset and to commonwealth ideals was not blind: he was skeptical of such as "kneel upon your grace's carpets and devise commonwealths as they like, and are angry that other men be not so hasty to run straight as their brains crow." Indeed, Smith's submission of a memorandum on the disastrous effects of debasement of the coinage had already led to some loss of favor, and it is conjectured that the increased leisure in the summer of 1549 that this entailed produced the writing of the *Discourse,* with its original and forward-looking analysis of the rationale of governmental action on economic and social issues.[96] Smith himself was to survive, unlike his patron; so too was another of Somerset's supporters, William Cecil, who, despite a period of imprisonment, displayed considerable dexterity and was by September 1550 a principal secretary. Indeed, in view of the elements of continuity between Wolsey and Cromwell, Cromwell and Somerset, and Somerset and the early years of the reign of Elizabeth I, perhaps it is time to recollect the Tudor precept about a measure and a mean, and to avoid overheightened contrasts in terms of commitment to commonwealth ideals.

Certainly, the near-identity in midcentury of religious and of social idealism, in the context of an increasingly influential Protestant ethos, is demonstrated in such prominent divines as Thomas Cranmer, Hugh Latimer, Nicholas Ridley, John Hooper, John Bradford, Thomas Becon, and Thomas Lever. Cranmer, who virtually exemplifies the transition from Erasmian to Protestant commonwealth ideology, was perhaps, as archbishop of Canterbury, somewhat circumspect in his declarations of support. Hugh Latimer, once bishop of Worcester, was at one time identified by Elton himself as nominal leader of the Commonwealthmen in the 1540s.[97] Although *not,* as is now known, the Latimer referred to in the Aucher letter cited earlier, he was always particularly outspoken in his condemnation of economic exploitation of the poor. Incidentally, J. D. Alsop, in establishing that the "Commonwelth of Kent called Lattymer" was not the cleric, became convinced "that there was popular 'commonwealth' activity in 1549 linked, at least in part, to Somerset."[98] Latimer's close friend Ridley, bishop of Rochester in 1547 and of London three years later, was actively engaged in endeavors to improve the provision for relief of poverty in the capital. Of his chaplains, Bradford (notwithstanding his contrition noted earlier) devoted much of his time to personal charity, while another, Lever, came close to Latimer in the power of his preaching against social and economic injustice. Thomas Becon, chaplain to Cranmer and to Somerset himself, reached many of the literate public through successful publications of his sermons. John Hooper, also chaplain to Somerset in 1549 and then bishop of Gloucester in 1550, was as radical and uncompromising in his social and economic strictures as he was in his declaration of his religious faith—for which, like several others just named, he suffered martyrdom.[99]

These men are sometimes dismissed as moralizing sermonizers with little practical knowledge of economic problems and even less grasp of potential solutions. But this is the very point at issue. Social and economic relationships in mid-Tudor England were still considered as subject to a moral code; judgments were not made solely on grounds of efficiency. What is of crucial importance is the fact that they actively besought the direct intervention of government in order to procure a Christian commonwealth, to which they in turn rendered something far more than formal lip service. Their breaking from the Catholic Church of Rome in no way diminished their belief in a unitary society, but may well have *increased* their estimate of the social and economic responsibilities of the temporal rulers of the body politic—in sharp contrast with Stephen Gardiner's far more limited assessment of the scope of governmental responsibility.

Mention must just be made of another of Cranmer's chaplains, John Ponet, Gardiner's successor as bishop of Winchester, whose crucially important political writing will demand our attention later, before we turn to two particularly zealous pamphleteers on behalf of commonwealth ideology: Henry Brinklow and Robert Crowley. Brinklow, a former Grey Friar who became a London mercer, was a radical Protestant reformer in the same mold as Tyndale, Frith, and Simon Fish. His particular preoccupation, in several tracts published in the 1540s prior to the accession of Edward VI, was with the failure to employ confiscated church wealth to the common good—such as in the setting up of hospitals for the sick poor and of free schools. Crowley, an Oxford-educated printer and preacher, published a small spate of works between circa 1549 and 1551 that, in the tradition of *Piers Plowman* (which he also published), exemplified the survival of traditional moralising about what he saw as the injustice and profit-seeking commercialism of contemporary society. J. W. Allen considered Crowley a typical exponent of this strain of commonwealth thinking, but no one has ever sought to attribute to him any constructive influence upon governmental action.[100]

As to the degree to which such influence may convincingly be proven, and indeed as to the very extent of commonwealth-type legislation itself during the reign of Edward VI, a note of caution has been sounded. But this is not at all surprising. Somerset's effective tenure of power was brief, while the rehabilitation of Northumberland has not sought to make of him a conscious and committed reformer of the social and economic aspects of the commonweal. Paradoxically, his eagerness, for whatever motive, in the further "protestantisation" of church leaders led him to promote some who proved to be most bitterly critical of the secular aspects of his policy. A. G. Dickens has computed that before its dissolution in 1536 the Reformation Parliament had enacted about seventy social and economic statutes.[101] Clearly, given the distractions of both chief ministers with other issues, such a total is not to be expected from the short-lived Parliaments of Edward VI. Yet, both in statutes and in royal proclamations, commonwealth terminology remains as prominent as it had been during—or, for that matter, before—the era of Cromwell's dominance. But sadly, we encounter also the oft-expressed lament of commonwealth idealists that Members of Parliament were anything but zealots for the public, as opposed to their own private benefit.

Consideration of Edwardian social and economic policies is often focused on two perennial commonwealth preoccupations since the time of Wolsey: enclosures and the problem of poor relief. The most discussed of Somerset's endeavors is his establishment of an Enclosures Commission. Although the royal proclamation "Announcing Enclosure Inquiry" (1 June 1548) does not in fact employ the term commonwealth, its denunciation of "insatiable greediness" and expression of the monarch's "pitiful and tender zeal to his most loving subjects, and specially to the poor" is unmistakably indicative of the influence of such ideals. The edict "Enforcing Statutes against Enclosures" (11 April 1549) *is* explicit in its declaration that thereby "there was a great hope conceived that the commonwealth of this realm should have been renewed and restored," the execution of such statutes being "so goodly and necessary for the commonwealth." Indeed the proclamation "Pardoning Enclosure Rioters," while ordering martial law against such future offenders (14 June 1549), is unrepentant in its allusion to the "godly zeal and love to the commonwealth of the realm, by the advice of his dearest uncle Edward, Duke of Somerset," as motivating the attempts at enforcement of anti-enclosure legislation.[102] John Hales, Somerset's principal agent in this work, was not entirely without effective influence. Certain suggestions in his paper on "Causes of Dearth" were carried through Parliament in November 1548; these included a tax on sheep that angered the Protector's brother, the Lord Admiral, and that was nullified when Somerset fell. But Hales bequeathed bitter accounts of the fate of his other legislative projects: "for re-edifying houses decayed, and for the maintenance of tillage and husbandry," for the establishment of a compulsory ratio between sheep and cows so as to secure an adequate supply of dairy produce, and "for regrating of victuals and other things."[103] Nonetheless, a royal proclamation "Pricing Victual" was issued on 2 July 1549. This detailed attempt "to set and tax reasonable prices of all kinds of victual" again alludes to "the principal and continual charge of the commonwealth and tranquillity of this realm, for the which Almighty God hath given to his majesty power to rule," and to the "good advice of his most dear uncle, Edward, Duke of Somerset."[104]

Undoubtedly more notorious is the Law of 1547 (1 Edw.VI, c.3) that, alongside prescribing enforced apprenticeship for the needy young and enjoining charitable collections on Sundays for the impotent, included more draconian measures. These included branding sturdy vagrants with the letters V and S—with forced labor and finally slavery to follow repeated offences. Elton's attribution of this measure to the temper of the House of Commons itself, in the context of a near-panic suggested by Dr. C. S. L. Davies as induced by the return of 48,000 men from Boulogne, and the impact of enclosures, seems convincing. Davies's ascription of such "*a priori*" and impracticable measures directly to commonwealth influence remains puzzling.[105] The most cursory reading of the many effusions of commonwealth idealists in this field yields an impression of a wish for discriminating but overwhelmingly humanitarian relief.

The law 3 & 4 Edw.VI, c.16 repealed such clauses "as tendeth to make vagabonds slaves." But traditional policy toward enclosures was temporarily reversed by a re-enactment of the permissive Statute of Merton, while taxes recently imposed on sheep were abolished. Latimer, in a sermon before the King in Lent 1550 was scathing about the first of these. Enactment that it was a felony to break down even unlawful enclosures, to enforce rights of common or right of way thereon, or even to meet in a number of twelve or over for the purpose of abating rents or the price of victual, surely still warrants Conyers Read's describing as infamous the session of Parliament from November 1549 to February 1550.[106] By now both Somerset and Hales (together with Smith) were imprisoned, and it seems almost perverse not to discern a setback to commonwealth ideology.

Yet under Northumberland continued lip service to such ideals continued to be paid. Proclamations prohibiting the export of victual (3 July 1550) and the spreading of rumors of coin abasement (24 July 1551) reiterated the "zeal and affection by his highness borne towards the commonweal, . . . having charge from God to see his commonwealth well governed." Several others condemned persons "minding only their own lucre without respect of the commonwealth." Indeed, an edict of 11 May 1551 pictured the "good purposes of the King's majesty with his council, travailing to do the commonwealth good," while that "Ordering Destruction of Seditious Bills against Privy Council" (20 May 1551) deplored such attacks as "defacing their well-doings in the commonwealth."[107] One wonders whether service to the commonweal had become something of a factional propaganda weapon! Certainly the commonwealth literature by now betrayed bitter despair and utter disillusionment about Northumberland, well illustrated in Crowley's *Fable of Philargyrie The Great Gigant* (1551) and in the anonymous *Respublica* (1553), with its sharply implied contrast with what was hoped-for from the reign of Mary Tudor.

During that reign, of course, the religious issue became dominant in quite a different direction. Interestingly, a clause in an early statute declares it "most necessary in every *Christian Commonwealth* [my italics], to provide that Tranquillity and Peace may be preserved amongst the People, and specially in Holy Church." The Proclamation "Announcing Injunctions for Religion" on 4 March 1554 contains an explicit assertion of the *moral* duty of government, in "remembering our duty to Almighty God to be to foresee as much as in us is may be that all virtue and godly living should be embraced." But perhaps most strikingly Erasmian in tone are the words of the preamble to the very first statute of Mary's reign, asserting that "the State of every King, Ruler and Governor of any Realm, Dominion or Commonalty, standeth and consisteth more assured by the Love and Favour of the Subjects toward their Sovereign Ruler and Governor, than in the Dread and Fear of Laws made with rigorous Pains."[108] In similar vein, Thomas North's introduction to his translation of Antonio de Guevara's *The Diall of Princes,* which he dedicated to Mary in 1557, repeated the principle of devotion to the commonweal—together with the Erasmian precept that "the prince that for his common wealth taketh care, hath not one moment of an hour quiet," for "even as by the yard, the merchant measureth all his ware; so by the life of the Prince, is measured the whole common weal."[109]

Such words would have sounded hollow to many of the most prominent of Edwardian commonwealth idealists—such as Latimer, Ridley, Hooper, Bradford, and Cranmer—who endured martyrdom for their doctrinal beliefs. John Hales fled abroad, as did Bishop Ponet, who produced in exile a supremely important political tract. Yet although its expression in a matrix of Protestant religio-social idealism is clearly not to be expected, the reign of Mary Tudor was not devoid of continued concern with economic problems. The continuity in office of some who professed commonwealth ideals is exemplified by Cecil and by Smith. It was to Cecil that a London merchant, William Lane, had dispatched an analysis of the effects of coinage debasement in 1551, while a projected bill for conversion of pasture to tillage had been entrusted to him a year later. In Mary's Parliament of 1555, two bills designed to check enclosures were handed to him after their first reading.[110] Sir Thomas Smith's continued interest led, circa 1554, to his memorandum "For the Understanding of the Exchange." As for actual regulatory legislation, in respect of ensuring proper standards of manufacture Robert Tittler points to 1 & 2 P and M, c.7 (on Retail Trade) and the "Weavers' Act" of 1555 (2 & 3 P and M, c.11) as important measures, and indeed describes 4 & 5 P and M, c.5, "touching the making of Woollen Cloths" as "perhaps the most comprehensive cloth-making legislation of the century."[111] Finally, whatever other errors were made by Mary, compared with those of preceding Tudors, her hands were clean of monetary debasement. One attempt to gainsay such recognition by citing the "spike years" of 1555–1556 for grain prices betrays a surprising confusion of "monetary" and of "real" factors in those years of spectacularly disastrous harvests.

Occasionally, the statutes deplore such as act "to the great Detriment of the Commonwealth" and in one instance those who pursue "their private Wealths and Commodity [ignoring] the Commonwealth of the Handicraftsmen, and other poor People." One Marian Proclamation confirms the impression that the concept was also used for propaganda purposes: the edict of 27 January 1554, "Offering Pardon to Supporters of Wyatt," condemns those who "under the pretense of the benefit of the commonwealth of the realm" intend only "the confusion of this commonwealth."[112] Certainly one must reiterate that it is inaccurate simply to *identify* commonwealth ideology with Protestant religious ideals. Thus, the anonymously written morality, *Respublica,* performed in London at Christmas 1553, is specifically concerned with the economic and social effects of the misgovernment of the previous few years. In particular, the oppression of the poor commons by such characters as Insolence, Avarice, and Adulation is specifically related not only to the debasement of the coinage but also to recent systematic raids upon the lands and incomes of the bishops. In a piece of supreme irony, the decay of Christian conduct that has allegedly followed misgovernment is attributed *not* to any failure to live up to Protestant social ideals—as it is by such as Fish, Brinklow, and Crowley—but to the evil side effects of doctrinal innovation, which had been identified by Erasmus himself as severing a crucially important link between faith and works.[113]

Objectives of Government

The continuity of commonwealth ideology into the reign of Elizabeth I will concern us in the next chapter; but Professor S. T. Bindoff's description of the "Considerations delivered to the Parliament 1559" as "conservatively, even reactionarily, paternalistic in outlook"[114] suggests an issue of considerable relevance. That is, whether the midcentury had seen a change in balance away from inherited notions toward some concept of *innovative* governmental action. Undoubtedly, some beliefs remained constant: the maintenance of social stability, embodied in the organic analogy of society; the preservation of equity, always eschewing equality; and the paramount duty of government to take all necessary action. But there is also some evidence of a challenge to the rigidly hierarchical constituent of social stability, of appeals to government for innovative or even permissive action in agriculture, industry, and commerce, along with a counter-suggestion that there were limits to any governmental duty to act as the moral and social conscience of the commonwealth.

The greatest single field of appeal to the godly prince to protect traditional standards was that of agriculture. If the *extent* to which enclosure occurred has been questioned, there can surely be no dispute about the recurrent outcry against sheep farming, evictions, misuse of commons, and the evocatively termed rack-renting. "Overall" statistics mask the impact of enclosure largely concentrated in the open-field corn-growing heartland of England. The alleged naïveté of "moralizing sermonizers" is perhaps equalled by acceptance either of the complete accuracy of recorded statistics or of the effective protection realistically achievable in the Common Law Courts to the aggrieved tenant or user of the commons. In Heywood's morality, *The Spider and the Flie,* the first-named points to the theoretical protection of the law of "copyholders"; but the wretched Fly's rejoinder that "the law is ended . . . as folk are friended" has the ring of truth.[115] The impression that there was a very real problem during these decades was shared by government itself, as the actions of Wolsey, Cromwell, and Somerset abundantly demonstrate.

Nor were the protests always muddle-headed: the subjects of complaint included extortionate entry fines, rack-renting, engrossing of farms, and over-stocking of the commons. John Hales himself instructed the Enclosure Commissioners of 1549 as to "what is meant by this word inclosure. . . . It is meant thereby, when any man hath taken away and enclosed any other men's commons, or hath pulled down houses of husbandry, and converted the lands from tillage to pasture." Action was solicited on frankly religious grounds, as in Tyndale's plea that "Christian landlords be content with their rent and old customs. . . . Let them not take in their commons, neither make parks nor pastures of whole parishes," or in the *Primer* of Edward VI which pleaded that "they, remembering themselves to be thy tenants, may not rack, and stretch out the rents of their houses and lands; nor yet take unreasonable fines and incomes."[116] Naturally, the reaction of authority derived not only from such pressures but also from apprehension of the alleged effects of depopulating enclosure in terms of a diminishing food supply, a weakened realm, and outbreaks of rebellion.

Fears of destruction of the balance of the economy and of spreading unemployment also motivated attitudes in craft and industrial matters. In general, moralizing here deplored increasing commercialization and what were seen as its baleful spinoffs: a swallowing up of the craftsman by the capitalist employer, excessive profits, refusal to accept the enforcement of standards, and plain dishonesty in manufacturing and marketing practices. Governmental action was usually designed to protect the guilds and their traditional approach as well as the corporate towns within which control was easier than in the countryside. Of course, most of the realities of economic development in an expanding market were pulling the other way, against controls. Yet between 1509 and 1559 over forty statutes concerned with the maintenance of manufacturing standards were enacted; enforcement of such measures was entrusted to the guilds or to such local officers as JPs or mayors. For along with protection of the guilds went a wish to arrest the decay of some older corporate towns and to check the shift of some industry into the countryside. Occasionally, governmental intervention sought directly to fend off unemployment, as when Sir Thomas Audley encountered clothmakers who threatened that enforcement of certain standards would cause them to cease production. Audley in turn warned them "that they might perform the Act if they had good will and zeal to the commonwealth, and if by obstinacy or wilfulness they left their clothmaking, any murmur or sedition among the people for want of work would be laid to their charge."[117]

Suspicion about standards of manufacture was matched by that concerning the greed and deceits involved in the marketing of products. Despite its dismal record of successive debasements of the coinage in 1526, 1542–44, 1545, 1546, 1549, and 1551, government was concerned almost throughout with the need to control prices. An almost medieval obsession with the alleged maneuvres of men who bought to sell again was fully shared by authority. All too obviously, a widening market increased both the opportunity for exploiting the gap between producer and consumer and the difficulty of enforcing any controls. Again, repeated appeals were made, as in Bishop Hooper's cry to Cecil in 1551: "For the love and tender mercy of God, persuade and cause some order to be taken upon the price of things." Nor will it do to dismiss such appeals as the futile complaints of those who cried out against realities. For there is massive evidence that the government shared the fears engendered and also the belief that it could and should take effective action. Persistent attempts to regulate both prices and the behavior of middlemen are recorded in scores of royal proclamations as well as in Statutes of the Realm. Grain, meat and other foodstuffs, wood, and coal are all included as causing concern.[118]

Finally, in this brief sampling of governmental responses to appeals to enforce traditional values, I revert to a constant preoccupation of commonwealth writers, the concept of the social hierarchy. Wolsey's attempt to preserve sartorial distinctions understandably increased the unpopularity of one who was himself derided in the scurrilously anticlerical *Burial of the Mass* as "Carter of York, the Vile butcher's son." Cromwell's effort to make sumptuary legislation "an instrument of social control" provoked a similar response. But Henry VIII himself took an interest in instigating the statute of 1533 that condemned "excess in apparel" as tending to "the subversion of good and politic order in knowledge and distinction of people according to their estates preeminences dignities and degrees."[119] Later proclamations, statutory enactment under Edward VI, and indeed continued efforts under Elizabeth I, attest this constant concern.

Yet oddly enough, although admittedly by minority voices, one also finds a questioning of whether the preservation of social stability does in fact require a total prohibition of social mobility. No less a person than Cranmer, dismissing as a criterion of admission to the grammar school at Canterbury the assertion that only gentlemen's children are "meet to have knowledge of government and rule in the commonwealth," remarks first that he has "seen no small number of them very dull," and secondly that many gentry had their origins "from a base and low parentage," being elevated by God to high authority. Ten years later Sir John Cheke, exhorting the Norfolk rebels, used the prospect of social betterment as an argument against egalitarianism: "for many mean men's children do come honestly up."[120] With considerable ingenuity, Morison's *Remedy for Sedition* (1536) coupled a stern assertion of the duty of obedience to legitimate authority and an avoidance of Anabaptist-type equality with an advocacy of the principle of careers open to talent. Both, he urged, are related to the criterion of loyal and efficient service of Crown and commonwealth. Scorning the complaints of the Pilgrims of Grace against base-born councillors, he credits Henry VIII himself with wishing "all his subjects to contend, who may obtain most qualities . . . and this only to be the way to promotion, and here nobility to consist." Elsewhere he asks rhetorically "were there ever more rewards for virtue?"[121] One need not take all this too seriously to recognize a clear realization of the fact of social mobility. While still a minority view, it signifies a changing assessment of this aspect of society. Insofar as there was to be more social mobility, and yet the fear of class hatred as leading to social dissolution was to be allayed, then reliance on the secular power as guarantor of stability must increase as reverence for a divinely ordained and rigid social hierarchy diminished.

By midcentury, the concept of governmental duties toward the commonwealth was increasingly subject to innovatory notions in regard not to the social distribution but to the production of wealth. These included pleas for a *relaxation* of traditional attempts at regulation both of production and of marketing, but also appeals for direct governmental help in introducing and nurturing new sources of production and employment, often as "projects." One has noticed skepticism as to the efficacy of a proclamation concerning cheese and butter: for Nature will never "consent that a pennyworth of new shall be sold for a farthing." The offending edict was cancelled, as had earlier been "An Act for the true making of Pynnes" within a session of its enactment, because of great "scarcity of Pins within this Realm." Such efforts were subject to the charge of creating the very dearth they were designed to mitigate.[122] Thus, Arthur B. Ferguson has pointed to the occasional realisation of a need for "compromise between a realistic recognition of the dynamism inherent in economic life and the conservative ideal of a static social organism," leading indeed to "an appreciation of the role of government in society that is more nearly modern than medieval." Equally indicative of changing ideas about the economic dimension of the commonweal were the urgent pleas for governmental support of specific projects. Admittedly, this was often special pleading by private interests. But beyond dispute the language of the commonwealth was often successfully deployed. Discussing "the Constructive Phase of Projects, 1540–1580," Joan Thirsk is quite specific: "Nor should we underrate the effectiveness of pamphlets and propaganda, the exhortations of the Commonwealthmen, and the official prodding of politicians and Privy Councillors in establishing projects."[123]

Considerations of security and power were also involved. In particular, the deliberate fostering of native manufacture of consumer goods would both create employment and increase the wealth of the realm. Yet the present writer would not dissent from Dr. Thirsk's admonition that such "plans for economic development should not be separated from the social ideals which underlay them, and which forged strong links between Commonwealthmen and the projectors."[124] A persistent advocate of the encouragement of "works of husbandry to increase plenty of victuals and the works of artificiality to increase plenty of money" during Cromwell's era had been Clement Armstrong. The *Discourse of the Common Weal* itself contained many pointers toward a program for projects. Even more specifically, in 1553 William Cholmeley sought royal support for his scheme for dyeing cloth in England. Contemporaneously, Somerset himself, and then Cecil after his master's downfall, patronized a short-lived establishment of Walloons at Glastonbury, to encourage diversification by the introduction of the weaving of lighter types of cloth.[125]

Citing an undated list of industries considered most suitable for employing the poor, Joan Thirsk conjectures that "because of that last phrase, it may be associated with the Commonwealthmen and perhaps with the period of Somerset's rule."[126] This indeed reminds us of one aspect of social policy that may well illustrate best of all how traditional beliefs evolved in response not only to changing economic circumstances but also to ideological, and especially religious, developments: the problem of poverty and of poor relief. Here the shift in emphasis away from indiscriminate almsgiving as a personal testimony of Christian faith, toward an advocacy of systematic provision for the poor and indeed elimination of the causes of poverty within an efficiently ordered commonwealth, was very gradual. Even Crowley could still write "though the beggars be wicked, thou shalt have thy reward," and the "Homily of Almsdeeds and Mercifulness Toward the Poor and Needy" still remind the rich that the poor man was the way to heaven.[127] Yet the notion of poverty as an affliction willed by God was increasingly supplemented if not supplanted not only by fear of those who were sturdy vagabonds by choice but also by the realization that a great deal of contemporary poverty had identifiable causes that might well evoke resentment and disorder. This transition in thinking was accelerated by the impact both of Erasmian humanism and of the social teachings of the emergent Protestant churches.

Among the crucial features of what occurred, the adoption of the ecclesiastical unit of the parish as the regional vehicle of Poor Relief is symbolic both of the retention of the idea of charity as a religious duty and of the supervision of its application by temporal authority. Next, the gradual shift in balance through successive statutes from a simple exhortation to almsgiving as a Christian duty toward the device of compulsorily levied poor rates is again indicative. So, too, is the evolution of a systematic and discriminating administration of the funds thus made available. Finally, although a substantive element of punishment of the wilful, obdurate, and disorderly is always present, the later emergence of a recognition of the duty and of the practicability of providing employment for those who are both able and willing to work but lack the opportunity, completes a logical progression. This takes until the second half of the sixteenth century; but the commonwealth literature from the 1530s onward anticipates, sometimes to an impractically idealist degree, most later developments.

As early as 1530 draft poor law proposals formerly attributed to William Marshall, but more recently claimed for the lawyer Christopher St. Germain, indicated an early grasp of the need for systematic state action that was so prominent in commonwealth-type thinking. Indeed, Guy contends that St. Germain's proposals for "quite astonishing legislation for large-scale public welfare, and his creative originality gives him a clear claim to be named true custodian of the Tudor Commonwealth." Included was a proposal to tackle unemployment through a scheme of public works, such as roads and harbors, fortresses and water-courses.[128] Henry Brinklow and Simon Fish concurred with "certain bishops . . . of the new learning" described by Cranmer as urging that at least some of the confiscated church wealth should go to "the founding of hospitals, where poor and impotent people should have been sufficiently provided for with physicians and surgeons which should have ministered physic and surgery freely, not only to them but also to all other poor folk within this realm."[129] Starkey, Crowley and Latimer were as one in identifying a duty of government to ensure the provision of full and useful employment. Thomas Becon, contemplating the spectacle of a daily increase in the number of beggars, regretted that society "do not only not provide any means to exile and banish this *absurdity* [my italics] out of the commonweal, but also suffer them to live comfortless."[130] Even the much-condemned statute of 1547—of which Slack remarks that it was neither a paper plan imposed by government nor yet a case of "allowing social theorists to have their heads"[131]—included the last attempt to grapple with the provision of employment for the adult poor before the 1570s. A statute of 1555, while introducing weekly collections for the relief of the poor, also reflects a temporary reversion in Mary's reign toward a Catholic attitude that begging was not necessarily evil or a subject of shame in its provision that "a poor Man licensed to beg shall wear a Badge on his Breast and Back openly."[132] Finally, it is worth observing that municipal schemes foreshadowed many principles of later enactments. A declaration addressed to the Privy Council by the citizens of London in 1552 asserted that the solution lay in "making some general provision of work, wherewith the willing poor may be exercised; and whereby the froward, strong and sturdy vagabond may be compelled to live profitably to the commonwealth."[133] This was to be followed a few years later by the establishment of the Bridewell institution, a model of many other "Houses of Correction."

One must not conclude this sketch of attitudes and policies toward the social and economic aspects of the commonwealth without noting, with the usual wisdom of hindsight, that certain of the objectives urged upon and sometimes shared by the Crown and its ministers were sometimes contradictory—as in the preservation of the guilds alongside industrial expansion and innovation. Moreover, not everyone agreed upon this burgeoning responsibility of government. Hugh Latimer might indeed cry out "for God's sake make some promoters," defined as "men of godly discretion, wisdom and conscience, to promote [that is, inform upon] transgressors, as rent-raisers, oppressors of the poor, extortioners, bribers, usurers."[134] But

I have already cited Stephen Gardiner's derision of what he saw as the attempt of his Protestant enemy Martin Bucer to burden temporal power with a duty of enforcement of Christian precepts in social and economic affairs, which he believed should remain the province of the church. Yet Gardiner's was a minority voice. Most of his contemporaries, Christian humanist as well as Protestant religio-social idealist, in reply to the question "Am I my brother's keeper?" would have answered "Yes!"

Meanwhile, in his concern with potential disturbances of the commonwealth, Gardiner's was far from being a minority voice. In turning now to political aspects of mid-Tudor ideology, some crucial touchstones may be identified. First, the voice of Erasmus rather than that of Machiavelli enunciated accepted canons of behavior in the exercise of power. Admittedly, Machiavellian touches have been identified in Morison, in William Thomas, and in Gardiner himself. But conventionally the exercise of political authority was thought of primarily in terms of religious accountability and social obligation. Power that was held in trust from God must be used for the good of society, itself defined in terms of the well-being of the prince's subjects. These in turn were bound by a paramount duty of obedience. The prince was accountable to God; the subject was accountable to God's image in his ruler. Significantly, mid-Tudor discussion of a potential breakdown of such obligations was almost always cast in terms of social apprehension rather than in that of the unthinkable notion of political participation by the commons. And linked with the specter of social subversion was that of religious heresy.

This virtually inextricable involvement of religious with political thinking can hardly be overemphasised. When, in tracing the political aspects of commonwealth ideology, one encounters a questioning of some of its traditional assumptions, it will be within the context of *religious* developments. Essentially, I shall be concerned not with "political rights" in any modern sense at all, but with the notion of "good order and obedience" as ordained by God, as the very basis of the commonwealth itself. Richard Morison's *Exhortation* in 1539 declared that "obedience undoubtedly is the knot of all common weals, this broken they must needs run all headlong to utter destruction." The *Book of Homilies* of 1547 was typical in its insistence that "the violence and injury that is committed against authority is committed against God, the common weal, and the whole realm." But the divinely sanctioned nature of royal authority had two sides. Tyndale was clear that "the law is God's and not the king's. The king is but a servant to execute the law of God, and not to rule after his own imagination." In the long run the notion thus emerged that the prince might be accountable not only to God in an afterlife but also to and through God's agents in this! But in mid-Tudor England the message, overwhelmingly, was that "Christ taught us plainly that even the wicked rulers have the power and authority from God."[135]

The interaction of political with religious issues is exemplified in the impact in the 1530s of the Breach with Rome upon accepted attributes of kingship. Cromwell's Injunctions to the Clergy included an admonition to preach "that the king's power is within his dominion the highest potentate or power under God." The transition in addressing the monarch from the designation "Your Grace" to that of "Your Majesty" and then even "Your Sacred Majesty" reflects in part at least the increased prestige deriving from Henry VIII's assumption of the headship of the church in England. Skinner dates from this step the royal claim to be regarded as the sole object of a subject's political allegiance. The basis of Shakespeare's later allusion to the divinity that "doth hedge about an anointed king" was surely established at this time. Such allegiance is combined with commonwealth terminology in the assertion of a royal proclamation in 1536 that "there is nothing more odious to God nor more pernicious and hurtful to the commonwealth than the contempt and inobedience of people against their sovereign lord."[136]

Naturally, the reality of the exercise of power involved not only the prince but also his under-officers. Here again, a two-way obligation applied. It became the prince to choose as his ministers and other servants those who would be faithful both to him and to the rightful expectations of his people. The influential writings of Erasmus were particularly insistent upon this aspect of the duties of kingship. But frequency of endorsement of such views was equaled by that of complaints of the failure of magistrates faithfully to perform their duties. Thus, in a society where local power in general equated with ownership of land it is naïve to look for meticulous administration of anti-enclosure legislation. Accordingly, William Baldwin, in *A Myrroure For Magistrates* (1559), echoed an ominous caveat anticipated by Cranmer in his remark that "when kings and chief rulers suffer their under officers to misuse their subjects, and will not hear nor remedy their people's wrongs when they complain, then suffereth God the Rebel to rage."[137]

The question of rebellion will concern us later. Meanwhile, what *were* the justifiable expectations of the subject? Put plainly, even in the most humanitarian type of commonwealth literature the subject had but one fundamental right: the right *to be governed well*. The passive voice is rigorously indicative. The notion of participation by the lower orders in the political process did not occur to the Tudor mind. This right to be governed well was itself conceived of almost totally in social and economic terms. An expression of popular protest if this ideal was betrayed was sympathetically endorsed in many a pamphlet and sermon. But any attempt to oppose or usurp the power of established authority was anathema. Indeed such action was thought of not as an attempt to participate in the political process but as designed to destroy it. Anarchy was held to be the natural aspiration of the commons.

Starkey was in no doubt that "the people in every common weal be rude and ignorant, having of them selves small light of judgement, but ever in simplicity, as sheep follow the herd, so follow they their masters." Sometimes the pastoral vein was cast aside, and the vulgar people, the rude multitude, were cast as "a beast of many heads, which doeth nothing as reason and right judgement would."[138] But perhaps the starkest expression of the contempt and the fear engendered by the lower orders is in William Thomas's Machiavellian discussion, written for Edward VI, of "whether it be better for a commonwealth that the power be in the nobility or in the commonalty":

> Neither do I mean, that for the dangers rehearsed, the commons should be so kept down, as the wretched commons of some other countries be. But I would their discipline and education should be such, that the only name of their prince should make them to tremble.... For if they have but so much liberty as to talk of the prince's causes, and of the reason of laws, at once they shew their desire not to be ruled: whereof groweth contempt, and consequently disobedience, the mother of all errors.[139]

Thomas is perhaps extreme in thus dismissing the plaintive bleat of "People," a character in the anonymously written *Respublica:* "ye'll give folk leave to think?" But he represents mainstream thinking on the axiomatic duty of obedience. This the corporeal analogy was supremely suited to convey. Sir John Cheke followed his admonition to the rebels of 1549 that as "the child is bound to the private father... be we not all bound to the commonwealth's father?," with the obvious analogy: "If the members of a natural body all follow the head, shall not the members of the political body all obey the king?" Earlier, in *A Remedy For Sedition* (1536), Sir Richard Morison had likened realms without laws to forests of wild beasts, for "when every man will rule, who shall obey?" It follows then that "they rule that best can, they be ruled that most it becometh so to be." And certainly, he observed elsewhere, "it far passeth Cobbler's craft" to discuss affairs of state. Thomas Cranmer was in no way exceptional in stating that "though the magistrates be evil, and very tyrants against the commonwealth, and enemies to Christ's religion; yet the subjects must obey *in all worldly things.*"[140] But the qualification here italicized is crucially important, and will eventually open the door to a very different approach.

The publication dates of several sources cited remind us that they often appeared in response to specific outbreaks of disorder or rebellion. Christopher Morris did not go too far in attributing to Tudor propagandists "an almost hysterical attitude towards rebellion." Morison may well have blustered that "God hath joined with the majesty of a king such a fear" that successful treason was unthinkable, and have identified the visitation of the north country with a pestilence as divine retribution for the recent rising, but in truth Tudor society went in constant dread of insurrection and its consequences. Colorful recollection of events prior to its establishment was an ever-handy weapon for publicists of the Tudor dynasty. The preamble to the statute of 1534 "for the establishment of the King's succession" exemplifies the fear of a reversion to conjectured anarchy.[141]

Nor were examples always either retrospective or theoretical. Apart from the news of such dreadful events in Germany as the Peasants' Revolt (1525) and the Anabaptist occupation of Münster (1535), mid-Tudor England was to yield its own crop of serious uprisings: the Pilgrimage of Grace in Yorkshire and Lincolnshire in 1536, and the Rising in the West and Ket's Rebellion in Norfolk in 1549. After a very real possibility of civil war was twice averted, first by Somerset's decision not to fight for his power in 1549 and then by the total collapse of Northumberland's attempt to do so after enthroning a puppet queen in 1553, Queen Mary was herself confronted by Wyatt's Rebellion, which reached the gates of London itself a year later. Even the much-hailed accession of Elizabeth was to be followed by the Rising of the Northern Earls in 1569.

Nicholas Udall's *Answer to the articles of the commoners of Devonshire and Cornwall,* in 1549, includes a measured exposition of the case against any purportedly justifiable revolt:

> Were there never so many private griefs . . . yet if every private person should be officer for himself . . . then where is a king without whose power no common weal can long prosper? Where is the force of laws without which no policy can flourish? Where is the authority of magistrates without whom the public peace and tranquillity cannot be preserved?

An exhortation to all menne to take hede and beware of rebellion, written by the Catholic John Christopherson, chaplain to Mary Tudor, in 1554, is remarkably similar in its ideas and approach, and sometimes even in its imagery, to the earlier works of Cranmer and of Cheke. The message that social dissolution will benefit no one emerged in very different form in John Heywood's *The Spider and the Flie* two years later. The Ant (the sage observer in this allegory) enunciates the most cogent of reasons why the Flies (the commons) must beware of insurrection:

> Flies have had ever cause to mislike war most
> Whoever had the right, the flies the field lost.
> To one score spiders slain, flies twenty score,
> And much of their offspring lost for evermore.

But what if they should win? Why then,

> When flies have killed spiders that stay the rude rout,
> Then fly against fly common cut-throat most stout;

and social anarchy ensues.[142]

Thus the catchphrase *Vox populi, vox Dei* was interpreted quite literally. To voice a protest was one thing; but for the people to take into their own hands the "rod of correction" was quite another. The reluctant understanding occasionally extended to those whose action was provoked by unendurable economic destitution stopped well short of condonation. Morison was starkly realist in his concession that extreme poverty almost always entailed disorder. But even the more humanitarian Hooper discerned a mixture of motives in depicting how "the poor man, partly provoked by necessity and need, and partly of unchristian hatred and disdain he hath at his neighbour's wealth and prosperity, conspireth [to oppose] magistrates and superior powers, take away and usurp every man's goods, he careth not how." Beyond question, this endemic nightmare of Tudor England, that reaction to economic distress might burst out in rebellion, became reality most often in the middle decades of the century. A letter to the Emperor in July 1549 relates how the peasantry are assembling in various places, with growing sympathy for their just cause. As yet, they commit no violence on any person, but "say that the violent usurpation of their rights committed by the nobles compels them to seek some remedy for the extreme need in which they now are, having no pastures for their cattle and sheep as they once had, and many being reduced to a diet of bread and water. . . .[143]

The unknown author of a perceptive tract addressed to Somerset himself in 1549 pointed to unemployment, poverty, and hunger as inevitably occasioning disorder, for

> surely there is nothing that will sooner move the people unto Sedition than the dearth of victual. What fair means or what threatening, what strait Laws or what weapons can pacify or keep quiet the hungry multitude. . . . For what Faith and allegiance will those men observe towards their prince and governor which have their children Famished at home for want of meat. For the people for the most part do impute the cause of Dearth unto the Rulers.[144]

A powerful if melodramatic statement of the factors that allegedly drove men to rebellion—though he himself would not condone it—is that of Robert Crowley in *The Way to Wealth, wherein is plainly taught a most present Remedy for Sedicion,* written in 1550 and printed a year later. The poor, says Crowley, would impute sedition to "the great farmers, the grasiers, the rich butchers, the men of law, the merchants, the gentlemen. . . . Yea, men that live as though there were no God at all! . . . Cormorants, greedy gulls; yea, men that would eat up men, women and children, are the causes of Sedition!" Raising of rents and entry fines, and enclosure of commons in the countryside are equalled in rapacity by the greed of landlords in the towns. Neither custom nor statute can restrain such oppression. "No remedy therefore, we must needs fight it out, or else be brought to the like slavery that the French men are in! These idle bellies will devour all that we shall get by our sore labour in our youth, and when we shall be old and impotent, then shall we [be] driven to beg. . . ." Better therefore to die like men.[45]

Yet as a rule, total submission even in face of extreme injustice was enjoined, as by Tyndale, who counselled the giving of "now a capon, now a pig, now a goose" to oppressive bailiffs or landlords. Thomas Becon, while conceding that "the belly hath no ears," still advised the poor that they should "rather starve and die for hunger, as poor Lazar did, than to trouble a commonweal . . . rather take that cross patiently." The Catholic Christopherson drew an equally clear distinction: those "oppressed with taxes, and tributes, with polling and pilling, with rents raised, and with pastures enclosed: such perhaps have cause to complain, but no cause at all to make rebellion."[146] Indeed, during the crisis of 1549 even Cranmer could tone down humanitarian sympathy with the conjecture that "the chief authors of all these tumults be idle and naughty people, which nothing have, nor nothing or little will labour to have." Certainly, the evidence of several proclamations against "Movers of Sedition and False Rumours" suggests that government was genuinely apprehensive of the danger from agitators and "runagates."[147]

What inspired the greatest dread was not the quite unreal notion of any democratic control or exercise of power but the more frightening specter of social dissolution. In face of this the speculative humanist was soon replaced by the practical politician in the writings of More when he sketched the danger from such as behave "with contempt of God and all good men, and obstinate rebellious mind against all laws, rule, and governance, with arrogant presumption to meddle with every man's substance, with every man's land, and every man's matter nothing pertaining to them." Not only property rights but also the whole concept of due degree and order stood threatened by claims to have all in common. Crowley, despite his eagerness to put the case for the commons, was clear that in the last resort "the devil should never have persuaded thee that thou mightest revenge thine own wrong! . . . To revenge wrongs is, in a subject, to take and usurp the office of a king, and consequently, the office of God."[148]

This appeal to religion is crucially indicative. Even the most radical-sounding of commonwealth idealists, despite their scathing indictments of contemporary ills and of the greed and failure of those responsible, never sought to change the structure of society by condoning rebellious action. In the last analysis, the rebels themselves and those whose oppression provoked their insurrection stood condemned by reference to the same organic ideal. Thus, in order to discover any attempt at the justification of passive or of active disobedience of lawfully constituted authority, one must turn to an issue still held to include and indeed to transcend all mundane political, social, and economic considerations: that of religious faith. Our final task in this chapter is therefore to consider this supremely important dimension of commonwealth thought.

The teachings of religion underpinned all the assumptions of society and its governance. The pulpit utterances of preachers and also—for literate society—their often well-read printed exhortations reflected and helped to mould much of public opinion. Government itself was keenly aware of the propaganda value of such voices and equally sensitive to the dangerous and inflammatory potential of allegedly misguided religious oratory. The conservative-minded Stephen Gardiner could even brand Erasmus's *Paraphrases* as potentially subversive. All this derives from the continuance into mid-

Tudor England of the notion of a unitary society. Church and commonwealth were still considered to be co-extensive, membership of one entailing membership of the other. This is clearly indicated in a royal proclamation of 8 July 1546, "Prohibiting Heretical Books," which declares the monarch's resolve "to purge his commonwealth of such pernicious doctrine." Early in the reign of Edward VI, an edict "Prohibiting Unlicensed Preaching" expressed a determination "that one and a most godly conformity might be had throughout all this realm."[149]

Any concept of a church as a voluntary association, limited in its membership and in some sense "withdrawn from the world," whose relations with the temporal power were at best matters for negotiation, lay in the future—though not far distant. Already, in Robert Barnes's *Supplication* a distinction was drawn between "the whole multitude of the people" and the true church of the faithful, who were saved.[150] This line of thinking was to go much further. But as yet the great body of accepted opinion considered that the subject of the realm was a member of the church. What was taught by that church, in turn, was not a subject for debate—or at least not by ordinary, untutored people. The modern notion that the origin and content of religious faith, or even the very existence of any authoritative source thereof, are freely debateable would have scandalized mid-Tudor England. What was then at stake was possession of the authority that purported to be the custodian of revealed religion. It was still thought possible to identify definitive religious truth and then, this once established, to prescribe and indeed enforce its acceptance by the members both of Church and of commonwealth.

In relating religious to social and economic developments two things stand out: the striking continuity between the teachings of the Catholic Church and those of Protestantism and incipient Puritanism; and the narrower but frighteningly deeper concern lest religious innovation and heresy entail a threat to many of the assumptions of the established social order. Outspoken preaching, in the tradition of *Piers Plowman,* against economic malpractice and social injustice was nothing new. But it now became of greater importance, and was subject to more critical scrutiny, against a background not only of accelerated economic and social change but also of doctrinal and administrative innovation within religion itself. Ultimately, the impact of such innovation was to challenge a fundamental assumption of a unitary society. But that effect was both fiercely resisted and for long delayed. The loyally Henrician Morison asserted the political unity ordained by God in every Christian commonwealth. The traditional association "of true obedience" in church and state was defended, from Gardiner to Richard Hooker's assertion toward the end of the century that "the Church and the commonwealth [are] one society." This position was maintained not only by Catholics and Anglicans but also by all the prophets of the Magisterial Reformation. Luther, Zwingli, and Calvin were as one in their appeal to the godly prince to enforce the true religious faith within his realm. Precise definitions might vary, but their identification of the true church with the commonwealth endured. So, too, did the plea to the godly ruler to enforce the moral, social, and economic values that their religious teachings entailed—as when Calvin urged Protector Somerset "to punish vice, and to reprove slanders," so that "the people be kept in good and honest discipline."[151]

Significantly, in this as in their doctrinal urgings, the English Protestants saw themselves not as innovators but as preaching a return to the purity of the truly Christian code of an earlier age. In Tyndale, Frith, Brinklow, Crowley, and Hooper, the organic interdependence of the members of the body politic, the belief in due degree and order, the ideal of measure, and the condemnation of any conscienceless pursuit of wealth reflected total continuity with the teachings of the Catholic Church. Over fifty years ago, M. M. Knappen identified these exemplars of an "early, semi-medieval phase of Puritanism."[152] Occasionally, Protestants were ready to condone social mobility, for individuals thus called by God, but usually their notion of one's calling or vocation was totally medieval. Or again, Bucer's advocacy of the rectitude of taking moderate interest won little support among mid-Tudor Protestants. On this issue, as on that of the gradual emergence of a more discriminating approach to the administration of poor relief, changing emphases do not correlate with any simple Catholic/Protestant doctrinal divide. Just as the cities of northern Italy had long evolved a far more sophisticated approach toward "usury," so now among the influential and innovatory writings on the relief of poverty were those of the Spanish Erasmian, Juan Luis Vives.[153]

Yet this general impression that continuity of teaching about social and economic relationships remained almost unaltered by doctrinal innovation, while its *efficacy* was often undermined by harsh realities, needs one important codicil. It was not always true of those most notorious representatives of the Radical Reformation, the Anabaptists. While it is quite unfair to ascribe to such "sectaries" a general wish to have all in common or to abolish the magistracy, a "lunatic fringe" did preach and even attempt to implement such notions. Their fellow-Protestants did not hesitate to condemn these

2: FIRST FLOWERING: THE MID-TUDOR COMMONWEALTH

extremists—whose ill-repute they rightly identified as a tar-brush to be used against their own position. Becon condemned "the jay-like janglers of God's word, and brainless babblers of the gospel," while Veron (translator of Zwingli's successor Bullinger) deplored those who sought in the Scriptures "but a carnal and fleshly liberty" that purportedly gave them license to defy temporal rulers and magistrates. Lever, picturesquely, referred to "clouds without any moisture of God's grace, tossed about with contrary winds of strange doctrine; trees passing summer time without any fruits of good works . . . wild waves of the sea frothing forth unshamefast brags, and wandering stars without constancy in judgement and opinion, [who] labour by wresting of the Scripture to pull themselves from under due obedience." Admittedly, to speak of having all things common in the sense of rendering all superfluity to the poor "doth derogate or take away nothing from the authority of rulers. But to will to have all things common, in such sort that idle lubbers . . . might take and waste the gains of labourers without restraint of authority, or to have like quantity of everything to be given to every man is under pretence to mend all, purposely to mar all."[154]

Lever's indignant denial that all this is but the evil fruit of the provision of the Scriptures in English echoes Tyndale's protest in *The Obedience of a Christian man:*

> Even so now (as ever) the most part seek liberty; they be glad when they hear the unsatiable covetousness of the spiritualty rebuked; . . . when tyranny and oppression is preached against; when they hear how kings and all officers should . . . seek no other thing save the wealth of their subjects; and when they hear that they have no such authority of God so to pill and poll as they do, . . . because the heads will not so rule, will they also no longer obey, but resist and rise against their evil heads, and one wicked destroyeth another. Yet is God's word not the cause of this, neither yet the preachers.[155]

'Liberty" is here employed in a pejorative sense (as also in the term "libertine"). But Tyndale's rebuttal did not satisfy such as Gardiner, whose *Answer to Bucer* (1541) contained a near-classic statement of the Catholic-conservative reaction to any free discussion of religio-social issues. He warned preachers "not to cite to the people such texts from Scripture, as not being brought forward in their proper place, or not being unfolded fully, beguile the people into the refusal of obedience." Assertions that "subjects are only entrusted to the prince's fostering care and protection, and are not subject to princes in any other way than for the sake of God" are not inherently false, "but they are spoken in such a way as to seem in favour of the people, and to tend to anarchy."[156]

This resolve to stifle discussion of dangerously radical political and social ideas is in full accord with Gardiner's limited concept of the functions of government within society that we encountered earlier. It also embodies a shrewd perception of precisely that gap in the defenses through which the flood of unwelcome development was to come. Others shared such apprehensions. Starkey had pointed to the danger from "unwise masters, foolish teachers of religion, indiscreet preachers" whose utterances might lead to "the ruin of all civil order . . . whereof good and true religion is the most stable and sure foundation." The realist politician Paget, deploring the disorders of 1549, wrote to Somerset urging that "society in a realm doth consist and is maintained by means of religion and law." What then might ensue when "the use of the old religion is forbidden by a law, and the use of the new is not yet printed in the stomachs of the eleven of twelve parts of the realm"? Indeed the final pages of Smith's *Discourse of the Common Weal* are devoted to the harmful effects of doctrinal controversy—which may well include "these uproars of the people."[157]

Before we turn, not to the detail of doctrinal controversy but to the circumstances in which it opened the door first to the advocacy of nonresistant disobedience and then to that of active resistance to commands seen as contrary to God's law, there is one other aspect of mid-Tudor religious developments that merits attention. The administrative and financial implications of what some would term the annexation of church power and possessions by Henry VIII had considerable economic and social significance. Former exaggerated estimates of the direct effects of monastic dissolutions upon enclosures and poor relief are now greatly discounted. But equally the Protestant idealist hopes both of sweeping doctrinal reform and of the socially ameliorative use of confiscated wealth were dashed. Instead, what often appeared as a lack of genuine religious zeal was accompanied by shameless misappropriation of ecclesiastical wealth under color of reformation. Disappointed hopes of the coming of a "godly order in Church and State" had led the "Puritan ecclesiast," Sir Francis Bigod, to rebel as early as 1537.[158] After the "Catholic Reaction" and the Six Articles of 1539 came the execution of Robert Barnes and of the great political hope of those who still looked for doctrinal and social reform, Thomas Cromwell. The literature and sermons of the following decade or so are filled with the bitterness of the commonwealth idealists. Brinklow contrasts the disposition of church wealth in England with "the godly and politic order of the

Christian Germans [who] put it to the use of the common wealth, and unto the provision of the poor." The anonymous author of *The prayse and commendacion of suche as sought comenwelthes* (circa 1548) asks the scathing if rhetorical question: "Who in these days are such oppressors, such grasiers, such shepherds, such enhancers of rents, such takers of incomes, as those which profess the Gospel?[159]

Yet despite such bitter chagrin, the early English Protestants preached nonresistance to legitimate authority. Rebellion against an anointed prince breached a fundamental assumption of society. But what if that prince should endeavor to subvert the religious truths upon which society itself was built? The reservation of a right to disobey commands that were against "the law of God" was always there beneath the surface. Its progressive emergence from the 1520s onward, first in passive then in active form, owed much more to circumstances than to doctrine. Thus while the exiled Catholic Pole was moving towards an advocacy of limited obedience, the Protestant Tyndale could only pray, at the point of martyrdom: "Lord, open the King of England's eyes." Yet Tyndale himself had written that "the king is but a servant to execute the law of God."[160] Thus, if a divinely appointed ruler might not be resisted, neither must his commands against God's law be obeyed. Christopher Morris rightly observed that Tyndale's stance should most properly be described as that of "Passive Disobedience"—a distinction borne out by later developments. Even the obdurate Hooper, while in no doubt that "if the higher powers command anything contrary to God's word, they should not be obeyed," was clear that this must be "without all violence, force or rebellion." His fellow martyr Hugh Latimer agreed that "I may refuse to obey with a good conscience yet for all that I may not rise up against the magistrates, nor yet make any uproar; for if I do so, I sin damnably. . . . Yet I may not obey their wicked laws to do them."[161]

Thus far it seems clear that the true subject may not, even for conscience sake, rebel against the ruler of the commonwealth. But while Hooper, Latimer, Cranmer, and others endured martyrdom for their principles, other Protestants—exiled during the reign of Mary Tudor—evolved a very different approach. This, while as yet severely circumscribed within the need to defend religious truth, was gradually to change the whole conception of the nature and duty of obedience within a commonwealth. Bishop Ponet's *Short Treatise of politike power, and of the true Obedience which subjectes owe to kynges and other ciuile Gouernours* (1556) has rightly been considered a seminal work, in some respects a precursor of that of John Locke. Since the exercise of politic power derived from God is subject to natural law then any claim, urges Ponet, to *absolute* power must be a usurpation. "Kings, princes, and other politic Governors, be subject to God's laws, and the politic laws of their countries." Such laws being the sinews of the body politic, extremes of racking or of shrinking must be avoided: "for too much maketh the governors to forget their vocation, and to usurp upon their subjects: too little breedeth a licentious liberty and maketh the people to forget their duty." Predictably, Ponet assigns these caps to papist and Anabaptist heads respectively.[162]

There follows the crucial assertion that, since rulers may err, "men ought to have more respect to their country than to their prince: to the common wealth, than to any one person. For the country and common wealth is a degree above the king." He is now ready to put and reply to the question: "Whether It Be lawful to depose an evil governor, and kill a tyrant?" Since rulers hold their authority of the people, and what is thus delegated may be revoked, it follows that "Kings, Princes and other governors, albeit they are the heads of a politic body, yet they are not the whole body. And though they be the chief members, yet they are but members: neither are the people ordained for them, but they are ordained for the people." Ponet follows this unexceptionable Erasmian declaration with a breathtakingly novel and audacious use of the corporeal analogy. Invoking the familiar point that a law of nature counsels the amputation of an incurable member lest it destroy the whole, he argues that "common wealths and realms may live, when the head is cut off, and may put on a new head."[163] Without forgetting the immediate circumstances of their expression, such views are of striking relevance not only to the immediate question of religious compliance but also to the wider theme of political obedience. Whereas Morison had expounded obedience to authority as the only safeguard of existing liberties and property rights against the "monster with many heads," Ponet would make a ruler's respect for at least certain designated rights into a condition of the continuance of his power. Perhaps Ponet was to Morison as, in the following century, Locke was to Hobbes.

In 1558 Christopher Goodman, John Knox's fellow exile in Geneva, published his *How Superior Powers Oght to be Obeyd*. In obvious sympathy with Ponet, he attacks any "preaching of unlawful obedience and yielding to ungoldy Rulers": for obedience which is against God is really disobedience. While the religious context of this assertion is equally clear, some sweeping consequences follow. Thus, "it appertaineth not only to the Magistrates and all other inferior officers to see that their Princes be subject to God's Laws, but *to the com-*

mon people also" (my italics). In pursuance of this duty, the commons "ought not to suffer all power and liberty to be taken from them, and thereby to become brute beasts, without judgement and reason, thinking all things lawful, which their Rulers do." Indeed, they "may lawfully punish their Magistrates as private persons transgressing the Lord's precepts." Nevertheless, despite the potentially revolutionary implications of what he wrote about a right of rebellion on *religio*-political grounds, Goodman, like Ponet before him, was adamant that these were the *only* grounds of such action. Ponet had deplored any "inward grudge, and secret malice between the members, that is, the Nobility and Commons," and attributed to traitorous papists any attempts to rouse the commons against their superiors. Goodman now laments the contrast between the people's readiness "to arm yourselves against your superiors, to defend your commons and earthly commodities with holden from you, by the greedy desire of new upstart gentlemen" and their culpable reluctance to do so in order to defend "spiritual possession."[164]

Clearly, William Turner, another exile for religion's sake, still spoke for them in his insistence that "the common people indeed, which is not indued with the spirit of God, is as it were a wild beast with many heads."[165] Indeed, to look ahead, on this issue of obedience within the commonweal one may discern two very different strands of thought that both derive from the crises and disorders of the midcentury. As far as religion is concerned, henceforth both Protestants and Roman Catholics will, when occasion demands, enunciate a right of active resistance, extending to tyrannicide, against a monarch's ungodly commands. Yet the point is fairly made that this was construed almost as a religious *duty* incumbent on the Christian subject, not as an individual *right* in any general sense. Conversely, in respect of the preservation of what were seen as the social and economic foundations of the commonwealth, and of property rights in particular, then *Vox populi, vox Dei* was to remain a very circumscribed notion. Popular action was thought all-too-likely to subvert, rather than to protect, the existing order!

There is therefore something of an irony in the fact that, in terms of what was expected of government toward the active furtherance of the social and economic well-being of the ordinary people, these decades had witnessed a genuine flowering of commonwealth idealism. Deriving in part from Erasmian humanism, taken up and nurtured by socially conscious early Protestantism, envisaged as a logical corollary of the assumption of the headship of the church by the temporal ruler, and given a special urgency by the contemporary conjunction of serious economic problems, the image of the mid-

Tudor commonwealth became a focus of discussion of and a vehicle for expression of social ideals in a way that was not equaled until the middle decades of the seventeenth century. As yet, there was still a near-consensus that only within and through the collectivity of church and Christian commonwealth could the individual achieve his full potential. In lamenting that "even so now (as ever) the most part seek Liberty," Tyndale was but enunciating the late-medieval assumption that, freed of constraints, the individual would reject all social and moral standards: there loomed side-by-side the dreaded heresy of Spiritual Liberty[166] and the specter of social dissolution. In this, yet again, he and his fellow Protestants conformed to the stance of the Catholic Church—which may be seen as "optimistic" only in the sense that salvation in the afterlife was at least open to all, *not* in its assessment of innate human potential, left to itself, within this world. The Christian commonwealth, as yet, alongside the Christian church, remained the custodian not of human "rights" or "liberties" in any modern sense but rather of the obligations of Christian conduct.

3
"The Dormant Years"?: Elizabeth I and the Early Stuarts

IN TERMS OF THE GENERAL DEVELOPMENT OF BRITISH POLITICAL AND SOcial thought, the description of the period between 1558 and circa 1639 as "the dormant years" is of course too sweeping. G. P. Gooch's assertion that "the accession of Elizabeth was the signal for the cessation of political thinking" now seems wide of the mark. The questing and insistent exploration of the social and economic implications of the ideal of the commonwealth that had characterized the mid-Tudor decades undoubtedly waned. Usage of the term "commonwealth" continued, as did appeals to the power and the duties of its ruler; but the parameters within which such discussion took place tended to contract. A near-moratorium ensued on any advocacy of the more extensive exercise of a ruler's functions in the pursuit of humanitarian social and economic reform. Professor Patrick Collinson has observed that discussion of " 'Commonwealth matters' . . . embraced a concern for the nation's security and destiny which was politico-religious rather than socio-economic," often in the context of a recurrent "Elizabethan Exclusion Crisis" in respect of Mary Stuart.[1] For the period as a whole, debate became more specifically politicized, apparently concerned with the mechanics of the exercise of power rather than with attributed social objectives—but with a continual intrusion of fundamentally important religious issues, and the ultimate emergence of basic problems pertaining to individual property rights.

The crucial long-term religio-political debate was between those who would stress the identity of church and commonwealth, or sometimes envisage a commonwealth of which the church was the religious and the state (a term increasingly in use) the temporal aspect, and those who rejected such assertions. Inevitably, this brought into question the derivation and extent of royal power first in religious and then, by implication, in political affairs. From this there derived at length not only the notion of religious toleration but also, more generally and perhaps indeed more notably, the "contractual" school of political thought. Not all of these issues were entirely new: Bishop Ponet's awkward questions cited earlier were quite soon to be taken up by Allen and Parsons, Romanist apologists, and his contention that a commonwealth may live after cutting off its own head and replace it with another was to constitute first a real danger and ultimately a sharp reality.

The organic analogy of society for long retained its popularity, occasionally with eccentric usage. But the emphasis was increasingly directed toward the position of the head of the body politic, in political and religious terms, rather than to the social and economic hopes and grievances of the members of that body. Broadly speaking, discussion of the commonwealth does become predominantly politicized, with little evidence of any speculative analysis of the social order. Those optimistic *socio*-political expectations that had flourished in the mid century decades, nurtured at least in part by consideration of the hoped-for after-effects of royal assumption of the headship of the church in England, lapsed into suspect quiescence. But those challenging *religio*-political questions posed in the same decades by those who questioned the rectitude and implications first of that very assumption and then of its temporary abandonment, were thereafter never far beneath the surface—whether in "Papist" or in "Puritan" minds. But widespread recognition of any right of active resistance to what was perceived as unlawful governmental action—let alone of any right of ordinary subjects to participate in governance—will be slow to emerge, and will ultimately do so only when hedged about with all sorts of conditional restrictions. Crucially, when this at last occurs, in the middle decades of the *seventeenth* century, it is in conjunction once more with a ferment of social and economic speculation. The witches' brew that had alarmed so much of respectable opinion in the mid-Tudor era is once more on the boil—this time with the addition of a couple of more frightening ingredients.

An outline even of basic trends over a period of eighty years encounters problems of subdivision. In the reign of Elizabeth I, some historians discern a change after about 1580, while others attach more importance to the accession of James I. Again, while some historians can identify no clear-cut emergence of well-nigh *inevitable* causes of civil war during the thirty-five years following that accession, to others these had clearly been present even before 1603. The year 1603 sees no sharp change in accepted opinion about the social and economic aspects of an established ideal, with continuity of concern for the preservation of traditional values and continued exercise of paternalist intervention in economic affairs, continued preoccupation with that theme of decay within the commonwealth encountered well before Elizabeth's demise, and the perennial spectre of the "beast with many heads." Thus, many Stuart tracts still have a Tudor flavor. Insofar as the very different personality of the monarch evoked diminishing respect for the head of the body politic, then dynastic change may well have quickened those dangerous religio-political currents that already swirled around the bases of the existing order. For the eighty-year period as a whole, limited in scope as any conscious exposition and development of the concept of the commonwealth may well have been, the religious and political background remained anything but static.

Elizabeth I

At the outset of Elizabeth's reign, John Hales the Commonwealthman, returned from exile, touched on some crucial issues in his loyal "Oration" to the Queen. Thus, just as any person "may not renounce his right in that which toucheth the commonwealth," so the Marian parliamentary statutes had been wrong in renouncing royal headship of the church, for "this style and title *more toucheth the commonwealth and realm of England* [my italics] than the king." Yet conservative continuity is evident within the quiescent ideology of the social and economic aspects of the commonwealth. An early Elizabethan royal progress through London encountered at the Little Conduit a pageant depicting two hills. On one, barren and stony, there sat at the base of a withered tree, clad in "homely and rude apparel, crookedly, and in mourning manner, . . . Ruinosa Republica, alias A decayed Commonweale,"—in total contrast with the neighboring depiction of "a flourishing Commonweale."[2] The device was commonplace. But alongside the causes listed of a healthy commonwealth—fear of God, wisdom and mercy in princes and magistrates, and obedience in their subjects—there was but little allusion to social and economic grievances. This typified much of subsequent discussion, at least as far as it was published.

For this one may suggest several reasons, both in "real" and in "ideological" terms. A recent critique of earlier historians of the "Mid-Tudor Crisis" concludes that "there was, indeed, a crisis [but] that it was in one way bleaker even than they had imagined"—an allusion to the demographic impact of the virulent epidemics that raged for a couple of years after 1556 and that had indeed been noticed by historians long ago. Ironically, insofar as population pressure had helped to drive prices up and wage rates down, this disaster had a silver lining. To the extent that the previously frightening upsurge in prices had ensued from reckless debasement of the coinage by the Crown itself, this was now in process of correction. Again, the wretched harvests of 1555 and 1556 were followed by an abundant yield in 1558. It has indeed been remarked that even the weather seemed to turn in favor of Elizabeth: there was but one poor harvest between 1563 and 1572. One crucially indicative statistic is the contrast between the disastrous doubling in the price of foodstuffs that had occurred between 1540 and 1560 and the leveling off, followed by gentler inflation, that characterized the reign of Elizabeth until its final decade.[3] Thus, until these final years, the frightening conjunction of social and economic with religious crisis that had been the background to so much of the "commonwealth" literature during the midcentury was absent almost throughout the reign. Yet if those real factors that had given an edge of urgency to so much of that writing now receded, recollection among the well-to-do of the disorder and rebellion that they had produced did not. For many decades such retrospective fears were to inhibit discussion of those aspects of the commonwealth ideal that might in any way be misinterpreted as critical of the existing social order and above all as a threat to property rights.

Of course, Elizabeth's reign was not devoid of economic problems; nor did her ministers abandon policies of paternalist intervention. In many royal proclamations, which attest avowed objectives, one notes the presence of traditional commonwealth terminology in a social and a religious context. The early years of the reign saw many allusions such as that to a "good ordered Christian commonweal." Interestingly, by 1588 we encounter a specific bracketing of "this state and commonweal," while significantly in the following year the Marprelate publications were deemed "untrue and slanderous to the *state*" (my italics).[4] As for the duties of the ruler of the unitary society thus envisaged, edicts on the coinage include a reference to her "having a perpetual care . . . to relieve the common hurts or griefs of her subjects" and to her duty "to preserve always the weal, surety, and honour of this realm before her own private weal or state." The distinction implied is made specific in an edict condemning those guilty of "seeking their own singular gain and advantage contrary to all reason and the commonwealth of her majesty's good and natural subjects." Most of the edicts thus far cited relate to the early years, but professed adhesion to the ideal endured throughout the reign. As late as June 1600, there was the quintessentially Erasmian declaration of Elizabeth's concern for "the poorer sort of her people (of whom her majesty is no less careful than of the richest, seeing Almighty God doth expect from her an account of all those whom He hath chosen her to be the ruler here on earth)."⁵

As for the substantive content of these proclamations, traditional social and economic objectives loom large. In this they typify Elizabethan policy. So does the massive Statute of Apprentices of 1563, with its "endeavour to freeze society, . . . to preserve good order and offer everybody a place in life."⁶ If indeed throughout the reign one perceives "the aspirations of governments anxious to preserve their humanist credentials with a little social engineering in the interests of the common weal,"⁷ such engineering was fundamentally conservative, exemplified in efforts to enforce the Statutes of Apparel. Though only one new enactment occurred, in 1563, proclamation after proclamation expressed concern about excess in apparel leading to "the disorder and confusion of the degrees of all estates." Such transgressions, "specially in the inferior sort," demanded "the redress of so grievous and pernicious a sore in this commonwealth." Opposition to another great target of earlier Tudor moralists, "excessive building," surfaced in 1580 and 1602, but in the context of overcrowding, fear of plague, of shortage of food, and of disorder, within the capital city of the realm.⁸

Equally conservative were the occasional expressions of concern about abuses in marketing, excessive prices, and the activities of such "greedy cormorants" as sought inordinate gain "by means of engrossing, or otherwise by forestalling or regrating" of grain. Against a worsening economic background in 1596, injunctions to justices of the peace to take action against such appear in a proclamation "Enforcing Orders against Dearth."⁹ Yet action in respect of agricultural production—from which all food derived—is not much in evidence. Elton finds that, apart from the codification of the 1563 Act of Tillage, there was an absence of any major legislation between 1559 and 1581.¹⁰ The meagre representation of this issue in the royal proclamations (although an edict in 1569 concerned "Enforcing Statutes on Tillage and Enclosures") contrasts with a fair number devoted to aspects of manufacture—in particular to the processing of and trade in wool. Occasional discouragement was attempted of activity undertaken "to the great damage of the commonweal," such as the sowing of woad on fertile ground.¹¹ But what attracted most attention in the later years of the reign was what had now become the perversion of the device of "projects."

In this context Joan Thirsk sees the expansive phase of the mid-century as followed, after 1580, by "the Scandalous Phase." Therein, while some devices were adopted by local authorities to assist in poor relief, others were simply exploited by speculators or by the Crown itself. The continuity discerned in the policies of Sir Thomas Smith and Sir William Cecil, which upheld "the ideals of the Commonwealthmen" in the promotion of projects had now been undermined and "the path they had blazed was losing its way in a dense, thorny thicket."[12] The language of the commonwealth was now most urgently employed *against* monopolies and patents. For the making of money by the prevention of competition rather than by genuine innovation was the issue. In the notorious outcry in Parliament in 1601 one speaker declared nothing "more Odious to the Subject, or more Dangerous to the Common-Wealth, than the Granting of these Monopolies," while another deplored how "the Principal Commodities both of Town and Country, are ingrossed into the Hands of those Blood-Suckers of the Common-Wealth."[13]

If one reverts from the fate of this formerly innovative aspect of commonwealth thinking to another major touchstone of such ideology, poor relief, a rather patchy impression emerges. The legislation of 1563 was basically a compendium of ideas and methods that had appeared in previous decades. Surveying the endeavors of private initiative and of official sanction in respect of failed and successful Elizabethan bills, Elton observes that, despite the enactments of 1563, 1572, and 1576, "no one revived the ambitious plan for a major scheme of public works" that had been mooted in the 1530s. The only really innovatory step was the collection of the first compulsory poor rate after 1572—already foreshadowed by local initiatives. Margo Todd cites a draft circa 1580 that conveys a typical set of humanitarian yet efficiency-conscious approaches—but it remained unpublished. By an act of 1576 JPs could take action to provide pauper employment in the towns and undertake correction of the workshy in counties; but Slack concludes that in practice little was done before 1603.[14]

Before leaving this social and economic aspect of commonwealth ideology, which had lain at its heart in mid-Tudor England, one must consider the case that its perceived waning in the middle and later decades of the reign of Elizabeth I was "something of an optical illusion." Clearly, it did not disappear. I have noted not only continued lip service in official promulgations but also some continuity of personnel who demonstrated adhesion to commonwealth ideals. Yet if one can make a meaningful distinction between a commonwealth and a paternalist approach, the balance shifts toward the latter. Certainly the crises and disorders of the midcentury had left a legacy of distrust of any radical socioeconomic speculation that could be seen to imply the dreaded descent from equity into equality. The sharpening of such fears is clearly expressed in a minor spate of proclamations commencing with that of 5 November 1591, "Placing Vagrants under Martial Law," which alludes to "the common wandering abroad of a great multitude" of subjects. Research suggests that such fears reflect the stark reality "of the rising tide of pauper migration . . . in an economy which was unable to employ a growing population." The "terror of the tramp" was not the invention of the social historian.[15]

To this issue I shall return in later discussion of the "crisis of the 1590s." Meanwhile, throughout the literature of Elizabeth's reign, alongside a general tendency to use the word "commonwealth" sometimes as a synonym but more often as a persisting social ideal devoid of any questioning and potentially threatening overtones, one finds repeated and very pointed reminders of what it *could* be taken to imply. By 1582 one Elizabethan could observe urbanely (albeit in Latin) to his countrymen that they were living in Smith's *Republica*, not in More's Utopia or in Plato's polity—and dismiss such unreal fantasies.[16] But the fear of the "many-headed monster," whose twin aims of anarchy and egalitarianism were no less frightening for being contradictory, was never far beneath the surface. Contemporaneously, Sir Philip Sidney's *Arcadia* (written circa 1579–83) included a fearful sketch of the anarchy that erupted when "the many-headed multitude" escaped restraint and "every man commanded, none obeyed." Sidney's fears, and those reflected in such very different works as Edmund Spenser's *Faerie Queene*, Sir Walter Raleigh's *Maxims of State*, and Shakespeare's *The Tempest*, will again require detailed treatment later. Understandably, Bradshaw has remarked that the intellectual ethos reflected in More's *Utopia* "is light years removed from that of *Arcadia* and *The Faerie Queene*. It may well be questioned if what happened to the commonwealth ideal in the meantime could be called progress."[17]

The terminology of the commonwealth continued to appear in published works throughout the reign of Elizabeth, sometimes indeed in their titles. So, too, did the organic analogy of society. But they were used pre-eminently to underline the duty owing to the prince, as head of the body politic, and the heinous nature and dreadful consequences of any disobedience by its lesser members, rather than as vehicles for the advocacy of social and economic improvement in any humanitarian sense. Lawrence Humphrey's *The Nobles, or of Nobility* (1563) typifies a deeply conservative assessment of both the status and the obligations of the traditional ruling class. The English translation (by Thomas Norton, 1570) of the *Catechism* of Alexander Nowell, dean of St. Paul's, is typical in deploring the hurt of conspiring "against the commonweal, against the country, the most ancient, sacred, and common mother of us all, . . . and against the prince, the father of the country itself, and parent of the commonweal." The translator himself, as joint author of *Gorboduc* in 1561, had enunciated the principle that

> Though kings forget to govern as they ought,
> Yet subjects must obey as they are bound.[18]

In 1581, one "Charles Merbury, Gentleman" published *A Briefe Discourse of Royall Monarchie, as of the best Common Weale*. Though not highly regarded by historians of political thought, this may reflect its author's diplomatic experience abroad (indeed, the introductory address to the Queen is in Italian!) and a knowledge—though not a clear understanding—of Bodin, and is not without interest. After repeating his titular assertion that "Royall Monarchie" is necessary to fashion "a most perfect common weal," Merbury essays a definition. "A common weal therefore is, An order of government observed in a city, or in a country, as touching the Magistrates that bear rule therein." He then distinguishes between those just commonwealths "which tend only unto the advancement of the common profit" and those wicked versions "tending altogether unto their own private commodity." While "commonweal" here is not simply a synonym for "realm," it is most certainly not identified with the "commonalty." It is an evil day "when the multitude of the common people, and of the baser sort (as of handicraftsmen, and such other) have the managing of public affairs: using, or rather abusing such their authority unto the oppressing of the nobility, and advancing of the commonalty: favouring always those, that are of the poorest and meanest condition at their own foolish fancy, without all order or discretion." The rule "of the mechanical people, (called *Democratia*) is always in confusion: she envieth the rich, and malices the mighty. . . . She is no better than a universal confusion, a horrible monster of many heads without reason, and a tempestuous Sea tossed with boisterous winds in every place and at every season."[19]

Nonetheless, Merbury reiterates the precept "that all good common weals have always an especial care, and tenderness over the subjects, as good fathers have over their children." The contrast between a good ruler and a tyrant is almost luridly expressed: "the one embraceth equity, and justice: the other treadeth both God's law, and man's law under his feet." As for his subjects, the evil ruler "gnaweth the bones, and sucketh out the very blood, and marrow of them with unlawful taxes, tolls, and confiscations." While advocating the continuity of dynastic rule, as avoiding the "troubles and dangers incident unto Elections," Merbury still rejoices that "our Prince is subject unto laws both civil, and common, to customs, privileges, covenants, and all kinds of promises, so far as they are agreeable unto the law of God. . . . Wherein we neither diminish the liberty of the subject, supposing all laws to be good, or ought to be good: Neither do we inlarge too much the Powers of the Prince, as to make him lawless, subject neither to God his law, nor man's law."[20]

Merbury's conventional priorities typify his age. Yet an earlier, more urgent version of the commonwealth ethos occasionally surfaces. As late as 1580 an extended exposition of traditional social values, still coupled with the type of moralizing that had been the staple of much midcentury literature, was published by Thomas Lupton. *Siuqila. Too good, to be true* extols the virtuous behavior of the people of Mauqsun. (Siuqila is a clear, though hardly euphonic, reversal of *aliquis,* elsewhere, as is Mauqsun of *nusquam,* nowhere.) Despite its fantasy setting the work is in effect an extended attack on contemporary English society, whose laws are likened "to a Spiderweb, which the Humble Bee doth break and rush through at pleasure, but the little weak and small flies are catched therein." Lupton attacks evil-living bishops: by means of friendship and even bribery many are put "into that holy and sacred function that are meeter to be Swineherds, than spiritual shepherds." Particularly reprehensible are those who preach in "gaudy attire"—for in Mauqsun *all* apparel is controlled. As for the hearers of their sermons, too many have recourse not to alms but to bear- and bull-baiting, players, and tumblers. Rather than succor their needy and naked neighbors, they feast greedily at the tavern—"the fourth part of which superfluous dinner or Supper would have succoured a score of them well a seven-night." Not that there is no poverty in Mauqsun, but the poor are patient, being "so well instructed in the Scriptures." In England, alas, our beggars remain idle and ungodly, despite the enactment of harsh punishment for idle rogues. As for constructive provision for the poor and deserving unemployed, "we have very good statutes ordained for them both, but if the statute for the said provision were as well prosecuted, as the statute for punishing rogues in some places is executed, then godly exercise should be more used: Idleness the root of all evil would soon be banished."[21]

In contrast with this latter-day fantasy—arguably as much a utopian as a commonwealth-type tract—it is perhaps appropriate to turn to the best-known and often-cited exposition of the Elizabethan concept of the commonwealth. Sir Thomas Smith, author of *De Republica Anglorum* (written circa 1565), had almost certainly already written perhaps the most original of those mid-Tudor commonwealth tracts encountered earlier: *The Discourse of the Common Weal.* Indeed his modern editor conjectures that Smith's failure to publish his *De Republica Anglorum* reflects his own awareness of its limitations. Yet his *Discourse* also remained unpublished until Elizabeth Lamond's researches in 1893, whereas the other work *was* printed posthumously in 1583.[22] The point of greatest significance in our context is surely the striking contrast in approach between two works—both by the same acute observer reflecting the preoccupations of the society in which he lived—written only sixteen years apart. The questing physiology of the first has now been transmuted into the calm anatomy of the second. The quite daring speculation of 1549 has given way to sober acceptance of the established order.

The book's subtitle, "The maner of Gouernement or policie of the Realme of Englande," is fairly indicative of its content. The descriptions of the functioning of governance, and of parliamentary procedure, are outside our present scope. But important passages touch on the notion of the commonwealth. In particular, "a commonwealth is called a society or common doing of a multitude of free men collected together and united by common accord and covenants among themselves, [that is] the society civil or common wealth." Again, although his book is sometimes considered as merely descriptive, Smith himself is clearly aware of the dynamic element in government and society: thus "it doth appear that the mutations and changes of fashions of governments of commonwealths be natural, and do not always come of ambition or malice: And that according to the nature of the people, so the commonwealth is to it fit and proper." This early recognition of the principle of evolution is the more impressive in the light of Smith's oft-cited conclusion that what he had delineated is "not in that sort as Plato made his common wealth, or Zenophon his kingdom of Persia, nor as Sir Thomas More his Utopia—feigned common wealths, such as never was nor never shall be, fantasies of Philosophers . . .—but as England standeth and is governed at this day the xxviii of March Anno 1565."[23]

My last example of general treatments of the commonwealth theme appeared a generation later, in 1600. Thomas Floyd's *Picture of a perfit Common wealth* envisages "a living body compact of sundry estates and degrees of men: this body is composed of two sorts, namely of the soul the worthiest wight, and of the members or parts. The soul is the king or supreme governor [for] no Commonwealth can be rightly a common wealth, without a king: so the body is no living body without the soul." If this quasi-mystical note is reminiscent of Clement Armstrong in the 1530s, later points remind one of Merbury. Equating "Common wealth" with "*Respublica, quasi res populica,* the affairs of the people" and with a civil society "disposed by order of equity, and ruled by the moderation of reason," Floyd discusses types of government. Although conceding that "Democracy is a popular regiment, tending to the common good, [there] is no Common wealth more loose than that wherein the common people have most liberty, which is their wished desire." Uproar and sedition ensue. "Wherefore there can no greater danger ensue, or happen to a Common wealth than to tolerate the rude, and common sort to rule, who . . . are always noted to be unconstant and wavering, tossed with every sudden blast." Rightly are they likened to the ugly Hydra and called the monstrous beast of many heads.[24]

After an early example of the analogy of the beehive, "which do make choice of the chiefest Bee, to be a king [*sic*] over all the hive, by which the whole swarm are led and guided," many traditional precepts are conveyed, accompanied by slightly more emphasis on the ruler's social duties. Thus, "kings ought to be the shelters to poverty, their seats the sanctuaries for the distressed"; a monarch must "listen and consider the complaint of his people without respect of person." The treatments accorded to liberality, idleness, and covetousness are quite conventional, as is the counsel of measure and moderation—with perhaps unintended humor when Floyd declares that "it is the point of a charitable minded man, to invite the poor, courteously to entertain them, and speedily to let them depart"! His lengthy work concludes with an appeal to equity and with a final caveat against the consequences of the "licentious liberty" that want of government may breed.[25]

Perhaps it is now appropriate to reflect that developments in political thought in England cannot be isolated from significant trends across the Channel. Jean Bodin's *Six Books of the Commonwealth* (1576) and François Hotman's *Franco-Gallia* (1573), works of outstanding importance within the very different context of events in France, were not without impact in England. Bodin alluded more than once to More's best-known work—even though he referred to it as "*Commonwealth*" and again as "*Republic*"! Certainly his own definition of a commonwealth as "the rightly ordered government of a number of families, and of the things which are their common concern, by *a sovereign power*" (my italics), and of sovereignty itself as "that absolute and perpetual power vested in a commonwealth" raised questions that would not long be absent from English discussion—though more openly in the Stuart than in the Tudor era. Interestingly, Richard Knollys, in his translation of 1606, still preferred in general to render Bodin's key term as "commonwealth" rather than as "state." Assuredly, Bodin's assertions that "the true nature of a people is to seek unbridled liberty without restraint," and that "the rich understand by equality, proportional equality, the poor, absolute equality," attest common concerns in both countries. But if Bodin appealed to one strand of English thought then Hotman's *Franco-Gallia*, written against the background of the Huguenot cause in France and purveying a "theory of popular sovereignty," was to prove congenial to those concerned to justify resistance.[26] The *politique* deduction that insistence upon religious conformity was ceasing to be a *necessary* condition of the unity and peace of the commonwealth, but was instead becoming almost a prescription for prolonged internal conflict, came much earlier in France than in England—which was spared any "Wars of Religion" until the seventeenth century.

Nevertheless, when I seek to identify one specific aspect of the ideology of the commonwealth with which Elizabethan debate was predominantly concerned, it proves to be the assertion of the unity of church and commonwealth in England. The official understanding of the position is typified by an unequivocal reference in a royal proclamation of 11 June 1573 to "this Church and commonwealth of England." The royal position was not devoid of social overtones: inherited fears of the Anabaptists surfaced in 1560 in a deportation order, while fifteen years later a warrant *Pro haereticiis comburendo* led to the martyrdom of two Flemish members of that sect. But the wider religio-political issue was clearly enunciated right at the end of Elizabeth's reign (in a proclamation of 5 November 1602) in the queen's derision at any suggestion "that we have some purpose to grant toleration of two religions within our realm, where God . . . doth not only know our innocence from such imagination [that] would not only disturb the peace of the church but bring this our state into confusion." Jesuit designs "to steal away the hearts especially of simple and common subjects from us their sovereign [are] not to be endured in the rule or policy of any well governed commonwealth."[27] Through much of the reign the Crown's position was challenged not only from the "Papist" but also from the "Puritan" side, and in the context of this debate the advocacy of a right of disobedience and of a limitation of royal sovereignty in *religious* matters emerges once again.

Pre-eminent among those who sought to demonstrate the virtual identity of church and commonwealth was Richard Hooker. While it has been contended that his definition of a commonwealth is effectively identical with that of Smith, the first four books of Hooker's *Laws of Ecclesiastical Polity* were not published until 1593, a generation after Smith wrote his work. (Indeed, publication of the remaining books was not completed until the mid-seventeenth century.) It might well be suggested that the two men were concerned with different sides of the same coin. But Hooker wrote to defend a position that was under attack—indeed a recent editor of his work identifies "his perception of the age as a perilous one".[28]

Hooker declares "the law of a commonweal," which is apparent in the law of reason, to be "the very soul of a politic body, the parts whereof are by law animated, held together, and set on work in such actions as the common good requireth." He asserts the identity of church and commonwealth, membership of the one entailing that of the other. Indeed, Christopher Morris attributes to him a reversion to "the medieval conception of a Christian Commonwealth, of which Church and State were two different aspects." Certainly Hooker's recoil from any recognition of a right of dissent is constant. His distaste for "turbulent wits" who resist authority is primarily directed against religious dissent, but the social undertones are near the surface. Significantly, some half-dozen pages in his preface are devoted to the threat from Anabaptists who, concerned at first "to beat down all dominion . . . had at length both Consuls and kings of their own erection, [ending] by enriching themselves with all kinds of spoil and pillage." Sadly, "he that goeth about to persuade a multitude, that they are not so well-governed as they ought to be, shall never want attentive and favourable hearers." Admittedly, in considering the origins of government, Hooker's proviso that men's "troubles would be endless, unless they gave their common consent all to be ordered by some whom they should agree upon" may be seen as foreshadowing "social contract" theory—if only as something morally and philosophically implied. Yet his assertion that "laws they are not therefore which public approbation hath not made so" is speedily hedged about with qualifications involving *virtual* assent through agents. He also hastens to explain that "the just authority of civil courts and Parliaments is not therefore to be abolished, because sometime there is cunning used to frame them according to the private interests of men over potent in the commonwealth."[29]

While Hooker was fully aware of contemporary social problems and of shortfalls in social justice, his own priorities are clearly set out (albeit in Book 8) in one crucial sentence: "A gross error it is to think that regal power ought to serve for the good of the body and not of the soul, for men's temporal peace and not their eternal safety; as if God had ordained Kings for no other end and purpose but only to fat up men like hogs and to see that they have their mash." Above all, he urges, "if the Commonwealth be Christian . . . this very thing doth make it the Church." Again, "in a free *Christian* state or kingdom . . . one and the selfsame people are the *Church* and the *Commonwealth.*" Though not printed until 1648, his conviction that there is not "any man a member of the Commonwealth which is not also of the Church of England" is his lodestar throughout the work. Hence his perpetual concern to "teach that the greatest honour to a State is perpetuity, [and that] alterations in the Service of God, for that they impair the credit of Religion, are therefore perilous in Commonweals."[30]

The marriage of religious with social apprehension was present in works ranging from the *Defense of the Apologie of the Churche of Englande* (first printed in 1567 and eight hundred pages long in its 1570 edition) by Bishop Jewel of Salisbury, with its derisive reference to "your Anabaptists, and Schwenkfeldians," to *A Defence of the Government Established in the Church of England for Ecclesiasticall Matters* (1587, and a more substantial 1400 pages in length, fully meriting Martin Marprelate's sardonic injunction: "Oh look over Dr John Bridges!"). Bridges shared Jewel's disdain for the Anabaptists, while his concern that "the good politic laws for the poor's relief" were not put into effect was heightened by the fear that the Elders and Deacons proposed by the sectaries would simply nurture "the breeding of greater multitudes in this land."[31]

The main concern both of Jewel and of Bridges was to defend the established ecclesiastical order. But when one turns to by far the biggest gun in the Anglican battery, John Whitgift, archbishop of Canterbury, one finds that his *Answere to a certen Libel intituled, An admonition to the Parliament* (1572) devotes proportionately even more space to associating religious dissent with social and political anarchy. The manifold and horrible heresies ascribed to the Anabaptists are linked with their "maintaining of licentiousness and lewd liberty," their wish "to be free from all laws, and to do what they list," their belief in holding all things in common, and their seeking "to overthrow common weals, and states of government." (Much of this is in fact derived from Bullinger, Zwingli's successor in Zurich, and the example of Germany is cited.) An unholy—and unlikely—alliance is then identified in that "it is manifest, that the Papists and they *jointly seek* [my italics] to shake, nay to overthrow the self same foundations, grounds, and pillars of our Church." Such dissidents will, if permitted, "not only with schisms and factions tear in sunder this Church of England, but in time overthrow the whole state of the commonwealth." The ultimate charge against these men, to whom "this name Puritan is very aptly given," is that they "would have all brought to such a popularity."[32]

In 1573 another substantial tome by Bridges declared *The Supremacie of Christian Princes* "in all causes so well Ecclesiastical as temporal." The obedience owed "is not only in temporal and civil matters: but in making us apt for the word of doctrine, in which all ecclesiastical matters are comprehended." He thus derides "the Papists' pretence of zeal to God to disobey their Prince." In phraseology reminiscent of that of Hooker (though the sentiment is also Erasmian) Bridges declares that "a Christian Prince regardeth further than the body, or than the natural or politic man. For being a Christian Prince, he regardeth them as Christian subjects." He greets with horror the contention "that Christian Princes may be deposed from their estates by the Bishops, and their kingdoms given to others, when their government hurteth the truth of the faith and the soul's health whereto they are ordained." Such advocacy of cutting "the knot of a subject's obedience" brings manifold perils—including "some suspicion of being a Millenary heretic"![33]

Another voice raised against change was that of Edwin Sandys, later archbishop of York. Preaching before Queen Elizabeth, he warned against "great alterations upon such light advice, these new commonwealths, however they be shadowed with the plausible name of reformation" of the church.[34] At far greater length, Thomas Bilson, bishop of Winchester, attempted a reasoned survey of the religious aspects of a Christian commonwealth in *The True Difference between Christian subjection and unchristian rebellion,* also published in 1585. Rebutting Jesuit attacks, Bilson is clear about the right of the prince to declare and also to enforce at least outward compliance with the true faith. Yet his advocacy of what resembles a Divine Right of Kings in *ecclesiastical* affairs is combined not only with that of a moderation in administering correction, which echoes Erasmus and anticipates the son of Bishop Sandys, but also with some significant political observations that have been seen as smacking of contractual theory, and indeed led J. W. Allen to ascribe to Bilson a "breaking away from the doctrine of royal supremacy as based on a strict identification of Church and Commonwealth." Certainly Bilson insists that "private men may not bear arms against a tyrant," nor may the pope depose a monarch. Moreover, given the circumstances, "Goodman's opinion which *himself hath long since disliked* [my italics], is in no way serviceable for your seditions." Nevertheless, kings have obligations, while the nobles may upon occasion "interpose themselves for the safeguard of equity and innocence." Therefore, if a prince should seek to "change the form of the common wealth" toward tyranny or "neglect the Laws established by common consent [then] if the Nobles and commons join together to defend their ancient accustomed liberty, regiment and laws, they may not well be counted rebels."[35]

Finally, in this sampling of works that were concerned to defend the unity of royal power in things temporal and spiritual, with a very keen eye to the potential social and political implications of dissent in doctrinal and disciplinary matters, one must note those of Richard Bancroft—described as the most active foe of Puritanism from the 1580s on, becoming bishop of London in 1597. Among the "false prophets" impugned in *A Sermon Preached at Paules Crosse* on 9 February 1588 are "Papists, Libertines, Anabaptists, the Family of Love." There is an intriguing reference to "the late obstinate heretic Francis Ket, who was within these two months burnt at Norwich," and there are several allusions to "Martin" (Marprelate). But most striking in this general context is the way in which a passage of social protest that might have been lifted verbatim from Brinklow, Crowley, Latimer, or Lever at the midcentury is here put into the mouths of the Anabaptists, designed to stir up their "brethren of the poorer sort." These are allegedly invited to "consider how in the apostles' time the faithful had all things in common [yet now must] groan under the heavy burden which is laid upon you. Your landlords do wring and grind your faces for the maintenance of their pride in apparel, their excess in diet, their unnecessary pleasures, as gaming, keeping of hawks and dogs, and such like vanities. They enhance your rents, they take great fines, and do keep you in very unchristian slavery and bondage." Little trace in Bancroft of Crowley's sneaking sympathy for this case; to him "the whole manner thereof is wholly Anabaptistical, and tendeth to the destruction and overthrow of all good rule and government." He does concede the danger also to church and to society of such as "are cormorants, and seek to fill the bottomless racks of their greedy appetites," but over all the swish of the Anabaptist tar-brush prevails.[36]

In respect of more narrowly *politico*-religious issues, Bancroft sets the Papist view that "where we had before a spiritual Pope, now the civil magistrate is made a temporal Pope," alongside Martin Marprelate's contention that "no petty Popes ought to be maintained or tolerated in any Christian common-wealth," with its alleged corollary that "his Majesty is a petty Pope: therefore his Majesty is not to be tolerated in a Christian common-wealth." Especially interesting is Bancroft's version of recent events in Scotland, and of King

James's reaction to the Presbyterians who "trod upon his sceptre, and laboured to establish an ecclesiastical tyranny of an infinite jurisdiction." The king, "perceiving withal, that the newly erected government was the mother of all faction, confusion, sedition, and rebellion: that it was an introduction to Anabaptism and popularity: that it tended to the overthrow of his state and Realm and to the decay of his crown, overthrew their presbyteries, and settled the Bishops again to their places."[37] (Bancroft, a zealous supporter of the "No bishop, no king!" principle, was to be archbishop of Canterbury from 1604 to 1610.)

In short, concludes Bancroft, those such as Harding and Cartwright "attribute in effect no more to his Majesty, and all other civil magistrates in those causes, than the Papists do." In an obvious allusion, "if this reformation (said one of them) be not hastened forward by the magistrate, the subjects ought not any longer to tarry for him, but to do it themselves." Warning his readers against "a wonderful new fangledness," he counsels them against being "carried about like little boats with every wind of doctrine by the deceit of men." Five years later he renewed his attack on certain *Daungerous Positions and Proceedings* taken "under pretence of Reformation, and for the Presbyterial Discipline." Again he couples the "seditious doctrine of Rheims" with that deriving from Geneva to the south and from Knox to the north—with their obvious implication of righteous tyrannicide.[38]

These "dangerous positions"—"Puritan" and "Papist"—concerning the relationship between religious and political power in the commonwealth demand consideration. In 1554 John Knox had already posed *Certain Questions* as to "whether obedience is to be rendered to a Magistrate who enforces idolatry and condemns true religion." His *First Blast of the Trumpet against the Monstrous Regiment of Women* (1558) is of special interest in that, within a pejorative and contrived exposition of the standard analogy, he incorporates a condemnation of female tyranny as "expressly against God and the profit of the Common-wealth." For a woman to bear rule is "repugnant to Nature; contumely to God." If the body "lacking the head can not be well governed, neither can the Common-wealth lacking Man." But, just as in nature there is sometimes the birth of monstrous bodies, "no less monstrous is the body of that Commonwealth where a Woman beareth empire; for either it doth lack a lawful head . . . or else there is an idol exalted in the place of the true head." Thus "women may and ought to be deposed from authority." There follows an important observation: "Neither yet does the foolish consent of an ignorant multitude, be able to justify that which God so plainly hath condemned."[39]

Such urgings were no more pleasing to Queen Elizabeth than those of Ponet. Knox, like Buchanan, reflected a Franco-Scottish background. But menacingly nearer home a persistent attack upon the "Anglican" position in England itself may be traced from Henrician times. Anthony Gilby, a Cambridge divine, in his *Admonition to England and Scotland* (also 1558), amidst much moralizing, is in no doubt about the error made under Henry VIII when the English people "so made you your King a God, believing nothing but that he allowed." "This monstrous boar must needs be called the Head of the Church, displacing Christ our only Head." In *A View of Antichrist* (1571) his tenure therein did not deter him from attacks upon "our English Church unreformed." The assault on "Popish abuses yet remaining in the English Church," notably in "Antichristian apparel,"[40] was continued in the following year by John Field and Thomas Wilcox in an *Admonition to the Parliament.* Yet their protest that the authorities "slanderously charge poor men (whom they have made poor) with grievous faults, calling them Puritans" is accompanied by a denial "that we mean to take away the authority of the civil Magistrate and chief governors."[41]

Its appearance signalled the commencement of a bitter controversy; but before considering this in the context of this general study, some crucial parameters must be established. For the *Admonition*'s combination of an attack on "Popish abuses" with a denial of any intent to upset the political and social order masked what were *ultimately* to emerge as crucial differences when the Separatists entered the arena. Between Anglicans, Presbyterians (J. W. Allen's "Disciplinarian Puritans"), and Romanists there were significant doctrinal and ecclesiological differences; but they all believed in an essential unity of church and commonwealth, while disagreeing over who should control it, and they all believed in a hierarchical society. The Separatists or Independents did not. They moved toward a denial of the identity of church and commonwealth—although admittedly they also believed that the code of Christian conduct expected voluntarily within the church of the chosen should also be imposed by the magistrate upon society as a whole. They also preached nonresistance. But in the mid-seventeenth century their abandonment of this principle was to trigger events that proved far more important for political development than the present disputes over dogma.

Meanwhile, Whitgift's response to the *Admonition* considered earlier led to a further exchange of diatribes, a notable participant wherein was a Cambridge professor, Thomas Cartwright, who published *A Replye to An answere made of M. Doctor Whitgifte* in 1573. Cartwright clung to the conventional corporeal analogy, observing "that the church and common wealth do embrace and kiss one another, . . . seeing they be like unto Hypocrates twins which were sick together and well together." But his prescribed priorities could not have pleased Whitgift. For "the breaches of the common wealth have proceeded from the hurts of the church, and the wants of the one from the lacks of the other. Neither is it to be hoped for that the common wealth shall flourish until the church be reformed." He is anxious to affirm that "we speak not against civil government." But he scorns Whitgift's alleged contention "that the church must be framed according to the common wealth"; indeed, "the church being before there was any common wealth, and the common wealth coming after, must be fashioned and made suitable to the church"! Well might Cartwright have been called Calvin's chief English disciple. The duty of the magistrate was to enforce the godly discipline enunciated by the church and thus render every realm a Christian commonwealth. But, unlike the Separatists, Cartwright was willing to "tarry for the magistrate," while his advocacy of an elective principle within the church had no taint of political or social egalitarianism.[42]

Just as Whitgift provoked Cartwright, so in 1587 Dudley Fenner published *A Defence of the godlie Ministers* "against the slanders of D. Bridges." While ready to accept the *lawful* authority of the queen, Fenner, expressing solidarity with Bishop Hooper, is clear that "to devise new rites and ceremonies for the Church is not the Prince's vocation." Bridges's slanders can only lead to "the heartening of the papists" and of such as "swarm with Deaneries, double benefices, pensions, advowsons, reversions, &c," and oppress "such as can hardly with what they have clothe and feed them selves and their families." He rebuts the charge "that we urge the alteration of the state both of Church and common wealth. . . . But we would have both bettered by adding *the perfection of Discipline*" (my italics). As for the imputation of "the enlarging of the people's government . . . , we cannot enlarge that which is not. We give unto them an approbation in some special matters by their free consent. . . . But government or carriage of matters we give not to them but to the Ministers or Elders only." Yet Fenner cannot refrain from social comment: "the Bishops' livings, pomps, and superfluities should be turned to the sufficient maintenance of the Ministry and Schools: which would be a wonderful advancement of godliness and learning, the sinews of the common wealth." More specifically, there must be "deacons for the care of the poor" and "Church-servants to attend on the poor."[43] Clearly, some midcentury commonwealth social priorities lingered.

A more serious threat to the seamless unity of church and commonwealth that those such as Whitgift and Hooker so desired was the thinking advanced by Robert Browne in 1582 in a work that evoked pointed allusions: *A Treatise of Reformation Without Tarrying for Anie,* purportedly printed in Middelburgh. Browne, conceding a general authority to the queen in church and commonwealth, then promptly modifies it. For magistrates may "do nothing concerning the Church, but only civil, and as civil Magistrates, . . . but only to rule the common wealth in all outward justice. . . . And therefore also because the church is in a commonwealth, it is of their charge: that is concerning the outward provision and outward justice." But "to force a submission to Ecclesiastical government by laws and penalties belongeth not to them . . . neither yet to the Church." For God's "rule in his Church is not the rule of man."[44] Despite ambiguities, the implications of the Separatist stance for the nature of the commonwealth seems clear. While it remains the Christian duty of the magistrate to protect the church and to enforce Christian values within society, the notion of a mutually comprehensive church and commonwealth is abandoned. Perhaps more accurately, the church is disassociated from the emergent concept of the state.

Henry Barrowe's *A Brief Discovery of the False Churches* (1590) has some familiar moralising in its condemnation of such "idle Bellies" as Collegiate Priests who should be dispossessed "and turned to some honest Trade, or Profession of living in the Common Wealth," and of university drones who spend their lives "in Vanity, Folly, and Idleness," as well as the gluttonous rich who "exceed in monstrous and vain Apparel" and waste money on building and on dogs. Alike condemned is "greedy Covetousness in purchasing and joining not only Field unto Field, but Town unto Town." When he turns to those who oppose reform in the church he is not surprised that "those that lived under a Monarchical State were not backwards to persuade the Magistrates that [such reform] would breed an Innovation, if not a Subversion, of the whole State . . . , that it would innovate and alter the Frame of the Government of the Common Wealth, and draw it into an Aristocracy or Democracy." Thereafter, comparing Christ's *church* to a human body, Barrowe himself condemns unnatural conjunctions: "what kind of strange and monstrous Body would they make unto Christ, by knitting into him strange Members, such as belong not to his Body?" But most important of all is the insistence that "God hath put difference (though no disagreement) betwixt the Church, and the Common-Wealth."[45]

In 1593 there appeared *The Examinations of Henry Barrowe, John Grenewood and John Penrie*, which had taken place at Lambeth in 1586. Conceding recognition of the queen as "supreme governor of the whole land," Barrowe nonetheless denies to her—or to anyone else—the power to make any laws for the church other than those present in Christ's Word. But he admits indeed that "no man may intermeddle with the prince's office, without lawful calling thereunto; and it is therefore utterly unlawful for any private man to reform the state," just as his fellow martyr Penry disclaims any intent to essay "the anabaptistical inversion of all good order in the church." Greenwood again reiterates the crucial principle that "the whole common wealth is not a church."[46] Unlike Browne, who survived imprisonment, both Barrowe and Penry were hanged as traitors in 1593. Yet despite their lurid prophecies of woe, neither had taught violent resistance to the magistrate.

Indeed to find such advocacy we must turn to the "Papist" assailants of the Elizabethan church, whom its defenders had sometimes bracketed with the "Puritans." Skinner, in a wider context, has argued that "the main foundations of the Calvinist theory of revolution were in fact constructed entirely by their Catholic adversaries." German Lutherans had in fact anticipated both, but it is true that a sample of the admittedly briefer output of Romanist critics of the Anglican Church presents a fascinating mixture of concurrence as well as divergence of argument. Most directly relevant is *An Apologie and True Declaration of . . . the two English Colleges* (at Rome and Rheims) printed abroad in 1581. Its author, William Allen, was the chief organizer of Roman Catholic missions to England and was made cardinal in 1587. He treads a perilous tightrope in condemning a tendency of the Sects to rail against their sovereign and thus rebel against the commonwealth, as a certain harbinger of rebellion also against Christ and his church. Such heretics are "the bane of all Kings and Commonweals." Yet he himself is soon to explain that "the Parliament is a mere temporal Court . . . being derived from the Prince and Commonwealth civil, unto whom neither by the law of God, nor of nature" do matters of religious definition appertain.[47]

As for the church, "which is Christ's mystical body or Commonwealth . . . no earthly Commonwealth can give or order it to their Prince." While Allen disclaims any general intent to resist the temporal laws of the realm, disobedience is *not* always treasonable. If enactments are heretical then it is surely a grievous sin "when a whole

State agreeth upon any iniquity, . . . the crown being not a spiritual dignity but a temporal: the person of a Prince not spiritual but a temporal: the Realm not a spiritual Commonwealth, but a temporal." He deplores incitement to rebellion—"a popular practice, most common now in the world among Protestants, as it always hath been a means to advance sedition." Yet "the revolt from the Catholic Church is a greater fault by manifold, than defection from any earthly king or Commonwealth." Allen's *True, Sincere, and Modest Defense of English Catholics* (1584) reiterates the conviction that "the state, regiment, policy, and power temporal be in itself always of distinct nature, quality, and condition from the government ecclesiastical and spiritual commonwealth," but also asserts that 'the spiritual hath right to correct the temporal." Heaven forbid "that the Christian religion is no otherwise admitted in commonwealths but so far as it serveth for policy and the advancement of the prince or temporal state. And God grant this be not the mark our Protestants and politiques shoot at. . . ."[48]

Even more sweeping propositions were advanced by Robert Parsons, a Romanist with as much talent for plots as for missions. Writing as "Doleman," his *Conference About the Next Succession to the Crowne of Ingland* (1594) seized upon a genuine cause of national concern in order to speculate on the nature and powers of the commonwealth. Ponet and Goodman would have writhed in chagrin at seeing so many of their arguments now deployed in the Catholic cause. Thus succession to power by claim of blood descent is established neither by divine nor by natural law, "but only by human and positive Laws of every particular common wealth, and consequently, may upon just causes be altered by the same." Indeed, forms of government themselves subsist "according as each common wealth has chosen and established," while divers monarchs "have been lawfully chastised by their common wealths for their misgovernment." For "government was ordained for the benefit of the weal public and not otherwise. . . . A common wealth is nothing else but the good government of a multitude gathered together to live in one"; its particular forms of government are determined neither by God nor by nature.[49]

Parsons goes further: "there can be no doubt, but that the common wealth hath power to chuse their own fashion of government, as also to change the same upon reasonable causes." Not only is it true that "all common wealths have prescribed laws unto their Prince," but English history in particular furnishes the example of how Richard III "was lawfully also deposed . . . by the common wealth, which called out of France Henry Earl of Richmond to chastise him." Whatever one's reservations about the accuracy of this delightful inversion of the usual appeal to history by Tudor propagandists, the principles enunciated are clear: "that common wealths have chastised sometimes lawfully their lawful Princes [and] that the common wealth which gave them their authority for the common good of all, may also restrain or take the same away again, if they abuse it to the common evil." For the prince's authority is but "a power delegate, or power by commission from the common wealth," based implicitly upon an "agreement, bargain and contract between the king and his common wealth at his first admission." Little wonder that, when any presumptive successor may appear unfit or pernicious, "the common wealth upon just occasions hath extended her authority to alter the natural course of succession by birth." Parsons concedes the potential danger "when not the true common wealth, but some faction of wicked men should offer to determine this matter." But this risk is dwarfed by another consideration, strikingly similar to that encountered in Hooker: the "highest end that God and nature appointed to every common wealth was not so much the temporal felicity of the body, as the supernatural and everlasting of the soul. [For] the highest and chiefest end of every common wealth is *Cultus Dei*, the service of God and religion."[50]

His involvement in plots against Elizabeth exposed Parsons to understandable denigration—then and later—by loyal English subjects. But it now seems hard to deny him a significant place in the history of political thought. Certainly his book evoked two spirited if somewhat belated rejoinders. John Hayward's *Answer to the First Part of a Certaine Conference, Concerning Succession* (1603) warns that "sometimes Democratical government doth draw to a pure anarchy; and so doth the interregnum of elective principalities," and dismisses any "power of people to choose or change or limit government [or] to dispossess the prince." If the ruler "enjoin us those actions that are evil; we must show our subjection by patient enduring." Only God may remove kings. Parsons's contention "that as a natural body hath authority to cure the head if it be out of tune, and reason to cut it off often-times, if it were able to take another; so a body politic hath power to cure or cut off the head, if it be unsound," is indeed the voice of "a foolish physician." Few princes hold their state by the people's grant. Concurring that "in popular governments there is nothing but sedition, trouble, tumults, outrages and injuries upon every light occasion," Hayward professes puzzlement that Parsons should then contend "that the power of a prince is given to him by the common wealth, with such conditions and exceptions, as if the same be not kept, the people stand free." Appealing more to historical precedent than to first principles, Hayward doubts "that God always approveth the will and judgement of the people. . . . In matters of this moment, the orderly course of proceedings is only by Parliament." Parsons's views can only prove to be "a nursery of war in the common-wealth."[51]

Equally specific is *The Right to Succession to the Kingdom of England*, "Against the Sophisms of Parsons the Jesuit." Written in Latin in 1603, and dedicated to James VI by a fellow Scot, the lawyer Sir Thomas Craig, this did not appear in print until an English version appeared a century later. Within a lengthy confutation of "Doleman," Craig makes the crucial point that "the prevalent faction assumes always the specious name of the Commonwealth. . . . But if the Commonwealth is to be resisted as long as it does open injustice, or manifestly offends God, and *endangers the Realm*" (my italics), what greater danger can threaten than exclusion of the lawful heir? Here again, as in Hayward, "commonwealth" is no simple synonym for "realm"—which, as a factious body, it may endanger. Moreover, do "the Meetings, Conventions and Dissolving of the Seditious People, or Tumultuating Mob, deserve to be honour'd with so honest a name as that of the Commonwealth is?" Surely those mobs that dethroned Edward II and Richard II, or Wat Tyler's men, cannot really be taken to represent the commonwealth![52]

Though limited in its discussion of the commonwealth itself, the attack made on "Doleman" by Peter Wentworth a few years earlier has a poignant irony. For this resolute parliamentarian was in the Tower when Parsons's book appeared—incarcerated for nearly five years for daring to assert, in the face of royal interdict, the right of Parliament to debate the succession. Wentworth exemplifies what Collinson sees as "the other, non-adulatory face of Elizabethan politics" and the fact that an ideology of resistance in the last resort was held in check not abandoned. Occasionally, "when it came to the crunch, the realm took precedence over the ruler." In 1576 Wentworth had deplored a conduct of Parliament in which he "saw the liberty of free speech, the which is the only salve to heal all the sores of this common wealth, so much and so many ways infringed" as to render it "a very school of flattery and dissimulation and so a fit place to serve the Devil and his angels in and not to glorify God and benefit the commonwealth."[53]

Yet surely pride of place as the most forthright discussion of the balance between the interests of Crown and of commonwealth must be given to *The Discoverie of a Gaping Gulf* (1579) by John Stubbs—for which he and his publisher thereafter sat in the Commons minus their right hands. The gulf consists of a proposed French marriage—dangerous, *inter alia,* as yoking us with a nation that has "newfangled and stirring commonwealth heads, lusting after innovation." Stubbs himself, while distinguishing between the queen's natural body and "her body politic and common-weal body," insists that the latter "can no more be removed from the commonweal than the head from the body." But he also counsels Elizabeth "to abide the advice and consent of all her estates not to conclude her marriage" before consulting Parliament and the laws of the commonweal. For "much more shall the high sin of a highest magistrat, done and avowed in open sun, kindle the wrath of God and set fire on church and commonweal."[54]

Wentworth's own *Pithie Exhortation to her Maiestie* regarding the succession (partly written circa 1587) was published posthumously and surreptitiously in 1598, together with *A Discourse . . . of the true and lawfull successor to her Maiestie,* composed in reply to Parsons. His dilemma reveals the swirling cross-currents in contemporary religio-political thinking. For this champion of parliamentary rights, given his Puritan sympathies, could not possibly concur with "Doleman's" theory of *popular* rights lest it further the papist cause. Thus, his own carefully circumscribed version of a contract dismisses the notion that a people, having "by common and voluntary consent" ceded governmental power to one who is "willing to preserve their laws," may still imagine "that that power doth yet rest in themselves." Wentworth's has justly been termed a "livre de circonstance"; but assuredly he was not devoid of principle—which cost him his life.[55]

Meanwhile, several publications of the 1590s reflect not only the problem of the royal succession but also an increasing awareness of widespread social and economic discontent. Christopher Haigh, while eschewing exaggeration, attributes to the years 1594–98 "a political and social disequilibrium which seems to have been worse than the crisis of 1555–8," and Professor Ashton concurs as to a "note of crisis and desperation." Roger Manning, more widely, discerns "late-Elizabethan crises which appear to have persisted between approximately 1590 and 1610." Contributory factors to a general malaise included an incidence in the 1590s of enclosure disorders of nearly double the average number for the previous twenty years, together with the outbreak of food riots. These last are related in particular by Buchanan Sharp, rejecting what he terms an "Arcadian" picture of rural England, to "the existence of a large rural industrial proletariat living on wages . . . and dependent on the market for food." Moreover, between 1581 and 1602, as its population virtually doubled, the city of London apparently endured thirty-five outbreaks of disorder.⁵⁶

Noteworthy in what has been called an epidemic of disorder was the Enslow Hill Rebellion of 1596 in Oxfordshire. This "poorly-organized and abortive conspiracy," coinciding with a particularly disastrous harvest, was nothing like as dangerous as the Midlands Revolt of 1607. But its leaders threatened violence against the gentry and planned to march on London. Thus, while several historians envisage most food riots almost "as extreme forms of petitioning," while even enclosure disorders often followed traditional rituals, both effectively achieving their objective if they "provoke ameliorative action by the government," they discern at the turn of the century a more sinister face to an explicit articulation of social conflict, involving "what can only be called class hatred of the wealthy." Yet in this gray area between ritualised socioeconomic protest and readiness to take up and use arms against what were increasingly clearly seen as exploiters, none find evidence for "the roots of radicalism or revolutionary behavior."⁵⁷

Nonetheless, if any period in the eighty-year span of this chapter bids fair to mirror the mid-Tudor crisis (which, despite attempts to argue it out of existence, the present writer still unrepentantly discerns in the *conjunction* of dynastic, political, religious, social, and economic crises of threatening proportions), it would surely be the years that straddle the turn of the century. The looming possibility of a disputed accession to the throne with potential repercussions in the spheres of religion and of foreign policy, serious trouble in Ireland, the return from that arena of the last of the Tudor "overmighty subjects" in the person of Essex, foreign war, and the emergence once more of major social and economic problems: the pattern is reminiscent. The considerable preoccupation of Elizabeth's last two Parliaments with poor relief, and the measures taken in 1597–98 and 1601, reflect the impact of three successive harvest failures, of industrial slump, and of another sudden and frightening upsurge in the prices of consumables. The position was further worsened by the impact on prices of war, as well as by new outbursts of depopulating enclosure in several counties that evoked predictable popular reaction and new legislation in 1597.

The literature evoked does *not* reflect the combination of religio-social indignation with euphoric expectations that had characterized the mid-Tudor era; it is typified by works whose very titles reflect a preoccupation with decline and future forebodings in what might almost be envisaged as a Tudor *fin de siècle*. *Solon His Follie, or A Politique Discourse, Touching the Reformation of common-weales conquered, de-*

clined or corrupted (1594) was written by Richard Beacon, who had served as a royal attorney in Munster, Ireland. It seeks to establish that "a Reformation of a declined common-weal" is nothing but the restitution of a politic body resembling that of a natural body. Indeed, "this refomation universal of the whole state and body of the common-wealth is nothing else but a thorough and absolute mutation and change, of ancient laws, customs, and manners of the people, and finally of the common-wealth itself, unto *a better form of government*" (my italics). Yet Beacon later concludes that "commonweals do participate with the quality and nature of all other creatures, in that first they have their being, their progression, their continuance, their perfection, and lastly their declination." Whatever the motivation of this work, with its dedication to the queen, it is of interest in its combined acceptance both of the evolutionary principle and of a pessimistic if logical application to the commonwealth itself of the terminal stage of the corporeal analogy.[58]

In 1595 the anonymously written *Polimanteia, or The meanes lawfull and unlawfull, to iudge of the Fall of the Common-wealth*, "against the frivolous and foolish conjectures of this age," was dedicated to the Earl of Essex! The preface of this second, oddly titled and obscurely motivated work declares that "we are fallen into the barren age of the world." In his musings upon "those things which concern the ruin of Government, or change of a Common wealth," tending to debase good laws and also harm the Church, its author has much to say about Bodin. But alas, his quest for the means whereby "to judge of the change, or ruin of Common wealths" leads to no very clear conclusion and is at best indicative of a pessimistic state of mind.[59]

The apparently prevalent conviction that all was not well is paraded at some length in the peculiarly titled *Preparative to Contentation* (1597) by John Carpenter. A major theme in its survey of contemporary obstacles to such contentment is identified in those pages devoted to "The Image of Anarchy." The author reproves rebellious souls, for Christ "was far from that purpose [they dream of] to destroy and abandon laws, orders, and governments, either in the church or in the Commonwealth." Christ himself "was no seditionary." Thus, if an evil prince makes ungodly commands we may lawfully speak or write against them, but "not so much as any little occasion be thereby ministered to schism in the Church, or Sedition among the people. . . . Men ought to pray to God for redress, and not to rebel." This clear survival of passive *dis*obedience reflects Carpenter's dread of such as "cease not to enhazard the safety of our established Common-wealth." His more positive prescriptions are traditional. Among them "Equity hath a place [as] one of the daughters of Justice.... And in this shall be seen that moderate liberty, and that moderate subjection, which Plato commended." The happy mean is wedded to the cause of social stability when, as "a comfort for the poor believers," the author extols the virtues of poverty, and counsels that, "labouring truly in our vocations, ... we augment not the present grief by our excessive carefulness how to live in time to come"![60]

A more impressive source than these obscure pamphleteers of a growing malaise in the 1590s is found in the *Essays, or Counsels Civil and Moral* (1597) of Francis Bacon. These include a treatment "Of Seditions and Troubles" that identifies two primary sources of such ills: "much poverty, and much discontentment." Significantly, if "poverty and broken estate in the better sort be joined with a want and necessity in the mean people, the danger is imminent and great. For the rebellions of the belly are the worst." Other potential "causes and motions of sedition are, innovation in religion, taxes, alteration of laws and customs, breaking of privileges, general oppression, advancement of unworthy persons, strangers, dearths, disbanded soldiers, factions grown desperate." Perhaps the list bespeaks the courtier as well as the social analyst—and indeed Bacon flirted with the Essex faction.[61]

Yet his remedial proposals are totally traditional: "the opening and well balancing of trade; the cherishing of manufactures; the banishing of idleness; the repressing of waste and excess by sumptuary laws; the improving and husbanding of the soil; the regulating of prices of things vendible; the moderating of taxes and tributes and the like." Nor is it surprising, after Bacon's warning that any "over-proportion to the common people" of a "multiplying of nobility" is dangerous, to find that "above all things good policy is to be used, that the treasure and monies in a state be not gathered into few hands. For otherwise a state may have a great stock, and yet starve. And money is like muck, not good except it be spread. This is done chiefly by suppressing, or at the least keeping a strict hand upon the devouring trades of usury, engrossing, great pasturages, and the like." The program is strikingly reminiscent of the ideals of mid-Tudor commonwealth men.[62]

A very different contemporary composition is of unusual interest and sometimes underestimated significance, in that its author envisaged a restoration of the realm to Rome. *A Memorial of the Reformation of England* (1596), by none other than Robert Parsons, considers the needs of the "two principal branches of a Christian and Catholic Commonwealth." One historian points to the Romanist ecclesiastical context of its prescriptions—but what else could be expected?

Certainly Parsons's yoking of "the Temporal good of the Commonwealth" with the assertion that, for "Christian Sheep and Subjects, all Princes are to be accounted in respect of their Souls" is quintessentially Erasmian and seems closer to Hooker than to Gardiner. In consideration of the tasks confronting a "Council of Reformation" the corporeal analogy persists—from the prince, now both head *and* heart, to "the Commonalty being the Body and Bulk of the Realm [and] greatly to be cherished." As for the nobility, their education is crucially important, in order "that their Prince and Commonwealth might afterwards employ them worthily in occasions and affairs that shall be offered, and not be forced to prefer others of far meaner birth for the defects and insufficiency of the nobility." Yet the gulf between Parsons and such as Morison and Cranmer on this issue is not absolute. Thus, "men are not lightly to be permitted to pass . . . to the State and Condition of a Gentleman, without particular merits to be allowed of by the Prince . . . and not only by way of wealth, as of late years hath been accustomed."[63]

Specific social and economic reforms proposed include the traditional and the innovative. The suggestion "that all racked Rents be brought back to the old proportion, or somewhat near the same," so as to avoid the extremes of poverty and wealth observable in other countries, has a familiar ring. It is not surprising that the Commission is to enquire as to "what Oppressions, Injuries, Vexations, Laws, or other injuries have been laid down upon the Commonalty . . . by the Heretical Estate of these late years, or by bad Landlords, Nobles, or Gentlemen of Puissance, to the end it may be remedied." The Commonalty should itself by reduced "to their old simplicity, both in Apparel, Diet, Innocency of Life, and plainness of Dealing and Conversation, from which Heresy hath distracted many." The achievement of this nostalgically envisaged Catholic Commonwealth is to be furthered by a device encountered earlier (in the shape of "Conservators of the Commonweal"), namely that "some such Officers as the Romans called the Censor to look that no Man lived idly, nor brought up his Children without some Exercise or means to live." But far more novel is a proposal "that nothing should be taken from labouring Men's wages for [the] time spent in hearing Mass, so that the loss would fall only upon the richer sort that are better able to pay"!

The plea for legal reform—since "divers parts of our Common Law, brought in by the Normans, . . . do favour much of Tyranny" as against all Natural Law—would find a place in any Protestant Commonwealthman's program. But by contrast, the reiterated commendation of "exercise in Piety and works of Charity" envisages individual actions enjoined by the clergy and "divers Companies and Societies also . . . erected among the common People," rather than any systematic recourse to state provision. Nevertheless, the existence of "the multitude of Thieves that rob and steal upon the Highways in England, more than likely in any other Country . . . is a great infamy to our Government, and hurt to the Commonwealth," demanding both punitive and remedial action. Yet most eye-catching of all is the proposal

> that in every City or great Shire Town, there should be set up a certain poor Man's Bank or Treasury that might be answerable to that which is called *Monte della Pieta,* in great Cities of Italy; to wit, where poor Men might either freely or with very little interest have Money upon Sureties, and not to be forced to take it up at intolerable Usury, as oftentimes it happeneth, to the utter undoing and general hurt of the Commonwealth; and for the maintenance of these Banks, some Rents or Stocks of Money were to be assigned by the Council of Reformation, out of the common Purse. . . .[64]

Much of this suggests a caveat against the imposition of too rigid a pattern in respect of alleged doctrinal or ecclesiastical determinants of contemporary assessments of governmental social and economic responsibilities within a Christian commonwealth. Thus, Collinson, while warning of the danger of an anachronistic identification of "an Anglicanism not yet conceived and of an alien puritanism not yet clearly discerned," goes on to emphasise the sociological "conservatism not only of protestantism but of the puritanism which was in continuity with it."[65] Indeed, the emergence of contrasting attitudes on the issue of poor relief derived primarily from consideration of the increasingly threatening realities of the position. Not surprisingly, the troubles of the 1590s evoked an increasing number of reflections on this problem. These demonstrate an ever-increasing perception of what Slack describes as "the dichotomy between the deserving and undeserving poor," and that "the poor who had to be managed were a large and substantial part of the social order." Most crucial was a growing recognition, alongside a persistent belief that the poor were fitting objects of Christian charity, that the size and gravity of the problem now cried out for systematic social intervention. The Reverend Henry Bedel, writing in 1572, could still appeal to an "exercise of faith to give to the poor, . . . not for merit, but in duty, because the poor are left among us for this cause," while condemning the hard-hearted rich who preferred to give to dogs or feed themselves until they were sick. But by 1597 Henry Arthington, while castigating the rich who would open neither ears or purses to the poor, along with unreasonable oppressing landlords and extorting userers, identifies some claimants for relief as having "misspent much good time in idle roguing up and down, and would not work." In making a distinction between the impotent poor and those who are able to work, he proffers the reflection that "if begging had been lawful, Christ would have said, You shall have Beggars always with you, instead of the poor."[66]

Robert Allen's *Treatise of Christian Beneficence* (1600) commends a recent "gracious Statute" for its "denial of disordered succour [to] a monstrous and sottish multitude, as neither regarded Church nor commonwealth. [Thereby] all loitering drones and lubbers be forbidden to be fatted abroad, so no diligent Bee or painful Labourer be suffered for want of necessary relief toward his over great family and charge of children, specially in time of sickness, or in times of dearth . . . to pine away and perish." While endorsing merciful relief of the needy "specially such as approve themselves to be of the household of faith," Allen insists that a gift must be given with discretion, lest niggardly covetousness "degenerate into over licentious prodigality . . . for ostentation and vain glory." Assuredly, "for the poor to live idly, in a christian commonwealth, and . . . bring up their children in idleness," is sinful. "And the civil magistrate should fail greatly in his duty, and so sin against God, if he should not by his authority provide against it."[67] Whatever the relative weight of doctrinal influence or of hard realities, of pity or of fear, the general trend seems clear.

Yet any depiction of late-Elizabethan social attitudes would be incomplete without reversion to the theme of the hydra-headed monster, already noticed in Sidney's *Arcadia*. In Spenser's *The Faerie Queene* (1596) the Knight Artegall, "Champion of true Justice," dispenser of Equity, and believer that "all change is perilous," does combat with a Giant. His foe, clearly an ancestor of the Levellers, boasts that he will all "Lordlings curb, that commons over-awe," distribute the wealth of the rich to the poor, and weigh all in his scales and reduce them to an absolute equality. Predictably, the vulgar then about him flock, "like foolish flies about an honey crock," expecting unrestricted freedom, and his defeat produces a scenario of mutiny and civil war. Again, Thomas Nashe's *The Unfortunate Traveller* (1594) includes a sketch of a visit to Münster, where "very devout Asses, . . . such as thought they knew as much of God's mind as richer men," ran amok, led by "an Anabaptistical Brother named John Leiden."[68]

On the stage, Shakespeare's *Henry VI, Part 2* reminded the audience how "Jack Cade the clothier" had resolved "to dress the commonwealth, and turn it, and set a new nap upon it," promising that "there shall be in England seven halfpenny loaves sold for a penny, [and] all the realm shall be common." All the lawyers will be killed, and "the pissing-conduit run nothing but claret wine this first year of our reign." Interestingly, Annabel Patterson, in *Shakespeare and the Popular Voice,* discerns alongside an apparently contemptuous dismissal of the noisy crowd a readiness to incorporate "a cultural tradition of popular protest," and even, in *Coriolanus* (reflecting the impact of the Midlands Revolt of 1607), "a remarkably daring analysis of the socio-political system." Yet in *The Tempest* Gonzalo's anarchic vision may surely be located in the realms of fantasy:

> I' the commonwealth I would by contraries
> Execute all things; for no kind of traffic
> Would I admit; no name of magistrate;
> Letters should not be known; riches, poverty,
> And use of service, none . . .
> No occupation; all men idle, all.

In a land devoid of sovereignty, "all things in common nature should produce without sweat or endeavour."[69]

Finally, I turn to another figure whose career spanned two reigns (though with an ultimately disastrous change of fortune in 1603) for one more pejorative account of what the term "commonwealth" might mean. Sir Walter Raleigh, in his *Maxims of State,* defines the state itself as "the form and set order of a commonwealth" and then goes on to sketch the possibility of its degeneration into "a government of all the common and baser sort, and therefore called a commonwealth *by an usurped nickname* [my italics]. There all respect their own, and not the public good, and therefore are called bastard governments." Far preferable "is the government of a state by the choicer sort of people, tending to the public good." He concedes, cautiously, that "some part of the government is or ought to be imputed to the people, [for] where the multitude is discontented, there must needs be many enemies to the present state." Nonetheless he persists that "a commonwealth is the swerving or depravation of a free or popular state, or the government of the whole multitude of the poor and baser sort, without respect of the other orders." If some blurring of terminology is evident, there is none in his unequivocal declaration that, all too often, "the common people suppose there ought to be an equality in all other things." Hence, perhaps, his advice to watch the number of the poor, to keep them out of cities, and to provide employment.[70]

Yet we cannot leave it there. Raleigh was not alone in his recognition that "the diseases and alteration of a commonwealth doth not happen all at once, but grows by degrees, which every common wit cannot discern, but men expert in policy." But he *was* unusual in his inclusion of some modern-sounding pieces of analysis and of some prescriptions that are breathtaking in their anticipation of the distrust of government that will surface fully decades or even generations later. These include the election of "magistrates from among the commons by lot or balloting," their tenure of office to endure for a short time and once only and to include an obligation "to give an account of their behaviour and government, and that publicly before the commons." None should be chosen "for their wealth's sake"; indeed the tendency of "the rich to conspire against the state" points to the need to beware of "an oligarchy." Moreover, there must be "public salaries and allowances of their magistrates, judges, & c., and yearly dividends for the common people, and such as have most need among them."[71] Whether or not such ideas, written at the turn of the century, should be dismissed as a Utopia-like *jeu d'esprit* or as a maverick anticipation of what was to come, it is surely significant that this work was published in 1642.

Raleigh's own fortunes were eclipsed in 1603. Not so those of the concept of the commonwealth, although insofar as the corporeal analogy persists then the importance of the replacement of Elizabeth as head of the body politic by James I cannot lightly be discounted. Thus, one may usefully pause to take stock. Overall, social and economic speculation in any positive sense—as distinct from expression of endemic fear of the lower orders—had waned. But consideration of the religious and political characteristics of the commonwealth had *not* stood still. Morris's assertion that "no more was heard for half a century of Ponet's revolutionary ideas" must at least be reduced in its time span, while as for Gooch's verdict that the accession of Elizabeth marked the cessation of political thinking, then assuredly the prospect of her demise without a Tudor heir had for well over twenty years evoked its re-emergence.[72] Many publications were indeed creatures of circumstance; but fundamental considerations were repeatedly interwoven with arguments that were admittedly *parti pris*.

Unexpected cross-patterns emerge—as when Ponet re-surfaces in Parsons. Yet this is not really surprising. For fundamental reservations about the relationship between the temporal commonwealth and the church could be expected from both "Papist" and "Puritan" critics of Hooker's ad hoc but legitimized status quo. But the arguments advanced were almost always against the *identity* of church and commonwealth as presently existing, rather than against the general political and social order. Nevertheless, the clear emergence of early versions of a contract theory of the origins of royal power, with inescapable corollaries as to limitation in its exercise, points ahead to future developments. Morris suggested of William Allen that "here the Catholic, by adopting the idiom of Natural Law, has half anticipated the Whig theory of civil government." On the other side of the fence, J. W. Allen has observed that "when Whitgift says he can see no real difference between Church and Commonwealth, when Hooker says that the law as determined by public authority is the act and deed of every member of the Commonwealth, they have come very near to committing themselves to the Hobbesian doctrine." Certainly, some crucial subjects of debate in the crisis of the mid-seventeenth century were clearly enunciated a couple of generations earlier—though their implications were not yet acted out. It may sound close to *lèse majesté* to remark of Gloriana that "she inherited chaos, lived long enough for it to go away, and died before it returned,"[73] but it is not far from the truth.

The Early Stuarts

Nonetheless, the contention that the groundswell of catastrophe in motion from the outset of the Stuart era had its springs located in Tudor times jostles with the opinion that, as late as 1640, civil war was not inevitable. Much contemporary debate on those political, constitutional, and religious issues that presaged armed conflict was avowedly devoted to the exercise rather than the origins of princely and of parliamentary powers. But fundamental disagreements about the one inevitably involved the other, with obvious relevance for the evolution of the concept of the commonwealth. One historian has described the seventeenth century as "the greatest age of English political thought."[74] Yet of the rather sweeping assertion that it witnessed the transition away from a concept of society and of governance cast primarily in terms of communal *obligations,* toward one that concentrated more particularly upon individual *rights,* it must be said that in the early decades of that century this was not overwhelmingly in evidence. Meanwhile, in terms of *social* ideology the picture of the commonwealth emerging from the writings of this era remains traditional. The absence of innovative speculation goes side by side with continued dread of social subversion.

Insofar as we may take quite literally the claim of James I about the proclamations of his reign that "most of them myself doth dictate every word," then the notion of the commonwealth to which he at least paid lip service displays total continuity with that of his Tudor predecessors. The term itself recurs both as a synonym for "realm" and as indicating an ideal of public welfare. Also reiterated is the princely duty to exercise "the Christian care which all Kings are bound by the Law of God and nature to take over all their people," and in particular "to give remedy to any thing that is found hurtfull to the Commonweale of His people." Equally clear, since "two things, the true service of God, and happiness of the State do commonly concur together," is the royal duty in respect of doctrine to ensure "the steadfast maintaining of things by good advice established." Such Papists as Gerrard and Garret are "pernicious to our Person, State, and Common wealth," while Jesuit and Seminary enemies "under pretense of zeal make it their only occupation to persuade disobedience and to practise the ruin of this Church and Common-wealth." Equally typical is the distaste expressed for "excess of lavish and Licentious Speech of matters of State . . . which are no Themes or subjects fit for vulgar persons or common meetings" (this, apparently, drafted by Bacon). Indeed "our proceedings in Church and Common wealth" are unfit subjects for such presumptuous discussion, since vulgar people's minds "do not see clearly into things."[75]

Despite this last sentiment, the assertion that "absolutist ideas were expressed far more frequently in early Stuart than in Tudor England," indeed that the accession of James I "accelerated the shift towards absolutism," needs very careful exegesis. Authority exercised without overmuch opposition—as reflecting a fundamental community of interest between the monarch and the "political nation"—feels no need for clarity of definition. But when challenged, then recourse to justificatory exposition of its basis as well as of its exercise may well produce assertions more frightening than earlier realities. While many would urge that the publicly recorded aspirations of James I sounded more absolutist than those of his predecessor, few would maintain that *effectively* he exercised unchallenged a greater power. One foremost scholar has concluded that "he was certainly more moderate and 'constitutional' than Queen Elizabeth."[76]

It remains true that the cumulative criticisms and opposition that the rule of the first two Stuarts engendered served to nurture and develop principles that proved to be of fundamental importance in the future development of the notion of the commonwealth. Collinson has remarked that "in the history of religion the passing of Elizabeth made very little difference." But the discontent aroused in some quarters by the Crown's exercise of its powers as governor of the church accelerated a process that had commenced in Tudor times, even though the achievement of individual religious liberty lay as yet in the distant future. Again, what often started as protests against alleged illegalities in the Crown's financial policies developed into a discussion of the whole basis of individual property rights, and indeed of individual economic liberties as opposed to obligations, which also had far-reaching implications for the concept of the commonwealth. Christopher Hill's observation of the presence of "commercial concepts" like contract and balance in political and religious as well as economic thought, exemplifies the near-impossibility of strict separation of the interacting elements in a public debate that was conducted in Parliament and the Law Courts as well as in specific publications. But it is almost certainly in discussion of the religio-political dimensions of the commonwealth that we may discern the clearest signs of impending change. It has been suggested that it was "on the ground of religion that the battle for intellectual freedom was, at this time, fought." The qualification "intellectual" is significant; a much more recent survey has concluded that, insofar as the exercise of power by the Crown was concerned, "apologies for active resistance were rare, at least until 1640."[77]

A sampling of that literature that devoted space to discussion of the nature and problems of the commonwealth reveals no sharp divergence between early Stuart and Tudor preoccupations. Assuredly, almost all of Robert Burton's prescriptions in his attempt in his *Anatomy of Melancholy* (first published in 1621) to "make an Utopia of mine own, a new Atlantis, a poetical common-wealth of mine own," could have been penned three-quarters of a century earlier. In envisaging hospitals of all kinds, purpose-built as distinct from any conscience-saving afterthought of extortion, some provision from the common purse of freely available surgeons and physicians, control of depopulating enclosure and tyrannizing landlords, and a prohibition of all beggars and vagabonds made feasible by the provision of work for the idle and of help for the infirm, Burton is totally reminiscent of mid-Tudor commonwealth idealism. There is also present the occasional slightly challenging provision, as in the declaration that there shall be "no impropriations, no lay patrons of church-livings," and in the provision that an annual rendering of account must be made by all office-holders, while Burton will allow "no private monopolies, to enrich one man, and beggar a multitude." But degree is to be maintained, attire suited to each calling must be worn, and "my form of government shall be monarchical."

For "Utopian parity is a kind of government to be wished for, rather than effected, *Respub. Christianopolitana,* Campanella's City of the Sun, and that new Atlantis, witty fictions, but mere chimeras."⁷⁸

Just as representative of old-fashioned moralizing is *The Isle of Man*: "or The Legal Proceedings in Man-shire against Sinne" (1627), in which Richard Bernard arraigns "the chief Malefactors disturbing both Church and Common-Wealth." Wilfull-Will—alas, a gentleman born—admits that "I took it for granted, that my Gentry stood in idleness, pleasurable delights, hawking, hunting, and haunting Taverns, drinking of health, whiffing the Tobacco-pipe, putting on of new and variety of fashion. . . ." Such conduct might more readily be expected of "new Upstarts, never having had the right breeding of true Gentry." "Master Common-weal," Wilfull-Will's accuser, then goes on to condemn such as have monopolized commodities, enhanced prices, corrupted justice by bribery, and proceeded to "depopulate our whole Parish of Wealth" by setting a shepherd and his cur in place of good housekeepers. Such as these bear the real guilt for the shifts to which the poor are driven: stealing corn, wood, or coal, plucking wool from sheep, robbing orchards, stealing geese and hens, and so forth, so as to "make us poor people hateful to God and man." Apart from the allusion to tobacco, this could have come straight from Robert Crowley.⁷⁹

Several publications that were more particularly concerned with princely power within the commonwealth present the reader with a curious amalgam of traditional precepts and uneasy consciousness of impending change. Edward Forset, a JP in occasional charge of the Tower, was described by Allen over fifty years ago as one of "the most original and distinguished of the political thinkers of the period 1603 to 1642," but has more recently and less kindly been dismissed as having written "an idiosyncratic and rather foolish work"! Rambling and idiosyncratic his *Discourse of the Bodies Natural and Politique* (1606) assuredly is, but it is not without interest. In treating of "Sovereigns and Sovereignty" Forset expresses the usual abhorrence both of misrule and of anarchy, together with the mutual expectation of prince and subject respectively, "to rule well, and to be well ruled." But in his exposition of "the soul of sovereignty" one is taken aback by learning that "the favourites of a prince may be resembled to the fantasies of the Soul, wherewith he sporteth and delighteth himself": subjects must beware of spiteful envy! Ingeniously also, while the head is naturally imbued with a fellow-feeling of the body's griefs, the judgment of physicians "that most of the diseases of the head are originally arising and caused from the body" must therefore surely prescribe that "subjects have a cause to bear with a Sovereign's faults"![80]

Yet inherited concepts of equity, due degree, and moderation accompany Forset's explanation of "why the body politique is called a Common wealth." It is not "that all the wealth should be common; but because the whole wealth, wit, power, and goodness whatsoever, of every particular person, must be conferred and reduced to the common good." Thus the state (a word that recurs) must not ignore grief or pain but ensure that "the plenty of some be not the cause of penury unto others." The analogy of disease is pursued at length in expounding the duties of magistrates—"the State's Physicians." But unskilled meddling is disastrous, as is "this odious injury of the subjects' over much enquiring and spying into the Sovereign," as into sacred and unsearchable majesty. Despite all this, Forset himself asserts another notion met with earlier: "the natural body hath his infancy, his youthfulness, his confirmed, declining, and decrepit age: so hath each Commonwealth his beginning, his enlarging, his puissance, his drooping, his decay and downfall."[81]

Much easier to assess than Forset's book is that published in 1609 by Joseph Hall. Its run-of-the mill encomium of monarchical rule is notable chiefly for a striking throwback to the sentiments of William Thomas in the assertion, regarding subjects, "that they should reverence, and seek the face of the Prince; not cursing the King so much as in their thought, nor the rich in their bedchamber; but fearing the Lord, and the King, and not meddling with the seditious, which only seek evil."[82] Less straightforward are the contents of the dialogue format of John Floyd's *God and the King*, translated from Latin into English and printed overseas in 1620. Indeed, so obliquely conveyed is its message that an explanatory note, "The Printer to the Reader," was appended. Yet if the stance adopted by its Jesuit author is not always easily discerned, his insights into developing problems of what would now be termed religio-political theory are worth attention. Floyd is clearly aware of the dangers of the teachings of such as Hotman, Beza, Goodman, Knox, and Buchanan—"whereby they make Monarchy subject to the people's pleasure, no more sure of his state, than weathercocks that must turn with the wind."[83]

The proposition that "Kings have their authority from the people, and the people may take it away again, as men may revoke their letters of Attorney" is considered, as are the demands of "these fiery Gospellers, as his Majesty calleth them" for the introduction of a popular state in matters of church doctrine and discipline. Some parliamentary Puritans are credited with making "bold to propose the changing of the government of the realm from Monarchy into

Democracy," and the question is posed: "Doth not this doctrine, that Princes are made by the consent of the Commonwealth, impair the Majesty of Kings?" Yet as against all this the counter-assertions "that Kings have authority immediately and only from God, that neither Tyranny, nor Heresy, nor Apostasy can release subjects of their obedience" provoke the contention that "this *new doctrine* [my italics] of Princely absolute Sovereignty . . . makes the Common-wealth so miserable, and the people such bondmen to their Prince."[84]

Perhaps of special interest is the analysis in the addendum of the three opinions or positions now held in England: "The first of Puritans, who will have God without Kings, or else such a King that must depend on the people's beck. . . . The second is of Politicians, who have no more Christianity, than Parliamentary decrees breathe into them. These will have King without God, or at least King and God, that is, God so long and no longer than the King shall please. . . . The third opinion is of the Catholics, whose whole motto is, God and the King: in the first place they worship God; in the second the King, to whom they give all Allegiance and subjection as far as Religion and conscience will permit."[85]

Such arguments did not afflict the position of the royal theorist on monarchy, James I, though this was indeed more balanced than is sometimes asserted. Addressing Parliament in 1610, he declares that "the state of monarchy is the supremest thing upon earth; for kings are justly called gods for that they exercise a manner or resemblance of divine power upon earth." Yet this must be seen in context; for James goes on to explain that "a King governing in a settled Kingdom leaves to be a King, and degenerates into a Tyrant, as soon as he leaves off to rule according to his Laws." His power is held of God, to edify not to destroy. "And it were an idle head that would in place of physic so poison or phlebotomise the body as might breed a dangerous distemper or destruction thereof." It is indeed "seditious in subjects to dispute what a king may do in the height of his power, but just kings will ever be willing to declare what they will do, if they will not incur the curse of God." Nonetheless, significantly, all "Members of the Common-weal ought to be forced (if otherwise unwilling) to contribute liberally . . . to the preservation of it"— especially in cases where church and commonwealth might otherwise perish together.[86]

Little of this is outside mainstream traditional thinking thus far encountered in apologists for the monarchical commonwealth. But as royal powers became increasingly subject to question in the following reign, so the assertions made in their defence became more sweeping. Charles I himself was perhaps readier to take forthright and often ill-advised action than to discuss his monarchical rights, but aggressive spokesmen were not lacking, especially among the ranks of the clergy. The Reverend Robert Sibthorp's *Apostolike Obedience* (1627), addressed to the monarch but also to "the Church and Common-weale of England," is adamant that "Christian liberty hath not freed us from Civil Obedience." In face of the threat that "an Anarchy confounds all, which we will avoid in a Christian Commonalty," Sibthorp enunciates nonresistance: "he that resisteth the Prince, resisteth the power and ordinance of God." The roll call cited of those whose teachings would allegedly confound a commonwealth ranges from Bellarmine, Parsons, and Sanders on the one hand to Knox, Buchanan, and Goodman on the other. Interestingly, the unity of church, state, and commonweal is best achieved by an acceptance of division and limitations of functions: "the People must not be busy-bodies to pry into the Prince's duty, the Laity into the Clergy's, or the Jurors into the Judge's."[87]

In the same year, Roger Mainwaring, bishop of St. David's, preaching on *Religion and Alegiance* before Charles himself—"the sacred and supreme Head of two Bodies, the one Spiritual, the other Secular"—is equally explicit. Declaring "religion the stay of polity; . . . the root of all virtues; the foundation of all well-ordered Commonweals," he goes on to assert that royal power "is not merely human, but Superhuman." Assuredly, it "is not a Derivation, or Collection of human power scattered among many; but a participation of God's own Omnipotency." Accordingly, "though any King in the world should command flatly against the Law of God, yet were his Power no otherwise at all to be resisted, but for the not doing of His will in that which is clearly unlawful." Those who suffer for their principles, having eschewed the resistance that would render them "odious traitors," may comfort themselves with the thought that they now "become glorious Martyrs"![88]

Pre-eminent in defending a concept of the unity of church and state that came increasingly under attack was William Laud, archbishop of Canterbury. His policies have been seen as engendering an overlap of ecclesiastical and secular personnel and functions that inevitably involved the obloquy of the one with the other. His utterances, designed to exalt both kingly power and episcopal authority, to assert the unity of church and commonwealth and to brand his adversaries as contemplating revolution in them both, produced in effect increasing unity of opposition. In the reign of James I he had already preached that "the Commonwealth can have no blessed and happy being but by the Church," and that "when we kneel down to pray, we must not forget the State." He now declared in 1626 that those "that would overthrow *sedes ecclesia* . . . will not spare (if ever they get power) to have a pluck at the Throne of David." By 1637, at the condemnation of Bastwick, Burton, and Prynne before Star Chamber for anti-episcopalian agitation, he finds it manifest that "the intention of these men and their abettors was and is to raise a sedition."[89]

Ultimately, Laud was to suffer what one historian has termed judicial murder. Yet earlier the rigorous policies that he helped to promulgate had produced their own victims. One of these, Sir John Eliot, imprisoned briefly in 1626 and then again from 1629 until his death in 1632, has retrospectively emerged as one of the profoundest thinkers of his era—posthumously as well as retrospectively, because his works were not published until the late nineteenth century. *De Jure Maiestatis: or Political Treatise of Government*, written, like his other composition, while a prisoner in the Tower, blends much that is traditional with the occasional strikingly searching insight that explains why he chose to remain a prisoner of principle. Commencing with the definition that "a Common wealth is nothing else but a right and exercise of Sovereign power over their Subjects," unchallenged by "either superior or equal power," Eliot derides the notion "that the people do make themselves a King." He scorns such as Hotman and warns that "if the people be allowed right to punish their prince, this opens a gap to all liberty, licence, rapine, spoil, rebellions. . . ." Moreover, since "nothing doth more conduce to the happiness and quiet of the Common wealth than religion," the monarch must prevail therein: for it is vain "to expect health from a Physician whom we will obey in but half of his prescriptions." Yet the king, "in abrogating laws, he must proceed with good conscience, for the evident utility of the Common wealth." Above all, "he must not exercise his prerogative over the goods of his subjects [unless] the safety of the State requires it."[90]

Such codicils explain the identification of Eliot as a bridge between a typically organic Tudor theory of the commonwealth and the emergence of a concept of *individual* property rights. These issues are further explored in his other work, *The Monarchie of Man*. Acknowledging that "of all Governments, Kingdoms are the best," Eliot is soon at pains to stress that royal power must be deployed "for his Subjects, for the common use and benefit." In a perhaps significantly mercantile analogy, "the Pilot is the Prince, the ship is the commonwealth, the Mariners, the officers subordinate, and magistrates; the goods and merchandise, the people." The first of several references to Bodin is followed by the warning "that Subjects are not more bound to the obedience of their Sovereign, than Sovereigns to do Justice to their Subjects." In stressing "the rights and interests of the commonwealth" a lengthy exposition of law cites Plato's assertion that "nothing but ruin can be the fortune of that Kingdom where the Prince doth rule the laws, and not the laws the Prince."[91]

Allusions to Fortescue, Plato, and Bodin again lead up to Eliot's enunciation that "monarchy is a power of government and rule for a common good and benefit, not an institution for private interests and advantage." The supreme objective is surely "the public utility and good." Yet clearly within the commonwealth there exist diverse interests; how these may be reconciled "is the great secret that we search for: the true course and method by which this reformation may be made, is the great difficulty we have." Here, in these supremely important passages, there emerges a dilemma that was to become ever clearer: that of reconciling collective responsibilities with individual rights. Again, our form of government "requires not an absolute submission and obedience in all things to be commanded, and at all times, . . . but a free and voluntary submission for the public utility and good." For the *bonum publicum* is "the true end and object of the Monarchy of man," whose members "must first intend the common good and benefit, and so descend by degrees unto our selves." Eliot is fairly seen as conveying a glimpse of a crucial debate of the future.[92]

Perhaps the same claim may be made for a striking passage in *A Relation of the State of Religion* by Sir Edwin Sandys, himself the son of the prelate cited earlier. Thus far, most writings considered on the place of religion in the commonwealth have been directed toward the supposedly crucial need for religious unity—unity both as to belief and in respect of relationships between church and state. Notions of toleration, of acceptance of diversity, or indeed of complete religious liberty were not new; but the early-sixteenth-century writings of those such as Castellio had awakened few chords of sympathy on the English side of the Channel. Even now, Sandys himself sought the suppression of an unauthorized printing of his composition in 1605. Yet, after his depiction of centuries of ruthless persecution he poses the question:

> Seeing there is no appearance of ever forcing an unity, unless Time, which eateth up all things, should bring in great alterations: it remaineth to be considered, what other kind of unity poor Christendom may hope for, whether unity of Verity, or unity of Charity, or unity of persuasion, or unity of authority, or unity of Necessity . . . A kind of men there are, . . . not many in number, but sundry of them of singular learning and

piety, whose godly longings to see Christendom re-united in the love of the Author of the name above all things, and annexed in brotherly correspondence and amity [urge that] these flames of controversy might be extinguished or slaked.[93]

Few in number they may have been, and unrepresentative of their era, but once again we counter impressive insights. An early work of pre-eminent importance is that of Leonard Busher. *Religious Peace: or, A Plea for Liberty of Conscience* was republished in 1646, with the expression of a hope that the "Brethren of the Presbyterian way" will abate their misguided persecution. But the original had been "long since presented to King James, and the High Court of Parliament" in 1614. In this short but passionately written tract Busher appeals to the head as well as to the heart. His reminder that Christ himself did not command persecution is followed by an exposition of the evil effects within the state of dissembling in order to comply with enforced uniformity. In contending that religious persecution may indeed ruin its own avowed objective, he cites an incident from the reign of Edward VI, who, "being urged by his bloody Bishops to subscribe to the burning of a woman called Joan Butcher, he answered, will you have me to send her quick to the devil in her error?"[94]

In advocating both "permission of conscience, and liberty of the gospel in our land of great Britain," and scorning the fiat that "all within the land be forced to be of the church as the Bishops and their ministers would still have it," Busher turns his adversaries' argument upon its head by urging that if toleration be permitted then "the commonwealth of his Majesty's Kingdoms will flourish and prosper. . . . For if the holy laws of God's word be practised . . . then Treason and Rebellion, as well as burning, banishing, hanging, or imprisoning, for differences in religion will cease." Nor is there lacking a social dimension to this elysium: "then shall not men, women, and youth be hanged for theft: then shall not the poor, lame, sick, and weak ones be stocked and whipped, neither shall the poor, stranger, fatherless, and widows be driven to beg. . . . Then shall not the great defraud and wrong the small, neither the rich oppress the poor by usury and little wages." J. W. Allen envisaged this dream of social justice as foreshadowing the Fifth Monarchy Men and the Quakers, but it is also reminiscent of mid-Tudor idealism; the really new element is the contention that the application of the Gospel spirit in social relationships derives from truly Christian diversity rather than from enforced uniformity.[95]

In 1615, published "without name or place" (though apparently printed in Holland), appeared a work entitled *Persecution for Religion Judg'd and Condemned*. This Anabaptist tract is notable for its insistence not only that *any* worship of God, let alone any particular form of worship, is meaningless if it be *enforced*, but also that religious freedom is in no way harmful to the state. Alluding to "his Majesty's own divers testimonies, that no man ought to be persecuted for his religion, be it true or false, so they testify their faithful allegiance to the king," the author willingly proffers such loyalty. *But* "the sword of the magistrate [prevails] only upon the outward man, and cannot convert a soul from going astray, nor beget faith."[96] As for the fears expressed that if "all religions should be suffered . . . there would be such divisions as would breed sedition and innovation *in the state*" (my italics), the author identifies a familiar switch from defeated scriptural argument "to conceits, and imaginations of sedition, innovation, and the like." This he counters with a point met with earlier, that "he that playeth the dissembling hypocrite with God" will hardly show dependable allegiance to a monarch. Better to recognize that "the statute law of the land requireth only civil obedience." He is willing to "acknowledge unfeignedly, that God hath given to magistrates a sword to cut off wicked men, and to reward the well-doer. But this ministry is a worldly ministry."[97] Thus early in the seventeenth century, this is a long way from Hooker.

Very similar arguments are set forth in *An Humble Supplication* "to the King's Majesty," made by "Loyal Subjects, ready to testify all Civil Obedience," unjustly called Anabaptists and persecuted for religion's sake, printed in 1620. Thus, "the vileness of persecuting the body of any man, only for the cause of conscience, is against the word of God and law of Christ." Indeed "it is no prejudice to the commonwealth if freedom of religion were suffered, but would make it flourish." But a much more ominous note is sounded when, not content merely to cite Chrysostom's view that the untutored mind may readily grasp the Scriptures, the tract declares that "those that fear and obey God, and so have the Spirit of God to search out and know the mind of God in the scriptures, are commonly, and for the most part, the simple, poor, despised, &c." Those endowed with worldly learning are for the most part in error![98]

The advocacy of religious toleration as expedient and, perhaps more fundamentally important in its implications, of religious liberty as a principle, was slowly to gather strength. Indeed by December 1648 the Council of Officers at Whitehall was formally to debate "whether the magistrate have, or ought to have, any compulsive and restrictive power in matters of religion?"[99] Meanwhile, there remains one other aspect of religious thought in the decades preceding the Civil War that merits close attention: the relationship between doctrinal developments and evolving social attitudes or indeed the nature of a commonwealth-type vision of society. Here Collinson has observed that "puritanism is not adequately described as a body of doctrine or as a set of religious and moral principles." Calvinist theology, which permeated the Jacobean church, "had broad implications for the sustenance of the existing political and social order, with which it was assumed to be entirely coherent." Indeed, "the conscious thrust of puritan doctrine was towards the redemption of the existing order, . . . social amelioration not social change, . . . the old world regenerated, not the world turned upside down."[100]

In *Christian Humanism and the Puritan Social Order* Margo Todd has advanced the thesis that post-Tridentine Catholicism rejected Erasmian social precepts—which I have earlier noted as major contributants to the emergence of the ideal of the Tudor Commonwealth—leaving Protestants, and in particular Puritans, as their standard-bearers. Here some caution is surely advisable. The seventeenth-century English Jesuit cited as endorsing indiscriminate almsgiving was after all but echoing the early Tudor Puritan, Robert Crowley. Nor was emerging perception of the idle poor as "ulcers and drones of the Common-wealth" confined to one doctrinal standpoint. Dr. Todd herself cites the "selective but substantial survival of humanist social ideology in seventeenth-century Anglicanism . . . in the joint sponsorship of the Books of Orders of 1630–31 by the most staunchly conformist of the hierarchy and the most zealous of Puritans." Again, Roger Mainwaring, no favorer of Puritans, could still extol the Erasmian precept that "in every well-ordered Commonwealth, as by Distributive Justice, each person hath a share in the Profits and Honours therein."[101]

Nonetheless, it is true that two favorite exemplars of Puritan social thought, William Perkins and William Gouge, furnish impressive evidence of continuity not only with Erasmian but also with mid-Tudor commonwealth ideology. In *A Treatise of the Vocations or Callings of Men*, composed at the turn of the century, Perkins relates the concepts identified to the common good—for which indeed they are "ordained and imposed on man by God." Not only is it decreed that every person, of every degree, "must have some personal and particular calling to walk in," but it is also essential "that the works of our calling be profitable not only to the doers, but to the commonwealth." As a general rule, "let every man abide in that calling wherein he was called" and to which he is suited; yet "a change of calling is a lawful going from one calling to another . . . but upon right and weighty causes . . . private necessity and the common good." A calling is not a passport to self-seeking; from the vice of covetousness there flows a sea of evils into church and commonwealth. Unsurprisingly, Perkins lists the misdeeds of merchants and tradesmen, and discerns in landlords "racking of rents, taking immoderate fines, enclosing of grounds that have lain common time out of mind." Whatever one's calling, work is essential: "it is a foul disorder in any commonwealth that there should be suffered rogues, beggars, vagabonds, [who] are as rotten legs and arms that drop from the body." Again one meets the opinion that "the statute made in the last parliament for the restraining of beggars and rogues is an excellent statute."[102]

God having ordained the society of man with man, "partly in the commonwealth, partly in the church and partly in the family," each of these must be considered as a body—the third of significance not only in itself but also as a training ground for the virtues needed in the other, wider spheres. While the emphasis placed upon the importance of Christian family life did not originate with Erasmus, it seems to be the case that the particular recognition that he gave it endured more especially in Puritan social thought. In his compendious treatment *Of Domesticall Duties* (1622), William Gouge identifies the family as "a seminary of the Church and common-wealth. It is as a Bee-hive, in which is the stock, and out of which are sent many swarms of Bees . . . into the Church and common-wealth." In fact, "a family is a little Church, and a little common-wealth, . . . whereby trial may be made of such as are fit for any place of authority, or of subjection in Church or common-wealth." Gouge echoes Perkins in his endorsement of the notion of God-given vocations or callings "in Common-wealth, Church, or family."[103]

Such considerations suggest that it is appropriate, finally, to review the development of early Stuart thinking about the social and economic dimension of commonwealth ideology. Alongside the slowly emerging indications of a questioning of former religious and political assumptions, what signs are evident of equivalent developments in social and economic thought? Despite the indications of continuity in mainstream commonwealth ideology encountered at the outset of the Stuart century, economic and social as well as political and religious developments could make for change. One must therefore at least allude to important if gradual trends in respect of population, of prices, wages and living standards, and of the balance of the economy as between agriculture, industry, and commerce. First, while the sixteenth century had witnessed something approaching a doubling of the population of England, the seventeenth was to record a proportionate increase of at most 25 percent.[104] Ironically, Robert Gray's *A Good Speed to Virginia,* in 1609, looks back nostalgically to a mythical age "when our Country was not pestered with a multitude" and its common lands "lay free and open for the poor Commons to enjoy." Alas, in the present absence of preferment and employment for all, "there is nothing more dangerous for the estate of common-wealth than when the people do increase to a greater multitude and number" than it can support. One remedy for such a demographic menace to the commonwealth assuredly is emigration to such settlements as Virginia—though the author confides his own ability to participate "neither in person nor in purse"![105]

Meanwhile, though generalization in this field is hazardous, the catastrophic imbalance between the inflation in prices and movements in wages that had characterized so much of the previous century now at least abated. Yet despite such secular trends, in the short run people still went hungry and sometimes starved. Whatever the statistical indications in respect of the "background" or "shallow" poverty identified by Slack as against "deep" or "crisis level" distress, the incidence of disastrous harvest failures produced familiar reactions. Indeed, he himself concludes that "the background level of poverty obviously deteriorated down to 1620; and there seems no reason to assume any improvement before 1650."[106] Admittedly, the balance of the economy itself was to change. Agricultural efficiency improved, while the industrial and commercial sectors both expanded and diversified. Yet enclosures involving loss of rights or eviction, and the severe unemployment that a market-related slump in some aspect of industrial demand might involve, alike produced distress and its associated problems. A plentiful harvest was little consolation to a would-be consumer without purchasing power. Thus, we need look for no striking Tudor/Stuart divide in contemporaries' apprehension of economic problems.

In the long run the inherited values of commonwealth ideology will become increasingly subject to pressures for modification, either in the light of a changing perception of priorities, as in the sphere of poor relief, or—more crucially—in that of clamant demands for unrestricted individual freedom in the use and pursuit of property and wealth within agriculture, industry, and trade. But it is the events and consequences of the midcentury, rather than the accession of the Stuart dynasty, that will mark the watershed, particularly in respect of the approach of government to the economic and social needs of the commonwealth. I have already touched on James I's declarations of intent; as for his successor, before whom

Roger Mainwaring preached on the principle of distributive justice,[107] J. F. Larkin finds much to commend in his endeavors—despite the obvious mistakes.[108] The conscious social policy of the early Stuarts consisted of the paternalism—alternatively defined by Joyce Appleby as "a style of government that has been called patrimonial"[109]—bequeathed to them by the Tudors. Larkin urges that during the Eleven Years' Rule without Parliament Charles I "attempted systematically to relieve the poor and indigent," but Slack, in tracing the long pedigree of the three Books of Orders of 1630–31, points out that the social policies thus promulgated were "no sudden or eccentric innovation" but rooted in earlier endeavors at "English public welfare." Their sternest critics could hardly deny to the first two Stuart monarchs a recognition of the avowed pursuit of several objectives in economic and social policy of which committed commonwealth sympathizers would have approved. But in general, their approach was defensive in that it feared social change and mobility, as all-too-likely to exacerbate unemployment, vagabondage, unrest, and disorder. This is not surprising, for what has been termed a permanent background of potential unrest erupted into actual and quite menacing outbreaks of disorder in 1607, 1622, and 1626–31.[110]

The fear of dearth expressed in several Jacobean edicts was engendered as much by fear of potential disorder as by humanitarian principles. Even an order that brewers "make their Beer and Ale not too strong" was concerned not only "that the poorer sort may have the greater proportion for their money" but also with curbing excessive use of malt. Several proclamations against the making of starch condemned the use for purposes of vanity and pride, "as it is used by inferior persons," of grain "which might have served in time of dearth, for the relief of the poorer sort." But the major cause of concern was the marketing process itself. A proclamation against the transportation of corn and grain attributed a situation in which "the poor must needs suffer extreme want [to] the greedy covetousness of Buyers and Hoarders of Corn." Another, directed toward a necessary "Reformation of the great abuses in Weights and Measures," enjoined the pursuit and prosecution of forestallers, ingrossers, and regrators as conducive to "the service of Our Common Wealth." Such efforts continued under Charles I, an early edict condemning those who drove up the price of victuals as "oppressors of the Common-Wealth." The period of personal rule saw attempts to set maximum prices and improve regulations for the baking and sale of bread. A lengthy proclamation of 28 September 1630 ordered action by mayors and justices of the peace to see "the Markets duly supplied with Corn and the poor first served," suppressing the abuses of "Ingrossers, Badgers, Broggers," and so forth, to do so.[111] Archbishop Laud's assertion in Star Chamber that the dearth of 1630–31 was "made by man and not by God"—if only partly true—bespeaks a continuing acceptance of a duty of government to identify and to curb "market forces."

The turn of the century had witnessed the recurrence of another problem that in Tudor England was a virtual test case of commitment to commonwealth ideals: that of checking depopulating enclosure. In 1604 a member for Northamptonshire complained to Parliament about "the depopulation and daily excessive conversion of tillage into pasture." Three years later the county was the center of a Midlands Revolt against enclosure and rack-renting. A proclamation in May 1607 for the suppression of anti-enclosure rioters claimed "that we have been careful to prevent such Enclosure and Depopulation." Yet in the six counties on which the subsequent Enclosure Commission reported, of the total area enclosed between 1578 and 1607 some two-thirds were enclosed between 1598 and 1607. John Martin envisages the outbreak as "the last peasant revolt in England," and Roger Manning concurs that something more than "a series of enclosure riots" was involved. These contentions gain force from the fact that some thousands took part and that in a major clash on 8 June forty or fifty peasants were killed. The participants' procedure in tearing down enclosing hedges and the banks on which they were often set, so as to fill up adjacent ditches and level off the ground was to furnish the language of protest with a new term. A report describing how "these fellows who term themselves levellers were busy digging," and the contemporaneous manifesto of the "Diggers of Warwickshire"—in which they professed "the good of the Commonwealth till death"—pointed to another.[112]

While the outbreaks spread, in particular to Leicestershire, *A Sermon Preached at North-Hampton* by Robert Wilkinson on 21 June is significant in its combination of condemnation of the greed that had provoked "Rebellion and Riot" with keen apprehension of what might ensue—a combination often noted in the mid-Tudor literature. Concurring with the "just complaints of the poor," Wilkinson declares that in truth the enclosers "were no sheep, they were hogs by their rooting"—and should therefore be ringed. But while condemning "these *Anthropophagi*, these devourers of men under a name of *right and property*" (my italics), such as would "*grind the faces* of the poor," he also warns that "desperate estates breed desperate minds." At first, indeed the rebels may "profess nothing, but to throw down enclosures, though that were indeed no part of the common power; but afterward they will reckon for other matters. They will account with Clergy men, and counsel is given to kill up Gentlemen, and they will level all states as they leveled banks and ditches."[113]

Governmental reaction was predictable. The perceived threat to the social order took massive precedence over any claim by the rebels to be defending the Crown's accepted, but increasingly ineffective, agrarian policy. A proclamation dated 28 June employed the analogy of the "course which the best Physicians use in dangerous diseases" to justify the bloody suppression of the main rising. It also claimed that "the said Inclosures (lawful or unlawful) were all for the most part made" before 1603. The subsequent royal commissions of enquiry, from August to October 1607, cast grave doubts upon this claim, and indeed "netted a number of big fish." But their powers were to enquire and report—not to redress or punish. Nevertheless, a number of indictments and prosecutions were undertaken, in Star Chamber and other courts, though these were usually followed by the infliction of far-from-draconian penalties upon those who were unable to evade the charge of depopulating enclosure. Occasional attempts to enforce the tillage laws continued to be made. But Martin sees this era as marked not only by the last peasants' revolt but also by the last futile efforts by government to check "agrarian capitalism."[114]

In truth, the sporadic attempts of this and of the following reign to protect open-field agriculture ran counter to an increasingly rapacious tide. Given the demand for food of a still-growing population, agricultural improvement—including consolidation of holdings for better arable exploitation—was a genuine issue. The early 1620s saw at least a tacit recognition of this. Yet the early years of non-parliamentary rule witnessed a revival, in response to rising prices, of prosecution of "depopulating enclosers." Laud's activities on the Enclosure Commission then established evoked unpopularity reminiscent of that of Wolsey. J. P. Kenyon suggests that "the most important single cause of Star Chamber's unpopularity was the role it was called upon to play in the 1630s in the enforcement of the king's fiscal and social policies." But it has been contended that what ultimately emerged was a device to license enclosures and raise revenue—while the Crown itself was sometimes involved.[115]

Another traditional touchstone of humanitarian commonwealth attitudes is treatment of poverty. Here we have noted Slack's conclusion that the background darkened, while Charles I's resort to "unparliamentary rule" virtually coincided with the onset of an economic crisis reflecting a combination of bad weather and wretched harvests, rising food prices, and unemployment in textiles. Christopher Hill declares that "the poor were treated as utterly rightless"—the forcible deportation of destitute children from London to Virginia in 1618 revealing the other side of the coin to Gray's bland appeal noticed earlier.[116] Yet when it is asserted that only the harsher aspects of the Elizabethan Poor Law were applied, the fault may hardly be assigned solely to the Crown, short-sighted and wrong-headed as it may sometimes have been. Admittedly, fear of the hungry poor driven desperate underlay a near-obsession with the expansion of building in London as increasing that city's population, "specially of the meaner sort, as can hardly be either fed and sustained, or preserved in health or governed," which surfaced in a dozen proclamations under James I and continued in the following reign. But the Book of Orders of April 1630 also included regulations that have been seen as part of "a protracted campaign to improve provision for public health in London."[117]

As far as the *relief* of poverty is concerned, it is true that governmental action consisted largely of appeals for the enforcement of *existing* legislation; but in this it was surely not far wrong. The Poor Law, which had been enacted as a virtual codification of the experience of Tudor England, was for generations to remain the basis of action. Its weakness lay not in any failure to identify the causes of poverty or to discriminate between the types of treatment most appropriate for each, but rather in a reliance upon enforcement by local agencies of very variable quality and motivation—a consideration that should give pause to endeavors to relate its efficacy too closely to any doctrinal exposition. Occasionally, both James and Charles looked back nostalgically in enjoining the gentry not to live in London but to stay at home and exercise charitable hospitality. For "the poor sort are unrelieved, and not guided or governed as they might be in case those persons of quality and respect resided among them." Such appeals may be set in the context of Felicity Heal's conclusion that concern with "the threat to traditional values" became most acute during these decades.[118]

Perhaps more significant is the evidence, in books and sermons alike, of the continuation of a process identified earlier of what some would term a hardening of attitudes and others an insistence on a clear-headed approach. A Latimer-like condemnation of greed and of the abuse of wealth by its owners as causing poverty continues. The exploitation of the poor is condemned in a sermon by Thomas Carew of Suffolk, in 1603. Taking as his text the evocative injunction "Go to now ye rich men, howl and weep for the miseries that shall come upon you," his "Caveat for craftsmen and Clothiers" pleads for the application of the "rules of equity . . . in giving of wages." The preacher condemns employers who "keep their riding Horses and their Dogs fat, but . . . their workfolks both very poor and lean"—and often "pay them with bad or dear commodities." Such indeed "do evil in setting the poor awork": for "this abridgement of wages is a cause of all the misery of the poor." Again, the Reverend Jeremy Dyke of Essex, preaching at Paul's Cross in 1619, launched a completely traditional *Counterpoison against Covetousnes*—which he defines as being "to desire beyond the bounds of sufficiency, . . . a desire of more than enough." This it is, become "an Epidemical disease," which produces "a man of many callings and possessions [who] hath but a little time for sleep, and none at all for God." This it is which leads to such a "whole crowd of abominations . . . as defrauding, overreaching, . . . extortion, inclosures, depopulations, . . . detention of the labourers' wages, engrossers, corn-hoarders," and so on.[119]

In 1621 the Reverend Bezaleel Carter, preaching in Suffolk, ranks the loss to the commonwealth "when a dogged Dives dies" as literally equal to that ensuing from the demise of a dog. But he scorns vainglorious charity as well as such teachings of "Papistical beggary" as those which "extol and praise Penury and Poverty as a state of perfection." Yet although "against Anabaptistical community" he is ready to "defend no other property of goods than may stand with the communion of saints. Though thy goods be thine, yet they are not so thine, but that the poor have a letter of Attorney from God, to have their use as well as thyself." In the same year, *Greevous Grones for the Poore,* printed for Michael Spark, seeking "the public Honour and profit of this Christian Commonwealth," lists the taking in of copy-hold lands, the surcharging of the commons, and the adding of land to land, by landlords as causes of poverty. He protests that "the Impotent with the lame foot is to be defended and sustained by every member of the body of this Commonwealth"—but abhors "Waspish and Dronish Beggary."[120]

Robert Sanderson, bishop of Lincoln (also in 1621) sounds a harsher note, declaring "sturdy Rogues and vagrant towns-end Beggars the very scabs, and filth, and vermin of the Common-wealth." Deploring "indiscreet and mis-guided charity," he declares that "he that helpeth one of these sturdy Beggars to the stocks, and the whip, and the house of correction, not only deserveth better of the Common-wealth; but doth a greater Charity in the sight of God, than he that helpeth him with meat, and money, and lodging. . . . For he that giveth any Alms to an Idle Beggar, robbeth the truly poor." Most crucially, this forthright cleric was in no doubt that "we have splendid laws"; but alas "those Laws are now no Laws for want of due execution." In *The Poor Mans Advocate, or A Treatise of Liberality* (1637), the Reverend William Whately commends not "a scant, backward, niggardly giving, but a constant, cheerful, discreet, and upright giving," for "the poor ye shall have always with you." But he is equally clear that "these men that be able to work, and out of sluggishness will not, are exempted from the number of those to whom the Lord would have our hands open to give. To feed them is to fat vermin, as it were, to feed mice, rats, and polecats, yea it is to feed vice itself."[121]

In general the early Stuarts deemed endorsement of existing legislation adequate. A statute of 1623 was devoted to "the Reviving and Making perpetual" an Elizabethan "Act for erecting of Hospitals, and Abiding and Working Houses for the Poor" (39 Eliz. I, c.5). A proclamation in February 1628 pointed to existing provision "both for the suppressing and punishing of this sort of lewd and incorrigible people and for the relief of the indigent and impotent poor, to which good Laws nothing can be added but the careful and due execution thereof." On 17 May 1629 another such edict commanded that laws to hand "for the relief of the indigent and impotent poor, for binding out Apprentices, for providing of Stocks [of material], and for setting the poor on work, be duly and carefully put in execution." Other proclamations deplored the "neglect of the due execution of the Laws." The best-known Book of Orders, issued in January 1631, set out directions for the relief of the poor, ordered action by the justices of the peace, and established a Privy Council commission to supervise endeavours.[122] It seems difficult not to concede that in this sphere, given the constraints of reality, especially in administration, early Stuart attempts to continue the more idealistic aspects of the commonwealth tradition were often on a hiding to nothing.

Concern for poverty driven desperate redoubled at times when, as in 1622–23, a familiar pattern occurred of a poor harvest being followed by high food prices, leaving less money for other consumer purchases and exacerbating a coincident slump in textiles.[123] In the increasingly important industrial sector the Stuarts, like their predecessors, were torn between encouragement of expansion, which was seen as conducive to national self-sufficiency or as generating employment, and the equally traditional protection of manufacture in corporate towns—allied with suspicion of potentially disruptive innovation. Insofar as this last attitude stunted any growth of prospects of employment it was of course counterproductive. Larkin again credits Charles I in particular with genuine attempts to protect the consumer and indeed the national interest by intervention in respect of trade and of standards in leather, wool, and silk. But sadly, despite the frequent presence of the terminology of the interests of the commonwealth, action through patent and proclamations was all-too-often almost blatantly fiscal in its intent—most notably in respect of the marketing of tobacco and wine, and the manufacture of starch and soap. The Cockayne Project, introduced in a proclamation of 7 December 1613 "for the true Working and Dying of Cloth," designed to enforce standards, increase employment, and yield both inducements for the Crown and profits for its promoters, was perhaps the most notorious of such devices.[24] Joan Thirsk, in the context of projects overall, designates the period 1601 to 1624 as the "Scandalous Phase, Part II." Nonetheless, as late as 1624–27 she discerns in John Stratford's scheme for a transformation of the idle poor from a burden to an asset to the commonwealth by means of flax cultivation and linen manufacture, the tone "of a Commonwealthman of an earlier age."[125]

Undoubtedly, declared social purposes were sometimes pushed aside by the fiscal needs of the Crown, as when controls such as those of the aulnagers, purporting to maintain standards in cloth production, were sometimes waived for cash. R. H. Tawney's verdict that "in spite of its lofty declarations of a disinterested solicitude for the public welfare, the social policy of the monarchy was as slipshod in execution as it was grandiose in design" still holds for many modern historians. Yet others would not deny to it any sincere motivation or real impact. Robert Ashton, while identifying an "incongruous mixture of fiscal advantage and genuine paternalism," remains convinced that "the immediate impact of the Orders was spectacular."[126] Moreover, if policy was sometimes vitiated by the intrusion of baser interests, its execution was often hamstrung by administration that was at best amateurishly incompetent and at worst deliberately obstructive. Justices of the peace, and sometimes town authorities, could nullify the clearest of instructions not only through inertia but often because of a clear apprehension that their selfish interests were involved. Crown policy was sometimes perceived, rightly or wrongly, as directed to its own financial gain or to that of a particular vested interest that had its ear. But those forces—whether they be described as contenders for economic freedom or as selfish business interests—that were outraged by royal grants to favorites were often equally aggrieved by genuinely paternalist restrictions. It has indeed been observed that "the more active policy of state intervention in the sixteen-thirties," in response at least in part to the troubles of 1628–31, intensified friction between the Crown and men of property.[127]

By now indeed there are a few signs of a conviction that the proper task of government is not to control the market, and restrict the operation of natural economic forces, but rather to hold the ring for the free operation of individual action. Whether one regards it as but a rationalization of acquisitive instincts, or as a slow but genuine formulation of an economic philosophy of private enterprise, these decades witness the emergence of an attitude toward private property and toward the role of government that heralds a sea-change in the whole conception of the position of the individual within, and the nature of his obligations to, the commonwealth. Inevitably, this affects the very nature of the concept of the commonwealth itself. The merchant Edward Misselden, writing on *The Circle of Commerce* (1623) in defense of free trade, opens the door to a vista of changing social criteria when he asks: "What else makes a Common-wealth, but the private wealth . . . of the members thereof in the exercise of Commerce?" Not only is it lawful "for Merchants to seek their *Privatum Commodum* in the exercise of their calling" but it might also well be urged that "there's none more fit to make a minister for a King, than an expert or judicious Merchant." Look at Venice, Genoa, and the United Provinces![128]

The balance between the overlapping elements within the contemporary phrase "religion, liberty, and property" starts to change. It is not necessary to concur with Joyce Appleby's contention in *Economic Thought and Ideology in Seventeenth-Century England* "that the modern concept of political freedom grew out of a prior reorganization of economic life" in order to recognize the commencement of a reassessment of the obligations of the individual to society. Undoubtedly, the influence of economic interests, and pre-eminently that of increasingly powerful market forces, contributed to a process whereby "the concept of a social goal greater than the sum of private ones appeared less as an eternal verity and more as a vestigial notion."[129] Admittedly of long gestation, the evidence in a few early Stuart writers of the start of that development is clear. Of course, the recognition in Tudor times—as by Sir Thomas Smith and Sir John Mason—that economic motives might be more fruitfully channelled than dammed, and that market controls might often be self-defeating, serves as a caveat against the attribution of total novelty. Nor were former values speedily abandoned.

Gerald de Malynes, a currency specialist writing on commerce in the early 1620s, drew from his recognition that in their pursuit of gain merchants might forget the good of the commonwealth the conclusion that for this reason "Princes and Governors are to sit at the stern of the course of Trade and Commerce." But others were beginning to suggest that such direction and intervention was not only wrongheaded but simply wrong. Misselden, again, challenged: "Is not gain the end of trade? Is not the public involved in the private, and the private in the public?" Thomas Mun, a Director of the East India Company, contemporaneously identifying England's *Treasure by Foreign Trade,* was another astute analyst of market forces.[130] Thus, it is argued that the seventeenth century witnessed "the Moral Economy in Retreat," as the individual became "subsumed in a depersonalized aggregation." Yet such a process was hotly contested throughout the decades before the outbreak of Civil War. The effort to establish a recognition of interest as merely the pricing of money, at once commercially essential and morally neutral, was assailed in several books on usury, though one author conceded that such recognition "hath corrupted all England."[131]

There is as yet ample evidence of the survival of religious and moral criteria in the approach to social and economic issues. Thus the preamble to the Book of Orders of 5 January 1631 deplores the way in which "public services for God, the King and the Commonwealth" go by default because of negligence in administration. As well as enjoining provision for the poor and setting to work, and punishment of abuses in manufacture, pricing, and marketing, the Orders require action in respect of "breakers of houses, common thieves and their receivers; haunters of taverns or alehouses; those that go in good clothes and fare well, and none knows whereof they live; those that be night walkers," together with "the suppressing of that odious and loathsome sin of drunkenness." A striking turn of phrase condemns that "licentious liberty [which] makes so many delight to be rogues and wanderers." Again, in July 1635 a proclamation prescribed enforcement of the statute 21 James I, c.20 "for the suppressing of profane Swearing and Cursing" in the interests of "the Weale-public of this Realm."[132] Thus the assertion that Catholic and Anglican had now agreed "that a change in behaviour and mode of life is neither possible nor the proper concern of the authorities," leaving Puritans alone to carry onward the banner of Erasmian reform, seems rather sweeping.[133]

Perhaps at least as valid in the context of any changing assessments of the *moral* responsibilities of the government in the commonwealth are the conclusions suggested by Joan Kent's survey of the attitudes of members of the House of Commons toward the regulation of "Personal Conduct" in late Elizabethan and early Stuart England. The evidence on such touchstone issues as excess in apparel, drunkenness, swearing, profaning of the Sabbath and absence from church, and bastardy, suggests an interesting if tentative pattern. First, prohibitive or penal legislation gained the most wholehearted approval when it was directed to economic and political considerations—pre-eminently, preservation of public order—rather than to moral reformation purely as such. Secondly, members sometimes feared that regulations considered appropriate for the meaner sort might be taken to apply to gentlemen—although in fairness one member took the opposite line in opposing legislation designed as "a mere cobweb to catch poor flies in."[134]

Yet perhaps of greater long-run significance are the signs of objection to "purely moral regulation by the secular arm of the state"—as in one member's assertion that "every evil in the state is not to be met with in a law. And as it is in the natural, so it is in the politic body, that sometimes the remedy is worse than the disease."[135] A superficial resemblance to the position of Stephen Gardiner may be discerned—until one remembers that whereas Gardiner would leave moral offenses to the church what we now see is nearer to a rejection of *any* regulation of individual morality. But these were minority voices; as yet on this issue it was William Laud who voiced mainstream opinion—although indeed it was for his blending (some would say, confusion) of ecclesiastical with secular functions that he was, and has been, criticized. In the widest context, there seems to the present writer only minimal evidence of any abandonment as yet of the inherited notion that the unitary church and commonwealth are responsible for the enforcement of a moral as well as a social order.

In conclusion, what may be said overall of the position reached by 1639—a date approximately indicating the onset of the near-disintegration of the early Stuart monarchical order? Certainly one may hardly speak of any meaningful *development* of the ideal of the commonwealth during the eighty-year span of this chapter. In social and economic terms it is fair to write of continued lip service, with some evidence of real if sporadic attempts to maintain traditional social standards and to continue paternalist intervention in economic activities. But the impression is one of waning hopes for social amelioration, and of a hardening of the arteries—to employ a favorite contemporary similitude. In terms of the religious aspect of the commonwealth, there is much evidence of opposition—from more than one quarter—to the policies of established ecclesiastical authority. Yet such opposition sought but a change in the control and the exercise of this authority. Few voices openly questioned the need for such authority and for an essential unity of church and commonwealth. Archbishop Laud still spoke for nearly all when he declared that "whoever he be, he must live in the body of the Commonwealth and in the body of the Church"—just as did Pym in asserting that "it is the end of government that virtue should be cherish'd, vice suppressed."[136] Most notably, while rejecting Laud's—and Hooker's—concept of unity, the Independents or Separatists stood alongside the Romanists, Anglicans, and Presbyterians in appealing to the disciplinary power of the godly prince to uphold the moral and social standards of the commonwealth. Collinson has pointed out that "for more than a hundred years, mainstream puritanism stood out against separatism," and that few Elizabethan or Jacobean Puritans "had any intention of reconstructing, still less of turning upside down the world they inhabited."[137] Yet it is instructive to recollect that, while a couple of Elizabethan Anabaptists were condemned for heresy, both Campion on the one hand, and Penry and his friends on the other, were done to death for treason. Clearly, government was far from complacent about the dangers perceived as lurking beneath the surface.

The same impression holds when one looks at the early Stuart era and indeed at sometimes more overtly political issues. But any talk about pent-up forces waiting to be unleashed needs careful qualification. It may first be fruitful to consider the emergent usage, from the Elizabethan era onward, of the word "state." Is it going too far to discern in its increasing popularity, not quite as an equivalent for "commonwealth" but rather as indicative of the governmental and above all of the coercive authority of the Crown and its ministers, a qualitative if only implied distinction of some significance? For this more limited concept—or rather perhaps its agents—could more credibly be attacked than could the more rounded concept of the commonwealth. Certainly the idea of a *monarchical* commonwealth remained the norm and was subject to little question. Well might Charles I, desperate for money, describe opponents of his demands in a proclamation of 7 October 1526 as "malevolous persons, who under pretence of common liberty, factiously intend nothing but the ruin both of Religion and the State."[138] But in fact such martyrs for political principle, or as some would say for an early defence of "civil liberties," as Wentworth or Eliot were both fervent defenders of the ideal of the commonwealth and loyal to the monarchy. It was the specific exercise of certain coercive powers that they deplored. Nor, in hailing parliamentary defenders of civil liberties under Charles I, should it be forgotten that the hated adversaries, Laud and Strafford, were done to death by procedures equally repugnant to any modern concept of their nature.

Moreover, when Sir Edward Coke concerned himself with "the Grievances of the Commonwealth," his voice was not that of the

Tudor moralist deploring social injustice. Rather was it that of the defender of individual liberties, often involving rights of private property, against the allegedly high-handed policies and actions of the Crown and its ministers, and on occasion that of wounded *amour propre* after his loss of favor. While Stephen White perhaps runs ahead of events in alluding to the term commonwealth as an "ominous and ideologically-laden catchword," his contention that Coke was equating the "limited, private interests of particular groups or classes [with] the collective well-being of all English subjects" goes to the heart of the matter.[139] Coke was involved with the issue of individual liberties versus the state, not with the more fundamental social issues that had preoccupied "commonwealthmen" in the mid-Tudor era and were soon to do so again. Nor, while such liberties were assuredly important, did he look forward to the demand for a widening participation of the ordinary citizen (however defined) in the political process as a condition of the safeguard of such liberties that was shortly to emerge—let alone to its occasional correlative of greater social egalitarianism. Indeed, the issues just raised point toward a different age. In the next chapter I shall trace the ferment of ideas that erupts in midcentury when these incipient pressures—political, religious, social, and economic—that we have encountered combine once more to produce a crisis in the commonwealth. The shape that this will take will indicate that, in terms of the formulation of ideas, the previous era had not been altogether dormant.

4
Full Blossom: The Mid-Seventeenth-Century Commonwealth

THE ATTRIBUTION OF THE TERM "FULL BLOSSOM" TO THE MIDDLE DECades of the seventeenth century is doubly apposite. Not only did the nature of the commonwealth once more emerge as the focal point of political, religious, and social debate, but for a short while England itself formally became a Commonwealth. The conjunction of political and religious uncertainty with social ferment and genuine economic distress that had characterized the mid-Tudor decades now returned. Against this background occurred what is probably "the most extraordinary outpouring of political philosophy that the modern world had seen."[1] The political historian and the constitutional analyst would distinguish between the "constitutional revolution" that preceded armed conflict, the Civil Wars themselves, and the events of the Interregnum—culminating in the Restoration of Charles II. But in the realm of ideology with which I am concerned the period as a whole has a certain unity as a virtually continuing crisis not only of Stuart monarchy but also—and more fundamentally—of English government, religion, and society.

Amidst the harsh realities of this era there bursts forth once more a strain of idealist optimism, in terms of an eager expectancy of social, economic, and religious reforms, with an intensity not witnessed since the mid-Tudor decades. The overwhelming majority of those who discussed such issues did so in terms of their relationship to the commonwealth. Nor was this merely a conventional peg to which such debate could be attached. For very many who combined their pleas for social and religious reform with an advocacy of what they saw as an as yet unfinished *political* revolution did so in the passionate conviction that this would help to translate the *ideals* of the commonwealth into realities within contemporary society. Indeed, in tracing the evolution of that concept the mid-seventeenth century stands out as a supremely important watershed. Political, religious, social, and economic issues remain its fundamental concerns. But the balance of emphasis as between the concept of organic unity and that of individual liberties starts to change. The advocacy of an extension of individual political rights is often accompanied by novel speculation as to their function as necessary guarantors of the discharge by government of *enhanced* social and economic responsibilities toward the well-being of individual members of society. The notion of society's organic nature persists, but within changing parameters. As for the religious dimension of the commonwealth, while the rectitude as well as the control of a unitary ecclesiastical authority comes under attack, an insistence upon the relevance of religious values for all social relationships remains almost undiminished.

Accordingly, this chapter will first consider the political and constitutional aspects of commonwealth thinking, related in turn to emerging tensions between organic unity and individual liberty, to the forms of government advocated, and finally to the rights and duties of the people in a commonwealth. Next, discussion of religion will focus on two major issues: religious liberty, and the continued insistence upon the ideal of a Godly Commonwealth. Finally, consideration of social and economic debate will include that on "Equity or Equality," the proliferation of pleas and of actual schemes for governmental control or intervention, and— foreshadowing a parting of the ways—the issue of *individual* social and economic rights.

"Of Government and Obedience"

In terms of political thinking, an increasingly urgent apprehension of the imminence of armed conflict forced into the open a widespread expression of ideas that had for decades been tentative. This often involved selective republication—as of Ponet. Between 1646 and 1651 in particular there took place an almost frantic debate as to what form of government should replace an allegedly discredited monarchy, while Cromwell's death in 1658 was followed by an equally urgent discussion as to whether the republic should in turn be displaced by a restored monarchy. But the whole period was a forcing-house for the germination and growth of political ideas unequalled in previous or in subsequent British history. Hobbes, Harrington, and Winstanley stand out in any history of political thought but they do not dwarf a number of lesser but still significant figures whose contributions, while often written in response to an immediate perception of a political or constitutional problem rather than as systematic expositions, are of major importance. Also of striking significance are the records of the Putney and Westminster Debates of the Officers of the New Model Army. Moreover, the extensive freedom of the press during the 1640s meant that what some may have muttered darkly in Tudor England was now set down in print in millenarian works.[2]

Amongst emergent topics of crucial import, the shift *not* toward the elimination of the concept of the collectivity of the commonwealth but rather toward identifying its primary raison d'être as that of the guarantor of the rights or liberties of individual constituent members has already been noticed. Professor Gunn suggests that by the midcentury the significantly different term "the public interest" was "gradually replacing the 'common good' of scholastic philosophy and the *salus populi* favoured by Roman law." Next, one may perhaps discern a general (though not all-pervasive) shift of emphasis toward envisaging individual rights more and more in political, economic, and social, and rather less in formally religious terms. Some sixty years ago William Haller suggested that "as the Revolution moved on, both the objects of revolutionary effort and the terms of revolutionary thought and expression, became less peculiarly religious and theological." Finally, it is revealing to identify in commonwealth ideology an uneasy distinction—sometimes sensed rather than enunciated—between private civil liberties, individual political rights, and private economic interests. Certainly the mid-seventeenth-century commonwealth idealist endorsed the first almost without question, was often increasingly favorably disposed toward the second, but almost always persisted in subordinating the third to the concept of organic unity. Sir John Eliot's apprehension noted earlier that "the great secret that we search for" in the commonwealth is the reconciliation of existing diverse interests with the supreme objective of "the public utility and good" emerges ever more clearly.[3]

In discussions of the nature of the commonwealth itself, its origins and purpose, the device of the organic analogy remained commonplace. Its use in variant forms for opposing purposes was not new. In 1642 the royalist Henry Ferne identified "the distractions and convulsions of the whole Commonwealth, as the distempers in a natural body" and likely to cause its dissolution. Contemporaneously, Henry Parker, replying to Charles I, conceding that head and members must live and die together in the natural body, contended that "it is otherwise with the Head Political, for that receives more subsistence from the body than it gives," while in 1647 John Cook reversed the usual order of things in commending that "all the members of the body have a care of the head."⁴ In 1654 John Hall's lengthy discussion *Of Government and Obedience,* misliking the trend of events, described how "in Democracy the head is made of many; and, by a monstrous deformity, made bigger than the body," and pointed to the Civil Wars as "this grand disease of the politique Body." Five years later William Sprigge, in *A Modest Plea for an Equal Commonwealth Against Monarchy,* attacking the hereditary nobility, asked whether such "swelling Tumours and unhandsome men of Greatness do ill become the face of a Commonwealth, . . . were it not better they should be pared off, than our state rendered of a monstrous or prodigious shape?" In the same year an anonymous attack on Harrington's proposal expressed the malevolent hope that "it should miscarry, and be strangled at its birth"!⁵

Alongside this analogy, the ideal of devotion to the general good was equally persistent. Philip Hunton, writing in 1643, declared that "the end of Magistracy is the good of the whole Body, Head and Members conjointly . . . the good of Society is the ultimate end," while in 1659 Marchmont Nedham in his *Interest will not lie* could still insist "that the real good of the Nation consists not in the private benefit of single men, but the advantage of the Public."⁶ But when one looks in some detail at discussions of the origin and purpose of government, at notions of sovereignty, and at ideas about civil, political, and religious liberty and about the relationship between private and public interests, it is hard to resist the impression of entering another age.

A House of Commons resolution of 4 January 1649 solemnly declared "That the people are, under God, the original of all just power"—being careful to add that the Commons in Parliament assembled, as representing the people, "have the supreme power in this nation."⁷ The radical analysis of Anthony Ascham in *The Original & End of Civil Power* (also 1649) starts with the declaration "that the People are the Womb of all Powers." This he modifies slightly in asserting that "the People (under God) are the Efficient cause, and Original of all just Powers." But most notably, Ascham is clear that the fact that "this or that form of Government is not of divine unalterable institution, but originally an Ordinance or Creation of man" is obvious to anyone "that hath not been born and bred up in a Bottle." Moreover, all such forms of government arise from the people's voluntary submission for the conservation of their mutual rights, which, together with "the People's good and welfare," is the purpose of government—"beside God's glory, which is the ultimate end of all things." Rulers thus become "the Guardians and protectors of private rights"; but in discharging this duty "upright and public spirits would disburden themselves of the clogs of private Interest."⁸

Other writers also clung to the notion of the public good. In his treatment of "the Public good, Common good, or Commonweal," John Hall (in 1654) declared that "by Happiness of a Kingdom, we understand that whole stock of pleasures and benefits of all sorts wherewith each Kingdom is furnished: and withal, the fit application and distribution thereof, according to the general capacities and numbers of the subjects." In particular, productive workers who provide food and clothing for us, "we truly call Commonwealths-men: forasmuch as they do by their occupations make real improvement without the loss of others"—unlike certain present seekers after power! In short, "the public or whole good of the kingdom is not to be estimated by every private possession, but by all in general."⁹ Alongside this notion of commutative or distributive justice one also finds the persistence of that of the precept *"Salus populi, suprema lex."* An anonymous tract of 1658 still identified "the safety of the People [as] being the Supreme Law." But Thomas White's book, entitled *The Grounds of Obedience and Government* (1655), having defined the governor's duty as being directed "as far as it is fitting for the Common-wealth and peace; he being nothing but the instrument of the common good," proceeds to resemble Jean-Jacques Rousseau in conceding that "the vulgar sort are so easily led by fancy, that they understand not the common good, nor what they should wish."¹⁰

The nature, location, and exercise of sovereignty or "sovereign power" are often envisaged in relation to the possibility of at least some involvement of the people. For Ascham, "without doubt there remains in the Body of the People an unresigned Sovereignty, which is their ultimate Reserve against the Irregularity, or overflowing Tyranny of the Magistrates." John Hall asserts that "Sovereignty is the supreme judge and disposer of the Public interest."¹¹ But Matthew Wren, in his *Monarchy Asserted* (1659), an attack on Harrington's *Oceana,* declares that "it is an Error to think . . . that the Generality of a People are infected with a Desire of Sovereign Power." Richard Baxter's *A Holy Commonwealth* (1659), purportedly written in rebuttal of James Harrington, enunciated that "the Sovereign Power is the Law-giver, and therefore can change them at his pleasure. Our brutish, impious rout . . . have not the Sovereignty if they cannot make and abrogate Laws."¹²

An anonymous *Copy of a Letter written . . . by A true Commonwealthsman, and no Courtier* (1656) is unequivocal in its assertion that "there cannot be any Political Government longer than there is an apparent Sovereignty somewhere abiding." But the nature and limitations (if any) of sovereignty as such involve a vexed debate concerning individual civil, political, and religious liberties. John Milton's ringing assertion, in *The Tenure of Kings and Magistrates* (1650) that "no man who knows ought can be so stupid to deny that all men naturally were born free, being the image and resemblance of God himself," is given more substantive content when he goes on to declare it "manifest that the power of Kings and Magistrates is nothing else but what is only derivative, transferr'd and committed to them in trust from the People, to the Common good of them all, in whom the power yet remains fundamentally."[13]

In John Hall's chapter "Of Liberty," "the true Liberty of Subjects will appear to be in the removal of all external impediments which cross his desires, without regard of more public utility"; indeed, "to say the Liberty of a Subject is none other than a contradiction: for wherein he is a Subject, he is not at liberty; and wherein any is at liberty, he is not a Subject." While the first of these comments appears to point to a concept of civil liberty, the second raises many questions. Rather clearer is the balanced approach of Thomas White: "Wherein then consists the Liberty of every Subject? in not being controll'd in his *private* affairs [my italics] . . . No more is it to be esteem'd Liberty, to have the privilege to subtract himself from the service of the Common-wealth. They are therefore seditious spirits, who, using the name of Liberty, provoke the Subject against the Magistrate."[14] A brief tract, reputedly by Harrington, asserts that "the distinction of Liberty into Civil and Spiritual, is not ancient, but of latter date," before going on to observe that "where there is a power that can usurp civil Liberty, there is no Commonwealth": but this is in the context of an uncomfortable *Discourse upon This Saying: The Spirit of the Nation is not yet to be trusted with Liberty; lest it introduce Monarchy, or invade the Liberty of Conscience* (1659). Ascham, who—as we have noted—sees rulers as the guardians of private rights, is clear that "by the People I mean every single or particular person within any Nation or Kingdom, high and low, noble and ignoble, rich and poor, bond and free, without any limitation or restraint." Given this definition, his subsequent observation that "all Sovereignties and Royalties are virtually in the People," and that "it cannot with any Reason be imagined, that the People can pass away irreversibly their particular Rights by this Consent of theirs" to the appointment of rulers, seems sweeping.[15]

John Cook's *Redintegratio Amoris* (1647) agrees "that by nature all men are born free," although it is also "a ground in Nature that wise men should govern the ignorant." All government derives from necessity and reason, from divine sanction and popular concurrence. "All lawful authority is derived from the people," who cannot by any covenant enslave themselves. Thus "no Government is divine . . . but that which is just and rational"; it is certain "that free people in their right wits never covenanted against the Law of God or Nature, nor meant to inslave themselves to the lusts of one or more whom they elected or consented to be their Governor." Thus far this seems to resemble a familiar "right to be governed well"; but Cook now goes on to a conclusion directly contrary to the Tudor consensus: "Anarchy is better than Tyranny." For "nothing is more lawless than that Law that would endanger the Public Welfare. . . . I conceive it far better to have no Government at all than a Tyrannical one." Not surprisingly, "there is in the people a sufficient power reserved to preserve themselves from slavery and oppression, if those whom they have chosen to infranchise them should be infringers of their liberties."[16] But as yet all of this could be taken to point only to residual sovereignty as a guarantor of the preservation of *civil* liberties. The whole question of popular participation in the exercise of any form of *political* liberty will later concern us at some length, as will also developments in ideas about the individual's *economic* liberties.

Meanwhile, we must first consider an issue which, a topic of academic discussion in Tudor England, now became an urgent theme of mid-seventeenth-century debate: whether a monarchical or a republican form of government is better for the commonwealth. Certainly, the position of monarchy as such remained a focal issue of much debate throughout the midcentury. The reluctance of some royalists to abandon total nonresistance to legitimate authority is typified by Henry Ferne's *The Resolving of Conscience,* dismissing any right of a subject to take up arms. Ferne, a fellow of Trinity College, Cambridge, who became a chaplain to Charles I himself when Civil War broke out, identified the monarch as "the Father of the Commonwealth," in this work published at Cambridge in 1642. He concedes that while the power of government is of God, laws are established for the people's security. Yet the idea that "power was every where from the people at first" must not be used to justify a right of resistance that may cause civil war. Ferne, one of the ablest royalist writers, paints a graphic picture of what may ensue if the people should presume to "say to their rulers . . . *Ye take too much* upon you, or as Cade and Tyler, boast themselves reformers of the commonwealth, overthrow King *and Parliament* [my italics], fill all with rapine and confusion."[17]

Dudley Digges, a fellow of All Souls and another devoted royalist, who died of camp fever in Oxford in October 1643, had not long published *The unlawfulnesse of a subject's taking up arms*, which ran through several editions among admiring supporters of the Crown and reappeared in 1662. Deploring the means by which the seduced multitude are misled by those purporting to make the yoke of government rest more easily, Digges warns against "an empty name of liberty; and . . . the so much applauded equality." Nonresistance is the only firm base, for "the King is *Dei minister,* not the people's servant, nor their creature." In reality, "*Populi salus suprema lex* is the engine by which the upper rooms are torn from the foundation and seated upon fancy only, like castles in the air. For the safety of the people is really built upon government." Sadly, those who "contribute their forces to destroy this Kingdom in behalf of the Commonwealth . . . are so far deceived, as to be made unhappy instruments to advance private interests with public hurts."[18]

This work had in fact been evoked by a brief tract published in May 1642 by Henry Parker of Lincoln's Inn: *Observations upon some of His Majesties late Answers.* Despite his disclaimer of any wish to see innovation concerning monarchy, Parker is clear that kingly right is held "by way of trust." Accordingly, if the monarch should act "to the danger of the State: In such cases they conceive there is a power in them [Parliament] to secure the State without his concurrence." In rejecting any claim to arbitrary and unbounded power the reader is invited to contemplate "the Asanine Peasants of France . . . whose Wooden shoes and Canvas Breeches sufficiently proclaim what a blessedness it is to be born under a mere divine Prerogative."[19] Another well-respected attempt at a reasoned justification of Parliament's case was Philip Hunton's *A Treatise of Monarchie* (1643). Hunton, a scholar of Wadham College, Oxford, and an adherent of Cromwell, argues that "the Sovereignty of our Kings is radically and fundamentally limited." Indeed, "it is acknowledged to be a Monarchy mixed with Aristocracy in the House of Peers, and Democracy in the House of Commons." In particular, "the two Estates in Parliament may lawfully by force of Arms resist any persons . . . advising or assisting the King in the performance of a Command illegal and destructive to themselves, or to the public." Little wonder that the book was reprinted in 1689:[20]

While Henry Ferne appears to be Hunton's immediate adversary, in 1646 Hunton was to be attacked by Sir Robert Filmer. While Filmer's prewar composition, *Patriarcha,* was not published until 1680, its views are reflected in several works printed in 1648. In *The Anarchy of A Limited or Mixed Monarchy* (April) he depicts monarchy as thereby crucified "between two thieves, the pope and the people." A detailed critique of Hunton (and later Parker) concludes that "mixed monarchy, just like the limited, ends in confusion and destruction of all government." In August Filmer published extracts from Bodin, again vigorously monarchical. Of two works printed in 1652 the *Observations Concerning The Original Of Government* (February) regrets Hobbes's use of the term "commonwealth," for thereby many ignorant men "understand a popular government, wherein wealth and all things shall be common"—though Filmer himself used the word almost interchangeably with commonweal, his preferred alternative. In general, Filmer's assertions alarmed even moderate monarchists.[21]

In equally forthright fashion, John Cook, solicitor to the Commonwealth, chief prosecutor of Charles I, executed as a regicide in 1660, was ready in 1651 to label *Monarchy No creature of Gods making*. Thus, "monarchs that assume an absolute Supremacy to do what they list are not creatures of God's ordination . . . but God permits such to be, as he suffers sin to be." By 1659, understandably, the monarchists rallied. Matthew Wren's *Monarchy Asserted* attacked Harrington's *Oceana* and derided any notion of power deriving from or being entrusted to "the People, being composed of Ignorance, Obstinacy, and Tumult."[22] The briefer and anonymous *Englands Monarchy Asserted, and Proved to be The Freest State, and The Best Commonwealthe* considers it "the sole and only Government ordained by God," and sighs for earlier "blessed Halcyon times"—before "Fanatic Saintship" picked the people's pockets! Its author derides "every wild and brain-sick fancy of our Republican Candidates . . . for this Utopian thing, of a Common-wealth." For by now the debate was conducted not only in terms of monarchical limitations but also of an overt advocacy of a republic. The oddly titled *Chaos: or . . . a Frame of Government by way of a Republique* (anonymously published in 1659), while restricting the right to vote, safeguarded its secrecy by commending the use of "a Box or Chest with a hole in the top, locked or sealed with three several Locks or Seals," and advocated annual parliamentary elections.[23]

In respect of such elections, the franchise and the electoral system had very probably become fairer—or at least more extensive—under the Commonwealth than was again to be the case until the late nineteenth century. Sir John Plumb has observed that in this regard the political nation was proportionately larger in the mid-seventeenth century than a hundred years later.[24] As to the role of Parliament within the commonwealth, in 1642 Henry Parker was confident that "we hold the Parliaments in England as the Apples of our eyes; and we know that all liberty must stand or fall with them"; yet even he conceded that, concerning the people, "some things they have reserved to themselves out of Parliament, and some things in the Parliament." By 1647 Laurence Clarkson, later allegedly a leading Ranter, was ready to identify "the inslaved Communality" as being "above the Parliament. . . . For from you they derived their Authority." Indeed he upbraided them with their negligence in suffering "the Parliament to deprive you of the power that Justice Equity had intrusted you withal."[25]

J. C. Davis sees this tract as urging the need for something more fundamental than mere constitutional change.[26] Meanwhile, the concept of constitutional change was itself now widely grasped. Ascham, in 1649, had conceded in two major works the inevitability of changes in form of government. Such changes were not always welcome or treated with respect. In 1650 Henry Nevile published *Newes from the New Exchange, or the Commonwealth of Ladies,* a somewhat bawdy depiction of women "in the posture of a Free-State," which included an allusion to an attempt "to erect a new Commonwealth among the Monkies" in America.[27] More seriously, some anticipated Pope's "For forms of government let fools contest; Whate'er is best administered is best." Anthony Ascham's *Of the Confusions and Revolutions of Government* (1649) concluded that "the difference which is betwixt Monarchy, Aristocracy, and Democracy, is no more than is betwixt one Jacobus piece of Gold, twenty two shilling, and forty four six-pence, . . . of the same intrinsic value." The striking, though anonymous, *Plea for limited Monarchy* (1659) stressed "how necessary it is to distinguish betwixt the Form and Essence of a Commonwealth." Its author alleged that under Protector Cromwell "our Architects of a Common-wealth . . . agreed in the necessity of subverting all our Fundamentals," and looked back nostalgically to a prewar era when "our former Government, eminently, included all the perfections of a Free-State, and was the Kernel, as it were, of a Common-wealth, in the shell of Monarchy." Even the unknown author of *Englands Monarchy Asserted,* while deriding "the Good old Cause-mongers," held that "a Free State, or Common-wealth" had no necessarily antimonarchical connotations.[28]

The author of *A Copy of a Letter written to an Officer in the Army, by A true Commonwealths-man* (1656) reflected bitterly that "there was a time indeed when Monarchy and Tyranny, Parliaments and Liberty, were thought to be the same, but the experience of our condition under that long, long, Parliament, and that little one since, hath rectified our judgements." Indeed "we shall therefore find Tyranny to be most cried out upon by the people under Elective government, and Insurrection and Civil War oftenest raised upon that score." Indeed, in political as well as idealist social and economic terms, there emerged a significant body of opinion (not confined to the Levellers) that came to think of the Protectorate as, in effect, the Commonwealth betrayed. Nevertheless, the author's conclusion that "were this Nation polled, not one in twenty but would desire their old Government again," is perhaps less realistic than that of the chameleon-like political theorist, Marchmont Nedham, in 1659, that "a great part of the Nation may be said to be Neuters; not addicted to any one Party."[29] The anonymously published *A Commonwealth and Commonwealthsmen Asserted and Vindicated* (1659) related alterations in government to changes in the balance of property, as "most politely and politiquely demonstrated by the Excellent Mr. Harrington." But William Sprigge, in the same year, while believing that "no Government can be fixed in this Nation, but according to the Balance of Land," looked back and lamented: "into how many several forms and moulds of Government have we of late been cast? How many new experiments have we made . . . and all to no purpose?" Yet what the nation must *not* now do is to "patch up a sorry half potch'd Commonwealth, upon the old, crazy, and rotten foundations of Monarchy as heretofore." A seriocomic *New Litany for these Times* (anonymous, 1659) expressed delight at England's hoped-for liberation from "changing of Governments, no man knows why."[30]

The most notable change in the official *form* of government had been initiated by the parliamentary abolition of the kingly office, followed in May of 1649 by "An Act Declaring and Constituting the People of England to be a Commonwealth and Free-State." On 2 January of 1650 all men over the age of eighteen were required to declare allegiance "to the Commonwealth of England as it is now established, without a king or House of Lords."[31] In 1649 Henry Robinson's *A Short Discourse between Monarchical and Aristocratical Government*, disdaining "that Tyrannical Power which was exercised by the late King," and asserting that "there is no more divinity in one Government more than another," expresses his contentment that "Aristocracy, (or this Government of a Common-wealth the Parliament have set up) is the most even, and just Government, . . . it being a middle State between Popular Anarchy, and Prerogative Tyranny." The nation must now beware, not only lest it it be reduced to the former tyranny but also lest it "run into Levelling Confusion."[32] In May 1650 Marchmont Nedham, an agile political theorist, published *The Case of the Commonwealth of England Stated*, in which he expounded "the equity, utility, and Necessity of a submission to the present government." In extolling the need for government, in the interests of "public equity, for the administration of justice, encouragement of virtue, and punishment of vice," Nedham warned against such as "are in some sense mere anarchists," pointed to the danger from Levellers and Diggers, and expressed approval of "Mr Hobbes." Some three years later he also supported the Instrument of Government, which has been described as England's first written constitution.[33]

Against this background one may hardly eschew a few reflections on the status of Oliver Cromwell as a "Commonwealth Statesman." In a message to the Speaker after his victory at Dunbar, he exhorted the Commons to "relieve the oppressed, hear the groans of poor prisoners in England; be pleased to reform the abuses of all professions; and if there be any one that makes many poor to make a few rich, that suits not a Commonwealth"—objectives that would have pleased any mid-Tudor idealist. Again, in his speech in July 1653, justifying the dissolution of the Rump, he spoke of "finding the people dissatisfied in every corner of the nation [with] the non-performance of those things that had been promised."[34] For Cromwell looked for action to improve the spiritual and social standards of the nation, not for revolutionary erosion of its bases. In speaking of the Levellers in 1649 he insisted to the Council that they were "necessitated to break them." Retrospectively, in September 1654, he looked to the danger that the magistracy of the nation was "not almost trampled under foot, under despite and contempt by men of Levelling principles." For "did not that Levelling principle tend to the reducing all to an equality? Did it think to do so, or did it practise towards it for propriety and interest? . . . It was a pleasing voice to all poor men, and truly not unwelcome to all bad men." In 1647 and again in 1649 he had taken resolute action to suppress mutinous Leveller elements in the army.[35]

As for the constitutional format best suited to the nation, in September 1651 Cromwell was ready to consider "whether a Republic, or a mixed monarchical government will be best to be settled." Indeed, Austin Woolrych has suggested that what are sometimes referred to as a series of constitutional experiments are more accurately described as "a succession of expedients, each rather hastily cobbled up to fill a hiatus in legitimate government or to avert a threatened breakdown." The experiment of "Barebone's Parliament" was short-lived, as Cromwell apprehended the danger from such as "tell us that liberty and property are not the badges of the kingdom of Christ," being deceived by "the mistaken notion of the Fifth Monarchy." Professor Roots has pointed to the dilemma confronting Cromwell as he strove "to achieve some sort of stability before the radicalism in the army and reaction outside of it had time to destroy the tottering fabric of the State."[36]

Believing that "the suppressing of vice and encouragement of virtue [is] the very end of magistracy," Cromwell justified the expedient of the Major-Generals.[37] Woolrych identifies an enduring belief in a godly reformation, involving "the propagation of the gospel by a zealous preaching ministry, liberty of conscience, the reform of the law, a clean-up of the administration . . . and greater concern for the poor, the hopelessly indebted, and the unemployed." But his suggested "conflict between radical puritanism and conservative constitutionalism within the breast of Oliver Cromwell" was perhaps not over-sharp.[38] Cromwell believed above all in religious and in civil liberty. But religious freedom proved to be "a fecund and reckless mother of sects," and Cromwell saw the danger from all extremes: "Every sect saith, Oh! Give me liberty. But give him it, and to his power he will not yield it to anybody else." Again, "is there not yet upon the spirits of men a strange itch? Nothing will satisfy them, unless they can put their finger upon their brethren's consciences, to pinch them there." Anabaptists, Presbyterians, and Fifth Monarchy Men alike would "cut the throats of them that are not of their forms." Equally clearly, in respect of civil liberties, which above all included property, he perceived the danger not only from the Levellers and the Diggers but also from the zealotry of those whose would-be rule as Saints threatened both liberty and property.[39] In his approach to the problems of the commonwealth, the influence of Cromwell, warts and all, still demonstrated some adherence to the precept of a measure and a mean.

Cromwell's concern for the preservation of the social order impinges on the third major theme in our consideration of mid-seventeenth-century political ideology: the status of the people in the commonwealth. Some continuity of the belief that their role should remain passive, accompanied by enduring dread of the "many-headed hydra" should they attempt to take action, has already been encountered. The consensus of opinion in the political nation is typified by Ascham—himself no friend of monarchy, who was indeed assassinated in 1650 while Commonwealth resident to the king of Spain. "Democracy reduces all to equality, and favours the Liberty of the people in every thing: but withal it obliges every man to hold his neighbours' hands, it is very short sighted, permits every one in the ship to pretend to the helm, yea in a tempest. . . . If this supreme power fall into the hands of a heady and of an unconstant multitude, it is lodg'd in a great animal, which cannot be better than in chains."[40] Clearly there is no concept of general participation in self-government in this vision of democracy as a near-neighbor to anarchy.

Yet contemporaneously we also find the clear emergence of a body of thought that would endow the ordinary people (however defined) with political rights, as distinct from passive social expectations. Significantly, recent scholarship has established that this must be seen in the context of an already existing trend toward the extension of the political nation—interpreted not only in terms of an intelligent interest but also in those of the actual size of the electorate—during the years *prior* to 1642. Derek Hirst has estimated possession of the franchise by as many as one-third of all adult males. Admittedly, Manning points out that many of the enfranchised "were too ignorant, or too poor, or too dependent to cast their votes" against the rich and powerful.[41] Yet this in turn goes far to explain the type of limitations of the franchise that many who were in principle in favor of democratic rights sought to impose. Moreover, surprisingly detailed consideration was often given to the means by which the people's political rights were to be exercised. Despite the common and accurate assumption that such ideas and devices proved to be well ahead of their time, this period is a crucial watershed in the development of political aspects of commonwealth ideology.

As yet, widespread though not universal lip service to the idea that all just power and all forms of government originate in the people was normally subject to two implicit codicils: that they never seek to influence, far less participate in, its exercise; and that they never try to take it back. Henry Parker, writing in 1642, declared that "power is originally inherent in the people"; but in 1644 his *Jus Populi* followed the assertion that "the Parliament is indeed nothing else but the very people itself artificially congregated, or reduced by an orderly election" with the explanation that this "differs in many ways from the rude bulk of the universality." More sharply, an anti-Baxter tract published in 1660 included the assertion that "supposing therefore Power to have originally been in the People, . . . it will not at all upon pretence of misuser entitle them to snatch it back. . . . If the people are still Judges of what is to be the public good, and have the Power of the Sword, they are what they were before they were, no Subjects."[42]

Clearly, one is on the verge of the great debate most strikingly rehearsed, if not initiated, by Thomas Hobbes—whose contribution demands specific treatment later. Does governmental power exist as the result of a once-and-for-all abandonment of a brutal "state of nature," becoming *after its establishment* the effective font of any individual rights and liberties? Or is it merely the guarantor of previously existing individual rights, its own continued existence conditional upon the respect it thereto renders? Does any successful rebellion against purportedly lawfully constituted authority inevitably entail reversion to the brutish realm of anarchy? Or is it a necessary if regrettable means of safeguarding natural individual rights against a power that in effect is but seeking to impose such a condition from above? An early stirring of this debate, within a restricted and deeply religious context, has already been encountered a century earlier in Ponet and in Goodman (who is cited by Milton).[43] Now, in changing circumstances, it will assume an increasingly secular aspect, with implications for the means of *exercise* of power that would have surprised its mid-Tudor harbingers.

An impressive and reasoned discussion of the right of resistance is found in *The Grounds of Obedience and Government,* addressed to Sir Kenelm Digby by Thomas White in 1655. White, a much-travelled student of St. Omer, Valladolid, and Douai, who apparently knew and engaged in fierce argument with Hobbes, declares that "government is, naturally, a power or right of directing the common affairs of a multitude, by a voluntary submission of the community's wills to the wills of the Governors, whom they trust." These "Trustees" derive their authority solely from "this resignation of the people's will." Accordingly, a ruler may not "dispense of one chip or dispense in one the least law, farther than he apprehends it as fit and necessary to the good of the Common-wealth." Conformably, the purpose of the subject's obedience "is the public good or the good of the Commonwealth"—not forgetting "the good he is to receive out of the Commonwealth."[44]

In answer to the question of when a subject may resist government, this "cannot be done, but when the occasion is greater than the value of the public peace and good of the Commonwealth." Occasional grievances or private motivations will not suffice. As for the issue of "wherein consists the power and liberty of the subject," White is clear that, while the people's authority derives from "force of nature," if the power that they used to institute government is now exercised to dissolve it, there looms the spectre of a relapse into anarchy. Hence the only circumstance that justifies rebellion is a total abandonment of the ruler's promises. For behind the justifiable case for the liberty of the subject there always lurks the "wilfulness of an ignorant rabble." Nevertheless, he is determined to resist what he terms the lawyers' argument, that "the People cannot speak their minds freely. I answer, certainly, they not only can, but cannot choose but speak their minds, in the case we put." In conclusion,

White—whom I may fairly identify as an early student of what he dubs "the science of Politicks"—is adamant that "the title of the Magistrate begins and dies with the good of the Common-wealth," recognizing that people may rightly, when "*forced by natural changes, violate the promises made to their Governors, cast them off when they think them pernicious.*"[45]

Not surprisingly, Henry Ferne, in *The Resolving of Conscience* (1642) upon the question of whether, "supposing the King will not discharge his trust but is bent or seduced to subvert Religion, Laws, and Liberties," that then "subjects may take Arms and resist," had a very different opinion. For "the life of a Commonwealth [is] not so endangered by Tyranny as by factions, divisions, tumults, power of resistance on the subjects' part." In no circumstances is it justifiable for "a Christian to run the hazard of damnation by resisting." A self-entitled "true Commonwealthsman," in 1656, descries the specter that "upon the death of every Elected Prince, the whole State and Government, and every man's future therein, must be left in tottering condition, whilst (during that inter-regnum) every man may do what seems good in his own eyes; and so be as in a state of Anarchy."[46]

Even John Hall, at one time retained by Cromwell for pamphleteering services, writing *Of Government and Obedience* in 1654, identified "the tyranny of Anarchy, which is of all tyranny the worst, for every man is herein oppressed of his neighbour," and indeed declared "Anarchy to be the absence of Monarchy." He pointed to the danger of "relying again upon our understanding and interpretation of Law and Right." But alongside such traditionalism he proffers the interesting insight that, despite the fact that statesmen always purport to act in their commonwealth's name, "these terms of *Commonwealth* and *Public* good are but bare political notions, not living creatures, . . . and that they are not otherwise manageable, or to be represented or collected into a sum or total, than as in relation to the persons therein intrusted. . . . From which it plainly appears that men are but deluded with this notion of a Commonwealth." For there may be "as many Commonwealths and Republics as there are parties and factions."[47]

Occasionally, ambivalent attitudes, or testimony to the fact that "circumstances alter cases," surface in the same writer. John Milton, in *The Tenure of Kings and Magistrates* (1650), was clear that "since the King or Magistrate holds his authority of the people, both originally and naturally for their good in the first place, and not his own, then may the people as oft as they shall judge it for the best, either choose him or reject him, retain him or depose him *though no Tyrant* [my italics], merely by the liberty and right of free born men, to be govern'd as seems to them best." Yet elsewhere he warned against "the envy and almost infinite prejudice likely to be stirr'd up among the vulgar sort" and would never "justify what enormities the Vulgar may commit in the rudeness of their zeal." Almost a decade later, in *The Readie & Easie Way to Establish a Free Commonwealth* (1659), he deplores the prospect of a restoration of the monarchy "which the inconsiderate multitude are now so mad upon." It is dreadful to contemplate the defeat of "the good old cause [through] this general defection of the misguided and abus'd multitude."[48]

Thus, among royalists and republicans alike, whatever lip service was paid to the people as the notional origin of political power, few were ready to credit them with the intelligence and responsibility required in its exercise. For not far beneath the surface there lurked a fear of what might ensue, in terms of social order, once the dyke of government and authority was breached. Indeed the instinct, selfishly motivated as it was, was not entirely wrong, as what has been termed "a long-buried stream of social discontent" burst forth once more and those who had been excluded from the political nation demanded recognition.[49] The social overtones of such requests are manifest in a cynical pamphleteer's query about the Civil Wars: "Is not all the Controversy Whose Slaves the poor shall be?"[50] Thus a pamphlet published in 1648 warned fellow Levellers to

> beware that ye be not frightened by the word *anarchy*. . . . 'Tis an old trick of the profane Court and against the liberties of the people, who, whensoever they positively insist for their just freedoms, are immediately flapped in the mouths with these malignant reproaches: "Oh, ye are for anarchy. Ye are against all government. Ye are sectaries, seditious persons, troublers both of church and state, and so not worthy to live in a commonwealth."

Against such a background there now entered into the field of political debate a reasoned exposition of the right of political participation by those to whom it had thus far been denied.[51]

It cannot be too heavily stressed that the advocacy of an extension of the political rights of the people was *not* confined to the Levellers. In this respect I shall later be concerned with James Harrington—indeed Wildman's *The Leveller* has been described as "in many ways more Harringtonian than Lilburnian."[52] But the term "Leveller," often deliberately confused with "Digger," was the usual weapon of pejorative attack by conservative opponents. A spate of pamphlets poured forth in advocacy of reform, but one of its earliest platforms may be found in the justly famous debates of the General Council of the Army, held at Putney in October–November of 1647. While others such as Petty—who asserted "that all inhabitants that have not lost their birthright should have an equal voice in election"[53]— and John Wildman made notable contributions, the nub of the debate is best seen in the head-on clash between Colonel Rainborough and the conservatively minded Ireton. Rainborough's crucial avowal of his belief "that the poorest he that is in England hath a life to live, as the greatest he; and therefore . . . that every man that is to live under a government ought first by his own consent to put himself under that government; and I do think that the poorest man in England is not at all bound in a strict sense to that government that he hath not had a voice to put himself under," is a major triggerpoint in a crucially revealing discussion of liberty and property.[54]

Ireton's rejoinders, that no one, directly or indirectly, shall influence the affairs of the kingdom unless he has "a permanent fixed interest" therein, that any such proposals will take away a "fundamental part of the civil constitution," lead up to his own avowal: "All the main thing that I speak for, is because I would have an eye for property."[55] Rainborough, in turn, would fain enquire how it is that the franchise, if a fundamental part of the constitution, has come to be the property of some men and not of others, and ends in the derisive outburst: "Sir, I see that it is impossible to have liberty but all property must be taken away." As I shall later show, there were those who would indeed take this to its logical conclusion! But within the immediate context of the Putney Debates, Ireton's declared wishes for more regular parliaments and a better electoral distribution "amongst the fixed and settled people of this nation" do not suffice to allay Rainborough's suspicion that the soldiers have but fought to be slaves to different rich men.[56]

Though published as late as 1659, a tract entitled *The Leveller*, attributed to Wildman, is equally revealing in its retrospective assessment. Thus, "if the People durst but look behind them upon the Bug-bear from which they fly, they would be ashamed of their own childish fear of the Levellers' Designs, to make all men's estates to be equal, and to divide the land by telling Noses." For surely "no number of men out of Bedlam could resolve upon a thing . . . so brutish and destructive to all Ingenuity and Industry as to put the idle useless Drone into as good condition as the laborious useful Bee . . . if all the land were distributed like a three-penny-dole."[57] When the author moves on from rebuttal of this unfair depiction to the declared objectives of those described as Levellers, he enunciates principles and prescriptions that embody a major shift in balance within commonwealth ideology—and that are in fact directly anticipatory of some which were enshrined in the Constitution of the United States of America. "First, they Assert it as Fundamental that the Government of England ought to be by Laws, and not by Men." Next, "all Laws, Levies of Money, War and Peace, ought to be made by the people's deputies in Parliament, to be chosen by them successively at certain periods of time." Thirdly, this being done, "then every man of whatever Quality or Condition . . . ought to be equally subject to the Laws. . . . Great Thieves and little must alike to the Gallows." Number four, again strikingly anticipatory, urges "that the People ought to be formed into such a Constant Military posture, by and under the commands of their Parliament, that by their own strength they may be able to compel every man to be subject to the Laws"—there must be no recourse to mercenaries. Not surprisingly, the author concludes by referring to the fact that "the late Lord Protector, knowing these Foundations of Freedom to be inconsistent with his Designs, hath often mentioned the Levellers' Plots with malice, scorn, and scandal; and now of late generally, whosoever asserts the People's Liberties and right of Government by Law and not by Will, is branded as a Leveller."[58]

At this point it is indeed appropriate to consider the seminal contribution of the Levellers to the development of the political aspect of commonwealth ideology. Their leaders—John Lilburne, William Walwyn, and Richard Overton, among others—declared themselves to be "Commonwealth's men" and asserted their devotion to the commonwealth ideal. Walwyn was firmly within an inherited tradition in defining "the end of Government being to promote virtue, restrain vice, and to maintain to each his own."[59] Though scholars' interpretation of the movement is not free from controversy, there is much agreement that the Levellers were primarily concerned with political remedies for what they discerned as contemporary evils. Within the context of commonwealth thinking they represent a significant attempt, first, to widen the base and extend the scope of the *political* dimension of such ideology, and secondly to establish a meaningful connection between that extension and the notion of the *social* duties of government. Over fifty years ago, A. S. P. Woodhouse declared that the Levellers "are at bottom individualists, distrusting the state and thinking in terms of safeguards." Much more recently, Brian Manning suggests that they "saw the solution to economic and social problems in political and constitutional changes which would divorce wealth from power."[60] Although a direct relationship between political exclusion and economic exploitation is clearly and fully implied in much of their literature, it seems obvious that they were primarily concerned with political remedies. As for the socioreligious aspect of their teachings, it has been contended that Walwyn's "professed aim was the good of the commonwealth rather than of the communion of saints," and indeed that Lilburne sought "not dissident communions of saints but an all-inclusive community of citizens."[61]

The writings of the Levellers have been characterized as those of "plain men speaking to plain men,"[62] not only in respect of their style and content, but also in their conscious wish to enlarge the political nation. Broadly speaking, their contribution to the vision of an ideal commonwealth that they expounded may be related to an emphasis upon a connection between natural law and the rights of man, the development and interpretation of the concept of a social contract, and an advocacy of democratic liberties. They were firmly grounded in an inherited commonwealth tradition in their belief in equity. But, while stopping well short of the socioeconomic egalitarianism advocated by the Diggers, their appeals to "the Law of Nature" were often couched in terms of a natural *equality of human rights*. Overton was certain that "by natural birth, all men are equally and alike born to like propriety, liberty and freedom"—possessing indeed inalienable rights. Equality before the law, and equal freedom of expression, were much emphasized. Thus, Lilburne would "desire that all alike may be levelled to, and bounded by the law," and condemned control of printing as "an Arbitrary unlimited Power, *even by a general Ordinance of Parliament*" (my italics).[63]

Yet surely most important, and the most strikingly novel element in their philosophy, was the marriage of their concepts of social equity and of individual social and political rights so as to produce that of equality of citizenship. In particular, neither a vague acceptance of "no Authority being of God, but what is erected by the mutual consent of a People,"[64] nor lip service to any merely nominal right of removal in the last resort, would satisfy Leveller aspirations. Two bedrock principles may fairly be identified: that no government (whether monarchical or parliamentary) has any right to abrogate inalienable individual liberties; and that, as the only effective safeguard against any such attempts, the people have a right of active participation in the selection and control of the institutions and the personnel of government. It seems difficult to dissent from Joseph Frank's verdict that "the central purpose of the Leveller party was to establish a constitutional democracy in England," based upon individual freedom and responsibility, and looking to administrative decentralization and a constitutional bill of rights.[65] Most certainly, their yearning for democratic, individualist rights stands in marked contrast with that of the Fifth Monarchy Men for an elitist enforcement of religio-social values.

As to the genesis of the Levellers, Lilburne, Overton, and Thomas Prince, in *The second Part of Englands New-Chaines Discovered* (1649), accuse their enemies of "framing a Name for them which of all others is most distasteful to the People.... The word *Leveller* was framed and cast upon all those in the Army (or elsewhere) who are against any kind of Tyranny."[66] I have already noted the use of the term during the enclosure disorders in 1607 and 1618, but an identifiable Leveller group only emerged in the early months of 1647. Support indeed relied heavily on sections of the army and of London artisans. Never more than a small minority, the extent of general and unrecorded sympathy with some at least of their objectives may hardly be quantified. The peak of Leveller influence came between the royalist military defeat and the Instrument of Government in 1653. It is suggested that by January 1649 they seemed to be on the verge of realizing a democratic constitutional revolution. If so, the bloodily resolute action of Cromwell in May turned the tide; Ian Gentles sees the Burford mutiny as "the most serious internal challenge faced by the regime until 1659," after which "monied men and magistrates heaved a huge sigh of relief." In contrast with the army, Bernard Capp concludes that the Leveller movement "seems to have made little impact on the navy."[67]

Many Leveller tracts, while embodying fundamental principles, may directly be related to political and social disillusionment with the fruits of royalist military defeat. In October 1645, Lilburne's *Englands Birth-right Justified Against all Arbitrary Usurpation, whether Regall or Parliamentary* attacked the present disregard of all equity, efforts to curb press freedom, arbitrary monopolies, neglect of the poor, and decay of trade. The tract questions the "nature of a Parliament man's place," deploring such as—whether because of interest and office or of poverty—"dare not speak freely for the Commonwealth, nor displease such and such a faction." Proposals to "make the present Parliament an everlasting Parliament, and the War a never ending War," merely for personal gain, appal the author. In the same month, William Walwyn, deploring *Englands Lamentable Slaverie*, is equally clear that "a Parliamentary authority is a power intrusted by the people (that chose them) for their good safety and freedom."[68] One of the fullest expressions of Leveller disillusionment with Parliament as it was in 1646 is Overton's *Remonstrance of Many Thousand Citizens*. This is particularly interesting in its assertion that "what-ever our Fore-fathers were; or whatever they did or suffered, or were forced to yield unto; we are men of the present age, and ought to be absolutely free from all kinds of exorbitancies, molestations or Arbitrary Power"—truly a remarkable declaration of the case for *evolving* civil and political liberties. Sadly, he argues, present members behave more like a House of Peers than a House of Commons in their clinging to and exercise of power: their efforts to control religion being reminiscent of the Norman Yoke, while the laws of the nation remain unworthy of a free people and ignore both right reason and common equity.[69]

The same author's *Appeale* in 1647 "from the degenerate Representative Body the Commons of England . . . to the Body Represented, The free people in general" is equally radical. The present "trustees" have forfeited their trust: "an Appeal from them to the people is not Anti-parliamentary, Anti-magisterial, not *from* that Sovereign power but *to* that Sovereign power." For surely "obedience doth not bind us to cut our own throats." We have not fought against the King "to pluck off the *Garments of Royalty* from oppression and tyranny, to dress up the same in *Parliament Robes*." Nor is it "the part of the just and merciful Freemen of England to behold the Politic Body of this commonwealth fallen among a crew of thieves." Indeed, "every rational honest Commonwealth's man is in duty bound even from the just principles of divinity, humanity, and reason . . . to endeavour the extirpation and removal of such usurpers and oppressors."[70] *The Bloody Project . . . promoting of a causeless Warre* (1648), attributed to Walwyn, repeats the phraseology of *The mournfull Cryes of many Thousand poor Tradesmen* (also 1648) in identifying the apparently fundamental issue as that of "whose Slaves the poor shall be."[71] In the following year, *The Hunting of the Foxes*, probably by Richard Overton, is explicit: "We have not the change of a Kingdom to a Common wealth; we are only under the old cheat, the transmutation of Names, but with the addition of new Tyrannies to the old. . . . And the last state of this Common wealth is worse than the first."[72]

In turning to the Levellers' positive prescriptions for changing these conditions, one finds that these concentrate upon fundamental institutional, or perhaps more accurately constitutional changes—most notably in relation to the franchise, the electoral system, and the provision of accountability by those agencies entrusted with authority. Interestingly, a Leveller petition of January 1648 relates "the Ancient Liberty of this Nation" to the right of "all the *Freeborn* people" (my italics) to participate in the election of Members of Parliament, sheriffs, and justices of the peace. It advocates that "that Birth-right of all English men be forthwith restored to all which are not, or shall not be legally disfranchised for some criminal cause, or are not under twenty-one years of age, or servants, or beggars." Much has been written about whether and why the Levellers stopped short of universal suffrage,[73] but insofar as any common criterion covered their exclusion of women, children, felons, beggars, and servants it appears to be that of fitness to cast a truly independent vote.

The nearest thing to a formal or "official" presentation of the Leveller case may be found in the "Agreements of the People." That proposed in November 1647 "by the Agents of the five Regiments of Horse" has been described by one American historian as anticipating the fundamentals of his country's constitution. It includes proposals that arrangements of the people "for the election of their Deputies in Parliament ought to be more indifferently proportioned, according to the number of the Inhabitants." Thereafter, the people should "choose themselves a Parliament once in two years" to enact laws, decide on offices and courts, appoint and call to account magistrates, make war and peace, and treat with foreign states.[74] The second *Agreement of the People,* dated at 15 December 1648, is much more comprehensive and has been termed an "astonishing anticipation of modern constitutional ideology."[75]

Reiterating the point about uneven distribution, this document names a detailed list of just under three hundred electoral districts. As for the franchise, those in receipt of alms are disqualified: electors shall be "such as are assessed ordinarily towards the relief of the poor; not servants to, or receiving wages from any particular person." A quorum of 153 elected members is prescribed for the passing of any statute; a council of state shall be appointed by and answerable to the representatives; to forestall factions or corrupt interests, no member of that council of state, no military officer, and no one in receipt of public money is eligible for election—and no lawyer who is either elected or appointed shall "practise as a Lawyer during that trust." Most notably, "we do not empower our Representatives to continue in force or make any Laws, Oaths, and covenants whereby to compel by penalties or otherwise, any person to any thing in or about matters of Faith, Religion or God's Worship." Equally emphatically, nothing shall be done to "take away the foundations of Common Right, Liberty or Safety contained in this Agreement, nor shall level men's Estates, destroy Propriety, or make all things common."[76] A third document has been identified as a direct outgrowth of Leveller agitation. In *A Petition* from Fairfax and the General Council of Army Officers (1649) there are some differences—as in the number of elected representatives—but its electoral principles, safeguards against corruption, and prohibition of any levelling of men's estates are reminiscent in principle and often in phraseology of the preceding document to which it alludes.[77]

What may be said in assessment of the political and constitutional importance of the Levellers? Frank describes the movement as "an evanescent phenomenon, . . . the biological sport of the Interregnum," but concedes that although as such it was consigned to almost immediate oblivion "it had lived long enough to generate certain ideological pressures which did not entirely disappear."[78] It is true that in the near future it generated an anti-Leveller reaction, the damaging effect of which upon its cause may not over-fancifully be compared with that of the French Revolution upon the cause of parliamentary reform at a later date. But in the long-run context of developing commonwealth ideology one must not underestimate the fact that, effectively, these men deliberately appealed to a section of society that had thus far largely been excluded from the political nation and was not used to appeals through the printed word. As I shall show, their ideas were driven underground but not extirpated. While no lineal descent can be proven, a striking similarity will be demonstrated between some of their ideas and those of the eighteenth-century Commonwealthsmen. Haller indeed concludes that the abortive Agreements of the People "contained ideas which were destined to become the revolutionary common-places of the future," and Wolfe that "the first two Agreements and the three great Leveller petitions, anticipated the patterns of democratic pressure that inaugurated the American republic and the English constitutional reforms of the nineteenth century."[79]

In the short run, anti-Levellerism—what one historian has described as "the reaction of the men of 1642"—was triumphant. Marchmont Nedham, in 1650, in a chapter "Concerning the Levellers," derided the *Agreement of the People* of May 1649 as perilous to the Commonwealth in opening the door to the tumults of annual elections, at the mercy of the brutish multitude. Nor did he scruple to confuse the Levellers with the Diggers.[80] Again, an anonymous "true Commonwealths-man," in 1656, pronounced anathema upon "this Levelling plea": "Do they think fit indeed, that every person and every family engaged in this Cause, should enjoy an arithmetical proportion of power and advantage with that of their superiors, both in electing and being elected? Why, then must the poorest Cottager and Mechanick of all come in with their equal voice to choose, and also with his equal turn or rota for being chosen."[81]

Others who wrote scathing critiques of the Levellers include William Prynne and Henry Parker.[82] But the allusion to the rota should serve to remind us that novel constitutional proposals were not confined to their ranks. For the term is above all associated with the outstandingly significant writings of James Harrington, in which three themes may be singled out: the nature and purpose of the commonwealth; the advocacy of an extension of the political nation; and the mechanisms by which the political nation may exercise its rights. Harrington's approach was not narrowly confined to constitutional mechanics. His great work, *The Common-Wealth of Oceana* (1656), declares that "a Common-wealth is nothing else but the National Conscience." Together with the assertion that "the interest of the Common-wealth is in the whole body of the People," this places him firmly within the context of an inherited tradition. Perhaps his own most distinctive contribution to the further development of commonwealth ideology was his insistence that the exercise of that conscience must be more widely and actively diffused among the body of the people. It is in this sense, *not* in that of any egalitarian implications, that his repeated references to the objective of an equal commonwealth must be interpreted. Most certainly he disdains those who would plaster over the reality of arbitrary and unlimited power simply "by virtue of the name Commonwealth."[83]

Harrington's vision of an ideal commonwealth is determined by his own interpretation of antecedent social developments,[84] by his insistence not only that the form of government must reflect the social structure but also that it must be a government of laws and not of men, and by his detailed prescriptions for the active involvement of the people in the political process. These are succinctly combined in his own definition: "An equal commonwealth is a government established upon an equal agrarian [law] arising into the superstructures or three orders: the senate debating and proposing, the people resolving, and the magistracy executing, by an equal rotation or interchangeable election, through the whole suffrage of the people given by the ballot."[85] A lightly fictionalized interpretation of the development of relations between Crown, nobility, and people from the time of Henry VIII leads to his conclusion that "the Balance of the Common-wealth" has shifted, reflecting the changes in ownership of land. In Harrington's stress upon balance we see the survival of the notion of a measure and a mean: "the Agrarian [Law] by the Balance of dominion preserving equality in the Root." But neither this nor such other statements as that "a Commonwealth that is internally equal hath no internal cause of commotion" implies complete equality in the distribution of property. A strong and healthy nobility is essential to balance the power of the people in "the natural mixture of a well-ordered Common-wealth." Indeed, Harrington finds it inconceivable "that an whole People should turn robbers or Levellers."[86]

If the Agrarian Law is one pillar of *Oceana*, then "the Ballot by an equal rotation conveying it into the branch, or the exercise of Sovereign power" is the other.[87] In *The Censure of the Rota Upon Mr Milton's Book* (1660) Harrington upbraids his opponent that "though you brag much of the People's managing their own affairs, you allow them no more share of that in your Utopia."[88] The devices of the ballot and the rota derive from Harrington's fundamental insight, which some would take to be his greatest single contribution to the history of political thought: that since "they that make the laws in Common-wealths are but men, the main question seems to be how a Commonwealth comes to be an empire of laws not of men?"[89] To this he returns again and again, as in *The Prerogative of Popular Government* (1658): "Whether a Commonwealth be Rightly Defined to be a Government of Laws and not of Men." What can only be interpreted as a distrust of any permanent possession of power is clearly seen in *The Censure of the Rota* (1660) Here Harrington contends "that a Common-wealth is like a great Top, that must be kept up by being whipt around, and held in perpetual circulation, for if you discontinue the Rotation, and suffer the Senate to settle, and stand still, down it falls immediately." Again, in a novel and ingenious resort to the traditional corporeal analogy: "I am most certain that these little Pills the Ballots are the only Physic that can keep the Body Politic soluble, and not suffer the humours to settle."[90]

Oceana, declaring that the foundation of "an equal Commonwealth" is "equal rotation" in governmental participation alongside the Agrarian Law that establishes a balanced distribution of property, explains that "equal rotation is equal vicissitude in government, or succession into magistracy, . . . succeeding others through the free election or suffrage of the people."[91] But the precise extent of the franchise remains a gray area in Harrington—although it has been suggested that his "failure to specify a minimum qualification, other than property itself, for the exercise of the franchise in Oceana places him nearer to Rainborough than to Ireton." Indeed J. G. A. Pocock concludes that "the franchise itself seems quite unequivocally to be extended to all in Oceana who are not servants. . . . But the people are distinguished into horse and foot by a property qualification for the former of £100 a year in land, goods or money."[92] There is a note of caution in Harrington's perception that "there is a mean in things: as exorbitant riches overthrow the balance of a commonwealth, so extreme poverty cannot hold it nor is by any means to be trusted with it," as also in his realist's observation that "a people, when they are reduced unto misery and despair, become their own politicians."[93]

Alongside his insistence that a people should be governed by laws and not by men stands Harrington's notion that a free people should bear arms as a guarantor of last resort of their liberty. These principles were permanently to be enshrined in the Constitution of the U.S. and also to figure largely in the writings of mid-eighteenth-century English Commonwealthsmen. More immediately, it is significant that, just as the apogee of Leveller agitation between 1647 and 1649 bespeaks their disappointment with the immediate fruits of Civil War, so too the fact that almost all of Harrington's political writings appeared between September 1656 and March 1660 attests another realization. That is, that neither the title of Commonwealth nor the facade of republicanism suffices in itself to secure a satisfactory form of government. Behind Harrington's apparently conventional reiteration that "a commonwealth is but a great family; and a family is a little commonwealth"[94] there lies a total rejection of any *paternalist* interpretation of society, if paternal be taken to mean any tenure of power other than by totally accountable trusteeship.

Very different is the picture to emerge from another work declaredly "occasioned by the disorders of the present time": *Leviathan* (1651) by Thomas Hobbes. Designed "to set before men's eyes the mutual Relation between Protection and Obedience,"[95] the content and terminology of this masterpiece are also of significance (if differently orientated) within the evolution of the concept of the commonwealth. Hobbes has recourse throughout to the inherited corporeal analogy, alluding to "the Nutrition, and Procreation of a Common-wealth," to its ills and diseases that include those "that proceed from the poisons of seditious doctrines" and those analogous with epilepsy and pleurisy. Indeed he contends that "the Sovereign is the public Soul, giving Life and Motion to the Commonwealth; which expiring, the Members are governed by it no more than the Carcass of a man by his departed (though Immortal) Soul."[96] Yet at the very outset Hobbes defines "that great Leviathan, called a Common-wealth or State [as] but an Artificial Man," endowed with artificial joints and nerves, with Sovereignty "an Artificial Soul." In his depiction of "the Causes, Generation, and Definition of a Common-wealth" Hobbes is so explicit that his condemnation in most conservative circles is not surprising. For he insists that it is *men* who "have made an Artificial Man, which we call a Common-wealth," equipped with "Artificial Chains, called Civil Laws." Having thus appointed "one Man, or Assembly of men, to bear their Person, . . . the Multitude" thus united is called a Commonwealth. Thus then, the generation 'of that great Leviathan, . . . of that Mortal God to which we owe under the Immortal God our peace and defence."[97]

Despite the artificial creation of this Leviathan, the organic analogy survives triumphant in Hobbes's insistence that, once created, sovereignty is unitary and indivisible, and that the overthrow of the ruler involves dissolution. "Then is the Common-wealth Dissolved, and every man at liberty to protect himself."[98] Thus, a century on from Ponet and Goodman, the concept of the "body politic" conveys a very different message. Not for Hobbes the prospect of such a body, artificial though it be, with a power to cut off its head and put on another. Ponet and Goodman, despite the deeply religious context of their thinking, had opened the door to the entry of a theory of individual rights as the basis of a social contract. Now, ironically, the more secular approach of Hobbes will have nothing to do with any antecedent individual rights: he reverts to an earlier interpretation in insisting that the downfall of the ruler entails the dissolution of the body politic and reversion to jungle law.

Conceding that there are several kinds of commonwealth, such as monarchy, democracy, and aristocracy, and appearing to reject any *necessary* equation of democracy with anarchy, Hobbes is quite adamant about individual liberties. "To resist the Sword of the Common-wealth, in defence of another man, guilty or innocent, no man hath Liberty; because such Liberty takes away from the Sovereign the means of protecting us;" and is therefore destructive of the very essence of Government. In short, only the law preserves and guarantees individual liberties—and that in the hands of the ruler. There is no law *of* liberty. Individual rights are derivative from, not antecedent to and a condition of the continuance of, a ruler's authority. "And they that go about by disobedience, to do no more than reform the Common-wealth, shall find they do thereby destroy it; like the foolish daughters of Peleus . . . which desiring to renew the youth of their decrepit Father, did by the Counsel of Medea, cut him in pieces, and boil him, together with strange herbs, but made not of him a new man." Most notably, in a complete inversion of the position later taken by John Locke, "where there is no coercive Power erected, that is, where there is no Common-wealth, there is no Propriety; all men having Right to all things"—for where there is no Commonwealth, nothing is unjust![99]

Well might Hobbes be described as having written with brutal lucidity. Indeed, to Kenneth Minogue's over-sweeping contention that "it is quite wrong to interpret Hobbes in terms of the political conflicts of his own time" I must add the fact that such lucidity did not appeal to many of his contemporaries.[100] Although the third part of *Leviathan* is entitled "Of a Christian Common-wealth," those who sought for a divinely sanctioned base of a hoped-for restored and rejuvenated monarchy would find no more to encourage them than the seeker after a theory of individual rights. In place of the supernaturally sanctioned authority appealed to both by the advocate of Divine Right and by the supporter of natural and inalienable human rights,[101] Hobbes seems almost to make Leviathan itself a god. If Hobbes may be considered a maverick in his contemporary context, he is certainly such in the context of evolving commonwealth ideals. His contention that "as for other Liberties, they depend on the Silence of the Law"[102] is doubly symbolic. Despite a lengthy treatment of religious and ecclesiastical issues, the reader of *Leviathan* will find little exposition of any divinely imposed responsibility of the commonwealth to take positive action for the social and economic well-being of its subjects. And even within its own parameters the book should check any temptation to impose upon the history of political thought any pattern of smooth progression towards a belief in natural and inalienable human rights.

Yet the general drift of commonwealth ideology during these crucial midcentury decades is toward just such a philosophy—now increasingly envisaged not merely in the limited terms of protection by the law and the absence of unjust constraints. The notion now emerges that only through individual freedom in a more positive sense can full political, religious, and economic potential be realized. Yet the relationship between the diverse aspects of commonwealth citizenship remains complex. The 1640s and 1650s find commonwealth idealists appealing not for diminished but for *increasing* governmental intervention in social and economic problems. These years saw the last and fullest flowering of the social and economic idealism of the mid-Tudor era but also prefigured concepts of collectivist intervention. As for the religious strand in commonwealth ideology, the connection between a "Puritan Revolution" and the emergence of individual religious, civil, and political liberties was as fortuitous as it was incontestably significant.

In identifying a pattern for these decades, older historians often wrote of Civil Wars followed by a Puritan revolution. More recently, the concept and the terminology of a "second revolution" have sometimes been employed.[103] But, whether one writes of an anti-monarchical civil conflict followed by a Puritan revolution, or seeks to delineate an anti-monarchical rebellion followed by abortive yearnings for a genuine revolution, one thing remains clear. To some skeptical and radical contemporary minds, what occurred in the 1640s was a quarrel about the arbitrary power of the king, which the victors then proceeded to share among themselves—not without further squabbles. In such frustrated social and economic reformers historians have identified the harbingers not only of political democracy but also of the philosophy of collectivism or even neo-socialism. Yet, novel as these interpretations may appear, these advocates of reform still proffered a vision of the commonwealth that was almost always cast in religious terminology.

"The Godly Commonwealth"

Any attempt at a clear division between political and religious, or for that matter between religious, social, and economic issues would be anachronistic. Most certainly an appeal to government to ensure social and economic justice on the grounds of *religious obligation* persisted—even when the exact nature of the ecclesiastical organization required to crystallize that obligation was at savage issue. Further, it may well be contended that demands for individual *political* rights were fuelled by a belief that their achievement was a means of eliciting such action. Yet, in endeavoring to identify the more specifically religious aspects of mid-seventeenth-century commonwealth ideology some crucially important issues stand out. Were there significant developments of the notion of religious liberty, as distinct from the perennial dread of religious licence? Was there any shift away from envisaging the commonwealth in fundamentally religious terms toward a more secular concept? Or is it more accurate to say that appeals to the "Godly Commonwealth" to guarantee prescribed standards of moral, social, and economic behavior strengthened rather than diminished? Cross-currents abound. Thus, many of those pamphleteers who assailed not only the prelates of the Catholic cause but also those perceived as their heirs, the Presbyterians, in denying *any* right to enforce religious uniformity, were also foremost in appealing to government to secure for its subjects acceptable Christian social standards. The range not only of published discussion of religious issues but also of the social origins of its participants has rightly been termed amazing.

Discussion of organized religion as an aspect of the commonwealth ranged from the type of skeptical and anticlerical abuse which dates right back to the later Middle Ages, to an advocacy of freedom of conscience and of religious toleration that is striking in its depth of thinking and urgency. A suggested "common distinctive characteristic of all the sects was refusal to recognize the historic church."[104] Sometimes, rejection of organized ecclesiastical constraints went hand-in-hand with abhorrence of predestination and a conviction that justification was free to all. Sometimes, anticlericalism was accompanied by derision of formal and above all of university education. To Gerrard Winstanley, "their Churches are the successors of the Jews' Synagogues, and are houses of bondage; their Universities are successors of the Scribes' and Pharisees' houses of learning." He condemned "selfish tythe-taking Preachers, and all others that preaches for hire." To many of the sectarian writers, organized religion appeared not so much as the custodian of established religious truth as the ecclesiastical arm designed to delude the poor people in the interests of the social establishment. Thus, when a poor man complains, pleading the scriptural injunction that the poor and the meek shall inherit the earth, "the tithing Priest stops his mouth with a slam and tells him that is meant of the inward satisfaction of mind which the poor shall have, though they enjoy nothing at all." Indeed, they "tell the poor People that they must be content with their Poverty, and they shall have their Heaven hereafter. But why may we not have our Heaven here . . . ?" Sadly, while people imagine a Heaven or fear a Hell after death, "their eyes are put out, that they see not what is the birthright, and what is to be done by them here on Earth."[105]

Winstanley was far from alone in expressing such sentiments. Robert Greville, Lord Brooke, in his *Discourse opening The Nature of that Episcopacie, which is exercised in England* (second edition, 1642), attacks the bishops' arrogation of "a Dictator-like power, to direct our judgements [and] to contradict our Reason, and force our consciences." Most crucially, "they affirm Civil Monarchy cannot stand without the Church. Thus they delude Silly People." Little wonder, in theology, "to see those things that are purely *Indifferent*, made *absolutely necessary*, to the insupportable burden of all men's consciences." On a wider canvas, one recognizes a familiar point when he cites the judgment of one who "had now served thirty years in Parliament, and in all that time never knew but Two or Three Bishops stand for the Common-wealth." Clearly, unity of church and state as a necessary condition of a stable commonwealth is at issue. But those who oppose it are *not* antireligious. For in the United Provinces they "let every Church please her self in her own way, so long as she leaveth the State to her self. And how religion doth flourish there. . . ."[106]

William Walwyn, in *The Compassionate Samaritane* (1645), derided "the Bishops, those Drones and Caterpillars of the Commonwealth," but was also in no doubt that "the Presbyters, as it is conceived, will be more violent, as slaves usually are when they become masters." An outstandingly strident note was sounded by "R.H.," a Quaker, in 1659, when he deplored the earlier link between "Popish Prelates" and "Civil Authority": "It's the Mother of Harlots and abominations, the Strumpet, the strange Woman Jezebel, that deceives the people with her fornications, the worldly Teachers, State-Ministers"; such are not of Christ's ministry.[107] Two Digger tracts in 1649 describe the priesthood as conducting "their sorceries only for their filthy lucre and bellies' sake," being but jugglers who "invent a thing they call Religion"—effectively, state-worship. Such works as *A Modest Reply* (published anonymously in 1659) tended to be fewer in number in their defence of "a National Clergy" and their plea that "when the Laws of a Christian Common-wealth have settled an honourable maintenance upon the Clergy, we doubt not but this is very acceptable to God."[108]

The swelling tide for religious liberty attested by the pamphlet literature raised more problems than it solved. To the Presbyterians, it meant the overthrow of the episcopal system, with its attendant "papist dregs," and the installation of full "reformed" religion. But the imposition of godly standards and the suppression of noxious heresy would remain the bounden duty of a national Presbyterian church—whose theology included predestination in the rigorous form that was anathema to many contemporary consciences. To the Independents, religious liberty meant freedom from the Presbyterian as well as the prelatist yoke: "new presbyter is but old priest writ large." Frequently, a belief in complete religious toleration was expressed, as opposed to the freedom to impose one's beliefs on others for which the Presbyterians were chided. Yet compliance with godly discipline by a sect's own voluntary membership was combined with an appeal to the magistrate to enforce Christian social standards. Finally, a persistent dread of the consequences should the human spirit be completely cast adrift from Christian doctrinal moorings ensured that few would equate religious liberty with licence—though many would avail themselves of this handy tar-brush against their adversaries.

As early as 1644 the much-travelled merchant and writer on economic issues Henry Robinson published, anonymously, his tract of *Liberty of Conscience*. His assertion that "the compelling of a man to any thing against his own conscience, especially in matters of faith, is a doing evil" goes far to justify the claim that he was perhaps the first Englishman to enunciate this principle with clarity. He goes on, first, to distinguish between necessary limits in *civil* obedience and matters of religious conscience, and secondly, to urge that "God will not have men persecuted for matter of Religion, lest under colour thereof the persecuting of his dearest Saints should seem more justifiable."[109] The royalist defeat saw Parliament emerge as the immediate adversary. Thus Richard Overton, in his *Remonstrance* already cited, informed its members that "it is not for you to assume a Power to control and force Religion, or a way of Church Government, upon the People, because former Parliaments have so done."[110] Another advocate of *The Necessity of Toleration in Matters of Religion* (1647) was the little-known Samuel Richardson, perhaps an army preacher and certainly an admirer of Cromwell. His case, posed in the form of questions, includes the query "whether corporal punishments can open blind eyes, and give light to dark understandings?" Or again, "whether it be not better for us that a patent were granted to monopolize all the corn and cloth . . . which yet were intolerable, as for some men to appoint and measure out to us what and how much we shall believe and practise in matters of religion?" Significantly, not only is it God's way to have religion free, but "it is best for the public peace to give every one content," since "it is not in the power of man to suppress errors." He upbraids his adversaries, "how have you laboured for to have power to go to the old trade of persecution"! "Better that the sword be in the hands of the advocates of Christians, honest and faithful Fairfax and Cromwell. . . ."[111]

The turn of the year 1648–49 saw a small spate of contributions to the debate. Indeed, at Whitehall the Council of Army Officers formally tabled the question of "whether the magistrate have, or ought to have, any compulsive power in matters of religion?"[112] The anonymously written *No Papist nor Presbyterian* demanded that "all penal Statutes against non-conformists in Religion may be forthwith repealed." Not only should there be "a free and unmolested exercise of Religion, at least in private houses, for all sorts of People that profess *Christ,* none excepted," but the authors assert "that no person be disabled from bearing any Office in the Common-wealth, for any opinion or practice in Religion, *though contrary to the public way*" (my italics). Add to all this the fact that liberty of conscience must not exclude Papists, and Don Wolfe's contention that this tract represents "a social awareness two centuries remote from public acceptance" is persuasive.[113] Third among this clutch of treatments of the issue, some proposals submitted by John Jubbes on behalf of the Common Council of London contain as Article XIV the declaration "that whereas God the Creator and Father of Spirits is Omnipotent and unlimited by man, giving to every one a various and different Spirit, of which no man is certainly Master, . . . therefore ought Liberty of Conscience to be granted to all godly Conscientious walkers. . . ."[114]

Debate about this issue continued throughout the life of the Commonwealth. In 1652 Henry Robinson, again, appealed to Parliament to "be pleased then to Proclaim an absolute Liberty of Conscience, with a Toleration of all differing opinions, provided they reproach not one another" and avoid the "Bug-bear words of Heresy or Blasphemy." At the very end of the period, in his *Readie & Easie Way to Establish a Free Commonwealth,* Milton asserted that "the whole freedom of man consists either in spiritual or civil liberty." Therefore, "he who cannot be content with this liberty to himself, but seeks violently to impose what he will have to be the only religion upon other men's consciences . . . bears a mind not only unchristian and irreligious, but inhuman also and barbarous." Accordingly, all civil states, above all a free Commonwealth, "would do much better, and remove the cause of much hindrance and disturbance in public affairs, much ambition, much hypocrisy and contention among the people, if they would not meddle at all with Ecclesiastical matters."[115]

In such works as these one sees foreshadowed the gradual abandonment of the insistence that the commonwealth, if it is to remain whole, must cherish and indeed enforce unity of belief in matters religious. Toleration and protection of religious diversity would become the *duty* of the commonwealth as its characteristics are thought of more and more in terms of individual liberty. There remains of course the codicil contained in Walwyn's appeal to "all who love the peace and unity of Commonwealth's men," that "Liberty of Conscience be allowed for every man, . . . and no man be punished or discountenanced by Authority for his Opinion, unless it be dangerous to the State."[116] Moreover, just because such liberties were still envisaged as essentially Christian, the appeal to the rulers of the commonwealth to enforce acceptable standards in social and economic affairs does not recede but is enhanced.

Meanwhile, a belief in total liberty of worship remained a minority viewpoint, as was uneasily attested in several works that combined the assertion of freedom in matters doctrinal with sharp attacks upon the Presbyterians. *An Apologeticall Narration* submitted to Parliament in 1643 evinces a fairly early realization by the Independents of a looming threat from "that which is the contention of these times, the *authoritative Presbyterial Government* in all the subordinations and proceedings of it." This more especially since they "do professedly judge the Calvinian Reformed Churches of the first reformation from out of Popery to stand in need of a further reformation in themselves"![117] For his part, John Goodwin is perturbed that "the gleanings of Independency (so called) will not hinder the vintage of Presbytery." He depicts the Presbyterian way as one "which conjures all men's gifts, parts, and industry into a synodical circle, and suffer them only to dance there, as it may possibly shut the doors against some errors and blasphemies."[118]

Lilburne's *Copie of a Letter*, addressed to Prynne in January 1645, rejects his abuse "of men whom they falsely label Sectaries, that have in the uprightness of their hearts without Synodianlike ends striven for the Common-wealth," and finds much in Prynne's writings reminiscent of Papists or Jesuits. But the most striking exposition of the anti-Presbyterian case is surely Richard Overton's *Arraignment of Mr. Persecution* (also 1645). Dedicated to "his Holynesse, Sir John Presbyter," its approach is reminiscent of both John Bunyan and William Turner, with its device of the "Roman Fox" clad in an English episcopal habit. This worthy is now, "lest all Trades should fail, become a zealous Covenanter, in the godly shape of a Presbyter [as] a new cheat to cozen the world," and will become as fat as any bishop. Had these fellows "but as much power as Queen Mary's Clergy, their Reformation would conclude in fire and faggot." "The Trade of Presbyter is the best Trade in England, all are taxed and it goes free," while poor men have not bread to feed their children.[119]

The note of social criticism thus sounded was often linked with the vexatious issue of religious licence. In Overton's same tract Sir Symon Synod is made to declare that "this fellow Liberty-of-Conscience is a Free-willer, a loose Libertine, one that opens a gate to all manner of profaneness [and] a Confuter of our mighty champions Mr. Prynne, Edwards, &c." Such would permit "every mechanic illiterate fellow to turn Preacher." Certainly there were enough genuine examples of would-be propagation of varieties of religious licence, often mixed with appeals for social disintegration, to provide a substantial reservoir of tar with which to smear the conservatives' adversaries. The moderate Robert Greville, Lord Brooke, attacking episcopacy in 1642, had written of Anabaptists, heretics, and atheists, while even the greatest of the "mechanick preachers," John Bunyan, felt constrained in 1658 to utter the caveat to extremists: lest "thou wilt Ranter-like turn the Grace of God unto wantonness."[120]

The Ranters resembled the dreaded Free Spirits or devotees of Spiritual Liberty of the late Middle Ages. A. L. Morton identifies an often incongruous combination of "a pantheistic mysticism and a crudely plebeian materialism." Some held indeed that the performance of allegedly sinful acts was *necessary* in order to demonstrate one's freedom from an artificial yoke. Little wonder that the line between the Ranters' own exposition of their views and such scurrilous parodies as *The Ranter's Last Sermon* is sometimes difficult to discern. Its author's assertion that they taught "that it was quite contrary to the end of Creation to Appropriate anything to any Man or Woman; but that there ought to be a Community of all things" was fair comment and lends weight to the suggestion that the Ranter was dreaded not so much as a heretic as he was as a social deviant. Davis contends indeed that the Ranters existed more as a myth in the minds of fearful conservative propagandists than as a dangerous reality in terms of numbers—much less a coherent movement. "There was no Ranter movement, no Ranter sect, no Ranter theology." He finds Laurence Clarkson, who once described himself as "the Captain of the Rant," more convincing as a one-time Ranter than Abiezer Coppe, whom he identifies as a millenialist.[121] Yet Coppe hardly needed a label to sound frightening and incur imprisonment. A former student at Merton, his *Fiery Flying Roll* (1649) appeals to "the Eternal God, who am Universal Love, and whose service is perfect freedom, and pure Libertinism." In this, and in the *Second Fiery Flying Roule* that accompanies it, Coppe disdains mere "sword-levelling, or digger-levelling" as inadequate; for God, the mighty Leveller, is coming "to Level in good earnest." Davis has not gone unchallenged; among many rejoinders that of Gerald Aylmer insists that the Ranters "were enough of a movement for the threat to seem a credible one." Appealing to scattered pockets of the urban lower orders, devoid of organization or discipline, they posed a minimal threat to society; but they purveyed a frightening glimpse of the spawning nihilism of the abyss. In 1656 James Nayler, himself a member of a Quaker sect far removed from its present-day pacific image, and assuredly no hireling of a conservative "yellowpress," gave the lie to an opponent: "Thou sayest our principles are but the principles of the old Ranters, which is as far removed from them both in principle and practice as light and darkness."[122]

Despite Nayler's indignant repudiation, the Quakers were often bracketed with the Ranters in public apprehension. Richard Baxter indeed perceived elements of difference, but also alleged ominous similarities when he described them as "but the Ranters turned from horrid Profaneness and Blasphemy to a Life of extreme Austerity on the other side." But they also claim "the Light which every man hath within him to be his sufficient Rule, and consequently the Scriptures and Ministry are set light by." An average of estimates of their numbers puts them at fifty thousand, perhaps as numerous as the Romanists and certainly more so than the Fifth Monarchy Men or the Baptists. Their ostentatious contempt for social deference is seen as motivating the savage punishment inflicted on Nayler by the Parliament of 1656 at least as much as his imputed blasphemy. Indeed, Ivan Roots has remarked that "Nayler's case raised religious, legal, constitutional, humanitarian and intellectual issues that blasted all artificial categories."[123]

The towering prophet of denunciation of all the sects was Thomas Edwards, whose evocatively entitled *Gangraena* is his frightening monument. In his defense of the Presbyterian-Calvinist conception of a properly ordered commonwealth against "the mischief of Ecclesiastical Anarchy, the monstrousness of the much affected Toleration," Edwards starts with a list of 176 heresies and eventually ends with nearly 300! His diatribes are directed "against Seekers, Anabaptists, Antinomians, Brownists, Libertines [and all other] whirlegig spirits," as a greater threat than the Cavaliers to the Parliamentary cause. In consequence of this "many headed monstrous Hydra of Sectarism, . . . this land is become already in many places a Chaos, a Babel, another Amsterdam, yea worse; we are beyond that, and in the highway to Munster." In face of this, misguided toleration "is the grand design of the Devil." Alongside doctrinal chaos stands "their holding of Popular Government, the power and experience of Church Government to be in the hands of the people, and not of the officers." Robinson and Lilburne are singled out for obloquy.[124]

In a *Second Part of Gangraena* the sectaries are depicted as "Libertines and loose persons who have a desire to live in pleasure and enjoy their lusts, and to be under no Government." Their "principles would bring in an universal Anarchy, both upon Church and State, overthrowing all Ministry, settled Government, and order in the Church." Yet a *Third Part* continues the sorry compilations, listing such heresies as "that all shall be saved at last," that "Adultery is no Sin, and that Drunkenness is none either, but a help to see Christ the better by it." The upshot of their plea "for Laws according to right reason, and for natural primitive rights" would be "to set up an Utopian Anarchy of the promiscuous multitude, and the lusts and uncertain fancies of weak people for Laws and Rules." For "in a word, nothing pleases them, not the Government nor any part of it; not the Laws, their design is to have all pull'd down, to have a total change made, that being *abrasa tabula* they might write in it what they pleased [in] the new modelling of Church and Commonwealth."[125]

Meanwhile, in endeavoring in more constructive fashion to shape what they saw as the "Godly Commonwealth," the Puritan ranks presented a wide spectrum of beliefs about that unity between the political and religious aspects of society that had been so much emphasized by their prelatist adversaries. Many now saw the duty of the state as confined to safeguarding an individual's right *not* to conform with any prescribed form of worship. But they all believed that any vision of a Christian commonwealth should include official concern both for public morality and for social justice. This latter, a long-term element in commonwealth ideology, now re-emerges in more insistent and sometimes more radical fashion. But it is important to remember that while concern for public morality and a demand for Christian standards in economic and social relationships sometimes overlapped, they were not identical. Inevitably, propagandists for radical social and economic change fell foul of the more conservatively minded custodians of the existing social and moral order.

Certainly, it has been suggested that the evidence of official action during the Commonwealth and Protectorate is fuller for concern for religion and morality than it is for ameliorative economic and social edicts. The Long Parliament in session in February 1647 set down an "Ordinance concerning the growth and spreading of Errors, Heresies, and Blasphemies, and for setting apart a day of Public Humiliation" acknowledging such. In May of the following year, punishments enacted for a clear list of blasphemous doctrinal errors extended to pain of death—but were not followed by draconian enforcement. Of two statutes in the summer of 1650, that of August declared certain "Execrable Opinions derogatory to the honour of God, and destructive to human society." Enunciating a parliamentary duty "to propagate the Gospel in this Commonwealth," to nurture "Reformation in Doctrine and Manners," and to uphold "the necessity of Civil and Moral Righteousness among men," this act repeated the resolve to take "strict and effectual proceedings against them, who should abuse and turn to Licentiousness, the liberty given in matters of Conscience." A long list of abhorrent sins included not only blasphemy, but also stealing and cheating, adultery and fornication, drunkenness, and swearing.[126] Some would have gone further. William Prynne's *Sword of the Christian Magistracy* (1647) had besought enactment of the death penalty against those guilty of religious innovation.[127] As I shall show, the hope of government by the godly was to founder at least in part upon the questions of who the godly were and of what was the nature of their vision.

The irony has been observed, in identifying an element of continuity in concern for public morality, that "Archbishop Laud had, in his moral concerns at least, been thoroughly puritanical".[128] Now, in the 1650s, Oliver Cromwell emerged as the great hope of those who looked for a combination of religious toleration and moral leadership. He himself was clear that "as for profane persons, blasphemers, such as preach sedition, the contentious railers, evil speakers who seek by evil words to corrupt good manners, . . . punishment from the civil magistrate ought to meet with them"—for his sword must not be borne in vain. Specifically, regarding the Major Generals, on 5 March 1656 he declared "the suppressing of vice and encouragement of virtue the very end of magistracy."[129] Their efforts at moral regulation have, of course, encountered a very mixed reception from historians—as well as from contemporaries. Alehouses were a major target, while in the realm of poor relief increased concern with the provision of almshouses for the infirm and of outdoor relief for the needy was accompanied by condemnation of those responsible for bastard births. Insofar as Cromwell is to be considered in the line of "commonwealth" statesmen of the old tradition, this emphasis upon the religious and moral responsibility of government is perhaps his outstanding characteristic. But he was never in danger of confusing a moral crusade with social revolution.

Alongside those who feared the latter were those who dreaded the dictatorship of a self-appointed religious elite—which did not lack for advocates. John Eliot, an emigrant minister in New England, where the rule of the Saints had already been installed, declared in *The Christian Commonwealth* (London, 1659), that "the Lord Jesus will bring down all people to be ruled by the Institutions, Laws and Directions of the Word of God; not only in Church Government and Administrations, but also in the Government and Administration of all affairs in the Commonwealth." Few were quite so explicit, but Richard Baxter (who corresponded with Eliot) published *A Holy Commonwealth* in the same year. Although he was later (1670) in part to disavow his book, Baxter was serious in his lengthy attempt to envisage on a national scale the imposition of the godly discipline that he had himself essayed in Kidderminster. While this, not confutation of Harrington, was his prime purpose, it is significant that Baxter sought to replace any propertied elitism with an elite based on godliness.[130]

His definition of "theocratical" government—which, under Richard Cromwell, he fleetingly believed to be attainable—is important. The nub of his thesis is "that the Church and Commonwealth should be very near commensurate, and that proved ungodly persons should neither Choose nor be Chosen" in the representative process. "Those Politicians therefore that say a Commonwealth in its own nature doth not participate of moral good or evil . . . do fundamentally err." Indeed, "the more Theocratical, or truly Divine any Government is the better. . . . In a true Theocracy, or Divine Common wealth, the Matter of the Church and Common-wealth should be altogether or almost the same, though the form of them and administrations are different." Both are essential to the national welfare. Yet it must never be forgotten that it is "the badness of men" that corrupts all forms of government and subjects the public good to the private. Not surprisingly, Baxter would wish to "see the Foundations of Parliament Reformed, by an exclusion of truly Unworthy persons from the Elections . . . so that we were out of danger of having Impious Parliaments chosen by an impious Majority of the people." This typifies his "sense of the mischief of Democracy" and his disdain for such as "would make Democracy the only Government that hath the stamp of God." As for the franchise, "Nature maketh Infants and Idiots uncapable: and women choose not members of Parliament. Servants are commonly judged incapable, and so are the poor [because] they are not free in their elections." But the rich must also be excluded, if rascally and criminal! Crucially, "Common wealths are not always to follow a Major Popular Vote." For sadly, "the rabble vulgar multitude are for the greater part not only void of solid Piety and Prudence . . . but enemies to it." Like all men, they are "biassed and Ruled by a private selfish spirit, till saving grace makes God their Centre"—otherwise they would "rather there were two Stars fewer in the Firmament, than one Cow less in their pastures."[131]

Baxter's concern with mundane social issues is far less evident in this work, in which he was concerned to justify the establishment of government by the godly, than was to be the case in the last treatise he wrote—which will be considered later. But much of Puritan opinion urged that even when salvation and a near-Christian perfection of conduct could be expected only by and from the elect, godly discipline in moral and social issues should be applied to *all*. Woolrych has pointed to a "continuing tension between radical millenarian Puritanism and moderate constitutionalism." Long ago, Haller concluded that certain elements "were moving from the start, not toward the democracy of the Levellers, but toward the rule of the saints of the Barebones Parliament." Nor is this the retrospective pattern-making of historians. Nothing could be more explicit than the challenge directed to Fairfax by some Fifth Monarchy Men in 1649: "How can the kingdom be the saints', when the ungodly are electors, and elected to govern?"[132] The Fifth Monarchists have been defined as "a political and religious sect expecting the imminent Kingdom of Christ on earth, a theocratic regime in which the saints would establish a godly discipline over the unregenerate masses and prepare for the Second Coming."[133] Their immediate program included a readiness to appeal to arms, if necessary, and millenarian social changes. More than one historian has identified the Nominated (or "Barebones") Parliament of 1653 as the high point of "normative Puritanism in power," with the Saints within fleeting touch of supreme political authority. But although the Fifth Monarchists therein exercised an influence out of all proportion to their numbers, their projects for social, legal, and economic change—which will be discussed later—sufficed at last to polarize the assembly and produce its sudden termination.[134] Cromwell considered them as sincere men deluded by a mistaken notion, pretending a special spirituality. "But for men to entitle themselves on this principle, that they are the only men to rule . . . and give laws to people; to determine of property and liberty, and everything else upon such pretence as this is truly" quite intolerable. Looking back, they themselves declared bitterly: "were not the last Parliament dissolved, for that they would rule as Saints (or part of the fifth monarchy, for Christ)?"[135]

Before proceeding to those social and economic issues to which I have alluded, what general conclusions may be proffered on those who wrote about religion in the commonwealth? In general, the belief in a dogmatic creed of revealed religion remained. Few would have accompanied Winstanley in his declaration that "I use the word Reason instead of God in my writings," or in his reference to "the Spirit of Reason, which I call God." But more might have joined him in discerning a conspiracy by the "zealous professors" of organized religion "to keep down those risings of the spirit in the poor . . . that threaten their titles and their special privileges."[136] Indeed, it might well be argued that insofar as religious liberty was nurtured by these revolutionary decades, it was as an unintended by-product of the movement initiated by those who rebelled against royalist episcopacy. Thus, the king defeated and indeed put to death, the fierce debate about the use that was to be made of "Parliament's" victory was conducted almost as much in religious and social as in political terms.

Sabine suggested of the Leveller and Digger movements that both "were nearly as much religious as they were political,"[137] while J. F. McGregor sees the former as "turning the principle of religious liberty into a secular theory of natural rights."[138] Their adherents, like the advocates of the *principle* of religious toleration, made up small minorities. But the religious "sectaries" more narrowly defined saw with increasing clarity that a uniformity enforced by Calvinist Presbyterians would hardly be more attractive than that prescribed by episcopacy, and thus were driven to commend religious liberty if only on the grounds of expediency. Yet, and notably, those very sectarians who offended against the Presbyterian conception of the proper ordering of church and state in the commonwealth, while rejecting any unitary authority in matters religious, often outstripped their adversaries (albeit in a much more radical direction) in their appeal to government to implement what they saw as a truly Christian social and economic ethos.

Equity or Equality?

The intensity of this appeal derived in part from an economic and social crisis sufficient in itself to generate a surge of discontent. Historians point to the conjunction of high prices, low wages, bad harvests, increased taxation, and the imposition of free quarter. Three consecutive poor harvests in 1647–49 were more immediately traumatic in effect than the long-term rise in prices, which in fact levelled off by the 1650s. In response, the emigration rate surged to a level unequalled until the late nineteenth century.[139] Contemporaries were in no doubt about the scale of the crisis. Samuel Hartlib in 1649 depicted people "constrained to feed upon beasts' blood and Brewers' grains boiled together," and alleged a year later that some were driven to eat dogs and cats.[140] News sheets from many parts of England described near-famine conditions. Both Parliament and the Common Council of London were concerned lest rioting ensue. Yet this was but the culmination of an existing trend. In 1645 Lilburne alluded to a petition to the mayor of London, which pleaded "that the Poor is in great necessity, wanting wherewith to set themselves on work, their Children uneducated, and thereby prepared to wickedness and beggary."[141]

The conjunction of social and economic distress, political uncertainty, and religious turmoil that had contributed to a searching discussion of the nature of governmental responsibilities in the commonwealth in the mid-Tudor decades has quite clearly recurred. But there is one crucial difference. The fear that *any* successful opposition to the existing political establishment must necessarily open the floodgates to social anarchy has at least in part abated. Many would contend that the Civil War derived from a split *within* the existing political nation. Only after a royalist defeat became increasingly probable did a surge of hope among the politico-social radicals, and conversely of fear among the propertied classes, become a major—perhaps *the* major—issue. Cromwell now stood as the bulwark not only against such as Lilburne but also against the Digger Winstanley, who proposed a revolution in the very economic structure of society. Winstanley chided "you that were the Gentry [that] when you were assembled in Parliament, you called upon the poor Common-People to come and help you, and cast out oppression." But although its top be lopped, "oppression is a great tree still, and keeps off the sun of freedom from the poor Commons."[142] This almost resembles a seventeenth-century version of "the Revolution betrayed"! The disenchanted envisaged such betrayal in political, religious, but perhaps most dangerously of all, in social and economic terms.

Accordingly, the real content of the term "commonwealth" once more becomes the focus of intense debate. Aylmer has suggested that its adoption as a formal title "was a kind of compromise with the English past, and seems to have been thought less doctrinaire than the word republic."[143] But I have cited expressions of a wish for something more than a change of name—and this extended to a social and economic as well as to a political level. Moreover, such discussion sometimes was cast in terms of individual rights as well as traditional communal obligations. Thus Joseph Lee, writing in 1654 about enclosures, urged that the commonwealth "is but the *summa totalis* of sundry persons in several figures."[144] The question of whether the commonwealth is beginning to be envisaged less as an organic entity and more as the sum of individual social and economic rights will recur in the context of several themes that will now be explored.

Foremost in the minds of many who clung to the organic similitude of society was the notion of hierarchy. Despite his reluctant willingness to behead an anointed king, Cromwell himself has been seen as "essentially a traditionalist and a believer in a hierarchical society." He would presumably have approved of John Dury's declaration, in a sermon before the House of Commons in November 1645, that although "every one of us is made his brother's keeper, [yet] the feet cannot effect the office of the head, nor the hand of the feet. . . . Let every man abide in the sphere and calling wherein God hath set him."[145] Three years later John Cook, the regicide, was to write—in words that could have come straight out of a mid-Tudor tract—that "the God of order hath appointed several degrees of men, and set them in their several stations; the rich to be liberal to the poor, and the poor to be serviceable to the rich. . . . I am not of their opinion that drive at a parity to have all men alike, 'tis but a Utopian fiction, the Scripture holds no such thing." Even Harrington's assertion that wherever "a man from the lowest may not rise unto the due pitch of his unquestionable merit, the commonwealth is not equal," is but reminiscent of Morison's conditional approval of such social mobility in the 1530s.[146]

Far more worrying to respectable society was increasingly open expression of what can only be described in modern terminology of class envy or even hatred. How else may one explain Nayler's denunciation of the "cruel covetous oppressors, who grind the faces of the poor needy," ignoring the law of God in their quest for riches, so long as they can "keep within the compass of the laws of the nation"? Again, William Covel answered his own question: "How came you Poor Ones by your poverties and miseries? . . . Ever since the people did choose Kings, and put their Images on Silver and Gold . . . to buy the Poor's labours for half the worth"—with their exploitation defended by the law.[147] In face of this, Abiezer Coppe—through university educated and not himself a member of the "meaner sort"—rejoices in his expectation that God, the mighty Leveller, will "confound it into a parity, equality, community; that the neck of horrid pride, murder, malice, and tyranny, &c may be chopt off at one blow." The rich must regard the poor as equals: "make them one with you, or else go howling into hell. . . . Bow before those poor, nasty, lousy, ragged wretches, . . . account nothing your own, have All Things common." The message is clear in his blood-curdling peroration: "Howl, howl, ye nobles, howl honourables, howl ye rich men for the miseries that are coming upon you." Nor would the worries of those thus addressed have been allayed by the intention attributed to a Fifth Monarchy Man (who believed in an elitism of a different type) to make the "Rulers of the Earth . . . sit bare-breeched upon Hawthorn-Bushes"![148]

Perhaps the most ingenious exposition of an alleged alliance between class exploitation and religious hypocrisy, together with engaging remedial suggestions, is in *Tyranipocrit*, anonymously published (possibly in Rotterdam) in 1649. Its thesis is that "the rich artificial thieves do rob the poor, and that under a feigned show of justice, and a seeming holiness," ascribing the result to "God's providence"—all with the active connivance of laws and lawyers. This "contract of Matrimony betwixt Tyranny and Hypocrisy" has produced "Tyranipocrit." Yet surely the true intent of God would "give unto every man with discretion so near as may be an equal share of earthly goods." Now "if the Rulers of this world cannot make all the poor rich, yet they can make the richest poor, for their sin is not so much in that some men are too poor, as it is that some are too rich." Therefore, "once in a year, or oftener, thou must examine every man's estate, to see if they have not made their goods uneven, and if they have, then thou must make it even again." Not surprisingly, the author of what reads almost like a parody of itself has definite views about the recent conflict. Therein "the Tyrants were divided, and did fight for the tyranny, for all of them were Tyrants, and did rob the poor people.... They have killed their king, and shared his tyranny amongst them."[149]

More temperately, Peter Chamberlen, in *The Poore Mans Advocate* (1649), advised: "Provide for the poor, and they will provide for you. Destroy the poor, and they will destroy you. And if you provide not for the poor, they will provide for themselves." For they perceive that "the riches of the rich are oftentimes but Trophies of their dishonesty, of having rob'd the poor, or couzen'd the Commonwealth." Even the comparatively restrained John Bunyan depicts the different fates in the next world of the rich and the poor, and marvels "to see how the great ones of the world will go strutting up and down the streets."[150] The Digger tract, *Mere Light Shining in Buckinghamshire* (1649) advances an ingenious variation of the notion of the calling by divesting it of hierarchical connotations and equating it with *work*. Thus, the people's oppressors are depicted as "altogether out of God's way . . . because they live without a Calling, and so are idle . . . and so but Vermin in a Common-wealth and by their own Law ought to be put in a house of Correction." *The True Levellers Standard,* advanced by John Taylor in the same year, went further in enhancing the dignity of labour, enunciating the Digger belief that "he that works for another, either for Wages or to pay him Rent, works unrighteously."[151] Admittedly, all these may be dismissed as minority opinions; but they were all set down in print, and the reaction engendered in the ranks of those against whom they were directed suggests that they should not too lightly be dismissed. Well might Alan Everitt conclude that "the civil wars and Interregnum dealt a death-blow to the age-old conception of society as a hierarchy of interdependent orders, and went far to replace it by the notion of society as a series of independent and necessarily antagonistic classes."[152]

Such considerations are clearly related to the concept of social justice that, however defined, will help determine contentment with one's lot. Here there is no doubting the accuracy of Margaret James's observation that "during the Civil Wars and Interregnum a long-buried stream of social discontent burst forth to horrify those who were content to drift with the main stream of political reform."[153] In this context the crucial issues of the rights and obligations of property, the problem of poverty and its relief, and projected law reform, may best be approached by considering the concepts of equity and equality. Significantly, while the ideal of equity in social and economic relationships persists as a fundamental yardstick, we may now identify a body of opinion prepared at least to correlate it with some notion of equality.

Quite often, the connotations of equity remain fully traditional. John Hall, whose ideas I have already noted, declared that "justice and Equity, so far as it concerns a Commonwealth, is to be that way and course which is most advantageous to public utility. . . . And therefore is that maxim avowed as the ground of Law and Equity in a popular State, *Salus populi suprema lex.*" This precept is often combined with that of the inherited insistence on moderation and measure. John Cook's *Redintegratio Amoris* (1647) counseled that "men must not make an immoderate gain of their professions, because every man is bound to regard the public welfare more than his own private ends." The notions of balance and of moderation run right through Harrington: "there is a mean in things: as exorbitant riches overthrow the balance of a commonwealth, so extreme poverty cannot hold it nor is by any means to be trusted with it." Thus when Harrington speaks of "a Commonwealth that is internally equal" he envisages an equitable balance, not egalitarian sharing of possessions.[154]

But William Walwyn's plea for "what is agreeable to common equity and true Christian liberty" points to more novel ideas. He himself was to protest that "as for my turning the world upside down, . . . it's not a work I ever intended." But others certainly did. Rainborough's rejoinder, when accused in the Putney Debates by Ireton of resorting to a "Law of Nature" that would confer equal rights to everything was intended in rebuttal,[155] but was now to be taken by Winstanley and the Diggers to its unintended but arguably logical conclusion. Of course, the position they adopted in so doing remained that of a very small minority.

A much more traditional position in respect of property rights was that of Samuel Richardson, probably a Baptist, in *The Cause of the Poor Pleaded* (1653). While stressing the Christian obligations of property, in that "it is not a sin to be rich, but it is a sin to keep riches when others and the Saints suffer and perish for want of them," he also realized that "if some who have great estates should sell them, and give all away, it would soon come to nothing." John Cook, in his *Unum Necessarium* (1648) repeats the medieval view "that God suffers some to be poor, that rich men may have occasion to do good." Admittedly, goods "were said to be in common among the Primitive Christians," but amid present realities to "drive at a parity is a senseless opinion." Nonetheless, the notions of balance and equity persist: thus, if a poor man driven desperate steals a loaf, "in this case I conceive he hath not offended the Law of God, . . . because the Law of property must not derogate from the Law of nature, much less abrogate it."[156]

Thus modified by this obligation of charity, the institution of private property possessed, in many eyes, another crucial—and justificatory—connotation. The anonymous author of *Some Grave and Weighty Considerations* relating to the election of representatives for "the approaching Parliament" of 1659, advises that electors "should chuse men of considerable estates and interest in the Nation, such being more concerned to vindicate the Laws, Rights and Liberties of the people (for they have more to lose) than men of beggarly and broken fortunes."[157] Yet this very realization of the connection between land-holding and political power sometimes led to the expression of a need for balance in the possession of property. I have already noted Harrington's views, and in this connection William Sprigge's *Modest Plea for an Equal Commonwealth* (1659) has some particularly interesting comments. Sprigge, having disavowed any sympathy with efforts "to break down the hedge of Propriety, by a promiscuous and injurious levelling of Estates," expresses "an apology for Younger Brothers" and proposes the reinstitution of gavelkind. He poses the question of those who have displaced the nobility only to seize their estates: "will they not be our Masters if they be our Landlords?" Hence, in order to preserve a balance, should not there be "an Agrarian fixed, for stinting and setting bounds to the vast unsatiable desires that are found in greedy men"?[158]

Meanwhile, such suggested limitations would not satisfy other proponents of change who would equate the evocative term younger brother with all poor common people, cheated out of all land and forced to work for wages, and who would in fact equate *equity* with *equality*. Winstanley urged that "in the light of reason and equity . . . the Land of England now ought to be a free Land, and a common treasury to all her children, otherwise it cannot properly be called a Common-Wealth." Accordingly, "when this universal law of equity rises up [then] every one shall put to their hands to till the earth. . . . There shall be no buying or selling, no fairs or markets, but the whole earth shall be a common treasury." Again, the authors of the Digger tract, *More Light Shining in Buckinghamshire* appealed to the example of a scriptural commonwealth: "they were gathered into a family and had all things common; yet so, that each was to labour and eat his own bread. And *this is equity* [my italics] . . . for it is not lawful nor fit for some to work, and the other to play. . . . And he that did not like this, is not fit to live in a Common-wealth." Strik-

4: FULL BLOSSOM: MID-SEVENTEENTH-CENTURY COMMONWEALTH 191

ingly, the emphasis on the equal duty to work seems as strong as is that on equality of possessions. For this is "the Rule of Equity, to do to all men as they shall do to others."[159]

At this point, the divergent views on property of the Levellers and the Diggers invite brief comment. Despite Edwards's comparison of Lilburne with John of Leyden and Cromwell's assertion that the Levellers had the support of all poor and all bad men, but of no others, the Levellers were *not* against all private property rights. Harrington's definition that "by levelling, they who use the word seem to understand: when a people rising invades the lands and estates of the richer sort, and divides them equally among themselves" did not apply to the Levellers.[160] Yet perhaps the claim of the Diggers to be the *true* Levellers opened the door to such confusion. *A Declaration Of some Proceedings* directed against Lilburne and his associates in 1649 is typical in its ascription of a wish to attack all property with "your levelling fury." The Levellers' recourse to the Laws of Nature would allegedly produce "the Doctrine of Parity or levelling, bringing all men's Estates to an Equality." The authors observe that, since "the rich may be oppressed as well as the poor, propriety is to be preserved to all." Significantly, "it is not the Parliament's work to set up a Utopian Common-Wealth, or to force the people to practise abstractions, but to make them as happy as the present frame will bear."[161]

In fact the Leveller declaration of *The Legall Fundamental Liberties of the People of England* (1649) employs the long-respectable phrase "distributive Justice" and is at pains to rebut those who would attach to them "all the erroneous tenets of the poor Diggers at George hill in Surrey"—including their misleadingly entitled book "called *The true Levellers Standard.*" As for the Diggers themselves there is no doubt as to Winstanley's conviction that it is a contradiction in terms to look for a free political system in a society where personal property and its economic implications and relationships put some men effectively within the power of others. In this sense it is fair to speak of his advocacy of a communistic commonwealth. The *New Law of Righteousness* (1649) states plainly that "the common-people shall never have their liberty [until] the earth becomes a common-treasury as it was in the beginning." If a man calls any piece of land his own, let him work alone thereon. For "did the light of Reason make the earth for some men to ingross up into bags and barns, that others might be oppressed with poverty?"[162] *The True Levellers Standard Advanced* (1649), by John Taylor, "shewing the cause why the common people of England had begun, and gives consent to dig up, manure, and sow corn upon George-Hill in Surrey," repeats the assertions that "the great Creator Reason made the Earth to be a Common Treasury," and that "this Civil Propriety is a Curse" that breaks the Seventh and Eighth Commandments. *An Appeal to all Englishmen* (1650) urges them "to take possession of your own Land, which the Norman Power took from you and hath kept from you about 600 years."[163]

Clearly, while many still clung to the idea that the rich property owner existed to relieve the poor, others openly questioned whether this was indeed divinely ordained. Many had by now written off what they saw as a specious justification of private property that was in reality all too often ignored. This should not be pushed too far, for private philanthropy had been an impressive feature of social life in the first forty years of the century.[164] But against a background of growing recognition of individual rights the relationship envisaged was increasingly considered to be bemeaning. Moreover, poverty itself was by now frequently ascribed not to divine prescription but to the mistakes or misdeeds of individuals and the malfunctioning of society itself. Thus the appeal to the government of the commonwealth not only to relieve the symptoms of poverty, but also as far as possible to eliminate its causes, was now repeated with increasing urgency. Such urgency was fully justified. One detailed survey has concluded that the second quarter of the century was probably among the most terrible eras through which the country has ever passed. In particular the impact and legacy of the Civil Wars in terms of social distress exposed the inadequacy of hospital provision and of poor relief.[165] In these circumstances, with reliance upon Christian charity administered by individuals through private philanthropy increasingly inappropriate, would-be reformers of several types appealed to governmental intervention.

These appeals were not limited to the relief of poverty, narrowly defined. They must be seen in the context of heightened expectations of an expansion of the social functions of government as a fruit of Parliamentary victory in the Civil Wars. But here a caveat is necessary first against any tendency to speak in terms of over-heightened contrasts, and secondly against any temptation to equate projects with performance. Margaret James's view that, in contrast with Stuart paternalism, the "Puritan" victory ushered in a harsher attitude toward the poor, has probably been superseded by J. P. Cooper's more recent contention that the "Commonwealth's intentions were at least as good as those of the Privy Council before 1640; in some places they were better."[166] But "intentions" is the crucial word; and in terms of achievement local variations were probably more important than any doctrinal pattern. Certainly many projected reforms were mooted, some even accorded official consideration, designed to improve what would now be termed the quality of life of ordinary people. These included the provision of medical and hospital services, educational facilities, changes in taxation, and reform both of the law itself and of its administration.

In respect of the relief of poverty, the literature continues to illustrate that uneasy amalgam of attitudes encountered earlier. Thus John Cook, while endorsing the Christian duty of the rich to show charity, is clear "that the Magistrate ought to provide bread for every honest poor man." Bernard Capp points out that "the saints emphasized the duty of the magistrate to provide work for the poor" and argued that "there should be no beggar in Israel" or in any well-governed commonwealth.[167] But in this of course they were but continuing earlier protests against the nonenforcement of what had been a clear constituent of Elizabethan legislation. *Stanleyes Remedy: or The Way to reform wandring Beggers* (1646) is in no way novel in finding it "very lamentable that poor Rogues and Beggars should be whipped or branded according to law . . . while no place is provided for them to set them to work." The crucial issue is identified by Samuel Hartlib's declaration in *Londons Charitie* (1649) that "I wish all people would consider whether this be not rather a public work than a private?" He appeals to "Parliament, who are the father of the Common-Wealth, therefore of the poor."[168]

William Sprigge, writing in 1659, combines several issues in stressing the need "of raising a stock, and employing such, as by reason of poverty are not able to set their industry on work, that none may be permitted to eat the bread of idleness, nor the voice of the poor and needy be any longer heard in the Land." Repeating a point encountered more than a century earlier, but now in a different context, he observes that despite confiscation of royal and of some church lands there is "yet no provision made for the poor, not one Work-house erected for setting the industry of the poor on work." Sprigge's charge that uncharitable deafness to "the cries of the poor is one of the crying sins of this Land"[169] suggests not an abandonment of Christian charity but rather a transfer of the responsibility for its implementation from an individual or ecclesiastical to a corporate, indeed a national, entity. A Leveller-inspired Petition to the Commons in 1648 had demanded that "the too long continued shame of this Nation, viz. permission of any to suffer such poverty as to beg their bread, may be forthwith effectively remedied." But it also included an expression of suspicion of funds misused in its request "that the Poor be enabled to choose their Trustees, to discover all Stocks, Houses, Lands, &c. which of right belong to them, and their use." Predictably, Winstanley insisted that the laws of the commonwealth should ensure that people "may not beg, nor be forced to steal through want, and so be hanged by the Kingly and Lordly Law."[170]

Distinctive Digger prescriptions for the provision of employment for the poor are among a range of suggestions that I shall consider later. But before so doing, four particular aspects of reformist agitation mentioned earlier merit consideration. Perhaps most notably, a spate of humanitarian suggestions for the free provision of medical treatment unequalled since that which occurred in the mid-Tudor era may fairly be described as anticipating "welfare state" provisions. Charles Webster, in *The Great Instauration,* relates these and other projects to the climate of opinion generated by "the social reformers of the Puritan Revolution."[171] But even before the outbreak of conflict the vision of the *Kingdome of Macaria* (1641, long attributed to Samuel Hartlib, but thought by Webster to be the work of Gabriel Plattes) included "an house, or Colledge of experience, where they deliver out yearly such medicines as they find"—although, indeed, alongside such provision for medical research its author continued the age-old tendency to look to the parson to double as a physician.[172]

The end of the decade saw quite specific demands for medical reforms. The Leveller manifesto *No Papist nor Presbyterian* (1649) included the prescription "that the excessive Fees of Physicians may be regulated and reduced, whereby the poor for a small and reasonable Fee may have the benefit of their skill." A year earlier in *Unum Necessarium,* John Cook, whose interest in the relief of poverty embraced concern for improvement in medicine and in his own legal profession, had gone further and proposed that "Physicians, Surgeons and Apothecaries might be assigned in *forma pauperis,* as well as Lawyers, Attorneys, &c."[173] But one of the fullest and most advanced proposals was that advanced by Henry Robinson in 1652: "That Physicians and Surgeons be appointed . . . at the Public charge, who may be obliged once a day to visit and administer . . . without any fee or consideration, but what the state allows them. And lastly, that Hospitals be erected . . . to which it may be free for all poor people to repair for taking Physic . . . at the sole charge and attendance of the Hospital." In 1659, when the Good Old Cause was well-nigh lost, William Covel was still to appeal to Parliament "that the rich may pay according to their Estates whereby to maintain the Impotent and aged poor in Hospitals; and that in every Parish an Hospital may be erected."[174]

Many of the equally advanced suggestions for extending and improving the provision of education for ordinary people are associated with Hartlib's circle. *The Advice of William Petty to Mr Samuel Hartlib* (1648), whose author forecast that "the Art of Printing will spread knowledge, so that the common people, knowing their own rights and liberties, will not be governed by way of oppression," is of special interest. Petty advised

> that there be instituted *ergastula literaria,* literary work-houses, where children may be taught as well to do something towards their living, and to read and write. That all children of above seven years old may be presented to this kind of education, none to be excluded by reason of the poverty or inability of their parents; for likely it hath come to pass, that many are now holding the plough which might have been made fit to steer the state.

Again, this seems irresistibly reminiscent of the utterances of some mid-Tudor idealists. Petty had also some comments to make on the methodology of education itself, deriding the "parrot-like repeating heteroclitous nouns and adverbs."[175]

Between 1648 and 1653 several works appeared on educational and vocational reform. Hartlib is described as regarding himself during these years as "the official parliamentary agent for educational affairs," and his hopes were possibly highest when the Committee for the Advancement of Learning set up by Barebone's Parliament received a scheme for a national educational system on which he had worked with John Dury. Another acquaintance, Henry Robinson, whose advocacy of religious toleration was cited earlier, proposed in 1652 "that Public Schools where there are none already be erected . . . to which all poor people may be free to send their Children, whether boys or girls, to be taught gratis, both to write and read at least"—with the novel addition to the curriculum, since we are a seafaring nation, of swimming for all! Webster has suggested that, unlike Winstanley whose less specific ideas on educational reform were directed to promoting radical social equality, the schemes of these men were more vocational and utilitarian in intent—as when Dury's *The Reformed-School* (1651) gave emphasis to "profitable employments which may fit them to be good Commonwealth's men."[176]

If free provision of medical treatment and of education were seen as positive contributions toward alleviating distress and poverty, some current taxes were identified as increasing their incidence. Particular resentment was aroused by what the Quaker, Richard Hubberthorn, described as "that great oppression of tithes." A decade earlier, in *Several Proposals* (1648) the Independent John Jubbes proposed "that annually there may be an equal Tax in every Parish . . . as well of Lands as Goods" so as to eliminate this evil.[177] Such notions were not devoid of religious undertones, but when in 1653 the Saints' Parliament stood on the brink of radical reform the vote against tithes was seen as a vote against *property* and precipitated its demise. Margaret James sees tithes as a crucial issue during the whole era, evident in all "left-wing political and religious parties," and contributing at length to the Restoration. If tithes were an age-old grievance, a tax introduced by Parliament itself to help finance the war emerged as a new, since it fell for the most part on items of popular consumption. Thus a *Petition* of January 1648 went near to propounding the principle of regressive taxation in urging that the "burthensome Tax of the Excise lies heavy only upon the Poorer and most ingenious industrious People," and that the rich "bear not the least proportionate weight of that burden."[178]

Yet bulking even larger in the list of grievances was discontent with the law and its administration. From the Levellers and the Diggers to the Fifth Monarchy Men, all were agreed on this. Cromwell himself identified "one general grievance in the nation. It is, the Law"—not only in terms of its administration, for "there are wicked abominable laws."[179] As to their origins, John Hare's *St. Edwards Ghost: or Anti-Normanisme* (1647) is typical in its demand "that our Laws be divested of their French rags." John Taylor, in *The True Levellers Standard* (1649) sees "all those Binding and Restraining Laws that have been made from one Age to another since the Conquest [as] but the Cords, Bonds, Manacles, and Yokes that the enslaved English, like Newgate Prisoners, wear."[180] As for those responsible for administering the law, Lawrence Clarkson writes of lawyers as "the Locusts and Caterpillars of your Kingdom," while Hubberthorn associates Lawyers and Priests as having "made merchandise of people's souls and estates." To Henry Robinson, "of all learning certainly that of the Lawyers is the most vain, not only unnecessary, but mischievous, destructive to a Commonwealth. . . . Their learning is but Law-cheating, juggling, pocket-picking." Predictably, Digger tracts join in the condemnation of "the horse-leech Lawyers [who] are as profitable as maggots in meat, and Caterpillars in Cabbages"—especially when "out of this rubbish stuff are all our Creatures called Judges"! Why then, in default of action by Parliament, "may not the Soldiers as well pull the Judges out of Westminster Hall, and take all their rusty Records, Laws, &c and make a fire on them, so that we may have honest, godly Laws, according to the Scriptures and Reason"?[181]

As for the content of the laws, *Tyranipocrit* declares that "when any laws, lawyers, offices, or officer become prejudicial to the Commonwealth, then they must be taken away, because then they are perverted from their right end" so that "the rich artificial thieves do rob the poor, and that under a feigned show of justice." *A Letter to Lord Fairfax* (1649) puts the question of "whether all Laws that are not grounded upon equity and reason, not giving a universal freedom to all, but respecting persons, ought not to be cut off with the King's head?"[182] *A New-Years Gift* (1650) is clear that "as your Government must be new, so let the Laws be new [in] a Reforming Commonwealth." *The Law of Freedom* (1651) insists that "we must either be subject to a Law, or to men's wills." But the law must apply to all. For "when the Will of officers rule above Law, that Government is diseased with a mortal disease." The task of Parliament "is to abolish all old Laws and Customs, which have been the strength of the Oppressor, and to prepare, and then to enact new Laws for the ease and Freedom of the people, but yet not without the people's knowledge." This must be done according to the principles of "Reason and Equity."[183]

Alas, as in the case of so many of the reforms demanded by commonwealth idealists, consideration and preparation was one thing, enactment another. Parliament did not lack for proponents of moderate reform, some of them highly placed and influential, as was Cook himself. Reform of the law was seriously considered by committees both of the House of Commons and of the Saints' Parliament. In 1653 Cromwell appointed William Sheppard, author of over a score of books on legal issues, as a Clerk of the Upper Bench, and in 1656 he became Serjeant-at-law. Despite such interest, Hirst records only very moderate measures to improve procedures to accompany the high caliber of the judicial appointments made. Aylmer concludes that "the hope of a salaried legal profession, with means-tested legal aid for all, which was demanded by some pamphleteers in the 1640s, was probably a lost cause by 1653."[184]

All in all, it is fair to compare the list of shattered hopes for several aspects of social reform now experienced by commonwealth idealists with that of their predecessors in the 1540s; the fruits of royalist defeat proved almost as illusory as those of the monarchical takeover of church land. But the range and nature of proposals made to eliminate a major cause of poverty by providing employment merit further consideration. Alongside suggestions to make a reality of existing legal provision for public stock or workplaces one finds a total difference of opinion as to the part that should be played by private enterprise. Whereas a Leveller appeal for improvement of the condition of the poor looked to "better wages for their labour" and increased employment prospects in manufactures and herring fisheries, the Diggers looked to the abolition of "this cheating device of buying and selling": a system of cooperative "Storehouses" will "make idle persons to become workers."[185]

The duty of government to make public provision of work was often urged. *Stanleyes Remedy* (1646) included "houses of Instruction or Correction" and pleaded that workhouses be set up in all large parishes. Peter Chamberlen's *The Poore Mans Advocate* (1649) proposed the financing of a joint or public stock from the proceeds of royal and delinquents' land, wastes, and commons.[186] Hartlib's *Londons Charitie inlarged* (1650), having alluded to the danger from the type of wandering rogues who, denied alms by a surly farmer, "care no more to set his Barn and Ricks of corn on fire than to light a pipe of Tobacco," suggests remedies. For those who are "willing to work at home with their children," hemp and flax should be supplied. He also sketched some features of a "Work-house"; these include for its inmates three meals a day: "for Supper, 4 ounces of bread, half a pint of beer, one Herring with a Turnip, and sometimes broth in cold weather." In particular, poor children there trained "will have a benefit by it, because they are like to be made serviceable for the Commonwealth." Henry Robinson, whose religious and humanitarian interests were accompanied by real business experience, combined objectives in his proposal for the erection "of Work-houses in all Cities and great towns . . . whereto all People . . . that cannot provide better for themselves, may have recourse, and be set to work. . . . This will not only keep multitudes of People from stealing and other lewd courses, but much increase the Manufacture and Handicrafts workmanship of the Nation. . . . This Work-house might likewise take care of all Children, boys or girls, which are found in the streets, as also lame and blind people."[187]

Such furnishing of what would later be described as indoor relief was accompanied by other devices. Thomas Lawson, as late as 1660, in *An Appeal to the Parliament,* anticipated the modern "labour exchange" in his proposal "to settle a Poor man's office, First, where Handy-crafts-men and Labourers that want Work, and such as want Workmen, may enquire"—and also "where all Poor People that are in distress . . . may make their Conditions known." William Covel, a year earlier, having demanded that "some rich men give out of their abundance some lands or goods to raise a Stock," went further in envisaging its use to give work within a "Society" whose members shall use "no buying or selling amongst themselves [so that] in time there will be less use of money, and less buying and selling." Additionally, in every parish there must be "Societies for youth, and manufactures for those that are able to work."[188] Another at least partial anticipation of Robert Owen appears in *A Way Propounded to Make the Poor . . . happy* (also 1659) by Peter Cornelius Plockboy. Though proudly identified by his modern editor as the "pioneer of the first cooperative commonwealth," Plockboy is at pains to stress that in each proposed "little Common-wealth" of industry, "every one may keep his propriety" and that "those that come into our society shall not be bound to make their goods common."[189]

Much nearer the mainstream of contemporary thinking were the additional suggestions made, again, by Henry Robinson. In order to generate employment by the advancement of trade and industry, his program includes action to improve navigable rivers, advance fen drainage, nurture woollen manufacture, secure lower interest rates, and help shipping, seamen, and fisheries. To "enlarge our Foreign Plantation" and overseas trade, the nation should "keep a Correspondent, or Banker in Paris, Antwerp, Amsterdam, Rotterdam." But "above all other Engines or Instruments, the greatest pre-eminence is due to a Bank," which must control money, import and export of coin, and so on. More traditionally, action must be taken to improve standards and ensure "that all deceitfulness in Spinning, Carding, Weaving, Dyeing, with all frauds . . . destructive to Trading, be enquired after and prevented in the future." (Here Joan Thirsk has pointed out that this constant quest of the Tudor and Early Stuart monarchs was in fact again revived during the Interregnum by the Council of Trade in 1651.) Another device encountered earlier, in a very different context, is Robinson's proposal to "Erect Lombards or Banks of Love for furnishing all people with moneys at Interest upon pawns, personal or Land security, at reasonable rates . . . [especially] for all poor people that shall desire it as far as 20s. at one time upon pawn gratis, to be repaid at six months, or the pawns to be sold."[190]

How to advance the Trade of the Nation, and employ the Poor by William Goffe, which appeared in 1641, before the outbreak of civil war, is particularly interesting in its combination of sound business acumen with a humanitarian attitude toward the poor. Thus, in the case of unskilled workers, "where the Price is beat down to so low a Rate that the slow Workmen cannot maintain themselves" what ensues is but "oppressing the oppressed." Better by far to provide both training in skills and employment—especially if one is to outwit the foreign competitor who now profits by manufacturing from our own unwrought materials! In particular, "Fishing-factories" should be set up near many ports, to produce ropes, sail-cloth, and timbers.

More generally, all charity should "be laid out in unwrought Goods": in every parish a large Work-house must be erected, "to teach the People to work." Similarly, *A Cleare and Evident Way For enriching the Nations . . . And for setting very great Numbers of Poore on Work* by "I.D." (1650) extols the virtues of manufacture, foreign trade, shipping, and fisheries. Again, the United Provinces are held up as the example; hence the insistence "that the Commodities should receive their full Manufacture in these dominions."[191]

In this context, developments in agriculture also attracted comment. *A Discovery of Infinite Treasure* (1639) by Gabriel Plattes advanced the challenging theme that "he that found out the way of fertilizing of Land with Lime or Marl (though by accident) did a more charitable deed in publishing thereof: than if he had built all the Hospitals in England." This treatise on the benefits of agricultural improvement in raising living standards, reducing poverty, and supporting a larger population—in short on good husbandry as the very legs and pillars of the commonwealth—also makes two relevant but different general points. First, "among all my Observations in the works of nature I could never find so exquisite a Model or resemblance of a well ordered and flourishing Common-wealth, as is an hive of Bees. . . . For first they are all industrious, and suffer no drones [sic]. Secondly, they are all bent to work for the general good." Very different is his point "that in these Ages, Inventions to save the number of men's works are not profitable to a Commonwealth overcharged with people, but rather the contrary."[192]

A similar point recurs in the context of fierce contemporary debate on enclosures and indeed on the general effects of increasing rationalization and commercialization of agriculture and of trade in foodstuffs. John Cook condemned engrossers of corn and urged that "charity consists as much in lending and selling to the poor at a moderate price, as in giving." John Moore, a minister of religion in Leicestershire, attacked such as "enhance Corn, and hoard it up to raise the rates of the poor that buy," in *The Crying Sin of England, Of not Caring for the Poor* (1653). In this, the first of his anti-enclosure tracts, Moore is principally concerned with the alleged effects of eviction and depopulation. If it be "the shame of a well governed Common Wealth to suffer so many idle Beggars, [then] how great a shame is it for a *Gospel Magistracie* [my italics] not to suppress Make-beggars, which make such swarms of Beggars?" Such men as, upon enclosure, "treble the price of their Land; and this they get by flaying the skin off the poor."[193]

Yet in the extensive discussion of agricultural reform that Webster discerns during the "Puritan Revolution," religious advocacy was also enlisted in favor of enclosure. *A Vindication of the Considerations concerning Common Fields,* published in 1654 by "Pseudonismus," asserts that "God is the God of order, and order is the soul of things, the life of a Commonwealth; but common fields are the seat of disorder, the seed plot of contention, the nursery of beggary."[194] In a similar *Vindication of A Regulated Inclosure* (1656), Joseph Lee, also a minister of the gospel, rebuts Moore's arguments, disdains any necessary connection between enclosure and rack-renting, and goes on instead to question the motives of such as "overstock their Commons, and plough up their neighbours' Land." Nor does he miss the chance to say that "there is a profane and levelling spirit now abroad in the world that cries out against government, and speaks evil of dignities. . . . True liberty of conscience [is] a liberty from sin, not a liberty to sin." Unabashed, Moore returned to the charge forthwith in *A Scripture-Word Against Inclosure* (1656). Therein he condemned those who declaim "May I not make the best of mine own," whereas, by way of contrast, "in common fields they live like loving neighbours together for the most part, till the spirit of Inclosure enter into some rich Churl's heart."[195]

This last sentence suggests a general issue that was to become an increasing preoccupation within commonwealth ideology: the nature of the balance between individual economic freedom and collective social rights. The realization of its nature was not new; it was most clearly enunciated by Sir John Eliot in the late 1620s.[196] But the suggestion has been made that it was these midcentury decades that constituted the watershed of changing attitudes. To what extent can one convincingly identify a shift away from the type of mutual responsibility explicit in the organic analogy of a Christian commonwealth of the Tudor era, toward a more secularly argued philosophy of individual rights of which the state was either (*pace* Hobbes) the creator or (*pace* Harrington) the obligated guarantor? Certainly the first of these continued to be the object of full and detailed lip service in very much of commonwealth-orientated discussion during these years. Indeed it is fair to discern in much of the literature a surge of enthusiasm, sometimes verging on euphoria, as to the prospects of governmental intervention in social and economic affairs so as to make a reality of the vision of a truly Christian commonwealth. But there is a distinct parallel with events of a century earlier, in that this was shot through with expressions of bitter disillusion.

Amidst the spate of undoubtedly sincere proposals of these decades, Aylmer has observed that "how much of this came anywhere near to being achieved . . . is a very different matter." Hugh Kearney goes so far as to suggest that "the final battle was won and lost in the Barebone Parliament," and Webster concludes that the social realities of the Interregnum were a far cry from the optimistic models of the idealists. The near-comprehensive program for social welfare, economic improvement, and intellectual reform did not materialize. But, retrospectively, was this realistically to be expected? Cromwell was not the first statesman professing commonwealth ideals to find himself distracted by governmental problems and the fear of threatened or actual rebellion inside the realm together with embroilment in foreign war without. Significant straws in the wind were the withdrawal of the last anti-enclosure bill from Cromwell's second Parliament, and the lapse of a legal reform requiring the use of English at the Restoration.[197]

The failure to make significant progress in the evolution of an efficient system of poor relief—as distinct from sporadic efforts at more enthusiastic enforcement of existing provisions—was particularly disappointing. In this crucially important context, Winstanley's resolve to abolish private property may perhaps be seen as a natural reaction to the contemporary tendency in some quarters to divorce the ownership of property from any necessary obligations of charity or indeed from any social connotations. All in all, despite the full flowering of the commonwealth ideal during these decades, the case is at least arguable that the success of its propagandists in eliciting a real governmental response to their humanitarian pleas and projects was rather less than that of their mid-Tudor predecessors.

Amidst such a ferment of discussion it is not surprising that a utopian strain has been identified alongside proposals that were at least purportedly realistic. Indeed Charles I himself alluded to "the new Utopias of religion and government into which they [his opponents] endeavor to transform this Kingdom." J. C. Davis, in his *Utopia and the Ideal Society*, points to the idiosyncratic *Nova Solyma . . . or Jerusalem Regained* of Samuel Gott (which was not translated until 1902), but of more immediate relevance is his contention that Winstanley moved from "the optimism of the perfect moral commonwealth theorist" to the position of "a utopian." While not everyone would accept his categorizations, Davis was not the first to discern such an element in Winstanley. Some time ago, Perez Zagorin saw him as demonstrating "two classic types of utopian outlook."[198] Without venturing into what is something of a semantic minefield, two points of mundane relevance may be made: first, some elements of his (and of general Digger) thinking anticipated Owenism; secondly, insofar as his hopes depended upon a change of heart in individual motivation they stand in stark contrast with the mid-Tudor analysis of Sir Thomas Smith, which aimed to enlist and direct quite selfish human motives within an existing economic framework.

A caveat against any temptation to create too simplistic a pattern is sounded by the combination of demands both for some aspects of individual economic freedoms *and* for paternalist social justice in a Leveller Petition to the Commons in September 1648. This requests "that you would have freed all trade and merchandizing from all monopolizing and engrossing by companies or otherwise. That you would have laid open all late enclosures of fens and other commons, or have enclosed them only or chiefly to the benefit of the poor. That you would have ordered some effectual course to keep people from begging and beggary in so fruitful a nation as, through God's blessing, this is." The same amalgam appears in Lilburne's *Foundations of Freedom* (1648), which includes provision that it shall not be in the legislators' power "to continue or make any laws to abridge any person from trading unto any parts beyond the seas unto which they are allowed to trade, or to restrain trade at home. They shall not continue or make a law to allow any person to take above six pound per cent for loan of money for a year."[199]

Certain of these requests are reminiscent of earlier instances of a willingness to regard the free market not as a moralist's nightmare in which all Christian values would disappear, but rather as a normal aspect of the natural order that it would be folly to flout. Most notably, Joyce Appleby contends that "the affirmation of a moral order where economic activities were means to social ends" now waned. "With this loss of a social vision to inform specific economic laws, political intrusion required justification on utilitarian grounds," while simultaneously the freedom of an individual to look after his own acquired its own moral basis as an aspect of increasingly emphasised personal freedom. Again "Liberty and Property" emerge as twin determinants. With the emphasis within and by the market upon efficiency and utility, then social relations themselves became increasingly directed "by economic processes rather than tradition, authority, or moral precepts."[200]

A growing tendency to judge market relationships by economic and functional criteria rather than by moral imperatives had a long-run impact on notions of the role of government in the commonwealth. The previously rarely challenged assumption of a duty to intervene in economic activities in the interest of the common good came under threat. Not only the efficacy but also the rectitude of such intervention was now queried—as was the definition of "the common good." As this was thought of more and more as made up of the sum of individual satisfactions, so the scope for private initiative expanded—including alleviation of poverty by the provision of employment. Increasingly, state intervention was expected not to restrict man's cupidity but to nurture national economic development. Of course, not all of this was new, and special pleading for specific commercial or financial interests had long worn the garb of the national interest. Whether it be seen as embodying a basic philosophical change, or as reflecting an emergence of a midcentury balance within the economy between population and food production (in "normal" years) that produced changing attitudes toward enclosure, this trend did not go unopposed. Indeed, while retrospectively identifiable, it was largely masked in these decades by one final mighty surge of advocacy of the older idealist plea for governmental action for collective moral and social objectives. The overwhelming majority of commentators still besought control—or if necessary the harnessing—of individual economic activities in the interests of amelioration of the lot of the weaker members of society.

Yet a change in balance of emphasis is unmistakable. Professor Gunn, in *Politics and the Public Interest in the Seventeenth Century*, identifies a gradual shift "from recounting a king's duty to his people to defending the people's right to look to their own interests." Although as yet the common good was seen as qualitatively different from private profit, self-interest was acquiring a measure of respectability. In the words of a striking contemporary declaration, "every man is an island . . . and hath somewhat which he may call his own, and which he not only lawfully may, but also out of duty to God [ought] to defend from acts of violence."[201] Thus, the strictly circumscribed duty of the citizen to act to protect the true religious faith has now been transmuted into an obligation to protect his own individual rights. Significantly, both those who appealed to government to preserve the traditional organic social image *and* those more concerned with the definition of individual economic rights advanced the establishment of political participation by the people as a means of securing what they sought.

Gunn concludes that whereas "prior to this time it had been the fashion to integrate social duties into the order of the universe . . . by postulating an artificial uniformity," now "Harrington's whole position rested upon the claim that his commonwealth would secure the interests of all, and the public interest was derived from those of individuals."[202] Yet Harrington's assertion that "a Commonwealth is nothing else but the National Conscience" must never be forgotten. He attempted to adhere to the criteria of equity of earlier commonwealth idealists against the background of the changing social structure of the mid-seventeenth century. But this he hoped to do by innovatory political and constitutional measures which in fact prefigure those of the eighteenth century "commonwealth-men" and of the authors of the Constitution of the United States of America—all of whom were to look back on him in reverence.

In assessing the intense political, religious, social, and economic speculation of this era, a more useful touchstone than any doctrinal or even utopian pattern is indeed its relationship to the ideal of the commonwealth—after all, for over a decade the formal title of the nation. In the short-lived conjunction between the earlier emphases upon the social duties of the commonwealth as transcending selfish individual interests, and the newly emerging vision of individual political participation both as a guarantor of the performance of such duties and as a condition in itself of the full development of each citizen's potential, the midcentury decades witnessed its fullest flowering. True, one may discern a paradox. The subject's merely passive right to be governed well gives way to a philosophy of individual rights—with the correlative implications both of more *limited* government, to safeguard civil and religious liberties, and of political participation to ensure political freedom. Yet simultaneously, the plea for more extensive social and economic protection of the subject in the interests of humanity and of equity leads in many writers to an *increasing* emphasis upon the obligation of governmental intervention.

From paradox emerged disintegration. What to some, disillusioned and disappointed both before and after 1660, appeared as shattered ideals, to others bore the guise of nightmares warded off. Hirst observes that property owners might well have concluded that the greatest threat to their possessions "came not from the crown but from another direction."[203] The fact that to many people the term "commonwealth" itself embodied their fears goes far to explain the Restoration and its consequences. The dual effect of its imputed association with egalitarianism and social disorder, and of an increasingly secular analysis of economic processes, is such that the more restricted version of commonwealth ideology that will survive into the eighteenth century will look to individual political, religious, and economic liberties. Not for many decades will the collectivist social vision of the mid-Stuart commonwealth idealist, who believed himself indeed to be his brother's keeper, emerge once more for serious consideration.

5
Recession and Reparation: 1660–1727

A COMMONWEALTH: IDEAL OR NIGHTMARE?

IN TRACING THE FORTUNES OF THE COMMONWEALTH IDEAL AND OF "commonwealth's men" the immediate hammer-blow to the "Good Old Cause" delivered by the Restoration is evident. Few would question "the success of the propertied classes and ecclesiastical hierarchy in suppressing or driving underground revolutionary and democratic ideals." Of course, this era was not one of undisturbed tranquillity. If Venner's second and not inconsiderable Fifth Monarchist rising of 1661 may be dismissed as a last splutter of failed millenarian hopes, the following decades were nonetheless studded by the threat and sometimes reality of violence. The Exclusion Crisis of 1679–81, which some contemporaries feared as a rerun of 1640–42, was followed by the Rye House Plot (1683). James II's accession was soon followed by Monmouth's Rebellion in June 1685, and the monarch was dethroned some three years later. William III was threatened by several genuine assassination plots, most notably in 1696. The reign of Anne witnessed, in the Sacheverell Riots of 1710, the second-worst outbreak of the eighteenth century, while that of George I was menaced by the Jacobite incursion of 1715 and the Atterbury Plot of 1722. Not until the mid-1720s (hence the date chosen for termination of this chapter) was it true, suggests Sir John Plumb, that "the English political system had begun to assume the air not only of stability but also of historical inevitability."[1]

Yet a fundamental difference between this period and the mid-seventeenth-century decades is valid. First, the genuine political and religious issues that continued in acrimonious and sometimes dangerous dispute were not now accompanied by the combination of economic discontent and social distress that had helped to produce both rebellion and a ferment of commonwealth-type speculation during the 1640s and 1650s. The persistent instability discerned was that of political rather than social life. Secondly, the one successful rebellion against established authority, in 1688–89, reflects the absence of any split of real magnitude within the political nation such as had engendered war in 1642—though the full implications of the appeal to William of Orange merit thought. Admittedly, interpretation of these events as producing a "conservative revolution" may well be more convincing in retrospect than it would have been clear to contemporaries. Yet the achievement of the "Reluctant Revolutionaries" underlined rather than jeopardized the implicit understanding of the Restoration Settlement. Charles I's infringements upon the liberties (especially the property rights) of those who saw themselves as the political nation had led to civil war and revolution—which for some years had threatened to get out of hand. No such risk was run by those who took action against the repeated indiscretions of James II: they welcomed the assurance that William of Orange "did not come over to establish a Commonwealth."[2] The evocatively titled draft, "Now is the time: a Scheme for a Commonwealth," proves on inspection to be a very moderate proposal for representative reform, and certainly neither antimonarchical nor a radical call to action. In particular, Douglas Hay suggests "the Glorious Revolution of 1688 established the freedom not of men, but of men of Property."[3]

Thus, when the era is identified as "one of the great periods of fermentation in English history," the ingredients of that ferment, reflected in published debate, were political, constitutional, and religious—not social or economic. Professor Holmes has elsewhere urged persuasively that the nation's economic condition, defined in terms of the balance between population growth (now checked, in marked contrast with earlier eras) and general agrarian productivity and availability of employment, gradually improved. Nearly thirty years ago, W. G. Hoskins, writing on the importance of harvest fluctuations, observed that "of the eight harvests between 1683 and 1690, seven were good"; the relative cheapness of food continued into the early 1690s, as part of a secular trend toward rising corn production (enabling the actual export of grain) since the mid-seventeenth century.[4] Against this background, the threat of imminent social upheaval, so frightening in midcentury, having been contained or perhaps crushed, the political nation was free to bicker over the terms of the distribution of power within its own ranks. Such bickerings were at times in themselves disruptive enough, and Plumb has indeed characterized the period between 1675 and 1725 as constituting a prolonged struggle to *achieve* political stability. Yet the increase in size of that political nation—defined as those whose franchise entitled them to participate in general elections, which were soon to occur with unexampled frequency, totalling seventeen within one forty-three-year period—which in Queen Anne's reign had reached a figure of about 250,000 (about one in five of all adult males) was in itself a safety valve of great significance.[5]

What were now the fortunes of the notion of the commonwealth itself? In terms of official usage, its absence from the statute book is unsurprising. But how far did it persist as a yearned-for objective? Long ago, Iris Morley's study of "the English Revolutionary Movement, 1660–1685" suggested that the government "never succeeded in stopping the secret flow of sedition." More recently, Richard Ashcraft, identifying a vocal and often organized minority, has argued cogently for the survival of Leveller ideas "as a subterranean element of Restoration political life." Admittedly, especially after the intensification of persecution of religious nonconformity, motivation was often primarily antipapist. Despite its text of *Salus Populi, Suprema Lex,* Robert Ferguson's *Appeal from the Country to the City* (1679) reads as a diatribe against the spectre of Romanist rapine and murder. But there is also ample evidence of neo-Leveller support for opposition during the Exclusion Crisis of 1679–81 and the plotting of the early 1680s.[6]

Indeed, the sea-green colors of the duke of Monmouth's men date from the funeral of Thomas Rainborough (vice admiral of the navy)—victim of cavalier assassins—in November 1648. Thereafter, the colors worn in his honor became Leveller "party colours," appearing in the Green Ribbon Club (circa 1677). Their best-known standard-bearer was possibly John Wildman, inveterate plotter against Oliver Cromwell and Charles II alike (when not in prison or in exile), and supreme survivor. Wildman was associated with Shaftesbury, formerly a member of Cromwell's Council of State and understandably accused of being "against the King and for seditions and factions and for a commonwealth." Most notably, there now seems to be no doubt as to the extent of the commitment of the philosopher John Locke to the political objectives, and even to the plotting, of this dissident group. It may well be contended that the Good Old Cause stood more of a chance of re-emergence during the Exclusion Crisis of 1679–81—the background to some of the writings of Sidney, Neville, Tyrrell, and Locke himself—than was ever to be the case in 1688–89. Ashcraft suggests that "the exclusion elections produced a greater polarization of the nation along class-divided lines than anything had done since the Civil War itself, with fears being expressed of "a new race of Levellers" and of the rule of "mean men and servants." He is, moreover, in no doubt as to the reality of the Rye House Plot in 1683, either in respect of its aims or of the extent to which its support—active or tacit but complicit—extended.[7]

As for Monmouth's Rebellion itself, whatever the motives of many of the rank and file, there is no disputing the presence of "commonwealth" sympathizers among his direct entourage—which included Wildman, "Ferguson the Plotter," and Fletcher. Peter Earle's examination of *Monmouth's Rebels* finds that they numbered at least some republicans who believed in "a free state or commonwealth"—though most of those local recruits who hankered after "the Good Old Cause" may well have done so on religious grounds. Perhaps not many historians would go so far as Iris Morley in describing Sedgemoor as the last battle of the Civil War, at which "the Leveller sea-green went down for ever into the mud of a Somersetshire ditch." Yet it is worth pondering the last speech of Colonel Richard Rumbold, thereafter condemned and executed. Enunciating his belief in a contract theory of government, which allows to "the people also as much property as to make them happy," and accepting also "that God hath wisely ordered different stations for men in the world," he nonetheless attests his belief that "none comes into the world with a saddle on his back, neither any booted and spurred to ride him."[8]

It may be argued that, despite his popularity with the lower orders, had Monmouth triumphed the expectations of many of his supporters might well have been as completely dashed, as were those of some of William of Orange's adherents in 1688–89. Yet in terms of the survival of midcentury commonwealth, and especially of neo-Leveller, principles and hopes, one may suggest that it was the defeat and death of many of their principal adherents during the 1680s, rather than the Restoration of 1660, that marked their terminal decline. This was in turn confirmed by the events and the aftermath of the Glorious Revolution. Pamphleteering by those such as Wildman and Ferguson persisted. But the widening split between such radicals and the more moderate Whigs, determined to carry with them their Tory counterparts, ensured that the establishment of a commonwealth was never even a remote possibility. Admittedly, William himself expressed the fear "that the Commonwealth party was the strongest in England," and even in the summer of 1689 suspected the intentions of some of the troops in London and "now discovered plainly there was a design for a Commonwealth"; but there is little evidence of any substantial basis for such apprehensions.[9]

Predictably, commonwealth terminology is not present in postrevolutionary statutes. Yet use of the word continued, though sometimes with ambivalent connotations, throughout the whole era. Even

Samuel Parker's virulent diatribe against "our Dissenting Zealots" in 1669 employed it as a synonym for "realm." In 1670 Leonard Willan's *Exact Politician, or Compleat Statesman,* while sensitive of the potential "Distemper of Incendiaries," looked for devotion to "the affairs of a Common-wealth under what Government soever," even alluding to "Free Common-wealths." In 1694 Locke's cautious friend, James Tyrrell, used it, sometimes interchangeably with "kingdom," but was anxious that his readers should "see I am none of those Common-Wealths men who maintain any such desperate Doctrines." Ofspring Blackall, chaplain to Queen Anne, juxtaposed "Country, State, Kingdom or Commonwealth," but certainly surprised some hearers of his sermon before the queen by accepting the notion of change and hazarding a speculation "that Government, which was at first an Absolute, and afterwards a Limited Monarchy, will become a perfect Commonwealth, transferring the whole Government upon the People." Yet an alternative term was gaining ground. By 1718 the Reverend John Jackson, author of many religious works, was to refer more than once to the "Christian State" where earlier one would have looked for commonwealth.[10]

Overall, in terms of an earlier ideal, this period was indeed one of "recession and reparation": what survived into the eighteenth century was an impoverished version of what had been in the heyday of the mid-seventeenth-century era. Schematically, one may perceive an irony: whereas under the early Stuarts the concept of the commonwealth essentially embodied *monarchical* duties in terms of social and economic equity, it now becomes equated with adherence to what were thought of as republican, though not necessarily antimonarchical *political* virtues. Writers alluding to the midcentury included some few who looked back with nostalgia, a far larger number who wrote in retrospective horror, and finally those who still defended an ideal expressed in much more restricted and cautious terms. What had happened was never forgotten. As late as 1699 a printing of the *Memoirs of Denzil Lord Holles,* written in exile in St. Mère Eglise some fifty years earlier, contained the notorious if intemperate depiction of what could still occur when "the meanest of Men, the basest and vilest of the Nation, the lowest of the People, have got the Power into their hands."[11] "Undoubtedly, the absence of much overt articulation of potentially revolutionary social ideas derives from just such recollections—fairly held or not.

Historians have in general identified the Commonwealthmen of the late seventeenth and early eighteenth centuries as displaying more taste for compositions relating to politics than for actual participation. But this must not be pressed too far. In his study of *Parlia-*

ment, Policy and Politics in the Reign of William III, Henry Horwitz identifies Members of the Commons who had by late 1691 acquired "the character of Commonwealth men," and cites a rumor in the following year that on one occasion "the Jacobites and Commonwealthmen joined together" to defeat a parliamentary bill. No fewer than twenty of those who had sat in the Covention Parliament were later to be considered suspect as "Commonwealthmen." As late as the end of William's reign, some still harbored the suspicion that certain of the Whigs hankered after the establishment of a "commonwealth." The protestation expressed in the early 1690s that whoever criticised the Court, voiced grievances, or was deemed to be "but lukewarm towards the state," could expect to be traduced as either "a Commonwealth's man" or "a plain Jacobite," was still justified.[12]

Pejorative connotations long persisted, as in the caveat in 1681 against such restless spirits as indulge "in commending and slyly insinuating the good old days of the late times, the plenty, power, riches and reputation of their dear Commonwealth." The anonymous *Dialogue betwixt Whig and Tory* (1692) condemned those who allude to "that Sham of a Commonwealth" in order unjustly to slander their opponents as being "Commonwealthsmen, Haters of Monarchy, &c." Surely such unfair smears can only affront "all common Sense and Reason; for whoever hath either of these will know a Commonwealth to be a Chimera impracticable . . . [and] that where there is not an Equality in the Conditions and Estates of a People, it is impossible for the People or Nation to erect a Commonwealth." Indeed, "whoever will look over what pass'd here in England from the year 1648 to the year 1660 will be yet more convinc'd of the Truth of this Assertion, and of the Nonsense of any Commonwealth Design in this Nation." Significantly, in the author's opinion, "perhaps there was never at any time so many Men of strong Inclination for a Commonwealth-Government as then, nor of greater Abilities to effect such a Design." But the combined opposition of nobility, gentry, and "dignified Clergy" reduced the effort to confusion and disorder, ensuring a restoration of monarchy. The legend remains, to serve as the dust that courtiers "threw into the People's Eyes, when they would make them blind to arbitrary Power and Popery." Thus, "when-ever you make your false Attack upon our Commonwealth, . . . your real Aim is at our Liberties and Properties." Yet the author remains worried by any signs of "Commonwealth Designs amongst the People." So does Jonathan Swift, who warns (circa 1693) that popular disenchantment with the present regime might become dislike "to that degree, as to wish for a Common-wealth."[13]

Thus, the publication in 1660 of *New Atlantis. Begun by Lord Verulam . . . and Continued by R. H. Esquire* was something of an anachronism. Dedicated to "My most Sacred Sovereign Charles II," setting forth "A Platform of Monarchical Government," deploring the recent "Inter-regnum of tyranny and oppression," and acutely aware of the danger of anarchy, its unknown author sees nothing incongruous in continuing Bacon's sketch in the first Atlantis of "a frame of laws or of the best state or mould of a commonwealth"—a term employed without pejorative implications. Indeed the contents of "The Second Part" often embody the values of an earlier age in envisaging an ideal society that allows "no poor, no Beggars, or idle Vagrants," that controls marketing so as to prevent "the vending of bad and unwarrantable Mechandise," that prevents engrossing and forestalling, that discourages excess in attire and immoderate usury. Even the criticism of contemporary England as too severe "in the grievous and capital punishment of *Petitlarcenies*" and as suffering "great Men in office, first to rob, spoil, and oppress the Common People" and then to punish even the theft of a sheep to which they are driven by destitution by hanging or the galleys, is unmistakably reminiscent of earlier social criticism.[14]

This publication may perhaps not unfairly be termed a maverick. In general, insofar as there is any evidence of continuity with midcentury commonwealth thinking, it is in terms of political principles and rarely in those of social idealism. Yet intriguingly, in the writings of George Savile, marquis of Halifax, before and after the Revolution of 1688, we find frank discussions of the *moral* implications of the ideal of the commonwealth. In *The Character of a Trimmer* (1681–84) he eschews such barbarous extremes of interpretation that declare "that Monarchy is a thing which leaveth men no Liberty, and a Common-wealth such a one as alloweth them no quiet," but then urges that while "Monarchy is liked by the People for the bells and Tinsel, . . . the Rules of a Common-wealth are too hard for the Bulk of Mankind to come up to: that form of Government requireth such a spirit to carry it on, as doth not dwell in great numbers." His *Rough Draught of a New Modell at Sea* (1694), in pondering the prospects for "the next revolution" and considering "whether England is likely to be turned into a Commonwealth," decides that by "all appearances, it is very improbable." Having put the question of "whether instead of an inclination or leaning towards a Commonwealth there is not in England a general dislike to it," he considers the perquisites to the building of a commonwealth that are lacking in this present age: "I mean Virtue, Morality, diligence, Religion, or at the least hypocrisy." All this leads to "a plain and a Natural inference that a

Commonwealth is not fit for us, because We are not fit for a Commonwealth."[15]

Occasionally, both before and after the Glorious Revolution, there is evidence of a residual belief that the commonwealth ideal was neither irredeemably tainted nor necessarily incompatible with monarchy. Sir Philip Warwick's *Discourse of Government,* written in 1678 by a politician and historian, writing within the parameters of the traditional analogy of the body politic, declared that "the Common-weal must be best advanced, when it is served by men who are best affected unto the established Government." In 1694 Matthew Tindal declared the duty of government to protect the commonwealth against its enemies.[16] Indeed, in *The Original Power of the Collective Body of the People of England* (1702), Daniel Defoe identifies "that Bug-bear which so many *pretend* [my italics] to be frightened at, a Commonwealth." Nevertheless, he himself commends, as "an absolute Security" against this spectre, what he discerns as a natural preference of the nation for monarchy. Significantly, the recent revolution witnessed no sign of "the least Inclination in any Party towards a Commonwealth." Surely, considering their chastening experience "during the short Government of Parliament in England, which was erroneously called a Commonwealth, . . . the people of England can never chuse a Commonwealth Government, till they come to desire less Liberty than they now enjoy; that is, till they come to be blind to their own Interest." This latter argument had also been employed by Roger North, writing in the 1680s, when he invited his readers to contemplate "by how much nearer the State hath warped towards what some call a common-wealth, by so much hath tyranny got ground, and the true liberty of the people sunk down."[17]

Assuredly, whether they be deemed convinced, chastened, or cowed, those forces from below that had sought a commonwealth envisaged in terms of greater political democracy or of social equality, have fairly been described as almost astonishingly inert during the opening decades of the most conservative age in British history. Yet despite the ascription of commonwealth ideals almost solely to "a handful of intellectuals or idiosyncratic political independents,"[18] by the turn of the century what may be termed a "sanitized" version of the commonwealth was vigorously defended by those determined to rid the term of its pejorative associations, and who helped to lay the basis of an eighteenth-century revival of the creed. Most notable in this respect were the philosopher Toland, a protégé of Shaftesbury and of Molesworth, and Molesworth himself.

Writing circa 1701, John Toland—described in a reprint in 1757 as "the Slave of no Party"—was concerned to combat what he considered the baleful efforts of Charles II "to possess the Royalists with Apprehensions of a Commonwealth." He contrasts absolutist versions of monarchy with those that "have been called Commonwealths, where the common Good of all was indifferently designed and pursued." Commending a mixed form of government, he argues that "in this sense England is undeniably a Commonwealth, though it be ordinarily styled a Monarchy. . . . Such as are afraid therefore that England should become a Commonwealth, may be suspected not to understand their own Language; and those who talk of making it one, may dream of turning it into an Aristocracy or Democracy, but can never make it more a Commonwealth than it is already." Yet, sadly, people have often been deluded by a device introduced by Charles II, *The Art of Governing by Parties* (the title of the book itself), allied with that by which "all the Dissenters from the Established Church were made to pass for Commonwealths Men; nor could a Man escape that Imputation who grudged the King any Power, though never so dangerous." In *The State-Anatomy of Great Britain* (1717), Toland deplores the way in which the public "are informed there is a strong party of Republicans, or Commonwealth's men in England," which threatens the King. "There is no such party at all, nor, as I verily believe, one single Commonwealth's man in the sense you understand them; that is, men who are either for an Aristocracy or a Democracy." Nor is there any danger from "Republicans, or Commonwealth's men, by which they mean men of levelling and Democratical Principles." Reiterating "that our Monarchy is the best form of a Commonwealth," Toland insists that "our envy'd Liberty then, you see, is not Anarchy nor Licentiousness, but a Government of Laws enacted for the common good of all the people, by their own consent and approbation, as they are represented in Parliament."[19]

Perhaps even more impressive, and certainly better known, is the work of Robert Molesworth. His preface to *An Account of Denmark* (1694) commences by identifying want of liberty as "a disease in any Society or Body Politick," and then changes the analogy in considering "how many grievous Tempests (which as often threatened Shipwrecks) this Vessel of our Commonwealth has undergone." Surely, some "method to preserve our Commonwealth in its legal state of Freedom, without the necessity of a Civil War once or twice every Age" is a paramount necessity! But it is the preface to his translation of Hotman's *Franco-Gallia* (first appearing in the 1721 edition, although perhaps composed a decade or so earlier) that Molesworth's justly famous rebuttal of the slanders directed at the notion of the commonwealth is found. He scorns "the heavy Calumny thrown upon us, that we are all Commonwealth's-Men: which (in the ordinary Meaning of the Word) amounts to Haters of Kingly Government," and goes on to define his notion "of a real Whig (for the Nominal are worse than any Sort of Men)." Thus,

> A true Whig is not afraid of the Name of a Commonwealthsman, because so many foolish People, who know not what it means, run it down: The Anarchy and Confusion which these Nations fell into near Sixty Years ago, and which was falsely called a Commonwealth, frightening them out of the true Construction of the Word. But Queen Elizabeth, and many other of our best Princes, were not scrupulous of calling our Government a Commonwealth, even in their solemn Speeches to Parliament.[20]

Before considering the political opinions of Molesworth, Toland, and others in more detail, one other aspect of the re-emergent ideal of the commonwealth demands attention. It is asserted that this was essentially a shrunken vision, restricted to political and religious liberties (and these often thought of in a negative sense), with negligible concern for any socially ameliorative functions of government, and conceived of primarily or even solely in terms of the independent individual interests of its members: all this reflected in a steadily diminishing appeal to the organic analogy of society. Perhaps this should not be taken too far. Caroline Robbins has rightly declared of Molesworth that "his chief preoccupation was political, not social." Yet near the end of his preface to *Franco-Gallia* occurs an impassioned enunciation of the "Articles of my Whiggish Belief":

> The supporting of Parliamentary Credit, promoting of all publick Buildings and Highways, the making all Rivers Navigable that are capable of it, employing the Poor, suppressing Idlers, restraining Monopolies upon Trade, maintaining the Liberty of the Press. . . . And if all these together amount to a Commonwealthsman, I shall never be asham'd of the Name, tho given with a Design of fixing a Reproach upon me.

Little wonder at the contemporary description of this as "one of the noblest things in the language."[21]

In respect of the nature of individual rights, J. A. W. Gunn points to a trend toward "analysis of society in terms of interests, and an increased awareness of the social implications of self-interest." William Kennedy, in the context of *English Taxation*, identified the emergence "in the actual legal and economic organisation of society, of ideas of unrelated rights and the motive of self-interest" with the state conceived of primarily "as an instrument for protecting the rights of the members." Quite clearly, the notion of "the body politic" endures. Contemporary revulsion against Hobbes was tempered by a stark realization of the implications of any collapse of government. Sir John Bramston's *Autobiography,* while explaining with engaging candor that should the exiled James II return, he thought England's "allegiance will also return to him," insists that "when the Government is fixed, obedience becomes necessary to it, and conscience obliges private persons to yield obedience, as well as prudence and safety to prevent anarchy and the rabble from spoiling the noble and wealthy." Another such an expression of "plain Common sense" is the author's avowal in an anonymous tract of 1696 that "I am to consider my self not merely as a single Person, but as related to the Body of the Nation, as one of Many." An equally brief treatment of *The Behaviour of Christians* when confronted by revolutions in government (1706), declares that "the propriety we have in our Goods is not from a natural Right, but from a positive Right which cannot subsist but in the Society. As soon as we quit a Society, which we do when we disown its Authority, we have no longer any Right to our Goods."[22]

This crucial issue of "propriety" or property, to which I shall return when considering Locke, was bound up with that of "private interests." In 1703 a London doctor, Peter Paxton, whose anonymously published *Civil Polity* was commended by Locke, conceded the existence of "one Politick Body, yet that Body being composed of a Multitude of distinct Persons, each of whom separately considered hath a peculiar Interest, which he will always regard." The Reverend Thomas Burnett, in 1716, declared that "by the Happiness of Society is to be meant chiefly the Security of every ones Right and Properties [which] every one should enjoy as his own." His fellow cleric John Jackson concurred as to "the public Good being nothing but the natural Rights of private particular Persons," while "Liberty, Property and Religion are the great natural Rights." Lawrence Braddon of the Middle Temple, in 1721, was certain that "Private Interest now is, what it always was, the main Spring which gives Motion to the most Considerable Designs. . . . [For] every Man is in Duty bound by all Lawful Means, consistent with the Publick Good, to advance his own Private Interest."[23]

Thus, the notion of a commonwealth imposing moral values upon the conduct of its members, especially in economic activities, was increasingly attacked. Mandeville encapsulated this trend in terms so extreme as to achieve much contemporary notoriety. The analogy of the beehive was encountered in an earlier chapter, but, crucially, what Mandeville depicted was a *grumbling* hive—devoid of any concerted and cooperative effort toward a commonly perceived objective. The contention that in that hive

> The worst of all the Multitude
> Did something for the Common Good

makes no assumption of any individual altruism in the service of the community. Indeed, even honesty is dismissed along with self-denial, for only fools would strive "to make a Great an Honest Hive." Rather does the secret lie in permitting the self-interest of one to profit from catering to the greed of another. While Mandeville did not preach doctrinaire nonintervention, mechanism not motive was to be the subject of any regulatory action:

> This was the State's Craft that maintain'd
> The whole of which each part complain'd:
> This, as in Musick Harmony,
> Made Jarrings in the main agree.

Well might one modern editor discern "a combination of philosophical anarchism in theory with utilitarianism in practice."[24] Yet, as so often in the history of ideas, the element of novelty must not be overstressed. The anonymous author of *The Grounds of Sovereignty and Greatness* (1675) had suggested that "some Art should be found out, for the regulating Cupidity; and this Art is the Politick Order, or State-Government." Again, E. F. Heckscher, in writing of the process by which "the welfare of the state was substituted in place of the amelioration of the individual," in furtherance of which "people should be taken as they are," pointed not only to Mandeville but back to some of the ideas in *The Discourse of the Commonweal*.[25] But here a supremely important distinction must be made: Sir Thomas Smith's book is permeated by a sense of social justice as an objective, the total absence of which in Mandeville is indicative that we have entered another age.

Indeed, urges Kennedy, this age sees a progressive abandonment of the sixteenth-century notion of the state "as an instrument for the general regulation and defence of the whole community." Other scholars concur that debate was concerned with the rights of the individual within society rather than with the individual's subordination to any idealized conception of the common good. Discussion of natural rights was colored more and more by pragmatic recognition of contemporary circumstances, and much of the literature was evoked by actual or potential crises. In general, concludes Hill, "the English conception of liberty came to be a negative one: the Englishman's freedom means being left alone."[26]

Most notably, within the political debate to which I now turn, the range of civil and political liberties envisaged did not include any right of democratic participation in self-government—even amongst those accounted "commonwealthmen." But before discussing in this context the commonwealth theme as such, a word is needed about the complex background of party politics, with which its relationship was far from simple. Most recent scholarship is in no doubt as to the reality and significance of the Whig and Tory parties, at least from the middle of the reign of Charles II onwards, nor as to the fact that party strife remained as bitter, and often personally dangerous, after the Glorious Revolution as before.[27] In this later era, greed for office and its fruits, and cutthroat personal rivalries, sometimes played as prominent a part in such conflict as any deeply held political principles. The frequency of general elections prior to the Septennial Act of 1716 and the size of the electorate gave every incentive to a spate of polemics and propaganda. After enactment of that statute, observes Professor Speck, "the Whigs did not so much control the electorate as evade it"; in time this proved conducive to the emergence of a political nation *manqué*. The emergence of the "New" (as opposed to the "Old," "Real," or "True") Whigs, whose singleminded pursuit of office left little room for even a tenuous attachment to traditional commonwealth principles, will be dealt with later. Eveline Cruickshanks points out that "since most voters voted Tory . . . a redistribution of seats would have amounted to electoral suicide for the Whigs"—hence a lack of enthusiasm for reform of the representative process![28]

It will therefore be both convenient and meaningful to make a broad distinction between surviving Commonwealthmen of the pre-1688 era, whose principles remained rooted in the middle decades of the century; two great writers (Halifax and Locke), whose works effectively straddle the events of the Glorious Revolution itself; and a number of postrevolutionary political thinkers of genuine interest and importance who may be considered as establishing the tradition of the eighteenth-century Commonwealthmen. Edmund Ludlow, whose *Memoirs* (not printed until 1698, though probably written a quarter-century earlier) reflect his experience in midcentury, was in fact forward-looking in his commendation of a separation of powers and the institution of a supreme court—anticipating American constitutional ideas. Yet he was perhaps unrepresentative of the first type of "survivor" in the Carolingian era in the sense that he remained in exile before returning to a hostile reception in 1689.²⁹ More immediately significant was Henry Neville, who had been politically active during the interregnum but whose focus of interest now shifted from the concept of the ideal commonwealth to that of the English constitutional monarchy.

Neville's *Plato Redivivus: or, a Dialogue concerning Government* (1681) affords a splendid example of this transitional phase in commonwealth ideology in a search for renewed respectability. His use of the analogy of the body politic, of its distemper or diseases and the remedies required of "the true physician"—now equated with Parliament—is broadly traditional. But he combines a reference to "the good government of England, which was before this time (like the law of nature) only written in the hearts of men," with a Hobbes-like assertion "that necessity made the first government. For every man by the first law of nature [had a] right to everything"— property rights deriving only from government and laws. Yet he is clearly Harringtonian in his subsequent implication that consciousness of political rights derives from the possession of property. The change in the distribution of property in recent centuries thus implies that "you must bring the government to the property as it now stands." When Neville says that "the natural part of our government, which is power, is by means of property in the hands of the people," his definition of "the people" in this context seems obvious.³⁰

As for types of government, "the extreme of democracy, which is anarchy," ensues when the people claim more than their share in the system and, "assuming debate in the market-place, making their orators their leaders, [proceed] to alter all the orders of the government when they please." The root cause of "all this disorder is the admitting . . . the meaner sort of people, who have no share in the territory, into an equal part of ordering the commonwealth." This is not consistent with "a well-regulated democracy." He is distressed at "both prince and people being so ready to cry out upon forty-one, and to be frightened with the name of a commonwealth; even now when we think popery is at the door." But sadly he recollects how "a civil war has miscarried in our days; which was founded (at least pretendedly) upon defence of the people's own rights," which led only "from one tyranny to another, from Barebone's parliament to Cromwell's reign. . . . Therefore this remedy will either be none, or worse than the disease." Toward the end of the book its author reaches this chastened conclusion: "I believe that we are not ripe yet for any great reform."³¹

More important than Neville was Algernon Sidney, who had actually fought at Marston Moor but had opposed both the execution of Charles I and what he saw as the arbitrary rule of Cromwell. In exile after the Restoration he survived two attempts on his life by royalist agents. His return to England in 1677 and re-entry into public life led to effective leadership of surviving republicans and more advanced Whigs but also, almost inevitably, to arrest and execution in 1683 for probable but not fully proven complicity in the Rye House Plot. He assisted Penn in drafting the important Constitution of Pennsylvania, and Gooch saw him as encapsulating "the transition between the thinkers of the Interregnum and Locke."[32] His lengthy *Discourses concerning Government,* written in 1681–83, were not published until 1698 (appropriately, by John Toland), and thereafter were most notably admired by the successful American revolutionaries of 1776.

Not highly original in content, the work's significance lay in its reasoned restatement of the case that men's natural rights empowered them to scrutinize and if necessary oppose the government under which they lived. Admittedly, "such as enter into Society must in some degree diminish their Liberty," but "this remains to us whilst we form governments, that we ourselves are judges how far 'tis good for us to recede from our natural liberty." On the basis as much of historical precedent as of theory, Sidney believed in "governments mixed," with elements of monarchy, aristocracy, and democracy, contriving to combine an explicit assertion of a right of rebellion with acceptance of elitist government. Caroline Robbins lays emphasis on Sidney's constant appeal to the public good and the public interest, but his assertion that the people themselves could identify that interest appears to be restricted to a vaguely formulated right of appeal in the last resort. Nonetheless, immediately prior to execution, he declared his belief "that God has left nations the liberty of setting up such governments as best pleased themselves" and his witness "for that *Old Cause* in which I was from my Youth engaged."[33]

The two great political philosophers whose thinking and writings in effect bestride the Revolution of 1688–89, George Savile, Viscount Halifax, and John Locke, must be related to the commonwealth tradition with some care. The first, cited earlier in this chapter, stood both above and beyond party, with his astringent and empirical approach and his soubriquet "The Trimmer." Rejecting the Tory sneers that "a Trimmer is worse than a Rebel," the peroration of his masterpiece (which Gooch considered the greatest political pamphlet of the seventeenth century) points out that "our Church is a Trimmer between the frenzy of Phanatick Visions and the Lethargick Ignorance of Popish dreams; that our Laws are Trimmers between the excesses of unbounded power, and the Extravagance of Liberty not enough restrained." As to the lower orders, "there is a Soul in that great Body of the People, which may for a time be drowsy and unactive, but when the Leviathan is roused, it moveth like an angry Creature, and will nether be convinced nor resisted. . . . Our Trimmer therefore dreadeth a General Discontent, because he thinketh it differeth from a Rebellion only as a spotted fever doth from the Plague." He had a pessimistic assessment of the prospect for any commonwealth in his own times.[34]

Some recent interpretations of Locke, who appealed much more than did the skeptically conservative Halifax to first principles, relate him to "revolutionary politics" prior to 1688. J. H. Franklin describes him as dabbling in conspiracy. More crucially, he believes that his abstract presentation of the social compact "is egalitarian in format, and could easily be interpreted more generously."[35] Locke eschewed the democracy of some midcentury commonwealth men and was assuredly no social egalitarian. Nevertheless, his ideas were *not* widely popular with the post-Revolution establishment, and the assumption that he was totally content to identify the people with the propertied class is now doubted. Book II of his *Treatises of Civil Government* (1690), "Concerning the True Original, Extent and End of Civil Government," establishes the criteria of "the commonwealth" and "the public good." In a very important amendment of the Hobbesian derivation from a state of nature, Locke is clear that "the liberty of man in society is to be under no other legislative power but that established by consent in the commonwealth." That commonwealth itself "seems to me to be a society of men constituted only for the procuring, preserving and advancing their own civil interests." Of those interests or rights that of property, the subject of a fairly long chapter, appears indeed to be preeminent, but its nature repays scrutiny. In the preservation of such rights, "where there is no law there is no freedom. For liberty is to be free from restraint and violence from others. . . . It is not, as we are told, 'a liberty for every man to do what he lists.' " Moreover, the organic analogy survives in Locke's depiction of how "the members of a commonwealth are united, and combined together into one coherent living body"—of which the legislative is "the soul."[36]

His exposition of the purposes, form, and limitations of a commonwealth and of its government starts with the blunt annunciation that "the great and chief end, therefore, of men uniting into commonwealths, and putting themselves under government, is the preservation of their property." The term "commonwealth" itself must be understood to "mean not a democracy, or any form of government, but any independent community." Within such an entity, the legislative power must remember always that its exercise "is limited to the public good" and "the fundamental law of Nature" according to "established and promulgated laws." Above all, "the preservation of property being the end of government," it may never be infringed without consent. Again, "the people alone can appoint the form of the commonwealth [and retain] a supreme power to remove or alter the legislative." For if trust is once betrayed, power must "devolve into the hands of those that gave." In dismissing Hobbes's claim that the dissolution of any form of government necessarily involves a consequent disintegration of the social order, Locke indeed appears as the inheritor of the mid-seventeenth-century commonwealth notion of political liberty.[37]

Yet before leaving Locke, one must take cognizance of two crucially significant aspects of recent interpretation. First, it has been contended that, unlike his more cautious friend Tyrrell, his stated conviction that "every man has a 'property' in his own person" (a notion reminiscent of Leveller debate) betrayed a sympathy "for a radically wider membership of political society." If so, this was never made explicit; Locke's belief in a certain natural equality of men never led him to promulgate political, let alone social, egalitarianism. Secondly, in a closely argued monograph James Tully suggests that for Locke, property is "a right to one's *due* rather than to one's *own*," and that "the agreement to institute conventional property succeeds the establishment of political society." Logically, therefore, the social origins of private property entail social limitations and obligations upon its owner. Pre-eminent among these is that of charity, which "gives every man a title to so much of another's plenty, as will keep him from extreme want."[38] Thus subsequent erosion of an emphasis in earlier commonwealth ideology upon the *obligations of property* and on the justice of its regulation in society should not in fairness be laid at the door of John Locke.

Some Remarks upon Government by "A.B.N.T." (January 1689) affords interesting if more mundane insights into moderately progressive thinking at this point. Its author fears that the notion of mixed monarchy is now so riveted in people's minds that "all things will again settle upon its old Basis, and the Government be rebuilt with all its irregularities." Endorsing the notion of a contractual origin of government, he insists that "the People must necessarily be supposed to have still a Reserve of Power [because] our General and Original Rights cannot totally be swallowed up by any Compact that can be made to settle Liberty and Property." Significantly, "Democracy does properly and naturally reduce all to equality, and most carefully consults the People's Liberty and Property, but withall, *it obliges every Man to hold his Neighbour's hand* [my italics], and when it falls it does with great difficulty recover its feet again." The author cites Sir William Temple's observation that "monarchies do indeed seem most Natural, but Common Wealths the more Artificial sorts of Government."³⁹

These comments, reminiscent of Halifax's point that an ideal commonwealth demands of its citizens more than they can give, are followed by an unusual usage of the corporeal analogy. "The Constitutions of our Government, as it now stands, placing the Dominion in the King, whilst the Property is in the People, does in this commit a sort of Violence upon Nature, in separating the Soul from the Body, the Power from the Possessions," and thus occasions "frequent Distempers and Convulsions in the Body Political." This Harringtonian analysis leads on to discussion of faults in parliamentary representation, in respect of suffrage, constituencies, and procedure. Thus, exclusions from "an Electing Vote" detract from the claim of Parliament to represent the people. As for the free exercise of the vote, the author commends the decision of the borough of Lymington "to Elect by Ballot," providing a differently colored ball for each candidate, the choice cast into "a close Box made for that purpose." This "very much assists that freedom which ought to be in Elections. No man in this way need fear the disobliging of his Landlord, Customer, or Benefactor; for it can by no means be discerned how he gave his Vote."⁴⁰

This tract took the form of two letters addressed "to Members of the Great Convention." Another significant pointer to public apprehension of potentially divergent courses is found in *The Late Proceedings and Votes of the Parliament of Scotland* (1689), contained in an address delivered to the King. This states plainly that "there is no more required to the freeing both of Scotland and England from the Common-wealths Men, and from all Republican Principles, but that His Majesty persevere in preserving unto his People their Rights and Liberties." Equally surely, wrongful actions by evil ministers will "withdraw nine parts of the People in six Months from their Love of Monarchy, and . . . force them upon wishing for a Common-Wealth."⁴¹ Clearly, for many, the term "commonwealth" still had indelible antimonarchical associations. Yet others continued resolutely to defend what they saw as moderate commonwealth principles. Before considering these, it is essential to allude, however briefly, to the party political background of these years.

The development of political parties between 1689 and 1725 precludes the attribution of any simple relationship between Whigs and Commonwealthmen. While Professor H. T. Dickinson writes of a "group of Real Whigs or Commonwealthmen," or again of "Commonwealthman or radical Country Whigs," Plumb sketches a Tory program (at this stage led by Harley and Davenant) that displays more empathy with commonwealth ideals than was shown by the "New Whigs." Indeed, it has been urged that it was the Tory country interest that opposed the Excise as a tax upon the poor, although Linda Colley dismisses any picture of "the embattled squirereach's superior social concern" or any attempt "to cast the Tories as forlorn paternalists." There is no real incompatibility of these positions. The key lies in what happened during these decades to the Whigs—variously described as "New" as against "Old," "Real," or "True." Broadly speaking, as the Whigs identified their interests with those of what has been termed "a new synthetic oligarchy" and with the singleminded and ruthless pursuit of office and power, their former principles became attenuated. Thus, Plumb concludes that the Whig Party "divorced itself completely from radical ideology, keeping merely the shibboleth of religious toleration. . . . After 1694, all truck with moderate radicalism goes."[42]

This last phrase begs a question. For some decades historians have written of radicals and radicalism in the early eighteenth century. Yet Colin Bonwick has pointed to the absence of "radical" as a descriptive term among contemporaries before the 1780s. More recently, Clark has challenged the alleged anachronism of "a particular and loaded account of the evolution of a radical ideology." Yet he also equates the "Commonwealthmen" with "radical Whigs," while Bonwick writes of "Commonwealth radicals."[43] Perhaps an adjectival use of the word is safer than its use as a noun! Above all, one need not retrospectively extrapolate the values and objectives of a later age, at least in the context of the present study. Those who still clung to elements of a commonwealth ideology looked *back* to a mid-seventeenth-century set of beliefs that included not only something approaching manhood suffrage, but also many of the social constituents of what would later be seen as the philosophy of the "Welfare State."

Meanwhile, the dialogue in *The True Picture of a Modern Whig* (1701, second edition), by Charles Davenant, economist and politician, conveys a scathing parody of what happened to the Whigs. It soon enunciates "the Principle of us Modern Whigs to get what we can, no matter how. . . . [For] if you talk or think of the Publick Good, you will never become a right Modern Whig." Such as have benefited from the Revolution by seizing all opportunities of bribery and corruption to advance their own interests, displaying contempt alike both for the mob and the House of Commons—until of late "Pox take it, our Villanies grew so rank that at last Parliament began to Smoke us. . . ." And "as for the Old Whigs in King Charles's time, many of 'em are dead, some of 'em are retir'd, being asham'd to see their Party play the Knave as soon as ever they get into Power." Here is bitter if biassed confirmation of Gunn's conclusion that "far from ending the corruption begun under Charles II, the Glorious Revolution had extended it."[44]

Against this background it is not fanciful to discern once more a familiar scenario of disappointed commonwealth expectations, envisaged this time not in terms of far-reaching social and economic amelioration, nor in those of radical constitutional reform, but simply in the shape of greater probity and rectitude in public affairs—whether on the part of ministers or of elected representatives. Among those basic principles espoused by those who saw themselves, or are identified by historians, as within the commonwealth tradition, the protection of individual liberties—civil, political, and religious—clearly ranks first. "Protection" implies a fear of attack, the sources of which were seen in any untrammeled exercise of power and especially in the threat of standing military power. Next perhaps should be listed the scrupulous discharge both by elected representatives and by responsible ministers of their obligations to the political nation from which their authority was held in trust. Here the perennial objects of suspicion were "Placemen" and venal Parliaments. Hence the recurrent attempts, in the reigns of William and Mary and of Queen Anne, at enacting Place Bills, with ultimately partial success, together with demands for more frequent, indeed annual general elections. But Commonwealthsmen combined a Harringtonian suspicion that office tainted and power corrupted with a resolute conviction that only the possession of sufficient personal property could help ensure that those involved would put the general good before personal advantage. This belief extended also to the electorate itself—a point encountered in discussion of Leveller debate on the franchise now recurs in a different context. The fear that Crown patronage would but replace royal prerogative as a threat to liberty led to a wish for some measure of parliamentary reform. But this did not extend to a radical increase in the size of the political nation itself, which would only give the vote to those considered too limited in their intelligence and too venal in their motivation to use it responsibly.

Among those Commonwealthsmen or Old Whigs who wrote against a background of increasing disenchantment with the new regime, Robert Molesworth was outstandingly important. In works encountered a few pages earlier he enunciates some fundamental principles. His suspicion of all perpetual authority leads him to urge "that no People in their right Wits . . . can be supposed to confer an absolute Dominion, or to give away the freedom of themselves and their Posterity for all Generations. . . . The People can no more part with their legal Liberties, than Kings can alienate their Crowns." Neither can Parliament legislate in perpetuity, particularly when "any Law grows apparently mischievous to the whole Body that made it. . . . The acts of one general Parliament, though a free one, are not perpetually obliging." Equally important, "our Constitution is a Government of Laws, not of Persons," so that "Allegiance and Protection" are mutual obligations. Moreover, "a right Whig looks upon frequent Parliaments as such a fundamental Part of the Constitution that even no Parliament can part with this Right. High Whiggism is for Annual Parliaments, and Low Whiggism for Triennial, with annual Meetings'." After delivering the shrewd observation that "the Honey-Moon of Government is a dangerous Season" for the liberties of the people, Molesworth moves on to an issue of crucial concern: "A Whig is against the raising or keeping up a Standing Army in Time of Peace." Admittedly, in some circumstances, "a Whiggish Army is the Guardian of our Liberties": best therefore to restore the ancient custom of "the arming and training of all the Freeholders of England."[45]

The emergence of this almost as a touchstone in political ideology is perhaps symbolized in the reprinting no fewer than eight times in the eighteenth century of John Trenchard's *History of Standing Armies in England*. The Scot Andrew Fletcher, who had sailed with Monmouth and then after exile joined William of Orange at The Hague, pubished *A Discourse Concerning Militia's and Standing Armies* (1697, effectively reproduced in many sections of *A Discourse of Government* . . . a year later). Reflecting on "how precarious our Liberties are, and how from having the best Security for them we are in hazard of having none at all," he scorns reliance on "Mercenaries, and Men that had no other Interest in the Common-wealth than their Pay." Surely the example of what has happened in Europe should demonstrate that "Standing Mercenary Forces kept up in time of Peace" lead in those states depending upon them to a change "from Monarchies to Tyrannies," whereas "the Subjects formerly had a real Security for their Liberty, by having the Sword in their own hands."[46]

Trenchard was to be a major force behind *Cato's Letters*. Meanwhile Walter Moyle, an admirer of Sidney, Neville, and Locke, and a mutual friend of Trenchard and Davenant, has been seen as rather more advanced than Molesworth. His *Essay upon the Constitution of the Roman Government,* written in 1698 but not printed until 1726, helped to set the fashion of incorporating transparently coded commentaries uon contemporary dangers within a treatment of Roman history.[47] After discussion of types of monarchy, which concludes "that Elective Monarchy is less dangerous to the Liberties of the People," Moyle declares "that eternal Principle, that Equality of Possession makes Equality of Power"—which of course, as already noted, does *not* imply a literal egalitarianism. What it does convey is the belief "that Land is the true Centre of Power, and that the Balance of Dominion changes with the Balance of Property, [as] so fully demonstrated by the Great Harrington in his Oceana." Moyle's other great concern is to commend "Laws against canvassing and soliciting for Places, which destroy'd the Freedom of Election" and to applaud "voting by the Ballot, which was an Expedient found out to preserve the Freedom of Elections, . . . the only Barrier which hinder'd the Autocracy from subverting the popular Government." For "nothing sooner dissolves a Commonwealth than the Continuance of Authority too long in the same Hands. It likewise subverts that successive change of Magistracy, which is the fundamental Constitution of all equal Governments, where the whole Community ought to have their turns of commanding and obeying." Again, in moving to the decline of Roman government, he makes the interesting assertions that "there were no Seditions after the Commonwealth became more equal," indeed that "seditions do not proceed from the nature of Commonwealths in general"—it is the "Reformation of Governments which are so unequal in their Constitution" that occasions tumult and violence.[48]

At about the turn of the century John Toland—who declared that commonwealth principles, properly understood, were in no way antimonarchical—related what in his opinion had gone wrong to *The Art of Governing by Parties* (circa 1701). As applied in religion and politics, in Parliament, on the bench, and in the ministry, "this Party-Business is all the while but a mere Blind, for Matters go on just as they did." Sadly, "Men of Peace and publick Spirit are in Matters of State branded with the name of Trimmers." For a sorry catalogue of bribes, embezzlements, and abuse of patronage in granting places, "no Remedy can be so proper as annual Parliaments"—for surely no one can afford annual bribery! Admittedly, triennial parliaments are a step forward, but representation remains unequal. "The only remedy against all the Mischief of Parties, is a Parliament equally constituted." *Some Reasons for Annual Parliaments* (1693) had envisaged the reluctance of greedy candidates to bribe electors "if they are sure to be laid aside like Almanacks, at the next Annual Election." *The Danger of Mercenary Parliaments* (1722), written when Toland was terminally ill, appealed to electors to spew out "these noxious Vermin to the Common-wealth."[49]

Yet Toland was no democrat, and he insisted that "by *Freemen* I understand men of property, or persons that are able to live of themselves; and those who cannot subsist in this independence, I call *Servants*": with due allowance for the different background, this is almost back to the Anglo-Saxon world of "the free and the half-free"! In their mingled contempt for and fear of the vulgar people, as unfit to participate in the political process, there was little difference between most Commonwealthmen, the more compliant Whigs, and the Tories. William Atwood, a Whig lawyer and friend of Tyrrell, in 1690 rejected any assertion (perhaps by Locke) that any dissolution of a social contract entailed "a mere Commonwealth, or absolute Anarchy, wherein every body has an equal share in the Government, not only Landed-men, and others with whom the Balance of Power has rested by the Constitution, but Copy-holders, Servants, and the very *Faeces Romuli*," and hence "a deplorable Confusion." Sir Philip Warwick's *Discourse of Government* (1694) expressed a very low estimate of the commonalty: "their passions being strong, and their judgments weak." In his *Bibliotheca Politica* (also 1694), James Tyrrell, more cautious than Locke, makes it very clear that "when I make use of the word people, I do not mean the vulgar or mixt multitude." Mindful of Wat Tyler, he condemns rebellion "by the meaner sort, or Scum of the People," often deluded and incited "by some turbulent Demagogues." Accordingly, the right of resistance in the last resort does "by no means allow the Rabble or Mob of any Nation to take Arms against a Civil Government, but only the whole Community of the People, of all Degrees and Orders, commanded by the Nobility and Gentry thereof."[50]

Daniel Defoe alike recoils from the specter of "the People assembled in a Universal Mob to take the Right of Government upon themselves," and insists that "I do not place this Right upon the Inhabitants, but upon the Freeholders. The Freeholders are the proper Owners of the Country . . . and the other Inhabitants are but Sojourners, like Lodgers in a House." His *Hymn to the Mob* (1715) is devoted to the danger threatened from "the New Dictator of the Street"—for "when Mob goes mad beware the State"! Admittedly,

> Of all the Mobs with which this Land is curst,
> Mobs for Religion are the worst,

but he goes on to

> speak of Party-Mobs, and Mobs of State;
> When Politicians stand in need of Fools,
> And use the Mob as Workmen use their Tools

—as at elections, to "insult the Voters, fright Men from the Poll."[51]

Yet in his abhorrence of the mob Defoe is not blind to danger from another quarter. *The Freeholder's Plea,* published earlier, in 1701, is directed against "Stock-Jobbing of Parliament Men." Deploring the way in which both "Religion and the State have felt the plague of Contention, eating into the very Entrails of the Nation," he concentrates upon "this new Trade of Jobbing for Elections." He fears lest thereby the "Election of Parliament-Men [will] come under the absolute Management of a few Hands." And as for its effect: "they who will Buy will Sell, [and] be capable of selling our Trade, our Religion, our Peace. . . ." Defoe is equally scathing on what was to be a principal concern of some eighteenth-century reformers: "That all the Free-holders of a County shou'd be represented only by two Men, and the Towns in the same County . . . by above Forty, as it is in Cornwall." Surely it is unjust and ludicrous that "the remains of a good Old Town, now lying in Heaps," should have parliamentary representation while thriving towns of more recent origin do not?[52]

Meanwhile, the right of resistance in the last resort itself became the subject of debate. *Vox Populi, Vox Dei* (1709) declared that "Absolute Passive-Obedience is a Damnable and Treasonable Doctrine," citing the example of Magdeburg and the authority of Luther and Melanchthon. Thomas Bradbury, a congregational minister, in *The Ass: or the Serpent* (1712) identified the notion as "laid in Stupidity," asserting, more ominously, that " 'tis better being crush'd at once, than condemn'd to a miserable Existence."[53] But the issue evoked the fiercest contention, even between clerics. Benjamin Hoadly, bishop of Bangor, insisted that "Submission cannot be a Virtue" if it condones the harming of "the public Interest"; but in *The Voice of the People, no Voice of God* (1710) Francis Atterbury, bishop of Rochester, later exiled for his Jacobitism, adopted another perspective. After citing Wat Tyler and Jack Straw he claimed that "it was the Voice of the People, rais'd in frequent Mutinies and Sedition, that began the Rebellion against King Charles the First." In general, "the Voice of the People is the Cry of Hell, leading to Idolatry, Rebellion, Murder, and all the Wickedness the Devil can suggest." Significantly, Gunn points out that, divorced from its tone and intent, most contemporary Whigs would have accepted the substance of Atterbury's assessment.[54]

Certainly those who are accounted Commonwealthmen did not combine with their suspicion of authority, hatred of corruption, and zealous defence of individual liberties, any wish to amend the political nation itself by giving power to the people. Thomas Gordon explained that "by the people I mean not the idle and indigent rabble under which name the people are often understood and traduced, but all who have property without the privileges of nobility." Gordon is best known for his collaboration with John Trenchard in the weekly writing (1720–23) of *Cato's Letters*. Often reprinted, these afford detailed insights into the philosophy of the "Independent Whig"—an alternative title by now as appropriate as "Commonwealthman." Liberty is "the inalienable Right of all Mankind," which cannot be renounced for oneself or one's heirs. Its preservation is the sole purpose of entry "into political Society" and has wide implications. Thus, Cato declares that "every Man's Religion is his own," eschews bigotry (although remaining virulently anti-papist), and deplores that fact that "Men often make War upon Truth, Conscience, and Honesty, in behalf of their Religion." In fact, "no Religion at all is better than a mischievous Religion." Since liberty is "the divine Source of all human Happiness" it must never be infringed by government; "the Good of the Governed being the sole End of all Government," acting as "the Trustees of the People upon the Interests and Affairs of the People." Thus "the only Secret therefor in forming a Free Government, is to make the Interests of the Governors and of the Governors the same." But Cato sees no solution to the problems of mechanism and of motivation involved "but by the frequent fresh Elections of the People's Deputies"—for, alas, "the Possession of Power soon alters and vitiates their Hearts."[55]

Suspicion of the exercise of power is endemic in the Letters. Assuredly, the imperfect minds of men "ought never to be trusted with a Power that is boundless." For "Power is like Fire . . . as dangerous as useful; [accordingly] all should proceed by fixed and stated Rules." Liberty must always be jealous of power, and too many restraints are scarcely possible. Arbitrary power may derive from excessive inequality or from military force. The sovereign specific is therefore government by law, and "the Benefit and Safety of the People constitutes the Supreme Law." "The Prince has only the sovereign Execution" of the Law, being "only the chief Servant of the State." But, sadly, "the World is governed by Men, and Men by their Passions." Thus, laws exist not only to safeguard individual liberties against would-be tyrannical government, but also to recognize and to curb selfish passions—"so wicked and merciless a Thing is Self-Interest" unchecked. So long as "every Man loves himself better than he loves his whole Species . . . Concord and Security are preserved by the Terror of Laws, and the Ties of mutual Interest; and both the Interest and Terror derive their Strength from the Impulse of Self-Love." Thus may "the two great Laws of human Society, . . . those of Equity and Self-preservation" redress the balance between principle and passion.[56]

"Generally speaking, when ever there is Power, there will be Faction; and wherever there is Money, there will be Corruption." Such "Crocodiles and Cannibals" as stock-jobbers and the "South Sea" directors exploit "instead of nourishing the Body-Politick." But the bowels of Jack Ketch (the public hangman's soubriquet) yearn for them in vain. "It is safer for a great Man to rob a Country, than for a poor Man to steal a Loaf. . . . Faction on one Side, and Riches on the other, have, as it were, made a Lane for the Great Criminals to escape." Moreover, wicked and corrupt ministers, exploiting "Parties in the Commonwealth," will suborn first electors and then their representatives so as to produce "an Interest distinct from that of the Body of the People." Thus, "every private Subject has a Right to watch the Steps of those who would betray their Country." Nor is Cato frightened by "the Word Mob," finding it "certain that the whole People . . . are the best Judges, whether Things go ill or well. . . . Every Cobbler can judge, as well as a Statesman, whether . . . he is paid for his Work; whether the Market, where he buys his Victuals, be well provided." Moreover (expressing a sentiment that seems to be oddly reminiscent of Rousseau), "the People would certainly be in the Interests of Truth and Liberty, were it not for external Delusion and external Force! . . . They have no Interest but the general Interest." "Political Jealousy, therefore, in the People, is a necessary and laudable Passion." A whole Letter expounds "the Right and Capacity of the People to judge of Government"—the basis indeed of "our late happy Revolution."[57]

Yet Cato was emphatically no egalitarian: his aim was equity. His contention that "Liberty can never subsist without Equality, nor Equality be long preserved without an *Agrarian* Law, or something like it" was directed against any excessive concentration of riches. For despite a certain initial equality of human beings, he is in no doubt that the first sign "of Inequality is in human Nature, and the next in the Nature of Society. . . . Some Inequality there must be; the Danger is, that it be not too great: Where there is absolute Equality, all Reverence and Awe, two Checks indispensable in Society, would be lost." Equity, moreover, safeguards minority rights, by preventing "a Conspiracy of the Many against the Minority. . . . It is a mistaken Notion in Government, that the Interest of the Majority is only to be consulted." Significantly, in his glowing valedictory tribute in the republication of the Letters in book format, Gordon described John Trenchard as "against all levelling in Church and State, and fearful of trying Experiments upon the Constitution. . . . As passionate as he was for Liberty, he was not for a Commonwealth in England. He neither believed it possible, nor wished for it." Clearly, in Cato the term "commonwealth" itself has a double connotation—the first, as an alternative for the term "state," at present embodied in a constitutional monarchy, and the second, which looks back to the seventeenth century—according to the context in which it is used. The Commonwealthmen were the heirs of Harrington, not of Rainborough—much less Winstanley. Conceptually, it may be admitted that "an Equality of Estate will give an Equality of Power; and an Equality of power is a Commonwealth or Democracy." But this can not be rushed through a hasty agreement of men, before Nature has prepared the way. The time has not yet come for an egalitarian commonwealth.[58]

Religion and Morality

This last issue will recur in the context of the fate of the social and economic dimension of commonwealth idealism. But first I must consider the fortunes of another and fairly recently emergent principle: that of religious liberty. The advocacy of such freedom for the individual on grounds of principle encountered continued opposition, but that of religious toleration on those of social and political expediency grew ever stronger. Some, although a minority, continued to demand full *civil* rights as well as religious liberty at least for Protestant Nonconformists. Sadly, the whole topic was entrammeled with political considerations. In particular, religious dissent—fairly or not—was daubed with the regicidal and levelling tar-brush of the mid-seventeenth century.

Charles II himself, from exile, had proffered "liberty to tender consciences" as an inducement to those wavering as to his restoration. But several dissenting tracts in 1661 attest to speedy disillusionment. A *Humble Petition* pleading for Anabaptists in Maidstone Gaol alluded to the liberty promised, and declared it unlawful for Christian magistrates to "root out the contrary-minded in religious matters, although idolaters." Another *Plea for Toleration* by a Baptist appealed to Breda, disavowed Venner, and praised "your excellent proclamations against swearing, debauchery, and drunkenness." But the imposition of "articles of faith, or rules of worship . . . both punishes sincerity and persuades hypocrisy"; it persecutes the truth and encourages dissembling.[59] Almost simultaneously, *Sion's Groans for her Distressed* derides "those whose strongest argument for the support of their religion is, Take Him, Jailor." Most notably, "if it shall still be objected, that it is inconsistent with the safety and well-being of any nation to allow or tolerate any more ways of worship than one: we answer, experience hath taught the contrary to several countries of Europe: as France, and the United Provinces, and several countries of Germany." *A Discourse Concerning Liberty of Conscience,* by Peter Pett (also printed in 1661) is explicitly concerned "about what Liberty in this kind is now *Politically Expedient* [my italics] to be given." Anabaptists should not be punished merely "for their opinion of Administering Baptism," while even Fifth Monarchy Men may be tolerated if they do not behave seditiously. Most striking perhaps is the proposal temporarily to tolerate Quakers on the ground that "a speedy punishing so numerous a party would not be prudent." The author's primary justification for liberty of conscience is "the necessary connexion between Civil Liberty and that which is Spiritual." Significantly, once such liberty is granted, it is "hardly possible for any civil Wars to happen on account of Religion"—though we must still be wary of the "toleration we allow Papists"![60]

Alas, the answer to these pleas was the Clarendon Code (1661–65), which at the very least imposed the severest civil disabilities upon Dissenters. Indeed the whole period was possessed by the two great phobias identified by Geoffrey Holmes as bequeathed by earlier conflicts: fear of Puritan fanaticism and dread of Popery. The first was virulently expressed in Samuel Parker's *Discourse of Ecclesiastical Politie* (1669), roundly asserting "the Authority of the Civil Magistrate over the Consciences of Subjects in Matters of External Religion." Misguided toleration gives free rein to "our Dissenting Zealots" to peddle "Schismatical Non-conformity . . . among little and unlearned People." The author, bishop of Oxford, urges that "the remiss Government of Conscience has ever been the most fatal miscarriage in all Commonwealths. Impunity of Offenders against Ecclesiastical Laws, the worst sort of Toleration." For "there are some Sects whose Principles, and some Persons whose Tempers will not suffer them to live peaceably in any Common-wealth." Most crucially, these "Melancholy Religionists" attack the "management of Publick Affairs [and] reflect upon the Wisdom and Ability of their

Superiors." Undoubtedly, "the Factions of Religion are ever the most Seditious."[61]

This diatribe received a speedy and direct chapter-by-chapter rebuttal in *Truth and Innocence Vindicated* by John Owen, one-time chaplain to Oliver Cromwell. The author deplores "this unparalleled heap of Revilings" and "Intimations of Sanguinary affections" toward Nonconformists. Surely "the interest of Kings and Rulers, of all Governments whatever, the good and welfare of private persons, lies in nothing more than in preserving Conscience from being debauched in the conducting principles of it; and in keeping up its due Respect to the immediate Sovereignty of God over it in all things." In an illustration of how religious and commercial notions sometimes overlapped, Owen scorns Parker's rejection of the claim "that Liberty of Conscience would be mightily conducive to the Advance of Trade" by asserting that this is too high a price to pay for something "destructive of the Ends and Interest of Government."[62]

As for the endemic suspicion of Popery, the bloody-minded consequences of the ludicrous "revelations" of the Popish Plot in 1673 lingered on. In 1677 the poet Andrew Marvell published (in Amsterdam) *An Account of the Growth of Popery, and Arbitrary Government in England,* urging that "there has now for diverse Years a design been carried on, to change the Lawful Government of England into an Absolute Tyranny, and to convert the established Protestant Religion into down-right Popery." Standing out against this "Conspiracy against our Religion and Government," which involves a "Scrutiny all over the Kingdom, to find out men of *Arbitrary Principles,* that will Bow the knee to Baal," Marvell discerns "an handful of Salt, a sparkle of Soul, that hath hitherto preserved this gross Body from Putrefaction. . . . Although so small a Scantling in number, that men can scarce reckon of them more than a Quorum."[63]

Toward the end of the reign of Charles II, Lord Halifax, in *The Character of a Trimmer,* observed that, despite its foundation upon eternal verities, in the present circumstances "the Consideration of Religion is so twisted with that of Government that it is never to be separated." Yet he insisted also that, since there can be no true religion without charity, a cool as well as prudent consideration of an element of toleration was most advisable. Nonetheless, with equal perception, in *A Letter to a Dissenter* (1687), against the background of James II's first Declaration of Indulgence, and fully apprised of its disingenuous objectives, "the Trimmer" warns his nonconformist readers that "wine is not more expressly forbidden to the Mahometans, than giving Heretics Liberty is to the Papists." Effectively, he counsels Protestant Dissenters as to the wisdom of "enjoying quietly" the merely de facto liberty they now possess. For by active and misguided advocacy of this Indulgence, seeking "to rescue your selves from the Severity of one Law, you give a Blow to all the Laws by which your Religion and Liberty are to be protected."[64] Halifax's clear-headed appraisal, as so often, encapsulates the realities of the contemporary position. Quite simply, the undoubtedly genuine contention that complete religious liberty was in no way a threat either to the cohesion or to the peace and security of the commonwealth, was vitiated by political considerations and by what were perceived, rightly or wrongly, as threats to national interests. Even the "religious toleration" that ensued after the Glorious Revolution demands the closest scrutiny and definition. The point is fairly made that, in context, the word "toleration" itself is indicative of an almost grudging decision to refrain from active persecution rather than of any open-hearted recognition of genuine equality.

Yet the years 1689–91 also witnessed, in successive appearances of John Locke's *Letters Concerning Toleration,* one of the noblest and most specific advocacies of the principle of individual freedom in religious matters within the commonwealth. Locke's declaration that "Absolute Liberty, Just and True Liberty, Equal and Impartial Liberty" is society's objective, is followed by a definition of "the Business of True Religion." It "is not instituted in order to the erecting of an external Pomp, nor to the obtaining of Ecclesiastical Dominion, nor to the exercising of compulsive Force; but to the regulating of Mens Lives according to the Rules of Virtue and Piety." How ludicrous then for burning zeal in enforcement of doctrinal orthodoxy "with Fire and Faggot" to wink at vice and wickedness! Locke's assessment of the place of religion within society is enunciated in several crucial passages. "The Commonwealth seems to me to be a Society of Men constituted *only* [my italics] for the procuring, preserving, and advancing of their own Civil Interests. . . . [Hence] the Care of Souls is not committed to the Civil Magistrate, any more than to other Men." "A Church then I take to be a voluntary Society of Men, . . . a free and voluntary Society. No body is born a Member of any Church." In particular, "no private Person has any Right . . . to prejudice another Person in his Civil Enjoyments, because he is of another Church or Religion." Finally, of special relevance in our context, "the Commonwealth of the Jews . . . was an absolute Theocracy: nor was there, or could there be, any difference between the Commonwealth and the Church. . . . But there is absolutely no such thing, under the Gospel, as a Christian Commonwealth." Christ himself "instituted no Commonwealth."[65]

Thus far have we moved, in Locke, away from the Erasmian concept of the duty of the ruler within the "Christian Commonwealth." But more mundanely, many of those who now published their opinions on the supremely significant gray area between religion and politics were more concerned with the civil obedience of the subject in this world than they were with the fate of his soul in the next. A grudging toleration might fall short of recognition of unrestricted freedom of worship, while this latter in turn was seen as a very different thing from the granting of full civil and legal equality, with all its correlative implications for political influence. While a radical minority wished to extend full civil rights along with religious liberty to Protestant Dissenters, it has been contended that *interest* was more of a constant in determining attitudes than was purely ideological commitment. Not only present-day interests but also historical associations, real or alleged, were involved—and sometimes indignantly repudiated.

I noticed earlier the eagerness of this era's Commonwealthmen to dissociate themselves from memories of the egalitarian political and social aspects of the Interregnum. Not surprisingly, many Protestant Dissenters now strove to free their cause from the taint of Puritan intolerance and republicanism. This was the background to the appearance in 1702 of what is rightly termed a piece of inimitable irony, by which many were for some time deceived until—its true import once grasped—the author was fined, pilloried, and imprisoned. Daniel Defoe's *The Shortest Way with the Disenters* regrets the failure of James I to send all the Puritans to the West Indies—which would have obviated the butchery of one king, the deposition of another, and the mockery of a third. Further, he asks, "what Peace, and what Mercy did they shew the Loyal Gentry of the Church of England in the time of their Triumphant Common-wealth?" Yet still they survive to threaten the realm and the church. Surely "Her Majesty did never promise to maintain the Toleration, to the Destruction of the Church"? "This is the time to pull up this heretical Weed of Sedition, that has so long disturb'd the Peace of the Church, and poisoned the good Corn." Dismissing an expression of distaste (Locke's?) for "Fire and Faggot," the tract points to the analogy of the apparent cruelty in the killing of snakes and toads, whereas "the Poyson of their Nature makes it a Charity to our Neighbours to destroy those Creatures" to prevent the evil they may do. In what way is the Papist with seven sacraments worse than a Quaker with none at all, or an Enthusiast better than a Jesuit? Alas for the Church of

England: "what with Popery on the one Hand, and Schismaticks on the other; how has she been Crucify'd between two Thieves."[66]

Much more explicit in its message was *The Rights of Protestant Dissenters* (1705, second edition), by John Shute, Viscount Barrington, whose great achievement was later to be his contribution to the repeal of the Occasional Conformity and Schism Acts—which purported to block the loopholes through which Dissenters had entered civil and political life despite the limitations of the Act of Toleration. After an outright disavowal of "the Rebellious Principles of the last Age," the author defines religious toleration: "A Toleration is the Exemption of a peaceable Man, who is thought to be mistaken in matters of Religion, from all sorts of Penalties and Force: And all Mistakes are peacable ones that are not injurious to our Civil Interests. . . . A Toleration is no Toleration that is not absolute and impartial." Part II of the book, "Being a Vindication of their Right to an Absolute Toleration," goes on to argue "(1) That the Admission of Dissenters to public Employments is not inconsistent with the Safety of the State, nor (2) with the Safety of the Church." At pains to dissociate Dissent from reputedly seditious commonwealth notions, Barrington rejects the charges of Sir Humphrey Mackworth (who also clashed with Defoe) and flings at him the recollection of his own seditious ancestry. In particular, he scorns the accusation that despite their feigned loyalty to the queen, Dissenters "are Enemies to the English Constitution, and bear an implacable hatred to Monarchy, and are great Friends to a Commonwealth," proposing to "increase the Liberties of the People." Ingeniously, Barrington proceeds to urge that "if there were any Commonwealthsmen in England, and the Dissenters were of that number, it would be *dangerous* to exclude 'em from offices, whilst there are any Churchmen stand possess't of 'em that are for Arbitrary Power." For such are "equally destructive to a Limited Monarchy."[67]

The force of this contention that a balance of religious interests would at the very least reinforce a purely constitutional balance has been noted. But it cut no ice with many contemporaries. As late as 1719 verses addressed to Lord Stanhope lamented how "the *Dissenting* Protestant" continued to be blamed

> For Crimes long since, and Madness not his own . . .
> Past woes are call'd to mind and present fears,
> And Forty One still rattles in our ears.

In 1709 Henry Sacheverell, to whom church and state were "so happily intermixt that 'tis almost impossible to offer a violation to the one, without breaking in upon the body of the other," had envisaged "heterodoxy in the doctrines of one [as] inferring rebellion and high-treason in the other." Toleration was not meant to "cherish such monsters and vipers."[68]

Despite such slanders, writers in what remained of a mainstream commonwealth tradition were adamant in advocacy of religious liberty. John Toland, whose *Christianity not Mysterious* (1696) derided "those Fooleries superadded" to the Gospel message as pseudo-mysterious doctrines and asserted that I "acknowledge no Orthodoxy but the Truth," rejects the notion that is "as false in it self, as common among shallow Politicians, that tis necessary for a Government to have but one Religion." Robert Molesworth, dealing with religious issues, maintains that "the thriving of any single Person by honest Means, is the thriving of the Commonwealth wherein he resides." Accordingly, "a true Whig thinks that all opinions purely spiritual and notional ought to be indulg'd." But this does not preclude the punishing of injustice, violence, and immorality. Moreover, ever mindful of property rights, "a Minister's Tithes are as much his Right, as any Layman's Estate can be his."[69]

One notices here, as in Locke, the combination of a commendation of religious liberty with a continued insistence on the duty of government to nurture virtue and punish vice. But does an abandonment of the duty of the ruler in the commonwealth to enforce doctrinal orthodoxy entail a gradually weakening assessment of his moral, social, and economic obligations? The case of Mathew Tindal exemplified the complexity of this issue. In *An Essay Concerning the Power of the Magistrate . . . in Matters of Religion* (1697) Tindal approves of the people's "Right to invest the Magistrate with a Power in those Matters of Religion which have an Influence on Human Societies, but not in others that are merely Religious." He goes on to declare it "the Magistrates Security, as well as Duty, to grant an impartial inviolable Liberty of Conscience." Nonetheless, as to a ruler's social duties, "in becoming their Governor, he has obliged himself to promote their Happiness and Welfare, [giving] impartial Encouragement to all that are Virtuous and Industrious." This seems clear enought, but oddly, some years later, Tindal defended Mandeville—whose notions will be discussed later.[70]

Meanwhile, though some have seen this aspect of commonwealth ideology as becoming increasingly tenuous, one must take note of what Dudley Bahlman has termed *The Moral Revolution of 1688*, as producing "a tremendous enthusiasm for a reformation of morals." William and Mary and Queen Anne alike expressed concern. One contemporary clergyman pleaded for the efforts of the magistrate lest the nation "be overrun with a torrent of impiety." This was quite literally paralleled by another torrent: the increase in distillation of gin from over eight thousand gallons in 1694 to over six million some forty years later attests a problem that was to persist into the midcentury. Little wonder that Latitudinarian churchmen and Dissenters cooperated in trying to procure enforcement of the measures already enacted against drunkenness and swearing, while in 1698 the Commons petitioned William to issue another proclamation against vice. Jonathan Swift's *Project for the Advancement of Religion and the Reformation of Manners* (1709) condemned the "Wickedness of the Age," "because the Ruin of a State is generally preceded by an universal Degeneracy of Manners, and Contempt of Religion." The "Quality" and "the Vulgar" alike stand condemned in a catalogue of drunkenness, whoredom, fraud and avarice, atheism, blasphemy, a dissolute theater, and "pernicious Books . . . under the Pretence of free Thinking." Significantly, Swift appeals to the example of "the present Queen," from whose Court higher standards might permeate the nation, while he commends the institution of "the office of Censors [as] anciently in Rome."[71]

The initial establishment in London in 1690 of a "society" for the reformation of manners and morals was widely imitated. Low churchmen and Dissenters approved the concentration on morals and ethics without overmuch concern for theology, which might arguably be seen as suited to the religious temper of the age. A favorite text of sermons delivered to such bodies was: "Am I my brother's keeper?" Yet their impact, while not negligible, was of only twenty years' duration. Laurence Braddon, in 1721, remarked that "the Societies for Reformation of Manners met with great Discouragements, and could not produce what they desired." The appeal to informers to initiate prosecutions recorded in their minutes—incongruously reminiscent of Latimer's mid-Tudor appeal for "promoters"—awakened bitter resentment: sadly, "the informer soon became the symbol of the socities." Arguably, their very existence could be taken as "a criticism of Church and state, a criticism which the reforming preachers and pamphleteers made explicit." In face of this, the societies sometimes met with a reaction reminiscent of that which had followed the Restoration. Despite a perception that morality might serve as a social cement, and that lewd and vicious persons often displayed a levelling tendency, one contemporary identified the societies as but "seedlings of the good old cause and sprouts of the Rebellion of '41."[72] More generally, Daniel Defoe spoke for many in his *Poor Man's Plea* (1698, second edition), concerning proclamations and statutes "for a Reformation of Manners, and suppressing Immorality in the Nation," protesting to its rulers that such edicts have little "effective Power to punish *you* for your Immoralities, as they do us." Deploring commitment to the stocks or houses of correction for immorality, Defoe derides—in reminiscent phraseology—what he calls "Cobweb Laws, in which the small Flies are catch'd, and great ones break through." For in displaying bad behavior, "the Gentry are the Leaders of the Mob." Yet he grudgingly concedes that the societies are not devoid of beneficent effect. Finally, in 1709 Henry Sacheverell disputed any right "under the sanctified pretence of reformation of manners to turn informer, . . . *turn the world upside down* [my italics], . . . and dogmatically censure, rebuke, or advise in our neighbour's proceedings that don't belong to us, neither lie under the verge of our cognisance." Cato also rejected governmental meddling "with the private Thoughts and Actions of Men" that do not injure others. "Let People alone and they will take Care of themselves. . . . What is it to a Magistrate how I wash my Hands, or cut my Corns; what Fashion or Colours I wear, or what Notions I entertain, or what Gestures I use, or what Words I pronounce?"[73] By many, an earlier insistence on the ruler's responsibility for the moral and spiritual welfare of his subjects was now resented.

Equity and Social Justice

Turning to a wider issue, what views developed on the *moral* aspect of individual conduct in economic relationships and, contingently, about the duty of governance to intervene in the interests of equity and social justice? What now became of that idealist socioeconomic dimension of commonwealth ideology that had reached a maximum of expectation in the mid-seventeenth century? It has been argued that, despite occasional commonwealth-type appeals to channel self-interest into the common good, late-seventeenth-century philosophy replaced preoccupation with the duty and nature of governmental ameliorative intervention, which had been the basis of Tudor social theory, by a concern for individual rights devoid of corresponding social duties.[74] On the evidence of actual public policy, including statutes, there is little doubt of the justice of this generalization. But perusal of that literature that is in the commonwealth tradition points to the need for careful qualification. A number of tracts, by no means always utopian or even nostalgic in character, attest the survival, if only in a minority of thinkers, of earlier social and economic ideals.

I mentioned earlier the "royalist Utopia" of *New Atlantis*. The economic and social objectives of the "Providorans" and "Corregidorans" within R.H.'s ideal society are seen by Davis as reflecting not only those of an earlier era but also as indebted to Burton and to Hartlib. Measures to increase output and productivity—through enclosure, drainage, afforestation, fishing, and canal development—went side by side with a residual suspicion of the working of a free market. Above all, any possibility that those driven desperate by poverty would pose a threat to social stability must be eliminated by governmental intervention. A note of more radical nostalgia occurs in *The Ass: or the Serpent* by the Dissenter Thomas Bradbury. Attacking the luxury of the well-to-do and deploring the taxation of the poor, he also regrets the meekness shown by the latter in face of tyranny and laments the failure of "the Good Old Cause"—though it is not clear exactly what constituents of that cause still elicit his approval.[75]

Two anonymously published works that appeared within a couple of years of each other at the turn of the century exemplify the changing currents of ideas. *The Free State of Noland* appeared in a truncated version in 1696 but was completed, as promised, five years later. J. M. Patrick identifies it as projecting the utopian ideas "of an advanced and progressive Whig . . . applied to a hierarchical society." Certainly it is devoid of egalitarian idealism. Despite the claim "to be an unexclusive Aristocracy: Or, an Aristocracy and Democracy mixt together . . . whose Basis and Foundation is as large as the whole People," what is portrayed is in effect a plutocracy. The author is certain that "a Community that hath nothing fixt and stable, but all is in rotation, is like a Windmill without a Post. And there was never any such in the World." Harrington seems also to be clearly indicated as "a late English Author, who hath left us the Model of a Common Wealth. But his Model is merely Democratical: A Levelling sordid Democracy. For he chiefly aims at Equality, which in plain English is Levelling." Despite its inaccuracy, the message is clear. Yet at the same time the author is emphatic that "all Elections must be perform'd by private suffrage, which is the true Conserver of Liberty." A projected third printing, with treatment added of militia, highways, and the poor, apparently did not materialize.[76]

In almost total contrast (unless it be the blackest of self-parodies!) stands *An Essay Concerning Adepts,* published "by a Philadept" in 1698, "Adepts look upon all men to be Brethren and Equals . . . [and therefore] conclude that there should not be such an unequality among Christians as there is." Christian Adepts propose that "inferior Subjects . . . might well live all in common, with relation to the possession of the goods of the Earth and inferior Offices." The author envisages a scheme whereby "a Body of Christians, *excepting the higher among them* [my italics], lived in Community together, much as they do in Colleges." The earth being equally divided among them—"not Geometrically but according to the goodness of the Soil"—then all would be equally obliged to labour. Under the government of a lord of the manor, each parish should yearly choose its inferior officers. After the proviso that all dwelling-houses shall be exactly alike, there follow copious regulations for virtually every aspect of life—including a detailed prescription of diet. Next a note of severe anti-frivolity is sounded. "No Songs must be allowed on the Subjects of Love, nor drinking." Later in the work the reader encounters the provision that those convicted as "habitual profane Swearers have their Tongues bore through with a hot Iron"! This is in the context of a tirade against gaming and tippling-houses that includes the significant assertion "that the greatest Zeal shall consist in using force and the Arm of Power, not against Speculative Errors but against Vices and known Sins."77

Reverting to the central theme of the tract, "if there was an Equality among men . . . there would be no Thieves then as there is now, for there would be no occasion to Steal. . . . All men would have enough." This the author follows with an impassioned depiction of the present plight of the poor that might have come straight out of the writings of any mid-Tudor or mid-Stuart commonwealth idealist. Men labor as slaves and still see their children hungry. "Regard what miserable Victuals they feed upon, Bread as black as Soot and heavy as Lead, with . . . not a piece of Flesh-meat once in an Age, but often eat what some Dogs would not touch, when they see daily others fare sumptuously." With rags for clothing and no shoes for their feet, they may burn with fever without medical help and die in torment. Whatever its provenance, the book has no idealized picture of long-suffering poverty: "Poverty ordinarily makes those weak Christians ungentle and Peevish, always cross and angry; and causes them to live most unchristianly." Impossible in face of this to justify our wines, perfumes, and rich attire. Yet Adepts would not force all men to live in common. Sufficient, as yet, "that a Provision may be made that the poor may live more comfortably; . . . that a fixed rate may be Publicly set . . . to most things that are Sold, to avoid as much as possible Cheating and Lying in Buying and Selling; . . . that Physicians and Lawyers, as well as Divines, may have set stipends, that Justice and Physic may be Common and dispensed Gratis to all Men." After further pages on the need for austerity on the one hand and for setting all the poor on work on the other, the author concludes with the enigmatic observation concerning Adepts, that "I my self never saw one, that I know"!⁷⁸

Whatever its motivation, the voice of idealist social protest so strongly heard within the utopian context of this work was quite untypical of its age. Geoffrey Holmes has pointed out that the hundred or so pamphlets in the aftermath of the Sacheverell Riots are devoid of significant allusions to the plight of the poverty-stricken in London. Indeed, J. R. Jones is in no doubt that there was no challenge to the supremacy of the gentry and the clergy "from below, from their inferiors in the form of popular radicalism."⁷⁹ In general, those who contributed most clearly to the survival of commonwealth values in respect of civil, political, and religious liberties thought in a social context in terms of *individual* interests—with primacy accorded to property rights, to the virtual exclusion of the social duties to which an earlier era had attached so much importance. There was a shrinking of the commonwealth ideal. The former appeal *to* government to enforce an acceptable Christian moral code in social and economic relationships was replaced by a suspicion *of* government that saw any intervention not as an humanitarian guarantor of social rights but as an infringement of individual economic liberties. Arguably, increasing insistence on the rights of the political nation accompanied diminishing recognition of social responsibility for the rest of society. Caroline Robbins concludes that discussions of "the distribution of wealth . . . were pretty closely limited to . . . the old question of the stable state, and were not much concerned with the welfare of the individual as such."⁸⁰ Perhaps Molesworth's socio-economic objectives smack more of "Public Works" than of the "Welfare State."

Yet changes in social philosophy were not rapid. Thus, Willan discerned a potential conflict "betwixt publick and private Interests," Swift warned against MPs who might "prefer their own private Gain and Advancement before the publick Good," Toland urged that a representative must "lay aside all private Capacities [so that] he Votes for the whole Common-wealth," and *Vox Populi* insisted that a ruler "is more careful of the Publick-Good and Welfare, than of his own private Advantage." Yet that school of thought that identified economic processes with the natural order, not needing governmental intervention or social engineering, was becoming more assertive. Joyce Appleby cites the writer in 1696 who, describing sureties for good behavior as stronger bonds than conscience, religion, or honor, explains that "in these we are sure there may be Hypocrisy, but in Interest we know there is none." For such, "the commonwealth had become an aggregation of private wealth." Suspicion of the market as an inducement to breaches of a moral code gave way to veneration of an impersonal and effective regulator, conducive to optimum economic efficiency. The acquisitive instinct itself is no longer a lamentable tendency but an essential trigger to maximum use of resources. Yet it is oversimple to describe the work ethic as losing its religious provenance in thus becoming market-orientated. Margaret Jacob's monograph identifies an objective of Newtonian and Latitudinarian philosophy as the Christianization of social relations in an existing market society, indeed "to synthesize the operations of a market society and the workings of nature" so as to justify "the right of the individual to pursue his self-interest . . . for the benefit of the whole; nature is integral and harmonious."[81] More mundanely, in terms of state activity, the emphasis within mercantilism is now clear: government must nurture prosperity by procuring an environment favorable to enterprise. Accordingly, protection of "national" interests accompanied relaxation of industrial controls. Thus, guild and apprenticeship regulations often atrophied, while guilds themselves sometimes disappeared from certain towns. Hill discerns "a complete reversal of economic policy."[82]

Changing social attitudes are best exemplified in relation to the two great touchstones of earlier commonwealth idealism: property and poverty. In respect of the first, the mutinous rejoinder of some to the strictures of the mid-Tudor and mid-Stuart moralist—"May not I do what I list with mine own?"—had now become a confident assertion. Along with this went resolute defence of possession itself, as statutory punishment of theft became draconian. The reign of William and Mary saw the enactment of the death penalty for such crimes as shoplifting or the stealing of furniture by lodgers. Douglas Hay identifies "a system of criminal law based on terror" that, "more than any other social institution, made it possible to govern eighteenth-century England without a police force and a large army"—although, admittedly, the very prospect of such punishment sufficed without large-scale enforcement.[83] The ethos of the age was Baconian or Harringtonian, not egalitarian.

Yet minority voices still insisted on the social obligations of the property-owner and, indeed, of the businessman. Unsurprisingly, three cogent advocates of such duties may fairly be described as throwbacks to an earlier Puritan ideology. Isaac Barrow's sermon of 1671 perpetuates sixteenth-century standards. "For our goods . . . are indeed none of them simply or properly our own, so that we have an absolute property in them. . . . They are committed to us as Stewards." Indeed, "inequality and private interest in things . . . were the by-blows of our fall; sin introduced these degrees and distances; it devised the names of rich and poor; it begot these ingrossings and enclosures of things." Thus, poverty by God's Providence is *not* in itself contemptible, and "equity doth exact no less" than charitable relief. Again, as late as 1680, in his *Life and Death of Mr Badman*, John Bunyan's antihero beguiles his creditors and deceives his customers "by deceitful Weights and Measures." Condemning hucksters who buy up victuals wholesale before "making a prey of the necessity of the poor by retailing at unreasonable rates," along with "those vile wretches called Pawn-Brokers," Bunyan declares such miscreants "the pest and Vermin of the Common-Wealth." He does not hesitate to assert that "it is not lawful for a man to make the best of his own" if this entails exploiting one's neighbor's ignorance.[84]

In October 1691 (only two months before his death, the work remaining unpublished until the present century) the Reverend Richard Baxter wrote *The Poor Husbandman's Advocate to Rich Racking Landlords*. Baxter does not scruple to warn his readers that "the oppression of the poor Husbandmen in Germany by the Rich, made them hearken to Munzer and other seducers that bid them endure their slavery no longer." He goes on to declare that "the Husbandmen are the Stamen [i.e., warp] of the Commonwealth. All the rest do live by them"—yet their double burden of work and of poverty is made unbearable. The source of evil rack-renting lies in those whose "*Atheistical misconceit of their propriety* [my italics] hardeneth them. They think they may please themselves with their own as they list. As if they know not that there is no Absolute Propriety but God's." Pleading for a reduction of one-third in many rents, Baxter appeals to landlords "that you will regard the public welfare of the nation above any few particular cases." The landlords' own expenditure might readily be reduced if they would retrench their "needless and sinful charges for superfluities, prodigality and fleshly lust."[85] Again, this could have come straight out of a sermon by Latimer or Lever, but many now looked, like Mandeville, to such expenditure as generating employment!

As for the obligation of Christian charity traditionally linked with private property, the early modern era had witnessed a tendency—still within the Christian humanist tradition—to shift the discharge of that obligation from individual alms-giving to organized relief. The Elizabethan Poor Law that had emerged in response to the continued urging of humanitarian moralists combined with a realization of changing circumstances as yet remained the framework of relief and punishment. Whatever one's opinions as to the spirit and the success with which this system had been implemented in early and mid-Stuart decades, insofar as statutory enactment is an index of public attitudes there is not much dispute as to trends after 1660. The Act of Settlement of 1662, admittedly reflecting a period of dislocation, has been seen as enshrining the assumption "that a pauper was idle, vicious, and rightless."[86] Movement of the poor was controlled, minimal rates of relief were prescribed within the parish of settlement, and the workhouses were designed as places only of last and desperate resort.

The traditional link between property and poverty was changing its nature: what was commended was not so much the distribution of superfluities as Christian charity but rather the use of wealth and property to generate employment. This change was not rapid. The skeptical opinion that indiscriminate charity served only to nurture idleness was in no way new. But an at least purportedly analytical approach to relationships between population, employment, and national wealth was now gaining ground. Too much should not be made of this. The modern economic historian delineates the interaction of a number of crucial variables in helping to determine living standards. These include trends in population, supply of natural resources, the quality of techniques of production both in agriculture and in industry, and the levels of capital and enterprise available to secure their application. Such sophisticated analysis should not be looked for at the turn of the seventeenth century. But such notions as the relationship between population and employment opportunities, the impact of what would now be called comparative wage costs, and the significance of training and skills within the workforce, as well as the regularity and intensity of employment as influencing comparative productivity, are clearly identifiable. Most notably, in respect of the *supply* of a labor force, late Tudor and early Stuart fears that population was increasing too rapidly and outstripping both availability of employment and the means of subsistence had by the later decades of the seventeenth century given way to a desire for a larger population. This may well reflect the justice of the contention, regarding "population, economic resources and opportunities for respectable employment, . . . that between, roughly 1680 and 1714 they were brought into balance."[87] Certainly the tendency of an earlier age to urge that surplus population should emigrate now gave way to an advocacy of strictly disciplined treatment of the available working force as a means of maximizing its useful output.

Discussion of the provision of useful employment has of course been noticed in the early commonwealth literature. The Tudor and early Stuart eras had also seen a gradual acceptance that many of the destitute were victims not of divine providence but of defects in the economic functioning of the commonwealth that it was a duty of government to help correct. But by now the wheel has turned a full, if malignant circle: the pauper is seen neither as reflecting the will of God nor of some economic malfunction within society, but rather as the victim of his own sinful idleness—in which he should not be encouraged to wallow. Despite occasional evidence of continued allegiance to the more Christian aspects of its social and economic content, in this sense it is accurate to speak of a recession of the commonwealth ideal. Certainly the priorities of those described as Commonwealthmen have shifted. Thus, Caroline Robbins has urged that while "not insensitive to the state of the poor ... on the whole, Molesworth was inclined to blame poverty in part on original sin or idleness, and in part on inadequate political liberty."[88]

Within the writings of those who were primarily concerned with economic developments, and in particular with the problems of poverty and of employment, it is instructive to observe the swing and sway throughout these decades first as between an humanitarian and a draconian approach, and secondly between an appeal to public intervention and an advocacy of reliance on private initiative. An interesting assortment of motives appears in the brief tract entitled *Provision for the Poor* (1678) by R. Haines. Its subtitle alludes to "Reasons for The Erecting of a Working-Hospital in every County ... to Promote the Linen Manufactory." Such institutions, in which "the Engine ... may be used, which cannot be in private families," will greatly relieve parishes oppressed with the charge of supporting the poor. In particular, "these Working Hospitals will put an end to all vexatious and chargeable Suits and Controversies by which much money is spent between Parish and Parish, for settling and placing such as are chargeable." They will educate children in thrifty and industrious habits, for "undoubtedly Idleness in Youth is the Seed-plot of the Hangman's Harvest." The author is one of many to draw the contrast with Holland: the existence of such "Public-Work-houses" there in every city is the reason why "to one Pickpocket, Cutpurse, &c. in Amsterdam, there are a hundred in London; and to one sturdy Beggar in Holland (in time of Peace) there are four hundred in England."[89]

Not everyone would support the appeal to intervention by public authorities. One anonymous tract in 1675 alludes with tantalizing brevity to private profit-seeking as producing services as useful "as could proceed from the present Charity-State Government"! But the two were not considered mutually exclusive. In 1681 Thomas Firmin, a friend of Locke, wrote on the basis of his own experience in having "erected my Work-House ... for the Imployment of the Poor in the Linen Manufacture" that has relieved hundreds of poor families. *Some Proposals For the imployment of the Poor* describes the begging that follows idleness as "dishonourable to the Nation, and to the Christian Religion." Indeed this "wicked Trade of Begging [is] the great scandal of the Government of this Nation." Firmin is scathing about "those profligate Wretches called the running Camp, which every day pester our Streets; they are a People that one would think come from the Suburbs of Hell itself, a Dishonour to human Nature, a Shame to the Government." But for the deserving destitute he would institute "Fathers of the Poor" (as is reputedly the case in Dutch and French cases) to inspect their needs so that they do not perish at home for want of food, fire, physic, or clothing.[90]

As for the obdurately idle, "if any will not work, neither let them eat." Thus parishes should "set up a School in the nature of a Workhouse, to teach their poor Children to work in," remembering that "it matters not so much what you employ these poor Children in" as long as they are not inured to idleness. Yet as to the educational content of their training, "why, I pray, must a poor Boy that is destined for a Mason, Bricklayer, Shoemaker, or the like honest and necessary Trade, be taught to write as if he were designed for a Master in that Art; or so far in Arithmetic as if he were designed for a Merchant?" Enough, surely, that they are taught to read the Bible and acquire rudimentary skills in writing and arithmetic. Even within the context of the relatively humanitarian approach of Firmin, well might Charles Webster conclude that after the Restoration the idealistic educational schemes of the midcentury idealists were "relegated to the sphere of utopian phantasy."[91]

A Discourse touching Provision for the Poor by Sir Matthew Hale, published in 1683, is of quite exceptional interest, as being written by a former Lord Chief Justice. At the outset its author commends such provision as an act not merely of piety, but also "of great Civil Prudence and Political Wisdom . . . Where there are many very Poor, the Rich cannot long or safely continue such." At present, England sets a poor example, despite the existence of "very severe Laws against Begging [and] against Theft, possibly more severe than most other Nations." Continuing his criticism, which is all the more striking in view of its provenance, Hale asserts that "the prevention of poverty, idleness, and a loose and disorderly Education, even of poor Children, would do more good to this Kingdom than all the Gibbets, and Cauterization, and Whipping posts, and Jails." After reviewing "the Laws at present in force for the Relief and Imployment of the Poor," he concludes that the major defects consist in lack of consistent, or indeed of general application. Thus, "it is rare to see any Provision of a Stock in any Parish for the relief of the Poor." The remedy proposed is the creation within each county of "several Divisions" of associated parishes, which will then be able to afford a workhouse and the necessary stock. This will ensure that "no Person will have need to Beg or Steal"—although the author concedes that "there are a sort of idle People that will rather beg than work." Moreover, "the Wealth of the Nation will be increased, Manufacture advanced," and trade encouraged.[92]

Experience of a different sort is reflected in the writing of John Cary, a merchant of Bristol. *An Essay on the State of England*, published in that city in 1695, includes a section on the problems of labor. This touches on contemporary discussion of whether the allegedly high cost of English labor has some effect, the question of whether "the People of England [can] live on such low Wages as they do in other Countries," and the significance in this context of skills. As for begging by "swarms of idle Drones, [this] is now become an Art or Mystery, to which Children are educated from their Cradles," demonstrating abilities that "if better employed might be more useful to the Common-Wealth." Idleness derives from innate sloth and from the abuse of defective laws. Suggested remedies include the expansion of manufactures in well-run workhouses. Yet also, at this late date, Cary concludes concerning emigration, that "hundreds by going to those Plantations have become profitable Members to the Common-Wealth, who had they continued here had still remained idle Drones." He, too, is concerned with the burden of relief and the need for "taking care that the Poor's Rates be made with more equality in Cities and Trading Towns than they now are."[93]

Experience both as a well-to-do cloth merchant and as a participant in a Quaker fund for employing the poor underlay the proposals for *A College of Industry*, published by John Bellers in 1696. Bellers, who was later involved in a Quaker proposal to petition Parliament on the topic, was not an egalitarian or a utopian. While dedicated "to the Children of Light, in Scorn called Quakers," commending both their diligence and the fact that their poor are less vicious than others, his tract is clearheaded in its perception of the nature of poverty. Despite the draconian-sounding injunction at the outset that "the Sluggard shall be cloathed with Rags. He that will not Work, shall not eat," it is not short of humanitarian ideals as well as business instincts and innovative proposals. Bellers has been seen as an early advocate of the notion that, intrinsically, labor is more important than money. As for the poverty-stricken, he is in no doubt about "the Cries and Miseries of some, and Idleness and Lewdness of others." Yet, "the Labour of the Poor being the Mines of the Rich," it is in the latter's interest "to take Care of the Poor, and their Education."[94]

Yet, and most crucially important for his case, "however prevalent Arguments of Charity may be to some, when Profit is joined with it, it will receive most Money, provide for most People, hold longest, and do most good." Hence his central proposal which (despite a possible resemblance to Pockboy) established his status as a fully recognised pioneer of the principles of cooperative production—a status attested by the action of Robert Owen in reprinting and distributing a thousand copies of Bellers's *Proposals*. For once established, within its own ranks, "this College-Fellowship will make Labour, and not Money, the Standard to value all Necessaries by." For "Money in the Body Politick is what a Crutch is to the Natural Body, crippled." Yet despite the assertion that "the Poor thus in a College will be a Community something like the Example of Primitive Christianity, that lived in common," any suspicion of egalitarianism is quashed when one learns that "beyond Reading and Writing, a multitude of Scholars is not so useful to the Public as some think; the Body requiring more Hands and Legs to provide for, and support it, than Heads to direct it."[95]

Nor is any roseate image conveyed in Bellers's *Essay Towards the Improvement of Physick* (1714), which enunciates a literal version of the necessary medicine of discipline: "except the Poor are kept always Imploy'd when they are Well, they will be too Irregular, and their Sick will be too Numerous for the Rich to provide for." Nevertheless, the same tract includes proposals for the provision in or near London of "Hospitals for the Poor: if not one Hospital for each Particular Capital Distemper." These shall include one hospital for the blind and one for incurables. Pauper corpses should be made available for dissection. Moreover, purveyors of medicines should be permitted to prescribe for "such incurable Patients as are willing to follow their Prescriptions"—success, if repeated, to be rewarded by the state with a gratuity and even placement as a hospital physician![96] Such propositions may explain why Bellers is sometimes classed as a utopian; but in the present writer's opinion, visionary and impracticable as they may sometimes have been, Bellers directed his ideas toward what he believed to be the foreseeable future rather than toward some unreal fantasy.

No visionary dreams preoccupied Richard Dunning. Deploring idle beggars in 1685, he asserted that "their not demeaning themselves as useful Members of the Common-wealth ariseth from the neglect of those that should regulate them." His longer *Bread for The*

Poor (1698), printed in Exeter, was equally preoccupied with the allegedly excessive costs of poor relief in Devon. In his search for cheaper measures, without either waste or want, Dunning dismisses those who, in "an attempt for the better Imployment and Relieving the Poor, say there must be a Stock, a large House, &c." For in Devon "there are Tradesmen in or near every Parish, who have Stocks already. . . . Therefore here is no great need of more Stocks, but of reforming the looser sort, so as to make them honestly industrious." What are the real causes of an undoubted problem? First, "Profuseness in Diet"; secondly, "Idleness"; thirdly, "Giving excessive Pay." More complicated and sophisticated analysis follows. Thus, "several of the Poor have ordinarily one House apiece . . . which would conveniently serve three or four of them, and the same Fire, Candle-light, and Attendance that now serves but one might serve three or four. . . . Only their Unwillingness to have their Idleness, Filching, and Profuseness in Diet discovered makes them extreme averse against such Cohabiting." A list of remedies ensues, including the payment of any relief not in money but in kind—despite the general antipathy of the recipients toward this method. Moreover, "whosoever Receives Parish pay, or any Contribution, is to expect to wear the Badge, that so the fear thereof may keep them Submissive and orderly."[97]

An extract from the writings of the merchant and economist Sir Josiah Child, published in the year of his death (1699) as *A Method Concerning the Relief and Employment of the Poor,* is in close agreement with the views of Hale, who is also printed. Rebutting the charge that "now Charity is deceased," the author proposes a recognition that "he that gives to any in Want does well, but he that gives to Employ and Educate the Poor, so as to render them useful to the Kingdom . . . does better." The present radical error lies in leaving each parish to relieve its own poor. He repeats the notion of association for this purpose, and would set up "Fathers of the Poor" to take over from the justices of the peace. Their powers would include that to "erect petty Banks and Lombards for the benefit of the Poor," but also authority to send certain of the poor "beyond the Seas."[98]

Much more challenging in their tone, if limited in specific proposals, are the anonymously published *Reflexions upon the Moral State of the Nation* (1701). Particularly concerned with education, the author would commit its direction "in its whole latitude to the Councils of a standing Body of Learned Men." But in discussing what should be done for "the Children of the poorer sort" he writes in emotive and most revealing terms. Working schools for each sort of manufacture should be set up for "all the issue of those poor *proletar-*

ian [my italics—surely an early use of the word] families, who have been suffer'd hitherto to live more like rats and weasels and such like noxious vermin, than Creatures of human race." The ragged retinue of beggars, accompanied by the doleful cry of cripples along our streets dishonor our misgovernment—as does the national loss though idle hands.

> For let the wealth of our Country . . . be search'd to the bottom of that Mine from whence it springs: and it will appear to have its first formation in the hands of the laborious poor, who for all their pains are allow'd oftentimes no greater share out of it than what will keep them from present Starving. 'Tis to the weariness and watchfulness of these most useful and necessary limbs of human Society, the very hands and feet, and *a good part of the brains too* [my italics] of the political body, that the *Drones* and *Epicures,* the mere *Guts* and *Garbidge* of Mankind owe all their ease and luxury: and upon a just balance of the Account on both sides, the true *Political Arithmetic* will state it so, that those who possess the greatest share of the riches of the World are most indebted to those that have nothing; and that the faithful diligence of honest and ingenious Poverty is really the richest Treasure and safest *Bank of Credit* in any Nation. So that Beggary is not so much the infelicity of those what practise it, as a damage and disgrace to the Government that permits it.[99]

Some of the ideas expressed have of course been encountered earlier, but rarely if ever in so sharp and explicit a form or—purportedly at least—so directly related to economic realities rather than to religio-social idealism. The analysis of this unknown neo-Marxist ahead of his time seems to point ahead to another age. Meanwhile, it may also give us pause to wonder as to what lay beneath the surface of the apparent quiescence of the lower orders in the Augustan Age. Yet his was indeed a lonely voice—at least in print. Most of his readers would have been more inclined to favor the thesis that perhaps received its most savage expression in Defoe's *Giving Alms no Charity* (1704): that many of the poor were idle from choice. Defoe writes in direct opposition to a bill proposed by Sir Humphrey Mackworth (which in fact passed through the Commons but was thrown out by the Lords) to establish in every parish a manufactory financed by a parochial rate. Whether exercised through workhouses or through "parish-stock," such publicly-financed assistance, he argues, is not only undeserved but is also counterproductive, contributing to the destruction of the nation's trade and hence to an actual increase in "the Number and Misery of the Poor."[100]

The proposition that "no Man in England, of sound Limbs and

Senses, can be Poor merely for want of Work" leads to the conclusion that " 'tis a Regulation of the Poor that is wanted in England, not a setting them to Work." While begging by the impotent is indeed "a scandal upon the Country," begging by the able is "a scandal upon their Industry." Bluntly, "the reason only so many pretend to want Work is that they can live so well with the pretense of wanting Work, they would be mad to leave it and Work in earnest." Defoe himself has had offers of reasonably waged employment spurned by a lusty beggar. The position is only worsened by self-defeating proposals and misdirected charity, which lead to "enriching one poor Man to starve another, putting a Vagabond into an honest Man's Employment." Workhouse labor and production is nothing but a source of unfair competition. On a broader front, while conceding the reality of poverty by casualty or infirmity, Defoe identifies the other causes as luxury, sloth, and pride, and then depicts their incidence in a notorious passage: Not only is it true "that English Labouring People eat and drink, but especially the latter, three times as much in value as any sort of Foreigners of the same Dimensions in the World," but there is also "a general Taint of Slothfulness upon our Poor, there's nothing more frequent than for an Englishman to Work till he has got his Pocket full of Money, and then go and be idle, or perhaps drunk, till 'tis all gone, and perhaps himself in Debt; and ask him in his Cups what he intends, he'll tell you honestly, he'll drink as long as it lasts, and then go to work for more." In conclusion, " 'tis the Men that wont work, not the Men that can get no work, which makes the numbers of our Poor."[101]

Such attitudes are mirrored in Bernard Mandeville's *Essay on Charity, and Charity-Schools* (1723). Reflections on the reality of Christian charity here give place to the comment that "thousands give Money to Beggars from the same Motive as they pay their Corn-cutter, to walk easy." Much hospital-building may be ascribed only to pride and vanity. So much for motives. As for effect: "Charity, where it is too extensive, seldom fails of promoting Sloth and Idleness, and is good for little in the Commonwealth but to breed Drones and destroy Industry. The more Colleges and Alms-houses you build the more you may." The welfare of society, and the plenty and cheapness of its provisions, depend on the supply of a workforce that is "sturdy and robust and never used to Ease or Idleness," soon contented as to the necessities of life and ready to perform coarse labor all day because driven by need. Therefore, we must not educate the Working Poor "beyond what relates to their Calling" (*sic*—the word has moved far from its original religious context!). In particular, educational provision for "the Children of the Poor . . . incapacitates them ever after for doing the Labour which is their proper Province." It is time to dismiss "an unreasonable Vein of Petty Reverence for the Poor." Explaining that comparative wage costs as between two competing manufacturing nations depend largely on hours of work performed and consumption of food required to maintain the workers involved, Mandeville concludes of the English poor that "by bringing them up in Ignorance you may [insensibly] inure them to real Hardships."[102]

There could surely be no more explicit an abandonment of an earlier insistence that the image of God was found among the poor. Admittedly, many of his contemporaries recoiled from much of what Mandeville wrote—and not only on humanitarian grounds. Embedded within the somewhat confusing presentation of Lawrence Braddon's book on *The Regular Government, and Judicious-Employment of the Poor* (1721) are some clear-sighted observations. First, Braddon defines "the Poor . . . in a very large and comprehensive Sense; for thereby I mean, Not only they, who are Maintain'd by their respective Parishes, but all they, who . . . must Work, or Beg, or be Maintain'd." In principle, "that Government is defective, which suffers any People to be idle, who are willing to Work." The social problem of how "our Ignorant and Seditious Populace will be converted" into a productive force is matched by the economic challenge of "how all the Capable, but now Idle Poor, might be employ'd, without depriving the now Industrious Poor of any part of their Work or Wages." The author's vague if grandiose proposals for a "Corporation" that will accomplish this, as well as being able to "lend Money upon Pawns" and establish Colleges of Instruction, are perhaps less striking than his economic analysis. Braddon considers the relationship between the price of materials, wage levels and wage costs, and the price of goods. Significantly, "where Men are poorly paid for their Art and Industry," not only must they and their families live miserably, but as "their Wages are lessen'd, they must reduce their Expenses, and consequently buy the less in Bread, Beer, Flesh, Butter, cheese . . . [which] must affect all the Landed-Men.[103]

This is a splendid exemplification not only of the continuity— alongside the harsher advocacy of what may fairly be termed an "if it isn't hurting, it isn't working" approach—of sympathy for *The Miseries of the Poor*, but also of a realization that remedial action by government was not only socially desirable but also economically expedient.[104] Long ago, Charles Wilson questioned the picture "of a ruthlessly materialistic class which did not merely neglect but actively exploited the poor," citing in particular Josiah Child as propounding "a theory that comes near to equating national prosperity with the effective value of its labour." Much more recently, Daniel Baugh concurs in questioning the universal acceptance of a body of economic thought that "endorsed poverty and pointed toward a policy of strict and oppressive regulation of the poor"—though dominant, this was challenged by an attitude that derived chiefly from Christian ethics and was accordingly less influential at a political level. We have indeed encountered continued expressions of the ideal of Christian charity and of a special concern for the poor. But in Braddon, as a Child, what modern scholars would perhaps call macroeconomic analysis begins to be harnessed to the same cause. The judgment some thirty years earlier in a seminal article by A. W. Coats, that "the distinction between the productivity and the money cost of labour appears to have been generally overlooked" prior to the mid-eighteenth century seems slightly overstated. Meanwhile, those who wrote in an avowedly Christian context were not always devoid of economic insight. In 1728 Isaac Watts, defending Charity Schools and their educational contribution against the attacks of such as Mandeville, was to declare that " 'tis not menial Servants, but Mechanicks and Manufacturers that increase the Commodities, and thereby the Riches of the Nation."[105]

The moral and political implications of Mandeville's assertions proved equally repellent to such as John Dennis, minor poet and playwright. His *Vice and Luxury Publick Mischiefs* (1724) was a direct refutation of *The Fable of the Bees,* and a fine example of the survival of an earlier tradition in its declaration that "as Moral Virtue depends upon Religion, the Constitution and Liberties of Great Britain depend upon Moral Virtue." Scorning the assaults of this "Champion for Vice and Luxury" upon the Charity Schools, Dennis suggests that " 'tis worth while to consider, who the working Poor are, whom he would have kept Ignorant, at the same time that he encourages them to be vicious." For they comprise "one Half of the Free-born Inhabitants of Great Britain, and, perhaps, above one Third of the Electors of our Representatives." What better recipe therefore for the introduction of "Aegyptian Bondage" than Mandeville's prescription for "keeping vast Multitudes of the Inhabitants poor and ignorant." Citing Tillotson in favor of his case for Christian education in the schools, he urges that, while "Want gives no Man a Right to another's Property," it certainly gives him a right to what should be common to all: knowledge. Overall, then, "Vice and Luxury are so far from being publick Benefits, that they are public Mischiefs; that they are Political Infections and Civil Plagues [that may] destroy the Liberties of a Free People." While citing Sidney,

Dennis makes it clear that he does not wish to be smeared with "the odious Name of a Republican, and pass for an Assertor of Democratical Government." Nevertheless, he finds it manifest that "the Liberties of Great Britain were never so Precarious as they are at present from the Vice and Luxury and Corruptions of the People." High time, surely, to recollect the virtue of Temperance, "situate in the Golden Mean," and also to reflect that "the Influence of Example is greater than that of Precept; especially the Example of Superiors upon Inferiors."[106]

Thus, while its terminology is no longer ubiquitous, many of the constituent elements of an earlier commonwealth ideology survive. Yet Mandeville's readiness to divest economic actions of any moral or religious implications is more typical of general trends. The adoption of efficiency in administration rather than Christian motivation as the criterion for assessment of charity is obliquely echoed in Cato's contention that "a Penny given by an Atheist to a Beggar, is better Alms than a Half-penny given by a Believer." As for the Charity Schools, "they destroy real charity . . . and pervert the benevolence which would be otherwise bestowed upon helpless widows and poor house-keepers" unable to maintain their families. They compete unfairly with honest tradesmen, providing subsidized and inefficient employment to "the dregs of the people" as well as "breeding up beggars to be what are called scholars" who then demand "to be maintained in idleness . . . for their fancied accomplishments."[107]

Cato's restricted notion of how the state "by laudable Ways makes the human Condition easier than it is elsewhere" is crucially indicative. "Where Property is precarious, Labour will languish"; but "where-ever there is Employment for People there will be People, [and] there will be always Industry where-ever there is Protection."[108] Such considerations of policy now tend to replace the matrix of religious and social idealism within which commonwealth ideology had formerly been set. As noted, the usage made of the term "commonwealth" itself often suggests reversion to a (sometimes suspect) synonym for realm, kingdom, or the increasingly popular state. Its survival in politics, redeemed with difficulty from residual mid-seventeenth-century obloquy, is limited to expression of a yearning for probity, fair elections and honest government, and to a commitment to individual liberties—most notably in property and in religion. But despite contemporary indications of determined rearguard action, insofar as economic, social, and even moral issues are concerned, the lingering taint of egalitarianism on the one hand and the economic rationale of a more secular age on the other, combine with changing circumstances almost to obliterate the idealism that had been the most striking characteristic of the mid-Tudor and mid-Stuart Commonwealthmen. Their eighteenth-century successors thought in terms of political rectitude, not in those of social amelioration.

6

Autumnal Fruits and Falling Leaves: The Eighteenth-Century Commonwealthman

Changing Perspectives

THE CURRENCY OF THE TERM "COMMONWEALTH" PERSISTED THROUGHout the remainder of the eighteenth century—from Moyle through David Hume's essay on the *Idea of a Perfect Commonwealth* to *Unanimity in all parts of the British Commonwealth* by his admirer David Williams in 1778, and even to John Cartwright's *The Commonwealth in Danger* and William Hodgson's advocacy of a *Commonwealth of Reason*, both in 1795. As late as 1796 the radical John Thelwall was to reprint Moyle's work of 1726. But sadly, the analysis that Moyle had applied to the normal life cycle of any particular commonwealth had by then become appropriate to commonwealth ideology itself: "As all natural bodies are born with seeds of dissolution in their own frame, so these great artificial bodies, commonwealths, are founded with such original flaws in their first constitution as, in some periods of time, corrupt and dissolve them." The diminishing popularity of the organic analogy of society or of the commonwealth is perhaps indicative. The conservative and skeptical rationalist Hume starts his treatment of the topic by contrasting forms of government "with other artificial contrivances, where an old engine may be rejected," and even Edmund Burke called landed proprietors "the ballast in the vessel of the commonwealth."[1]

The question must at least be asked as to whether, by the mideighteenth century, the term "commonwealth"—apart from occasional service in pointing to the specter of sociopolitical leveling—had in general usage reverted to a synonym for realm? Probably this goes too far, for the ideals of personal freedom and political liberty therein embodied never disappeared, and were indeed to receive new impetus in the later decades of the century. Yet even within limited political parameters, the contention that by the 1720s the terms Commonwealthman and Real Whig had become virtually indistinguishable remains significant. Within a wider perspective, adapting Moyle's analogy, it may well be argued that those roots of commonwealth ideology that had nurtured its growth in earlier centuries no longer found their necessary sustenance in either the circumstantial or the philosophical soil of Hanoverian England. Most crucially, assessment of the social duties of government had changed, reflecting the shift in balance between an emphasis on individual rights and recognition of collective responsibility. As for religion, the gradual abandonment of the idea that government must preserve the doctrinal unity of the commonwealth had opened the door to religious liberty—subject only to *political* considerations. Admittedly, much concern continued to be expressed about the moral standards of the age, but this was increasingly related to the preservation of good order in this world rather than to the prospect of salvation in the hereafter. In respect of the traditional commonwealth assumption of the duty of government to intervene in social and economic affairs so as to preserve Christian values in personal relationships—to enforce equity and curb the selfish exploitation of property rights where this involved the exploitation of the poor—the general ethos of the time ran in a contrary direction. Eighteenth-century Methodism has been described as "the Puritan ideal reborn, shorn of its political radicalism";[2] it might as accurately be said that now a concept of the commonwealth had re-emerged, shorn of its social idealism.

Such generalizations demand scrutiny. So, too, does the assertion that the term "commonwealth" became irrelevant to the sphere of practical politics—concern even with this shrunken ideal being found in the writings of those who sought to theorize about rather than participate in statecraft. Moreover, it is of course misleading to consider the eighteenth century as a unity. What has rather sweepingly been termed "the notorious complacency and conservatism of politics in the reign of George II"[3] was followed by a succession of crises, internal and external, during the decades after 1760. Throughout the first era, the ideal of the commonwealth remained the subject of sporadic discussion, with no prospect of its implementation in practical politics. The later crises served not only to revive attempts at realizing certain of its political prescriptions, but ultimately to reveal its effective disintegration. It will therefore be both pertinent and convenient to relate examination of its fortunes to each of the periods identified.

Before so doing it is essential to examine, however briefly, the political and constitutional as well as economic and social background to ideological discussion. The seventeenth-century trinity of constitutional and dynastic upheavals had been followed by an at-first precarious and then a gradually more stable equilibrium—whether one chooses to speak of stability or of stasis. While some historians have demurred at the description "Age of Oligarchy," it seems difficult to contest the justice of G. H. Guttridge's summation that "the reluctant revolutionaries of 1689 became the complacent conservatives of 1750, and to them Whiggism stood less for the principles which had produced the Glorious Revolution than for the society which it had inaugurated."[4] Certainly, those contemporaries who professed commonwealth ideals had little good to say about a governing establishment that allegedly owed its authority neither to real nobility of birth nor to any distinction in ability—nor yet to any genuine representation of the people's will. Springing from an alliance between power and wealth, it seemed hardly surprising that these— rather than any ideals—became also its objectives.

Surely beyond dispute, the striking expansion (both in absolute and in relative terms) of the size of the electorate that had distinguished an earlier era now ceased. Moreover, by the middle of the century a now proportionately diminishing electorate functioned only intermittently. Speck has written of "the circumvention of the electorate both by the Septennial Act and by the growth of oligarchy in the constituencies"—where the Last Determinations Act of 1729 had frozen existing franchises. When one adds to the real growth of population that dated from circa 1740 some recent sanguine estimates of increasing literacy, then the gradual re-emergence of a "political nation *manqué*," with an informed interest in political issues from which it was virtually excluded, cannot be ignored. The readiness of a few recent historians to accept the case for "virtual representation" was not shared by all contemporaries.[5] Virtual representation would continue to be tolerable only so long as its fruits remained acceptable. In the short or medium term, riot might serve as a sufficient safety valve for virtual representation; but this would not last forever.

It could be urged that the Riot Act of 1715 controlled the safety valve just as the Septennial Act subdued the electorate; yet the fact that the "Venetian Oligarchy" went in fear of riot but not of revolution is indeed indicative. Despite the continual and endemic suspicion of Jacobite plots until the midcentury, the dread of an overmighty monarch had almost been eliminated; but this had not yet been replaced by that of "democracy" as a genuine prospect. The riots that frequently occurred were triggered by the immediate impact either of economic hardship or of real or fancied grievances. These ranged from food prices, enclosures, excise, or even turnpikes to such pseudo-religious issues as evoked the Sacheverell, the Jewish naturalization, or the Gordon Riots. None of them was fueled by aspirations for a sociopolitical revolution. Much has been written about the objectives, organization, and conduct of eighteenth-century riots, particularly about the "moral economy" of the English mob. But there is general agreement that the professed purposes of the rioters were almost always conservative, not innovatory. It has plausibly been deduced that the general rectitude of the existing hierarchical social and political order was just as much taken for granted by those excluded from the political nation as it was by their oligarchical superiors.[6]

Any such quiescence must be related to several economic trends that characterized the period before circa 1760. Modern scholarship has identified a minimal overall population growth between 1660 and the early 1740s; thereafter, sustained expansion recommenced. Alongside increasingly efficient food production in the countryside and expanding employment opportunities in the industrial sector, this had thus far helped to produce a lengthy period of gradual improvement in *real* wages—except for one vital decade that will concern us later. Thus, apart from the occasional incidence of poor harvests or of short-term slumps in employment prospects, those long-term pressures on living standards that might in theory produce compelling demands for political or social change (as distinct from sporadic rioting) were not present. Paul Langford's conclusion that "with real wages at a relatively high level, poverty was attributed to temporary misfortune or culpable fecklessness" has a familiar ring.[7]

Hence the contention that up to the midcentury "the lower and lower-middling orders of society, though ready enough to appeal to a libertarian heritage, . . . were still inhibited by limited political consciousness and inbred social assumptions."[8] Nevertheless, there is considerable evidence, perhaps most notably in a number of publications in the years immediately following the debate (itself most revealing) on a proposed repeal of the Septennial Act in 1734, for a body of opinion that resented the sociopolitical arguments for continued exclusion from the political nation of "the people." Yet it remains the case that the almost total absence of idealism at the top of the social hierarchy, and of conscious pressure for change from the lower orders, goes far to explain the near-quiescence by the midcentury of the more challenging aspects of commonwealth ideology. This impression may be tested by the touchstone of commonwealth-type notions of equity and of social obligations of an earlier era: the concept of property. Here, almost symbolically, as the electorate (at least proportionately) shrank in size, so did the list of capital crimes against property increase. By 1740, even a child could be hanged for theft from the person of a handkerchief worth over one shilling. Between 1688 and the last quarter of the eighteenth century the number of capital offences quadrupled. Despite notorious instances of evasion by commonsense jurors, the intention of the "Bloody Code" is clear.

Little wonder at the identification of property as the only acceptable criterion of any claim to political participation, or that electors themselves "regarded their franchises, as indeed did the Courts, as a kind of personal property."[9] Little wonder either that the legislation enacted by the representative body was concerned not only to safeguard the ownership of property but also to increase individual freedom in its exercise by removing much of what was seen as the interfering paternalism of the Tudor and Stuart eras. But, while public and restrictive legislation waned, private and permissive or "enabling" legislation burgeoned. Enclosure and turnpike trust legislation, motivated by private profit thinly veiled under a cover of the advancement of the public interest (to be fair, no new conjunction!), was to advance alongside the abandonment of many industrial restrictions enforcing standards. In the economic as well as the political sphere the philosophy of individual rights attained its apogee in the Hanoverian years. Political liberty was sought, by the Commonwealthmen or Real Whigs, in order to guarantee civil and religious liberties, *not* as a device for ensuring the pursuit of social and economic equity, as had been the case for many earlier commonwealth idealists. The Christian conscience of society had not disappeared. But its resurgence in many manifestations either of individual philanthropic activity or of voluntary organizations dedicated to religious, educational, or charitable objectives is significant. In many minds, *governmental* intervention should be related primarily to the preservation of security and good order, its success to be measured by the criteria of expense and efficiency. Against the background of such general trends the evolution of commonwealth ideology may now be considered in more detail.

1727-1760

When historians of political thought look back to the period 1727-1760 for any evidence of democratic political or of ameliorative social thinking they often relate such discoveries to the context of "early radicalism" or to the development of "a nonconformist social conscience." Yet paradoxically it has also been suggested that by the mid-1740s "Jacobitism had accumulated so many of the social-cum-constitutional grievances on top of its original, dynastic premise, that it had insensibly become a neo-radical movement." Whether or not in some respect it may be considered as usurping or as overlapping the commonwealth ideology of the past, after the midcentury of course Jacobitism was virtually dead. By contrast, and whatever one's reservations as to the balance therein between lip service and the survival of a vigorous ideology, the commonwealth tradition and terminology endured. Thus, while Clark alludes to "a single generation of radicals" extending from Molesworth to Moyle,[10] so too the influence of the Commonwealthmen of the reign of George I extended into the midcentury decades and, together with writings of that era, pointed ahead to the work of Richard Price, David Williams, and John Cartwright. Moyle's work on the subject of *The Honest Elector,* written in collaboration with Anthony Hammond at the time of the passing of the Septennial Act, was republished in 1747, as was Toland some ten years later.

Another element of continuity—this time of ideas from an even earlier age—is found in the enduring appeal of the teachings of Harrington. Of particular, indeed peculiar interest is *A Dissertation on the Civil Government of the Hebrews* (1740) by the Nonconformist divine Moses Lowman. This interpretation of "the Hebrew Commonwealth," effectively confuses ancient Israel with *Oceana* in its commendation of agrarian laws designed to preserve the balance of the nation and of a rotation in office so as to preclude potential ministerial abuse. Lowman identifies the Hebrew government as designed "to serve the common and general Ends of all good Governments, to protect the Property, Liberty, Safety, and Peace of the several Members of the Community." Crucially, "Property is the natural Foundation of Power, and so of Authority. . . . If the Property be generally divided near equally among all the Members of the Society, the true Power and Authority of such Government will naturally be in all the Members." Thus, "the very Foundation of the Hebrew Constitution, was an equal Division of the Land." The devices of the Agrarian Law, rotation of the militia, and rotation of the representatives ensured that "the Balance of the Hebrew Government was so well fixed." Yet Lowman is keenly aware of the danger of "ambitious and restless Spirits" in all ages, and of the need to ensure that places in government are "rather places of Burthen than of Profit."[11]

Preoccupation with the allegedly corrupting influence of perceived oligarchical trends, in particular with an almost obsessive distrust of the influence of the executive over the legislature, continued throughout the midcentury. While *The Honest Elector,* appearing in 1747, with its "Unerring Reasons For the Prevention of Chusing Corrupt Members To serve in Parliament," contained a side-thrust at the joint-stock principle as a gateway to *commercial* corruption, its main concern was the dreadful dangers that threatened if the electoral system itself, "this Bulwark of our Liberties be undermined by Bribery and Corruption." Yet divergent views emerged about what oiled the wheels of the system. James Thomson's poetic sketch of *Liberty* (1736) deplored that

> Shameless pens for plain corruption plead,
> The hired assassins of the commonweal![12]

Samuel Johnson's verses, *London* (1738), scorned the devotion "to Vice and Gain" of those "whom Pensions can incite / To vote a Patriot black, a Courtier white." But contemporaneously William Arnall (in Walpole's pay!) could declare *Opposition no Proof of Patriotism* (1735) and ask "can government exist without places, and men to fill them?" The need for what John B. Owen terms "constitutional lubricant" was recognized by David Hume, writing of "Influence" in 1741 that "some degree and some kind of it are inseparable from the very nature of the constitution, and necessary to the preservation of our mixed government."[13]

Much of this debate coincides with that explored by Gunn in *Factions No More*: contention as to the danger from "factions" and as to the respectability of "parties." Perhaps appropriately, the field remains disputed by modern historians: thus, while Speck has suggested that "the rage of party was superseded by the strife of faction," Clark finds it obvious "that the old parties survived into the 1750s." In general terms, despite a traditional tendency to see opposing factions as inimical to stable government, and indeed as in some sense disloyal to the commonwealth, it may be argued that by now some perceived an analogy between the "grumbling hive" in economic affairs and the existence of political conflict. Just as the competitive pursuit of selfish commercial advantage helped to maximize profitable output, so a healthy rivalry between politicians might be a safeguard against the erosion of civil and political liberties. Indeed, Dorothy Marshall has suggested that "the growth of His Majesty's Opposition as a recognised part of the machinery of government is one of the major constitutional developments of the eighteenth century."[14] Of course, this development was of long gestation, and the debate on party continued until the time of Edmund Burke.

In a couple of contributions to *The London Journal* in 1732, "F. Osborne" pseudonymously conveyed a different interpretation of the commonly much-maligned "factions." He argued that "in Free Governments there are Factions of all Sorts" both in Church and in State: and "the Good of Free Governments with Faction is infinitely greater than the Good of Arbitrary Government without Faction." For "in those Countries where there is no Opposition, there is a Dearth of Liberty and publick Virtue." Again, in 1734, "all free Countries will always have Parties; . . . for all Power is subject to Abuse; and all Men in Power, even the best, if not check'd and controul'd will be apt to leap the Bounds of Law and Reason, so that Parties and Oppositions are often useful to the Publick." In 1743, in his preface to his translation of an extract from Polybius, Edward Spelman declared that "in all free Governments there ever were, and ever will be Parties." Indeed, parties "are not only the Effect, but the Support of Liberty," their contentions keeping ministers upon their guard and making the people "the judges of every contest." Two years earlier, in a typically judicious survey, David Hume, while pointing to the complications of "Court" and "Country" and to changes in approach consequent upon possession of or exclusion from power, asserted that "there are parties of *principle* involved in the very nature of our constitution"—though admittedly "these parties are very much fomented by a difference of *interest*," which may become the dominant motive to the heads of parties.[15]

Significantly, *A Dissertation upon Parties* (1735) has been seen by Professor H. T. Dickinson as perhaps the greatest work of Henry St. John, Lord Bolingbroke, to whom I must now turn. In his case an era of leading involvement in government had been abruptly followed by disgrace and a period of exile. Neither contemporaries nor historians display doubt about the defects of his character; yet as to the quality of his writings and ideology there was and is dispute. Nonetheless, Bolingbroke is one of the very few leading practitioners of politics in this era who may plausibly be included within the commonwealth tradition—although the gulf between theory and practice suggests that he be cast in the role of antihero of commonwealth ideology. Isaac Kramnick points to the reluctance of Caroline Robbins to include him in a commonwealth context at all.[16] Yet his writings, and those of a fairly close circle of friends and acquaintances such as Pope, Gay, and Swift, exemplify the survival into the midcentury of what one may designate as a retrospectively nostalgic version of the social and economic dimensions of commonwealth paternalism, alongside much of early eighteenth-century "Real Whig" political ideology. The existence in uneasy juxtaposition alongside "Tory paternalism" of elements that were to be seized upon by end-of-the-century radicalism points ahead to the ultimate disintegration of an earlier commonwealth ideology.

Bolingbroke's periodical, *The Craftsman*, first appeared in December 1726, soon after his return from exile, and for more than a decade was the spearhead of the anti-Walpole press. Much of the contents of such works as *The Spirit of Patriotism* (1736), the *Idea of a Patriot King* (authorized publication in 1749), and *Some Reflections on the Present State of the Nation* (1749) first appeared in its pages. Bolingbroke himself became the focus of a purportedly "Patriot" movement but, though he lived until 1751, his influence waned after Walpole's fall. An eclectic but inconsistent political philosopher, his concept of society, and of any form of contract on which it might be based, was a throwback to Elizabethan or even late-medieval notions of the commonwealth. Dickinson identifies an "aristocratic and paternalistic theory of government, that followed naturally from his theory of the Great Chain of Being, with its hierarchical order of society."[17] While his critics discern propaganda dressed up as history or philosophy (and this may hardly be denied in his anti-Walpole polemics), much of his writing is of particular relevance to a waning commonwealth ideal—to which he pays repeated tribute. It may well be argued that his own political frustration led Bolingbroke, himself no utopian, to propound at length an unrealistic, outdated, and utopian solution to society's problems, and that his nostalgic and paternalistic version of commonwealth ideology ran into another cul-de-sac alongside that of the Real Whigs.

Nevertheless, it is fairly urged that, while touching greatness neither as statesman nor as philosopher, Bolingbroke's significance as an outstandingly perceptive political analyst has often and ironically been obscured by historians' own perception of his personal ambition and lack of integrity—a pattern noted earlier in the canon of "commonwealth" statesmen, as has been the charge of diagnosis of the disease without prescription of an effective remedy. Much of traditional commonwealth imagery recurs in Bolingbroke's own pessimistic prognosis, especially in his preoccupation with what is identified as the decay or even dissolution of society. Thus over-powerful financial institutions are described as "monstrous members and societies in the Body politic, [possessing] bodies, but no souls, nor consequently consciences," while a letter in 1739 asks rhetorically "are we not in the dotage of our commonwealth, my Lord?" Bolingbroke echoed many who had gone before in declaring that "the best instituted governments, like the best constituted animal bodies, carry in them the seeds of their destruction: and, though they grow and improve for a time, they will soon tend visibly to their dissolution."[18]

His two outstanding works may not inaccurately be described as devoted, in turn, to shrewd analysis of current ills and to a nostalgic and unrealistic remedy. *A Dissertation upon Parties,* addressed to Walpole, attacks the joint evils of faction and corruption. An evil minister who chooses "to govern by division, and by faction" has established a corrupt dependency of Parliament upon the Crown. Within this regime of venality and prostitution, "abilities to serve the commonwealth will be an objection to preferment"! In face of attempts, by its prolongation, to corrupt Parliament, "the re-establishment of annual, or at least of triennial" elections is crucial. In principle, a mixed constitution, the "three estates balancing one another," is ideal. For "absolute monarchy is tyranny; but absolute democracy is tyranny and anarchy both." Nevertheless, Bolingbroke derides the fear that the House of Commons "should usurp more power than belongs to them, and establish a kind of democratic tyranny"; the real danger comes from "the adulation and servility of parliaments, which are the necessary consequences of corruption and dependency." Above all, "the collective body of the people . . . delegate, but do not give up; trust, but do not alienate their right and their power." Only the people's own degeneration can destroy the British Constitution.[19]

By 1738 Bolingbroke professes his conviction that this point of depravation has been reached, so that a "way of salvation will not be opened to us, without the concurrence, and the influence, of a Patriot King." He will recognize that God "has made our happiness dependent on society; and the happiness of society dependent on good or bad government"—a striking affirmation of commonwealth paternalism for the mid-eighteenth century. But, since "the safety of the commonwealth is ill provided for, if the liberty be given up, [and] the good of the people is the ultimate and true end of government," a Patriot King will distinguish "between his rights, and those of his people: he will look on his to be a trust, and theirs a property." By now, only such, the most powerful of all reformers "can save a country whose ruin is so far advanced," so that "a new people will seem to arise with a new king." Governing "like the common father of his people," he will espouse no party, for "party is a political evil, and faction is the worst of all parties. The true image of a free people, governed by a Patriot King, is that of a patriarchal family, where the head and all the members are united by one common interest."

Eschewing the spirit of faction, as was done "in the days of our Elizabeth," the monarch will unite his people, so as to "approach as near as possible to these ideas of perfect government, and social happiness under it."[20]

This is perhaps Bolingbroke's most important work, not in respect of any alleged impact on George III, but in its combination of immediate political discernment with a distinctive social philosophy. Contemporary decay is seen as a consequence not only of corruption and faction, but also of a rejection of an ordered hierarchy. Not believing that man entered upon a social contract primarily to protect his selfish property rights, Bolingbroke deplores the current emphasis upon individual interests at the expense of the common good. Frustrated in his efforts to create an effective Country Party, he now turns to a Patriot King who will accomplish reform not by institutional remodeling but by giving a moral example from above. It seems hard not to detect echoes—whether conscious or not—of Elyot and of Erasmus in such an appeal. Yet any tendency to dismiss Bolingbroke as a mere purveyor of frustrated nostalgia, or alternatively as "a frightened Harringtonian"[21] who realized that the balance of possessions had shifted beyond his *desiderata,* is over-hasty. First, much of his constitutional and political analysis was to resurface, with avowed tributes, in sources as diverse as David Williams, the SCI, Montesquieu, such Americans as Jefferson and John Adams—and even the mid-twentieth-century Conservative Party! Secondly, his criticisms of contemporary social values, and the grounds upon which they were based, were shared by a coterie of some distinction, including Alexander Pope, John Gay, and Dean Swift.

Pope, a personal friend of Bolingbroke, whom he often visited and to whom he dedicated his *Essay on Man* (1733–34), was in close sympathy with many of his philosophical ideas and certainly with his hierarchical concept of society. All things are subject to "the laws of *Order,*" joined in "that Chain which links the immense design." Ideally, based upon "Order, Union, full Consent of things"—

> The rich is happy in the plenty giv'n,
> The poor contents him with the care of Heav'n.

Within this integrated frame of society, God and Nature conspire to bid "Self-love and Social be the same." But alas, Pope does not feel able to extend his oft-cited injunction, "Whatever *is,* is *Right,*"[22] to the present political mores. Indeed, *The Dunciad* (1728) was a direct attack upon Walpole:

6: AUTUMNAL FRUITS AND FALLING LEAVES 269

> Tyrant supreme! shall three Estates command,
> And Make One Mighty Dunciad Of The Land!

Pope's *Epistle to Bathurst* (1733) deplored the influence and power of money; he shared with its recipient the fear "that this power had been institutionalized and enabled to command the commonwealth." Money can pocket states and fetch and carry kings. A splendid thrust alludes to

> Blest paper credit! last and best supply!
> That lends corruption lighter wings to fly.

Well might the poem be termed a Christian and aristocratic humanist reply to Mandeville.[23] Bathurst himself, in *Some Reflections on The Present State of the Nation* (1749), was to express a paternalist/commonwealth sentiment in scorning such taxes as excise, which bear hardest on poor laborers—whose masters, exploiting the product of their work, should pay the whole.

A lesser if still distinguished poet, John Gay, shared Pope's contempt for the vitiating effects of financial and commercial interests not only in respect of probity in government, but also as regards all the values of society. His best-known work, *The Beggar's Opera* (1728), lampoons an entire age in which the landed gentry and the poor are bracketed as victims of a corrupt and artificial milieu. A member of Macheath's crooked gang protests: "Why are the Laws levelled at us? are we more dishonest than the rest of mankind?" Peachum concedes that in one respect this may apply, "because, like Great Statesmen, we encourage those who betray their Friends." Elsewhere, Gay clearly associates Walpole and Mandeville in derision:

> A bee of cunning, not of parts,
> Luxurious, negligent of arts,
> Rapacious, arrogant and vain,
> Greedy of pow'r, but more of gain,
> Corruption sow'd throughout the hive—
> By petty rogues the great ones thrive.[24]

Closely akin to Bolingbroke and Gay in expression of distaste for, and in his case ridicule of, contemporary trends was Jonathan Swift. The Principal Secretary of the realm of Lilliput (one destination of *Gulliver's Travels*, 1726) explains the support of the monarch in excluding the party of "High-Heels" from office in favor of "low Heels." Significantly, he says, "we compute the Tramseckan, or High-Heels, to exceed us in Number; but the Power is wholly on our

Side." In a separate dispute, "the Books of the Big-Endians have been long forbidden, and the whole Party rendered incapable by Law of holding Employments," because of their heretical mode of opening eggs. Meanwhile, the ruler of Brobdingnag is appalled to deduce from his visitor's panegyric of his country "that Ignorance, Idleness, and Vice are the proper Ingredients for qualifying a Legislator. The Laws are best explained, interpreted, and applied by those whose Interest and Abilities lie in perverting, confounding, and eluding them," and that the lines of originally tolerable institutions have been blotted and erased by corruption.[25]

Walpole in turn had his own cohort of not negligible propagandists, including Thomas Gordon, whom he bought over. But perhaps the most forceful attack upon Bolingbroke was that uttered by Sir Robert himself in the debate on a proposed repeal of the Septennial Act in 1734. An excoriating passage depicts "an anti-minister, ... of so great and extensive parts" that he deems himself alone as fit to govern and suborns other disappointed and malicious men to spit out his venom. But of more general significance is the evidence in this debate of opinion about the correlation between the frequency of elections and the propriety or desirability of the people exercising any influence upon the legislature. Thus Sir John St. Aubyn remarks that "it has of late been denied, that the people have a right of remonstrating to us. It has been called an unjustifiable controul upon the freedom of our proceedings. But then, let them have more frequent opportunities of varying the choice of their representatives." In the ensuing exchanges charges of corruption and even an advocacy of annual elections were countered by depictions of "the nation in a continual ferment," and repeal was defeated. Walpole, alluding to "Faction and Sedition," conceded that "in monarchical and aristocratical governments, it generally arises from violence and oppression but in democratical governments, it always arises from the people's having too great a share in the government."[26]

Clearly, his sentiments were those of the majority of members. Again, in a debate in the Lords in 1738 on a motion for "Reduction of the Army," the lord chancellor declared that "it is only among the very dregs of our people, that these discontents, and this spirit of mobbing and rioting prevail." If such are allowed to "prescribe to, or controul the legislative authority of the kingdom ... not only our present establishment, but government itself must be at an end. Anarchy and confusion must ensue, and from that anarchy, as has been once our fate already, one of the worst sort of tyrannies will certainly spring up." Most dangerously, "many of our modern Jacobites have learned to disguise themselves, by assuming the characters of lovers of liberty." In a debate in the Commons on a "Motion for Annual Parliaments" in 1745, one speaker stated plainly that "my argument is founded upon the supposition of the people being generally in their nature corrupt."[27]

Yet a sampling of the discussion of such topics in the pamphlet literature of these decades yields a rather different picture. William Hay's *Essay on Civil Government* (1728) pursues a balanced approach. Thus, "in a Monarchy, the Liberty of the People is not so well secured; nor in a Commonwealth, their Tranquillity: the first . . . may degenerate into oppression and Tyranny; the last, into Faction and Anarchy." Again, it is not always "Equitable nor Prudent for the People to have recourse to Arms." A partial anticipation of Rousseau concedes that "in a Democracy, the People would certainly pursue their own Good if they knew it; but they are generally mis-led by Artifice and Insurrection to mistake it." Nonetheless, Hay remains faithful to many commonwealth values of an earlier era. "The Publick Good was the End for which men entered into Civil Society." Thus, government has a duty to enact "good Laws concerning Education, that their Subjects may receive an early Tincture of Virtue and Morality, and especially of Religion"—though without doctrinal prescription. A utilitarian as well as humanitarian reflection on capital punishment observes that thereby "a Member is taken from the Commonwealth, who by his Labour might continue useful" if corrected. Hay, an MP for twenty years, made two abortive efforts at statutory Poor Law reform.[28]

In 1737, however, George Fothergill, preaching at Oxford on the anniversary of the martyrdom of Charles I, pointed to *The Danger of Excesses in the Pursuit of Liberty*. His sermon made it clear that "Legal Liberty then is all that can be demanded by Members of Society." Deploring anything that sows "the seeds of Discontent, and fomenting Rebellion," Fothergill adduces the present solemn remembrance as demonstrating "the pernicious Consequences of Liberty pursued too far," urged on by "the Cry of the infatuated Multitude." He concludes with an encomium of the present Constitution, which proffers "a just Authority and a sober Liberty."[29] Yet in sharp contrast with this obdurate wish to batten down the hatches, a number of publications between 1740 and 1744, temperately expressed, demonstrate a train of thought that rejects both this contempt for ordinary people on the one hand, and a supine acceptance of the authority of Parliament as at present constituted on the other.

The Livery-Man: or, Plain Thoughts on Publick Affairs was anonymously published in 1740. Its objective was "to show that the People of Britain in general have an indubitable Right to canvass publick Affairs, to express their Sentiments freely, and to declare their Sense of any Grievances under which they labour." Its author is incensed to see "those Insects, which are bred out of the Corruption of Power, ... Folks who call themselves Friends to Liberty, treating the People daily in terms of Disrespect." Nor is he appeased by the explanation of these "Apologists for Power ... that they intend only the meaner Sort"—such as have no vote. "For after all, where are these mean People? Is there a Man in England who does not either drink Beer, wear Shoes, or now and then smoak a Pipe of Tobacco? Can he do any of these without contributing to the Support of the Government? and is it not a fair Compliment to the Government to say, that it is supported by the Mob? ... It follows that every the meanest Man in the Kingdom has an Interest in the Publick." It seems difficult not to detect echoes of Putney here. As to liberties as a birthright, do these not pertain to the son of the peasant, or of the honest man who lost his last shilling in 1720, as much as to infamous Directors who kept by means of perjury money obtained by fraud? The author scorns the charge of being "an Incendiary, a Disturber of the People." This should be laid at the door of those at the helm who "pursue only what they take to be their particular Interests"; in face of their example, little wonder that "the People, in a Fit of Madness, will immerse themselves in Luxury." Attributing the Revolution itself to liberty of the press, he finds it preposterous "to treat all Enquiries as Acts of Sedition." As for local assemblies, "the Design of these little Governments is not to raise petty Republicks, independent of the Commonwealth," but to secure local objectives—as in the City of London. The existence of genuine grievances "is the true Cause why Tumults are so frequent." It is fatuous to argue "that the Heats of Factions are injurious to the Nation, and that it is for the Good of the People, the People should be restrained ... [thus] treating the major Part of a Nation as if they were Children, and Children not over-sharp."[30]

Nor was this publication a solitary maverick. In the same year Hume-Campbell, earl of Marchmont, published *A Serious Exhortation to the Electors of Great Britain*. After computing the number of Placemen in the Commons, and their aggregate remuneration, he invites his readers to "judge whether their unanimous Support of the present Minister in every Measure for these twenty years is a proof of their Independency." In view of the approaching election, it must be stressed that "to instruct your Representatives ... is not only a Right the Electors of Britain have ever enjoy'd, but the ... prolonging [Parliament] for seven Years has made the Exercise of such a

Right more particularly expedient." Since the Revolution, "we shall find the Power of the Crown greatly increas'd . . . and the Freedom of the People much subjected, and sometimes explicitly restrain'd." Specifically, unless urgent need is clear, "the multiplying of Penal Laws ought to be avoided in a Free State." Predictably, the author laments "that Corruption which now like a Deluge seems to sweep all before it." But more challenging is his assertion that "the People are not only concern'd to guard against all Innovation in the Constitution, but they have always a Right to demand any Amendment in the Constitution, should they discover any Part defective."[31]

Yet again, two years later, John Campbell of the Inner Temple, in *The Case of the Opposition Impartially Stated*, finds it regrettable that "Opposition in the Style of some People is a Term Synonymous with Disaffection." He devotes several pages to the social and economic effects of the current existence of "a boundless Propensity to Pleasure, a prodigious Relaxation of Principles, and an Epidemic Corruption of Manners." Amongst "a People affected thereby, . . . instead of virtuous Industry, there prevails . . . a fraudulent dexterity in coining artificial Riches." Campbell points to the present unbounded licence, with libertinism of morals as notorious as licentiousness of speech. The common people have lost respect for dignity, while "the middle Sort are full of Jealousies and Suspicions." But this does not stop at a moralist's lament. The corruption of an evil example comes from above. He derides the volteface by which "what may be now styled the Clamour of the *Mob,* was t'other day the *Voice* of the *Nation.*" There follows a scathing denunciation of those who trumpet the folly of making the conduct of government known to the vulgar, "of putting it into the Power of that hot-mouth'd Beast the Multitude, to take the Bit in its Mouth. . . . For as Government concerns every Man, so it seems but natural that every Man should concern himself about Government, [for] the lowest Fellow in the Kingdom contributes out of what he gets to the public Service." Away then with talk of the mob, the rabble, the dregs of the people: such ogres are "mere Bugbears and Chimeras, a Sort of Rounheads and Bloody-bones, invented by political Nurses to fright their Children from squalling." In a country with freedom for people to enquire, there will be no recourse to insurrection—the only remedy under arbitrary government.[32]

Once more, such points are reminiscent of an earlier debate, and it may well be suggested that some of the discontent expressed in the midcentury was not devoid of sociopolitical undertones, however carefully these were expressed. But there seem to be no positive proposals for extension of the franchise as a means of procuring a remedy for society's ills. Another *Essay on Civil Government,* anonymously published in 1743, identifies the origin of all power as being in the people, and goes so far as to recognize democracy as a form of regular government in which "the liberty of the people seems to be most secure; for here laws are equally binding, . . . property is on a more equal footing." The assertion that "in proportion to the distribution of property will be the balance of power in a mixed government" seems a clear indication. But the author is an uneasy Harringtonian, influenced by notions of social justice. "By nature all men seem to be equal . . . but in a state of society this equality cannot be entirely kept." Nevertheless, "nothing seems more inconsistent with the natural equality of people, than the unequal division of property which prevails in most societies," especially since "very few governments at present seem to be built upon a regard to man's general rights, but to particular interests." Strikingly, he declares that "the real strength and riches of a country consists in the number of people, therefore it is reasonable that their good should be the chief spring to the conduct of their governors. It is from the people's labour and industry that kings are upheld in their grandeur." Here Erasmian commonwealth notions obtrude alongside Harrington. Predictably, in dealing with the present state of England, one encounters the evils of "luxury and corruption," and the threats of standing armies and long parliaments.[33]

In 1744 the hack writer James Ralph, later praised by Fox, devoted two volumes to the *Use and Abuse of Parliaments,* whose general drift may be discerned from his contention that the principal legacy of the Revolution has been "a surer and more infallible Way of Enslaving the Subject." What if princes, defeated by the former dread of Prerogative and wary of conflict with Parliaments, "should find it expedient to compromise the Affair with them, and agree to divide the Common wealth between them"? Would not our representatives then become our masters, and their constituents their slaves? Ralph is in no doubt as to the parliamentary response: "that to the Calls of the Crown they have always answer'd; that to the Cries of the People they have always been deaf." He concludes "that the Grand secret of G———t is to fleece with one Hand, and corrupt with the other; and that the sole Relic of the People's Power is the glorious Privilege, to sell themselves as often as they are favour'd with Leisure to make a new Election." After repeating Burleigh's maxim that England could be enslaved only by a Parliament, Ralph concludes that Crown influence is so great, the spirit of the Grandees so servile, and the hearts of the People so depraved, that "those who are dispos'd to go farthest in the Cause of the Common-wealth are on the Point of crying out, If the People will be enslav'd, let them be enslav'd!'"³⁴

Thus far, while the last few pages clearly put in question any picture of totally contented quiescence, the reader may feel that he or she has encountered much rhetoric but little by way of specific reform proposals. But this can not be said of the anonymous *Liberty and Right,* which appeared in 1747. Dickinson, who conjectures as to the possible authorship of John Campbell, observes that it made little impact at the time (which coincided with publication of *The Honest Elector*). The preface attacks the Septennial Act as "the severest Stab the Liberties of the People of England ever received." Opponents of a return to what was an ancient right of the people "are afraid that annual Parliaments should also produce annual Ministers." More sweepingly, the author deplores the ability of an alliance of Crown and ministers "to introduce a national depravity of manners, to reduce or over-come the native freedom of popular elections, and to subvert and destroy the honour and integrity of the popular representation." But this lament is now followed by specific proposals, commencing with an almost grotesquely elaborate procedure for selection by ballot not only of Members of Parliament but also of the *candidates* for election. Thereafter, a suggested property qualification for members, together with the exclusion of Placemen and prohibition of immediately successive representation, should ensure genuine independence of action, while a three-year life of Parliament (with one-third of its members replaced annually) should ensure accountability.³⁵

Interestingly, another scheme for reform is found in the writings of a philosopher of the first rank: David Hume. Political and social discussion figures notably in his *Treatise of Human Nature,* first published in 1740, and his *Essays, Moral, Political and Literary,* which were developed over the period 1742 to 1777. Most immediately relevant is his essay on the *Idea of a Perfect Commonwealth.* Its declared thesis is that "all plans of government which suppose great reformation in the manners of mankind are plainly imaginary. Of this nature are the *Republic* of Plato, and the *Utopia* of Sir Thomas More. The *Oceana* is the only valuable model of a commonwealth that has yet been offered to the public." Yet even here, the device of the rotation is inconvenient, while the "Agrarian" law is impracticable and unenforceable. Thirdly, and most significantly, "the *Oceana* provides not a sufficient security for liberty, or the redress of grievances," in that the Senate may outweigh the voted wishes of the people. Undeterred by his predecessors' failures, Hume propounds his own "form of government" for a "country proposed to be created into a commonwealth." Freeholders worth £20 a year in the county, and householders worth £500 in the town parishes, are to meet annually "and choose by ballot some freeholders of the county" as their representatives. Thereafter, by indirect elections according to a decimal pyramid, magistrates and senators are to be appointed—the senators "to be endowed with the whole executive power of the commonwealth" while the county representatives "possess the whole legislative power." Noteworthy amidst a welter of further detail is the provision that the newly elected senators appoint, "by an intricate ballot, such as that of Venice or Malta," executives—commencing with "a protector, who represents the dignity of the commonwealth."[36]

Detailed religious, legal, and military regulations follow, together with the claim that the plan resembles "the commonwealth of the United Provinces." But of more especial interest is Hume's explanation of the limited popular participation proposed. Thus, "the lower sort of people and small proprietors are good judges enough of one not very far distinct from them in rank or habitation," that is, at a parochial level; but they are quite unfit for county meetings or for electing higher officers, because "their ignorance gives the grandees an opportunity of deceiving them"! As for discussion, "a large assembly of 1,000, for instance, to represent the people, if allowed to debate, would fall into disorder." For "Cardinal de Retz says that all numerous assemblies, however composed, are mere mob." The continued fascination with the notion of an ideal commonwealth, this late and in such as Hume, is striking. But in his assessment of contemporary realities Hume is clear that "the chief support of the British government is the opposition of interests; but that, though in the main serviceable, breeds endless factions." He sees his proposals as preserving the good while removing the harm: *balance* remains essential. Hume lived until 1774 and became—despite acquaintanceship with Wilkes—increasingly fearful of the mob. An unpublished passage in a late revision of his *History* was to assert that "on the whole, Men in political Life cannot take a worse Measure of Right and Wrong than the Clamour of the People"; they must disregard "the usual Blindness and Malignity of the Populace."[37] The terror of the many-headed monster bequeathed by an earlier era was nurtured by contemporary incidents.

Another midcentury work of special relevance—although admittedly it only touches its cap to commonwealth terminology—is Thomas Pownall's *Principles of Polity* (1752), which has been credited with considerable originality though with little immediate impact. Pownall is principally concerned with individual rights, with property, and with balance. Admittedly, government inevitably "abridges every Individual of that Liberty, which in a State of Nature he is born to." But such liberty as is preserved must be defended, not only from any external threat, but also from "any injurious Attack within, *either of the People or the Government*" (my italics). "Thus it becomes the Interest of the Democratic Part, to be a constant Clog and Check upon the Measures of the administering Power. . . . Hence a Balance of Power, and a due Regulating of this Balance, is the Essence of this Constitution."[38]

But this is the limit of the "democratic" function. For if the bonds of government become too loose, then the "Seeds of Confusion and Anarchy" are sown by certain "boasted Principles of Liberty" as exercised by "the Mob and noisy Part of Mankind." For surely any "Multitude of People got together" must feel "their natural Incapacity to will or act." Fortunately, nature itself has taught the many to deduce from this the need for "Obedience to the Will of the Few, who could reason for them"; on this, Montesquieu is cited. Predictably, Pownall is disdainful about some schemes that have recently plagued the nation in "a mad Zeal for Innovation." It is the balance of property that is the base for a balance of power. Those who have "attempted to frame and model it artificially to their own Schemes . . . have all found their Schemes *Utopian* and their Legislature abortive." For "there is one Mistake which runs through all these *Utopian* Levellers . . . even down to Sir Thomas More. And it is: They see the natural Connexion that there is between the Balance of Power and the Balance of Property, but think this Balance is a mere artificial Thing, and must owe both its Nature and Existence to the Wisdom of the Legislator." Avoidance of such folly is surely the consideration "which distinguishes the *Utopian* from the Politician: And it is this which distinguishes Mr Harrington from the Wild-sharers." The book concludes with variations on the theme of "how improper Man is to be trusted with Power," and on the consequent difficulties in reconciling the rights of the state with the sacred civil liberties of the community.[39]

Not without interest as another illustration of a belief that the present equilibrium, however finely balanced, *must* be preserved, is *An Enquiry into the Foundation of the English Constitution* (second edition, 1753) by Samuel Squire, archdeacon of Bath. His "historical essay upon the Anglo-Saxon Government" incorporated as an appendix an "essay on the Balance of civil Power in England." The verdict on the effect of the Civil Wars of the mid-seventeenth century is significant: "The sovereign power being now fallen into the hands of the *People,* for want of wisdom in themselves, and honesty in their leaders... they found themselves, at the foot of the account, losers by the exchange, and in a more wretched situation than they were when the civil war commenced. Thereafter, "it was the *revolution* [of 1688–89] which gave the last and permanent establishment to the popular interest, and immoveably fixed the nodding balance of power to that side." In England's auspicious position, "the danger, therefore, to our present excellent establishment, if there really be any, [is] lest the *People,* or more properly their representatives," should become too powerful. "In short, a true and consistent *Whig* is a balancer, and a mediator."[40]

Such representative samples of mainstream establishment thinking may well exemplify Kenyon's allusion to "stasis." It might indeed be argued that, most certainly in contrast with mid-seventeenth-century developments, even the "commonwealthmen" had run into a constitutional and political cul-de-sac in their ideology. Yet we have also noted the clear expression of considerable political discontent, much of it with social undertones. Similarly, some caution is needed also in respect of the contention that a shrunken ideology of the commonwealth is most strongly exemplified in the sphere of religion. Gordon Rupp concludes that the "high-church dream" of "a true *Corpus Christianum* where Church and State were two facets of one Christian commonwealth," with the laity in Parliament supporting the clergy's exercise of spiritual discipline over the whole nation, had been rendered unattainable by the events of the previous half-century. It was neither rapidly nor wholly abandoned. As late as 1792 Edmund Burke was to declare that "in a Christian Commonwealth the Church and State are one and the same thing, being different integral parts of the same whole." Nonetheless, the notion of a unitary commonwealth gave ground, at best, to a consideration of relationships *between* church and state. Some of the harsher judgments made on the state of religion in early and mid-eighteenth century England have recently been tempered. It has been pointed out that neither the Evangelical movement nor the Methodist revival sprang from entirely barren soil within the church, while William Law's *Serious Call to a Devout and Holy Life* was to become a devotional classic. Yet it may also be urged that, under pressures both philosophical and political, the concept and standing of the church itself, together with those of organized religion, became diminished.[41]

Undoubtedly, political reliability rather than doctrinal orthodoxy was established as the criterion for episcopal advancement. The presence of the bishops as a voting phalanx in the House of Lords was much more important than any activity in Convocation—which largely lapsed. By the same token, the issue of religious liberty was viewed by many as a matter of expediency rather than as affecting any principle of faith. Latitudinarian Anglicans triumphantly observed that toleration led *not* to any flowering of the Dissenters' cause but accompanied a relative decline of this former bugaboo. Indeed, insofar as the Church of England felt any apprehension as to its ecclesiastical dominance this came first from Deism and thereafter from Methodist "enthusiasm." Yet repeated concern for the allegedly deplorable irreligion of the mass of the people is widely voiced, together with appeals for the enforcement of morality, both of these of course not unrelated to the endemic fear of social disorder—even if this engendered riot not revolution. In the context of our present enquiry, this persistent belief that moral discipline *was* a matter of public and indeed of governmental concern, sometimes linked with a residual notion of an integrated commonwealth, is as important as the issue of religious liberty.

Much religious discussion during this era was influenced by William Wollaston's *The Religion of Nature delineated* (1726 edition). With strikingly colored illustrations, this work ran to seven editions in the next thirty years. Charles Vereker suggests that its sentiments, whatever their doctrinal logic, had considerable appeal to lay minds. Wollaston contends that "the foundation of religion lies in that difference between the acts of men, which distinguishes them into good, evil, indifferent." God, "the Supreme Being," is indeed the author of nature, but since he is also "a Being of perfect reason" it will not do to follow nature slavishly. Man is a social creature and may well "part with some of his natural rights, and put himself under the government of laws" in order to gain their protection. But thereafter, "the end of society is the common welfare and good of the people associated." In each individual's judgment of this good, "ultimate happiness is the sum of happiness, or true pleasure, at the foot of the account"—an interesting choice of phrase. Wollaston was an Anglican clergyman, but his views were sufficiently close to Deism as to cause apprehension in those who professed doctrinal rigor. The same is true of Samuel Clarke, from whom Wollaston derived some of his tenets, and also of Matthew Tindal—whose political ideas we have already noticed. In 1730, at the age of seventy-five, Tindal published what has been called "the Bible of the Deists": *Christianity as Old as the Creation, or the Gospel a Republication of the Religion of Nature.* Insofar as Deism had a major impact on the philosophy of the period, then Stromberg's point about its near-allies Arianism and Socinianism is significant: a tendency to "slough off all dogma and stress only conduct."[42]

Deism perhaps reached its apogee at about this time, thereafter waning as a credo but retaining much influence. But the door to liberty of doctrinal speculation had long been opened from within the church by Benjamin Hoadly, bishop of Bangor (and ultimately of Winchester). Hoadly was convinced that Christ himself never purported to convey to anyone infallibility of interpretation of his message. No one therefore "hath authority either to make new laws for Christ's subjects; or to impose a sense upon the old ones, which is the same thing; or to judge, censure, or punish . . . in matters relating purely to conscience, or salvation."[43] Hoadly's provocatively expressed opinions evoked reactions (in common with his political notions encountered earlier). Yet clerical efforts at refutation produced what has been termed an accepted compromise in Bishop William Warburton's *Alliance between Church and State* (1736). Warburton was a friend and literary heir of Alexander Pope, whose *Essay on Man* enjoined the reader:

> For Modes of Faith, let graceless zealots fight,
> His can't be wrong whose life is in the right,

and the very title of his work may be seen as indicative. Warburton continues to admire "the beauteous Structure of a Commonwealth," and indeed speaks of "a Christian Commonwealth," and of "the Unity of its End." But he is clear that "the Care of the State extends only to the Body and its Concerns, and the Care of the Church only to the Soul." Inevitably, the civil magistrate "must seek for some Union or Alliance with the Church." This because "Society by its own proper Force cannot provide for the Observance of above one Third Part of moral Duties. [Accordingly] there must be added some other coactive Power . . . to keep Society from running back into confusion. But there is no other than the Power of Religion." Asserting "the Equity and Necessity of the alliance between Church and State . . . for the sake of public Utility," he goes so far as to say that "Ecclesiastical Jurisdiction . . . was given *solely for Reformation of Manners*." Not surprisingly, he rejoices that a "narrow, sour, ignorant Spirit of Bigotry, blessed be God, is no more. A learned one, of Liberty, and Christian Charity, universally prevails." Not everyone would concur with "universally," but there is much justice in a recent opinion that the religious liberalism of eighteenth-century society derived in part from "the benevolent negligence . . . of a tolerant, pluralist State." Yet far from benefiting therefrom, the older Nonconformist sects produced their own horrendous and disastrous dispute on Arian opinions, which one contemporary described as causing more damage than all the efforts of their adversaries. Little wonder that, across the board, Warburton himself discerned a "fatal crisis when religion hath lost its hold on the minds of the people."[44]

Yet insofar as that hold was bound up with the acceptance both of morality and of the social order, all shades of religious opinion concurred in deploring its loosening. Admittedly, the Societies for Reformation of Manners now petered out; the London Society published its last report in 1738. But concern with what some believed to be a virtual collapse of public morality did not. Paul Langford finds increasing concern with social problems in the literature of the 1740s, with "acute anxiety about the indiscipline and immorality of the lower classes, supposedly evidenced by the popular taste for gin and the rising level of crime." Whatever the justice of the second apprehension, there is no doubt about the first. The combination of rising real wages, good harvests, and a plentiful supply of raw material for the distillation of gin produced a soaring consumption of the spirit. Cheap food left more to spend on cheaper drink. This was a far cry from James I's concern that strong beer was too expensive. Nor was concern restricted to moralizing pamphleteers. Parliament produced the Gin Act of 1736, which proved to be unenforceable and itself provoked serious rioting. It took a combination of further statutes restricting retail outlets, together with the rising price of grain in the midcentury to reduce the problem. This was not an isolated target of parliamentary moral fervor: between 1739 and 1745 four statutes unsuccessfully attempted to restrict illicit gambling in the capital.[45]

I have already noted Defoe's expression of resentment that what were seen as mere peccadilloes in their betters were simultaneously identified as symptoms of social decay among the lower orders. Coincidentally or not, mounting concern about the irreligion of the poor, accompanying a spate of disorders between 1738 and 1740, provided the backcloth to the emergence of Methodism. Of course, John Wesley's career must be related not only to a wider evangelical movement in England but also to like developments in Wales. Certainly, Methodism included an avowed and specific appeal to the poor. On political issues, Wesley himself was clear that "the greater the share the people have in government, the less liberty, civil or religious, does a nation enjoy." In spite of this, and whatever opinions came to be retrospectively held about the allegedly conservative political and social teachings of Methodism, contemporaries often saw this burgeoning movement not only as a challenge to the existing clerical hierarchy, but also as conveying dangerous implications for social relationships. As early as 1744 Bishop Gibson attributed to Methodism "open Defiance of Government" and "open Inroads upon the National Constitution," in particular "by publick Advertisement to invite the *Rabble* to be their Hearers," often in open fields.[46] Whatever their careful qualifications, the utterances of many "field-preachers" proved just as suspect to the established hierarchy as had been those of Latimer and Lever to Gardiner. Even equality in sin could be perceived as dangerous! Ironically, such rioting as was directly provoked by Methodism took the shape of *hostile* mobs. Yet alongside a quite genuine distaste—on the grounds both of religion and of reason—for the "enthusiasm" of their meetings was a fear that the Methodists might engender social criticism that would threaten the established order.

This issue will again be of concern when I examine in some detail the development of social and economic perceptions in the commonwealth. But before so doing, two works are of special interest as straddling religious, social, and political values. *Discourses on all the Principal Branches of Natural Religion and Social Virtue* by James Foster appeared (in two volumes) in 1752. Foster identifies the community as "one grand and vast body . . . formed for the noblest purposes of reasonable life, intermingling benevolence, moral rectitude, and happiness. . . . In the outward *corporeal* structure, there are no jarrings or contrarieties; there is no such thing as a detached member." After such an utterly traditional analogy it is not surprising, later, to read that, despite the existence of certain "absolutely *unalienable*" rights that are common to all, there are nonetheless "certain *differences* and *inequalities*, likewise in the outward condition of mankind." This granted, since "all *equitable government* must be founded in *mutual consent*," the overall result must be "to dignify and enlarge the social character, and advance more completely the social happiness, of man." Indeed one chapter is largely devoted to "the Christian rule of Equity." Our impression of long-established values is confirmed when one finds that equity includes benevolence, and a recognition that those who are often regarded with contempt are in fact "the most natural, and proper, objects of our compassion. Having so many *inconveniences*, and *hardships*, to conflict with, and the strength of their minds enfeebled and broken, by the oppressions they labour under, our *generosity* should the rather incline us . . . to soften and alleviate their cases, and raise their drooping spirits." Yet, crucially, amidst all his concerns for social values and standards Foster is at pains to rebut "all the claims of civil government, to interfere in the concerns of religion and consciences."[47]

The Reverend John Brown's *Estimate of the Manners and Principles of the Times* appeared in 1757, and its appeal ensured a number of reprintings. His survey of "the public State and Welfare" envisages a nation "rolling on the Brink of a Precipice," beset by "a vain, luxurious, and selfish Effeminacy." For "the modern Spirit of Irreligion leads to rascally and abandoned Cowardice"—although indeed its prevalence "among the fashionable World" is not of universal applicability. But, alas, "the Principle of public Spirit *exists not*." In its place, "the great Chain of political Self-Interest was at length formed; and extended from the lowest Cobbler in a Burrough, to the King's first Minister. But a Chain of Self-Interest is indeed no better than a Rope of Sand, [and may] break into an Infinity of Factions." A scathing verdict on Walpole concludes (in anticipation of some modern critics) "that while he seemed to strengthen the Superstructure, he weakened the Foundations of our Constitution." Thus, through "Election-jobbing" and self-interest "the public Body is again weakened, or rather mutilated, in all its Limbs." Predictably, Brown condemns Mandeville's influence and applauds the efforts of the legislature to reduce gin-drinking. He deplores the impact of taxation upon the poor: "the Poor must indeed increase their Wages in order to subsist, yet this Increase never takes Place till they are compelled by the last Necessity or Want: The natural Consequence of which must be Murmur, Sedition, and Tumults." Yet, rejecting a traditional analogy between natural and political bodies, he salvages a note of hope in the reflection that "in Societies, of whatever Kind, there seems no such necessary or essential Tendency to Dissolution." A despairing nation may yet be saved by "Some Great Minister"! Brown himself committed suicide.[48]

In considering specific economic and social issues it must again be recognized that explicit avowals of an earlier commonwealth ideology so often associated with the corporeal analogy are as infrequent in this context as in that of religion. For insofar as this ideology had derived either from general trends in the philosophy of the age or from pressure on living standards in an era of socioeconomic crisis, both were wanting at least until the midcentury. The course of changes in population and in real wages throughout the eighteenth century is certainly not without controversy. But most historians would accept the suggestion that "the relatively high real wages of the 1730s and 1740s reflected demographic decline or at least stagnation," and were "accentuated by a series of fortuitously good harvests." Indeed, E. A. Wrigley has identified an upward secular trend in terms both of expectation of life and of real wages until the later eighteenth century.[49]

Against this background I have noted the assertion that the

"moral economy" of the mob and the reactions of those who governed alike reflect unspoken assumptions as to the parameters of political possibility. Indeed, E. P. Thompson has defined "one characteristic paradox of the century: we have a *rebellious* traditional culture." It seems to be contended that the "lower orders" harbored no articulate sense of social injustice, and certainly no revolutionary political pretensions, so long as they did not go too hungry too often. Thompson goes even further in his picturesque assertion that an allegedly "growing middle class," which some historians discern as nursing an increasing resentment at their exclusion from the political nation, were in fact "consenting adults in their own corruption."[50] At all events, they would hardly be advocates of social revolution. Standards of literacy were now much improved from the mid-seventeenth-century position; but amidst such general quiescence one would not find in the books produced for an expanding readership much trace of the urgent propaganda for social reform by government that had distinguished that earlier era.

In assessing the shifting balance in social philosophy between individual rights and collective duties, the older commonwealth touchstones of equity—property, poverty and poor relief, and the exercise and direction of governmental intervention in economic affairs—will still serve. In general, one encounters a further hardening of attitudes apropos the defence of property rights, the treatment of the poor, and the rectitude, objectives, and limitations of governmental controls. In respect of the first of these, Langford has remarked of Real Whigs or Commonwealthmen that, while often heterodox in theology, they whispered no word of heresy about the worship of property.[51] The need to defend one's property in face of taxation was an emotive notion. Walpole was ever-mindful of the advisability of caution in taxing land, and justified his proposals to extend the excise principle on the ground that the poorer segments of society must also contribute to its upkeep. An insistence on freedom to maximize the income from one's property in response to market forces will dominate the debate on governmental intervention.

Perhaps equally indicative was the attitude toward what was recognized as most important among productive resources: the potential labor force. Here, any residual commonwealth notion of the equitable distribution of the fruits of production was normally swamped by an emphasis on maximizing output—ostensibly, of course, in the national interest. Much of contemporary debate concerned the issue of whether low or high wages were the more conducive to cost-efficiency, together with the allegedly notorious indiscipline of a workforce insistent on honoring "Saint Monday" after a weekend of idle debauchery. Yet the contempt thus implied was *not* shared by all. While the occurrence of explicit commonwealth terminology is rare, Coats[52] cites several midcentury writers who displayed what we may term *humanitarian* utilitarianism—deriving from traditional Christian values but justified in the context of an essentially economic analysis of those factors seen as contributing to the strength of the state. Pre-eminence belongs to the timber merchant Jacob Vanderlint, in respect not only of the appearance of his work as early as 1734 but also of the perception of its contents. The title, *Money answers all Things,* conveys an apparent cynicism that totally belies its message. Its address "To the Merchants of Great Britain" is itself significant: for while Bolingbroke and his coterie purveyed a nostalgic appeal to the traditional *noblesse oblige* of the landed interest, Vanderlint is convinced by now this concerns nothing more than high rents, and that only by a clearheaded appreciation of market forces and an efficient application of productive processes can the living standards of ordinary people be enhanced. His alternative title, "An Essay to make Money Sufficiently plentiful Amongst all Ranks of People,"[53] conveys an assessment of the *use* of money that stands in total contrast with that of Alexander Pope noticed earlier. At times the reader is tempted not only to look back to Sir Thomas Smith but also forward to J. M. Keynes.

Vanderlint's initial identification of "reducing the present Rates of Labour" as a paramount objective is *not* accompanied by any admonition to drive down living standards. Rather, it is increased production "which will make the Price of the Labour of Working People much lower; for the Rates of Labour are always settled and constituted of the Price of Victual and Drink: And all Manufactures will be vastly cheaper; for the Value of all Manufactures is chiefly constituted of the Price or Charge of the Labour bestowed thereon." Moreover, " 'tis certain a poor People can't pay great Taxes, any more than they can pay great Rents," while the competitive edge necessary in face of foreign producers must not be acquired "by making the Poor fare harder, or consume less than their reasonable Wants in that Station require." Although he recognizes the impact of improvidence via the "Brandy-shops and Ale-houses," he insists that "there is a Necessity to lower the Necessaries of Life to about half the present Price, if we would reduce Labour only one fourth Part lower than it now goes."[54]

He now proceeds to more radical analysis: extolling the happiness of a community "that abounds most with middling People," he commends diffusion of property ownership. In particular, "the Cause of such general or national Luxury is solely owing to too great an Inequality of Property, by which too many are enabled to live excessively splendid, whilst the rest, having much less than they want, are too much depress'd and sunk." Of crucial importance, "a Decay of Trade is nothing else but the Bulk of the People wanting many Things which they ought to have, and which, for want of sufficient Employment and Business, it is out of their Power to procure." Vanderlint goes on to spurn the objection "that the working People will not now work above 3 or 4 Days in a Week, but get drunk the other 2 or 3 Days; and that this would be worse, if Necessaries were rendered so cheap." Encouragement to labor should replace such derision. Finally, reverting to rents, "the People have a just and reasonable Right to have so much more Land put to Use, as shall be needful and sufficient to give them full Employment, and subsist them comfortably; because every Person is, by Nature, as much entitled to all the Land he can cultivate and use, as he is to the Air in which he breathes. [For] Mankind are all by Nature born equal in this respect."[55]

While many of his sentiments would have been applauded in the mid-seventeenth century, commonwealth terminology is absent in Vanderlint. In Malachy Postlethwayt's *Britain's Commercial Interest Explained and Improved* (2 volumes, 1757), the corporeal imagery recurs, but "the strength of the body politic" is associated with "the resources of the state." Yet Postlethwayt echoes Vanderlint in deploring excessive luxury as "owing to too great an inequality of property. . . . The one side is idolized for their wealth, the other contemned for their poverty." Again, "were property to be diffused . . . the labor &c of people would not come so unreasonably low. The natural and just division of property will not only eradicate the luxury injurious to the state and to individuals, but extinguish vice and immorality therewith. For the too great inequality of property is the source of depravity, and general poverty." Nonetheless, one discerns no clearly egalitarian note: economic efficiency looms as large as social justice. Thus, "it is indispensably necessary to employ those we have in the best manner possible. That best employment consists in receiving from them all the assistance that can be gathered from their faculties, both mechanic and intellectual. . . . It is not enough for the public welfare that every poor inhabitant gets a livelihood; but the manner in which he gets it ought likewise to be useful to society in general." He condemns the contagion of idleness, which weakens the body politic, remarking of the workforce that "to multiply the days of that employment is to multiply the resources of the state."[56]

A slightly different perspective is adopted in the prize dissertation of William Hazeland of St. John's College, Cambridge, in 1756. *A View of the Manner in which Trade and Civil Liberty support each other* asserts that "the *Agrarian law,* by removing all the rewards of industry and application, must produce a general idleness and inactivity." But its fundamental message is that society has moved beyond the stage where, since "land was the only source of wealth," this law was advocated "as the firmest support of civil freedom." By now, "wealth in the subject, then, is the natural poise against arbitrary power in the state. . . . But Wealth is the peculiar gift of Trade." Thus Hazeland enunciates his thesis that trade promotes liberty "by the production of a monied interest, which emancipates the meaner people from their subjection to the land-owners who are otherwise their natural masters." Once more the argument of such as Bolingbroke and Pope is inverted. But more is to follow. Although Hazeland commends an equable, not equitable, distribution of property as necessary to free government, and a "modest inequality in the fortunes of free-citizens," he too condemns too great a degree of inequality on macroeconomic grounds. For

> where the whole people are rich or poor to an extreme, exceedingly the greater part must confine their wants to the bare supply of nature, and that at the cheapest rate she can be served. . . . If you suppose that the aggregate of wealth, which is possessed by the Grandees, and scattered by them on a refined luxury, will make up the other's defect, it is certainly a mistake. For wherever this immense disparity of condition subsists, the national wealth will always be less than in consequence of a more uniform dispersion. Where all the laborious part of a people are slaves, or hirelings, it is folly to expect the same increase.[57]

Admittedly, there is little ground on which to relate the relatively enlightened views considered in the last few pages to the context of commonwealth ideology. They have nothing in common with the version expressed by Bolingbroke's coterie, while that of the mid-seventeenth century—of which they are occasionally reminiscent—was by now irretrievably tarnished. Moreover, as Coats has pointed out, their expression is rarely encountered before the midcentury. In general, the shift in attitude toward the poor as between Hale and Child before and Dunning after the 1680s now went further. This is typified in Dorothy Marshall's discernment of "a transition between the solicitude which required that work should be found for the Poor and the harsh determination of the eighteenth century to compel the Poor to work." Much more recently, Speck has identified "a more ruthless approach to social problems on the part of the ruling class."[58]

This is strikingly exemplified in John Clayton's bizarrely titled *Friendly Advice to the Poor* (of Manchester) in 1755. Lamenting the continued spectacle in the streets of "distressed objects of every Kind, . . . notwithstanding the pious Liberality of the Rich," this divine finds the cause "but too plain and obvious. The Poor refuse or neglect to help themselves." They have an abject mind, a mean and sordid spirit. Writing "in the Spirit of Love," the author identifies specific causes of distress. First, coupled with idleness, is the poor's determination, "in a most unchristian Sense of the Words, [to] *take no Thought for the Morrow.*" Their shameful extravagance is directed toward "the Alehouse, the Distiller's, and the Tea-shop, . . . beguiled by the low Prices"! Next, their bad management and lack of economy is evidenced in their reluctance to work "above four Days in a Week," in their clinging to their "Play-days" and "slothful spending the Morning in Bed."[59] One almost suspects self-parody; indeed, bound with this work in the Bodleian's copy is *A Sequel* "by Joseph Stot, Cobbler. 1756," in which the tongue is unmistakably in the cheek.

Alexander Pope had parodied such attitudes in the *Epistle to Bathurst* (1733):

> The grave Sir Gilbert holds it for a rule,
> That 'every man in want is knave or fool':
> 'God cannot love (says Blunt, with tearless eyes)
> The wretch he starves'—and piously denies;
> But the good Bishop, with a meeker air,
> Admits, and leaves them, Providence's care.[60]

But in general those unable or unwilling to work were deemed a double affront to national efficiency—as both a wasted productive opportunity and a burden on the rates. This simplistic judgment helps to explain the approach to the problem of poor relief. With the addition of an act of 1723, which permitted parishes to combine in order to establish workhouses, the statutory machinery of poor relief remained basically that bequeathed by Elizabeth I. Much depended therefore on the attitudes and the efficacy with which it operated.

Here a distinction must be made between "outdoor" and "indoor" relief. Dorothy Marshall's conclusion that help given to the poor in their own homes represented "the least difficult and best executed branch of the Poor Law" is endorsed by K. D. M. Snell's allusion to "the generous and widely encompassing nature of relief." Their impression contrasts with William Law's more guarded contemporary verdict regarding the old and sick, that "the parish allowance to such people is very seldom a comfortable maintenance."[61] But more significant is the fact that Law's contemporaries were preoccupied not so much with outdoor relief as with the vexed issues of vagrancy and workhouse administration. Thus, the unknown author of *A Short View of the Frauds, Abuses, and Impositions of Parish Officers* (1744) is concerned, not with the welfare of the poor, but to expose "all the Mal Practices of the lower Sort of People to get themselves into Office, and to make Advantage thereby"—facilitated by the right of "the lowest and meanest Inhabitants" to attend the relevant meetings! All-too-often the system foundered between the Scylla and Charybdis of incompetent administration by amateur parish officers and of blatant exploitation if "farmed out" to contractors. As to its *objective,* Dorothy Marshall's judgment that the "method was to hold the workhouse over them *in terrorem* in order to force them to accept the smallest possible allowance" receives contemporary confirmation. Thus, Thomas Ruggles declared that "a parish workhouse is a parish bugbear, to frighten distress from applying for relief." Even more explicitly, *An Account of several Workhouses* (1725) explained that "the advantage of the workhouse to the parish does not arise from what the poor people can do towards their subsistence, but from the apprehensions the poor have of it. These prompt them to exert, and to do their utmost to keep themselves off the parish."[62]

Yet more discriminating and humanitarian discussion occurred in midcentury. Thomas Alcock's *Observations on the Defects of the Poor Laws* (1752), discussing charity, suggests that "a Law to enforce Relief tends to destroy the Principle it proceeds from, the Principle of Charity. All Virtue must be free: If you force Charity you destroy her." Moreover, regrettably, "the forced and expensive Way of relieving the Poor, has put many Gentlemen and Parishes upon contriving all possible Methods of lessening their Number"—by discouraging early marriage, discharge of servants in time to prevent "settlement," and pulling down of cottages. Yet any suggestion to revert to church responsibility is ludicrous—unless church lands and tithes are also restored. Of course, the lower sort do not help themselves by resorting to tobacco and snuff and in wasting time and money "in preparing and sipping their Tea," sometimes twice daily. All-in-all, "there is only one good Argument . . . in Favour of a Poor Tax, and that is, it forces open the Purses of the Covetous-Rich," especially since "at present, the Love of many waxeth cold.

As Poor Rates have increased, private Alms and Gifts have lessened." Thus, Alcock applauds parliamentary contemplation of the functions and types of hospitals, poorhouses and workhouses, which he proceeds to discuss—including the reflection that "surely Palaces are not proper for Paupers." Much moralizing on "Idleness, Drunkenness, Sloth and Luxury" concludes with a stark injunction reminiscent of Morison over two centuries earlier: "To tell a Man in extreme Want, and in no Way of getting a Livelihood, not to rob or steal, is almost the same Thing as to tell him not to eat or drink."[63]

Henry Fielding's writings on this issue gain added weight from his genuine if short-lived involvement with problems of crime and poverty as Bow Street magistrate. His *Proposal for Making an Effectual Provision for the Poor* (1753), in considering the contribution that all members must make to the well-being of "this Common-wealth" (a term that recurs), is clear that "to effect this is the Business of every wise and good Legislature." In particular, the poor, unlike the rich, "having nothing but their Labour to bestow on the Society, if they withhold this from it, they become useless Members"; Parliament must therefore "procure to such the Means of Labour; and secondly . . . compel them to undertake it." Depiction of the evil impact of the present mode of raising the taxation needed, and of the suffering of those who starve, freeze, beg, and steal, is followed by full "Proposals for Erecting A County Work-house &c." for Middlesex, which include provisions for an infirmary, with surgeon, apothecary, matron, and nurses, as well as a house of correction.[64]

Wider-ranging reflections are included in Fielding's *Inquiry into the Causes of The Late Increase of Robbers* (1751). His historical survey, paying tribute to Hale and Child, identifies a statutory provision for the poor that in intent compares favorably with other nations. But, alas, there exists "a most scandalous perversion of the design of the legislature" in respect of "the employment of the able poor." Apart from their treatment of "their office as a matter of private emolument," he believes that relieving the impotent poor is the only power "which hath much exercised the mind of the parish officers." Of the category of poor "unable to work," he advances the surprising conclusion that they are "so truly inconsiderable in number" that given the duty "so positively commanded by our Saviour," their relief "might be safely left to voluntary charity, unenforced by any compulsive law," or at best supplemented by a very inconsiderable tax. Provision of work for those "able and unwilling" is more easily said than done, but is "surely not above the reach of the British parliament." But the problem of the recalcitrant, which Fielding considers most numerous of all, evokes the lengthiest consideration.

Here he parts company with Child and approves of legislation to prohibit "all conspiracies for raising wages"; he himself is clear that cheap labor means cheap produce, enhanced consumption, and hence fuller employment. But sadly, many "if they cannot exact an exorbitant price for their labour, will remain idle." Again, the "houses of correction" established to correct the incorrigibly idle are often "no other than schools of vice, seminaries of idleness, and common-sewers of nastiness and disease." Such astringent perception of realities includes the observation that *public* executions are usually the occasions of triumphant bravado rather than of a terrible deterrent. Again, in considering the problem of vagabonds, he is certain that "in all cases of removal, the good of the parish, and not of the public, is consulted."[65]

J. Massie's *Plan for the Establishment of Charity Houses* (1758) was primarily directed to the relief of fallen women, but contained several general humanitarian reflections. Among the defects of the law is the fact that it "makes only a Cobweb Partition between Stealing and Begging." The principle of equity should apply in the raising of poor rates as well as their application. Above, all, Massie is in no doubt that, while charity is a religious duty, "the making of Provision for the Poor is the Business of Government." Another work specifically devoted to one type of institution, *Essay on Charity Schools* by Isaac Watts (1728), may well prompt reflection on a crucial aspect of the midcentury philosophy. Watts enunciates that "the great God has wisely ordained . . . that among mankind there should be some rich and some poor. . . . Nor is it possible according to the present course of nature and human affairs to alter this, . . . nor is it our design." Only a few years earlier, William Law had insisted that "it is not left to the rich to gratify their passions in the indulgences and pride of life, nor to the poor, to vex and torment their hearts with the poverty of their state." Thus, Rupp finds in Watts no vision "of the transformation of an advancing society" and points the contrast with Cranmer and Latimer, while Roland Stromberg emphasises that to the eighteenth-century mind, humanitarianism meant charity, not social engineering.[66]

Perhaps over-sweeping generalization should be avoided. Thus, Watts rebuts the gibe about the poor that "their Business is to Labour, not to Think." For "men of crafty and aspiring Minds know how to make use of Persons bred up in such gross Ignorance to carry on their own seditious Purposes." He urges that every Charity School should "have partly the Nature of a Work-House, as well as of a School," condemns any who would "eat the Bread of Idleness," and dismisses unnecessary niceties of learning. Yet he is also insistent that " 'tis not menial Servants, but Mechanicks and Manufacturers that increase the Commodities, and thereby the Riches of the Nation," and concludes with a stark warning that the poor must not be permitted to "become a Burden and a Nuisance to the Kingdom, if you have any Value for the Preservation of Property, for the Propagation of Virtue or Religion."[67] Yet it remains true that many sentiments displayed are reminiscent rather of the sixteenth century than of the mid-seventeenth-century era, and that forward-looking perceptions are functional and prudential rather than challengingly ideological. One looks in vain for the appeals to government of the type that had distinguished mid-Stuart commonwealth ideology.

What of the less challenging aspects of paternalism? Certainly, I noted in Bolingbroke and his circle an avowed nostalgia for supposedly traditional and "pre-commercial" values, but also in such as Vanderlint clear evidence that this came under challenge. Even financial procedures were in a way to be redeemed: Charles Wesley presumably saw no verbal incongruity in depicting the joyful amazement of the sinner when assured that he possessed "an *interest* in the Saviour's blood." Thompson, predictably, dismisses the whole vague notion of paternalism as a loose descriptive term that conveys "implications of warmth [but] confuses the actual and the ideal."[68] Genuine individual philanthropic effort during the middle decades of the century, notably in the establishment of new hospitals for the poor, makes blanket condemnation of the age over-harsh. Nonetheless, as far as concerns *governmental* intervention in social and economic matters, most contemporary trends would have appalled earlier commonwealth idealists. Consider three major features of Tudor and Early Stuart paternalism: attempted control of markets to ensure a "just price" and prevent exploitation of the poor in times of real shortage; the prevention of enclosures, which cause unemployment; and support of apprenticeship procedures allied with wage supervision, so as to hold the balance between employer and employee and maintain skills and standards.

The general trends identified earlier would obviate the need for frequent action on the first of these, but after the occasional bad harvest attacks by moralizers upon forestallers, engrossers, and regrators persisted. Speck cites the opinion, in 1758, "that the present dearness of corn arises principally from the avarice of farmers and iniquity of the factors, merchants, bakers and dealers in corn." Yet insofar as there was any attempt to impose the standards of a "moral economy" in this sphere, it came from spontaneous action rather than from government. Writing of the waning of "Tudor policies of provision . . . and of paternalist social control," Thompson ingeniously suggests that by the period 1700 to 1760 "there was a certain migration of the theory from the rulers to the crowd."[69] Ministers and Parliament alike were more concerned with optimum conditions in producers' and traders' markets in response to purportedly national interests.

In respect of enclosures, which overwhelmingly occurred after about 1750, the tides of revisionism and counter-revisionism have in turn swept over Goldsmith's "Deserted Village" and the Hammonds's *The Village Labourer*. On balance it seems impossible to dismiss the social impact upon the poor first of the increasing incidence of *total* wage dependency in face of market fluctuations; secondly, of the fragile safeguards of any proven *legal* rights to an allotment, in face not only of fencing costs but also of the qualitative justice of plot allocation; thirdly, of the loss of extremely important rights of common such as pasturage and fuel. Massie, in 1758, considered "the great Increases of Unemployed Poor . . . to be primarily caused by the Monopolizing of Farms, and the Inclosure of Common Lands." No one can dispute the very real contemporary perception by those involved of a very close correlation between the extent of enclosure and increasing per capita expenditure on poor relief—a perception endorsed by recent statistical scholarship. The facilitation of swathes of enclosure by legislation stands in striking contrast with the statutory endeavors of the Tudor and Stuart eras. The paucity in the Commons Journals of expression of opposition to these acts reflects the disappearance of commonwealth-type paternalism, which is the more remarkable in the light of the opinion by Arthur Young himself that "by nineteen out of twenty enclosure Bills the poor are injured and some grossly injured."[70]

Admittedly, much of what occurred was the result of long-term and overwhelming pressures—as were also the decline of the guilds and the decay of apprenticeship. But the point at issue is that here again governmental action, where taken, was designed to accelerate not to halt the process. Dorothy Marshall dated this acceleration from about 1720, while Langford observes that wage regulation, as a function of paternalistic magistracy, effectively lapsed. Yet intervention of a different kind had been in evidence in 1721: an agreement of journeymen tailors in London to demand higher pay and shorter hours was followed by a petition of master tailors against such "Combinations" and by an act (7 Geo.I, c.3) that declared associations for such purposes illegal and fixed maximum wages.[71]

Assuredly, much of earlier governmental intervention purporting to protect the poorer orders of society had been evoked by fear of social disorder as well as by the prescriptions of the ideal Christian commonwealth. In Hanoverian England, while the socioeconomic dimension of commonwealth ideology had attenuated almost to the point of oblivion, the specter of the rioting mob was ever-present. But one has noted not only that the trigger points of the most notorious riots were religious and political, but also that they were localized occurrences with no real sign of general social disorder, much less rebellion. Langford cites the observation in 1749 that the conduct and management of the "English Mob" often blends a "Spirit of Equity, Moderation, and even good Nature" and that such a spirit must not be further subdued "so as to leave inanimate the Body of the People." Professor Ian Christie sees food riots as but an extreme expression of popular pressure that "scored a relatively high degree of success" as part of "an essentially conservative process."[72] There seems to be no sign of endemic rebelliousness in search of a sweeping change in the social order, much less of any demand for a right of political participation in order to effect such change.

Yet ironically there now emerged, in the shape of Methodism, a widespread and articulate appeal to the lower orders that, while *not* directed toward militant action to improve their material circumstances, conveyed sufficient potential social overtones to alarm the establishment. Despite John Wesley's explicit support of the existing political and social hierarchy, he realized "that a fairer distribution of goods could alleviate hardship, and opposed as wickedly, devilishly false the idea that the poor were poor merely because they were idle." Methodist exhortations that their members should have a particular care of their sick, and should devote surplus wealth to the poor, may well have evoked uncomfortable recollections from earlier eras of the potential for misinterpretation of such urgings. That Methodism appealed overwhelmingly to the unpropertied is agreed. Dr. J. D. Walsh points to Wesley's explicit avowal of his mission to preach the Gospel to the poor. But in formulating a "radical ethic of charity" his enunciation that "everything about thee which cost more than Christian duty required thee to lay out is the blood of the poor" is as potentially inflammatory as any of the sermons of suspect preachers of earlier times. In 1744, apparently, he even contemplated "a scheme of voluntary Christian communism."[73]

George Whitefield, on occasion, strayed near to issues of class conflict, while Charles Wesley included in one of his hymns the couplet declaring that

> Our Saviour by the rich unknown
> Is worshipped by the poor alone.

Little wonder at the suggestion that such facets of the movement "roused traumatic recollections of the Commonwealth. Early Methodism was regarded as a potentially revolutionary rather than a conservative force." Nevertheless, while his appeal to the poor aroused suspicion, the crucial point must be reiterated that "Wesley wanted to vanquish sin, not social deprivation."[74] His *explicit* message did not threaten the status and property either of the established church or of a hierarchical society, despite any implicit criticism of the former's discharge of its functions or of the lack of Christian values in certain social relationships.

1760–1793

In 1760 the Reverend Alexander Jephson of Durham published *A Friendly and Compassionate Address* to Methodists, deploring "their Notion of the Community of Christian Mens Goods." He warned that "this levelling Principle would initially frustrate and destroy the End and Design which is aimed at thereby.... Such a wretched State of Poverty and Want would presently ensue, as would render the Poor ten times more unhappy." John of Leyden and Münster are recalled! Despite such continued suspicions, Methodism burgeoned further thereafter. But the year 1760 has a far wider significance in that many of our basic assumptions for the early and mid-eighteenth century were now to alter. It has been urged that the years following the accession of George III "were marked by recurrent political controversy and an almost permanent sense of instability and crisis."[75] The fact that the monarch himself became suspect of political designs that modern historians consider at worst not proven was a contributant factor. But the agitations and disturbances associated with the name of Wilkes reflected fears of infringement of civil liberties as much by Parliament itself as by the Crown and its ministers. Military defeat in America and events in Ireland not only sharpened debate on basic constitutional and political principles, but also reflected on the ability of the establishment to continue to govern successfully. Meanwhile, long-term economic and demographic developments helped to produce once more a discontented political nation *manqué* of considerable size, and ultimately to an increasing incidence of socioeconomic distress as a pressure making for change.

Four or five decades of rising real wages and cheap food now came to an end as population increase weakened the bargaining power of labor while simultaneously posing problems of food supply. The weather itself, which had in a sense assisted the successful establishment of Elizabeth I, now seemed to conspire against George III. A series of bad harvests between 1763 and 1774 led to an upsurge in price of food and of consequential disorder and rioting—occasionally of exceptional severity. A speech from the throne in October 1767 adjured Parliament to consider especially "the distresses of the poorer sort." The fact that parliamentary-supported enclosure during the third quarter of this century was predominantly of open-field arable land was most certainly a contributant to social discontent, as was the incidence of price inflation, which reached a level not seen for well over a century. Not surprisingly, there ensued "a spectacular deterioration in the relations of capital and labour . . . and a rash of industrial disputes and disorder unprecedented in their severity."[76] Yet although these decades saw the emergence of reasoned demands not only for "economical reform" in administration but also for changes in parliamentary representation including, ultimately, the extension of the franchise, such proposals were again almost devoid of the associated objective of economic and social amelioration that had so characterised mid-seventeenth-century commonwealth ideology.

Despite continuing usage of the term "commonwealth," the search for evidence of another full flowering of the commonwealth ideal—in all its dimensions—against the background of recurrent crises ends in disappointment. Several modern historians search the middle decades of the eighteenth century for early signs of radicalism rather than for residual commonwealth ideology. But this raises its own problems. What was "radical" in 1720 might not still be so in 1793. One may broadly distinguish three positions: those who wished to purify the existing political system, substituting "integrity" for "corruption"; those who aspired to make fundamental changes, primarily by extending the franchise; those who saw such changes as desirable not only in themselves but as a means to a *social* as well as a *political* end. Obviously, in individual positions there were no sharp dividing lines. In terms of the methods advocated for achieving change, these ranged from appeals and propaganda to a belief in petitioning and the formation of associations and, at the end of the century, an advocacy of a "convention" that could override existing institutions, if necessary by force. It is salutary to recollect that those who had eagerly professed the commonwealth cause in the mid-*seventeenth* century included a wing that may unhesitatingly be assigned to the "radical" extreme of the positions thus outlined, in terms both of political and social objectives and of willingness to resort to direct action in order to attain them.

Alongside the increasingly powerful groundswell of demands for political change during the later decades of the eighteenth century there is undoubted evidence of recurrent if sporadic outbursts of social discontent. Yet one essential constituent element is missing from those interacting factors that might arguably be expected to generate something resembling the eager "commonwealth" debate of such earlier eras: the political philosophy of the age had virtually abandoned any belief in the religio-social ethos of a unitary society, and in the duty of government to enforce the values and standards therein prescribed. By now the concept of the government of the commonwealth as its Christian conscience equipped with teeth had but few adherents. J. G. A. Pocock suggests that the commonwealth ideology, though "of vast importance in the history of thought, . . . was by now visibly out of touch with reality." Indeed, Langford, noting the currency of the awkward term "State," concludes that "its competitors were still more objectionable. 'Commonwealth' was already outmoded. It also had dangerous, mid-seventeenth-century connotations."[77]

Yet funeral rites should not too hastily be administered. Works by Nedham, Neville, Sydney, Locke, and Toland were reprinted by Thomas Hollis and the publisher Richard Baron,[78] though admittedly these may be seen as the last survivors of the Commonwealthmen of the first half of the century. Moreover, though it hardly played a part in practical politics, clear evidence of the survival of certain aspects of commonwealth ideology is not lacking in the voluminous writings evoked by the striking events of the next thirty years. This may most conveniently and pertinently be related, first, to the notion of the citizen's *civil* liberties; secondly, to perceptions of the nature and the unity of the commonwealth; next, to the issue of *political* liberties therein; and last but not least, to the concept of equity, or in modern terminology that of social justice, seen largely in economic terms. Inevitably, these overlap, while the shift in balance between them will be influenced by such events as American Independence and the French Revolution.

The escapades of John Wilkes served as pegs on which to hang real public concern with certain aspects of the civil liberties of the subject—notably aroused by the "Massacre" in St. George's Fields and the Middlesex Election of 1768. But they also demonstrate the difficulty of separating these from political issues as well as "the prevalence of bitter anti-monarchical, pro-republican sentiment."[79] In 1769 the Society of Supporters of the Bill of Rights was set up. In the same year Joseph Towers printed *Observations on Public Liberty, Patriotism, Ministerial Despotism, and National Grievances,* which extolled "the old Whig principles" and enunciated of Wilkes himself that "the question is not whether he be a good or a bad man, but whether the rights of Englishmen have not been violated." But a year later Samuel Johnson, alluding to *The False Alarm* engendered, excoriated Wilkes, identified "every artifice of sedition," and pointed to "the rabble" as supporters of the Society just named.[80] Nonetheless, a shift was by now taking place toward discussion of wider aspects of reform.

In 1767 John Almon published *The Honest Elector's Proposal* (echoing an earlier title), scorning the present delusion of "a vain and pretended *freedom of election*," vitiated by the threat of "*remember your bread*"! Almon's detailed scheme involves a box for each candidate into which electors cast their votes, in a private and curtained room: this "may be truly called *ballotting*." His demand for substitution of annual for septennial elections was repeated in number 12 of his *Political Register* (1768), which contends that "all men of property ought to be electors," and reiterates the earlier commonwealth contention that "man is ever liable to be intoxicated with" power, along with the French gibe "that we are *free* only *once* in *seven* years." Significantly, "the people (I do not mean the illiterate rabble, who have neither capacity for judging of matters of government, nor property to be concerned for) are the *fountain* of authority." The insistence that "a militia, properly regulated, is . . . the only natural defence for a free people" echoes another commonwealth preoccupation that will endure.[81] Almon was at least as much the last of the Commonwealthmen as the first of the radicals.

Joseph Priestley's *Essay on the First Principles of Government* (1768) concentrated on the distinction between civil and political liberty, with most emphasis upon "an inalienable right" to defend the former. But Edmund Burke's *Thoughts on the Cause of the Present Discontents* (1770) was more closely involved with problems of "popular elections . . . in a free state." Admittedly, "the frame of our commonwealth" does not permit of a democratic suffrage, but general accountability to Parliament is essential. The present "interior ministry" and "double cabinet" vitiates this; but Burke does not wish that "the House of Commons should be infected with every epidemical frenzy of the people," has "no sort of reliance upon either a triennial Parliament, or a place-bill. . . . To say nothing of the horrible disorders among the people attending frequent elections." Of course, "the interposition of the body of the people itself" would be a desperate remedy. Burke's much more limited prescription rests upon a rebuttal of court sneers about factions. For "when bad men combine, the good must associate; else they will fall." Adapting a traditional device, "commonwealths are made of families, free commonwealths of parties also." For "party is a body of men united for promoting by their joint endeavours the national interest upon some particular principle in which they are all agreed."[82]

While Burke may be considered a conservative among those who still employed commonwealth and indeed corporeal terminology, Catharine Macaulay's speedily issued rebuttal of his tract surely represents the transition to "radicalism" of its other devotees—although in truth nothing that she wrote would have affronted many mid-seventeenth-century idealists. Conceding its skill, she identifies "the obvious intent of this pernicious work" as against effectual reformation. A system of corruption originating at the Revolution has been bolstered by septennial Parliaments and by the financial devices "of this state engine." Burke himself is but another mouth of faction. What is really at issue is a dread of "the extension of popular powers." Macaulay proposes meetings and petitions to agitate for "the orthodox principle of rotation" and "a more extended and equal power of election, as a very important spring in the machine of political liberty"—the change in analogy is interesting. For "as democratical power can never be preserved from anarchy without representation, so representation can never be kept free from tyrannical exertions on the rights of the people without rotation." Not surprisingly, her ideas have been related to the seventeenth century.[83]

In 1771 Obadiah Hulme's *Historical Essay on the English Constitution* continued a traditional device in looking back to the myth of Anglo-Saxon democracy as well as forward to annual elections, a secret ballot, extension of the franchise, and the elimination of rotten boroughs. He also suggested that associations in every county should demand of candidates pledges to be honored if elected. In the same year, a work by David Williams, *The Philosopher: in Three Conversations*, is of particular interest not only as another early instance of similar proposals, but as a splendid if unintended exemplification of the relevance of commonwealth constitutional principles to the Constitution that later emerged in the United States. While cool about Wilkes, Williams concedes the significance of some issues raised: for behind ministerial abuse of authority lies the danger of arrogation of excessive power by a supposedly accountable representative body, and even the perennial bugaboo of commonwealth ideology: a standing army. The definition of the duty of government "to guard the interests, and to promote the happiness of the people" is reminiscent of earlier commonwealth ideology, as is Williams's recourse to the corporeal analogy. Yet we surely enter a new era with the assertion—of genuine originality—that when men come to understand their rights "there can be no restraint on them, from the claims of any magistracy. The rights of man may be said to be enlarged, as their capacities are enlarged. To know them, is ever a sufficient title."[84]

Yet he also makes clear that "when I said, the people were to chuse delegates and representatives, I meant, the people in general, of a fixed property, to a small amount." Williams also identifies the problem with which much progressive opinion was now grappling: how "to get the will of the people freely and properly expressed." He advocates the introduction of annual elections by ballot, not only of the Commons but also of *all* civil officers. Yet a paternalist confidence at one point as to the character of those locally elected is followed, at governmental level, by an assertion reminiscent of Hume and anticipatory of American thought in *The Federalist*: "in the regulations of government, the business of a legislator is to guard against all possible vices: he is never to give credit for the influence of any probable virtue." The omission of David Williams even from the index of the classical study of the eighteenth-century commonwealthmen is surprising. Yet he was essentially a maverick: his later urgings for a yet wider extension of the franchise were to be followed by a final conservative phase, reminiscent of Burke, in which his emphasis was overwhelmingly upon the organic, quasi-mystical unity of the body politic.

In the 1770s Williams is also an outstanding example of the realization that the *extent* as well as the liberties of the commonwealth are at issue. The problem of the colonies in North America, established and still largely populated by Englishmen who had now reached a point where they considered themselves to be the equals in all civil liberties of the citizens of the mother country, looms large in his anonymous work, *The Morality of a Citizen,* published in the year of the outbreak of hostilities. Its enigmatic and ambivalent tone understandably puzzled reviewers but was an accurate reflection of the dilemma of many who were sympathetic to commonwealth ideals and who despaired at the appeal to violence and the threatened disruption of what they still saw as potentially the greatest vehicle of political freedom: the British commonwealth. Nor is this the retrospective imposition of a pattern. Two years later Williams printed a pamphlet entitled *Unanimity in all parts of the British Commonwealth* (1778). While deploring English unwisdom and American intemperance, he is particularly angry at the colonists' deluded recourse to France—a child flying from its parents to the protection of a crocodile. Most crucially, "the British commonwealth (for I will still include America) is divided into several parts which may be considered as the several branches of the same family" and it is imperative for "the welfare of millions for many ages" that its two great divisions reunite. Williams exemplifies the fact that the main line of British reformist thought during the American Revolution derived from the commonwealth tradition, and also that its representatives yearned for reconciliation long after it had become a forlorn hope.[85]

Two years earlier his fellow Welshman, Richard Price, had also considered "the Justice and Policy of the War with America." Part 2 of *Observations on the Nature of Civil Liberty* (1776) was specifically devoted to America. Price, though employing less of commonwealth terminology than Williams, encapsulates the contention of that tradition that "we are not maintaining but violating our own constitution in America," that the rebels were contending for the civil and political liberties of *British* citizens, and that what was taking place was effectively a civil war within the British commonwealth. An early work of John Cartwright had gone further in 1774 by declaring *American Independence the Interest and Glory of Great Britain*. Concurring with one contemporary who "hath clearly and elegantly refuted the notion of parliamentary sovereignty," Cartwright urges that man's inherent and inalienable entitlement to liberty is in no sense derivative. Surely the Americans have this right, and ideally he "would consider the American governments, like that of Ireland, as sister kingdoms." In his definition of political liberty Cartwright is in the forefront of a suggested transition from "commonwealth" to "radical" prescriptions: his *Take Your Choice!* (1776) commended manhood suffrage, the ballot, annual elections, and equal electoral districts, while the 1780 edition added the abolition of the property qualification and payment of Members—though he was never an egalitarian or social leveller.[86]

Retrospectively, in his *Letters on Political Liberty* (1782), concern for preservation of the unity of the British Commonwealth having given way to that for the preservation of its political liberties, Williams reflects that had British arms succeeded then such as were "amused with the promises of being lords of America, would have seen the chains which had bound down upon their fellow-subjects rivetted on themselves, and despotism . . . would have enthroned itself in horrid majesty on the ruins of the commonwealth." Richard Price's *Observations on the Importance of the American Revolution* (1785) expressed his satisfaction at "the revolution in favour of universal liberty which has taken place." Meanwhile, the American troubles had an impact in Ireland. A feeling of empathy with the colonists, added to religious discord and deepening economic discontent, led to a movement for a truly independent Irish parliament on the one hand and to fear of invasion of Ireland by America's allies on the other. Relative calm between 1714 and 1760 had concealed a growing Irish national consciousness, now made more formidable by about 80,000 United Volunteers. Thus, William Jones of the Middle Temple, in 1780, pointed to "extorted concessions." David Williams, more hopefully, forecast that the need for "political bodies to have one soul, one spirit, one interest, should have their members united vitally" would be "exemplified in the consequences of political accomodation with Ireland."[87]

Williams also had much to say on one other aspect of the unity of the commonwealth to which I must now turn: on what had been quite literally an article of faith with some commonwealth idealists of a much earlier era, the notion of religious uniformity. But here of course his position was that of an advocacy of its abandonment. Since the early eighteenth century, the mainstream of commonwealth thought had been directed to the establishment of freedom of religious belief and worship—effectively as an essential civil liberty within a well-ordered commonwealth. Colin Bonwick discerns "a close correspondence between the goals of the Commonwealthmen and the political aspirations of Protestant Dissenters to obtain relief from discrimination based on confessional criteria." Writing in 1768, Joseph Priestley prophesied that "unbounded free ènquiry . . . may certainly be attended with some inconvenience, but it cannot be restrained without infinitely greater inconvenience." Indeed, already "religious knowledge is greatly advanced and the principle of universal toleration is gaining ground apace." But he also admitted that "toleration in England, notwithstanding our boasted liberty, is far from being complete. . . . It is not the law, but the mildness of the administration, and the spirit of the times, to which we are indebted for our present liberties." In 1782 the urbanely sceptical Soame Jenyns was to ask: "What has government to do with men's religion? . . . Nothing; provided men's religion has nothing to do with government: but our religious and political opinions are intimately connected."[88]

There lay the rub. While the Protestant Dissenters wished to be rid of any doctrinal test that would make them, administratively and politically, second-class citizens, there were still those such as William Hazlitt who identified their ministers as "a sort of Fifth-monarchy men"—though almost extinct. This was not wholly in jest. In 1772 Israel Mauduit, presenting *The Case of the Dissenting Ministers*, deemed it necessary to protest that Dissenters were not "wild Enthusiasts, and Fifth-monarchy men." Nor was any hoped-for progress in sweetness and light toward complete religious equality helped by the contention aroused by the Methodists, by residual and virulent anti-Romanism, and finally by contentious doctrinal dissension among the Dissenters themselves. While formal Deism had waned by the midcentury, the growth of unorthodox opinions about the Trinity within the older Nonconformist denominations was such as to vitiate attempts at a united front. Indeed, Edward Hitchin, also writing in 1772, declared himself convinced that "the Tenets of Pelagius and Socinus were never more propagated, nor the Notions of Deists and Fatalists, ever so prevailing as at this time."[89]

This was the unpromising background to the applications made by the Dissenting Ministers to Parliament in 1772–73 for the abolition of compulsory subscription to the Thirty-Nine Articles. At a crucial meeting within their own ranks, four of their number refused support on the ground that this would open the door to the extremists listed by Hitchin, and one (almost certainly David Williams) because he objected to "any Declaration of Faith, as a Term of Exemption from Penal Laws"! The failure of the dissenting petitions was shortly followed, in 1774, by the establishment by Theophilus Lindsey of the first church built in England for Unitarian worship, and then by David Williams's own particular version of religious worship, which a fellow nonconformist clergyman described as "a sanctuary for every strange being who takes it into his head to *run a muck*"![90] Ultimately, in 1779, Parliament conceded a declaration of acceptance of the Bible as the basis of the Christian faith as adequate for Nonconformist Ministers in place of the Thirty-Nine Articles. But sadly, for the cause of religious tolerance, the very moderate and limited Catholic Relief Act of 1778 was but a precursor to the dreadful Gordon Riots of June 1780. Yet again, renewed Dissenting efforts to secure toleration in 1787, 1789, and 1790—against the increasingly threatening (or encouraging, according to taste!) background of events in France—were followed by the "Church and King" or "Priestley Riots" in Birmingham in 1791.[91]

If the notion of a unified church and state as constituting the commonwealth, to which Burke defiantly clung, on the one hand, and the more limited notion of agreement within religious ranks upon the fundamental tenets of their faith, on the other, both now appeared as lost causes, what of the influence of religious morality within the workings of society? David Williams's doomed conventicle set out avowedly to preach morality without an underpinning of abstruse dogma. More generally, the skeptical Hume, in his *Dialogues Concerning Natural Religion* (1779), while convinced of "the absolute incomprehensibility of the divine nature," was equally certain about religion being "the ground of all our hopes, the surest foundation of morality." Indeed, "religion, however corrupted, is still better than no religion at all. The doctrine of a future state is so strong and necessary a security to morals"—infusing "the spirit of temperance, order and obedience."[92] A very different voice, that of the Anglican Robert Raikes in 1783, declared that "the aim of the Sunday School is the reformation of Society . . . one only practicable by establishing notions of duty and discipline at an early stage." Whether within the ranks of Christians, including notably the Methodists, or of those described by Stromberg as searching for "a moral order independent of any special or miraculous revelation," indeed for a "reduction of religion to morality," a conviction of the necessity of a moral code within the commonwealth endured. But the belief in a prescribed unity of faith either as essential to underpin this code or as a condition of a healthy commonwealth was now very much a minority opinion. Moreover, neither Stromberg forty years ago, nor James Bradley much more recently, accept any implication of a close correlation between "the radical or liberal tradition in religion with such a tradition in politics or social questions."[93]

Significantly, Albert Goodwin cites a pamphleteer of 1789 as explaining that "the grievance from which the Dissenters seek relief is a *civil* and not an *ecclesiastical* oppression: they complain of being injured as citizens." But it is now time to revert to a mainstream concern of this chapter, the increasing demand for *political* liberties. Remembering always the significant extent of overlap—in respect both of content and of time—it is probably true to say that by about 1779 the main focus of concern amongst would-be reformers has shifted from civil to political liberties. But we have already encountered—in Almon, Hulme, Williams, and Cartwright—the expression of increasingly advanced opinions on political liberty before the outbreak of American hostilities—let alone the impact of defeat. Some would give pride of place, not only as a source for subsequent writers but also in terms of early expression of many advanced ideas, to James Burgh's *Political Disquisitions: or, An Enquiry into public Errors, Defects, and Abuses* (2 volumes, 1774), which has been seen as "perhaps the most important political treatise which appeared in England in the first half of the reign of George III."[94]

Burgh exemplifies the difficulty of making any clear distinction between moderate and advanced reformers, or between "commonwealth" and "radical" ideas. His emphasis at one point upon the device of rotation seems clearly Harringtonian, while that upon annual Parliaments and on balloting is not novel. Yet he goes on to declare "exclusion by rotation . . . only a palliative, not a *radical* cure" (my italics). His approval of Catherine Macaulay's rejoinder to "a noisy declaimer in the house of commons" is indicative. He also cites Voltaire's gibe about freedom once only in seven years, and deplores the fact that "Members of Parliament no longer hold themselves responsible to the People." In defining the people, in the sense of those entitled to participate in the political process, Burgh opens the door to notions more advanced than those of the midcentury Commonwealthmen or indeed of some mid-Stuart Levellers. "It is commonly insisted on, that persons in servitude to others, and those who receive alms, ought not to be admitted to vote [because they] will be influenced by those on whom they depend." Yet "every man has what may be called property, and unalienable property" in his civil and religious liberties and in his family. "What is particularly hard upon the poor in this case is, that though they have no share in determining who shall be the lawgivers of their country, they have a very heavy share in raising the taxes which support government." Taxation on malt, beer, leather, soap, and candles, which falls chiefly upon the poor, must be set alongside the land tax. Thus, "no taxation without representation" acquires a new meaning, and "virtual representation" gives way to actual taxation![95]

Here again one recognizes points encountered earlier in this chapter. Thus, it is important to stress that John Brewer's contention that the American affair served to "help to alter the parameters of debate" and "acted as an ideological midwife" must not be taken too far. American success sharpened but did not initiate discussion; the roots of the movement for reform lay in the commonwealth tradition. Nonetheless, it would be perverse not to recognize the significance of the emergence of the Associations Movement in 1779 and of the Society for Constitutional Information a year later. The first of these is indelibly linked with the name of Christopher Wyvill; but E. C. Black's magisterial survey points out its virtually simultaneous emergence both in Yorkshire and in Middlesex. The establishment of a "Grand National Association for Restoring The Constitution," comprising "all men of property, all friends of liberty, all able commanders," with a committee in every county, had been mooted by James Burgh, and also by Cartwright. Wyvill, more cautious, expressed regret "if Gentlemen are hurt by the term *Association*." The movement spread quickly and other shires joined to produce the "Associated Counties."[96]

Yet Christie stresses that Wyvill himself "was no root and branch reformer" and Black concludes that social and economic theory has passed him by. Thus, when a meeting in March 1780 that declared for additional county members, annual Parliaments, and equal electoral districts was followed by a Westminster subcommittee plan that anticipated the entire Chartist program, the movement splintered. Those who wished merely for "economical reform" withdrew in fright, while such radicals as Jebb, Cartwright, and Thomas Brand Hollis found a home in the Society for Constitutional Information. Richard Pares points to the awakening fear of "an anti-parliament" as well as to the unfortunate verbal resemblance to the zealot Gordon's "Protestant Association." John Cannon cites the apprehension that "when once the mob and the middling people lose their respect for Parliament there is an end of all government and subordination." At least one historian has adduced the failure of the Association Movement as one mark of the final disappearance of the Commonwealthmen.[97]

If Wyvill represented the traditionalist and moderate within the ranks of would-be active reformers, John Jebb spoke for the more advanced element. His "Address to the Freeholders of Middlesex" in 1779 includes the traditional notion that "a people is free, when such constitutional checks exist, as render it impracticable for ministers to betray the public cause." But this is not enough: "the blessing of an equal, annual, and universal representation of the commons [is] the only effectual remedy for the increasing disorders of our distempered state." While skeptical as to the effectiveness of the counties petitioning a body that they are unable to coerce, he himself uses the term "convention" and his purposes have been seen as "entirely revolutionary" in floating the scenario of a national association as a putative sovereign assembly. Bonwick assigns him to "an extreme wing of commonwealth radicalism."[98]

Writing of these trends and of the emergence of the SCI, Carl Cone stresses that, a decade before the outbreak of the French Revolution, the movement's "origins were in the commonwealth tradition of the seventeenth century, and the members were fully conscious of the British ancestry of their radicalism." Certainly at the outset the SCI, established in April 1780, stood four-square upon a commonwealth tradition—reprinting Trenchard, Molesworth, and Fletcher, as well as Ponet and others noted earlier. Its members have been described as "heirs of the Lockeian and seventeenth-century commonwealth tradition." Yet the founder members included Cartwright, Jebb, and Brand Hollis, and their purposes were assuredly not antiquarian. It also printed and distributed, often freely, more controversial and immediately relevant material, such as *Two Speeches of Thomas Day* (another member) that, alongside an interesting allusion to "the continuance of the pernicious civil war," asserted that "annual Parliaments, and an equal representation, are the undoubted constitutional rights of the English people."[99]

His biographer insists that neither Cartwright nor the organization of which he was the leading founder wished to change the social order nor was in any way egalitarian. Yet another founding-member, Brand Hollis, chaired a meeting of a Westminster subcommittee that denounced property as "the grand enchantress of the world." Such opinions were almost certainly those of a minority of members. But a handbill that was distributed gratis by the SCI in 1782 declared that—excluding only infants, the insane, and the criminal—"liberty, or freedom, consists in having an actual share in the appointing of those who frame the laws," and indeed that "the poor man has an equal right, *but more need,* to have representatives in the legislature than the rich" (my italics).[100] *If* one dare attempt to locate a meaningful division within the ranks of the reformers, it may well be related to the welcome or rejection accorded to such an *arriere pensée* attaching to the notion of universal suffrage.

Thus, both the Association Movement and the SCI contained radical as well as more traditional elements. The advent of the French Revolution was at first to revive and then to dash the former's hopes. Meanwhile, the latter achieved only very limited success in certain measures of "economical reform," while the hopes pinned on Pitt the Younger, after some fleeting prospects of success, ended with the rejection of his very modest proposals for reform in 1785— described by Jonathan Clark in turn as "the last effort of the commonwealth tradition." Any attempts at classification are cut right across by two crucial issues engaging the attention of conservatives as well as radicals: the maintenance of social deference, and the problem of accurate identification of "the people's will." Thus, whatever their initially enthusiastic reaction to the French Revolution, Richard Price and David Williams never abandoned the concept of social deference: Price's own congregation at Stoke Newington all knew their place in respect of seating arrangements, while Williams shared to the full his contemporaries' vexation with "the servant problem"—and agonized at one stage about extending the franchise thus far! Certainly they "shared the values of a socially differentiated community." Again, right across the political spectrum writers were engrossed with either the mechanics or the propriety of a true representation of the people's will. David Williams grappled with the former in many of his works.[101] Far less well-known, Lewis De Lolme expressed the fear that, however ascertained, on occasion "a general will results, which is also void of reflection." But he also uttered the caveat that may not yet have lost its point: "to render ineffectual the silent, powerful, and ever active conspiracy of those who govern, requires a degree of knowledge, and a spirit of perseverance, which are not to be expected from the multitude." The cynical if entertaining Soame Jenyns identified the real problem in pushing forward the rights of "that important and misapplied term the people [as being] not what right they have to liberty, but what degree of it they are capable of enjoying, without accomplishing their own destruction." As to parliamentary representatives themselves, Cone's assertion that "the idea that members of the lower orders would ever be elected to the Commons was totally beyond eighteenth-century comprehension" is no gross exaggeration.[102] David Williams and Cartwright alike believed that, properly informed, the people would elect those best fitted by standing and experience as well as by intellect and character to speak on their behalf.

Undoubtedly, the swing back toward conservatism and against even moderate parliamentary and electoral reform occurred during the mid-, if not early, 1780s, long before the outbreak of the French Revolution. But equally surely the outbreak and then the course of revolution across the Channel served to polarize and harden positions. Richard Price's *Discourse on the Love of Our Country*, delivered in November 1789, contained many sentiments that would have been applauded by early-eighteenth-century Commonwealthmen. But his extension of congratulations to the National Assembly of France, his appeal to those in power to "consent to the correction of abuses, before they and you are destroyed together," and his hope for "a general reformation in the governments of Europe," awakened obvious fears. Most especially, the address evoked Edmund Burke's *Reflections on the Revolution in France* (1790). For time was to show that Price's symbolic gesture in addressing his discourse to the Society for Commemorating the Revolution (of 1688–89) was quite misplaced.[103] While the Glorious Revolution might well be interpreted—as it was by Burke himself—as defending the liberties of a status quo ante as an essentially conservative revolution, the French Revolution was soon to open floodgates.

Yet before looking in some detail at British reaction to events in France, most particularly at their contribution to the final splintering of commonwealth ideology, it is essential to turn once more to the social dimension, against the economic background of the last decades of the eighteenth century. This latter changed indeed during that period. Persistent distress amongst the poorer orders from the 1760s until the early 1780s was followed by what Christie discerns as "a steady improvement in the general social and economic conditions of the British people"—at least until the full impact was felt of war with France. In terms of statistics, the general price trend leveled off after an upsurge in the early eighties,[104] while in terms of social attitudes this was matched by signs of a more humanitarian approach. Again, consideration of three crucial aspects of commonwealth ideology—attitudes toward property, poverty, and the pursuit of equity through ameliorative governmental intervention—will prove informative.

Regarding property, it has been urged that Harrington's basic premise, that power followed property, had by now been accepted—devoid of qualification—as a total justification of the existing political and social order. In short, it had become a conservative device. Soame Jenyns found it axiomatic that "power and property always accompany each other, and power is government." Arguably, the strength of the presumptive link between property and *political* power was almost equaled by that of the belief in the unrestricted *economic* exercise of property rights. Parliamentary attitudes toward enclosures and industrial regulation may well exemplify this point. Yet Langford's conclusion that "the dual obsession of the age with property and customary rights made radical reform unthinkable,"[105] while most certainly valid in the realm of practicable policy, should not be taken too literally. A few minority voices concurred in Brand Hollis's skepticism about the grand enchantress of the age.

I have already noted expressions of discontent both with the *excessive* inequality of distribution of property and with neglect of its traditional social obligations by too many of its owners. But a far more sweepingly directed dissentient voice spoke out as early as 1775—although not reaching print until 1792. In that year Thomas Spence addressed, and was duly expelled by, the Philosophical Society of Newcastle on the question of "Whether Mankind, in Society, reap all the advantages from their natural and equal rights of property in land and liberty, which in that state they possibly may, and ought to expect?" His own reply, that "every man has an equal property in the land in the neighbourhood where he resides," has been seen as reflecting both Harrington and Locke, the former more particularly in respect of political implications, the latter in conceiving of property as "an extension of the person." Notably, in the late-seventeenth- and early-eighteenth-century commonwealth tradition, the application of this principle will obviate any need for a standing army, for "as all have property to defend, they are alike ready to run to arms when their country is in danger."[106]

It is worth stressing that Spence, to whose views I shall return in a wider context, spoke before American Independence, let alone the

French Revolution. So did William Ogilvie, a professor at Aberdeen, whose *Essay on the Right of Property in Land* was published in 1781. This radically inclined Harringtonian enunciates that "no individual can derive from this general right of occupancy a title to any more than an equal share of the soil of his country." "Agrarian laws" would obviate the present "abuses and pernicious effects of that exorbitant right of property in land." Fortunately, "the collective body of the people," endowed with power, may introduce change—although "it is only in purely democratic governments" that this may realistically be expected. Interestingly, Ogilvie's avowed objective, "a system of property in land wholly consonant to natural justice, and favourable to the greatest happiness of the greatest number of citizens", has a distinctly Benthamite flavor. Such may well be thought of as maverick opinion before the 1790s. Yet others deplored "the fatal gap between the very rich, and very poor," and were certain that "the great Author of our being never meant that Riches should prove the means of oppression."[107]

In respect of general attitudes toward labor, wages, and poor relief, one meets evidence of a more humanitarian approach coupled with an increasingly enlightened appreciation of realities that did not go entirely unreflected in the field of policy. In 1767 Nathaniel Forster, admittedly ready to avow himself "an advocate for the poor," was eager in *An Enquiry into the Causes of the Present High Price of Provisions* to pronounce the workers "the real strength and support of a state. And the greater or less happiness of their conditions perhaps its truest barometer." He derided the contention "that the poor will be industrious only in the degree that they are necessitous [as being] as false as it is inhuman." Five years later, Thomas Mortimer, in *The Elements of Commerce, Politics and Finances* (1772, reprinted 1780), exhorted employers to "Hold out an adequate reward." He was ready also to make qualitative judgments on the social usefulness of employments: concerning domestic servants, how ludicrous that "these slaves of idleness and panders to lust, are cloathed, fed, and better paid, than soldiers, sailors, or manufacturers, the vital arteries of the commonwealth"! Even Josiah Tucker, dean of Gloucester, no believer in mollycoddling the idle, could ask rhetorically "Is it not much cheaper to give 2s.6d. a Day in the rich Country to the nimble and adroit Artist, than it is to give 6d. in the poor one to the tedious, awkward Bungler?"[108]

As for labor's standard of living, the early 1760s saw several works devoted to the causes of its perceived deterioration. Forster pointed to a recent increase in the "quantity of circulating money"—alas, wrongly directed. For "luxury or a wanton consumption of any commodities . . . tends in the same degree to impoverish and starve the rest." Again, "in some instances of taxation the burthen falls almost entirely upon the labouring poor," while the monster of Avarice leads to the engrossing of farms and the unjust allocation of land enclosed. Predictably, in Soame Jenyns's treatment of the same topic, old attitudes persist. Rejecting the complaints that "this calamity arises from the artifices of monopolizers, regraters, forestallers, and engrossers, encouraged, or at least connived at, by ministers desirous of oppressing the people, and parliaments unattentive to their complaints," he looks to the increase in money but also to the National Debt and taxation. For "our people, notwithstanding the present scarcity, are still better fed than taught. . . . The lowest manufacturer and meanest mechanic will touch nothing but the very best pieces of meat, and the finest white bread; and, if he cannot attain double the wages for being idle, to what he formerly received for working hard, he thinks he has a right to seek for a redress of his grievances, by riot and rebellion." In 1773 Francis Moore's balanced and much more humanitarian assessment attributed "the Exorbitant Price of Provisions" to a genuine lack of sufficient supply. But he also derided such as, "enjoying themselves over a flowing bowl after a sumptuous dinner," assert that "the poor never lived better" or argue that "the higher we have the Price of Provisions, the more our poor are compelled to labour." He would wish that "the price of provisions and the price of labour should always rise or fall together."[109]

There remained the problem of the treatment appropriate for those unable or unwilling to work. In 1760, considering *The Manifold Causes of the Increase of the Poor*, Josiah Tucker advocated the incorporation of parishes for relief, the need for "equal Taxation for their Support," and "the Prevention of Law-Suits about their Settlements." But he was also wary of those "desirous of Parish-Pay, as a Pension to support them in Laziness and Indolence" and would wish to see, within the workhouse, "all Beggars, Rogues, and Vagrants . . . pounding Hemp, or Free-Stone . . . and to be whipped twice every Week" if recalcitrant. Nonetheless, he suggested that, if hired out, "the Poor themselves shall reap a Benefit from their Wages." In 1775 Richard Woodward, on the basis of experience in Dublin, expounded the *Expediency of a Regular Plan for the Maintenance and Government of the Poor*, "making my appeal solely to your interest, not (as I falsely might) to your benevolence and compassion." Despite such frankness, his book is not devoid of advocacy of "religious discipline" and attacks critics of Charity Schools. But his principal theme is that "voluntary contributions are not sufficiently certain," nor are they equitable for contributors. Congratulating a committee of the English House of Commons on proposing organization of parishes into counties, Woodward claims this as an Irish precedent. But in a crucially significant concluding passage, he poses the question of "Whether education should be provided for the infants, medicine for the sick, and a retreat for the aged, from a regular fund; or whether they should be abandoned to idleness, vice, disease, and famine? It affects national health, happiness, and manners; it is deeply interesting to the commonwealth." Such sentiments indeed bespeak a partial survival of the ideology as well as the terminology of the commonwealth.[110]

As for the actual implementation of policy, Dorothy Marshall's allusion to "the wave of humanitarianism which swept over the whole administration of the Poor Law in the last quarter of the century" has been endorsed by more recent scholars who discern a "positive sense of social responsibility." Statutory reform is linked with the name of Thomas Gilbert. His first Poor Law bill passed through the Commons but was rejected by the Lords as early as 1765. But growing consciousness of the need for change was voiced, for example, by the Member who declared in 1774 that "if we do not alter our laws of settlement we shall depopulate this country," and that "the quantity of executions at Tyburn owe part of their origin to our poor laws." The successful enactment of 1782, which commonly bears Gilbert's name, most notably provided for parishes to combine for the establishment of workhouses, and is seen as a major landmark in attitudes toward the poor. Meanwhile, alongside the efforts of individual philanthropy to help the unfortunate, occasionally there was voiced a proposal to nurture what would later be called "self-help." In 1772 a scheme for state-sponsored contributory sickness insurance survived the Commons but not the Lords. Some fifteen years later another abortive scheme sought to provide social insurance "by obliging the rich in a certain limited proportion to become contributors to the benefit of the poor, and to oblige the poor, while young and in health, to contribute towards their own support when disabled by sickness, accident, or age."[111]

Such schemes, though thwarted, exemplify what has been seen as "an increasingly open debate about the proper direction of social policy" from the 1760s on; yet all in all, it is difficult to dissent from the conclusion that "only occasionally and temporarily did the eighteenth-century State recall its paternalist antecedents."[112] Little now remained at an effective level of the notion of government as the social conscience of the commonwealth with teeth. Worse, whereas the early-eighteenth-century Commonwealthmen had expressed an almost pathological distrust of governmental intervention in economic and social affairs, these later decades became accustomed to the spectacle of such action, very often via parliamentary statute, in pursuit of partial or local commercial or financial interests.

Enclosure legislation is a case in point. The cry of protest that engrossing of farms was an evil "which can effectually be checked by authority only" had no hope of being heard. Admittedly, in the spate of statutory enclosure the legalities were usually scrupulously observed; but recognition of any *communal* property rights in the shape of access to and usage of the common was often sacrificed on the altar of definition of strictly individual property. Again, the earlier expressed objectives of maintenance of standards of manufacture, regulation of relations between employer and worker, and protection of the consumer were increasingly allowed to go by default rather than formally abandoned. The Statute of Apprentices was not in fact repealed until 1814, but by the 1760s and 1770s calls for enforcement were desperate and usually futile, although in 1773 the weavers secured a statute enjoining minimum wage regulation by Middlesex JPs. There was also occasional action to enforce legislation inherited from the Tudor era against engrossing, forestalling, and regrating, as in a royal proclamation of 1766. A speech from the throne in October 1767, following another bad harvest, asked Parliament to consider "the distresses of the poorer sort."[113]

Yet the general trend of what earlier commonwealth idealists would have considered—though not in that terminology—as dereliction by government of its duties in the field of social equity seems clear. Nowhere was this more so than in that form of intervention that to many seemed all too prevalent and socially unjust: the imposition of taxation. This was perceived to bear proportionately less and less on owners of landed property and more and more by way of indirect taxation of necessities upon the disposable income of the poorer members of society—almost as a concealed and regressive income tax. Nor were matters helped by the fact that by the 1780s, of a budget of about £13 million, some £9 million went to pay the interest on the National Debt. Nathaniel Forster, as early as 1767, considered it to be "universally allowed, that taxes upon luxury are of all others the more equitable." He therefore commended taxation of dogs and horses maintained for pleasure, not forgetting servants either! But most strikingly he proposed a capitation tax from which "the lower people were entirely exempt, or, what would be still better, had premiums in proportion to the numbers of which their families consisted."[114]

Such suggestions stood little chance of serious consideration. Yet we may fairly speak of a literature of protest long prior to 1789, remembering always that social protest did not often imply any disposition to social revolt. Christie has pointed to the near-dichotomy between consciousness of social grievances and the agitation for political reform between 1763 and 1785, observing that the riots that undoubtedly occurred "were not directed against the social system in general. In a real sense oligarchical government in late eighteenth-century Britain stood four-square on its foundations in the tacit consent of the people." Yet those who ruled were always uneasily aware of what might be. As early as 1765 Soame Jenyns was ready to understand why, when "the lowest of the people . . . feel themselves oppressed with poverty, and condemned to labour, and behold their superiors enjoying all the pomps and luxuries of life, it will be easy to persuade them, that they receive *greater benefits from government* [my italics] than themselves, and that, for that reason, they have a right to subvert it."[115]

Quite often within those writings that express social protest, the use of the corporeal analogy of society, the appeals already noticed on such issues as the relief of poverty and the recognition of the social obligations attached to ownership of property, and the occasional employment of commonwealth terminology, suggest the survival of elements of an earlier ideology—though without any connotations in terms of political change. The recurrent complaints against luxury are reminiscent not only of early-eighteenth-century commonwealth notions of the classical virtues in government and in general probity, but also of a much earlier insistence upon "a moderation and a mean." Yet sometimes, in context, such complaints come near to what would now be termed a coded indication of class exploitation. As early as 1767 the fear surfaces that there is a "fatal gap between the very rich, and very poor," that the nation "will soon be divided into these two extremes," and that "the few will soon begin to combine against the many."[116] This is twenty years before the outbreak of the French Revolution. But indisputably, the combined effect of the example of events across the Channel and of increasing economic hardship during the 1790s sharpened the tone of social criticism. Several publications made a direct connection between the discontent expressed and the need for political reform. Sometimes, alongside humanitarian concern, one meets a note of what can only be described as class conflict, at variance with mainstream commonwealth ideology.

This is clearly exemplified in a *Review of the Constitution of Great Britain* (1790) by John Oswald—who proudly declared himself a pike-bearer. Thus, the rich "have divided the earth among them

[and] the great mass of mankind must pine in perpetual indigence, in order that the unfeeling few may wallow in wealth"—while the poor may hang "for the horrid crime of cutting a cabbage." Infuriated by the description of "the *swinish multitude,* as the philanthropic Edmund Burke has dared to stigmatize the people," Oswald declares that "it is force alone that can vindicate" their rights. The much better known Mary Wollstonecraft, in *A Vindication of the Rights of Man* (1790), a direct attack on Burke, excusing what she calls the "Utopian reveries" of the elderly Richard Price, does not fall far behind Oswald's extremist views. "The demon of property has ever been at hand to encroach on the sacred rights of man"—a particularly daring heresy. Admittedly, "if the poor are in distress, [the rich] will make some benevolent exertions to assist them; they will confer obligations, but not do justice." Little wonder if "the poor consider the rich as their lawful prey." "Why cannot large estates be divided into small farms?" Meanwhile, in the cities, misery and mendicancy prevail. "How many mechanics, by a flux of trade or fashion, lose their employment?" What then were the outrages on one day, 6 October 1789, compared "to these continual miseries"?[117]

A gentler line is taken by Thomas Bentley, "a seeker of Christianity," in a broadsheet issued in July 1791. *The Rights of the Poor* (an interesting choice of title) demands "Free Schools [for] poor children of both sexes" whose parents are unable to cope—indeed, if necessary children should be taken from their parents to be brought up and taught a trade. The courts must enforce justice for the poor. Authority must intervene to rectify the present "disproportion between the present prices of provisions and the wages of the poor." This is indeed reminiscent of some mid-seventeenth-century commonwealth reformers. Much sharper in tone is Thomas Cooper's *Reply to Mr. Burke's Invective* (1792). He proposes to remedy the "Circumstances of national Ignorance, so prevalent among the lower Classes of Society [by] a well formed Plan of public *Education,*" as "an Act of national Justice." But he also commends Ogilvie's publication noted earlier, and condemns privileges as "the Hot-beds of Luxury, Idleness and Immorality . . . the fountain-head of luxurious Ostentation." In his impassioned peroration, Cooper asserts that "the whole of our conduct toward the Poor, seems to me a System of flagrant iniquity. . . . Having made them poor and kept them ignorant, we declare them unfit to be trusted, and thrust them out from any Participation of the most essential rights of Man and a Citizen." Indeed, "our sanguinary code of criminal Law . . . is converted into an Instrument of legal Murder against the poor." Equally explicit was J. T. Callender's declaration in *The Political Progress of Britain* (Edinburgh, 1792) that "what our most excellent constitution may be in theory, I neither know nor care. In practice, it is altogether A Conspiracy Of The Rich Against the Poor."[118]

In 1793 more polemics continued to appear. George Dyers's *The Complaints of the Poor People of England* lamented the "consequences of an imperfect Representation, particularly to the Poor," pointing to the effects of ignorance, to weaknesses in the law, and to the "Disproportion between Crimes and Punishments." William Godwin's very different and massive work reached only the elite. Not so the project commenced by Thomas Spence, who had now printed his lecture of 1775 in his own version of *The Rights of Man. One Pennyworth of Pig's Meat*, "or, Lessons for the Swinish Multitude" (1793–95) was designed as a weekly printing of extracts from instructive works. These included *Oceana*, Sydney, and William Sprigge's *Modest Plea for an Equal Commonwealth* (1659). Spence even included the mid-Tudor moralist's favorite (Isaiah 5.8) "Wo unto them that join house to house, that lay field to field. . . ." Yet his anticipation, to the tune of "Hearts of Oak," of the time when Britain's brave sons

> . . . Joining with Frenchman, all tyrants o'erthrow
> The oppress'd world releasing wherever they go,

bespeaks a very different era. As early as 1763 one MP had conjectured that "such is the levelling principle that has gone forth, that the people imagine they themselves should be judges over us."[119] John Reeves's establishment on 20 November 1792 of his "Association for the preservation of liberty and property against republicans and levellers" demonstrated that the conjecture had now become a nightmare.

Yet even those considered as extremists were sometimes loath to abandon commonwealth terminology. Spence himself described the French (Jacobin) Constitution of 1793 as that of "a Perfect Commonwealth." Indeed his depiction of "the Constitution of Spensonia, a country in Fairy-Land, situated between Utopia and Oceana," included the provision that "the general forces of the commonwealth are composed of the whole people"—a familiar requisite.[120] Again, William Hodgson, while imprisoned, wrote *The Commonwealth of Reason* (1795), a scheme for a type of egalitarian democracy.[121] Much more in the mainstream of those who professed to see in France a realization of many commonwealth ideals was James Mackintosh. His *Vindiciae Gallicae* (1791) speculates on the prospect of "a Revolution so unparallelled . . . spreading its influence throughout the *Christian* Commonwealth" (my italics). Mackintosh also takes up the issue of the grounds of enfranchisement, remarking that the poorest man "still pays a tax in the increased price of his food and clothes." Daringly, he too contends that "life and liberty are more sacred than property, and that the right of suffrage is the only shield that can guard them"—daringly perhaps only in a late-eighteenth-century context, for some would identify mid-seventeenth-century precedents for such ideas. Most notably, he reiterates a sentiment encountered earlier in David Williams: "It is not because we *have* been free, but because we have a right to be free, that we ought to demand freedom."[122]

Mackintosh wrote in direct rebuttal of Edmund Burke, whose *Reflections* he credited with having polarized opinion, and to whose ideas I now turn. Important in themselves, a comparison with those both of David Williams and of Thomas Paine yields crucial illustrations of the separating strands of commonwealth ideology, with which I may appropriately conclude this chapter. Burke believed not only in the organic unity of society, a traditionally conservative notion, but also and most specifically in the unity of church and state. He was not over-rigorous in respect of doctrinal orthodoxy. His contributions to the debates of 1772 and 1773, while fearful of "anything that tends to shake one of the capital pillars of the state," concluded "that toleration, so far from being an attack on Christianity, becomes the best and surest support." He wished to "see the Established Church of England great and powerful," but abhorred "the mutual hatred of Christian congregations." But one passage above all places him at the heart of an inherited commonwealth tradition:

> An alliance between Church and State in a Christian commonwealth is . . . an idle and a fanciful speculation. An alliance is between two things that are in their nature distinct and independent, such as two sovereign states. But in a Christian commonwealth the Church and the State are one and the same thing, being different integral parts of the same whole. . . . Religion is so far, in my opinion, from being out of the province or the duty of a Christian magistrate, that it is, and it ought to be, not only his care, but the principal thing in his care.[123]

Continuity and tradition, predictably, dominate his concept of politics. Debating "A Bill for Shortening the Duration of Parliaments" in May 1780, he finds it "always to be lamented, when men are driven to search into the foundations of the commonwealth." He was ever fearful lest "a violent and furious popular spirit would arise." Admittedly "to govern according to the sense and agreeably to the interests of the people is a great and glorious object of government. This object cannot be obtained but through the medium of popular election; and popular election is a mighty evil." Given that "the electors are corruptible, . . . easily overreached, easily seduced," he sees in triennial elections only "triennial corruption, triennial drunkenness," and so forth, which would undermine "the deepest and best-laid foundations of the commonwealth."[124] His *Reflections on the Revolution in France* (1790) reiterate the same principles. Perpetual reform or revolution are not the signs of a healthy body politic. In particular, Burke deplores "that monstrous fiction which, by inspiring false ideas and vain expectations, . . . serves only to aggravate and embitter that real inequality, which it can never remove." For "all men have equal rights, but not to equal things." Thus, "the science of constructing a commonwealth, or renovating it, or reforming it, is, like any other experimental science, not to be taught *a priori*." His "Appeal from The New to the Old Whigs" asserts that "what was done in France was a wild attempt to methodize anarchy." He scorns the "argument for supposing a multitude told by the head to be the people," and that then, "as such their will is to be law." For sadly, "arbitrary power is so much to the depraved taste of the vulgar . . . that almost all the dissensions which lacerate the commonwealth are not concerning the manner in which it is to be exercised, but concerning the hands in which it is to be placed." "The democratic commonwealth is the foodful nurse of ambition." But above all, Burke laments "the ruin which follows the disjoining of religion from the state, the separation of morality from policy."[125]

Although, ironically, his experiences in France led him to reach conclusions very similar to those of Burke, his personal bête noire, on several issues, David Williams presents us with a very different case study of the ultimate disintegration of commonwealth ideology. In his writings noticed earlier, and indeed up to and including his *Lectures on Political Principles* in 1789, his vision of the commonwealth combined acceptance of social inequality with pleas for social equity, but also with a steadily more explicit concept of political equality as a necessary guarantor of *all* rights. His adhesion to an organic analogy of society did not stop him from pushing a belief in religious toleration beyond limits that would have appalled Burke—and indeed did appal many of the Dissenters from whose ranks he had emerged. He displayed an old-fashioned commonwealth conviction that the pursuit of wealth *ad libitum* was reprehensible, alongside an attitude toward the education of the poor that would have repelled any mid-seventeenth-century idealist. Thus far his taste for daring experiment in the field of religious worship had not been matched by an active participation in the political arena—unlike Burke, he abhorred parties.[126] But now the impression made by his *Lessons to a Young Prince* (September 1790), together with his friendship with Brissot, gave him the opportunity to participate in a political experiment on a far wider stage than that of Margaret Street. In his interpretation of events in France, Williams scorns alike Burke's picture of "a bloody and ferocious democracy" and his fellow London Welshman Price's misplaced seventeenth-century radical-dissenting interpretation of what was happening. Williams's own prescription for the way in which, in his opinion, the French should now proceed sounds rather like a Rousseau-type concept of General Will dedicated to the preservation of Lockeian individual rights, with commonwealth/paternalist social overtones.[127]

The work ran through seven editions up to 1791, and a French translation was issued by the printer of the National Assembly in Paris in 1790. Thereafter Williams, in touch with both Pétion and Brissot, accepted an invitation from his Girondin friends, after acceptance of French citizenship, to visit Paris and act as an adviser in the drafting of the first republican constitution of France. French sources leave no doubt as to the importance of his contribution to the abortive Girondine constitution. The influence of commonwealth political thought upon the United States Constitution of 1787 has often been remarked; no doubt because it was abortive, its presence in the Girondine has elicited far less comment. But in February 1793 Williams, disillusioned and frightened by the increasingly violent turn of events, returned to England—a much chastened man. Thereafter he adopted political views that can only be described as neo-Burkeian conservatism. Unlike either Burke or Price (who died in 1791), Williams had seen at firsthand, in theory and in actuality, the difficulties in attempting to institutionalize the expression of "the people's will," and also what could so disastrously go wrong in attempting to implement it. He took refuge in a near-obsession with the organic analogy of society to a point of quasi-mysticism, abandoning hope of constitutional reform and reflecting that "the transition from Evil to Good, because suddenly attempted, often aggravates the Evil, instead of producing the Good."[128]

Another British adviser in the drafting of the Girondine had been Thomas Paine—who indeed spent some time in prison in consequence of Robespierre's antipathy. Paine's writings contain at least three elements of commonwealth ideology: suspicion of government per se; a demand for sweeping political reform; and the advocacy of welfare provision as a duty of government. But in his case they appear to be disparate elements, and although he expresses approval of the term *respublica* as the objective of government, Paine has little recourse to commonwealth terminology. His *Common Sense*, evoked by the American crisis in 1776 and written in support of the colonists, is noteworthy for its clear distinction between society and government: the latter "even in its best state is but a necessary evil; in its worst state an intolerable one." In this context, suggests Kramnick, "government was not a positive agent laying the foundation for a just or good society, let alone a welfare state." Beyond dispute, in both his major works, what has been termed his "fierce egalitarianism endeared Paine to the working man"; but it was an egalitarianism of opportunity, not of living standards.[129]

Part 1 of his *Rights of Man* (1791), combining a direct rejoinder to Burke with criticism of the British constitution, made an even greater impact. But Part 2, which followed in 1792, invites contrast with what appears to be his earlier insistent rejection of a one-time traditional commonwealth emphasis on the *moral* duties of government. The pages of computations and proposals in which Paine includes "a distinct provision" for the aged poor and public funding of education up to the age of fourteen would have gladdened the hearts of reformers in the "Great Instauration" of the seventeenth century. He deplores the spectacle of "old age working itself to death, in what are called civilized countries" and would pay, from taxation, £6 per annum and £10 per annum over the ages of fifty and sixty respectively. At one end of the age range, assuredly "a nation under a well-regulated government should permit none to remain uninstructed"; at the other, a fund is desirable to defray the funeral expenses of strangers far from home. As for taxation, Paine seizes upon current discussion of taxing luxuries to urge that "an overgrown estate . . . is a luxury at all times, and, as such, is the proper object of taxation." Indeed he even prints a "table of progressive taxation" on all estates above "clear yearly value of £50." Significantly, "the object is not so much the produce of the tax as the justice of the measure." The present "poor laws, those instruments of civil torture, will be superseded"; in lieu of the poor-rates (to be abolished) a remission of taxes to the poor of double their amount will be made. Whatever the provenance of these ideas, Paine has been seen as a precursor of the type of social justice that was ultimately to create the Welfare State rather than a legatee of commonwealth social ideology. Again, he regrets that "several laws are in existence for regulating and limiting workmen's wages. Why not leave them as free to make their own bargains as the law-makers are to let their farms and houses?" All confidence in this aspect of paternalism has gone.¹³⁰

Overall, Thomas Paine is more difficult than Burke or Williams to relate to the inherited commonwealth ideology, but is also perhaps the best illustration of what were by now its disparate elements. Many of his ideas on social welfare were not original in kind, but Cone asserts that "the *Rights of Man* preached social revolution." Cannon points to an "undeniable strain of class hatred" and to the contention that "by providing the missing link between parliamentary reform and social and economic progress" Paine elicited a mass response far surpassing that of Wyvill or Cartwright, but also the fear "that parliamentary reform would be but the prelude to social revolution." But who would say that this scenario had not existed in some mid-seventeenth-century minds? It pervades the Putney Debates. Perhaps Paine should have the last word: he concludes Part 2 of his greatest work by envisaging the growth of emerging buds on tree-twigs in February, a process that he believes to have begun. But he does not relate them to the tree of commonwealth.¹³¹

Conclusion

THE CHOICE OF 1793 AS A TERMINAL DATE FOR THIS STUDY, WHILE NOT OF course definitive, is in several ways appropriate. Some years ago Caroline Robbins concluded that the cumulative impact of the terror awakened by the Gordon Riots, the failure of Wyville's Associations, and the outcry evoked by suggested parallels between England's Glorious Revolution and the new order emerging in France, effectively "marked the end of the Commonwealthmen." Already, it is urged, there survived but a tenuous link between end-of-century radical ideology and that of the early-eighteenth-century Commonwealthmen. Other historians, largely equating the surviving commonwealth tradition with a genuine hope of political reform, insist that the cause had been lost by the early or mid-1780s—well before the impact of events across the Channel. Pocock asserts that "one reason for this failure was that the commonwealth ideology . . . was by now visibly out of touch with reality."[1]

Nevertheless, it would be unrealistic to minimize the impact of the course of events in France between 1789 and 1793 upon British opinion. The tide may well have turned against constitutional and political reform by 1785; but it was events in France after 1789 which brought it to the flood. Most crucially, within the context of this study, the revulsion correctly identified involved not only the prospect of *political* reform, but also the *social* dimension that, at least over the long-term time span, had been such an important constituent of commonwealth ideology. The "red fool fury of the Seine" now usurped the function of the earlier Leveller nightmare: not only did it help to put back the cause of political reform in England at least for a further quarter-century, but it also established that "whereas in the 1770s reform had not seemed to threaten property or status, it now reeked of revolution." Contemporarily, Arthur Young, in *The Example of France, a Warning to Britain* (1793) asserted that "the leading conclusion deducible from the French experiment . . . is this, *if persons are represented, property is destroyed*"; thus, "power in the hands *of the people*, by means of personal representation, has ruined France."[2]

This caveat, when set alongside the notion of a European or indeed an Atlantic revolution as in Palmer's thesis, reflects a bitter irony. Keith Baker, alluding to the emergence of the "notion of public opinion as a political tribune" in France, concurs with Gunn's conclusion that "the use of the term to describe the expression of the voice of the people in political matters first grew out of British experience." Indeed, in France, from Montesquieu to De Lolme and David Williams, the British example had been looked to. But now, while American Independence had stimulated the movement for political reform in Britain, those events in France that revealed certain challenging *socio*political implications confirmed its recession.[3]

Very recently, Gunn has traced the emergence and evolution of the comparative content in France and in England of the term "public opinion." In England "the centrality of Parliament" had long served to limit "the constitutional impact of the opinions current in the general population," the concept of virtual representation rendering highly suspect any attempt at the latter's intrusion at least until the 1784 election. Conformably, public opinion itself—in contrast with the notion of "interest"—"suggested tradition, collective behaviour and community standards." Most significantly, despite his "radical" phase and visit to Revolutionary France, even David Williams proved unable to free his mind from a deeply ingrained conviction that the people should follow the lead of an elite.[4]

Some years earlier, of course, Jürgen Habermas had also considered "the model case of British development" as anticipating the emergence and impact of public opinion in France. Despite some differences in interpretation, Gunn, who finds the term "opinion publique" in usage earlier than its English equivalent, stresses its early-eighteenth-century embodiment of totally traditional assumptions. His discernment in France by around 1791 of recognition of "the usefulness of the notion of a spirit whose defining quality seemed to be a concern for the social whole" almost invites identification with an earlier English "commonwealth" ideology. But by now "the French concept of public opinion was *radicalized*";[5] the events of 1789–93 swept away the anchor points of an earlier derivative British tradition.

There thus emerged that which had at the very least remained dormant throughout the eighteenth century, the specter of class warfare. How many people in England shared the hopes of the drunken yeoman who, in March 1793, coupled with his toast to Thomas Paine his own resolve to "go to my neck in Blood and Guts and Garbage for to be in the fore-front of the Battle for a Revolution" must forever remain an unknown quantity—but most certainly those in authority at least professed themselves greatly perturbed. By now, as Langford observes, "it was to be class oppression rather than corrupt self-interest that was at issue." Accordingly, reactions to and interpretations of events in France widened still further incipient splits within the ranks of those who desired political reform. Christopher Wyvill's *Defence of Dr Price, and the Reformers of England* (1792) deplored the fact that Paine's "counsel, to break up and destroy the noble fabric of our Constitution, and rebuild a new political edifice on the plans of America, seems to be conveyed in the most dangerous shape [that] might tend to excite the lowest classes of the People to acts of violence and injustice."[6]

Arguably, an expectation of earlier commonwealth idealists that social amelioration for the lower orders would be interwoven with political reform had now returned—but in the shape of a nightmare for the upper levels of the social hierarchy. Cone points to the virtual disappearance after a meeting in May 1794 of the SCI, suggesting that "with it the old Commonwealthman doctrinairism vanished from the reform arguments. . . . The end of the SCI was the end of a phase in English thought that had begun with the Levellers." Yet agreement on what are generally accepted as Leveller social and economic objectives had never been manifest within the ranks of the SCI. Something resembling a dichotomy now emerged between humanitarian radicals whose outcries against social injustice resembled much of what had been written in the 1640s and 1650s, and such as David Williams who, having made his peace with the establishment, decried such interference with natural economic forces as intrusive attempts to educate the children of the poor above their station in language that would have gladdened Mandeville. Thomas Holcroft, who had earlier visited Williams's Margaret Street conventicle, was now in prison, whence he penned (in 1795) an impassioned depiction of the plight of the poor in face of the well-to-do: "Why are the rich tyrants? Because the poor are humbled, and terrified till they dare not speak." Significantly, Holcroft protests that the labels of Jacobin and of Leveller have now become interchangeable in the language of denigration.[7]

Meanwhile, though historians may write of the end of the Commonwealthmen, the usage of commonwealth terminology continued. In 1795 John Cartwright's *The Commonwealth in Danger* insisted that the British realm had formerly been in its essence a republic or commonwealth and must now revert to this status by means of necessary reforms. Cartwright's vision of reform no longer coincided with that of more extreme exponents of the ideal commonwealth such as Spence or Hodgson, already briefly noticed. But the line of demarcation is not sharp: Hodgson's insistence on rulers "as the servants of the commonwealth," on rotation of office-holding, and on citizen-soldiers, was completely within an older commonwealth tradition, while issues of Spence's *Pigs Meat* were full of extracts from seventeenth- and eighteenth-century Commonwealthmen.[8]

The year 1793 has another significance. The Jacobin constitution that emerged in June—which was promptly shelved—has been described by Maurice Duverger as still bourgeois, and was attacked by one deputy as lacking adequate safeguards for the well-being of the poor. But Albert Goodwin has pointed to the Declaration of Right, which was its preamble, as making important contributions to "the conception of the welfare state. The purpose of society was declared to be the happiness of the people, public assistance the right of the infirm or unemployable, public education a general necessity."[9] Indeed, in ensuing months legislation was introduced to control prices and wages; Europe thus saw an attempt at "paternalism" not by a benevolent monarch but by what has been termed an "elective dictatorship." The spectacle of socially interventionist legislation alongside a major extension of the franchise will not have been lost in England, and rendered more suspect at least one major strand of recent commonwealth political ideology. To others, of course, such egalitarian indications were not unwelcome. It cannot be overemphasized that, whatever their intellectual provenance, Paine's proposals in Part 2 of his *Rights of Man* were published in 1792 and were in no way derivative from French experience; but knowledge of developments across the Channel surely deepened conservative dread of what he stood for.

The word "conservative" suggests one other exemplification of the splintering of the commonwealth tradition. Caroline Robbins reminds us that Edmund Burke "distrusted the ideologies of the Commonwealthmen and they distrusted him, even when circumstances brought them into the same camp."[10] Yet, ironically, Burke's fervent belief in the unity of church and commonwealth had been a major basis of the earliest commonwealth tradition. So, too, had been his utter conviction of the organic nature of the established social hierarchy. Oddly enough, this organicism was one of the few elements of his earlier ideology to survive in the much-chastened David Williams. Despite their personal antipathy and totally divergent opinions on religious issues, both men by now concurred on the danger of hasty and ill-considered attempts at either political or social reform. Paine never had any time for social deference, and furnishes little trace of commonwealth terminology; yet he it was who took up the challenge of the need for systematic governmental provision of help for the aged and unfortunate, together with educational services, in a way that would have enthused commonwealth idealists of the mid-seventeenth century—despite his rejection of the religious basis that essentially motivated their approach.

Of course this apparent disintegration of commonwealth ideology was no sudden and very recent phenomenon. From the outset the term "commonwealth" itself had sometimes meant different things to different men, and the most that one can hope to do by way of general retrospect is to sketch a few outstanding trends and turning points. For some two centuries after about 1450 the word was broadly taken to imply the well-being of society, considered as an entity. Admittedly, it was probably as often employed as a general synonym for "realm." But those who extolled the commonwealth as an ideal, and in particular as an objective of governmental policy, thought mainly in terms of the welfare of the members of society. And members indeed in a quite literally organic sense. In no way antimonarchical or antihierarchical, the ideal of the commonwealth could fairly be identified as comprising the Christian conscience of society. In its service, integrity and administrative efficiency, rather than institutional reform per se, were enjoined—in sources ranging from Erasmus to Pope—as a means to an end. It is true that there were always some who discerned in the term "*common*-wealth" a potentially sinister egalitarian connotation. But in general the accepted and beneficent ethos of paternalist care for the body politic, and in particular for its weaker members, for long endured.

If it may well be argued that the "revolution in government" and most particularly in the relationship between church and realm attributed to Thomas Cromwell both widened and deepened traditional perceptions of the scope and duties of the commonwealth, it may as cogently be urged that the first incipient signs of any questioning of such perceptions came with the challenge to nationwide acceptance and enforcement of religious uniformity. Yet, ironically, those who posed this very challenge, far from questioning the *social* duties of government, went on to expound an increasing emphasis thereon in what they conceived of as a truly Christian commonwealth. Their objectives were anti-episcopal but assuredly not antireligious. In partial consequence of this blossoming assertion of individual religious rights within the commonwealth, there followed those who thought in terms of what would in due course be seen as individual *civil* rights—to be envisaged largely in terms of property. Both of these trends contributed toward the opposition first to

James I and then to his son. Both also, in different ways, contributed toward the ultimate erosion of the first-phase organic ideal of the commonwealth.

Meanwhile, their convergence, and the civil war and revolution that ensued, helped to nurture a new and added dimension of the commonwealth ideal: the notion that some degree of political participation by the ordinary citizen was a necessary condition not only of his own fulfilment but also of the attainment of the requisite standards—civil, religious, social, and economic—of a Christian commonwealth. This, surely, in the mid-seventeenth century, marks the apogee of the commonwealth ideal. The ideology remained that of an organic and Christian society. Yet the vision of the social, educational, and generally humanitarian scope of governmental responsibilities was in many respects not again to be advanced until well over a century later. Nor was that of an individual's political rights and duties. Sadly, this full blossoming of the commonwealth ideal was short-lived, cultivated only by minority opinion, and most of its seeds fell on stony ground.

Thereafter, those extended individual political rights and enhanced social duties of government that had been yoked together as short-lived expectations swiftly became twin specters in the egalitarian nightmare of the upper echelons of society. The story of the late seventeenth and early eighteenth centuries is indeed one of striving to rid the now circumscribed commonwealth ideal of this double incubus, and of association with the real and imagined excesses of the past. Thus, the spartan but limited political ideology of these later Commonwealthmen, seeking to re-establish respectability, led them to repudiate both the organic notion of a unified state and church that had distinguished many of their Tudor namesakes, and the belief in an interventionist and socially ameliorative duty of government that had so distinguished the middle phase of the ideal. So far have things now moved in the context of the religious aspects of the commonwealth that at one point Jonathan Clark appears virtually to identify the eighteenth-century Commonwealthmen with Dissent.[11] Certainly their insistence upon political rights for virtually a century after 1688 was accompanied by an almost frantic dissociation from any idea of economic or social levelling. Thus, in the mid-eighteenth century, the paternalist commonwealth nostalgia of Bolingbroke and his circle looked back *not* to the dangerous political and social experimentation of mid-Stuart ideologues, but still further to the much more acceptable social pattern that they attributed to Elizabethan England.

Little wonder then, that while many of the ideas encountered in the writings of some late-eighteenth-century reformers may fairly be identified as disparate elements of a tradition reaching back over three centuries, they were by now no more than that. The mid-Tudor era had witnessed a conjunction of dynastic, religious, and economic crises that evoked the first major blossoming of a commonwealth ideology in response to perceived social needs. A century later, in several respects history went close to repeating itself, although by now that ideology was acquiring a new and extremely significant dimension that both reflected and in turn influenced changing political circumstances. But the winds of change in the late eighteenth century blew in a vastly different political, social, and religious climate, and served but to stir the leaves fallen from a no longer flourishing or fashionable tree.

It is worth observing that the continued insistence of many sincerely religious men upon a moral function of government had often accompanied their own denial of the notion of a national church with an orthodox code of belief as being coextensive with the commonwealth. But an increasing credence in a completely secularized concept of individual rights could not but hasten the disintegration of a commonwealth ideology that had for so long been embodied in an organic analogy of society. The slow decline in popularity of the term commonwealth itself reflected not only changing verbal fashions but also the continued erosion of the basis of the notion of a *Christian* commonwealth. The term indeed survived, but now not nearly as often in the mouths of statesmen as in the minds of some individual expressions of the conscience of society. At the heart of the sixteenth and mid-seventeenth centuries concept of the commonwealth there lay an acceptance of a religious and moral purpose as pervading and in a sense unifying society—preached by organized religion and enforced by the secular power. Government was endued with a moral duty to nurture values of conduct in all aspects of social relationships, in the interest of the quality of life of all members of the commonwealth. The early modern era saw the ultimate erosion of the conviction that this duty is part of a divinely imposed imperative. In terms of political participation and of provision of a range of welfare services, many of the objectives of commonwealth ideology have by now been achieved; but the problem of deriving any agreed moral purpose from a secularized philosophy of individual rights has not yet been resolved—indeed by many is repudiated—in the modern world.

Notes

DNB   *Dictionary of National Biography,* edited by L. Stephen and S. Lee. London: Oxford University Press, 1908–
EETS   Early English Text Society
Econ HR   *Economic History Review*
EHR   *English Historical Review*
PP   *Past and Present*
TED   *Tudor Economic Documents,* edited by R. H. Tawney and E. Power. 3 vols. London: Longmans, Green, 1953.
TRHS   *Transactions of the Royal Historical Society*

(Full references are found in the Bibliography)

Chapter 1. Genesis: Roots and Branches

1. Skinner, *Foundations of Modern Political Thought,* vol. I, *The Renaissance,* xiii.
2. Elton, *The Tudor Revolution in Government.*
3. John Locke, *Two Treatises of Civil Government,* 183.
4. Robert Molesworth, *The Principles of a Real Whig,* viii.
5. Robbins, *The Eighteenth-Century Commonwealthman,* 379.
6. Ibid., 4, 385.
7. Chrimes, *English Constitutional Ideas in the Fifteenth Century,* 304.
8. See *Revolution Reassessed,* ed. C. Coleman and D. Starkey, especially 18–25.
9. Gilson, in *EHR* 26 (1911), 512–25. See also Sir H. Nicolas, *Proceedings and Ordinances,* 6: 90–91.
10. *William Gregory's Chronicle of London,* 191.
11. Davies, ed., *An English Chronicle,* 81.
12. "Charges against the Duke of Suffolk," *Historical Manuscript Commission, Third Report,* appendix, 280.
13. See Elton, "Reform and the 'Commonwealth's Men' of Edward VI's Reign," 23–38; Starkey, *Revolution Reassessed,* 13–27 and 199–208; Elton, "A New Age of Reform?," 709–16, and "Tudor Government," 425–35.
14. Quoted in Owst, *Literature and Pulpit in Medieval England,* 550–51.
15. Troeltsch, *The Social Teaching of the Christian Churches,* 1:203.
16. Owst, *Literature and Pulpit,* 553–54.
17. Noonan, *The Scholastic Analysis of Usury,* 2.
18. Langland, *Piers the Ploughman,* 206.
19. Ibid., 213.
20. Occleve, *The Government of Princes,* 166.

21. Fortescue, *The Governance of England*, 114–17, 138–39; Starkey, *Revolution Reassessed*, 25.
22. *The Boke of Noblesse*, 21, 55, 56, 57, 60, 68, 70.
23. *The Curial made by maystere Alain Charretier*, 13.
24. 7 Edw. IV; Ric. III, preamble to statutes, 1483; Hen. VII, preamble to statutes, 1485, 3 Hen. VII c. ix, 11 Hen. VII, preamble to statutes, 12 Hen. VII c. v, 19 Hen. VII, preamble to statutes, 19 Hen. VII c. xvii.
25. L. K. Born, introduction to Erasmus, *Education of a Christian Prince*, 10–12, 32.
26. Ibid., 32.
27. Erasmus, *Enchiridion*, 1533; *Erasmus: Enchiridion Militis Christiani: An English Version*, 162.
28. Erasmus, *Education of a Christian Prince*, 154, 170, 175–76, 180, 182, 183.
29. Ibid., 148, 150, 178, 193, 212, 217, 236.
30. de Pisan, *Body of Polycye*, 3–6, 9.
31. Ibid., 11, 27–31, 33–34, 57, 150–51.
32. Dudley, *The Tree of Commonwealth*; Morris, *Political Thought in England: Tyndale to Hooker*, 15.
33. Deuteronomy 25.4.
34. Dudley, *Tree of Commonwealth*, vi, 16–17.
35. Ibid., 14.
36. Ibid., 22, 31–32.
37. Ibid., 32–34.
38. Ibid., 37–39.
39. Ibid., 40–47.
40. Ibid., 48–50, 58, 87–91.
41. Elton, *Reform and Reformation: England 1509–1558*, 2.
42. Skinner, *Foundations of Modern Political Thought*, vol. 2, *The Age of Reformation*, 55–56.

Chapter 2. First Flowering: The Mid-Tudor Commonwealth

1. Davis, *Utopia and the Ideal Society*, 10; Hanson, *From Kingdom to Commonwealth*.
2. Thirsk, *Economic Policy and Projects*, 27.
3. Starkey, *Dialogue between Pole and Lupset*; Ponet, *Shorte Treatise of politike power*; Humphrey, *The Nobles*.
4. Elyot, *The Governour*, 2:445.
5. Starkey, *Dialogue*, 55–57.
6. Starkey, *Exhortation to the people*, 11.
7. Becon, *The Fortress of the Faithful* (1550), in *The Catechism*, 593.
8. Cranmer, *Miscellaneous Writings and Letters*, 2:183.
9. Latimer, *Sermons and Remains*, 299.
10. Armstrong, printed in *TED*, 3:121.
11. Lever, *Sermons* (1550), 28, 47.
12. Hales, printed in Strype, *Ecclesiastical Memorials*, vol. 2, Pt. ii, 358; and also by Lamond, ed., *Discourse of the Commonweal*, lvii–lviii.
13. Slack, in Loach and Tittler, eds., *The Mid-Tudor Polity*, 96; see also his *Poverty and Policy in Tudor and Stuart England*, 24.

14. Starkey, *Dialogue*, 76–85; Gilpin, "Sermon" (1552), printed in W. Gilpin, *Life of Bernard Gilpin*, 12, 40.
15. Cheke, *The hurt of sedition*, printed in Holinshed, *Chronicles*, 3:1004–5.
16. Griffiths, ed., *The Two Books of Homilies*, 72.
17. Tyndale, *Works*, 1:138; Henry VIII, *Letters*, 167.
18. Elyot, *The Governour*, 1:1–3.
19. Hughes and Larkin, *Tudor Royal Proclamations. 1*, no. 218 (319).
20. Hales, printed in Tytler, *Edward VI and Mary*, 1:114–17.
21. *Literary Remains of King Edward the Sixth*, ed. J. G. Nichols, 480–81.
22. Morison, *Remedy for Sedition*, A.ii–A.iii.b, B.iv–B.iv.b, D.ii–D.ii.b, E.iii.b; *A Lamentation* (1536), B.iiii.b.
23. *The Two Books of Homilies*, 105.
24. Baldwin, *A Myrroure For Magistrates*, F.ii.a.
25. Cheke, *The hurt of sedition*, 1003.
26. In Lloyd, ed., *Formularies of Faith*, 188.
27. Edward Hall, *Chronicle* (1548), 699–700.
28. Gardiner, *Answer to Bucer* (1541), in *Obedience in Church and State*, 175, 179, 193, 209.
29. Gardiner, *A Machiavellian Treatise*, 142, 146.
30. Mason printed in Tytler, *Edward VI and Mary*, 1:341.
31. Brinklow, *Complaynt of Roderyck Mors* (c. 1542), 15; Starkey, *Dialogue*, 59–61.
32. See Clay, *Economic Expansion and Social Change*, 2:203–6, 222–50.
33. Guy, *The Cardinal's Court*, comment by Brendan Bradshaw, "The Tudor Commonwealth: Reform and Revision," 459.
34. Scarisbrick, "Cardinal Wolsey and the Common Weal," in *Wealth and Power in Tudor England*, ed. E. W. Ives et al., 45–46; Slack, *Poverty and Policy*, 116–17.
35. Hughes and Larkin, *Tudor Royal Proclamations. 1*, no. 75 (122–23).
36. Scarisbrick, "Cardinal Wolsey," 52, 62–63.
37. *Tudor Royal Proclamations. 1*, nos. 110, 113, 114, 119, 123; no. 110 (14/7/1526), p. 155; no. 119 (15/5/1528), pp. 174–75; Scarisbrick, 64–66.
38. Elton, *Reform and Reformation*, 69.
39. Scarisbrick, "Cardinal Wolsey," 65–67; see also P. Gwyn, *The Rise and Fall of Thomas Wolsey*, chap. 10.
40. Elton, *Reform and Reformation*, 58.
41. Ogilvie, *The King's Government and the Common Law*, 68, 70.
42. Guy, *The Cardinal's Court*, 123.
43. Scarisbrick, "Cardinal Wolsey," 67.
44. Bradshaw, "Tudor Commonwealth," 466.
45. Scarisbrick, "Cardinal Wolsey," 67.
46. Guy, "Wolsey, the Council and the Council Courts," 487.
47. Marius, *Thomas More*, x, 164.
48. Skinner, *Modern Political Thought*, 1:262.
49. See Morris, *Tyndale to Hooker*, 19, and J. W. Allen, *A History of Political Thought in the Sixteenth Century*, 154–56.
50. Hogrefe, *The Sir Thomas More Circle*, 98.
51. Bradshaw, "Tudor Commonwealth," 464–65. For a very different interpretation of *Utopia*, see Fenlon, "England and Europe," 115–35.
52. More, *Works*, 313; *Utopia*, 44–45.
53. *PP* 25 (1963): 3–58, and 29 (1964), 26–49; Bradshaw, "Tudor Commonwealth;" 463; for a balanced critique of Bradshaw, see Guy, "The Tudor Commonwealth: Revising Thomas Cromwell," 681–87. Most recently see G. W. Bernard, "Elton's Cromwell," *History* 83 (1998), 587–607.

54. *Letters and Papers, Foreign and Domestic, of the Reign of Henry VIII* 11,(1536): No. 1244, 504–6.
55. Elton, *Reform and Renewal: Thomas Cromwell and the Common Weal*, 36–37.
56. Beckingsale, *Thomas Cromwell*, 151.
57. Ibid., 152.
58. Elton, *Reform and Renewal*, 64, 92, 98.
59. Ibid., 67.
60. See Dickens and Jones, *Erasmus the Reformer*, 200–201; *Opus Epistolarum Des. Erasmi Roterodami*, Vol. 11, Epp. 3036, 3058, 3107.
61. Dickens and Jones, *Erasmus the Reformer*, 197–200; T. H. Mayer, "Faction and Idealogy," 1–25, sees little evidence of any close link between Starkey and Cromwell.
62. Elton, *Reform and Renewal*, 21.
63. Dickens, *The English Reformation*, 154–57.
64. 28 Hen. VIII, c. XIII.
65. *Life and Letters of Thomas Cromwell*, vol. 2:26–29.
66. Beckingsale, *Thomas Cromwell*, 68.
67. Bradshaw, "Tudor Commonwealth," 465; Guy, "Tudor Commonwealth," 681–87.
68. Elton, *Reform and Renewal*, 158.
69. Ibid., 81, 87.
70. *Tudor Royal Proclamations. 1*, no. 181 (265); no. 189 (281–83).
71. Elton, *Reform and Renewal*, 90.
72. Bradshaw, "Tudor Commonwealth," 465; Elton, *Reform and Renewal*, 123, 125.
73. Elton, *Reform and Renewal*, 169.
74. Ibid., 140–57; Plucknett, "Some Proposed Legislation of Henry VIII," 119–44.
75. Bateson, "The Pilgrimage of Grace: Aske's Narrative," 342.
76. Brigden, "Popular Disturbance," 257–78.
77. Preambles for 1539, 1540, and 1541.
78. *Tudor Royal Proclamations. 1*, no. 197 (280–81).
79. See Dickens and Jones, *Erasmus the Reformer*, 75; *The Letters of Stephen Gardiner*, 381, 383–84, 422.
80. Cooper, printed in Strype, *Ecclesiastical Memorials*, vol. 2, pt. ii, 124.
81. Printed in *Literary Remains of Edward VI*, 480.
82. *Tudor Royal Proclamations, 1*, no. 287 (393–403).
83. Letter to Pole, 4 June 1549, printed in N. Pocock, *Troubles Connected with the Prayer Book of 1549*, viii.
84. Elton, "Reform and the Commonwealth's Men of Edward VI's Reign," 23.
85. *Calendar of State Papers, Domestic Series, of the Reigns of Edward VI, Mary, Elizabeth, 1547–1580*, S.P. Dom. Edw. VI, 8, no. 56.
86. Elton, "Reform and the 'Commonwealth's Men,' " 24.
87. Lemon, S.P. Dom. Edw. VI, 8, no. 56 (fol. 103).
88. Bradford, *Writings*, 163.
89. Pollard, *England under Protector Somerset*, 215.
90. Ibid., 310.
91. Printed in Tytler, *Edward VI and Mary*, 1:114–17.
92. Printed in Russell, *Kett's Rebellion in Norfolk*, 16–17.
93. Bush, *The Government Policy of Protector Somerset*, 98; see also Jones, *The Tudor Commonwealth 1529–1559*, 34.

94. Slack, in Loach and Tittler, *The Mid-Tudor Polity*, 94.

95. Mary Dewar, "The Authorship of the 'Discourse of the Commonwealth,' " 388–400.

96. Dewar, *Sir Thomas Smith*, 3, 49–66.

97. Elton, *England under the Tudors*, 186.

98. Alsop, "Latimer, the 'Commonwealth of Kent' and the 1548 Rebellions," 379–82; Beer and Nash, "Hugh Latimer and the Lusty Knave of Kent: The Commonwealth Movement of 1549," 175–78, adduce further evidence that the Kentish Latimer claimed Somerset's sanction for his doings.

99. Source references in W. R. D. Jones, *The Tudor Commonwealth 1529–1559*, 37–38.

100. Ibid., 38–39; Allen, *Political Thought in the Sixteenth Century*, 137–38.

101. Dickens, *The English Reformation* (1st ed., 1964), 113.

102. *Tudor Royal Proclamations*, *1*, nos. 309 (427–29), 327 (451–53), 334 (462–64).

103. For resistance to reform see Jones, *The Tudor Commonwealth*, 202–6; on Hales see Lamond, ed., *A Discourse of the Commonweal*, lxii–lxv.

104. *Tudor Royal Proclamations*, *1*, no. 336 (464–69).

105. Elton, *England under the Tudors*, 207; C. S. L. Davies, "Slavery and Protector Somerset; The Vagrancy Act of 1547," 537–38.

106. See Jones, *The Tudor Commonwealth*, 40; Conyers Read, *Mr. Secretary Cecil and Queen Elizabeth*, 66.

107. *Tudor Royal Proclamations*, *1*, nos. 361 (495–96), 378 (528–29), 377 (526–27), 373 (520–21), 374 (522–23).

108. I Mary, c. III; *Proclamations*, *1*, no. 407 (35–38); I Mary, c. I.

109. Guevara, A, Fol41 verso, and a.ii.

110. See Jones, *The Tudor Commonwealth*, 144–45, and Read, *Mr. Secretary Cecil*, 67, 80, 109, 474.

111. See M. Dewar, "The Memorandum 'For the Understanding of the Exchange,' " 476–87; R. Tittler, "The Emergence of Urban Policy, 1536–58," in Loach and Tittler, *The Mid-Tudor Polity*, 84–85.

112. 1 & 2 P. & M, c.v, and 2 & 3 P. & M., c. XII; *Tudor Royal Proclamations*, *II*, no. 399 (26).

113. *Respublica*, 15, 23–24, 27, 31, 42, 50, 52; Nicholas Udall's authorship is suggested.

114. "Consideration," in *TED*, 1: 325–30; Bindoff, "The Making of the Statute of Artificers," in *Elizabethan Government and Society*, 80–81.

115. See Jones, *The Tudor Commonwealth*, 158–60; John Heywood, 96–108, 111–21.

116. Hales's "Charges," in Strype, *Ecclesiastical Memorials*, vol. 2, pt. 2, 361–62; Tyndale, *The Obedience of a Christian Man*, in *Works*, vol. 1:237; Edward VI, *Primer*, in *Writings of Edward VI*, 89.

117. Details and source references in Jones, *Tudor Commonwealth*; Audley's comment in *Letters and Papers . . . Henry VIII*, vol. 12, pt. 2 (1537), no. 737.

118. Full illustration in Jones, *Tudor Commonwealth*, 147–55; Hooper's plea is in Tytler, *Edward VI and Mary*, 1:365–66.

119. Jerome Barlow, *Burial of the Mass* (1528), 20, 57; Elton, *Reform and Renewal*, 121; 24 Hen. VII, c. 13; see Clay, *Economic Expansion and Social Change*.

120. Cranmer, *Miscellaneous Writings and Letters*, vol. II, 398–99; Cheke, *The hurt of sedition*, in Holinshed, 3:990.

121. Morison, A.ii.b and B.i.b; see also his *Exhortation to styrre all Englyshe men to the defence of theyr countrye* (1539), B.iiii.recto.

122. Sir John Mason, in Tytler, *Edward VI and Mary*, vol. 1, 341, 347; 5 Hen. VIII, c. 6 and 35 Hen. VIII, c. 13.
123. Ferguson, *The Articulate Citizen and the English Renaissance*, 382, 385; Thirsk, *Economic Policy and Projects*, 27.
124. Thirsk, *Economic Policy and Projects*, 17.
125. Armstrong's *Treatise* in *TED* 3: 116; Cholmeley, *The Request and Suite of a True-Hearted Englishman*, 2, 19.
126. Thirsk, *Economic Policy and Projects*, 30.
127. Robert Crowley, *Select Works*, 14–16; *Two Books of Homilies*, 385. Slack's *Poverty and Policy* is full, authoritative, and amply documented on the subject. See also A. L. Beier, *Masterless Men* (London and New York: Methuen, 1985).
128. See Elton, "An Early Tudor Poor Law," 55–67; Guy, "Tudor Commonwealth," 681–87, and *The Public Career of Sir Thomas More*, 151–56; Slack, *Poverty and Policy*, 118–19.
129. Cranmer, *Miscellaneous Writings and Letters*, 2:16.
130. Becon, *Early Works* (c. 1542–43), 40.
131. Slack, in Loach and Tittler, *Mid-Tudor Polity*, 102.
132. 2 & 3 P & M, c. 5.
133. "The Citizens of London to the Privy Council," in *TED* 2: 307–9.
134. Latimer, *Sermons* (1528–1552), 279.
135. Morison, *An Exhortation*, B.ii.recto; *Homilies*, 105–14; Tyndale, *The Obedience of a Christian Man*, in *Works*, 1:369; *Homilies*, 105–14.
136. Cromwell's *Life and Letters*, 2:26; Skinner, *Foundations*, 2:89, *Tudor Royal Proclamations*, I, no. 168 (244–45).
137. Baldwin, *Myrroure*, iii(a), H.i(a) and (b).
138. Starkey, *An Exhortation . . . to Unitie and Obedience*, 34.
139. Thomas, *Discourse*, in Strype, *Ecclesiastical Memorials*, vol. 2,·pt. 2, 372–77.
140. *Respublica*, 38; Cheke, in Holinshed, *Chronicles*, 3:988–90; Morison, *Remedy for Sedition*, A.ii–A.ii.b, and *A Lamentation in whiche is showed what Ruyne and destruction cometh of seditious rebellyon*, A.iii–A.iii.b; Cranmer, *Miscellaneous Writing*, 2:188.
141. Morris, *Tyndale to Hooker*, 72–74; Morison, *An Invective Ayenste the great and detestable vice, treason* (1539), a.v.(b)–a.vi.(b), D.iii(b), D.viii.(a)–(b); 25 Hen. VIII, c. 22.
142. Udall, in Pocock, *Troubles*, 146–74; Christopherson, A.iiii.(b), A.a.iiii(b), B.ii.(b), D.vii.(b), L.i.(b); Heywood, *Spider and the Flie*, 222, 238–39, 242, 262–63.
143. Morison, *Remedy*, D.ii–D.ii.b; Hooper, *Later Writings*, 97; letter printed in R. L. Palmer, *English Social History in the Making: The Tudor Revolution*, 33–34.
144. "Policies to reduce this realme of England unto a prosperous wealthe and estate," printed in *TED*, 3:325, 335–36.
145. Crowley, *The Way to Wealth*, in *Select Works*, 132–33.
146. Tyndale, *Works*, 2:295–96; Becon, *Fortress of the Faithful*, in *Catechism*, 601; John Christopherson, *An exhortation to . . . beware of rebellion* (1554), D.v.
147. Cranmer, *Miscellaneous Writings*, 2:189.
148. More, *The supplicacion of soules*, 313; Crowley, *Select Works*, 134.
149. *Tudor Royal Proclamations*, I, no. 272 (373–76), and no. 303 (421–23).
150. Barnes, *A Supplicatyon unto Henry VIII* (c. 1543), H.2 verso, H.4.
151. Hooker, *The Laws of Ecclesiastical Polity* (1593); *An Epistle from Calvin to the duke of Somerset*, trans. 1550, D.vi recto and verso.
152. Knappen, *Tudor Puritanism*, 401, 406.
153. Vives, *De Subventione Pauperum* (1526), trans. in *Some Early Tracts on Poor Relief*, ed. F. R. Salter.

154. Becon, *Early Works*, 347; Veron, *A most necessary & frutefull Dialogue*, B.iiii; Lever, *Sermons*, 27–28, 105.
155. Tyndale, in *Works*, 1:199–200.
156. Gardiner, in *Obedience in Church and State*, 205.
157. Starkey, *An Exhortation*, 34, 72–72, ii; Sir William Paget's letter in Russell, *Kett's Rebellion*, 17; *Discourse*, Lamond ed., 21, 131–41.
158. See Dickens, *Tudor Treatises*, 9–17, 43–51.
159. Brinklow, *The Lamentacyon of a Christen*, in *Complaynt of Roderyck Mors*, 116; Anon., *Prayse and commendacion* (c. 1548), A.iv.b.
160. See Zeeveld, *Foundations of Tudor Policy*, 107; Tyndale, *Works*, 1:369.
161. Morris, *Tyndale to Hooker*, 38; Hooper, *Later Writings*, 109; Latimer, *Sermons* (Everyman ed.), 311.
162. Ponet, *Polike power*, A.i–A.viii.b, B.iii–C.vi.b, C.viii–C.viii.b.
163. Ibid., D.vi, G.ib–G.vi.b.
164. Goodman, *Superior Powers*, 28, 43, 142, 148, 175–77, 197.
165. Turner, *The Huntyng of the Romyshe Wolfe* (c. 1555), E.viii.
166. See Cohn, *The Pursuit of the Millenium*, 177ff.

CHAPTER 3. "THE DORMANT YEARS"?: ELIZABETH I AND THE EARLY STUARTS

1. Gooch, *English Democratic Ideas in the Seventeenth Century*, 32; Collinson, "The Elizabethan Exclusion Crisis and the Elizabethan Polity," 73.
2. Hales in John Foxe, *Acts and Monuments*, 8:676–77; John Nichols, *The Progresses and Public Processions of Queen Elizabeth*, 49–51.
3. Loach, *A Mid-Tudor Crisis?*, 22–23; Fisher, "Influenza and Inflation," 120–29; Outhwaite, *Inflation in Tudor and Early Stuart England*, 9–15; Hoskins, "Harvest Fluctuations and English Economic History," 28–46.
4. *Tudor Royal Proclamations*, II, no. 458; III, nos. 699, 709.
5. Ibid., II, nos. 487, 491, 518; III, no. 803.
6. Elton, *The Parliament of England 1559–1581*, 267; see also R. Ashton, *Reformation and Revolution 1558–1660*, 100, 105.
7. Slack, "Poverty and Social Regulation in Elizabethan England," 236.
8. *Tudor Royal Proclamations*, II, nos. 542, 646, 649; III, no. 815.
9. Ibid., II, no. 541; III, no. 784.
10. Elton, *The Parliament of England*, 229; see Clay, *Economic Expansion and Social Change: England 1600–1700*, 2:231.
11. *Tudor Royal Proclamations*, II, nos. 560, 678.
12. Thirsk, *Economic Policy and Projects*, 33, 51–77.
13. Townshend, *Historical Collections*, 233–36.
14. Elton, *The Parliament of England*, 268–71; M. Todd, *Christian Humanism and the Puritan Social Order*, 126; Slack, "Poverty and Social Regulation," 222–23.
15. *Tudor Royal Proclamations*, II, nos. 740, 762, 796, 800, 809; Slack, "Poverty and Social Regulation," 229–30, 238.
16. Harvey *Marginalia*, 197.
17. Sir Philip Sidney, *Arcadia* (1587) yet Blair Worden, in *The Sound of Virtue* (228–32, 239, 252), points to Sidney's equal concern with the negligence of princes (the anonymous *Copie of A Letter* or "Leycester's Common-wealth" (1584) con-

demned a favorite's malignant influence); for Bradshaw; see "Tudor Commonwealth," 473.

18. Humphrey, B.vi, C.iii verso, X.ii verso; Nowell, *Catechisme*, 132–33; T. Sackville and T. Norton, *Gorboduc*, 60 (lines 50–51); on Norton "the Parliament Man," see M. A. R. Graves, "Thomas Norton," 17–35.

19. Merbury, *Briefe Discourse*, 1–5, 7, 9, 11–12.

20. Ibid., 10–11, 13, 14, 25, 37, 44.

21. Lupton, *Siuqila*, 9–11, 20, 21, 27, 33–34.

22. Mary Dewar, *Sir Thomas Smith*.

23. Smith, *De Republica Anglorum*, 57, 62, 144.

24. Floyd, *A perfit Common wealth*, 1–3, 11–14, 17–18, 19.

25. Ibid., 29, 40–41, 221–23, 239–40, 271, 186, 359.

26. Bodin, *The Commonwealth*, 1, 25, 75–76; See Skinner, *Foundations* 2:355, 310–13.

27. *Tudor Royal Proclamations, II*, nos. 597, 470, 740; III, no. 817.

28. Talbert, *The Problem of Order*, 41–42; A. S. McGrade, ed., *Ecclesiastical Polity*, xv.

29. Hooker, *Ecclesiastical Polity*, bk. I, 87; Morris, *Tyndale to Hooker*, 191; Hooker, preface, 41–47; bk. I, 89–90, 93, 99.

30. Hooker, bk. 8, 154, 184, 157, 130.

31. Jewel, *Defense of the Apologie*, 34; Bridges, *Defence of the Government*, 134, 1105, 1120.

32. Whitgift, *Answere to a certen Libel*, 1, 4, 5, A.iii recto & verso, 6, 17–18, 133, 139.

33. Bridges, *Supremacie of Christian Princes*, 668, 779, 850, 899, 913–14, 948.

34. Sandys, 1595, in *Sermons*, 95.

35. Bilson, *True Difference*, 512, 420, 515–16, 520–21; Allen, *Political Thought*, 177.

36. Bancroft, *Sermon Preached at Paules Cross*, 7, 14, 25–27.

37. Ibid., 67–68, 74.

38. Ibid., 82, 96, 105; *Daungerous Positions and Proceedings* (1593), 3–4, 14–15.

39. Knox, in *Works*, 381, 373, 388, 390–91, 414, 417.

40. Gilby, *Admonition*, printed in Knox, vol. 4, appendix, 563–64.

41. Field and Wicox, *Admonition to the Parliament* (1572), A.iii, B.ii, B.iii.

42. Cartwright, *Replye to An answere*, A.ii, 6, 144; Morris, *Tyndale to Hooker*, 161–64.

43. Fenner, *Defence*, B.4 recto, E.4 recto, F, G.4, 122, 128–30, 133.

44. Browne, *Reformation Without Tarrying*, 18, 26–27, 30.

45. Barrowe, *Brief Discovery*, 212, 222–23, 257, 271, 309–11, 374–75.

46. *Examinations* printed in *Harleian Miscellany*, 2:19–21, 28.

47. Skinner, *Foundation*, 2:321; W. Allen, *An Apologie and True Declaration*, 30 verso, 38 verso.

48. Allen, *Apologie*, 39 verso, 41 verso, 51 recto, 74 verso, 75 verso, 76 recto, 77 verso, 96 recto–verso, 106 recto; *True, Sincere, and Modest Defense*, 155–56, 203.

49. Parsons, *Conference About the Next Succession*, A.3 verso, I, 4, 9.

50. Ibid., 12, 22, 61, 37, 72–73, 119–129, 139–40, 200, 204, 207. See below, 112–114, for another significant, if very different, work by Parsons.

51. Hayward, *Answer to . . . a Certaine Conference*, D.3, G.I. verso, G.3. verso, H.iii, K.iv verso–L.i recto, L.ii, T.i verso, T.ii recto–verso.

52. Craig, *The Right of Succession*, 225–26.

53. Collinson, "The Monarchical Republic of Queen Elizabeth," 407–9, and

"*De Republica Anglorum*: Or, History with the Politics Put Back," 18–19; T. E. Hartley, ed., *Proceedings in the Parliaments of Elizabeth I*, 1:425–26.

54. Stubbs, *Discoverie of a Gaping Gulf*, 20, 46, 68.

55. See Neale, "Peter Wentworth," 35–54, 175–205, for sources and comment.

56. Haigh, *The Reign of Elizabeth I*, 21, 23; Ashton, *Reform and Revolution*, 177, 180–81; R. B. Manning, *Village Revolts*, 82–83, 187; Sharp, *In Contempt of All Authority*, 1–6; See also Guy, ed., *The Reign of Elizabeth I*, 1–19, 192–211.

57. Manning, *Village Revolts*, 1–3, 53, 55, 221–29, 238, 245–46, 319; Sharp, *Contempt of All Authority*, 10, 42, 264–65; Martin, *Feudalism to Capitalism*, 175–76, 224.

58. Beacon, *Solon His Folie*, 5, 19, 72.

59. *Polimanteia*, (3), B.2 verso, D.2 verso, K.

60. Carpenter, *Preparative to Contentation*, 141, 144, 161, 167, 295, 312, 316.

61. Bacon, *Essays* (c. 1597, printed London, 1892), 34, 36–37.

62. Ibid., 38–39. John Walter, in "A 'Rising of the People' " (133), points out that after his interrogation of the leaders of the Oxfordshire Rising of 1596 Bacon "became the main protagonist for procuring legislation against enclosures."

63. Parsons, *Memorial*, 197, 302, 255, 255–26, 257. See Todd, *Christian Humanism*, 218.

64. Parsons, *Memorial*, 235–36, 256–57, 89, 85; 248, 96, 260, 210–11, 95.

65. Collinson, *The Religion of Protestants*, ix, 187.

66. Slack, *Poverty and Policy*, 23, 31; Bedel, *A sermon exhorting to pitie the poore*, A.iv, B.ii recto and verso, C.ii verso, D.iv verso; Arthington, *Provision for the poore, now in penurie*, A.3 recto and verso, B.2 verso, B.3 recto.

67. Allen, *Christian Beneficence*, A.iii recto and verso, A.iv recto and verso, 6–7, 30, 33, 126–27.

68. Spenser, *The Faerie Queene*, book 5, 530–31, 539–41, 543; Nashe, *Unfortunate Traveller*, 284–91.

69. Shakespeare, *Henry VI, Part 2*, act 4, scene 2, lines 6–8, 73–77, 86–87; scene 6, lines 3–5; A. Patterson, *Popular Voice*, 1, 5, 32, 38, 135, 143 (more recently, her *Reading Holinshed's Chronicles* argues for "the Chroniclers' representation of active social protest" (188–89); Shakespeare, *The Tempest*, act 2, scene 1, lines 154–61, 163–67.

70. Raleigh, *Maxims of State*, in *Works*, 8:1–4, 30.

71. Ibid., 11, 28–29.

72. Morris, *Tyndale to Hooker*, 156.

73. Ibid., 133; Allen, *History of Political Thought*, 179; Haigh, *Reign of Elizabeth I*, 15.

74. Deane Jones, *The English Revolution, 1603–1714*, 319.

75. *Stuart Royal Proclamations*, I, p. v, nos. 65, 214; nos. 30, 35; no. 266; nos. 208, 123.

76. Sommerville, *Politics and Ideology in England, 1603–1640*, 47; J. P. Kenyon, *The Stuart Constitution*, 8.

77. Collinson in Haigh, *The Reign of Elizabeth I*, 194; Hill, *Century of Revolution*, 101; J. W. Allen, *English Political Thought, 1603–1660*, 1:203; Sommerville, *Politics and Ideology*, 75.

78. Burton, *Anatomy of Melancholy*, 58, 59, 60–64.

79. Bernard, *The Isle of Man*, 178, 180–81, 198–99, 210–13; on this "veteran preacher and controversialist," see Collinson, *Religion of Protestants*, 85, 133, 152–55.

80. Forset, *Discourse*, 3, 4, 49, 15, 27–28; Allen, *English Political Thought*, 83; Sommerville, *Politics and Ideology*, 49.

81. Forset, *Discourse*, 48, 63, 45, 71–85, 41.
82. Hall, *Solomons Politicks, or Common-wealth*, 132–33.
83. Floyd, *God and the King* (Cologne, 1620), 137–40, 13. This Jesuit served in the English mission field and suffered imprisonment before becoming professor of theology at Louvain: see *DNB*, 19:344–45.
84. Floyd, *God and the King*, 14, 16–19, also 23, 39.
85. Ibid., 139–40.
86. *King James His opinion and Judgement, concerning a Real King and a Tyrant* (1647 reprint), A recto-verso, A3 verso, Kenyon, *Stuart Constitution*, 12–14.
87. Sibthorp, *Apostolike Obedience*, (4), 6, 9, 3, 22, 24, 33.
88. Mainwaring, *Religion and Alegiance* (1627), 5, 10–11, 18.
89. See Kenyon, *Stuart Constitution*, 148, 153, 155, 165, Allen *English Political Thought*, 186; Hill, *Century of Revolution*, 79.
90. Eliot, *De Jure Maiestatis*, 4, 10–11, 60, 98, 133, 135, 117, 171.
91. Eliot, *Monarchie of Man* (1629–32), 9, 13, 28, 36–37, 38, 42, 47.
92. Ibid., 58, 71, 78, 80–81, 136–37, 104, 207, 227.
93. Sandys, *State of Religion* (written in 1599 and dedicated to Whitgift), 139–40. See Allen, *History of Political Thought in the Sixteenth Century*, 241–46.
94. Busher, *Religious Peace*, 7–8, 13.
95. Ibid., 22, 25, 32–33. On Busher, see Allen, *English Political Thought 1603–60*, 221–27.
96. 1662 reprint in Underhill, ed., *Tracts on Liberty of Conscience*, 95, 110, 113.
97. Ibid., 129, 139, 135, 121.
98. Anon., *Humble Supplication*, in Underhill, *Tracts*, 231, 192, 224, 202, 205, 199.
99. See Woodhouse, *Puritanism and Liberty*, 125.
100. Collinson, *English Puritanism*, 20; and *Religion of Protestants*, 82, 179, 148, 152–55.
101. Todd, *Christian Humanism*, 240, 253, 249; Mainwaring, *Religion and Alegiance*, Second Sermon, 45.
102. Perkins, in *Works*, 446–47, 454–55, 462, 449, 472, 464, 467–68, 455–56.
103. Ibid., 454; Gouge, *Of Domesticall Duties*, 1, 17–18.
104. See Clay, *Economic Expansion and Social Change*, 3; Wrigley and Schofield, *The Population History of England 1541–1871*, 178–79.
105. Gray, *Good Speed to Virginia*, B.2 recto-verso, B.3 verso, D.4 recto.
106. See Hoskins, "Harvest Fluctuations and English History, 1620–1759," (especially 19–20); Slack, *Poverty and Policy in Tudor and Stuart England*, 39–41, 53.
107. Above, page 129.
108. *Stuart Royal Proclamations, II, Charles I, 1625–1646*, x–xx.
109. Appleby, *Economic Thought and Ideology in Seventeenth-Century England*, 30.
110. *Stuart Royal Proclamations, II, Charles I, 1625–1646*, xi; Slack, "Books of Orders: The Making of English Social Policy," 1–22.
111. *Stuart Royal Proclamations, I*, nos. 91; 86, 107; 127; 182, and *II*, nos. II, 141.
112. See Gay, "The Midlands Revolt and the Inquisitions of Depopulation of 1607," 195–244; Kenyon, *Stuart Constitution*, 38; *Stuart Royal Proclamations, I*, nos. 71, 72, and p. 155 n. 2; Martin, *Feudalism to Capitalism*, 161–64, 168, 176; R. B. Manning, *Village Revolts*, 230, 235.
113. Wilkinson, *A Sermon*, B.3 verso, C.4 recto, D.i recto, D.2 recto–verso, F.2 verso.
114. Manning, *Village Revolts*, 246–52; Martin, *Feudalism to Capitalism*, 214–15. Buchanan Sharp, however, writing of food riots in general and in particular of "the

Western Rising, 1626–1632," asserts that governmental responses "were based upon no systematic working-out of social or religious ideas": *In Contempt of All Authority*, 43, 74, 155, 258.

115. Kenyon, *Stuart Constitution*, 119. For a contemporary tribute to the perceived reality of royal efforts to apply the principles of "distributive and Commutative Justice," see Powell, *Depopulation Arraigned* (1636), 3–4, 48, 119–20.

116. See Hirst, *Authority and Conflict: England 1603–58*, 169–70; Hill, *Century of Revolution*, 26.

117. *Stuart Royal Proclamations, I*, no. 87; Slack, "Books of Orders," 9.

118. *Stuart Royal Proclamations, II*, no. 159; Heal, "The Idea of Hospitality in Early Modern England,"—especially 68.

119. Carew, *Certaine godly and necessarie Sermons*, S.9 recto, T.4 verso, U.1 recto, V.3 verso, W.2 recto, X.7 recto; Dyke, *Counterpoison*, 13, 16, 27, 40, 45.

120. Carter, *Christ His Last Will and John His Legacy*, 52, 58, 83–86; Spark, *Greevous Grones for the Poore*, 9–11, 18, 22. For his indication of the Carew and Carter sources, I am much indebted to Patrick Collinson.

121. Sanderson, *XXXIV Sermons* (printed in 1664), 238, 246–48; Whateley, *The Poor Mans Advocate*, 4, 17, 107–8.

122. 21 Charles I, c.1; *Stuart Royal Proclamations, II*, nos. 85, 115, 114; Slack, "Books of Orders," 2.

123. For a detailed analysis of the interaction of such economic variables, see Supple, *Commercial Crisis and Change in England, 1600–1642*.

124. *Stuart Royal Proclamations, II*, xix–xx, and *I*, no. 135.

125. Thirsk, *Policy and Projects*, 78–105.

126. Ashton, *Reformation and Revolution, 1558–1660*, 277–78, 292; see Hirst, *Authority and Conflict: England 1603–58*, 170.

127. Hill, *Century of Revolution*, 37.

128. Misselden, *Circle of Commerce*, 17, 19.

129. Appleby, *Economic Thought and Ideology*, ix, 22.

130. Ibid., 43–47; Misselden, *Circle of Commerce*, 17.

131. Appleby, *Economic Thought and Ideology*, 52–53, 67–68.

132. Kenyon, *Stuart Constitution*, 497–501; *Stuart Royal Proclamations, II*, no. 200.

133. Todd, *Christian Humanism*, 253–55.

134. Kent, "Attitudes of Members of the House of Commons to the Regulation of 'Personal Conduct' in Late Elizabethan and Early Stuart England."

135. Ibid., 61.

136. See Barker, *Religion and Politics 1559–1642*, 3; also Russell, *Unrevolutionary England: 1603–1642*, 197, 191.

137. Collinson, *English Puritanism*, 31, 6.

138. *Stuart Royal Proclamations, II*, no. 55.

139. White, *Sir Edward Coke and "The Grievances of the Commonwealth," 1621–1628*, 18, 275–76.

Chapter 4. Full Blossom: The Mid-Seventeenth-Century Commonwealth

1. Sabine, introduction to *The Works of Gerrard Winstanley*, I.

2. See Woodhouse, ed., *Puritanism and Liberty*; Capp, *The Fifth Monarchy Men*, 36–37.

3. Gunn, *Politics and the Public Interest in the Seventeenth Century*, ix; Haller, *Tracts on Liberty in the Puritan Revolution, 1636–1647*, 1:4.

4. Ferne, *The Resolving of Conscience*, 26; Parker, *Observations upon some of his Majesties late Answers*, in Haller, *Tracts*, 2:183; Cook, *Redintegratio Amoris*, 44.

5. Hall, *Of Government and Obedience*, 86, 492; Sprigge, *A Modest Plea*, 76; Anon., *An Answer to a Proposition . . . of A Commonwealth or Democracy* (1659), (6).

6. Hunton, *A Treatise of Monarchy* (1644), 4; Nedham, *Interest will not lie*, 4.

7. Kenyon, *The Stuart Constitution*, 324.

8. Ascham, *Original & End of Civil Power*, A.3 verso, A.4 verso, (11)–(12).

9. Hall, *Of Government and Obedience*, 158–61.

10. Anon., *Some Grave and Weighty Considerations*, (14); White, *Obedience and Government*, 140, 153.

11. Ascham, *Civil Power*, (26); Hall, *Of Government and Obedience*, 75.

12. Wren, *Monarchy Asserted*, 21; Baxter, *A Holy Commonwealth*, title-page, 85.

13. Anon., *Copy of a Letter*, 25; Milton, in *Complete Prose Works*, 198, 202.

14. Hall, *Of Government and Obedience*, 117–18; White, *Obedience and Government*, 127–28.

15. Harrington (?), *Discourse*, (10), (11); Ascham, *Civil Power*, (3)–(5).

16. Cook, *Redintegratio Amoris*, 3–6, 30, 33, 45.

17. Ferne, *Resolving of Conscience*, 1, 14, 29, 30; see *DNB*, 18:372–73.

18. Digges, *A subject's taking up arms*, 1–3, 8—see *DNB* 15:70; see also Sanderson, "But the People's Creatures," 73–85.

19. Parker, *Some Few Observations*, (7)–(8), (13), (15); Allen, *English Political Thought*, 426; see *DNB*, 43:240–41.

20. Hunton, *Treatise of Monarchy*, 26, 32, 41; Allen, *English Political Thought*, 449; *DNB*, 33:312–13.

21. Filmer, *Patriarcha*, xi–xiv, xx, xxxiv; *Anarchy of a Limited or Mixed Monarchy*, 132, 157; *The Original of Government*, 186.

22. Cook, *Monarchy No creature of Gods making*, 1–2; Wren, *Monarchy Asserted*, 58.

23. Anon., *Englands Monarchy Asserted*, (6)–(7); Anon., *Chaos*, 38–39.

24. See Hirst, *Authority and Conflict*, 330–31; Plumb, "The Growth of the Electorate in England from 1600 to 1715."

25. Parker, *Some Few Observations*, (13); *Observations upon some of his Majesties late Answers*, in Haller, *Tracts*, 2:(8)/174; Clarkson, *A General Charge . . . in the Name of Justice Equity*, 2, 4.

26. Davis, *Fear, Myth and History*, 58–61.

27. Neville, *Newes from the New Exchange*, (2), 6.

28. Ascham, *Confusions and Revolutions of Governments*, 131; anon., *Plea for limited Monarchy*, (3)–(5); anon., *Englands Monarchy Asserted* (1660), (1)–(2), (6).

29. Anon., *A Copy of a Letter*, 23, 36; Nedham, *Interest will not lie*, 20.

30. Anon., *A Commonwealth and Commonwealths-men Asserted*, 2, 5; Sprigge, *A Modest Plea*, A6, 82, 13; anon., *New Letany for these Times*, (6).

31. Kenyon, *The Stuart Constitution*, 339–42; the second of these is the "Engagement."

32. Robinson, *Monarchical and Aristocratical Government*, (5), (11), (14), (20).

33. Nedham, *Case of the Commonwealth*, 1, 30–31, 98, 109, appendix. Nedham, whose pen could be hired, wrote against the background of the Engagement Act (1649–50), which demanded an oath of loyalty to the Commonwealth as a condition even of being permitted recourse to law.

34. See Woolrych, *Commonwealth to Protectorate*, 14; *Speeches of Oliver Cromwell*, 13.

35. *Speeches of Oliver Cromwell*, x, 30–31; see Ivan Roots, *The Great Rebellion 1642–1660*, 123, 144–47.

36. *Speeches of Oliver Cromwell*, 206; Woolrych, *Commonwealth to Protectorate*, 391; *Speeches*, 33–34; Roots, *The Great Rebellion*, 116.
37. *Speeches of Oliver Cromwell*, 78.
38. Woolrych, *Commonwealth to Protectorate*, 395, 397.
39. *Speeches of Oliver Cromwell*, 51, 66–67, 230; Roots, *The Great Rebellion*, 204.
40. Ascham, *Confusions and Revolutions of Governments*, 74.
41. See Plumb, "Growth of the Electorate"; D. Hirst, *The Representative of the People?*, 157; Stone, *The Causes of the English Revolution 1529–1642*, 172; B. Manning, *The English People and the English Revolution*, 413.
42. Parker, *Observations*, in Haller, *Tracts*, 1:(1)/67, and *Jus Populi* ("Published by Authority"), 18; Tomkins, *The Rebels Plea, or Mr. Baxters judgement*, 2.
43. Milton, *Complete Prose Works*, 250–51.
44. White, *Obedience and Government*, 47–49, 97; see *DNB*, 61:79–81.
45. White, *Obedience and Government*, 109–13, 120–23, 124–25, 176–77, 181, 183.
46. Ferne, *Resolving of Conscience*, title-page, 30, 50; anon., *Copy of a Letter*, 26.
47. Hall, *Government and Obedience*, 67, 80, 85, 93–94.
48. Milton, *Tenure*, in *Complete Prose Works*, 206; *Eikonoklastes* (1649 and 1650), *Complete Prose Works*, 339, 535; *Readie & Easie Way*, (12), (18).
49. James, *Social Problems and Policy During the Puritan Revolution, 1640–1660*, 90.
50. Anon., *The mournfull Cryes of many thousand poor Tradesmen* (1648), printed in Wolfe, ed., *Leveller Manifestoes of the Puritan Revolution*, 276.
51. Wildman (?), *A Call to all the soldiers*, in *Puritanism and Liberty*, 440.
52. Frank, *The Levellers*, 225.
53. *Puritanism and Liberty*, 53; See C. Thompson, "Maximilian Petty and the Putney Debate on the Franchise."
54. *Puritanism and Liberty*, 53.
55. Ibid., 53–57.
56. Ibid., 60–61, 71, 77.
57. Wildman (?), *The Leveller*, 4.
58. Ibid., 5–9, 15–16.
59. Walwyn, *The Compassionate Samaritane* (1644), in Haller, *Tracts on Liberty*, 3:(75)/(21).
60. *Puritanism and Liberty*, 98; B. Manning, *The English People*, 401.
61. Haller and Davies, eds., *The Leveller Tracts 1647–1653*, 23, 40.
62. Haller, *Tracts on Liberty*, 1:6.
63. Overton, *An Arrow against all Tyrants* (1646); Lilburne, *Englands Birthright Justified* (1645), in Haller, *Tracts on Liberty*, 1:113, and 3:(266–67)/(10–11).
64. *To the Supream Authority of England* (1648), in Wolfe, *Leveller Manifestoes*, 265.
65. Frank, *The Levellers*, 245, 248–49.
66. Lilburne, et al., printed in Haller and Davies, *The Leveller Tracts*, 178.
67. Haller, *Tracts on Liberty*, 1:116; Wolfe, *Leveller Manifestoes*, 325; Gentles, *The New Model Army*, 345, 348; Capp, *Cromwell's Navy*, 118.
68. Lilburne, *England's Birthright*, and Walwyn, *Lamentable Slavery*, in Haller, *Tracts on Liberty*, 3:266–67/(10)–(11), 288/(30), and 313/(3).
69. Overton, *Remonstrance*, in Haller, *Tracts on Liberty*, 3:354–55/(4)–(5), 361/(11), 363/(13), 365/(15).
70. Overton, *An Appeale*, in Wolfe, *Leveller Manifestoes*, 163, 174, 177, 179, 183.
71. Walwyn (?), *The Bloody Project*, in Haller and Davies, *Leveller Tracts*, 145.
72. Overton (?), *Hunting of the Foxes*, in Wolfe, *Leveller Manifestoes*, 358, 372.
73. *To the Supream Authority of England*, in Wolfe, *Leveller Manifestoes*, 269; B. Manning, *The English People*, 416–17; Sir Keith Thomas, in G. E. Aylmer, ed., *The Interregnum*, 57–78.

74. Wolfe, *Leveller Manifestoes*, 223, 226–27.
75. Ibid., 291–92.
76. Ibid., 295–97, 299–301.
77. Ibid., 331–54.
78. Frank, *The Levellers*, 2, 11, 244.
79. Haller, *Tracts on Liberty*, 1:118; Wolfe, *Leveller Manifestoes*, 398–99.
80. Nedham, *Case of the Commonwealth of England*, 96–99, 102–3, 109.
81. Anon., *A Copy of a Letter . . . by A true Commonwealths-man*, 7, 9.
82. See Sanderson, *"But the people's creatures,"* 118–19.
83. Harrington, *Oceana*, 37, 25, 32; *The Wayes and Means* (1660), title-page; *The Censure of the Rota Upon Mr Milton's Book* (1660), (13).
84. See Tawney, *Harrington's Interpretation of His Age*, 4.
85. Harrington, *The Prerogative of Popular Government* (1658), in *The Political Works of James Harrington*, 424.
86. Harrington, *Oceana*, 48–49, 53, 64, 135, 119, 155.
87. Ibid., 32–33, 85.
88. *The Censure of the Rota*, (14).
89. Harrington, *Oceana*, 21.
90. Harrington, *Prerogative of Popular Government*, 40I; *The Censure of the Rota*, (15).
91. Harrington, *Oceana*, 32.
92. Pocock, *Political Works*, 43, 67; Harrington, *Brief Directions* (1658), in *Works*, 590–91.
93. Harrington, *Oceana*, 66, 138.
94. Harrington, *Prerogative of Popular Government*, in *Works*, 414.
95. Hobbes, *Leviathan*, 391. The publication of this work must again be related to the "Engagement," which also elicited an embarrassed discussion by Filmer in his *Directions For Obedience to Government in Dangerous or Doubtful Times* (May 1652), ed. Sommerville, in *Patriarcha*, 281–86.
96. Hobbes, *Leviathan*, 130, 172, 175, 178.
97. Ibid., 87, 111.
98. Ibid., 174–75, 177–78.
99. Ibid., 96–97, 115, 180, 74.
100. Ibid., Minogue's introduction, xii, xxiii—though Nedham cited him in the appendix to *The Case of the Commonwealth*.
101. Hobbes, *Leviathan*, 199–329.
102. Ibid., 115.
103. See Taylor, ed., *Conspiracy, Crusade or Class Conflict*.
104. Haller, *Tracts on Liberty*, 1:35.
105. *The Works of Gerrard Winstanley*, 238, 194, 388–89, 409, 569.
106. In Haller, *Tracts on Liberty*, 2:(75)/31, (89)/45, (55)/11, (80)/36, (135)/91.
107. Walwyn, in Haller, *Tracts on Liberty*, 3:(73–74)/(17–19); R.H., *The Good Old Cause*, 8.
108. *Light Shining in Buckinghamshire* and *More Light Shining in Buckinghamshire* in Winstanley, *Works*, 619, 632; anon., *A Modest Reply*, (6)–(7), (17)–(22).
109. Robinson, *Liberty of Conscience*, in Haller, *Tracts on Liberty*, 3:(119)/(3), (122)/(16), (141)/(25); Haller, 1:67; *DNB*, 49:14–15.
110. Overton, *Remonstrance* (1646), in *Tracts on Liberty*, 3:363.
111. Richardson, printed in Underhill, *Tracts*, 255, 258–59, 253, 254, 173, 184.
112. Woodhouse, *Puritanism and Liberty*, 125.
113. Anon., *No Papist nor Presbyterian*, in Wolfe, *Leveller Manifestoes*, 305–10.

114. Jubbes, *Several Proposals for Peace and Freedom* (1649), *Leveller Manifestoes*, 311, 318.
115. Robinson, *Certain Proposals In order to the Peoples Freedome and Accomodation*, (6); Milton, *Readie & Easie Way*, (14)–(15).
116. Walwyn, *Compassionate Samaritane*, in Haller, *Tracts on Liberty*, 3:(67)/(5).
117. Goodwin, et al., *Apologeticall Narration*, in Haller, *Tracts on Liberty*, 2:330, 332.
118. Goodwin, *The Grand Imprudence of . . . Fighting Against God* (1644), in Haller, *Tracts on Liberty*, 3:(17)/((11), (29)/((23), (30)/(33).
119. Lilburne, in Haller, *Tracts on Liberty*, 3:(182)/(2), (186)/(6); Overton, ibid., 3:(207)/A3, (212)/1, (235)/25, (246)/36.
120. Overton, *Arraignement of Mr. Persecution*, (227–28)/17–18; Greville, *The Nature of that Episcopacie*, in Haller, *Tracts on Liberty*, 2:(140)/96; Bunyan, *A Few Sighs from Hell*, 250.
121. Morton, *The World of the Ranters*, 70, 90; J. F. McGregor, in *Radical Religion in the English Revolution*, 132; Davis, *Fear, Myth and History*, 18–19, 57, 74–75, 92, 123–24.
122. Coppe, *Fiery Flying Roule*, (1)/5, 2; see Aylmer, "Did the Ranters Exist," 219; also Davis, *PP* 129 (1990): 80 n. 3; Nayler, *Deceit Brought to Daylight* (1656), 1.
123. Morton, *World of the Ranters* 91; Reay, in McGregor and Reay, *Radical Religion*, 141, 163; Roots, *The Great Rebellion*, 207; the *Diary of Thomas Burton*, MP from 1656 to 1659, fears that "the Quakers grow numerous and dangerous," 1:22; 2:112–13.
124. *Gangraena* (1646, the Rota reprint, 1977), 9; part 1, A1 verso, A4 recto–verso.
125. Ibid., part 2, 185, 192; part 3, 10, 14, 217, 262.
126. *Acts and Ordinances of the Interregnum 1642–1660*, 1:913, 1133–36; 2:393–96, 409–12.
127. Prynne, in Haller, *Tracts on Liberty*, 1:78–79.
128. Hirst, *Authority and Conflict: England 1603–58*, 338.
129. *Speeches of Oliver Cromwell*, 67, 78.
130. Eliot, *The Christian Commonwealth*, A4; Baxter, *A Holy Commonwealth*, x–xi, xiv–xvii, xxvii.
131. Baxter, *A Holy Commonwealth*, 14, 63, 127, 129, 160; 77, 84, 105, 111, 127, 140.
132. Woolrych, *Commonwealth to Protectorate*, 4; Haller, *Tracts on Liberty*, 1:62; *Puritanism and Liberty*, 246.
133. Capp, *The Fifth Monarchy Men*, 14–15.
134. See Frank, *The Levellers*, 243; Capp, *Fifth Monarchy Men*, 14, 130; Woolrych, *Commonwealth to Protectorate*, 209, 233.
135. *Speeches of Oliver Cromwell*, 33; Woolrych, *Commonwealth to Protectorate*, 351.
136. Winstanley, *Works*, 47, 104–5.
137. Sabine, introduction to Winstanley, *Works*, 3.
138. McGregor, *Radical Religion*, 51.
139. See Aylmer, *Rebellion or Revolution? England 1640–1660*, 115–16; Hirst, *Authority and Conflict*, 290.
140. Hartlib, *Londons Charitie*, 4, and *Londons Charity inlarged*, 22.
141. Lilburne, *England's Birth-right Justified*, in Haller, *Tracts on Liberty*, 3:280/22.
142. Winstanley, *Works*, 357.
143. Aylmer, *Rebellion or Revolution?*, 131.
144. Lee, *Considerations Concerning Common Fields and Inclosures*, 39.
145. Aylmer, *Rebellion or Revolution?*, 133; Dury, *Israel's Call to March out of Babylon* (1646), 19, 20.

146. Cook, *Unum Necessarium: or, The Poor Mans Case* (1648), 36; Harrington, *The Art of Lawgiving* (1659), in *Political Works,* 677.
147. Nayler, *A Discovery of the First Wisdom* (1653), 33, 37; Covel, *A Declaration Unto the Parliament* (1659), (4).
148. Coppe, *Fiery Flying Roll,* 2, 4, 6–7; *Second Fiery Flying Roule,* 4, 19; see Capp, *Fifth Monarchy Men,* 19.
149. Anon., *Tyranipocrit,* 16, 31, 19, 38, 54, 56.
150. Chamberlen, *Poor Mans Advocate,* A4,12; Bunyan, *A Few Sighs from Hell* (1658), A4–A5, 7.
151. *More Light Shining,* in Winstanley, *Works,* 633; Taylor, in Winstanley, *Works,* 262.
152. Everitt, in Thirsk, *Agrarian History,* 4:465.
153. James, *Social Problems and Policy,* 90; see also Schenk, *The Concern for Social Justice in the Puritan Revolution,* 2.
154. Hall, *Of Government and Obedience,* 147, 159; Cook, *Redintegratio Amoris,* 73; Harrington, *Oceana,* 66, 135.
155. Walwyn, *A Helpe to the right understanding of a Discourse concerning Independency* (1645), in Haller, *Tracts on Liberty,* 3:(199)/(7); *Puritanism and Liberty,* 71.
156. Richardson, *Cause of the Poor Pleaded,* B3, A2, 4; Cook, *Unum Necessarium,* (1), 44.
157. Anon., *Some Grave and Weighty Considerations* (1658), title page, (13).
158. Sprigge, *A Modest Plea,* title page, A5, 65, 84–86.
159. Winstanley, *Works,* 322, 184; *More Light Shining,* in Winstanley, *Works,* 616, 638.
160. Harrington, *The Prerogative of Popular Government,* in *Political Works,* 460.
161. Anon., in Haller and Davies, *Leveller Tracts,* 93, 105, 130, 117, 120.
162. Anon., *Legall Fundamental Liberties,* in Haller and Davies, *Leveller Tracts,* 443, 449; *New Law of Righteousness,* in Winstanley, *Works,* 159, 195–97—see also Sabine's introduction, 58–70.
163. Taylor, *True Levellers Standard,* in Winstanley, *Works,* 251, 258; *An Appeale to all Englishmen,* in Winstanley, *Works,* 413.
164. See Webster, *The Great Instauration,* 361 and references.
165. Bowden, in Thirsk, *Agrarian History,* 4:621; Webster, *Great Instauration,* 260; James, *Social Problems and Policy,* 241–56.
166. James, *Social Problems and Policy,* 272, 301: "a general impression of harshness coupled with failure"; J. P. Cooper, "Social and Economic Policies under the Commonwealth," in Aylmer, *The Interregnum,* 128.
167. Cook, *Unum Necessarium,* (1); Capp, *Fifth Monarchy Men,* 148.
168. Anon., *Stanleyes Remedy,* 4–5; Hartlib, *Londons Charitie,* 6.
169. Sprigge, *A Modest Plea,* 42–44.
170. *To the Supream Authority of England,* in *Leveller Manifestoes,* 270; Winstanley, in *Works,* 432.
171. Webster, *Great Instauration,* 263.
172. *Macaria,* 5–6.
173. In Wolfe, *Leveller Manifestoes,* 308; Cook; *Unum Necessarium,* (3).
174. Robinson, *Certain Proposals,* (26); Covel, *A Declaration [of] the Causes of the Peoples Tumults,* (21).
175. *Macaria,* 13–14; Petty, *Advice . . . to Mr Samuel Hartlib,* 144.
176. See Webster, *Great Instauration,* 197, 210–11, 213–14; Robinson, *Certain Proposals,* (24)–(26); Dury cited in Webster, 214.
177. Hubberthorn, *The Real Cause of the Nations Bondage and Slavery* (1659), 4;

Jubbes, *Several Proposals for Peace & Freedom,* in Wolfe, *Leveller Manifestoes,* 318. See Hill, *Century of Revolution,* 163–65, for other examples.

178. *To the Supream Authority,* in Wolfe, *Leveller Manifestoes,* 270; M. James, "The Political Importance of the Tithes Controversy in the English Revolution."

179. *Speeches of Oliver Cromwell,* 99.

180. Hare, *St. Edwards Ghost,* 19; Taylor, in Winstanley, *Works,* 259.

181. Clarkson, *A Generall Charge Or, Impeachment of High-Treason* (1647), 6; Hubberthorn, *Real Cause,* 5–6; Robinson, *Certaine Proposals in order to a new Modelling of the Lawes, and Law-Proceedings* (1653), 7; *Light Shining* and *More Light Shining,* in Winstanley, *Works,* 615, 617, 637.

182. *Tyranipocrit,* 16; Winstanley, *Letter to Lord Fairfax* (1649), in *Works,* 288.

183. Winstanley, *New Yeers Gift* and *Law of Freedom,* in *Works,* 358, and 507, 529, 558–59.

184. See Webster, *Great Instauration,* 257–58, 261; *DNB* 52:63–64; Hirst, *Authority and Conflict,* 320; Aylmer, *Rebellion or Revolution?,* 125–27; Hill, *Puritanism and Revolution,* 67–87.

185. *To the Supream Authority* (1648), in *Leveller Manifestoes,* 270; Winstanley, *Law of Freedom,* in *Works,* 511–13, also 580–81.

186. *Stanleyes Remedy,* 2, 4; Chamberlen, *Poore Mans Advocate,* 3–4.

187. Hartlib, *Londons Charitie inlarged,* 4, 10, 14–17, 19; Robinson, *Certain Proposals,* (23)–(24).

188. Lawson, *Appeal to the Parliament,* 2–3; Covel, *A Declaration,* (10)–(11), (17), (21).

189. *Peter Cornelius Plockboy,* J. Dowie reprint, title pages, 6.

190. Robinson, *Certain Proposals,* (9)–(19); Thirsk, *Economic Policy and Projects,* 116.

191. Goffe, in *Harleian Miscellany,* 4:366–70; "I.D.," *A Cleare and Evident Way,* 1–18.

192. Plattes, *Discovery of Infinite Treasure,* a verso, 63, C verso, 75.

193. Cook, *Unum Necessarium,* (1); Moore, *The Crying Sin of England,* 7, 14.

194. Webster, *Great Instauration,* 473; anon., *Considerations concerning Common Fields,* in Thirsk and Cooper, *Seventeenth-Century Economic Documents,* 144.

195. Lee, *Vindication of a Regulated Inclosure,* 3, 29; Moore, *A Scripture-Word Against Inclosure,* (6), (12).

196. Above, p. 126.

197. Aylmer, *Rebellion or Revolution?,* 121; Kearney, *Scholars and Gentlemen,* 119; Webster, *Great Instauration,* 292, 518; Hill, *The Century of Revolution,* 148–51, 176–79.

198. Davis, *Utopia and the Ideal Society,* chapter 6; also pages 171, 180; Zagorin, *History of Political Thought in the English Revolution,* 55–57.

199. *Puritanism and Liberty,* 338–40, 364–65.

200. Appleby, *Economic Thought and Ideology in Seventeenth-Century England,* 70, 84.

201. Gunn, *Politics and the Public Interest in the Seventeenth Century,* 16–17, 44, 11: thus is Donne's "no man is an island" qualified!

202. Gunn, *Politics and the Public Interest,* 135, 144.

203. Hirst, *Authority and Conflict: England 1603–58,* 358.

CHAPTER 5. RECESSION AND REPARATION: 1660–1727

1. Hill, *Century of Revolution,* 250; Plumb, *The Growth of Political Stability in England,* 2; J. P. Kenyon in *Revolution Principles* (204) suggests that "stasis" is more

NOTES

appropriate than "stability," J. V. Beckett, in *Britain in the First Age of Party 1688–1750*, ed. C. Jones (1–18), sums up the debate.

2. *Life and Letters of Sir George Savile, Bart.*, 2:203; J. R. Jones, *Country and Court: England 1658–1714*, 4–5, 360; Plumb, *Political Stability*, I; Speck, *Reluctant Revolutionaries*; Clark's avowedly revisionist approach concurs that "1688 only preserved what 1660 was supposed to have re-established": *English Society 1688–1832*, 7.

3. Hay, et al., *Albion's Fatal Tree*, 18.

4. Holmes, *Religion and Party in Late Stuart England*, 3, and *Politics, Religion and Society in England 1679–1742*, 252–57; Hoskins, "Harvest Fluctuations and English History, 1620–1759," 22.

5. Plumb, *Political Stability*, xviii, 64, 27–29; Jones, *Country and Court*, 43; but see Clark, *English Society*, 8–41.

6. Morley, *A Thousand Lives*, title page, 60, 80–84; Ashcraft, *Revolutionary Politics and Locke's Two Treatises of Government*, ix, xiii–xiv; Ferguson, *Appeal*, I.

7. Morley, *A Thousand Lives*, 101 n.1, 138–41, 177, 193; Capp, *Cromwell's Navy*, 16–21, 26–28, 45; Ashley, *John Wildman*, 54, 103, 136–37, 215ff, 246–47; Ashcraft, *Revolutionary Politics*, 81, 86–87, 181–91, 235, 248, 340, 362, 369, 391–93.

8. Earle, *Monmouth's Rebels*, 10, 16; Morley, *A Thousand Lives*, 208, 220; *State Trials*, 11:880–81.

9. Horwitz, *Parliament, Policy and Politics in the Reign of William III*, 35; *Life and Letters of Sir George Savile*, 2:203, 222, 224, 226, 227.

10. Parker, *Discourse of Ecclesiastical Politie*, 2, 147, 155, 158, 271; Willan, *Exact Politician*, A.2 verso, 2; Tyrrell (see Kenyon, *Revolution Principles*, 36–37, 47–50, and Gough, "James Tyrrell.") *Bibliotheca Politica*, 145–46, 177, 179, 779; Blackall, *The Subject's Duty* (1705), 9, 31, 15–16 (see Kenyon, *Revolution Principles*, 119–21; Ashcraft and Goldsmith, "Locke," 786–87); Jackson, *The Grounds of Civil and Ecclesiastical Government*, 33, 37.

11. *Memoirs of Denzil Lord Holles*, 102.

12. Horwitz, *Parliament, Policy and Politics*, 98, 109, 210, 214, 277.

13. Thirsk and Cooper, eds., *Seventeenth-Century Economic Documents*, 406; anon., *Whig and Tory*, 376, 380–82; Swift, *The People of England's Grievances*, 2.

14. Anon., *New Atlantis*, a3, a4, (1), (18), 16, 27, 35, 41–42, 44, 45.

15. Halifax, *Character of a Trimmer* and *Rough Draft of a New Modell at Sea*, in *Works*, 1:184–85 and 301–3.

16. Warwick, *Discourse of Government* (published 1694), 121; Tindal, *An Essay Concerning Obedience*, 45.

17. Defoe, *Original Power*, 13; North, *Discourse on the English Constitution*, extract printed in *The Scholar Armed* (1795), 1:310.

18. Holmes, *Politics, Religion and Society*, 259; Clark indeed alludes to "the Commonwealthmen on whom modern scholarship has so unduly focussed" (*English Society*, 279).

19. Toland, *The Art of Governing by Parties* (1757 reprint), iii, 21–23; *The State-Anatomy of Great Britain*, 8–9, 11–14; on Toland, see below, pages 227–28.

20. Molesworth, *Account of Denmark*, a2, a6–7; also his preface to *Franco-Gallia*, v, vii–viii.

21. Robbins, *The Eighteenth-Century Commonwealthman*, 89; Molesworth, preface, to *Franco-Gallia*, xxxiv.

22. Gunn, *Politics and the Public Interest*, 153; Kennedy, *English Taxation 1640–1799*, 88–89; Bramston's *Autobiography*, 355; anon., *The Country Gentleman's Notion Concerning Governments*, 7–8; anon., *Behaviour of Christians* in *State Tracts of the Reign of William III* (1706), 2:163–64.

23. Paxton, *Civil Polity*, 56 (see also Gunn, "The Civil Polity of Peter Paxton"); Burnett, *An Essay upon Government*, 25, 12–13, 20; Jackson, *Civil and Ecclesiastical Government* (1718), 7–8; Braddon, *The Regular-Government, and Judicious-Employment of the Poor*, 24ff.

24. *The Grumbling Hive: or, Knaves turn'd Honest*, in *The Fable of the Bees: or, Private Vices, Publick Benefits*, 1:24, 36, lvi.

25. Anon., *Sovereignty and Greatness*, 20; Heckscher, *Mercantilism*, 2:286, 293.

26. Kennedy, *English Taxation*, 84, 89; Hill, *Century of Revolution*, 299.

27. See Holmes, *Politics, Religion and Society*, 2–4; Plumb, *Political Stability*, xiii–xv; Kenyon, *Revolution Principles*; and Cruickshanks, in *Britain in the First Age of Party*, 19–43.

28. Speck, 60–61, and Cruickshanks, 40, in C. Jones, *Britain in the First Age of Party*.

29. Robbins, *Eighteenth-Century Commonwealthman*, 47–48; *Memoirs of Edmund Ludlow . . . 1625–1672*, 2:99, 172.

30. Neville printed in *Two English Republican Tracts*, 75–76, 82, 184; 122, 85; 144–45, 132–33, 152–53.

31. Ibid., 101–2, 170, 177, 196.

32. See West, foreword to his edition of *Discourses Concerning Government*, xv–xxxvi; Gooch, *English Democratic Ideas*, 283–86.

33. Sidney, *Discourses*, 1, 248, 270; Robbins, *Eighteenth-Century Commonwealthman*, 44–45.

34. Gooch, *English Democratic Ideas*, 191; Halifax, *Character of a Trimmer*, 240–43.

35. Ashcraft, *Revolutionary Politics*, Franklin, *John Locke and the Theory of Sovereignty*, 121, 125.

36. Locke, *Two Treatises of Civil Government*, 117–18, 127, 129–41, 143–44, 225.

37. Ibid., 180, 183, 185–89, 192.

38. Ibid., 130; J. Richards, L. Mulligan, and J. K. Graham, " 'Property' and 'People': Political Usages of Locke and Some Contemporaries," 29, 33–37, 40–42; Tully, *A Discourse of Property*, 61, 98–99, 162–65; Locke, *Civil Government*, 30.

39. *Some Remarks upon Government*, 5, 8, 11, 12.

40. Ibid., 17, 24–26.

41. *Late Proceedings*, 11–12.

42. Dickinson, *Liberty and Property*, 106, 116; Plumb, *Political Stability*, 140–42, 149; xv, 134; Colley, "Eighteenth-Century Radicalism before Wilkes," 5; Kenyon, *Revolution Principles*, 203–5. For a revealing analysis of what happened to Whig "principles" in London, see G. S. De Krey, *A Fractured Society*, especially 50, 66–67, 178, 185–87, 237.

43. See Dickinson, "The Precursors of Political Radicalism in Augustan Britain," in C. Jones, *Britain in the First Age of Party*, 63–84; Bonwick, *English Radicals and the American Revolution*, xiv, 21; Clark, *English Society 1688–1832*, 3, 279.

44. Davenant, *The True Picture of a Modern Whig*, 5–7, 14–15, 29, 32–33; Gunn, *Beyond Liberty and Property*, 13.

45. Molesworth, *Account of Denmark*, b.8 verso–c.1 recto; *Franco-Gallia*, x, xvi, xviii, xxv–xxvi.

46. On this issue, see Schwoerer, *"No Standing Armies!"*; Fletcher, *Concerning Militia's and Standing Armies*, 14, 23; and *Discourse of Government*, 8, 36.

47. For full treatment of this device, see chapter 1 of Gunn, *Beyond Liberty and Property*.

48. Moyle, *Roman Government*, in *Works* (1726), 1:58, 63, 72–73, 93–97, 102, 112.

49. Toland, *Governing by Parties*, 63, 71; 45, 47–49, 103; *Annual Parliaments*, 10; *Danger of Mercenary Parliaments*, 6, 16–17.

50. See Dickinson, *Liberty and Property*, 89; Atwood, *The Fundamental Constitution of the English Government*, 100; Warwick, *Discourse of Government*, 123; Tyrrell, *Bibliotheca Politica*, advertisement, (1), 182, 672, 808, 780.

51. Defoe, *Original Power*, 17–18; *Hymn to the Mob*, 37, 14, 23, 30, 32.

52. Defoe, *The Freeholder's Plea*, subtitle, 3, 9, 13, 11, 15; 16–18.

53. Anon., *Vox Populi, Vox Dei*, 1, 25, 35 (on this tract see Kenyon, *Revolution Principles*, 123, 209–10, and Ashcraft and Goldsmith in "Locke," 787–94); Bradbury, *The Ass: or the Serpent*, 3, 17.

54. Hoadly, *The Measures of Submission to the Civil Magistrate Consider'd* (1706), 10 (see Kenyon, *Revolution Principles*, 116, 205, and Ashcraft and Goldsmith, "Locke," 787); Atterbury, *Voice of the People*, 6, 13; Gunn, *Beyond Liberty and Property*, 271.

55. Robbins, *Eighteenth-Century Commonwealthman*, 122; *Cato's Letters*, 2:214–16, 245, 227, 302, 80, 113; 252–54, 229 and 1:184, 97; 2:323–23, 238–39.

56. *Cato's Letters*, 1:185, 192, 255, 260–61; 2:16; 1:192–93, 66–67, 2:21; 1:259; 2:23, 54–55, 68–69, 77–84.

57. Ibid., 2:131; 1:12–15, 152; 2:22; 1:111–17, 86–87, 153, 178, 260; 2:34–43, 225.

58. Ibid., 2:16, 71, 246; 1:liv, lvi; Robbins, *Eighteenth-Century Commonwealthman*, 125.

59. Anon., *The Humble Petition and Representation of the . . . Anabaptists*, in Underhill, *Tracts*, 297–98, 305; Sturgion, *A Plea for Toleration of Opinions and Persuasions in Matters of Religion*, in Underhill, *Tracts*, 324–25, 327, 332.

60. *Sion's Groans* (by Jeffrey, Hanmon, and others), in Underhill, *Tracts*, 362, 376; Pett ("R.T."), *Discourse Concerning Liberty of Conscience*, title page, 7–10, 21, 24.

61. Holmes, *Religion and Party*, 8–11; Parker, *Ecclesiastical Politie*, title page, i, xii, xx, 2, 147, 149, 155.

62. Owen, *Truth and Innocence* (1669), 11, 69, 80. See also Parker, *Ecclesiastical Politie*, xxxvii.

63. Marvell, *Account of the Growth of Propery*, 3, 79, 153–54.

64. Halifax, in *Works*, 1:200–201, 251, 256–57.

65. Locke, *First Letter Concerning Toleration*, (iii), 1, 3, 6–7, 9, 14, 37.

66. Defoe, *Shortest Way*, 116–18, 124–26, 132–33, 250–52.

67. Shute, *Rights of the Protestant Dissenters*, 1:16, 37; 2:title page, 6, 14–17.

68. Verses cited in Robbins, *Eighteenth-Century Commonwealthman*, 229; Sacheverell, *The Perils of False Brethren* (1709), in Dickinson, *Politics and Literature in the Eighteenth Century*, 11–13; on Barrington and the concept of balance see Gunn, *Government and Opposition* 3 (1968), 223–40.

69. Toland, *Christianity not Mysterious*, xxiii, 6, 25, 158–73, 175; and *State-Anatomy of Great Britain*, 29. For Toland's contemporary notoriety as, allegedly, "the most notorious freethinker of all," see Jacob, *The Newtonians and the English Revolution 1689–1720*, 210–50; Molesworth, *Franco-Gallia*, xv.

70. Tindal, *The Power of the Magistrate*, 1, 11–12, 149; Gunn, *Beyond Liberty and Property*, 106–7.

71. Bahlman, *Moral Revolution*, 1, 7, 14–19, 23, 27, 37, 58, 65; Swift, *Advancement of Religion*, 7, 9, 21, 41, 54–55, 14–18, 20–21.

72. Bahlman, *Moral Revolution*, 70, 76, 79, v, 42, 46, 62, 83–84; Braddon, *The Regular-Government . . . of the Poor*, 40–41, and *The Miseries of the Poor* (1717), 57; *The Eight and Twentieth Account of . . . the Societies for Promoting a Reformation of Manners* (for 1721–22) cites a "total for Debauchery and Prophaneness [reported] in and near London during 32 Years past 84,720" (1).

73. Defoe, *The Poor Man's Plea*, title page, 4, 6, II; Bahlman, *Moral Revolution*, 94–95; *Cato's Letters*, 2:246–48.

74. Gunn, *Politics and the Public Interest*, 289–90.
75. Davis, *Utopia and the Ideal Society*, 2; *New Atlantis*, 28, 40, 35, 38, 40–41.
76. Anon., *Free State of Noland*, 4, 6, 9–10, 61; J. M. Patrick, "*The Free State of Noland*, a Neglected Utopia," 81, 88.
77. Anon., *An Essay Concerning Adepts*, 10, 13–14, 15–22, 38–40.
78. Ibid., 30–31, 32, 36–38, 51.
79. Holmes, *Politics, Religion and Society*, 230–31; J. R. Jones, *Country and Court: England 1658–1714*, 93–94, 359.
80. Robbins, *The Eighteenth-Century Commonwealthman*, 91.
81. Willan, *The Exact Politician* (1670), 10; Swift, *The People of England's Grievances* (c. 1693), 6; Toland, *Annual Parliaments* (1693), 6–7; *Vox Populi, Vox Dei* (1709), II; Appleby, *Economic Thought and Ideology*, 189, 151; Jacob, *The Newtonians*, 25, 51, 194–95, 200.
82. Hill, *Century of Revolution*, 204–5, 209–12, 263.
83. Hay et al., *Albion's Fatal Tree*, 18–19, 22, 56.
84. Barrow, *The Duty and Reward of Bounty to the Poor*, 71, 121, 126–28, 155–56; Bunyan, *Life and Death of Mr. Badman*, 93–97, 106, 116–18.
85. Baxter, printed as *The Reverend Richard Baxter's Last Treatise*, 20–22, 36–39.
86. Hill, *Century of Revolution*, 207.
87. Holmes, *Politics, Religion and Society*, 252–55; especially relevant to these issues is D. C. Coleman, "Labour in the English Economy of the Seventeenth Century."
88. Robbins, *Eighteenth-Century Commonwealthman*, 89, 114.
89. Haines, *Provision for the Poor*, title page, 3–6, 8.
90. Anon., *The Grounds of Sovereignty and Greatness*, 20; Firmin, *Some Proposals*, title page, 1, 20, 29: see G. S. De Krey, *A Fractured Society*, 58, for the high regard in which Firmin was held by the people of London.
91. Firmin, *Some Proposals*, 21, 2, 5; Webster, *Great Instauration*, 244.
92. Hale, *Provision for the Poor*, A2 recto–A3 verso, 1–7, 9, 11, 12, 20.
93. Cary, *Essay on the State of England*, 143–44, 152–53, 156–61, 164, 167.
94. A. Ruth Fry prints copious extracts from his works in *John Bellers 1654–1725*: introduction, 6–9; *College of Industry*, title page, 34–37.
95. Fry, *John Bellers*, 37, 39, 47–48; introduction, 25.
96. *Improvement of Physick*, in Fry, *John Bellers*, 113–15.
97. Dunning, *A Plain and Easie Method: shewing How the Office of Overseer of the Poor may be managed* (1685), 1–3; *Bread for The Poor*, title page, iii recto and verso, 1–3, 4–5, 9–10.
98. Child, *Relief and Employment of the Poor*, 2, 6–7, 10–11: closely repeating a chapter in his *New Discourse of Trade*, 1693.
99. Anon., *Moral State of the Nation*, 17–20.
100. Defoe, *Giving Alms no Charity*, title page, 160.
101. Ibid., 163, 166–67, 171, 173, 185–87.
102. Mandeville, *Essay on Charity*, 259, 261, 267, 286–88, 311, 313–14, 316–17.
103. Braddon, *Regular Government*, 5–6, 10, 20, 42, 77–79, 52–57.
104. Herein, in stressing the link between poverty and ignorance on the one hand and sedition and treason on the other, Braddon credits the Jacobites with wishing to prevent Poor Law reform for this reason: *Miseries of the Poor*, vii, xxix.
105. Wilson, "The Other Face of Mercantilism," 82–85; D. A. Baugh, "Poverty, Protestantism, and Political Economy: English Attitudes toward the Poor, 1660–1800," in *England's Rise to Greatness 1660–1763*, ed. S. B. Baxter, 76, 83; A. W. Coats, "Changing Attitudes to Labour in the Mid-Eighteenth Century," 46–47; Watts, *Charity Schools*, 39.

106. Dennis, *Vice and Luxury Publick Mischiefs*, title page, iv, xvi, xxiii, xxxii, xxxiii, xxxix–xl, xlviii, 5, 6–8, 25, 53, 72.
107. *Cato's Letters*, 1:244–45; 4:no. 133.
108. Ibid., 2:252, 308–9.

Chapter 6. Autumnal Fruits and Falling Leaves: The Eighteenth-Century Commonwealthmen

1. Moyle, 1796 reprint in Robbins, *Two English Republican Tracts*, 225–26; Hume, in *Hume: Theory of Politics*, 227; *Edmund Burke on Government, Politics and Society*, 317.
2. Plumb, *England in the Eighteenth Century*, 95.
3. Robbins, *Eighteenth-Century Commonwealthman*, 271.
4. Guttridge, *English Whiggism and the American Revolution*, 10–11.
5. On these issues see Speck, *Stability and Strife*, 4, 16, 21, 212–13; Plumb, "Political Man," in J. L. Clifford, ed., *Man versus Society in Eighteenth-Century Britain*, 7–9; Cannon, *Parliamentary Reform 1640–1832*, 42; Holmes and Szechi, *The Age of Oligarchy: Pre-industrial Britain 1722–1783*, 190; Clark, *English Society 1688–1832*, 8–41.
6. See Speck, *Stability and Strife*, 80–1; Holmes and Szechi, *Age of Oligarchy*, 171–79; E. P. Thompson, in *PP* 50 (1971) and in *Social History* 3 (1978), 154.
7. Holmes and Szechi, *Age of Oligarchy*, 134, 167–68; Wrigley, "Growth of Population in Eighteenth-Century England," 121–50; Schwarz, "Standard of Living," 24–41; Langford, *A Polite and Commercial People: England 1727–1783*, 123.
8. Holmes and Szechi, *Age of Oligarchy*, 52.
9. Owen, *The Eighteenth Century 1714–1815*, 101.
10. Holmes and Szechi, *Age of Oligarchy*, 92–93; Clark, *English Society*, 299.
11. Lowman, *Civil Government of the Hebrews*, 1, 8, 33, 47, 58–59, 233–34, 236–37.
12. Hammond and Moyle, *The Honest Elector*, title page, 9–10, 15; Thomson printed in Dickinson, *Politics and Literature in the Eighteenth Century*, 106.
13. Johnson in Dickinson, *Politics and Literature*, 99; Arnall in Dickinson, *Politics and Literature*, 93; Owen, *Eighteenth Century*, 101; Hume, in Dickinson, *Politics and Literature*, 106.
14. Speck, *Stability and Strife*, 4; Clark, "The Decline of Party, 1740–1760," 505; Marshall, *Eighteenth-Century England*, 150.
15. Osborne printed in Gunn, *Factions No More*, 114–15; Spelman, preface to *Several Forms of Government*, v–vi, viii–ix; Hume, "Of the Parties of Great Britain," printed in Dickinson, *Politics and Literature*, 105–6.
16. Dickinson, *Bolingbroke*, 238; Kramnick, *Bolingbroke and His Circle*, 2–3.
17. Kramnick, *Bolingbroke and His Circle*, 99–100; Dickinson, *Bolingbroke*, 171.
18. Kramnick, *Bolingbroke and His Circle*, 72, 35; Dickinson, *Bolingbroke*, 260.
19. *A Dissertation upon Parties* (1733), in *The Works of Lord Bolingbroke*, 2:5, 9–13, 15, 102–3, 118–20, 146–47, 150–51.
20. *The Idea of a Patriot King* (1738), in *Works*, 2:374–75, 379–81, 383, 391–92, 395–97, 401–2.
21. Kramnick, *Bolingbroke and His Circle*, 78–79, 169.
22. See Dickinson, *Bolingbroke*, 214–15; Pope's *Essay on Man* in *Poems of Alexander Pope*, vol. III.i, 11, line 1; 31, lines 129–30; 123, line 296; 87, lines 265–66; 126, lines 317–18; 51, line 294.

23. *The Dunciad* in *Poems*, vol. V, 403, line 601; *Epistle to Bathurst* in *Poems*, vol. III.ii, 93, lines 69–70; Kramnick, *Bolingbroke and His Circle*, 63, 220.
24. Gay, *Dramatic Works*, 2:23, 36–37, 64–65; Kramnick, 225.
25. Swift, *Gulliver's Travels*, 48–49, 132.
26. Cobbett, *Parliamentary History of England*, vol. 9, cols. 471, 402, 404, 430, 467, 474.
27. Ibid., vol. 10, cols. 555, 558; vol. 13, col. 1082.
28. Hay, *Essay on Civil Government*, 22, 15, 23, 29, 39, 45.
29. Fothergill, *The Dangers of Excesses*, title page, 13–14, 23, 28, 35.
30. Anon., *The Livery-Man*, 2–3, 6–8, 11, 18, 22, 34, 56, 62.
31. Hume-Campbell, *A Serious Exhortation* (1740), 13–14, 16, 22, 32, 53.
32. Campbell, *The Case of the Opposition* (1742), 3, 28–29, 34–35, 51–52.
33. Anon., *An Essay on Civil Government*, 9, 19, 132–34, 328, 338, 339.
34. Ralph, *Use and Abuse of Parliaments* (1744), vol. 1, 111; vol. 2, 714–17.
35. Anon., *Liberty and Right*, xi–xii; Dickinson, *Politics and Literature*, 115–19.
36. *Hume: Theory of Politics*, 229–32.
37. Ibid., 236–38, 239, 241; transcript, xxix.
38. Pownall, *Principles of Polity*, 3–4, 9.
39. Ibid., 10–11, 28–29, 30, 100, 102–3, 107, 130.
40. Squire, *Foundation of the English Constitution*, title page, 365, 379, 382, 396.
41. Rupp, *Religion in England 1688–1791*, 53, 75; for Burke, see pp. 317–18.
42. Vereker, *Eighteenth-Century Optimism*, 53–54; Wollaston, *The Religion of Nature Delineated*, 7, 45, 72, 110, 145, 147, 38; Stromberg, *Religious Liberalism in Eighteenth-Century England*, 38; see Rupp, *Religion in England*, 267–70.
43. Hoadly in *Politics and Literature*, 49; see Rupp, *Religion in England*, 88–101, and Speck, *Stability and Strife*, 95–96.
44. Pope, *Essay on Man*, 124, lines 305–6; Warburton, *Church and State*, 26, 104, 52–53, 13, 113, 132, 86, v; Langford, *Polite and Commercial People*, 292–93; Speck, *Stability and Strife*, 102–3.
45. See Langford, *Polite and Commercial People*, 123, 148–49, 296–97; Holmes and Szechi, *Age of Oligarchy*, 112–13.
46. Speck, *Stability and Strife*, 111; Gibson, in E. N. Williams, *Eighteenth-Century Constitution*, 376.
47. Foster, *Natural Religion and Social Virtue*, 2:2–3, 159, 185, 223–37, 295–97, 187.
48. Brown, *Manners and Principles of the Times*, 14–15, 29, 90, 55, 64, 111–12, 115, 119, 121, 134, 190, 195–96, 214, 221.
49. Langford, *Polite and Commercial People*, 146–47; Wrigley, "The Growth of Population in Eighteenth Century England," 129, 143, 146; Snell, *Annals of the Labouring Poor*, 37–38; for a less sanguine view, see Schwarz, "Standard of Living," 24–41.
50. E. P. Thompson, "Eighteenth-Century English Society: Class Struggle Without Class?," 154, 142.
51. Langford, *Public Life and the Propertied Englishman 1689–1798*, 2–3.
52. Coats, "Changing Attitudes to Labour."
53. Vanderlint, *Money answers all Things*, title page.
54. Ibid., i, 6–7, 21, 67–69, 85–86.
55. Ibid., 101–3, 105, 120, 122, 153–54.
56. Postlethwayt, *Britain's Commercial Interest*, 1: 36–37; 2:527, 533, 536.
57. Hazeland, *Trade and Civil Liberty*, 5–6, 10, 8, 17, 20–21, 23.
58. Marshall, *The English Poor in the Eighteenth Century*, 47; Speck, *Stability and Strife*, 78.

59. Clayton, *Friendly Advice to the Poor*, 3–6, 15–16, 21–23, 29, 36.
60. Pope, *Epistle to Bathhurst*, 99–100, lines 103–8.
61. Marshall, *English Poor*, vii; Snell, *Annals of the Labouring Poor*, 104–5; Law, *A Serious Call to a Devout and Holy Life* (1723), 80–81.
62. Anon., *A Short View*, 8, 45; Marshall, 132, 140; *An Account*, cited in Speck, *Stability and Strife*, 78.
63. Alcock, *Defects of the Poor Laws*, 11, 19, 40, 46–48, 52, 54–55, 72–76.
64. Fielding, *Effectual Provision for the Poor*, 4, 5–6, 8–10, 18–21.
65. Fielding, printed in *Complete Works* (London, 1889), 769, 771–77, 783.
66. Massie, *Establishment of Charity Houses*, title page, 55, 97, 107; Watts, *Essay on Charity Schools*, 14; Law, *A Serious Call to a Devout and Holy Life, 35;* Rupp, *Religion in England*, 308; Stromberg, *Religious Liberalism*, 151, 153.
67. Watts, *Charity Schools*, 15–16, 17, 28, 35, 39, 47.
68. E. P. Thompson, "Eighteenth-Century English Society," 137.
69. Speck, *Stability and Strife*, 53; E. P. Thompson, *Customs in Common*, 269.
70. Massie, *Charity Houses*, title page; chapter 4 of Snell's *Annals of the Labouring Poor* surveys the debate; Snell, 194–98, on poor relief expenditure; on parliamentary enclosure see J. L. and B. Hammond, *The Village Labourer*, vol. 1, 7, and Plumb, "Political Man," 8.
71. Marshall, *English Poor*, 183–85; Langford, *Polite and Commercial People*, 180–81; Snell, chapter 5: "The decline of apprenticeship"; 7 Geo. I, c.3 is printed in Bland, Brown, and Tawney, *English Economic Documents* (London, 1914), 622–24.
72. Langford, *Public Life and the Propertied Englishman*, 470; Christie, *Stability and Stress in Late Eighteenth-Century Britain*, 150–55.
73. Speck, *Stability and Strife*, 118; Walsh, "Elie Halevy and the BIrth of Methodism," 14, 16–17.
74. Walsh, "Elie Halevy," 17–19; Langford, *A Polite and Commercial People*, 253.
75. Jephson, *Friendly and Compassionate Address*, title page, 33–34, 36–37; *Polite and Commercial People*, Langford, 331.
76. Holmes and Szechi, *Age of Oligarchy*, 164, 167–69, 319; Langford, *Polite and Commercial People*, 442–4,449; Marshall, *Eighteenth-Century England*, 342 n.1, 388–89.
77. Pocock, *Three British Revolutions: 1641, 1688, 1776*, 274, 284; Langford, *Polite and Commercial People*, 701.
78. On Hollis and Baron, see Robbins, *The Eighteenth-Century Commonwealthman*, 259–69.
79. See Christie, *Wilkes, Wyvill and Reform;* Plumb, "Political Man," 15.
80. Towers, *Observations*, 5, 8; Johnson, *The False Alarm* (1770), 7, 16, 35.
81. Almon, *The Honest Elector's Proposal*, 5, 18–19, 21, 22–36, and *Political Register*, no. 12, 226–28, 233, 34, 238.
82. Priestley, *First Principles*, 17; Burke, in *Writings and Speeches*, 1:472, 478–80, 492, 517, 521, 526–27, 530.
83. Macaulay, *Observations on . . . Thoughts on the Cause of the Present Discontents* (1770), 5, 10–11, 14, 16–20; see B. and C. Hill, "Catharine Macaulay and the Seventeenth Century."
84. Hulme, *Historical Essay*, title page, 7, 23, 115–16, 145–47, 158–61; *The Philosopher* is fully surveyed in the present writer's *David Williams*, 11–21.
85. For lengthier comment on both these works, see *David Williams*, 67–71.
86. Price, *Civil Liberty*, title page, 32, 49; Cartwright, *American Independence*, 6–8, 13; see Osborne, *John Cartwright*, 11, 14, 17–19.
87. Williams, *Political Liberty*, 13, 29–30 (see *David Williams*, 75–87); Price, *American Revolution*, 9; Williams, *Lectures on Political Principles* (1789), 114.

88. Bonwick, *English Radicals and the American Revolution*, xv; Priestley, *First Principles*, 159, 188; Jenyns, *Disquisitions on Several Subjects*, 173.

89. Robbins, *Eighteenth-Century Commonwealthman*, 269; Mauduit, *Dissenting Ministers*, 51; Hitchin, *Free Thoughts on the Late Application of some Dissenting Ministers*, 10.

90. See *A collection of the several papers relating to the application made to Parliament in 1772 and 1773* (British Library 215.i.3) and *David Williams*, 42–46.

91. See Black, *The Asociation: British Extraparliamentary Organisation 1769–1793*, chapter 4, "The Children of Darkness."

92. Hume, *Natural Religion*, 128, 172, 219–20.

93. M. G. Jones, *The Charity School Movement*, 146; Stromberg, *Religious Liberalism*, 68, 119–20, 124; Bradley, "Whigs and Nonconformists," 1–27.

94. Goodwin, *The Friends of Liberty*, 78–79; Robbins, *Eighteenth-Century Commonwealthman*, 365.

95. Burgh, *Political Disquisitions*, book 1, 36–38, 129, 173, 180, 185; chapters 6 and 7 of Book 3 deal with Rotation and the Ballot respectively.

96. Brewer, *Party Ideology and Popular Politics at the Accession of George III*, 20, 215; Black, *The Association*, 32; Burgh, *Political Disquisitions*, 428–29.

97. Christie, *Wllkes, Wyvill and Reform*, 188; Black, *The Association*, 32; see also Guttridge, *English Whiggism and the American Revolution*, 113–16; Pares, *King George III and the Politicians*, 51–54; Cannon, *Parliamentary Reform 1640–1832*, 62.

98. Jebb, in *Works* (1787), 2:460, 480–42; Christie, *Wilkes, Wyvill and Reform*, 78–79; Bonwick, *English Radicals*, 7.

99. Cone, *The English Jacobins*, 62; Robbins, *Eighteenth-Century Commonwealthman*, 375; Black, *The Association*, 174; Day *Speeches* (1780), 10, 19.

100. Osborne, *John Cartwright*, 25–26; Hollis cited in Cannon, *Parliamentary Reform*, 82; SCI handbill, *Rights of the Commonalty* printed in Dickinson, *Politics and Literature*, 166–67.

101. Clark, *English Society 1688–1832*, 339; see Hecht, *The Domestic Servant Class in Eighteenth-century England*: Bonwick, *English Radicals*, 243.

102. De Lolme, *The Constitution of England* (English version, London, 1777), 203–4, 206 (De Lolme, a Swiss immigrant, whose perceptive analysis was praised by Bentham, in later life sought help from the Literary Fund); Jenyns, *Disquisitions on Several Subjects*, 153; Cone, *The English Jacobins*, 58–59.

103. Price, *Discourse on the Love of Our Country*, title page, 51, and appendix 13.

104. Christie, *Stress and Stability in Late Eighteenth-Century Britain*, 77; see Langford, *Polite and Commercial People*, 456, for tables.

105. Jenyns, *Disquisitions*, 159; Langford, *Polite and Commercial People*, 299.

106. Spence, printed in *The Rights of Man* (1793), 3, 11, 16; see Chase, *"The People's Farm": English Radical Agrarianism 1775–1840*, 32–36.

107. Ogilvie, *The Right of Property in Land*, 12, 20, 35, 97–98, 141, 175; Forster, *High Price of Provisions*, 42; Moore, *Considerations on the Exorbitant Price of Provisions*, 70.

108. Forster, *High Price of Provisions*, 55, 62; Mortimer, *Commerce, Politics and Finances*, 91, 95; Tucker, *Four Treatises* (1774), 2.

109. Forster, *High Price of Provisions*, 1, 40, 50, 115; Jenyns, *Thoughts on the Causes and Consequences of the Present High Price of Provisions* (1767), 2, 3–6, 12; Moore, *Considerations on the Exorbitant Price of Provisions*, title page, 69–70, 81.

110. Tucker, *Manifold Causes of the Increase of the Poor*, 10–11, 3, 6, 27, 33; Woodward, *Expediency of a Regular Plan*, 2, 7, 8–9, 33–35, 41–44, 90.

111. Marshall, *The English Poor*, 13, 153; Christie, *Stress and Stability*, 96; Snell, *Annals of the Labouring Poor*, 104–5; Brooke, *The History of Parliament: The House of Commons 1754–1790*, 268–69; Langford, *Polite and Commercial People*, 486–89, 497–98.

112. Langford, *Polite and Commercial People*, 457, 461.
113. Forster, *High Price of Provisions*, 115; Christie, *Stress and Stability*, 153; Marshall, *Eighteenth-Century England*, 388.
114. Langford, *Polite and Commercial People*, 644–46; Forster, *High Price of Provisions*, 50–53.
115. Christie, *Wilkes, Wyvill and Reform*, 223, and *Stress and Stability*, 35; Jenyns, *Disquisitions*, 159–60.
116. Forster, *High Price of Provisions*, 11, 42.
117. Oswald, *Constitution of Great Britain*, title page, 5–8, 16–17, 20–21, 48, 52; Mary Wollstonecraft, *Vindication of the Rights of Men*, 33–34, 8, 133, 148, 149, 151.
118. Bentley, *The Rights of the Poor*, single-sheet broadside; Cooper, *Reply to Mr. Burke's Invective*, 13, 20, 60–62, 66–67; Callender, *Political Progress*, 23, n.*.
119. Dyer, *Complaints of the Poor People*, 12–16, 22–28; Spence, *Pig's Meat*, no. 1 (1793), title page, 89, 98; Pares, *King George III*, 49.
120. Spence, printed in *The Important Trial of Thomas Spence* (1801), 71–72, as is *The Constitution of a Perfect Commonwealth: Being the French Constitution of 1793* (2nd ed., 1798); see Chase, *"The People's Farm,"* 32–33.
121. Hodgson's *The Commonwealth of Reason* defines rulers as "the servants of the commonwealth" and would make all positions of power "Revolutionary or Rotative." In a commonwealth (a term used throughout) based on "reason, liberty, fraternity, and equality," every citizen must be a soldier: v–vi, 18, 96.
122. Mackintosh, *Vindiciae Gallicae*, 224, 226–27, 305.
123. *Writings and Speeches of Edmund Burke*, vol. 7, 10 (1772), 25 (1773), 36 (1773), 43 (1792).
124. Ibid., vol. 7, 71, 72–73, 76, 79 ("Speech on A Bill for Shortening the Duration of Parliaments," 8 May 1780).
125. *Reflections on the Revolution in France*, 40, 65, 67; *Writings and Speeches*, vol. 4, 70, 173–74, 163–64, 202.
126. For exemplification of these points see Jones, *David Williams*, 102–9, 41–45, 184–85, 92–96.
127. Ibid., 109–12.
128. Ibid., chapter 6, "Citizen of France" and chapter 7, "Recessional: 'British Patriot.'"
129. Paine, *Common Sense*, 65, 47, 50.
130. Paine, *Rights of Man* (1791 and 1792), 219–28, 231–35, 237.
131. Cone, *The English Jacobins*, 104; Cannon, *Parliamentary Reform*, 120; Paine, *Rights of Man*, 254; on Paine's social thinking and the reactions thereby engendered, see Gregory Claeys, *Thomas Paine*, 80–82, 96–101, 124–25, 132–34.

Conclusion

1. Robbins, *Eighteenth-Century Commonwealthman*, 321–24; Osborne, *John Cartwright*, 27, 35; Cannon, *Parliamentary Reform*, 140; Pocock, *Three British Revolutions*, 284.
2. Plumb, "Political Man," 18; Young, *The Example of France*, 44 n. 46.
3. Palmer, *The Age of the Democratic Revolution*; Baker, *Inventing the French Revolution*, 168, 171, 181, 199.
4. Gunn, *Queen of the World: Opinion in the Public Life of France from the Renaissance to the Revolution*, 3, 45; on David Williams, see above pages 318–19.

5. Habermas, *The Structural Transformation of the Public Sphere*, 57–67; Gunn, *Queen of the World*, 123, 348; Habermas, 99.

6. PRO, Treasury Solicitors' Papers, II, 4053; Langford, *Polite and Commercial People*, 304; Wyvill, *A Defence of Dr. Price*, 60.

7. Cone, *The English Jacobins*, 213; Jones, *David Williams*, 155–56; Holcroft, *A Letter to the Right Honourable Wiliam Windham*, 2, 23, 39, 47–48.

8. Cartwright, *The Commonwealth in Danger*, 97: see Osborne, *John Cartwright* 47; Hodgson, *The Commonwealth of Reason*, v, 18, 96.

9. Duverger, *Les Constitutions de la France*, 58; Goodwin, *The French Revolution*, 156.

10. Robbins, *Eighteenth-Century Commonwealthman*, 322–33.

11. Clark, *English Society 1688–1832*, 293–94, 297, 302, 306.

Bibliography

Primary Sources

Anonymous. *An Account of Several Work-Houses.* London, 1725.
———. *An Agreement of the Free People of England.* London, 1649.
———. *An Agreement of the People.* London, 1647.
———. *An Answer to a Proposition.* London, 1659.
———. *The Case of the Armie, Truly Stated.* London, 1647.
———. *Chaos: or . . . a Frame of Government.* London, 1659.
———. *A Commonwealth, and Commonwealths-men Asserted.* London, 1659.
———. *A Commonwealth or Nothing.* London, 1659.
———. *A Copie of a Letter.* London, 1647.
———. *A Copy of a Letter . . . by A true Commonwealths-man.* London, 1656.
———. *The Country Gentleman's Notion Concerning Governments.* Nottingham, 1696.
———. *A Declaration of some Proceedings.* London, 1648/9.
———. *A Declaration of the . . . Poor Inhabitants of the town of Wellinborow.* London, 1650.
———. *A Declaration of the Wel-affected.* London, 1649.
———. *Decrees and Orders of the Committee of Safety of the Commonwealth of Oceana.* London, 1659.
———. *A Defence of Liberty against Tyrants.* A translation of the *Vindiciae Contra Tyrannos*, by Junius Brutus. Edited by H. J. Laski. London, 1924.
———. *A Dialogue betwixt Whig and Tory.* London, 1692.
———. *The Diggers Christmas-Caroll.* London, 1650.
———. *Englands Freedome, Souldiers Rights.* London, 1647.
———. *Englands Monarchy Asserted.* London, 1659/60.
———. *An Essay on Civil Government.* London, 1743.
———. *Foundations of Freedom; or an Agreement of the People.* London, 1648.
———. *The Free State of Noland.* London, 1696 and 1701.
———. *The Good Old Cause Explained.* London, n.d.
———. *The Grounds of Sovereignty and Greatness.* London, 1675.
———. *A Hue & Crie After the Good Old Cause.* London, n.d.
———. *The Humble Petition and Representation of the . . . Anabaptists.* London, 1660/1.
———. *King James His Opinion.* London, 1647.
———. *The Leveller: . . . concerning Government and Religion.* London, 1659.

———. *Light Shining in Buckinghamshire*. London, 1648.
———. *A Letter to a Friend concerning . . . Revolutions*. London, n.d.
———. *A Modest Reply*. London, 1659.
———. *More Light Shining in Buckinghamshire*. London, 1650.
———. *The mournfull Cryes of many thousand poor Tradesmen*. London, 1648.
———. *A Negative Voyce*. London, 1659.
———. *New Atlantis*. London, 1660.
———. *A New Letany for these Times*. London, 1659.
———. *No Papist nor Presbyterian*. London, 1648.
———. *The Livery-Man: or, Plain Thoughts on Publick Affairs*. London, 1740.
———. *Now is the Time: a Scheme for a Commonwealth*. London, n.d.
———. *A Petition . . . Concerning the Draught of an Agreement of the People*. London, 1648.
———. *A Plea for Limited Monarchy*. London, 1659/60.
———. "Policies to reduce this realme of England unto a prosperus wealthe and estate," 1549. Printed in *TED*, vol. 3.
———. *The Poor Orphans Court*. London, 1636.
———. *The prayse and commendacion of suche as sought comenwelthes*. London, c. 1548.
———. *Reflexions upon the Moral State of the Nation*. London, 1701.
———. *Respublica*. 1553. Edited by L. A. Magnus. London: EETS, 1905.
———. *Several Proposals for Peace & Freedom*. London, 1648.
———. *A Short View of the Frauds, Abuses, and Impositions of Parish Officers*. London, 1744.
———. *Sion's Groans for her Distressed*. London, 1661.
———. *Some Grave and Weighty Considerations*. London, 1658.
———. *Stanleyes Remedy*. London, 1646.
———. *To the . . . Commons in Parliament Assembled*. London, 1647.
———. *To . . . the Commons of England*. London, 1649.
———. *To the Right Honorable, the Commons of England*. London, 1648.
———. *To the Supream Authority of England*. London, 1647.
———. *To the Supream Authority of England*. London, 1648.
———. *Tyranipocrit*. Rotterdam, 1649. (Also printed in *British Pamphleteers*, edited by G. Orwell and R. Reynolds, vol. I. London: Allan Wingate, 1948.)
———. *The vanitie of the present Churches*. London, 1649.
———. *Vox Populi, Vox Dei*. London, 1709.
A.B. and N.T. *Some Remarks upon Government*. London, 1689.
Alcock, Thomas. *Observations on the Defects of the Poor Laws*. London, 1752.
Allen, R. *A Treatise of Christian Beneficence*. London, 1600.
Allen, William. *An Apologie and True Declaration*. Hainault (?), 1581.
———. *A True, Sincere, and Modest Defense of English Catholics*. 1584. Edited by R. M. Kingdom. Ithaca, Cornell University Press, 1965.
Almon, John. *The Honest Elector's Proposal*. London, 1767.
Arnall, William, *Opposition is Proof of Patriotism*. London, 1735.
Arthington, Henry. *Provision for the poore, now in penurie*. London, 1597.

Ascham, Anthony. *Of the Confusions and Revolutions of Governments.* 1649. Edited and introduced by G. W. S. V. Rumble. Delmar, NY: Scholars' Facsimiles and Reprints, 1975.

———. *The Origin and End of Civil Power.* London, 1649.

Atterbury, Francis. *The Voice of the People, no Voice of God.* London, 1710.

Atwood, W. *The Fundamental Constitution of the English Government.* London, 1690.

Bacon, Sir Francis. *Essays, or Counsels Civil and Moral.* London: Newnes, 1892.

Baldwin, William. *A Myrroure For Magistrates.* London, 1559.

Bancroft, Richard. *Daungerous Positions and Proceedings.* London, 1593.

———. *A Sermon Preached at Paules Crosse.* London, 1588.

Barlowe, Jerome. *Burial of the Mass.* London, 1528. Printed as *Rede me and be nott wrothe*, edited by E. Arber. London: English Reprints, 1895.

Barnes, Robert. *A Supplicatyon unto Henry VIII.* London (?), 1543. Facsimile printed in The English Experience No. 567. Amsterdam/New York: Da Capo Press, 1973.

Barrington, John Shute, Viscount. *The Rights of the Protestant Dissenters.* London, 1705.

Barrow, Isaac. *The Duty and Reward of Bounty to the Poor.* London, 1671.

Barrowe, Henry. *A Brief Discovery of the False Churches.* London, c. 1590.

———. *Examinations. . . .* London, 1593.

Baxter, Richard. *A Holy Commonwealth.* London, 1659. Edited by W. Lamont. Cambridge: Cambridge University Press, 1994.

———. *The Poor Husbandman's Advocate to Rich Racking Landlords.* London, 1691. Edited by F. M. Powicke. Manchester University, 1926.

Beacon, Richard. *Solon His Follie, or A Politique Discourse, Touching the Reformation of common-weales.* Oxford, 1594.

Becon, Thomas. *The Catechism . . . with other pieces.* Edited by J. Ayre. Cambridge, Parker Society, 1844.

———. *Early Works* (c. 1542–43). Edited by J. Ayre. Cambridge: Parker Society, 1843.

Bedel, Henry. A sermon exhorting to pitie the poor. London, 1572.

Bellers, John. Tracts printed in *John Bellers 1654–1725* by A. Ruth Fry. London, Cassell, 1935.

Bentley, Thomas. *The Rights of the Poor.* London, 1791.

Bernard, Richard. *The Isle of Man.* London, 1627.

Bilson, Thomas. *The True Difference between Christian subjection and unchristian rebellion.* Oxford, 1585.

Blackall, Ofspring. *The Subject's Duty.* London, 1705.

Bodin, Jean. *Six Books of the Commonwealth.* 1576. Abridged, translated, and with an introduction by M. J. Tooley. Oxford: Blackwell, 1967.

Bolingbroke, Henry St. John, Viscount. *A Dissertation upon Parties.* London, 1733–34.

———. *The Idea of a Patriot King.* London, 1738.

———. *A Letter on the Spirit of Patriotism.* London, 1736.

———. *Some Reflections on the Present State of the Nation.* London, 1749.

Bradbury, Thomas. *The Ass: or the Serpent.* London, 1712.

Braddon, Lawrence. *The Regular-Government, and Judicious-Employment of the Poor.* London, 1721.
Braddon, Lawrence. *The Miseries of the Poor.* London, 1717.
Bradshaw, ?. *English Puritanisme.* London, 1605.
Bramston, Sir John. *Autobiography.* Edited by P. Braybrooke. London: Camden Society, Old series, no. 32. 1845.
Bray, William. *A Plea for the Peoples Good Old Cause.* London, 1659.
Bridges, John. *A Defence of the Government.* London, 1587.
———. *The Supremacie of Christian Princes.* London, 1573.
Brinklow, Henry. *The Complaynt of Roderyck Mors.* London, c. 1542, Edited by J. M. Cowper. London: EETS, 1874.
Brooke, Humphrey. *The Charity of Church-Men.* London, 1649.
Brown, John. *Estimate of the Manners and Principles of the Times.* London, 1757.
Browne, Robert. *A Treatise of Reformation Without Tarrying for Anie.* London, 1582.
Bunyan, John. *A Few Sighs from Hell.* London, 1658.
———. *The Life and Death of Mr Badman.* London, 1680. Edited by J. Brown. Cambridge: Cambridge University Press, 1905.
Burgh, James. *Political Disquisitions.* London, 1774.
Burke, Edmund. *Edmund Burke on Government, Politics and Society.* Edited by B. W. Hill. London: Fontana, 1975.
———. *Reflections on the Revolution in France.* London, 1790. Edited by F. G. Selby. London: Macmillan, 1924.
———. *Writings and Speeches of Edmund Burke.* Vols. 1, 4 and 7. London: Bickers, 1920.
Burnett, Thomas. *An Essay upon Government.* London, 1715.
Burton, Robert. *The Anatomy of Melancholy.* 1651. London: Blake and Ridley, 1838.
Burton, Thomas. *Diary of Thomas Burton (1656–59).* Edited by J. T. Rutt. London, 1828.
Busher, Leonard. *Religious Peace: or, A Plea for Liberty of Conscience.* London, 1614; rpt. 1646.
Calendar of State Papers, Domestic Series, of the Reigns of Edward VI, Mary, Elizabeth. 1547–1580. Edited by R. Lemon. London, 1856.
Callender, J. T. *The Political Progress of Britain.* London, 1792.
Calvin, Jean. *Epistle to the duke of Somerset.* London, 1550.
Campbell, J. *The Case of the Opposition Impartially Stated.* London, 1742.
Carew, Thomas. *Certaine godly and necessarie Sermons.* London, 1603.
Carpenter, John. *A Preparative to Contentation.* London, 1597.
Carter, Bezaleel. *Christ His Last Will and John His Legacy.* London, 1621.
Cartwright, John. *American Independence the Interest and Glory of Great Britain.* London, 1774.
———. *The Commonwealth in Danger.* London, 1795.
Cartwright, Thomas. *A Replye to An answere.* London, n.d.
Cary, John. *An Essay on the State of England.* Bristol, 1695.
Cato's Letters. London, 1755. New York: Da Capo Press, 1971 (2 vols.).
Chamberlen, Peter, *The Poore Mans Advocate.* London, 1649.

Charretier, Alain. *The Curial made by maystere Alain Charretier.* Translated by William Caxton, 1484. Edited by F. J. Furnivall. London: EETS. Extra series, 54, 1888.

Cheke, Sir John. *The hurt of sedition*, 1549. Printed in Raphael Holinshed's *Chronicle*, vol. 3. London, 1808.

Child, Sir Josiah. *A Method Concerning the Relief and Employment of the Poor.* London, 1699.

———. *A New Discourse of Trade.* London, 1693.

Cholmeley, William. *The Request and Suite of a True-Hearted Englishman.* London, 1553. Edited by W. J. Thoms. Camden Miscellany, 2. London, 1853.

Christopherson, John. *An Exhortation to . . . take hede and beware of rebellyon.* London. 1554.

Clarkson, Laurence. *A Generall Charge.* London, 1647.

Clayton, John. *Friendly Advice to the Poor.* London, 1755.

Cobbett, William. *Parliamentary History of England.* London: vols. 5 (1809), 9 (1811), 10 (1812), 13 (1812), 18 (1813).

Colle(d)ge, Stephen. *Dying Speeches.* London, 1681.

Cooke, John. *Monarchy No creature of Gods making.* Waterford, 1651.

———. *Redintegratio Amoris, or A Union of Hearts.* London, 1647.

———. *Unum Necessarium: or, The Poore Mans Case.* London, 1648.

Cooper, Thomas. *An Admonition to the People of England.* London, 1589.

Cooper, Thomas. *A Reply to Mr. Burke's Invective.* London, 1792.

Coppe, Abiezer. *A Fiery Flying Roll.* London, 1649.

———. *A Second Fiery Flying Roule.* London, 1649.

Cornelius, Peter. *A Way Propounded to Make the poor . . . happy.* London, 1649. Edited by J. Downie. Manchester: Cooperative Union, 1934.

Coster, Robert. *A Mite Cast into the Common Treasury.* London, 1649.

Covel, William. *A Declaration Unto the Parliament.* London, 1659.

Craig, Sir Thomas. *The Right of Succession to the Kingdom of England.* London, 1703 (translation of the Latin original of 1603).

Cranmer, Thomas. *Miscellaneous Writings and Letters,* vol. 2. Edited by J. Cox. Cambridge: Parker Society, 1846.

Cromwell, Thomas. *Life and Letters of Thomas Cromwell.* Edited by R. B. Merriman. 2 vols. Oxford: Clarendon, 1902.

Cromwell, Oliver. *Speeches of Oliver Cromwell.* Edited and with an introduction by Ivan Roots. London: Dent 1989.

———. *Letters and Speeches.* Edited by S. C. Lomas. Vol. 2. London: Methuen, 1904.

Crowley, Robert. *Select Works.* Edited by J. M. Cowper. London: EETS, 1872.

Culpepper, Thomas. *A Tract against Usurie.* London, 1621.

Davenant, Charles. *The True Picture of a Modern Whig.* London, 1701.

Davies, David. *The Case of Labourers in Husbandry Stated and Considered.* London, 1795.

Davies, Rev. J. S., ed. *An English Chronicle.* London: Camden Society, Old series, no. 64, London: 1856.

Day, Thomas, *Two Speeches of Thomas Day.* London: SCI, 1780.

De Lolme, John Lewis. *The Constitution of England.* (English translation.) London, 1777.

De Pisan, Christine. *The booke whiche is called the body of Polycye*. London, 1521.
D'Ewes, Simonds. *Autobiography*. Edited by J. O. Halliwell. Vol. 2. London, 1845.
Defoe, Daniel. *Every-Body's Business is No-Body's Business*. London, 1725.
———. *The Freeholder's Plea*. London, 1701.
———. *The Shortest Way With the Dissenters*. 1702. Oxford: Blackwell, 1927/London, 1974. (Edition also contains: *The Poor Man's Plea* (1698), *The Original Power of the Collective Body of the People* (1702), *Giving Alms no Charity* (1704).
———. *Hymn to the Mob*. London, 1715.
Dennis, John. *Vice and Luxury Publick Mischiefs*. London, 1724.
Dickens, A. G., ed. *Tudor Treatises*. Wakefield: Yorkshire Archaelogical Society, Record Series, 125. 1959.
Dickinson, H. T., ed. *Politics and Literature in the Eighteenth Century*. London: Dent; and Totowa, NJ: Rowman and Littlefield, 1974.
Digges, Dudley. *The Unlawfulness of Subjects Taking up Arms*. London, 1662.
Dudley, Edmund. *The Tree of Commonwealth*. 1509–10. Edited by D. M. Brodie. Cambridge: Cambridge University Press, 1948.
Dunning, Richard. *Bread for the Poor*. Exeter, 1698.
———. *A Plain and Easie Method*. London, 1685.
Dury, John. *Israel's Call to March out of Babylon*. London, 1646.
Dyer, George. *The Complaints of the Poor People of England*. London, 1793.
Dyke, Ier(emy). *A Counterpoison against Covetousnes*. London, 1619.
Edward VI. *Literary Remains of King Edward VI*. Edited by J. G. Nichols. London: Roxburghe Club, 1857.
Edwards, Thomas. *Gangraena*. London, 1646. Rpt. Exter: The Rota/Exeter University, 1977.
Eliot, Sir John. *De Jure Maiestatis: or Political Treatise of Government*. 1628–30. Edited and printed from the manuscript by A. B. Grosart. 2 vols. London: private printing, 1882.
———. *The Monarchie of Man*. C. 1631. Edited and printed from the manuscript by A. B. Grosart. 2 vols. London, Chiswick Press, 1879.
Eliot, John. *The Christian Commonwealth*. London, 1659.
Elyot, Sir Thomas. *The Boke named the Governour*. 1531. Edited by H. H. S. Croft. 2 vols. London: Kegan Paul, 1883.
———. *The Image of Governance*. 1541. Edited, introduced, and printed (facsimile) by L. Gottesman, in *Four Political Tracts*. Gainesville, FL: Scholars' Facsimiles and Reprints, 1967.
Erasmus, Desiderius. *The Education of a Christian Prince*. Translation of *Institutio principis Christiani*. 1516. Edited by M. J. Heath. In *Collected Works of Erasmus* 27. Toronto, Buffalo, London: University of Toronto Press, 1986.
———. *The Education of a Christian Prince*. 1516. Edited by L. K. Born. New York: Columbia University Press, 1968.
———. *Enchiridion*. 1504. Translated by William Tyndale. London, 1533.
———. *Enchiridion Militis Christiani: An English Version*. Edited by A. M. O'Donnell. London: EETS, 1981.
———. *Opus Epistolarum Des. Erasmi Roterodami*. Edited by P. S. Allen, H. M. Allen, and H. W. Garrod. 12 vols. Oxford: Clarendon, 1906–58.

Fenner, Dudley. *A Defence Of the godlie Ministers.* London, 1587.
Fennor, William. *The Compters Common-Wealth.* London, 1617.
Ferguson, Robert. *An Appeal from the County to the City.* London, 1679.
Fern, Henry. *The Resolving of Conscience.* Cambridge, 1642.
Field, J., and T. Wilcox. *Admonition to the Parliament.* London, 1572.
Fielding, Henry. *An Inquiry into the Causes of The Late Increase of Robbers.* Printed in *Complete Works.* London, 1889.
―――. *A Proposal for Making an Effectual Provision for the Poor.* London, 1753.
Filmer, Sir Robert. *Patriarcha and Other Writings.* Edited by J. P. Sommerville. Cambridge University Press, 1991.
Firmin, Thomas. *Some Proposals For the imployment of the Poor.* London, 1681.
Firth, C. H., and R. S. Rait. *Acts and Ordinances of the Interregnum 1642–1660.* 3 vols. Abingdon, Oxon.: Professional Books, 1982.
Fletcher, Andrew. *A Discourse of Government With relation to Militias.* Edinburgh, 1698.
Floyd, J. *God and the King.* St. Omer, 1620.
Floyd, Thomas. *The Picture of a perfit Common wealth.* London, 1600.
Forset, Edward. *A Comparative Discourse of the Bodies Natural and Politique.* London, 1606.
Forster, Nathaniel. *An Enquiry into the Causes of the Present High Price of Provisions.* London, 1767.
Fortescue, Sir John. *The Governance of England.* C. 1470. Edited by Charles Plummer. Oxford: Oxford University Press, 1926 (1885).
―――. *De Laudibus Legum Anglie.* 1468–71. Edited, translated, and introduced by S. B. Chrimes. Cambridge: Cambridge University Press, 1949.
Foster, James. *Discourses on all the Principal Branches of Natural Religion and Social Virtue.* Vol. 2. London, 1752.
Fothergill, George. *The Danger of Excesses in the Pursuit of Liberty.* London, 1737.
Gairdner, James, ed. *William Gregory's Chronicle of London.* In *The Historical Collections of a Citizen of London in the Fifteenth Century.* London: Camden Society, new series 17, 1876.
Gardiner, Stephen. *The Letters of Stephen Gardiner.* Edited by J. A. Muller. Cambridge: Cambridge University Press, 1933.
―――. *A Machiavellian Treatise.* Translated and edited by P. S. Donaldson. Cambridge: Cambridge University Press, 1975.
―――. *Obedience in Church and State.* Translated and edited by P. Janelle. Cambridge: Cambridge University Press, 1930.
Gay, John. *The Beggar's Opera.* In *Dramatic Works,* edited by J. Fuller, Vol. 2. Oxford: Clarendon Press, 1983.
Gilpin, W. *Life of Bernard Gilpin.* London, 1752.
Gilson, J. P., ed. "A Defence of the Proscription of the Yorkists in 1459." *EHR* 26 (July 1911): 512–25.
Goffe, William. *How to advance the Trade of the Nation, and Employ the Poor.* 1641. Printed in *Harleian Miscellany.* Vol. 4. London, 1775.
Goodwin, John. *The Grand Imprudence of . . . Fighting Against God.* 1644. In J. Haller, *Tracts on Liberty,* vol. 2.

Goodwin, Thomas, and others. *An Apologeticall Narration*. 1644. In J. Haller, *Tracts on Liberty*, vol. 2.
Gordon, Thomas, and Trenchard, John. See *Cato's Letters*.
Gouge, William. *Of Domesticall Duties*. London, 1622.
Gray, Robert. *A Good Speed to Virginia*. 1609. Facsimile reprint in The English Experience, no. 253. Amsterdam/New York: Da Capo Press, 1970.
Griffiths, J., ed. *The Two Books of Homilies Appointed to be Read in Churches*. Oxford: Oxford University Press, 1859.
Guevara, Antonio de. *The Diall of Princes*. Translated by Thomas North. London, 1557. Printed in The English Experience, no. 50. Amsterdam/New York: Da Capo Press, 1968.
Haines, R. *Provision for the Poor*. London, 1678.
Hale, Sir Matthew. *A Discourse touching Provision for the Poor*. London, 1683.
Halifax, George Savile, Marquis of. *Works*. Edited by M. N. Brown. Oxford: Clarendon, 1989.
Hall, John. *Of Government and Obedience*. London, 1654.
Hall, Joseph. *Salomons Politicks, or Common-wealth*. London, 1609.
Haller, William, ed. *Tracts on Liberty in the Puritan Revolution 1638–1647*. New York: Octagon Book reprint of Columbia University Press, 1934.
———, and Godfrey Davies, eds. *The Leveller Tracts 1647–1653*. New York: Columbia University, 1944.
Hammond, Anthony, and Walter Moyle. *The Honest Elector*. London, 1747.
Hare, John. *St. Edwards Ghost*. London, 1647.
Harrington, James. *The Censure of the Rota*. London, 1660.
———. *Oceana*. London, 1656. Edited by S. B. Liljegren. Heidelberg, 1924.
———. *Political Works*. Edited and introduced by J. G. A. Pocock. Cambridge: Cambridge University Press, 1977.
———. *The Wayes and Meanes*. London, 1660.
Hartley, T. E., ed. *Proceedings in the Parliaments of Elizabeth I*. Vol. 1. 1558–1581. Leicester: Leicester University Press, 1981.
Hartlib, Samuel. *Londons Charitie*. London, 1649.
———. *Londons Charity inlarged*. London, 1650.
Harvey, Gabriel. *Marginalia*. Collected and edited by G. C. Moore Smith. Stratford upon Avon: Shakespeare Head Press, 1913.
Hay, William. *An Essay on Civil Government*. London, 1728.
Hayward, John. *An Answer to . . . a Certaine Conference*. London, 1603.
Hazeland, William. *A View of the Manner in which Trade and Civil Liberty support each other*. London, 1756.
Henry VIII. *The Letters of King Henry VIII*. Edited by M. St. C. Byrne. London, 1936.
Heywood, John. *The Spider and the Flie*. 1556. Edited by J. S. Farmer. London: Early English Drama Society, 1908.
Historical Manuscripts Commission. Third Report. Appendix 2. London, 1872.
Hitchin, Edward. *Free Thoughts on the Late Application*. London, 1772.
Hoadly, Benjamin. *The Measures of Submission to the Civil Magistrate Consider'd*. London, 1706.

Hobbes, Thomas. *Leviathan*. Introduced by K. Minogue. London: Dent, 1973.
Hodgson, William. *The Commonwealth of Reason*. London, 1795.
Holcroft, Thomas. *A Letter to the Right Honourable William Windham*. London, 1795.
Holinshed, Raphael. *Chronicles*. London, 1808.
Holles, Denzil, Lord. *Memoirs*. London, 1699.
Hooker, Richard. *Of the Laws of Ecclesiastical Polity*. Edited by A. S. McGrade. Cambridge/New York: Cambridge University Press, 1989.
Hooper, John. *Early Writings*. Edited by S. Carr. Cambridge: Parker Society, 1843.
———. *Later Writings*. Edited by C. Nevinson. Cambridge: Parker Society, 1852.
Howell, T. B. *A Complete Collection of State Trials*. Vol. 25. London, 1818.
Hubberthorn, Richard. *The Good Old Cause*. London, 1659.
———. *The Real Cause of the Nations Bondage and Slavery*. London, 1659.
Hughes, P. L., and J. F. Larkin, eds. *Tudor Royal Proclamations. I. The Early Tudors (1485–1553)*. New Haven and London: Yale University Press, 1964.
———. *Tudor Royal Proclamations. II. The Later Tudors (1553–1587)*, New Haven and London: Yale University Press, 1969.
———. *Tudor Royal Proclamations. III. The Later Tudors (1588–1603)*, New Haven and London: Yale University Press, 1969.
Hulme, Obadiah. *An Historical Essay on the English Constitution*. London, 1771.
Hume, David. *Dialogues Concerning Natural Religion*. 1779. Edited and introduced by N. K. Smith. Indianapolis/New York: Bobbs-Merrill, 1947.
———. *Hume: Theory of Politics*. Edited by F. Watkins. Edinburgh: Nelson, 1951.
Hume-Campbell, H., 3rd earl of Marchmont. *A Serious Exhortation to the Electors*. London, 1740.
Humphrey, Lawrence. *The Nobles or of Nobility*. London, 1563.
Hunton, Philip. *A Treatise of Monarchy*. London, 1689 (first edition, 1643).
Jackson, John. *The Grounds of Civil and Ecclesiastical Government*. London, 1718.
James I. *King James His opinion and Iudgement*. London, 1647 (1609 speech).
Jebb, John. *An Address to the Freeholders of Middlesex*. 1779. Printed in *The Works . . . of John Jebb*, edited by John Disney. 3 vols. London, 1787.
Jenyns, Soame. *Disquisitions on Several Subjects*. London, 1822. (Rpt. of original 1782 ed.)
———. *Thoughts on the Causes and Consequences of the Present High Price of Provisions*. London, 1767.
Jephson, Alexander. *A Friendly and Compassionate Address*. London, 1760.
Jewel, John. *A Defence of the Apologie of the Churche of Englande*. London, 1570.
Johnson, Samuel. *The False Alarm*. London, 1770.
Jones, William. *An Inquiry into the Legal Mode of Supressing Riots*. Together with *A Speech on the Nomination of Candidates*. London, 1782.
Jubbes, John. *Several Proposals for Peace and Freedom*, 1649. Printed in D. M. Wolfe, ed., *Leveller Manifestoes*.
Knox, John. *The Works of John Knox*. Edited by David Laing. Vol. 3. Edinburgh, 1864. Vol. 4. Edinburgh, 1855.
Lamond, E., ed. *A Discourse of the Common Weal of this Realm of England*. 1549. (Although the title-work is no longer attributed to John Hales, this edition prints several papers which are his.)

Langland, William. *Piers the Ploughman*. 1377–1379. Translated and edited by J. F. Goodridge. London: Pelican, 1959.

Larkin, J. F. *Stuart Royal Proclamations. II. Royal Proclamations of King Charles I, 1625–1644*. Oxford: Clarendon, 1983.

———, and P. L. Hughes. *Stuart Royal Proclamations. I. Royal Proclamations of King James I. 1603–1625*. Oxford: Clarendon, 1973.

Latimer, Hugh. *Sermons*. (1528–1552). Edited by G. E. Corrie. Cambridge: Parker Society, 1844.

———. *Sermons and Remains*. (Sermons 1552–1555 and Letters.) Edited by G. E. Corrie. Cambridge: Parker Society, 1845.

———. *Sermons*. Edited by Canon Beeching. London: Everyman, 1926.

Law, William. *A Serious Call to a Devout and Holy Life*. Edited and introduced by N. Sykes. London: Dent; and New York: Dutton, 1967. Rpt.

Lawson, Thomas. *An Appeal to the Parliament, concerning The Poor*. London, 1660.

Lee, Joseph. *Considerations Concerning Common Fields and Inclosures*. London, 1654.

———. *A Vindication of a Regulated Inclosure*. London, 1656.

———. *A Vindication of the Considerations Concerning Common-Fields and Inclosures*. London, 1656.

Letters and Papers, Foreign and Domestic, of the Reign of Henry VIII. Edited by J. S. Brewer, J. Gairdner, and R. H. Brodie. London, 1862–1932.

Lever, Thomas. *Sermons*. 1550. Edited by E. Arber. London: English Reprints, 1870.

Lilburne, John. Ten pamphlets printed in W. Haller, *Tracts on Liberty*. New York: Octagon, 1934.

Lloyd, C., ed. *Formularies of Faith put forth by Authority during the Reign of Henry VIII*. Oxford: Clarendon, 1825.

Locke, John. *Letter Concerning Toleration*. First, 1689.

———. *Two Treatises of Civil Government*. 1690. Introduced by W. S. Carpenter. London and New York: Dent, Dutton, 1955. (Rpt. of 1924 ed.).

Lowman, Moses. *A Dissertation on the Civil Government of the Hebrews*. London, 1740.

Ludlow, Edmund. *The Memoirs of Edmund Ludlow*. 1625–1672. Edited by C. H. Firth. Oxford: Clarendon, 1894.

Lupton, Thomas. *Siuqila. Too good, to be true*. London, 1580.

Macaulay, Catharine. *Observations on a Pamphlet, Entitled, Thoughts on the Cause of the Present Discontents*. London, 1770.

Mackintosh, James. *Vindiciae Gallicae*. London, 1791.

Mainwaring, Roger. *Religion and Alegiance*. London, 1627.

Mandeville, Bernard. *The Fable of the Bees*. 1705, 1714, 1729. Introduced by F. B. Kaye. 2 vols. Oxford: Clarendon, 1924. (This edition also contains *An Essay on Charity, and Charity-Schools*.)

Marvell, Andrew. *An Account of the Growth of Popery and Arbitrary Government in England*. Amsterdam, 1677.

Massie, J. *A Plan for the Establishment of Charity Houses*. London, 1758.

Mauduit, Israel. *The Case of the Dissenting Ministers*. London, 1772.

Merbury, Charles. *A Briefe Discourse of Royall Monarchie, as of the best Common Weale*. London, 1581.

Milton, John. *The Readie & Easie Way to Establish a Free Commonwealth*. London, 1659/60.

———. *The Tenure of Kings and Magistrates*. 1649/50. Printed in *Complete Prose Works*, edited by M. Y. Hughes. Vol. 3. 1648–1649. New Haven and London: Yale University Press, 1962.

Misselden, Edward. *The Circle of Commerce*. London, 1623.

Molesworth, Robert. *An Account of Denmark*. London, 1694.

———. *The Principles of a Real Whig*. Written in 1705, first published in 1721, as a preface to the second edition of his translation of Francis Hotman's *Franco-Gallia* (1574). Reprinted in its own right at the request of the London Association, London, 1775.

Moore, Francis. *Considerations on the Exorbitant Price of Provisions*. London, 1773.

Moore, John. *The Crying Sin of England, Of not Caring for the Poor*. London, 1653.

———. *A Scripture-Word Against Inclosure*. London, 1656.

More, Sir Thomas. *The supplicacion of soules . . . Agaynst the supplicacion of beggars*. 1529. Printed in *The Workes of Sir Thomas More Knyght*. London, 1557.

———. *Utopia*. Translated by Raphe Robinson. 1551. Edited by J. O'Hagan. London and New York: Dent, Dutton; Everyman, 1941.

Morison, Sir Richard. *An Exhortation to styrre all Englyshe men to the defence of theyr countreye*. London, 1539.

———. *An Invective Ayenste the great and detestable vice, treason*. London, 1539.

———. *A Lamentation in which is shewed what Ruyne and destruction cometh of seditious rebellyon*. London, 1536.

———. *A Remedy for Sedition*. London, 1536.

Mortimer, Thomas. *The Elements of Commerce, Politics and Finances*. London, 1772.

Moyle, Walter. *An Essay upon the Constitution of the Roman Government*. In *The Works of Walter Moyle Esq*. Vol. 1. London, 1726.

Nashe, Thomas. *The Unfortunate Traveller*. London, 1594. Printed in *Shorter Elizabethan and Jacobean Novels*. Vol. 1. Introduction by G. Saintsbury. London: Dent, Dutton; New York: Everyman, 1938.

Nayler, James. *Behold you Rulers*. London, 1658.

———. *The Condition and Portion of the People of England*. London, 1654.

———. *Deceit Brought to Day-Light*. London, 1656.

———. *A Discovery of the First Wisdom*. London, 1653.

Nedham, Marchmont. *The Case of the Commonwealth of England, Stated*. London, 1650. Edited by P. A. Knachel. Charlottesville: Folger Shakespeare Library/University of Virginia Press, 1979.

———. *Interest will not Lie*. London, 1659.

Neville, Henry. *Newes from the New Exchange, or the Commonwealth of Ladies*. London, 1650.

———. *Plato Redivivus: or, a Dialogue concerning Government*. London, 1681. Printed in *Two English Republican Tracts*. Edited by C. Robbins. Cambridge: Cambridge University Press, 1969.

Nichols, John. *The Progresses and Public Processions of Queen Elizabeth*. Vol. 1. London, 1823.

Nichols, J. G., ed. *The Boke of Noblesse*. 1475. London, 1860.

Nicolas, Sir Harris. *Proceedings and Ordinances of the Privy Council of England.* Vol. 6. London, 1837.

North, Regis. *A Discourse on the English Constitution.* London, 1795.

Norton, Thomas, and T. Sackville. *Gorboduc.* 1561–62. Edited by I. B. Cauthen. London: E. Arnold, 1970.

Nowell, Alexander. *A Catechisme.* Translated by Thomas Norton, 1570. Edited by G. E. Corrie. Cambridge: Parker Society, 1853.

Ogilvie, William. *An Essay on the Right of Property in Land.* London, 1781.

Occleve, Thomas. *The Government of Princes.* Edited by T. Wright. London, 1860.

Oswald, John. *Review of the Constitution of Great-Britain.* London, 1790.

Overton, Richard. Six pamphlets printed in William Haller, *Tracts on Liberty in the Puritan Revolution 1638–1647.* New York: Octagon, 1934.

Owen, John. *Truth and Innocence Vindicated.* London, 1669.

Paine, Thomas. *Common Sense.* London, 1776. Edited and introduced by I. Kramnick. London: Pelican, 1976.

Parker, Henry. *Jus Populi.* London, 1644.

———. *Some Few Observations.* London, 1642.

———. *Observations upon some of his Majesties late Answers.* London, 1642.

Parker, Samuel. *A Discourse of Ecclesiastical Polity.* London, 1670.

Parsons, Robert (as R. Doleman). *A Conference About the Next Succession to the Crowne of Ingland.* 1594. Rpt. Menston, Yorks.: Scolar Press, 1972.

———. *Memorial for the Reformation of England.* 1596. London, 1690.

Paxton, Peter. *Civil Polity. A Treatise Concerning the Nature of Government.* London, 1703.

Peel, Albert, ed. *The Notebook of John Penry 1593.* London: Camden Society, 1944.

Perkins, William. *A Treatise of the Vocations or Callings of Men.* N.p., c. 1600. Printed in *The Works of William Perkins.* Edited by I. Breward. Abingdon: Sutton Courtenay Press, 1970.

Pett, Peter. *A Discourse Concerning Liberty of Conscience.* London, 1661.

Petty, Sir William. *The Advice of W. P. to Mr. Samuel Hartlib.* London, 1648. Rpt. in *Harleian Miscellany,* Vol. 6. London, 1810.

Plattes, Gabriel. *A Description of the Famous Kingdome of Macaria.* London, 1641. (Plattes's claims to authorship are now thought more likely than those of Hartlib.)

———. *A Discovery of Infinite Treasure.* London, 1649.

Philadept, A. *An Essay concerning Adepts.* London, 1694.

Pocock, N. *Troubles Connected with the Prayer Book of 1549.* London: Camden Society, 1884.

Ponet, John. *A Shorte Treatise of politike power.* London, 1556.

Pope, Alexander. *The Dunciad.* In *Poems of Alexander Pope,* vol. 5, edited by J. Sutherland. London and New Haven: Yale University Press, 1965.

———. *Epistle to Bathurst.* London, 1733. In *Poems of Alexander Pope,* vol. 3, edited by F. W. Bateson, London and New Haven: Yale University Press, 1961.

———. *An Essay on Man.* 1733–34. In *Poems of Alexander Pope,* vol. 3, edited by M. Mack. London and New Haven: Yale University Press, 1964.

Postlethwayt, Malachy. *Britain's Commercial Interest Explained and Improved.* 2 vols. London, 1757.
Powell, Roger. *Depopulation Arraigned.* London, 1636.
Pownall, Thomas. *Principles of Polity.* London, 1752.
Price, John. *Walwins Wiles.* London, 1649.
Price, Richard. *A Discourse on the Love of Our Country.* London, 1789.
———. *Observations on the Importance of the American Revolution.* London, 1785.
———. *Observations on the Nature of Civil Liberty.* London, 1776.
Priestley, Joseph. *An Essay on the First Principles of Government.* London, 1768.
Ralegh, Sir Walter. *Works of Sir Walter Ralegh.* Oxford, 1829. (Vol. 8, *Miscellaneous Works,* contains "Maxims of State.")
Ralph, James. *Use and Abuse of Parliaments.* 2 vols. London, 1744.
Richardson, Samuel. *The Necessity of Toleration in Matters of Religion.* London, 1647. Printed in E. B. Underhill. *Tracts.* London: Hanserd Knollys Society, 1846.
———. *The Cause of the Poor Pleaded.* London, 1653.
Robinson, Henry. *A Short Discourse . . . in setting up the Government of a Common-wealth.* London, 1649.
———. *Certaine Proposals in order to a new Modelling of the Lawes.* London, 1653.
———. *Certain Proposals In order to the Peoples Freedom.* London, 1652.
Rotuli Parliamentorum. London, 1767–77.
Sadler, J. *A Word in season.* London, 1646.
Salter, F. R. ed. *Some Early Tracts on Poor Relief.* London: Methuen, 1926.
Sanderson, Robert. *XXXIV Sermons.* London, 1664.
Sandys, Edwin. *Sermons.* London, 1585. Printed and edited by J. Ayre. Cambridge: Parker Society, 1841.
Sandys, Edwin. *A Relation of the State of Religion.* London, 1605.
Savile, Sir George. *The Life and Letters of Sir George Savile, Bart.* Edited by H. C. Foxcroft. Vol. 2. London, 1898.
Sharp, Andrew, ed. *Political Ideas of the English Civil Wars 1641–1649.* London and New York: Longman, 1983.
Sidney, Algernon. *Discourses Concerning Government.* Edited by T. G. West. Indianapolis: Liberty Classics, 1990.
Sidney, Sir Philip. *Arcadia (The New Arcadia).* Edited by V. Skretkowicz. Oxford: Oxford University Press, 1987.
Smith, Sir Thomas. *De Republica Anglorum.* London, 1583. Edited by M. Dewar. Cambridge: Cambridge University Press, 1982.
———. *A Discourse of the Commonweal of This Realm of England.* Attributed to Sir Thomas Smith. Edited by M. Dewar. Charlottesville: University of Virginia Press, 1969.
Societies for Promoting a Reformation of Manners, Accounts. London, 1722.
Sparke, Michael. *Greevous Grones for the Poore.* London, 1621.
Spence, Thomas. *The Rights of Man.* London, 1793.
———. *One Pennyworth of Pig's Meat.* London, 1793.
———. *Political and Religious Tracts 1795–1803* (BL 900.h.24) contains several items by Spence, including *The Constitution of Spensonia . . . situated between Utopia and Oceana.*

Spenser, Edmund. *The Faerie Queene.* Edited by A. C. Hamilton. London and New York: Longmans, 1977.
Sprigge, W. *A Modest Plea for an Equal Commonwealth Against Monarchy.* London, 1659.
Squire, Samuel. *Foundation of the English Constitution.* London, 1763.
Starkey, Thomas. *A Dialogue Between Reginald Pole and Thomas Lupset.* C. 1535. Edited by K. M. Burton. London: Chatto and Windus, 1948.
———. *An Exhortation to the people, instructynge theym to Unitie and Obedience.* 1536.
Statutes at Large. London. Vol. 2, 1735 & 1763; Vol. 3, 1770.
Stock, Richard. *Sermon.* In *Historical Manuscripts Commission. Salusbury.* Part II (1910), p. 672.
Stubbs, John. *The Discovery of a Gaping Gulf.* London, 1579. Edited by L. E. Berry. Charlottesville: University of Virginia Press, 1968.
Sturgion, John. *A Plea for Toleration of Opinions and Persuasions in Matters of Religion.* London, 1661.
Swift, Jonathan. *The People of England's Grievances.* N.p., London, c. 1693.
———. *A Project for the Advancement of Religion and the Reformation of Manners.* London, 1709.
———. *Gulliver's Travels.* London, 1726. Edited by H. Davis. Oxford: Blackwell, 1965. Rpt. of 1959 ed.
———. *A Proposal for Giving Badges to the Beggars.* London, 1737. In *Directions to Servants and Miscellaneous Pieces 1733–1742*, edited by H. Davis. Oxford: Blackwell, 1959.
Sybthorpe, Robert. *Apostolike Obedience.* London, 1627.
Tawney, R. H., and E. Power, eds. *Tudor Economic Documents.* 3 vols. London: Longmans, Green, 1953.
Thirsk, Joan, and J. P. Cooper, eds. *Seventeenth-Century Economic Documents.* Oxford: Clarendon, 1972.
Tindal/Tyndall, Matthew. *An Essay Concerning Obedience to the Supreme Powers.* London, 1694.
———. *An Essay Concerning the Power of the Magistrate, and the Rights of Mankind, in Matters of Religion.* London, 1697.
Toland, John. *The Art of Governing by Parties.* C. 1701. Rpt. 1757.
———. *Christianity not Mysterious.* London, 1696. Facsimile rpt. New York and London: Garland, 1978.
———. *The Danger of Mercenary Parliaments.* London, 1722.
———. *Some Reasons for Annual Parliaments.* London, 1693.
———. *The State-Anatomy of Great Britain.* London, 1717.
Towers, Joseph. *Observations on Public Liberty, Patriotism, Ministerial Despotism, and National Grievances.* London, 1769.
Townshend, Heywood. *Historical Collections.* London, 1680.
Tucker, Josiah. *The Manifold Causes of the Increase of the Poor.* London, 1760.
———. *Four Tracts . . . on Political and Commercial Subjects.* London, 1774.
Turner, William. *The Huntyng of the Romyshe Wolfe.* C. 1555.
Tyndale, William. *The Works of William Tyndale and John Frith.* Edited by T. Russell. London, 1831.

Tyrrell, James. *Bibliotheca Politica*. London, 1694.

Tytler, P. F., ed. *England under the Reigns of Edward VI and Mary*. 2 vols. London, 1839.

Underhill, E. B., ed. *Tracts on Liberty of Conscience and Persecution 1614–1661*. London: Hanserd Knollys Society, 1846.

Vanderlint. Jacob. *Money answers All Things*. London, 1734.

Veron, John. Introduction to translation of Henry Bullinger's *A most necessary & frutefull Dialogue*. Worcester, 1551.

Vives, Juan Luis. *De Subventione Pauperum*. Translation in F. R. Salter, ed., *Some Early Tracts on Poor Relief*. London: Methuen, 1926.

Walwyn, William. Nine tracts printed in William Haller, *Tracts on Liberty in the Puritan Revolution, 1638–1647*. New York: Octagon, 1934.

Warburton, William. *The Alliance between Church and State*. London, 1736.

Warwick, Sir Philip. *A Discourse of Government*. London, 1694 (written in 1678).

Watts, Isaac. *Essay on Charity Schools*. London, 1728.

Wentworth, Peter. *A Discourse . . . of the true and lawfull successor to Her Maiestie*. London, 1598.

———. *A Pithie Exhortation to her Maiestie for Establishing her Succession to the Crown*. (Printed with the foregoing, but probably written c. 1587; see J. E. Neale, *EHR* 39 (nos. 153 and 154 [1924].)

Whately, William. *The Poore Mans Advocate*. London, 1637.

White, Thomas. *The Grounds of Obedience and Government*. London, 1655.

Whitgift, John. *An answere to a certen Libel*. London, 1572.

Wilkinson, Robert. *Sermon Preached at North-Hampton*. London, 1607.

Willan, Leonard. *The Exact Politician, or Compleat Statesman*. London, 1670.

Williams, David. *Letters on Political Liberty*. London, 1782.

———. *Lectures on Political Principles*. London, 1789.

———. *Unanimity in all the parts of the British Commonwealth*. London, 1778.

Williams, E. N. *The Eighteenth-Century Constitution 1688–1815*. Cambridge: Cambridge University Press, 1960.

Winstanley, Gerrard. Fourteen works printed in *The Works of Gerrard Winstanley*, edited by G. H. Sabine. Ithaca: Cornell University Press, 1941.

Wolfe, D. M., ed. *Leveller Manifestoes of the Puritan Revolution*. With introduction and commentaries. London: Nelson, 1944; New York: F. Cass, 1967.

Wollaston, William. *The Religion of Nature delineated*. London, 1726.

Wollstonecraft, Mary. *A Vindication of the Rights of Men*. London, 1790.

Woodhouse, A. S. P., ed. and intro. *Puritanism and Liberty*, being the Army Debates (1647–49). London: Dent, 1986 (with new preface by Ivan Roots).

Woods, Richard. *Norfolkes Furies*. London, 1615.

Woodward, Richard. *An Address to the Publick*. Dublin, 1775.

Wren, Matthew. *Monarchie Asserted*. Oxford, 1659.

Wyville, Christopher. *A Defence of Dr. Price, and the Reformers of England*. London, 1792.

Young, Arthur. *The Example of France, a Warning to Britain*. London, 1793.

SECONDARY SOURCES

Inevitably, this list is selective, including only those works that are actually cited or of direct relevance.

Allen, J. W. *English Political Thought 1603–1644*. London: Methuen, 1938.

———. *A History of Political Thought in the Sixteenth Century*. London: Methuen; New York: Barnes and Noble, 1951.

Alsop, J. D. "Latimer, the 'Commonwealth of Kent' and the 1549 Rebellions." *Historical Journal* 28 (1985): 379–82.

Appleby, Joyce O. *Economic Thought and Ideology in Seventeenth-Century England*. Princeton: Princeton University Press, 1978.

Ashcraft, Richard. "Revolutionary Politics and Locke's *Two Treatises of Government*." *Political Theory* 8 (1980): 429–86.

———. *Revolutionary Politics and Locke's Two Treatises of Government*. Princeton: Princeton University Press, 1986.

———, and M. M. Goldsmith. "Locke, Revolution Principles, and the Formation of Whig Ideology." *Historical Journal* 26 (1983): 773–800.

Ashley, Maurice. *John Wildman*. London, 1947.

Ashraf, P. M. *The Life and Times of Thomas Spence*. Newcastle upon Tyne: Frank Graham, 1983.

Ashton, Robert. *Reformation and Revolution 1558–1660*. London: Paladin, 1985.

Aylmer, G. E. "Gentlemen Levellers?" *PP* 49 (1970): 120–25.

———, ed. *The Interregnum: The Quest for Settlement 1646–1660*. London: Macmillan, 1972.

———. Introduction to "Winstanley, *England's Spirit Unfoulded*." *PP* 40 (1968): 4–8.

———. *Rebellion or Revolution? England 1640–1660*. Oxford: Oxford University Press, 1986.

———. "Review Article: Did the Ranters Exist?" *PP* 117 (1987): 208–19.

Bailyn, Bernard. *The Ideological Origins of the American Revolution*. Cambridge: Harvard University Press, 1967/77.

Bahlman, Dudley W. R. *The Moral Revolution of 1688*. New Haven: Yale University Press, 1957.

Baker, Keith M. *Inventing the French Revolution*. Cambridge: Cambridge University Press, 1990.

Barker, W. A. *Religion and Politics 1559–1642*. London: Historical Association, 1957.

Bateson, M. "The Pilgrimage of Grace. Aske's Narrative." *EHR* 5 (1890): 330–45, 550–73.

Baumer, F. le V. *The Tudor Theory of Kingship*. New Haven: Yale University Press, 1940.

Baugh, Daniel A. "Poverty, Protestantism, and Political Economy: English Attitudes toward the Poor, 1660–1800." In *England's Rise to Greatness 1660–1763*, edited by Stephen B. Baxter. Berkeley and Los Angeles: University of California Press, 1983.

Beckingsale, B. W. *Thomas Cromwell*. London: Macmillan, 1978.

Beer, B. L., and R. J. Nash, "Hugh Latimer and the Lusty Knave of Kent: The Commonwealth Movement of 1549." *Bulletin of the Institute of Historical Research* 52 (1979): 175–78.

Beier, A. L. *Masterless Men.* London and New York: Methuen, 1985.

Bindoff, S. T., et al. *Elizabethan Government and Society.* London: Athlone Press, 1961.

Black, Eugene C. *The Association: British Extraparliamentary Organization 1769–1793.* Cambridge: Harvard University Press, 1963.

Bonwick, Colin. *English Radicals and the American Revolution.* Chapel Hill: University of North Carolina Press, 1977.

Bowden, Peter. "Agricultural Prices, Farm Profits, and Rents." In *Agrarian History,* vol. 4, edited by J. Thirsk, 592–695. Cambridge: Cambridge University Press, 1967.

Bradley, James E. "Whigs and Nonconformists: 'Slumbering Radicalism' in English Politics." *Eighteenth-Century Studies* 9 (1975–76): 1–27.

Bradshaw, Brendan. "The Tudor Commonwealth: Reform and Revision." *Historical Journal* 22 (1979): 455–76.

Brewer, John. *Party Ideology and Popular Politics at the Accession of George III.* Cambridge: Cambridge University Press, 1976.

Brigden, Susan. "Popular Disturbance and the Fall of Thomas Cromwell and the Reformers, 1539–1540." *Historical Journal* 24 (1981): 257–78.

Brooke, J. *The History of Parliament: The House of Commons 1754–1790: Introductory Survey.* Oxford: Oxford University Press, 1968.

Burns, J. H., ed. *The Cambridge History of Political Thought 1450–1700.* Cambridge: Cambridge University Press, 1991.

Burrage, C. *The Early English Dissenters in the Light of Recent Research. 1530–1641.* 2 vols. Cambridge: Cambridge University Press, 1912.

Bush, M. L. *The Government Policy of Protector Somerset.* London and Montreal: E. Arnold, 1976.

Cannon, John. *Parliamentary Reform 1640–1832.* Cambridge: Cambridge University Press, 1973.

―――, ed. *The Whig Ascendancy.* London: E. Arnold, 1981.

Capp, B. S. *The Fifth Monarchy Men.* London: Faber and Faber, 1972.

―――. *Cromwell's Navy.* Oxford: Clarendon, 1989.

Caspari, F. *Humanism and the Social Order in Tudor England.* Chicago: University of Chicago Press, 1954.

Chase, Malcolm. *"The People's Farm": English Radical Agrarianism 1775–1840.* Oxford: Clarendon, 1988.

Chrimes, S. B. *English Constitutional Ideas in the Fifteenth Century.* Cambridge: Cambridge University Press, 1936.

Christie, Ian R. *Wilkes, Wyvill and Reform.* London and New York: Macmillan, 1962.

―――. *Crisis of Empire: Great Britain and the American Colonies, 1754–1783.* London: E. Arnold, 1966.

―――. *Myth and Reality in Late-Eighteenth Century British Politics.* Berkeley and Los Angeles: University of California Press, 1970.

―――. *Wars and Revolutions. Britain 1760–1815.* London: E. Arnold, 1982.

―――. *Stress and Stability in Late Eighteenth-Century Britain.* Oxford: Clarendon, 1986.

Claeys, Gregory. *Thomas Paine.* Boston and London: Unwin Hyman, 1989.

Clark, Jonathan C. D. *English Society 1688–1832*. Cambridge: Cambridge University Press, 1985.

———. *The Language of Liberty 1660–1832*. Cambridge: Cambridge University Press, 1994.

———. "The Decline of Party, 1740–1760." *EHR* 93 (1978): 499–527.

Clay, C. G. A. *Economic Expansion and Social Change: England 1500–1700*. 2 vols. Cambridge: Cambridge University Press, 1984..

Coats, A. W. "Changing Attitudes to Labour in the Mid-Eighteenth Century." *Econ. HR*, 2nd ser., 11 (1958–59): 35–51.

———. "Economic Thought and Poor Law Policy in the Eighteenth Century." *Econ. HR*, 2nd ser., 13 (1960): 39–51.

Coleman, Christopher, and David Starkey. *Revolution Reassessed*. Oxford: Clarendon, 1986.

Coleman, D. C. "Labour in the English Economy of the Seventeenth Century." *Econ. HR*, 2nd ser., 8 (1955): 280–95.

Cohn, Norman. *The Pursuit of the Millenium*. London: Secker and Warburg, 1957.

Colley, Linda. "Eighteenth-Century English Radicalism before Wilkes." *TRHS*, 5th ser., 31 (1981): 1–19.

Collinson, Patrick. "De Republica Anglorum: Or, History with the Politics Put Back." In *Elizabethan Essays*. London: Hambledon, 1994.

———. "Ecclesiastical Vitriol: Religious Satire in the 1590s and the Invention of Puritanism." In *The Reign of Elizabeth I* edited by J. Guy, 150–70. Cambridge: Cambridge University Press, 1995.

———. *The Elizabethan Exclusion Crisis and the Elizabethan Polity* (Raleigh Lecture). *Proceedings of the British Academy* 84 (1993): 51–92.

———. *The Elizabethan Puritan Movement*. London: Cape, 1967.

———. "The Monarchical Republic of Queen Elizabeth!" *Bulletin of the John Rylands Library* 69 (1986–87): 394–424.

———. *The Religion of Protestants*. Oxford: Clarendon, 1982.

Cone, Carl B. *The English Jacobins*. New York: Charles Scribner's Sons, 1968.

Cooper, J. P. "Social and Economic Policies under the Commonwealth." In *The Interregnum*, edited by G. E. Aylmer, 121–42. London: Macmillan, 1972.

Corfield, P. J. "Class by Name and Number in Eighteenth-Century Britain." *History* 72 (1987): 38–61.

Cruickshanks, Eveline. "Religion and Royal Succession—The Rage of Party." In *Britain in the First Age of Party*, edited by C. Jones, 19–43. London and Ronceverte: Hambledon Press, 1987.

Davies, C. S. L. "Slavery and Protector Somerset; the Act of 1547." *Econ. HR*, 2nd ser., 19 (1966): 533–49.

Davis, C. *Utopia and the Ideal Society*. Cambridge: Cambridge University Press, 1981.

———. *Fear, Myth and History*. Cambridge: Cambridge University Press, 1986.

———. "Fear, Myth and Furore: Reappraising the Ranters." *PP* 129 (1990): 79–103.

De Krey, Gary S. *A Fractured Society*. Oxford: Clarendon, 1985.

Derry, J. W. *English Politics and the American Revolution*. London, 1976.

Dewar, Mary. *Sir Thomas Smith*. London, 1964.

———. "The Memorandum 'For the Understanding of the Exchange': Its Authorship and Dating." *Econ. HR*, 2nd ser., 17 (1965): 476–87.

———. "The Authorship of the 'Discourse of the Commonweal.' " *Econ. HR*, 2nd ser., 19 (1966): 388–400.

Dickens, A. G. *The English Reformation.* 2nd ed. London: Batsford, 1989.

———, and Whitney R. D. Jones. *Erasmus the Reformer.* London: Methuen, 1994.

Dickinson, H. T. *Bolingbroke.* London: Constable, 1970.

———. "The Eighteenth-Century Debate on the Sovereignty of Parliament." *TRHS* 5th series, 26 (1976): 189–210.

———. *Liberty and Property. Political Ideology in Eighteenth-Century Britain.* London: Weidenfeld and Nicolson, 1977.

———. "Popular Politics in the Age of Walpole." In *Britain in the Age of Walpole*, edited by J. Black. London, 1984.

Dow, F. D. *Radicalism in the English Revolution 1640–1660.* Oxford: Blackwell/Historical Association, 1985.

Duverger, Maurice. *Les Constitutions de la France.* Paris: Presses Universitaires de France, 1944.

Earle, Peter. *Monmouth's Rebels.* London: Weidenfeld and Nicolson, 1977.

Eccleshall, Robert. *Order and Reason in Politics.* Oxford: Oxford University Press (University of Hull), 1978.

Elton, Sir Geoffrey. "An Early Tudor Poor Law." *Econ. HR*, 2nd ser., 6 (1953): 55–67.

———. *England under the Tudors.* London: Methuen, 1957.

———. "A New Age of Reform?" *Historical Journal* 30 (1987): 709–16.

———. *The Parliament of England 1559–1581.* Cambridge: Cambridge University Press, 1986.

———. *Reform and Renewal: Thomas Cromwell and the Common Weal.* Cambridge: Cambridge University Press, 1973.

———. "Reform and the Commonwealth's Men of Edward VI's Reign." In *The English Commonwealth 1547–1640*, edited by P. Clark, et al. Leicester: Leicester University Press, 1979.

———. *The Tudor Constitution.* Cambridge: Cambridge University Press, 1960.

———. "Tudor Government." *Historical Journal* 31 (1988): 425–35.

———. *The Tudor Revolution in Government.* Cambridge: Cambridge University Press, 1953.

Entreves, A. P. d'. *The Medieval Contribution to Political Thought.* Oxford: Oxford University Press, 1939.

Everitt, Alan. "Social Mobility in Early Modern England." *PP* 33 (1966): 56–73.

———. "Farm Labourers." In *Agrarian History*, vol. 4, edited by Joan Thirsk, 396–465. Cambridge: Cambridge University Press, 1967.

Fenlon, D. B. "England and Europe: Utopia and its Aftermath." *TRHS*, 5th ser., 25 (1975): 113–35.

Ferguson, Arthur B. *The Articulate Citizen and the English Renaissance.* Durham, NC: Duke University Press, 1965.

———. "Renaissance Realism in the 'Commonwealth' Literature of Early Tudor England." *Journal of the History of Ideas* 16 (1955): 287–305.

———. "The Tudor Commonweal and the Sense of Change." *Journal of British Studies* 3 (1963): 11–35.
Fisher, F. J., ed. *Essays in the Economic and Social History of Tudor and Stuart England*. Cambridge: Cambridge University Press, 1961.
———. "Influenza and Inflation in Tudor England." *Econ. HR*, 2nd ser., 18 (1965): 120–29.
———. "The Sixteenth and Seventeenth Centuries: The Dark Ages in English Economic History?" *Economica*, n.s., 24 (1957): 1–18.
Frank, Joseph. *The Levellers*. Cambridge: Harvard University Press, 1955. Rpt. New York: Russell and Russell, 1969.
Franklin, J. H. *John Locke and the Theory of Sovereignty*. Cambridge: Cambridge University Press, 1978.
Gay, Edwin F. "The Midlands Revolt and the Inquisitions of Depopulation of 1607." *TRHS*, n.s., 18 (1904): 195–244.
Gentles, Ian. *The New Model Army*. Oxford: Blackwell; and Cambridge, Mass. 1992.
Goldsmith, M. M., and Ivan Roots. Introduction to Rota edition of Edwards's *Gangraena*. Exeter: The Rota/Exeter University, 1977.
Gooch, G. P. *English Democratic Ideas in the Seventeenth Century*. 2nd ed., Edited by H. J. Laski. Cambridge: Cambridge University Press, 1927.
———. *Political Thought from Bacon to Halifax*. Oxford: Oxford University Press, 1933.
Goodwin, Albert, ed. *The American and French Revolutions, 1763–1793*. New Cambridge Modern History, vol. 8. Cambridge: Cambridge University Press, 1965.
Goodwin, Albert. *The Friends of Liberty: The English Democratic Movement in the Age of the French Revolution*. London: Hutchinson, 1979.
———. *The French Revolution*. London: Arrow/Hutchinson, 1959.
Gough, J. W. *Fundamental Law in English Constitutional History*. Oxford: Clarendon, 1971.
———. "James Tyrrell." *Historical Journal* 19 (1976): 581–610.
Graves, M. A. R. "Thomas Norton the Parliament Man: An Elizabethan M.P., 1559–1581." *Historical Journal* 23 (1980): 17–35.
Greaves, Richard L. *Enemies under his Feet*. Stanford, Calif.: Stanford University Press, 1990.
Gunn, J. A. W. "The *Civil Polity* of Peter Paxton." *PP* 40 (1968): 42–57.
———. *Politics and the Public Interest in the Seventeenth Century*. Toronto: University of Toronto Press; London: Routledge and Kegan Paul, 1969.
———. *Factions No More*. (Introduction to edited extracts.) London: Cass, 1972.
———. *Beyond Liberty and Property*. Kingston and Montreal: McGill/Queen's University Press, 1983.
———. *Queen of the world: Opinion in the Public Life of France from the Renaissance to the Revolution*. Oxford: Voltaire Foundation, 1995.
Guttridge, G. H. *English Whiggism and the American Revolution*. Berkeley and Los Angeles: University of California Press, 1963 (rpt. of 1942 ed.)
Guy, J. A. *The Cardinal's Court*. Brighton: Harvester Press, 1977.
———. *The Public Career of Sir Thomas More*. Brighton: Harvester Press, 1980.

———, ed. *The Reign of Elizabeth I: Court and Culture in the Last Decade.* Cambridge: Cambridge University Press, 1995.

———. "The Tudor Commonwealth: Revising Thomas Cromwell." *Historical Journal* 23 (1980): 681–87.

———. "Wolsey, the Council and the Council Courts." *EHR* 91 (1976).

Gwyn, Peter. *The Rise and Fall of Thomas Wolsey.* London: Barrie and Jenkins, 1990.

Gwyn, W. B. *The Meaning of the Separation of Powers.* New Orleans: Tulane University Press, 1965.

Habermas, Jürgen. *The Structural Transformation of the Public Sphere.* Translated by T. Burger. Cambridge: MIT Press, 1989.

Haigh, Christopher, ed. *The Reign of Elizabeth I.* London: Macmillan, 1984.

Hammond, J. L., and Barbara Hammond. *The Village Labourer.* 1911. 2 vols. London: Guild Books/Longmans Green, 1948.

Hanson, Donald. *From Kingdom to Commonwealth.* Cambridge: Harvard University Press, 1970.

Harris, R. W. *Political Ideas 1760–1802.* London: Gollancz, 1963.

Harte, N. B. "State Control of Dress and Social Change in Pre-Industrial England." *Trade, Government and Economy in Pre-Industrial England,* edited by D. C. Coleman and A. H. John, 132–65. London: Weidenfeld and Nicolson, 1976.

Hay, Douglas. et al. *Albion's Fatal Tree.* London: Allen Lane, 1975.

Heal, Felicity. "The Idea of Hospitality in Early Modern England." *PP* 102 (1984): 66–93.

Heckscher, E. F. *Mercantilism.* Translated by M. Shapiro. Revised ed. by E. F. Söderbund. London: Allen and Unwin, 1955.

Hill, B. and C. "Catherine Macaulay and the Seventeenth Century." *Welsh History Review* 3 (1967), 381–402.

Hill, Christopher. *The Century of Revolution 1603–1714.* Edinburgh: Nelson, 1961.

———. *Puritanism and Revolution.* London: Secker and Warburg, 1965.

Hirst, Derek. *Authority and Conflict: England 1603–58.* London: E. Arnold, 1986.

———. *The Representative of the People?* Cambridge: Cambridge University Press, 1975.

Hinton, R. W. K. "The Decline of Parliamentary Government under Elizabeth I and the Early Stuarts." *Cambridge Historical Journal* 13 (1957): 116–32.

Hoak, Dale E. *The King's Council in the Reign of Edward VI.* Cambridge: Cambridge University Press, 1976.

Hogrefe, Pearl. *The Sir Thomas More Circle.* Urbana: University of Illinois Press, 1959.

Holmes, Geoffrey. *Politics, Religion and Society in England 1679–1742.* London and Ronceverte: Hambledon Press, 1986.

———, and Daniel Szechi. *The Age of Oligarchy: Pre-industrial Britain 1722–1785.* London and New York: Longman, 1993.

Hone, J. A. "Radicalism in London, 1796–1802." In *London in the Age of Reform,* edited by J. Stevenson. Oxford: Oxford University Press, 1977.

Horwitz, Henry. *Parliament, Policy and Politics in the Reign of William III.* Manchester: Manchester University Press, 1977.

Hoskins, W. G. "Harvest Fluctuations and English History, 1620–1759." *Agricultural History Review* 16 (1968): 15–31.

Howell, Roger, Jr., and David E. Brewster. "Reconsidering the Levellers: the Evidence of *The Moderate.*" *PP* 102 (1984): 66–93.

Jacob, Margaret C. *The Newtonians and the English Revolution 1689–1720.* Ithaca: Cornell University Press; Hassocks: Harvester, 1976.

James, Margaret. "The Political Importance of the Tithes Controversy in the English Revolution, 1640–60." *History,* n.s., 26 (1941–42): 1–18.

———. *Social Problems and Policy During the Puritan Revolution, 1640–1660.* London: Routledge, 1930.

Jones, Clyve, ed. *Britain in the First Age of Party 1688–1750.* London and Ronceverte: Hambledon Press, 1987.

Jones, I. Deane. *The English Revolution, 1603–1714.* London: Heinemann, 1952.

Jones, J. R. *Country and Court, England 1658–1714.* London: E. Arnold, 1978.

Jones, Margaret G. *The Charity School Movement.* London and Edinburgh: F. Cass, 1964. Rpt. of Cambridge University Press 1938 ed.)

Jones, Whitney R. D. *David Williams: The Anvil and the Hammer.* Cardiff: University of Wales Press; Tuscaloosa: University of Alabama Press, 1986.

———. *The Mid-Tudor Crisis 1539–1563.* London: Macmillan, 1973.

———. *The Tudor Commonwealth 1529–1559.* London: Athlone Press, 1970.

Kearney, Hugh. *Scholars and Gentlemen.* London: Faber and Faber, 1970.

Kennedy, William. *English Taxation 1640–1799.* London: G. Bell, 1913.

Kent, Joan. "Attitudes of Members of the House of Commons to the Regulation of 'Personal Conduct' in Late Elizabethan and Early Stuart England." *Bulletin of the Institute of Historical Research* 46 (1973): 41–71.

Kenyon, J. P. *Revolution Principles.* Cambridge: Cambridge University Press, 1977.

———. *The Stuart Constitution.* Cambridge: Cambridge University Press, 1966.

Knappen, M. M. *Tudor Puritanism.* Chicago: University of Chicago Press, 1939.

Kramnick, Isaac. *Bolingbroke and His Circle.* Cambridge: Harvard University Press, 1968.

Lamont, William M. *Godly Rule: Politics and Religion, 1603–60.* London: Macmillan, 1969.

Langford, Paul. *A Polite and Commercial People: England 1727–1783.* Oxford: Clarendon, 1989.

———. *Public Life and the Propertied Englishman, 1689–1798.* Oxford: Clarendon, 1991.

Laski, H. J. *Political Thought in England: From Locke to Bentham.* Oxford: Oxford University Press, 1950.

Loach, Jennifer. *A Mid-Tudor Crisis?* London: Historical Association, 1992.

———. *Parliament and the Crown in the Reign of Mary Tudor.* Oxford: Clarendon, 1986.

———, and Robert Tittler, eds. *The Mid-Tudor Polity c. 1540–1560.* London: Macmillan, 1980.

MacCaffrey, W. T. *The Shaping of the Elizabethan Regime.* Princeton, Princeton University Press, 1968; London: Cape, 1969.

McConica, J. K. *English Humanists and Reformation Politics.* Oxford: Oxford University Press, 1965.

McGregor, J. F., and B. Reay, eds. *Radical Religion in the English Revolution.* Oxford: Oxford University Press, 1984.

Manning, Brian. *The English People and the English Revolution.* London: Bookmarks, 1991.

Manning, Roger B. *Village Revolts: Social Protest and Popular Disturbances in England, 1509–1640.* Oxford: Clarendon, 1988.

Marius, Richard. *Thomas More.* London and Melbourne: Dent, 1985.

Marshall, Dorothy. *Eighteenth Century England.* London: Longman, 1974.

———. *The English Poor in the Eighteenth Century.* London: Routledge, 1926.

Martin, John E. *Feudalism to Capitalism.* London: Macmillan, 1983.

Mayer, Thomas F. "Faction and Ideology: Thomas Starkey's *Dialogue.*" *Historical Journal* 28 (1985): 1–25.

Morley, Iris. *A Thousand Lives: An Account of the English Revolutionary Movement 1660–1685.* London: Deutsch, 1954.

Morris, Christopher. *Political Thought in England: Tyndale to Hooker.* Oxford: Oxford University Press, 1953.

Morton, A. L. *The World of the Ranters: Religious Radicalism in the English Revolution.* London: Lawrence and Wishart, 1970.

Neale, Sir John E. *The Elizabethan House of Commons.* London: Cape, 1949.

———. "Peter Wentworth." *EHR* 39 (1924): 35–54; 39 (1924): 175–205.

Noonan, J. T. *The Scholastic Analysis of Usury.* Cambridge: Harvard University Press, 1957.

Ogilvie, Sir C. *The King's Government and the Common Law, 1471–1641.* Oxford: Blackwell, 1958.

Osborne, John W. *John Cartwright.* Cambridge: Cambridge University Press, 1972.

Outhwaite, R. B. *Inflation in Tudor and Stuart England.* London: Macmillan, 1969.

Owen, John B. *The Eighteenth Century 1714–1815.* London: Nelson, 1974.

———. *The Pattern of Politics in Eighteenth-Century England.* London: Historical Association, 1962.

Palmer, R. Liddlesdale. *English Social History in the Making: The Tudor Revolution.* London: Nicholson and Watson, 1934.

Palmer, R. R. *The Age of the Democratic Revolution.* 2 vols. Princeton: Princeton University Press, 1959, 1964.

Pares, Richard. *King George III and the Politicians.* Oxford: Oxford University Press, 1963.

Parssinen, T. M. "Association, Convention and Anti-Parliament in British Radical Politics, 1771–1848." *EHR* 88 (1973): 504–33.

Patrick, J. Max. "*The Free State of Noland,* neglected Utopia from the Age of Queen Anne." *Philological Quarterly* 25 (1946): 79–88.

Patterson, Annabel. *Reading Holinshed's Chronicles.* Chicago and London: University of Chicago Press, 1994.

———. *Shakespeare and the Popular Voice.* Oxford: Blackwell, 1989.

Plucknett, T. F. "Some Proposed Legislation of Henry VIII." *TRHS*, 4th ser., 19 (1936): 119–44.

Plumb, Sir John (H.). "British Attitudes to the American Revolution." In *In the Light of History*, 70–87. London: Allen Lane, 1972.

———. *England in the Eighteenth Century.* London: Pelican, 1953.

———. *The Growth of Political Stability in England 1675–1725.* London: Macmillan, 1986.

———. "The Growth of the Electorate in England from 1600 to 1715." *PP* 45 (1969): 90–116.

———. "Political Man." In *Man versus Society in Eighteenth-Century Britain,* edited by J. L. Clifford, 1–21. Cambridge: Cambridge University Press, 1968.

Pocock, J. G. A. *Politics, Language and Time.* London: Methuen, 1972.

———. ed. *Three British Revolutions: 1641, 1688, 1776.* Princeton: Princeton University Press, 1980.

Pocock, N. *Troubles connected with the Prayer Book of 1549.* London: Camden Society, 1884.

Pollard, A. F. *England under Protector Somerset.* London: Kegan Paul, 1900.

Potter, G. R., ed. *The New Cambridge Modern History.* Vol. 1. *The Renaissance, 1493–1520.* Cambridge: Cambridge University Press, 1957.

Read, Conyers. *Mr Secretary Cecil and Queen Elizabeth.* London: Cape, 1955.

Richards, Judith, Lotte Mulligan, and John K. Graham. " 'Property' and 'People': Political Usages of Locke and some Contemporaries." *Journal of the History of Ideas* 42 (1981): 29–51.

Robbins, Caroline. *The Eighteenth-Century Commonwealthman.* Cambridge: Harvard University Press, 1961.

———, ed. and intro. *Two English Republican Tracts.* Cambridge: Cambridge University Press, 1969.

Roots, Ivan. *The Great Rebellion 1642–1660.* London: Batsford, 1966.

———. Introduction to *Speeches of Oliver Cromwell.* London: Dent, 1989.

Rudé, G. "The London Mob of the Eighteenth Century." *Historical Journal* 2 (1959): 1–18.

———. *Wilkes and Liberty.* Oxford: Oxford University Press, 1962.

Rupp, Gordon. *Religion in England 1688–1791.* Oxford: Clarendon, 1986.

Russell, Conrad. *Unrevolutionary England: 1603–1642.* London and Ronceverte: Hambledon Press, 1990.

Russell, F. W. *Kett's Rebellion in Norfolk.* London, 1859.

Sabine, G. H. *A History of Political Theory.* London: Harrap, 1966.

Sanderson, John. *"But the people's creatures." The Philosophical Basis of the English Civil War.* Manchester and New York: Manchester University Press, 1989.

Scarisbrick, J. J. "Cardinal Wolsey and the Common Weal." In *Wealth and Power in Tudor England,* edited by E. W. Ives, et al., 45–67. London: Athlone Press, 1978.

Schenk, W. *The Concern for Social Justice in the Puritan Revolution.* London: Longmans, Green, 1948.

Schwarz, L. D. "The Standard of Living in the Long Run: London, 1700–1860." *Econ. HR,* 2nd ser., 38 (1985): 24–41.

Schwoerer, L. G. *"No Standing Armies."* Baltimore and London: Johns Hopkins University Press, 1974.

Sharp, Andrew. *Political ideas of the English Civil Wars, 1641–1649.* London and New York: Longmans, 1988.

Sharp, Buchanan. *In Contempt of All Authority*. Berkeley, Los Angeles, and London: University of California Press, 1980.

Sharpe, Jim. "Social Strain and Social Dislocation, 1585–1603." In *The Reign of Elizabeth I*, edited by J. Guy, 192–211. Cambridge: Cambridge University Press, 1995.

Skinner, Quentin. *The Foundations of Modern Political Thought*. 2 vols. Cambridge: Cambridge University Press, 1978.

Slack, Paul. *Poverty and Policy in Tudor and Stuart England*. London and New York: Longman, 1983.

———. "Books of Orders: The Making of English Social Policy, 1577–1631." *TRHS*, 5th ser., 30 (1980): 1–22.

———. "Poverty and Social Regulation in Elizabethan England." In *The Reign of Elizabeth I*, edited by Christopher Haigh, 221–40. London: Macmillan, 1984.

———. "Social Policy and the Constraints of Government, 1547–58." In *The Mid-Tudor Polity c. 1540–1560*, edited by J. Loach and R. Tittler, 94–115. London: Macmillan, 1980.

Smith, Edward O., Jr. *Crown and Commonwealth: A Study in the official Elizabethan Doctrine of the Prince*. Transactions of the American Philosophical Society, n.s., 66, part 8 (1976).

Snell, K. D. M. *Annals of the Labouring Poor*. Cambridge: Cambridge University Press, 1985.

Sommerville, J. P. *Politics and Ideology in England, 1603–1640*. London and New York: Longman, 1986.

Speck, W. A. "The Electorate in the First Age of Party." In *Britain in the First Age of Party 1688–1750*, edited by Clyve Jones. London and Ronceverte: Hambledon Press, 1987.

———. *Reluctant Revolutionaries*. Oxford: Oxford University Press, 1988.

———. *Stability and Strife: England, 1714–1760*. London: E. Arnold, 1977.

Starkey, David, et al. *The English Court: From the Wars of the Roses to the Civil War*. London and New York: Longman, 1987.

Stephen, L., and S. Lee. *Dictionary of National Biography*. London: Oxford University Press, 1908–   .

Stevenson, J., ed. *London in the Age of Reform*. Oxford: Oxford University Press, 1977.

Stone, Lawrence. *The Causes of the English Revolution, 1529–1642*. 2nd ed. London: Routledge and Kegan Paul, 1986.

———. *Social Change and Revolution in England, 1540–1640*. London: Longmans, 1965.

———. "Social Mobility in England, 1500–1700." *PP* 33 (1966): 16–55.

Stromberg, Roland N. *Religious Liberalism in Eighteenth-Century England*. Oxford: Oxford University Press, 1954.

Strype, John. *Ecclesiastical Memorials*. Oxford: Clarendon, 1822.

Supple, B. E. *Commercial Crisis and Change in England: 1600–1642*. Cambridge: Cambridge University Press, 1959.

Talbert, Ernest W. *The Problem of Order*. Chapel Hill: University of North Carolina Press, 1962.

Tawney, R. H. *Harrington's Interpretation of His Age*. London: Humphrey Milford, 1941.

Taylor, P. A. M., ed. *Conspiracy, Crusade or Class Conflict?* Boston: Heath, 1958.

Thirsk, Joan, ed. *The Agrarian History of England and Wales.* Vol. 4. *1500–1640.* Cambridge: Cambridge University Press, 1967.

———. *Economic Policy and Projects.* Oxford: Clarendon, 1978.

———, and J. P. Cooper, eds. *Seventeenth-Century Economic Documents.* Oxford: Oxford University Press, 1972.

Thomas, Keith. "The Levellers and the Franchise." In *The Interregnum,* edited by G. E. Aylmer, 57–78. London: Macmillan, 1972.

Thompson, Christopher. "Maxmilian Petty and the Putney Debate on the Franchise." *PP* 88 (1980): 63–69.

Thompson, E. P. *Customs in Common.* London: Penguin 1991.

———. "Eighteenth-century English Society: Class Struggle Without Class?" *Social History* 3 (1978): 133–65.

———. *The Making of the English Working Class.* London: Pelican, 1968.

———. "The Moral Economy of the English Crowd in the Eighteenth Century." *PP* 50 (1971): 76–136.

Tittler, Robert. "The Emergence of Urban Policy, 1536–58." In *The Mid-Tudor Polity,* edited by J. Loach and R. Tittler, 74–93. London: Macmillan, 1980.

Todd, Margo. *Christian Humanism and the Puritan Social Order.* Cambridge: Cambridge University Press, 1987.

Toohey, Robert E. *Liberty and Empire.* Lexington: University Press of Kentucky, 1978.

Troeltsch, Ernst. *The Social Teaching of the Christian Churches.* Translated by O. Wyon. 2 vols. London: Allen and Unwin, 1931.

Tully, James. *A Discourse on Property.* Cambridge: Cambridge University Press, 1980.

Vereker, G. S. *Eighteenth-Century Optimism.* Liverpool: Liverpool University Press, 1967.

Viner, J. "Man's Economic Status." In *Man versus Society in Eighteenth-Century Britain,* edited by Clifford, 22–53. Cambridge: Cambridge University Press, 1968.

Walsh, J. D. "Elie Halévy and the Birth of Methodism." *TRHS,* 5th ser., 25 (1975): 1–20.

Walter, John. "A 'Rising of the People'? The Oxfordshire Rising of 1596." *PP* 107 (1985): 90–143.

———, Keith Wrightson. "Dearth and the Social Order in Early Modern England." *PP* 71 (1976): 22–42.

Webster, Charles. *The Great Instauration: Science, Medicine and Reform, 1626–1660.* London: Duckworth, 1975.

Wernham, R. B., ed. *The New Cambridge Modern History.* Vol. 3. *The Counter-Reformation and Price Revolution, 1559–1610.* Cambridge: Cambridge University Press, 1968.

White, Stephen D. *Sir Edward Coke and "The Grievances of the Commonwealth," 1621–1628.* Chapel Hill: University of North Carolina Press, 1979.

Williams, E. N. *The Eighteenth-Century Constitution, 1688–1815.* Cambridge: Cambridge University Press, 1960.

Wilson, Charles. "The Other Face of Merchantilism." *TRHS,* 5th ser., 9 (1959): 81–101.

Woolrych, Austin. *Commonwealth to Protectorate.* Oxford: Clarendon, 1982.

———. "Last Quests for a Settlement 1657–1660." In *The Interregnum,* edited by G. E. Aylmer, 183–204. London: Macmillan, 1972.

Worden, Blair. *The Sound of Virtue*. New Haven and London: Yale University Press, 1996.

Wrigley, E. A. "The Growth of Population in Eighteenth-Century England." *PP* 98 (1983): 121–50.

——, and R. S. Schofield. *The Population History of England 1541–1871*. London: E. Arnold, 1981.

Zagorin, Perez. *A History of Political Thought in the English Revolution*. London: Routledge and Kegan Paul, 1954.

Zeeveld, W. G. *Foundations of Tudor Policy*. Cambridge: Harvard University Press, 1948.

Index

Adams, John, 267
Agrarian law, 168–69, 190, 231, 275, 310
Agreements of the People, 166, 167
Agriculture, 63, 89, 131, 134, 200, 207, 261. *See also* Enclosure; Open Fields; Tillage
Alcock, Thomas, 289–90
Allen, J. W., 59, 99, 102, 118, 121, 127
Allen, Robert, 115
Allen, William, 86, 105–6, 118
Almon, John, 298, 304
Alsop, J. D., 58
American colonists, independence, 297, 300, 301, 304, 305, 309, 320, 323
American Revolution, 220, 301
Anabaptism/Anabaptists, 73, 78–9, 96, 97, 98, 100, 101, 115, 128, 142, 156, 178, 180, 233; tracts, 128, 232–33
Anarchy, 16, 72, 73, 74, 80, 91, 111, 124, 150, 151, 154, 157, 158, 160, 180, 212, 215, 219, 228, 270, 277, 299, 318. *See also* Mob, fear of
Anglo-Saxon government and society, 228, 277, 299
Anne, queen of England, 206, 208, 210, 225, 238, 239
Apparel, 65, 89, 104, 120, 212
Appleby, Joyce, 132, 139, 203, 243–44
Arbitrary power/absolutism, 92–93, 119, 123, 150, 153, 154, 227, 230, 234, 267, 318
Arianism/Socinianism, 279, 280, 303
Aristotle, 14
Armstrong, Clement, 36, 67, 95
Arnall, William, 264
Arthington, Henry, 114–15
Artificers/apprentices, 89, 137, 244, 292, 293; Statute of, 89, 313
Ascham, Anthony, 147–48, 149, 153, 156–57
Ashcraft, Richard, 208–9

Ashton, Robert, 109, 138
Associations, 296, 305–6, 307, 322
Atterbury, Francis, bishop of Rochester, 229–30; Atterbury Plot, 206
Atwood, William, 228
Aucher, Sir Anthony, 55, 58
Audley, Sir Thomas, 65
Aylmer, Gerald E., 179, 186, 197, 201

Bacon, Sir Francis, 112, 119, 212
Bahlman, Dudley, 238
Baker, Keith, 323
Baldwin, William, 39, 71
Bancroft, Richard, bishop of London, 100–101
Banks, *Monte della Pieta*, 114, 199, 251
Baptists, 180, 232–33
Barebones Parliament, 155, 183–84, 195, 196, 197, 202
Barnes, Robert, 53, 76, 80
Baron, Richard, 297
Barrow, Isaac, 244–45
Barrowe, Henry, 104–5
Bathurst, Allen, earl, 269
Baugh, Daniel, 255
Baxter, Richard, 148, 157, 179, 182–83, 245
Beacon, Richard, 111
Beckingsale, B. W., 47
Becon, Thomas, 36, 57, 58, 69, 75, 79
Bedel, Henry, 114
Bee-hive, analogy of, 95, 130, 200, 216–17, 264
Beer/ale, 132, 281
Beggars/vagabonds, 60, 68, 69, 91, 93, 115, 130, 136, 193, 200, 203, 212, 248, 250, 252–53, 291, 311. *See also* Charity; Poverty
Bellers, John, 249–50
Bentley, Thomas, 315
Bernard, Richard, 121, 337 n.79

383

INDEX

Bible of 1539, English, 49
Bigod, Sir Francis, 80
Bilson, Thomas, 99–100
Bindoff, S. T., 63
Black, E. C., 305
Blackall, Ofspring, 210
Bodin, Jean, 92, 95–96, 111, 125, 126, 126, 152
Bolingbroke, Henry Saint John, viscount, 265–68, 270, 285, 287, 292, 327
Bonwick, Colin, 224, 302, 306
Books of Orders, 1630–31, 129, 132, 135, 137, 140
Bradbury, Thomas, 229, 241
Braddon, Lawrence, 216, 239, 254, 255
Bradford, John, 55, 57, 58, 62
Bradley, James, 304
Bradshaw, Brendan, 34, 44, 45, 46, 50, 52, 91
Bramston, Sir John, 216
Breda, Declaration of, 232,
Brewer, John, 305
Bridewell, 69
Bridges, John, 98, 99, 103
Brigden, Susan, 53
Brinklow, Henry, 41, 58–59, 63, 69, 78, 80, 100
Brodie, D. M., 29
Brogan, Denis, 28
Brown, John, 282–83
Browne, Robert, 104
Bucer, Martin, 70, 78
Building, 39, 89, 104, 135
Bullinger, Johann Heinrich, 79, 98
Bunyan, John, 178, 188, 245
Burford Mutiny, 164
Burgh, James, 304–5
Burke, Edmund, 258, 264, 278, 298–99, 300, 303, 308, 315, 317–18, 319, 320, 321, 325
Burnett, Thomas, 216
Burton, Robert, 120–21, 241
Bush, M. L., 55, 56
Busher, Leonard, 127

Cabinet, 298
Callender, J. T., 316
Calling. *See* Vocation
Calvin, John/Calvinism, 78, 103, 129, 177, 180, 184

Cambridge, 150
Campbell, John, 273, 275
Campion, Edmund, 142
Cannon, John, 306, 321
Capital punishment, 127, 212, 244, 262, 271, 291, 312, 315
Capp, Bernard, 164, 193
Carew, Thomas, 135
Carpenter, John, 111–12
Carter, Bezaleel, 136
Cartwright, John, 258, 262, 301, 304, 305, 306, 307, 308, 321, 324
Cartwright, Thomas, 101, 103
Cary, John, 249
Castellio, Sebastian, 126,
Catholic Relief Act (1778), 303
Catholicism, social and economic teachings of, 16, 22–24, 77–78, 84, 129
Caxton, William, 25
Cecil, William, Lord Burghley, 34, 55, 57, 62, 65, 67, 90
Chamberlen, Peter, 188, 198
Charity, 23, 68, 113–14, 190, 192, 193, 202, 222, 245–46, 252, 253, 255, 256, 289–90, 291, 294. *See also* Beggars; Poverty
Charity schools, 253, 255, 256, 291, 311
Charles I, king of England, 123–24, 132, 134, 135, 137, 142, 146, 150, 152, 202, 207, 220, 229, 271, 327
Charles II, king of England, 144, 208, 212, 214, 218, 224, 232, 234
Charretier, Alain, 25
Cheke, Sir John, 37, 39, 66, 72, 74
Child, Sir Josiah, 251, 254–55, 287, 290, 291
Cholmeley, William, 67
Chrimes, S. B., 20
Christie, Ian, 294, 305, 308–9, 314
Christopherson, John, 74, 75
Church/Clergy, 30–31, 49–50, 174, 175, 278, 279, 317; land, wealth of, 18, 48, 69, 80–81, 103
Cicero, 14
Civil war, fear of, 150, 153, 214; mid-seventeenth-century, 118, 129, 140, 144, 147, 150, 160, 164, 170, 172, 185, 188, 192, 209, 277
Claeys, Gregory, 354n.131
Clarendon Code, 233
Clark, J. C. D., 224, 263, 264, 307, 327, 346nn.2 and 18

Clarkson, Laurence, 153, 179, 196
Clayton, John, 288
Cloth, manufacture of, 67, 138, 199; standards and regulation of, 62, 65, 199
Coats, A. W., 255, 285, 287
Cockayne project, 138
Coinage, debasement of, 51, 57, 62, 65, 88. *See also* Prices
Coke, Sir Edward, 142–43
Coleman, D. C., 349 n.87
Colley, Linda, 224
Collinson, Patrick, 85, 108, 114, 119, 129, 142, 339 n.120
Common law, courts of, 43, 64; projected reform of, 43, 113
Commons, House of, 140, 147, 151, 155, 165, 186, 197, 211, 225, 239, 267, 298, 312; defects of 229, 272. *See also* Electoral Procedures
Commons, (land), 61, 63–64, 75, 131, 136, 201, 203, 293, 313
Commonwealth, British, 13, 300–301; Christian values in, 16, 48, 50, 54, 58, 61, 84, 88, 98, 103, 181, 259, 280, 317, 326, 327, 328; formal establishment of, 1649, 15, 19, 144, 154, 186, 205; notion of a "Godly Commonwealth," 145, 173–85; unity, identity with Church, 50, 77, 85, 96–99, 102–6, 117–18, 119, 124–26, 141, 174, 177, 180–83, 235–36, 278, 297, 303, 317, 325, 327, 328
Commonwealth Men: mid-Tudor, 15, 18, 47, 49, 50–51, 55–59, 67, 112; eighteenth-century, 14, 16–17, 19–20, 170, 205, 210–11, 218, 224, 225–28, 230–32, 262, 284, 297, 298, 305, 308, 312, 322, 325, 327
Commonwealth Party, notion of, 54–55
Cone, Carl, 306, 308, 321, 324
"Conservators of the Commonweal," 52, 113
Constitutional amendment, evolution, 153, 273, 319
Convocation of Clergy, 278
Cook, John, 146–47, 149–50, 152, 186, 189–90, 193, 194, 197
Cooper, J. P., 192
Cooper, Thomas, 54, 315
Coppe, Abiezer, 179, 186

Copyhold tenure, 64, 136, 228
Corn, 65, 89, 132, 200, 207, 292
Corruption, 224–25, 227, 231, 256, 263–64, 267, 268–70, 272–74, 296, 299
Council, King's Privy, 69, 137, 192
Council of Army Officers, 128, 146, 161, 166, 176
Court, Royal, 25, 53, 239
Covel, William, 186, 194, 198–99
Cox, Leonard, 49
Craig, Sir Thomas, 108
Cranmer, Thomas, archbishop of Canterbury, 36, 57, 58, 62, 66, 69, 71, 73, 74, 75, 81, 113, 291
"Crisis" eras: mid-Tudor, 17–18, 86, 87, 110; late-1590s, 109–10; Exclusion Crisis, 206, 208
Cromwell, Oliver, Lord Protector, 143, 151, 155–56, 159, 162, 176, 181–82, 184, 185–6, 196, 197, 202, 208, 220
Cromwell, Richard, 182
Cromwell, Thomas, earl of Essex, 17, 21, 28, 34, 44, 46–53, 56, 57, 64, 65, 80, 326
Crowley, Robert, 58–59, 61, 63, 68, 69, 75, 76, 78, 100, 121, 129
Crown, British, financial policies of, 120, 138; influence, power and prerogatives of, 125, 225, 267, 272, 273, 274, 275, 295; succession to, 73, 85, 106, 108–9, 117
Cruickshanks, Eveline, 218

Dairy products, 60, 66
Davenant, Charles, 224–25
Davies, C. S. L., 60
Davis, J. C., 34, 45, 153, 179, 202, 241
Day, Thomas, 306–7
De Lolme, J. Lewis, 307–8, 323, 353 n.102
"Dearth." *See* Food and Drink; Harvests; Prices
Declaration of Indulgence, 234
Defoe, Daniel, 213, 228–29, 236–37, 239–40, 252–53, 281
Deism/Deists, 279, 303,
Democracy, 92, 107, 123, 151, 156–57, 163, 171, 173, 183, 214, 218, 219, 222–23, 241, 270, 271, 274, 299, 310, 316; definition of, 95, 232, 274; per-

versions of, 116, 147, 156, 219, 267, 318. *See also* General will, People
Dennis, John, 255–56
Depopulation, 44, 51, 64, 110, 133, 200
Dewar, Mary, 57, 94
Dickens, A. G., 49, 59
Dickinson, A. G., 224, 265, 266, 275
Digby, Kenelm, 158
Diggers, 133, 155, 156, 160, 163, 167, 175, 184, 188, 190–92, 194, 196, 198, 202
Digges, Dudley, 150–51
Dissent/Dissenters, 214, 233, 234–35, 236, 237, 239, 280, 302–3, 304, 318, 327. *See also* Baptists, Independents; Methodists; Presbyterians
Divine Right of kings, 71, 99, 123–24, 151, 172
"Doleman." *See* Parsons, Robert
Dudley, Edmund, 17, 28–32
Dudley, John, earl of Warwick, duke of Northumberland, 54, 56, 59, 61, 73
Dunning, Richard, 250–51, 287
Dury, John, 186, 195
Duverger, Maurice, 325
Dyer, George, 316
Dyke, Jeremy, 136

Earle, Peter, 209
Education, 59, 195, 248, 250, 251–52, 253–54, 271, 291, 312, 315, 318, 320, 324, 325
Edward II, king of England, 108
Edward IV, king of England, 24, 25
Edward VI, king of England, 21, 37, 38, 44, 53–60, 64, 66, 72, 76, 127
Edwards, Thomas, 178, 180
Electoral procedures, 152, 161, 165–67, 223, 227, 264, 270, 275, 276, 298, 299, 301; ballot, 117, 152, 169, 223, 227, 241, 275, 298, 299, 300, 301, 301, 304; franchise, 152, 157, 161, 165–67, 169, 183, 207–8, 224, 225, 260, 262, 276, 296, 298, 299, 301, 307, 317, 325
Eliot, Sir John, 125–26, 142, 146, 201
Eliot, John, 182
Elizabeth I, queen of England, 18, 34,57, 63, 66, 73, 86, 87–88, 90, 91, 96, 99, 102, 107, 117, 119, 215, 268, 288, 296

Elton, Sir Geoffrey, 21–22, 32, 34, 42–43, 46, 48, 50–52, 57, 60, 89, 90
Elyot, Sir Thomas, 14, 17, 35, 37, 45, 267
Emigration, 131, 135, 185, 246, 249, 251
Employment, 207, 261, 286; maintenance, nurturing of, 65, 66, 68–69, 137, 193–94, 197–99, 256, 290. *See also* "Projects"
Enclosure, 63–64, 75, 109–10, 131, 133–34, 164, 200–201, 203, 204, 262, 293; governmental policy toward, 42,44, 59–62, 89, 133–34, 292, 293, 296, 309, 313; commissions on, 36, 42, 55, 57, 59, 64, 133–34. *See also* Engrossing
Engagement, Act of, 154, 340 n.33, 342 n.95
Engrossing of goods and land, 42, 64, 89, 132–33, 136, 191, 200, 212, 245, 292, 311, 313
Enslow Hill Rebellion (1596), 110
Equality/egalitarianism, 15–16, 18–19, 38–39, 96, 116, 151, 187–88, 189, 190–92, 205, 221, 222, 231–32, 274, 320; economic and social, 187–88, 190–92, 241–42, 274, 286, 287, 309, 318; political, 227, 307, 318
Equity/Natural Justice, 15–16, 27, 33, 37, 136, 189, 190, 231–32, 262, 282, 284, 297, 318
Equity Jurisdiction, 38, 43–44
Erasmus, Desiderius, 26–27, 35, 40, 44–45, 49, 50, 51, 53, 54, 62, 63, 70, 71, 76, 99, 113, 129, 130, 267, 326
Essex, Robert Devereux, earl of, 110, 111, 112
Everitt, Alan, 188

Faction, 159, 231, 264, 267, 268, 270, 272, 276, 298
Fairfax, Sir Thomas, 166, 176, 183
Fenner, Dudley, 103–4
Ferguson, A. B., 67
Ferguson, Robert, 208, 209
Ferne, Henry, 146, 150, 151, 159
Field, John, 102
Fielding, Henry, 290–91
Fifth Monarchy Men, 127, 155, 156, 164, 179, 183–84, 186, 196, 233, 302
Filmer, Sir Robert, 151–52
Fines, entry, 64, 75, 130
Firmin, Thomas, 247–48, 349 n.90

Fish/fisheries, 198, 199, 200
Fish, Simon, 45–46, 58, 63, 69
Fletcher, Andrew, 226, 306
Floyd, John, 122–23, 338 n.83
Floyd, Thomas, 94–95
Food and drink, Englishmen's diet of, 242, 251, 253, 254, 311; marketing of, 65, 132–33, 200, 231; supply of, 64, 109, 135, 137, 185, 204, 207, 281, 295, 296, 311, 315. *See also* Prices
Forestalling, 89, 132, 189, 212, 292, 311, 313
Forset, Edward, 121–22
Forster, Nathaniel, 310–11, 313
Foster, James, 282
Fortescue, Sir John, 24, 126
Fothergill, George, 271
France/Frenchmen, 24, 75, 95, 96, 151, 233, 300, 303, 308, 309, 322, 323, 324
Frank, Joseph, 163, 167
Franklin, J. H., 221
Freehold tenure/freeholders, 226, 228–29, 276
French Revolution, 167, 297, 306, 307, 308, 310, 314, 316, 317, 318, 319, 322; National Assembly, 308, 319
Frith, John, 45, 58, 78
Fuel, 65, 293

Gardiner, Stephen, bishop of Winchester, 40, 53, 58, 70, 76, 78, 79–80, 113, 141, 282
Gay, John, 265, 268, 269
General will, concept of, 148, 231, 271, 307, 319
Gentles, Ian, 164
George I, king of England, 206, 263
George II, king of England, 259
George III, king of England, 267, 295, 296, 304
Germany/Germans, 105, 233
Gibson, Edmund, bishop of London, 281–82
Gilbert, Thomas, 312
Gilby, Anthony, 102
Gilpin, Bernard, 37
Gilson, J. P., 21
Gin/Gin Act, 239, 281, 283
Girondins/Girondine, 319
Godwin, William, 316
Goffe, William, 199–200

Goldsmith, Oliver, 293
Gooch, G. P., 85, 117, 220
"Good Old Cause," 153, 160, 194, 206, 208, 209, 220, 241
Goodman, Christopher, 82–83, 99, 106, 158, 171
Goodwin, Albert, 304, 325
Goodwin, John, 178
Gordon Riots, 261, 303, 306, 322
Gordon, Thomas, 230–32, 270
Gott, Samuel, 202
Gouge, William, 129, 130
Government, British: concern with morality, 20, 40, 54, 61, 63, 78, 113, 140–42, 181–82, 238–40, 259, 271, 279, 280, 281, 297, 304, 328; economic and social responsibilities of, 16, 25–27, 30, 40–41, 48, 58, 63, 88–89, 114, 119, 145, 155, 156, 162, 172, 175, 177, 185, 192, 201–5, 215, 240, 243, 259, 291, 292–93, 297, 313, 319, 327; religious responsibility of, 7, 107, 113, 155–56, 173, 177, 181–82, 185, 235, 271, 317, 328
Gray, Robert, 131, 135
"Great Instauration," 194, 320
Green Ribbon Club, 208
Greenwood, John, 105
Gregory, William, 21
Greville, Robert, Lord Brooke, 174, 178
Guevara, Antonio de, 62
Guilds, 64, 65, 69, 244, 293
Gunn, J. A. W., 146, 204, 215, 225, 229–30, 264, 323, 348 n.68
Guttridge, G. H., 260
Guy, John, 34, 41, 43, 44, 68

Habermas, Jürgen, 323
Haigh, Christopher, 109
Haines, R., 247
Hale, Sir Matthew, 248–49, 251, 287, 290
Hales, Sir John, 36, 38, 55–57, 60, 61, 64, 87
Halifax, George Savile, marquis of, 212–13, 218, 220–21, 223, 234–35
Hall, John, 122, 148, 149, 159, 189
Hall, Joseph, 122
Haller, William, 146, 167, 183
Hammond, Anthony, 263
Hammond, J. L. and Barbara, 293

388 INDEX

Hanson, D. W., 34
Hare, John, 196
Harley, Robert, earl of Oxford, 224
Harrington, James, 145, 147, 148, 149, 152, 154, 160, 168–70, 182, 186–87, 189, 190, 201, 204–5, 219, 227, 232, 241, 263, 277, 309
Hartlib, Samuel, 185, 193, 194, 195, 198, 241
Harvests, 88, 110, 131, 135, 137, 185, 207, 281, 283, 292, 296, 313
Hay, Douglas, 207, 244
Hay, William, 271
Hayward, John, 107–8
Hazeland, William, 287
Hazlitt, William, 302
Heal, Felicity, 135
Heckscher, E. F., 217
Henry VI, king of England, 21
Henry VII, king of England, 25, 29, 106
Henry VIII, king of England, 16, 29, 34, 36, 37, 51, 65, 66, 71, 102, 168
Heresy, 22, 45, 53, 70, 77, 113, 175, 177, 180, 181. *See also* Anabaptism, Lollardy
Heywood, John, 45, 64, 74
Hill, Christopher, 120, 135, 218, 244
Hirst, Derek, 157, 197, 205
Hitchin, Edward, 303
Hoadly, Benjamin, bishop of Bangor, 280
Hoake, Dale, 55
Hobbes, Thomas, 26, 82, 118, 145, 152, 155, 157, 158, 170–72, 201, 216, 219, 222
Hodgson, William, 258, 316, 325, 354 n.121
Hogrefe, Pearl, 45
Holcroft, Thomas, 324
Holles, Denzil, Lord, 210
Hollis, Thomas, 297
Hollis, Thomas Brand, 306, 307, 309
Holmes, Geoffrey, 207, 233, 243
Hooker, Richard, 78, 96–98, 99, 107, 113, 117, 118, 128, 142
Hooper, John, bishop of Gloucester, 57, 58, 62, 65, 74, 78, 81, 103
Horwitz, Henry, 211
Hoskins, W. G., 207
Hotman, François, 95, 96, 125, 214
Hubberthorn, Richard, 195, 196

Huguenots, 96
Hulme, Obadiah, 299, 304
Humanism, Christian, 26, 33, 44, 68, 83, 129
Hume, David, 258, 264, 265, 275–76, 300, 303–4
Hume-Campbell, earl of Marchmont, 272–73
Humphrey, Lawrence, 35, 91
Hunton, Philip, 147, 151, 152

Idleness, 37, 93, 115, 193, 247, 248, 249, 251, 251–53, 286, 288, 291
Independents/Separatists, 102, 104, 142, 175, 177, 178
Inflation, 88, 131, 296. *See also* Coinage; Prices
Injunctions to the clergy, 49–50, 71
Instrument of government, 164
Interest/self-interest, 126, 146, 147, 148, 151, 161, 203, 204, 215, 216, 217, 231–32, 240, 243, 244, 265, 283, 323, 324
Interregnum, 144, 167, 188, 199, 202, 212, 236
Ireland, 110, 295, 301–2
Ireton, Henry, 161, 169, 189
Italy, 78

Jacob, Margaret, 244, 348 n.69
Jacobins, 316, 324, 325
Jacobites, 206, 211, 260, 263, 270–71, 349 n.104
Jack Straw, 229
Jackson, John, 210, 216
James I, king of England, 86, 100–101, 108, 117, 118–19, 123, 124, 131, 135, 236, 281, 327
James II, king of England, 206, 207, 216, 234
James, Margaret, 188, 192, 344 n.166
Jebb, John, 306
Jefferson, Thomas, 268
Jenyns, Soame, 302, 308, 309, 311, 314
Jephson, Alexander, 295
Jesuits, 96, 99, 119, 236
Jewel, John, bishop of Salisbury, 98
John of Leyden, 115, 295
Johnson, Samuel, 264, 298
Jones, J. R., 243
Jones, Whitney R. D., 35, 54

Jones, William, 302
Jubbes, John, 176–77, 196
Justices of the Peace, 65, 89, 90, 132, 137, 138

Kearney, Hugh, 201–2
Kennedy, William, 215–16, 217
Kent, Joan, 140–41
Kenyon, J. P., 134, 278, 345 n.1
Ket, Francis, 100
Ket, Robert, rebellion of, 55, 66, 73
Keynes, J. M., 285
Knappen, M. M., 78
Knollys, Richard, 96
Knox, John, 82, 101–2
Kramnick, Isaac, 265, 320
Krey, G. S. de, 347 n.42, 349 n.90

Labour, attitudes toward, 246, 249–50, 252, 253, 284–85, 286–87, 290, 310–11; position of, 246, 295
Lamond, Elizabeth, 57, 94
Landlords, 23, 64, 75, 245. *See also* Rents
Lane, William, 62
Langford, Paul, 261, 281, 284, 293, 294, 297, 309, 324
Langland, William: *Piers Ploughman*, 19, 23, 59, 77
Larkin, J. F., 132, 137
Latimer, Hugh, bishop of Worcester, 36, 57–58, 60–61, 62, 69, 81, 100, 245, 282, 291
Latimer, the "Commonwealth of Kent," 55, 58, 333 n.98
Laud, William, archbishop of Canterbury, 124–25, 133, 134, 141, 142, 181
Law: Courts of. *See* Common Law, Requests, Star Chamber; projected reform of, 43, 52, 113, 193, 196–97, 202
Law, William, 278, 289, 291
Lawson, Thomas, 198
Leadam, I. A., 42
Lee, Joseph, 186, 201
Lemon, R., 55
Levellers, 115, 133, 154, 155, 156, 160, 161–67, 169, 170, 183, 184, 191, 194, 196, 197–98, 203, 305, 322, 324
Lever, Thomas, 36, 57, 58, 79, 100, 245, 282
Liberalitas/liberality, 23, 33, 39, 137
Libertines, 79, 84, 178, 179, 180

Liberty, 149, 150, 163–65, 171, 172, 214, 218, 220, 221, 225, 230, 235, 271, 274, 277, 301, 308; civil, 120, 142–43, 146, 149, 156, 205, 233, 262, 271, 277, 281, 295, 297, 298, 300, 326; political, 18, 143, 145, 146, 157, 160–63, 173, 205, 262, 297, 304, 307, 317, 327; religious toleration, 85, 96, 120, 126–28, 156, 166, 173, 175–8, 181, 184–85, 205, 232–38, 259, 278–9, 280, 281, 282, 302–4, 317, 318. *See also* Democracy; Natural Rights; People
Lilburne, John, 160, 162, 163, 164, 178, 180, 185, 203
Lindsey, Theophilus, 303
Living standards, 131, 261, 283, 285, 308–9, 310
Locke, John, 19, 26, 81, 82, 171, 208, 216, 218, 220, 221–22, 226, 228, 235–36, 238, 297, 309
Lollards/Lollardy, 18, 53
London, 69, 87, 89, 109–10, 135, 164, 176, 185, 209, 239, 243, 272, 293
Long Parliament, 181
Longland, John, bishop of Lincoln, 44, 47
Lords, House of, 151, 154, 165, 278, 312
Lowman, Moses, 263
Ludlow, Edmund, 218–19
Lupset, Thomas, 45
Lupton, Thomas, 93
Luther, Martin/Lutherans, 50, 53, 78, 105, 229

Macaulay, Catharine, 299, 305
McGregor, J. F., 184
Machiavelli, Niccolò, 70
Mackintosh, James, 316–17
Mackworth, Sir Humphrey, 237, 252
Magdeburg, 229
Mainwaring, Robert, bishop of Saint David's, 124, 129, 132
Major Generals, 156, 182
Malynes, Gerald de, 139–40
Mandeville, Bernard, 216–17, 238, 245, 253–54, 255, 256, 269, 283, 324
Manning, Brian, 157, 162
Manning, Roger B., 109, 133
Manufactures/industry, 198–200, 285; control of, 62, 64–65, 67, 137, 140,

313; standards in, 31, 51, 62, 64–65, 138, 199, 262, 313
Marius, Richard, 45
Marketing, 89, 138–39, 203, 243–45, 285, 293; control of, 65, 66–67, 132–33, 139, 203, 212, 242
Marshall, Dorothy, 264, 287, 288, 289, 293, 312
Marshall, William, 48, 68
Marsiglio/Marsilius, of Padua, 20
Martin, John, 133, 134
Martin Marprelate, 88, 98, 100
Marvell, Andrew, 234
Mary I, queen of England, 56, 61–62, 69, 73, 74, 81, 178
Mary II, queen of England, 225, 238, 244
Mason, Sir John, 40, 139
Massie, J., 291, 293
Mauduit, Israel, 302
Measure, concept of, 15, 37, 39, 112, 189
Medical relief/hospitals, provision of, 59, 69, 120, 137, 192–95, 200, 242, 250, 290, 292, 312
Melanchthon, Philip, 229
Merbury, Charles, 92–93, 95
Mercantilism, 244
Mercenaries, 162, 226
Merchants/middlemen, 65, 130, 139, 285
Methodism, 259, 278, 279, 281, 282, 294, 295, 303, 304
Middlesex Election of 1768, 297
Midlands Revolt, 1607, 110, 116, 133
Militia, 162, 170, 298
Milton, John, 149, 158, 159–60, 177
Ministers of the Crown, 69, 295, 298, 299
Minogue, Kenneth, 171
Misselden, Edward, 139, 140
Mob, fear of, 198, 228–29, 261, 273, 276, 277, 294
Molesworth, Robert, 19, 213, 214–15, 226, 227, 238, 243, 247, 263, 306
Monmouth, duke of, Rebellion of, 206, 208, 209, 226
Montesquieu, Charles Louis de Secondat, baron de, 268, 277, 323
Moore, Francis, 311
Moore, John, 200–201

More, Sir Thomas, 44–46, 76, 91, 275, 277
Morison, Sir Richard, 38–39, 52, 66, 70, 72–73, 74, 77, 82, 113, 186, 290
Morley, Iris, 208, 209
Morris, Christopher, 73, 81, 97, 117, 118
Mortimer, Thomas, 310
Morton, A. L., 178
Moyle, Walter, 226–27, 258, 259, 263
Mun, Thomas, 140
Münster, 38, 73, 115, 180, 295

Nashe, Thomas, 115
Natural law, 81, 113, 118, 150, 189, 190, 219, 222
Natural rights, 163, 172, 184, 216, 217–18, 220, 282, 298, 300, 301, 317
Nayler, James, 179–80, 186
Nedham, Marchmont, 147, 154–55, 167, 297, 340 n.33
Neville, Henry, 153, 208, 219, 226, 297
New Model Army, 155, 164
Nobility: aristocracy, 113, 147, 168; concept of, 27, 30, 39
Norfolk, Thomas Howard, duke of, 40
"Norman Yoke," 165, 192
North, Roger, 213
North, Thomas, 61
Norton, Thomas, 91–92
Nowell, Alexander, 92

Obedience, duty of, 34, 70–71, 76, 79, 81, 124, 151, 158–59, 171, 216, 229; passive disobedience, 76, 80, 81, 111
Occleve, Thomas, 24
Ogilvie, Sir Charles, 43
Ogilvie, William, 310, 315
Oligarchy, 117, 224, 260, 263, 314
Open Fields, 134, 201
Oswald, John, 314–15
Owen, John, 199, 234
Owen, John B., 264
Owen, Robert, 199, 202, 250
Overton, Richard, 162, 163, 164, 165, 176, 178
Owst, G. R., 23
Oxford, 151

Paget, Sir William, 56, 80
Paine, Thomas, 317, 319–21, 323, 324, 325–26

Palmer, R. R., 323
Papacy/popes, 100
Papists, 82, 83, 98, 99, 100, 101, 102, 105–8, 119, 123, 142, 176, 179, 233, 224, 236
Pares, Richard, 306
Parker, Henry, 146, 151, 152, 157, 167
Parker, Samuel, bishop of Oxford, 210, 233–34
Parliament, British, 42, 47, 48–49, 51, 59, 105, 108, 109, 120, 151, 152–53, 157, 164, 176, 185, 193, 197, 219, 223, 226, 267, 271, 274, 275, 293, 295, 303, 306, 317; defects, corruption of, 108, 223, 225, 229, 264, 267, 274, 299; proposals for reform of, 183, 225, 295, 321; annual or triennial parliaments, 152, 167, 225–28, 267, 270, 271, 275, 298, 301, 304, 305, 307, 318. *See also* Electoral procedures
Parr, Katherine, queen to Henry VIII, 53
Parsons, Robert, 86, 106–7, 109, 112–14, 117
Patrick, J. M., 241
Patriot King, notion of, 267–78
Patterson, Annabel, 116, 337 n.69
Paxton, Peter, 216
Peasants' Revolt, Germany, 1525, 38, 73
Pennsylvania, Constitution of, 220
Penry, John, 105, 142
People, the, 80, 108, 261, 271–72, 277–78, 322; definition of, 149, 219, 228, 230, 272, 273, 298, 300, 305; Fear of, grown disorderly, 46, 83, 91, 156, 160, 228, 229, 276, 324; *see also* Anarchy, Mob; residual power of, 16, 83,153, 157, 220, 222, 226, 231, 267, 273; implementation of the will of, 220, 270, 300, 307, 318, 319; *see also* General Will; sovereignty of, 147–50, 158–60, 163,165, 168, 210, 222, 274, 298, 310. *See also* Democracy
Perkins, William, 129–30
Pett, Peter, 233
Petty, William, 161, 195
Pilgrimage of Grace, 37, 47, 53, 66, 73
Pisan, Christine de, 27–28
Pitt, William, the Younger, 307
Place Bills/Placemen, 225, 272, 275, 298

Plato, 14, 27, 112, 126, 275
Plattes, Gabriel, 194, 200
Plockboy, Peter Cornelius, 199, 250
Plumb, Sir John, 152, 206, 207, 224
Pocock, J. G. A., 169, 297, 322
Pole, Reginald, archbishop of Canterbury, Lord Cardinal, Legate, 45, 81
Political nation, concept and size of, 152, 157, 160, 167–68, 207–8, 218, 225, 260, 261, 284, 295
Political parties, 218, 223–25, 227, 264–65, 267, 299. *See also* Tories, Whigs
Pollard, A. F., 55
Ponet, John, bishop of Winchester, 35, 58, 81–82, 83, 86, 102, 106, 117, 145, 158, 171, 306
Pope, Alexander, 153, 265, 268–69, 280, 285, 287, 288, 326
Population, 130–31, 207, 246, 260, 261, 283, 295; pressure of, 87–88, 91, 131, 134–35. *See also* Depopulation
Postlethwayt, Malachy, 286
Poverty: attitudes toward 23–24, 40, 60, 68, 114–15, 135–37, 174, 188, 192–94, 242, 246–47, 251–55, 282, 287–91, 315; as cause of revolt, 39, 40, 74–75, 112, 135, 169–70, 245, 283, 293; causes of, 68, 136, 192, 247, 286, 288; incidence of, 131, 135, 192, 308; relief of, 51–52, 68–69, 90, 93, 110, 114–15, 135–37, 182, 193–94, 245–46, 247–55, 271, 288–91, 311–12, 320. *See also* Beggars, Charity
Powell, Roger, 339n 115
Pownall, Thomas, 276–77
Preaching, influence of, 76, 79, 282, 294
Presbyterians/Presbyterianism, 101, 127, 142, 156, 173, 175, 177, 178, 180, 184–85
Price, Richard, 263, 301, 307, 308, 315, 319
Prices, 88, 110, 134, 135, 137, 185, 281, 285, 309; regulation of, 38, 40–41, 60, 65, 66–67, 132, 292. *See also* Inflation
Priestley, Joseph, 298, 302; "Priestley Riots," 303
Prince, Thomas, 164
Proclamations, Royal, 42, 51, 54, 60, 61, 62–63, 65, 76, 77, 89, 96, 132–34, 233, 313
"Projects," 66, 67, 89–90, 138

Proletariat, industrial, 109, 251–52
"Promoters," informers, 69, 239
Property, concept of, rights, limitations, 15, 23, 125, 133, 136, 139, 161, 166, 171, 189–90, 192, 202, 216, 219, 221, 222, 227, 243, 244–45, 259, 261–62, 268, 284, 285–86, 305, 307, 309–10, 313, 315, 317, 322, 326. *See also* Agrarian law
Protestantism, 33, 49, 57; economic and social ideals of, 63, 68, 77, 80, 83, 114. *See also* Calvinism, Dissent; Lutheranism; Puritanism
Prynne, William, 167, 178, 181
Puritanism, 77, 78, 99, 100, 102, 122–23, 128–30, 142, 172, 183, 244
Putney Debates, 146, 161, 189, 272, 321
Pym, John, 142

Quakers, 127, 175, 179–80, 233, 236, 249, 343 n.123

Radicals/radicalism, 224, 243, 262–63, 296, 298, 299, 301, 306, 310, 322, 323
Raikes, Robert, 304
Rainborough, Thomas, 161, 169, 189, 208, 232
Raleigh, Sir Walter, 91, 116–17
Ralph, James, 274–75
Ranters, 153, 178–79
Rastell, John, 39, 45, 52
Read, Conyers, 61
Rebellion/sedition, 46, 71, 73–76, 106, 108, 112, 132, 133, 221, 227, 229, 238, 271, 273, 294
Reeves, John, 316
Regrating, 60, 89, 132, 292, 311, 313
Rents/rack-renting, 51, 63, 64, 75, 113, 130, 201, 245, 285, 286
Requests, Court of, 43, 57
Resistance, right of, 16, 82–83, 86, 120, 158–59, 220, 228, 229
Restoration of 1660, 144, 196, 205, 206, 207, 209, 239
Revolution, "Glorious" of 1688–89, 207, 209, 212, 213, 218, 220, 224–25, 231, 235, 260, 272, 274, 278, 299, 308, 322
Richard II, king of England, 108
Richard III, king of England, 25, 106
Richardson, Samuel, 176, 189

Ridley, Nicholas, bishop of Rochester and London, 58, 62
Riot Act of 1715, 260
Rising in the West, 73
Rising of the Northern Earls, 73
Robbins, Caroline, 19, 20, 215, 220, 243, 247, 265, 325
Robespierre, Maximilien, 319
Robinson, Henry, 154, 175–76, 177, 180, 194, 195, 198, 199
Roots, Ivan, 155–56, 180
Rota/rotation, 167–69, 263, 275, 299, 304–5, 325
Rousseau, Jean-Jacques, 26, 148, 231, 319
Ruggles, Thomas, 289
Rumbold, Richard, 209
Rupp, Gordon, 278, 291
Rye House Plot, 206, 208–9, 220

Sabine, G. H., 184
Sacheverell, Henry, 237–38; "Sacheverell Riots," 206, 243, 261
Saint Aubyn, Sir John, 270
Saint Germain, Christopher, 68
Saint George's Fields, 297
Sanderson, Robert, bishop of Lincoln, 136–37
Sandys, Edwin, bishop of Worcester, London, archbishop of York, 99
Sandys, Sir Edwin, 99, 126–27
Scarisbrick, J. J., 42, 43, 44
Schwarz, L. D., 351 n.49
Scriptures, the, 47, 49, 79
Septennial Act, 218, 260, 261, 263, 270, 272, 275, 299
Settlement, Act of, 246, 247, 289, 312
Seymour, Edward, duke of Somerset, 28, 34, 38, 53, 54–56, 58, 59, 61, 64, 67, 73, 75, 78, 80
Seymour, Thomas, lord admiral, 60
Shaftesbury, Anthony Ashley Cooper, earl of, 208, 213
Shakespeare, William, 71, 91, 115–16
Sharp, Buchanan, 109, 338 n.114
Sheep/sheep farming, 51, 60, 63
Sheppard, William, 197
Shute, John, viscount Barrington, 237, 348 n.68
Sibthorp, Robert, 124

Sidney, Algernon, 208, 219–20, 226, 255, 297, 316
Sidney, Sir Philip, 91, 115, 335 n.17
Six Articles, 80
Skinner, Quentin, 14, 32, 45, 71, 105
Slack, Paul, 36, 42, 56, 69, 90, 131, 132, 134
Smith, Sir Thomas, 32, 34, 57, 61, 62, 80, 90, 94, 97, 202–3, 217, 285
Snell, K. D. M., 288–89
Social contract, 26, 97, 107, 109, 118, 171, 221, 222, 228, 268
Societies for Reformation of Manners, 239–40, 281, 348 n.72
Society: corporeal analogy of, 15, 22, 26, 33, 35–41, 82, 86, 91, 102, 145, 146–47, 169, 170, 201, 215, 221, 252, 266, 282, 300, 318, 319, 325; hierarchical concept of, 23–24, 27–28, 36, 38–39, 65–66, 186, 188, 261, 268, 294, 307, 325; stability of, social mobility, 31, 39, 66, 78, 186–7. *See also* Upstarts; Vocation
Society for Constitutional Information, 268, 305, 306–7, 324
Sovereignty, concept of, 95, 116, 125, 147–49, 151, 165, 170, 277, 301
Spark, Michael, 136
Speck, W. A., 218, 260, 264, 287–88, 292
Spelman, Edward, 265
Spence, Thomas, 309, 316, 325
Spenser, Edmund, 91, 115
Sprigge, William, 147, 154, 190, 193, 316
Squire, Samuel, 277–78
Standing armies, 225, 226, 274, 299, 309
Stanhope, Charles, earl of, 237
Star Chamber, Court of, 133, 134
Starkey, David, 21–22, 24, 34, 46
Starkey, Thomas, 14, 35–36, 37, 41, 45, 49, 52, 69, 72, 80
State: Church and, 85, 97, 104, 106, 124, 237–8, 278, 280, 303, 317, 327; concept of, 20, 33, 35, 85, 88, 116,119, 122, 124, 125, 142, 151, 177, 201, 210, 213, 216, 217, 228, 232, 277, 286, 297
Stewardship, concept of, 15, 40, 64, 244
Strafford, Thomas, Wentworth, earl of, 142
Stratford, John, 138
Stromberg, Roland, 279, 291, 304

Stubbs, John, 108–9
Sumptuary legislation, 39, 65–66
Supple, B. E., 339 n.123
Supremacy, Royal, Act of, 48, 71, 80, 86, 99, 102–5
Swift, Jonathan, 211, 239, 243, 265, 268, 269–70

Taverner, Richard, 49
Tawney, R. H., 138
Taxation, 27, 28, 52, 60, 185, 193, 195–96, 215, 224, 269, 283, 284, 305, 311, 313, 317, 320
Taylor, John, 188, 190–91, 196
Temple, Sir William, 223
Thelwall, John, 257
Thirsk, Joan, 34, 67, 89, 138, 199
Thirty-Nine Articles, 303
Thomas, William, 70, 72, 122
Thompson, E. P., 284, 292–93
Thomson, James, 264
Tillage, 51, 54, 62, 64, 89
Tindal, Matthew, 213, 238, 279
Tithes, 174, 195–96, 238
Tittler, Robert, 62
Todd, Margo, 90, 129
Toland, John, 213–14, 220, 227–28, 238, 243, 263, 297, 348 n.69
Toleration, Act of, 237
Tories, 209, 218, 224, 228, 266
Towers, Joseph, 297–98
Trade, benefits of, 140, 287; boom and slump in, 131, 137, 286, 316
Trenchard, John, 226, 230–32, 306
Tucker, Josiah, 310, 311
Tully, James, 222
Turner, William, 83, 178
Tyler, Wat, 108, 228, 229
Tyndale, William, 37, 46, 58, 64, 70, 75, 78, 79, 81, 84
Tyrrell, James, 208, 210, 222, 228

United States, Constitution of, 20, 162, 166, 167, 170, 205, 218, 299, 319
Udall, Nicholas, 73
Unemployment, 63, 131, 135
United Provinces, Holland, 139, 174, 200, 233, 247, 276
Upstarts, 39, 47, 65, 83, 121
Usury/Interest, 23, 31, 51, 78, 114, 140, 203, 212

Vanderlint, Jacob, 285–86, 292
Venner, Thomas, 206, 232
Veron, John, 79
Vives, Juan Luis, 78
Vocation, 78, 112, 129–30, 188
Voltaire, F.-M. A. de, 305

Wages, 131, 136, 185, 198, 199, 246, 249, 251, 261, 281, 283, 284, 285, 290, 291, 292, 293, 295, 310, 311, 313, 315, 320
Walpole, Sir Robert, 264, 266, 267, 268, 269, 270, 282, 284
Walsh, J. D., 294
Walwyn, William, 162, 164, 165, 174–75, 177, 189
Warburton, William, 280–81
Warwick, Sir Philip, 213, 228
Watts, Isaac, 255, 291
Webster, Charles, 194, 195, 200, 202, 248
Welfare state, concept of, 15, 20, 47, 224, 320, 325
Wentworth, Peter, 108, 109, 142
Wesley, Charles, 292, 294
Wesley, John, 281, 294, 295
Whately, William, 137
Whigs, 209, 211, 218, 220, 224, 228, 298; "New," 218, 224; "Old," "Real," "True," 19, 215, 218, 224, 225, 238, 258, 262, 266, 278, 284
White, Stephen, 143
White, Thomas, 148, 149, 158–59
Whitefield, George, 294
Whitgift, John, archbishop of Canterbury, 98, 102–3, 118
Wilcox, Thomas, 102

Wildman, John, 160, 161, 208, 209
Wilkes, John, 276, 295, 297, 298, 299
Wilkinson, Robert, 133–34
Willan, Leonard, 210, 243
William III, king of England, 206, 207, 209, 211, 225, 226, 238, 239, 244
Williams, David, 263, 268, 299–301, 303, 304, 307, 308, 317, 321, 323, 324, 325
Williams, Penry, 46
Wilson, Charles, 254
Wimbledon, Thomas, 22
Winstanley, Gerrard, 145, 174, 184, 190, 194, 195, 202, 232
Wolfe, Don M., 167, 176
Wollaston, William, 279
Wollstonecraft, Mary, 315
Wolsey, Thomas, archbishop of York, Lord Cardinal, Legate, 17, 41–44, 46, 47, 57, 64, 66, 134
Woodhouse, A. S. P., 162
Woodward, Richard, 311–12
Wool, 25, 62, 89
Woolrych, Austin, 155, 156, 183
Worden, Blair, 335n.17
Workhouses, 137, 193, 198, 200, 246, 247–48, 249, 252–53, 288, 289, 290, 291, 311, 312
Wren, Matthew, 148, 152
Wrigley, E. A., 283
Wyatt, Sir Thomas, 62, 73
Wyvill, Christopher, 305, 306, 321, 324

Young, Arthur, 293, 322

Zagorin, Perez, 202
Zwingli, Huldrych, 78, 79, 98